English Composition and Grammar
BENCHMARK EDITION

Complete Course

English Composition and Grammar

BENCHMARK EDITION

John E. Warriner

Complete Course

 Harcourt Brace Jovanovich, Publishers

Orlando   San Diego   Chicago   Dallas

THE SERIES:

English Composition and Grammar: Introductory Course
English Composition and Grammar: First Course
English Composition and Grammar: Second Course
English Composition and Grammar: Third Course
English Composition and Grammar: Fourth Course
English Composition and Grammar: Fifth Course
English Composition and Grammar: Complete Course

Annotated Teacher's Edition and Teacher's Resource Book for each above title.

CORRELATED SERIES:

English Workshop: Introductory Course
English Workshop: First Course
English Workshop: Second Course
English Workshop: Third Course
English Workshop: Fourth Course
English Workshop: Fifth Course
English Workshop: Review Course

Composition: Models and Exercises, First Course
Composition: Models and Exercises, Second Course
Composition: Models and Exercises, Third Course
Composition: Models and Exercises, Fourth Course
Composition: Models and Exercises, Fifth Course
Advanced Composition: A Book of Models for Writing, Complete Course

Vocabulary Workshop: Introductory Course
Vocabulary Workshop: First Course
Vocabulary Workshop: Second Course
Vocabulary Workshop: Third Course
Vocabulary Workshop: Fourth Course
Vocabulary Workshop: Fifth Course
Vocabulary Workshop: Complete Course

John E. Warriner taught English for thirty-two years in junior and senior high schools and in college. He is chief author of the *English Composition and Grammar* series, coauthor of the *English Workshop* series, general editor of the *Composition: Models and Exercises* series, and editor of *Short Stories: Characters in Conflict*. His coauthors have all been active in English education.

PHOTO CREDITS:

Key: T, Top; B, Bottom

Cover: HBJ Photo

Page 1, Spencer Swanger/Tom Stack and Associates; 2, John U.A.F. Neal/Photo Researchers, Inc.; IW1, Photography by Patricia Fisher, mural by Elizabeth Calomiris; IW2, Walter Smalling/Washington, D.C.; IW4, *The St. Petersburg Times* by Eric Mencher; IW5, Ray Metzker/Laurence Miller Gallery; IW6, HBJ Photo; IW8, Sepp Seitz/Woodfin Camp and Associates; IW9, Mark Sherman/Bruce Coleman, Inc.; IW9, Len Lahman; IW10, John McGrail; IW12, Matsumoto/Black Star; IW13, Aram Cesar/The Image Bank; IW14, Dan Carraco; IW16, Frank Grant/International Stock Photo; 337, John Lei/Omni-Photo Communications; 338, Steve Elmore; 409, Nick Waring; 410, R. Hamilton Smith from f/Stop Pictures; 697, D. Van deZande/Photri; 698, Gordie Corbin; 791, Chip Feise; 792, Max Hirshfeld.

Printed in the United States of America

ISBN 0–15–311736–2

To the Student

Now you are probably thinking, "Here we go again—another English class, another textbook." You are, of course, quite right. Since almost everything you do involves the use of language, schools make the study of English a required subject in every year, and in any English class, a textbook is an essential tool.

This textbook is designed to help you master the skills required for the effective use of standard English. Although the book will help you to *speak* better, its primary purpose is to help you to *write* better.

You have been learning to write almost as long as you have been going to school, which, at this point, may seem to you to be a very long time. To be sure, you have already studied many composition skills. This book reviews those skills while it carries you further into the study of more advanced skills which lead to better writing.

As your experience increases, your ideas become more sophisticated and consequently more difficult to express. Additional skills are needed. This textbook provides instruction in these skills and the opportunity to practice their use. Practice is important because you learn to write by writing. No one ever learned to write in any other way.

Your textbook is also designed as a useful reference book: it offers the solution to almost any writing problem you are likely to encounter. By familiarizing yourself with the contents and organization of the book, and by using the index freely, you can easily find out what you need to know, whether it is a question about punctuation or usage or sentence structure, or a suggestion about the form of an outline, of a bibliography, or of a business letter. Keep this book nearby whenever you write. Develop the habit of looking up the answers to questions that arise concerning the use of standard English.

J.W.

CONTENTS

2. Writing Paragraphs   35

3. Writing Expository Compositions 85

THE WHOLE COMPOSITION

4. Writing Expository Compositions 122

SPECIFIC EXPOSITORY WRITING ASSIGNMENTS

5. Writing Persuasive Compositions   169
LANGUAGE AND LOGIC

7. Writing a Research Paper 255
RESEARCH, WRITING, DOCUMENTATION

Part Two: COMPOSITION: Writing and Revising Sentences

10. Sentence Completeness   339

FRAGMENTS AND RUN-ON SENTENCES

11. Coordination and Subordination   345

RELATIONSHIPS BETWEEN IDEAS IN A SENTENCE

Part Three: TOOLS FOR WRITING AND REVISING

GRAMMAR

USAGE

MECHANICS

31. Punctuation   658
OTHER MARKS OF PUNCTUATION

32. Spelling   679
IMPROVING YOUR SPELLING

Part Four: RESOURCES FOR
WRITING AND STUDYING

33. The Library   699
ARRANGEMENT AND RESOURCES

Part Five: SPEAKING AND LISTENING

38. Discussion and Debate 793
TYPES OF DISCUSSION; ELEMENTS OF DEBATING

39. Public Speaking 808
PREPARING, DELIVERING, AND EVALUATING
AN INFORMAL SPEECH

Index 819

PART ONE

COMPOSITION:
The Writing Process

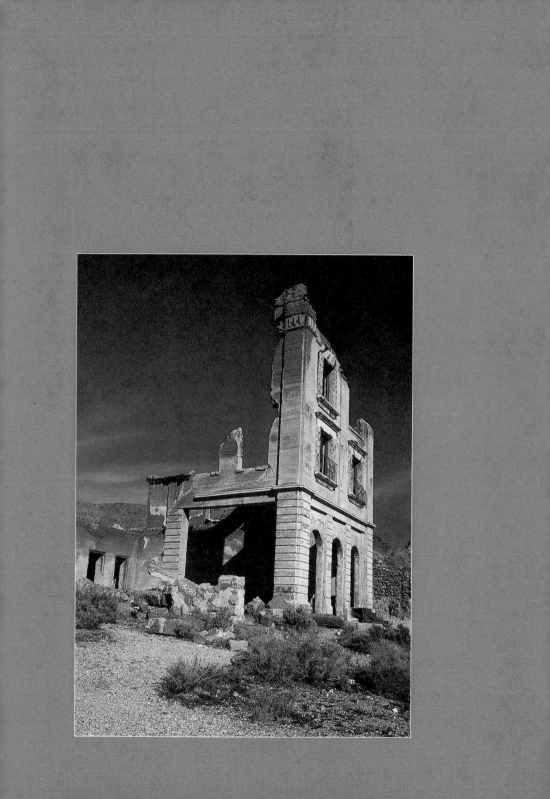

Writing and Thinking

THE WRITING PROCESS

Writing is not a single activity; it is not something that you can or should do in a single sitting, all at one time. Whenever you write, whether a paragraph or a composition, you are involved in an ongoing process of thinking, decision making, and rethinking. In this chapter, you will learn and practice the stages of the writing process and the many steps that make up each stage.

THE WRITING PROCESS

PREWRITING—Identifying your purpose and audience; choosing and limiting a subject; considering attitude and tone; gathering information; classifying and ordering information

WRITING A FIRST DRAFT—Expressing your ideas in sentences and paragraphs

EVALUATING—Judging the content, organization, and style of a draft

REVISING—Improving the content, organization, and style

PROOFREADING—Checking the revised version to correct errors in grammar, usage, and mechanics

WRITING THE FINAL VERSION—Preparing a final version and proofreading it

PREWRITING

During prewriting, the first stage in the writing process, you answer five important questions: Why am I writing? For whom am I writing? What will I write about? What will I say? How will I say it?

THE WRITER'S PURPOSE

1a. Have in mind a clear purpose for writing.

Every piece of writing has a purpose—sometimes more than one. Even when multiple purposes exist, however, a single purpose usually guides the writing. In an essay about what happened during your driving test, you may explain the test, but your main purpose is to tell a story about your experience.

> *Techniques for Prewriting.* As you begin to plan your paper, remember the four basic purposes for writing:
>
> - *Narrative* writing tells a story or relates a series of events.
>   A letter describing your first day at a new job
> - *Expository* writing gives information or explains.
>   A definition of a water table for an essay question
> - *Descriptive* writing describes a person, place or thing.
>   An essay describing the Grand Canyon
> - *Persuasive* writing attempts to persuade or convince.
>   A brochure encouraging eighteen-year-olds to vote

EXERCISE 1. Identifying Purposes for Writing. Identify the purpose (to narrate, to explain, to describe, or to persuade) for writing about each of the following topics. (Some items could have more than one purpose.)

1. What a penguin looks like
2. The history of the founding of Pennsylvania

3. A funny incident during a shopping trip
4. How to tune a guitar
5. Why high-school students should volunteer to help elderly people in the community

EXERCISE 2. Identifying Purpose in Writing.   Identify the writer's purpose in the following paragraph.

> David Gordon's new ballet, *Field, Chair, and Mountain,* uses ordinary folding chairs in a unique way. The dancers enter the stage carrying their own chairs. In the first section of the "chair" part of this ballet, the chair is each dancer's partner, giving support and balance as the dancers move in unison in a long series of graceful, intricate movements. Even in a romantic duet between the lead male and female dancers, a chair is central to the movements. Finally, the whole troupe dances in pairs, each pair with a chair. The graceful, innovative, sometimes humorous movements are danced to a nineteenth-century piano concerto by the Irish composer John Field.

CRITICAL THINKING:
Analyzing How Purpose Affects Writing

Analysis is a critical thinking skill that you use in two ways when writing: to break a whole into its smaller parts and to determine how the parts are related. During prewriting, you are examining the separate elements of your paper and their effects on each other. For example, you analyze how purpose affects both the content of your writing and the particular words you use.

Consider the differences in two paragraphs about the danger of ultraviolet light; one paragraph explains and one tells a story. The explanation includes scientific facts and uses fairly formal language. The narration includes interesting details and uses less formal language.

> Natural sunlight and some artificial sources of illumination can cause a host of visual difficulties. Ultraviolet light from the sun and from lamps can cause cataracts and retinal damage. Even during winter, when the amount of ultraviolet radiation reaching the earth's surface is greatly reduced, those such as skiers and skaters exposed to intense direct or reflected light can suffer harm. Dr. Morris Waxler of the Food and Drug Administration says that they should wear sunglasses that filter out ultraviolet light during exposure to the midday sun and to other strong sources.
>
> JANE E. BRODY

When I was seven and my brother thirteen, my parents took us for a vacation to Florida. We drove from the freezing January of Cleveland, Ohio, to the tropical sunshine of sunny Miami, making the trip in three days. The warmth and the ocean were unbelievable to us, straight from a gray, cold winter. My brother and I hurried to the beach and spent all of our first afternoon swimming, building sand castles, and—worst of all—lying on our stomachs at the shoreline while the waves washed delightfully over our legs. Of course, I didn't realize it, but I was absorbing enough ultraviolet rays to burn my legs badly. By evening, I was in considerable pain; by morning I could not walk. I spent the next three days in bed, recovering from that painful sunburn. And that's the last bad sunburn I've ever had. Now I always cover my fair, freckled skin with sunscreen, and I always limit my time in the sun. Nothing is worth the pain of a bad sunburn.

Persuasion and description also combine different details and language. Persuasive writing presents opinions, reasons, and evidence in formal, concise, clear language. Descriptive writing uses concrete and sensory details to create vivid images with less formal language and a freer writing style.

EXERCISE 3. Analyzing How Purpose Affects Writing.   Two purposes for writing are given for each topic below. Consider how each purpose would affect a piece of writing in two ways. First, decide what aspect of the topic you would write about. Then list at least three details you would include to develop the topic for each purpose. Be prepared to explain your answers.

1. *Topic:*   The worst natural disaster you have experienced
   Purpose: a. To inform   b. To describe
2. *Topic:*   The problem of adult illiteracy
   Purpose: a. To persuade   b. To tell a story

THE WRITER'S AUDIENCE

1b. Identify the audience for whom you are writing.

Audiences for your writing may vary widely in age and background; therefore, you cannot write in the same way for all audiences. Like purpose, audience affects both content and language. If your topic is a new type of word processing software, you will write about it differently for members of your computer club than for your other classmates.

EXERCISE 4. Identifying Purpose and Audience. Go to the library and find six different samples of writing. You may include magazine and newspaper articles, novels, and short stories. For each piece of writing, identify what you think is the writer's main purpose and who you think is the intended audience.

CRITICAL THINKING:
Analyzing How Audience Affects Writing

The following paragraphs were written for adults interested in the birds of the northern states:

> Until recently most students of migration focused on its mechanics, such as energetics, or navigation and orientation. Little was known about what happens to "our" birds during the months they are away from their breeding grounds. Where do they go? What dangers do they face? How do they live in their winter homes? Nature's grandest theatrical event remained largely mysterious.
>
> Now ornithologists who followed the birds into the tropics are able to answer some of those questions. One point, though it may ruffle our proprietary instincts, ought to be cleared up at once. A good many of the most familiar birds in our gardens and forests are not "ours" at all. Families such as the wood warblers, vireos, flycatchers, and tanagers are, for the most part, not northern birds that happen to fly south for a while to escape the wintry blasts. They are tropical birds that come north for a few months every year to raise a family and then return to their ancestral homes.
>
> FRANK GRAHAM, JR.

If you rewrote this information for fifth-graders, you would have to explain or omit some unfamiliar terms, such as *energetics, navigation, orientation,* and *ornithologists.* You might provide a brief background about migration, and you would omit the references to "our" birds and "proprietary instincts." You might also replace the rather flowery phrases *grandest theatrical event* and *ancestral homes.* Finally, you would generally simplify vocabulary and shorten sentences to make the information easier to understand.

Also be aware of purpose when analyzing audience, because the two are closely related. In persuasive writing, for example, you must carefully consider readers' beliefs and prejudices. Your answers to the questions on the following page will help you understand your audience and adapt your writing to that audience.

Techniques for Prewriting. Ask yourself the following questions about your audience:

- What information does the audience already know about the topic?
- What background or technical information might this audience need to understand the topic? What terms might be defined for them?
- What language and style are most appropriate for the audience: simple or complex words and sentences, casual or formal presentation?
- Does the audience have any bias (strong feelings either for or against) about the topic that could affect the writing? If so, what is the bias?

EXERCISE 5. Analyzing the Effects of Audience. Read the following item, in which four different audiences are given for one topic and purpose. Then write out answers to the questions that follow.

Topic: Why all high-school students should be required to take four years of a foreign language

Purpose: To persuade

Audiences: (a) twelfth-graders, (b) high-school foreign language teachers, (c) members of the local board of education, (d) local businesspeople

1. Which audiences would have greater knowledge of the topic? Less knowledge?
2. For which audiences would terms need to be defined? What terms might be defined for the audience(s)?
3. Which audiences would need background information? What kind of background information might be supplied for them?
4. Which audiences might have strong feelings for or against the subject? What might the feelings be? How would the feelings affect your writing?
5. For which audience would you choose to write? Why?

EXERCISE 6. Rewriting a Paragraph for Different Audiences. Select one paragraph from a high-school or college textbook or a reference book. Choose a topic that interests you—one you already have some background knowledge of or experience with. Then rewrite the paragraph for two of the following audiences. At the beginning of each version, be sure to identify the audience.

a. Fourth-grade students
b. Adults who have no previous knowledge of the topic
c. Exchange students from the Soviet Union

CHOOSING AND LIMITING A SUBJECT

1c. Choose a subject that is appropriate to your audience.

When choosing a subject, always consider your readers' knowledge and interests. While you could explain the concept of probability to third-graders—by giving extensive, simplified definitions—that subject is better for an older audience. The subject of probability, however, is not appropriate for every audience that can understand the concepts. You might choose it for a science-essay contest, but you would not choose it for your first contribution to the school newspaper. Make sure that your readers will be interested in your subject and that it is neither too complex nor too simple for them.

EXERCISE 7. Choosing a Subject Appropriate for an Audience. Consider the following subjects in relation to the five audiences listed below. Determine the audiences for which each subject would be appropriate. Be prepared to explain your answers.

Audiences: (a) readers of the local newspaper, (b) business owners, (c) parents, (d) your classmates, (e) senior citizens

1. How to make money in the stock market
2. How to get along with teen-agers
3. Planning a Thanksgiving dinner for thirty
4. The most valuable postage stamps in the world
5. How to do batik (a method of dyeing cloth)

1d. Limit your subject so that it can be adequately covered in the form of writing you have chosen.

A *subject* is a broad, general area of knowledge, such as "robots" or "art." A *topic* is a limited subject, such as "the use of robots in the home" and "Vincent Van Gogh's landscapes at Arles." A topic for a paragraph is necessarily more limited than one for a composition because a paragraph allows less space for developing the main idea. If you choose a topic too extensive for your form of writing, you cannot present it adequately to your audience.

EXERCISE 8. Distinguishing Between Subjects and Topics. Identify each item as either a general subject (*S*) or a limited topic (*T*) for a short composition.

1. How to prepare tacos
2. William Shakespeare
3. Efforts to save the endangered manatee
4. Better television programs
5. How to create a crossword puzzle

CRITICAL THINKING:
Analyzing a Subject

To find limited topics for writing, you may analyze a subject by dividing and subdividing it into smaller parts. Depending on the subject, the basis for your analysis may be time periods, examples, features, uses, causes, or types.

EXAMPLES 1. *Subject divided into examples*
      Subject: Dogs that are bred for hunting
    Main divisions: Retrievers
                Hounds
                Setters
                Pointers
                Spaniels

    2. *Subject divided into features or aspects*
      Subject: Dreams
    Main divisions: Why people dream
                 Types of dreams
                Interpretation of dreams
                Scientific study of dreaming

EXERCISE 9. Analyzing Subjects to Develop Topics. From the following list, choose three subjects and divide each one into at least five smaller parts. (Note: For each subject, different analyses are possible and correct.)

1. Congress
2. Team sports
3. Personality
4. American literature
5. Exploration

6. Pollution
7. Alcoholism
8. Popular music
9. Medicine
10. Precious metals

EXERCISE 10. Limiting a Subject to Develop Topics Suitable for Paragraphs. Choose one of the subjects that you analyzed for Exercise 9. Could each of these topics be covered adequately in a paragraph of about 150 words? If not, divide the topics further until you have at least three that can be adequately covered in a paragraph. List them, and save your paper.

TONE

1e. Consider your attitude toward your topic and its expression through tone.

Your attitude, or point of view, toward your topic is important because it affects both the details you include and the language you use in your writing. The expression of your attitude—whether approving, angry, humorous, or fearful—is called *tone.*

Consider the tone of the following movie review. Clearly the writer's attitude is negative, but what particular words and details convey her attitude and create the sarcastic tone? If you wanted to write a favorable review of the film, what changes in words and details would you make to alter the tone?

"Cross Creek," an account of a woman's struggle to become a writer, is given a supernal glow by the director Martin Ritt. The picture seems to be suffering from earthshine: everything is lighted to look holy, and whenever the score isn't shimmering and burnishing, nature is twittering. It's all pearly and languid, and more than a little twerpy—it's one long cue for "Oh, What a Beautiful Mornin'." Loosely based on Marjorie Kinnan Rawlings' semi-autobiographical tales about what she learned during her years in an orange grove in the Florida swamps, the movie opens in 1928. We're meant to admire Mrs. Rawlings (Mary Steenburgen), a Northerner, for her courage in leaving her home and husband and going down to Florida to write. But the script doesn't give even a hint of why she bought the grove (sight unseen), or why she thinks she'll find more propitious conditions for writing gothic romances in the subtropical marshland than she had in her bedroom or her study in New York. The filmmakers view her as a feminist ahead of her time—a heroine who gives up a social life and goes out on her own to face hardships. Yet the way they tell the story, she's almost immediately equipped with everything she has cast aside. When her jalopy gives out before she arrives at her property, it's said to be in hopeless condition, but the courtly and handsome hotelkeeper Norton Baskin (Peter Coyote), who drives her to her tumbledown shack, shows up again a day or two later bringing the car, which has been repaired so that it looks sparkling and new. Meanwhile, friendly neighbors have been dropping in, and Mrs. Rawlings has hired a young black woman, Geechee (Alfre Woodard), to clean and cook, and field hands to take care of the crops. The house is already transformed; it's gracious and orderly, and she's at her typewriter, with a potted gloxinia blooming nearby. She's ladylike, and the local people do everything for her. So what's so heroic about her—beyond her managerial skills?

PAULINE KAEL—*The New Yorker*

EXERCISE 11. Identifying Tone.   Bring to class five paragraphs from different sources, such as magazines, short stories, novels, and nonfiction books. Identify the tone of each paragraph and the author's attitude toward the topic.

GATHERING INFORMATION

1f. Gather information appropriate to your purpose.

Your purpose for writing largely determines the kinds of information you must gather. For example, to *describe* your grandparents' kitchen, you would need to provide vivid details for your readers: the utensils, the furniture and appliances, even the smells in the room. To *give information* about Haleakala National Park on Maui Island, you would provide facts about the park and about sightseeing within it.

No matter what kinds of details you need, however, you can learn techniques to make your information gathering easier. The methods discussed in the following pages show you both how to tap your own creativity and how to analyze a topic.

Direct and Indirect Observation

(1) Use your powers of observation to note specific details.

Whenever your observations are made through your own senses of sight, smell, sound, taste, or touch, they are called *direct observations*. In the following paragraph, Harry Crews's firsthand observation provides interesting details that create a vivid picture of a room.

> I went on down the hallway and out onto the back porch and finally into the kitchen that was built at the very rear of the house. The entire room was dominated by a huge black cast-iron stove with six eyes on its cooking surface. Directly across the room from the stove was the safe, a tall square cabinet with wide doors covered with screen wire that was used to keep biscuits and fried meat and rice or almost any other kind of food that had been recently cooked. Between the stove and the safe sat the table we ate off of, a table almost ten feet long, with benches on each side instead of chairs, so that when we put in tobacco, there would be enough room for the hired hands to eat.
>
> HARRY CREWS

Indirect observations are all those not made directly through your own senses. When you listen to other people telling about their experiences or read about other people's observations, you are making an indirect observation. Much of the information that you gather for writing comes through indirect observations.

CRITICAL THINKING:
Observing Specific Details

You cannot possibly remember every sensory detail of an experience, but you can improve your powers of observation. Concentrate on paying attention to specifics, and you will discover many interesting details for your writing.

EXERCISE 12. Improving Your Powers of Observation. Choose one of the following places, take a pencil and paper with you, sit (or stand) in one place for ten minutes, and list as many sensory details (sight, sound, smell, touch, and taste) as you can.

1. A shopping mall
2. The school cafeteria during lunch hour
3. The street outside your home at 6:00 A.M.
4. An empty field (or woods or vacant lot)
5. A bus stop or subway station

A Writer's Journal

(2) Keep a writer's journal to record your thoughts and feelings about your experiences.

A writer's journal can be a rich source of ideas for writing as well as a record of specific experiences. You may record any number of things in a journal: sudden insights, considered opinions, striking sights, overheard conversations, quotations from favorite books, and reactions to other people. A writer's journal should contain only what you want to share with others; however, you might also keep a private journal for your own use.

EXERCISE 13. Using a Journal Entry to Gather Ideas for Writing.
Read the following journal entries and then answer the questions that follow it.

> January 22. Not too often that frost hits southern Florida—sometimes the central part of the state, but not here. Temperature going down to 30 degrees tonight after two days of "Arctic" weather. Rest of the country having weird weather, too: -27° in Chicago with a wind-chill factor that makes it -80°. I'm glad I'm missing that. (Poor Uncle Bernie in Chicago.) Trying to save my vegetable garden. Draped all of the vegetables with black plastic. Mom helped me water the ground well without getting leaves wet. I feel sorry for the farmers with acres and acres. Can't use smudge pots here; don't even know where I'd find one. We've moved my two zebra finches to the kitchen, the warmest room in the house. They're so delicate they'd never survive the chill in the rest of the house. Hoping for the best tonight.
>
> January 23. Temperature went down to 29! A record for southern Florida. Vegetable plants are all frozen, but I tried my best. When the weather warms, I'll start again with tomato seedlings, eggplants, peppers. Farmers here lost most of their crops, and upstate citrus crops are badly damaged.

1. The journal writer decided to write a composition explaining how to plant a small vegetable garden. List at least three other topics, suggested by the entry, that the writer might have chosen.
2. Where would you look for information about the topics you listed in item 1?

Brainstorming and Clustering

(3) Use brainstorming and clustering to find writing ideas.

Both brainstorming and clustering are techniques that generate a free flow of ideas. You may use these techniques either to think of topics for writing or to generate specific details to develop a topic you have already chosen.

When you brainstorm you think of one specific subject or topic, and then write down every idea, word, or phrase that comes to mind as you concentrate on that subject or topic. The end result is a long list of words or phrases—the longer, the better—written under the subject or topic you started with. Relax, but work quickly, jotting down every idea that occurs to you, and do not stop until you have run out of ideas. Only then should you evaluate the items you have listed. Circle those that seem usable, and write down any others suggested by your evaluation.

One writer created the following list during a five-minute brainstorming on the subject "deer."

DEER

hunting deer
kinds of deer—tiny Key deer; white-tailed deer
deer endangered?
what happens to deer in winter—food supply?
deer need salt
Bambi and other deer stories
gentle, peaceful creatures
what do they harm? eat gardens, crops
relatives of antelopes? many African species?
sayings associated with deer—shy as a deer, run like a deer
social structure of deer—travel in groups? stay in families? how many
    born each year?
where are most deer living—what parts of the U.S.?
many road signs about deer crossing; urban areas?
life cycle of deer
males called bucks; females—does; babies—fawns

Clustering, or *making connections,* is like brainstorming, but the result is a diagram of related ideas, not an unordered list. The end result is a diagram (instead of a list, as in brainstorming) with ideas grouped together around the subject or topic you started with. Begin by writing your subject or topic in the center of the paper and circling it. As ideas come to mind, write them down, circle them, and draw lines connecting them either to the central idea or to each other.

Here is the subject "deer" as a clustering diagram. Notice that some of the ideas are related only to the subject "deer," not to other ideas.

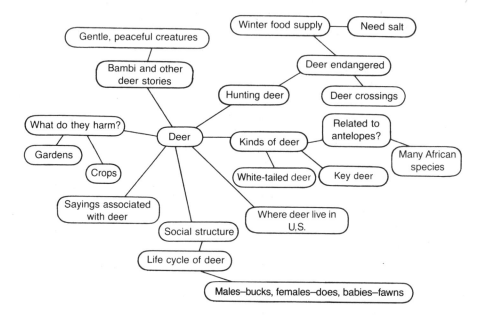

EXERCISE 14. Using Brainstorming or Clustering to Gather Information. Use either brainstorming or clustering to gather information about a topic you developed for Exercise 10 or for another topic.

Asking the 5 *W-How?* Questions

(4) Ask the *5 W-How?* questions to gather information.

The *5 W-How?* questions—*Who? What? Where? When? Why?* and *How?*—can help you gather specific details to use in your writing. Not every question will apply to every topic.

EXAMPLE *Topic:*   The founding of this city (community)
         Who?   Who founded this city?
         What?   What was here before the city was founded?
         Where?   Where was the first settlement built?
                     Where is the oldest part of the city?
         When?   When was the city founded?
         Why?   Why was the city founded at this particular place?
                     Why did the first people come here?
         How?   How was the city founded?

EXERCISE 15. Gathering Information by Asking the 5 *W-How?* Questions.   Use the *5 W-How?* questions to gather information about one of the following topics or a topic of your own. Write both your questions and the answers. (You may need to do research to find some answers.)

1. The records set by an outstanding athlete
2. An important change in your life
3. A solution to a problem in your community
4. The Civil War's major battle
5. An accident

Asking Point-of-View Questions

(5) Use different points of view to gather information.

Considering your topic from different points of view is another way to gather information. Three basic questions—What is it? How does it change or vary? What are its relationships?—will generate other questions specific to a topic.[1]

1. *What is it?* This first point of view focuses on the topic itself: what it looks like, what it does, and how it differs from others of its kind. The question *What is it?*—because it defines—is useful even for abstract ideas.

EXAMPLES   *Topic:*   My favorite place to be alone and think
[Where is the place? What does it look like? Why have I chosen it as my favorite place? What are my feelings when I am there?]

Topic: What is a democracy?
[How does a democracy work? What are its unique characteristics? What nations today are democracies?]

2. *How does it change or vary?* The second point of view focuses on how a topic changes over time. Its questions help you discover information about a topic's history and future, as well as how a topic keeps its identity even when it varies.

---

[1] This technique is based on ideas in *Rhetoric: Discovery and Change* by Richard E. Young, Alton L. Becker, and Kenneth E. Pike (New York: Harcourt Brace Jovanovich, 1971).

EXAMPLE *Topic:* What is a sonnet?
[When was a sonnet first defined? Are there different types of sonnets? How do they differ? What characteristics distinguish all sonnets from other poems? What are some famous early sonnets? What are some modern sonnets?]

3. *What are its relationships?* Using the third point of view, you analyze the topic's elements or aspects, considering how they are related to each other and to the topic as a whole. You may also consider how the topic is related to similar topics.

EXAMPLE *Topic:* Requirements for a successful speech
[What are the indispensable elements of a successful speech: content, organization, humor, presentation? Which element is most important? Least important? Or are they all equally important? How is a good speech like a good performance in a play?]

EXERCISE 16. Gathering Information by Asking Point-of-View Questions. Use the three point-of-view questions (What is it? How does it change or vary? What are its relationships?) to generate questions for two writing topics. You may use any topics in this chapter or choose new ones. Write all of the questions you think of as well as your answers.

CLASSIFYING INFORMATION

1g. Classify your ideas and information by grouping related ideas.

The next step in the writing process is to organize the ideas and details you have gathered. You must *classify* the information by deciding how items are related.

CRITICAL THINKING:
Classifying Ideas and Details

When you classify, you try to group similar details under a heading that explains what they have in common. Here is a classification of the writer's list of details for the subject "deer."

Types of deer in U.S.
    White-tailed deer of northeastern U.S.
    Key deer (Florida Keys)
    Black-tailed deer of the Pacific Coast
    Mule deer of the plains and western U.S.
Dangers to deer
    Natural dangers
        Lack of food (caused by flooding, winter)
        Animal predators
        Disease
    Dangers caused by people
        Hunters
        Cars

In the process of classifying, the writer has created more than one heading, so the relationship of the groupings has to be clarified. Two of the headings, "Natural dangers" and "Dangers caused by people," are actually subdivisions of a main heading, "Dangers to deer."

Classifying may also suggest missing details or reveal unnecessary ones. In this example, the writer has included in the outline several details that were not in the original list of brainstormed ideas—information such as other types of American deer. On the other hand, the writer chose to omit many details from the original list of brainstormed information because of the limited space of a short composition.

Techniques for Prewriting.   Use the following questions to help you classify a list of ideas and details.

- Which items have something in common? What is it? (Use the common element to write a heading.)
- Are some items or groupings more important than others? If so, which ones?
- Which items are subdivisions (examples, parts, etc.) of the main ideas? (If you have not listed any subdivisions for your main ideas, return to the information-gathering techniques.)
- Do some items not fit within your groupings? (Discard these for the present paper; you may use them later to develop another limited topic.)

EXERCISE 17. Classifying Ideas and Information.   Read the following list of ideas for a composition on cave-dwelling animals. Decide which ideas can be grouped together, and write a heading for each group. (Note: The headings are not in the list.) Then write the ideas under their proper headings. Put secondary headings under main headings if necessary. You may omit items that do not seem to fit.

a. cave-dwelling animals called *troglodytes:* salamanders, fish, insects, and crustaceans (shrimps, crabs, crayfish)
b. animals are blind—eyesight not useful in complete darkness
c. scarcity of food, must be brought in (by stream, bird droppings) from outside
d. animals have no pigment (all white)
e. no vegetation in caves; no light
f. weather not a threat—temperature fairly constant
g. environment usually small; fewer predators than at surface, less competition for food
h. high humidity, advantage for skin-breathing animals such as some salamanders
i. slower metabolism (rate of body functions) than surface animals; can exist on less food
j. troglodytes—fewer and larger eggs; newborns—better chance to survive
k. longer legs than surface relatives—can search for food more easily
l. *Ursus spelaeus*—extinct species of cave bear; fossils in caves

ARRANGING INFORMATION

1h. Arrange your ideas in order.

After classifying your ideas under main headings, you must consider the best order in which to present the information. With this sequence decided, you have an informal outline for your paper. Often your purpose suggests an order. Chronological order is appropriate, for example, when your topic is a step-by-step process, such as "preparing for a college-entrance examination." Arranging ideas in order of importance is more logical, however, if you are trying to persuade readers to visit residents of a nursing home.

In expository compositions background information is often necessary for the reader to understand what you have to say. Such background information, as well as technical terms that need to be defined for your audience, should be presented first. Then arrange your ideas in the order you think will be clearest and most interesting for your audience. (You will learn more about types of order in Chapter 2.)

REVIEW EXERCISE A. Following the Steps for Prewriting.
Prepare to write a paragraph or short composition on a topic of your choice. Choose a subject, and limit it to a suitable topic. Decide on your purpose and audience, and consider your attitude and tone. Using at least one of the techniques for gathering information, list specific details to include. Classify the details under main headings, decide on an appropriate order, and write the order down as an informal outline for your writing.

WRITING THE FIRST DRAFT

All of the prewriting steps prepare you for the second stage of the writing process, the actual writing of a first draft.

WRITING THE FIRST DRAFT

1i. Write a first draft, keeping your audience and purpose in mind.

Your goal in writing a first draft is not perfection, but the clear expression of your ideas in complete sentences. With your notes and outline in front of you, recall your purpose and audience. Then write freely. You will take time later to evaluate, revise, and proofread.

CRITICAL THINKING:
Synthesis

Synthesis is a creative process: the making of a new whole from smaller parts. All writing is therefore a synthesis: the combining of ideas and words into unique letters, essays, plays, or stories. Because writing is creative, the process itself often gives you new ideas. During a first draft you may rethink earlier decisions. You may alter your tone, delete a weak detail, arrange ideas more logically. Do not hesitate to use the discoveries that arise from synthesizing.

EXERCISE 18. Writing a First Draft. Using the prewriting notes you developed for Review Exercise A, write a first draft of your paragraph or composition.

EVALUATING

A draft, by definition, is not a finished piece of writing. All writers— professionals as well as students—must evaluate their first drafts to correct and improve them. To complete the writing process, you must be able to recognize the weaknesses, as well as the strengths, of your writing.

EVALUATING YOUR WRITING

1j. Evaluate your first draft.

Evaluating writing is the process of judging what works and what does not work. You are already evaluating when you make changes as you write a first draft. After you finish the draft, however, you must evaluate it as a whole, and this step requires distance: you examine the writing as if it were someone else's. You also judge the writing in its entirety: content, organization, and style. A thorough evaluation requires several rereadings of your first draft. By using different techniques, you can gain new insights from each review.

Techniques for Evaluating. To gain different perspectives on your draft, use the following techniques:

- Set your draft aside for awhile so that you are seeing it fresh.
- Read aloud, to "hear" what you have said. Listen for confusing statements, missing details, inappropriate language or tone.
- Have a classmate or someone else read your draft and comment on strengths and weaknesses. (Professional writers almost always have a friend or an editor who evaluates their writing.)

CRITICAL THINKING:
Evaluating Content, Organization, and Style

When you *evaluate,* you judge your writing on the basis of *criteria,* or standards, that can be grouped under three headings:

Content   What have you said?
Organization   How have you arranged your ideas?
Style   How have you used words and sentences?

The following Guidelines for Evaluating apply to almost any form of writing. With this checklist, you can identify problems in your draft and mark them for later revision.

GUIDELINES FOR EVALUATING

Content

Purpose
1. Do the paper's ideas and details support the primary purpose: to explain, describe, persuade, or tell a story?

Audience
2. Will the intended audience find the paper interesting? Does the paper contain adequate background information and explanations of terms?

Topic Development
3. Is the information sufficiently detailed for the audience's understanding? Is any information unnecessary?

Organization

Order
4. Is similar information presented together, or must the reader jump back and forth among ideas? Does the order of the information make the main idea clear?

Transitions
5. Are sentences smoothly joined by connecting words? Does one idea lead clearly to another, or does information seem to be missing?

Style

Tone
6. Does the choice of words and details effectively communicate the writer's attitude toward the topic? Does the paper sound serious enough, or light enough, for its purpose?

Sentence Structure
7. Do the sentences vary in length and structure to avoid monotony?

Word Choice
8. Are words precise and specific rather than general and vague? Is meaning clear rather than fuzzy? Are descriptive words vivid?

EXERCISE 19. Evaluating a First Draft. Read the following draft, intended for an audience of high-school students, and evaluate it using the guidelines on page 23. Number your paper as the guidelines are numbered, 1–8, and write *yes* if the guideline is met and *no* if it is not. Give at least one specific example from the paper to support each "no" answer.

Caves are dark, damp hollow places within the earth. Sometimes they are hollowed-out places in hillsides. Because no light can reach the inside of a cave and light is necessary for photosynthesis to take place, no plants grow inside of caves, and it is plants that we associate as a source of food for animals. You would expect that caves should be empty of animal life, but that is not true. Thousands of animal species live full-time in caves. They have a special name: troglodytes, or "cave dwellers." Many other species of animals live part-time in caves (bears, bats, some tropical birds), but this paper is about full-time cave-dwelling animals.

A cave isn't the easiest place in which to live, as you can probably imagine. It is dark all the time—*pitch* dark—because no light from the sun can enter the cave except at the cave entrance. There is also very little food in a cave—no plant food, as we have mentioned already. What little food there is must be "imported" from the outside. Usually, it comes into the cave from a stream or, if bats live in the cave, from droppings.

So why would any animal want to live in such a hostile environment? They do. One of the advantages to living in a cave, if you are a troglodyte, is that the weather poses no threat. Usually the temperature inside of a cave remains pretty much the same, unlike the surface world with its extremes of heat, cold, and storms. Life in a cave may be more peaceful than life on the surface, because there are usually fewer predators and less competition for the existing food supply. Some animals that require high humidity to breathe through their skins, like the salamander, are delighted by the high humidity inside of a cave; they never would make it in the outside world.

Troglodytes look different because of the adaptations they have made to living in total darkness. For one thing, most are blind or have no eyes at all and have lost the power to see because it has been unused for generations. Also, troglodytes are white because they have no pigment. Apparently, pigmentation has the purpose of protecting creatures from the effects of the sun. These cave-dwelling creatures have adapted to their environment in other ways. They have longer legs than their relatives on the surface, apparently to enable them to search more easily for food on the craggy surface of the cave walls. Also, their meatabolism rate is slower; this slower rate enables the cave-dwellers to get by with less food. They have adapted to their environment in one more way, too, in the way in which they reproduce. Compared to their surface relatives, they lay fewer eggs and the eggs are bigger. This means that the newborn creatures are bigger and more likely to survive in the challenging environment of the cave.

EXERCISE 20. **Evaluating a First Draft.** Using the Guidelines for Evaluating, evaluate your first draft from Exercise 18 or any other piece of writing. To write your evaluation, number your paper 1–8 and indicate whether each guideline was met. Explain why any guideline was not met. You may exchange papers with another student to evaluate one another's draft.

REVISING

When you evaluate your paper, you locate problems in your writing. When you revise, you find a specific way to correct each weakness in your paper.

REVISING YOUR FIRST DRAFT

1k. Revise your first draft.

Four basic revision techniques can correct most problems in writing: adding, cutting, replacing, and reordering.

> *Techniques for Revising.* To improve your evaluated draft, use the following techniques:
>
> - *Add:* add new information (ideas or details), sentences, or words
> - *Cut:* take out information, sentences, or words
> - *Replace:* take out information, sentences, or words and substitute something more relevant or appropriate
> - *Reorder:* move information, sentences, or words to another place in the paper

These four techniques can be used for problems in content (what you say about your topic), organization (how you arrange ideas about your topic), and style (how you use language to discuss your topic). Notice how one writer used these techniques to revise the following paragraphs. (See Revising and Proofreading Symbols on page 34.)

Topic:	The value of S.A.T. preparation courses
Purpose:	To inform
Audience:	Classmates and teacher

Many high-school ~~students~~ *seniors* enroll in S.A.T. prepara- — replace

tion courses. ~~They hope to improve~~ *in the hope of improving* their S.A.T. (Scho- — replace/reorder

lastic Aptitude Test) scores ~~that most colleges require as~~ *the second time around.* — reorder/replace

~~part of an entrance application.~~ Do these preparation — cut

courses ~~have any effect in improving~~ *actually improve* test scores? ~~Course~~ *Those who* — replace

~~givers~~ *give the courses* say "yes"; the Educational Testing Service, which — replace

administers the S.A.T.'s, says "not ~~really.~~ *much*." An indepen- *a recent* — cut/replace

dent study ~~recently released~~ analyzed a large number of *done at the University of Michigan's Center for Research* — add/replace

individual studies. *on Learning and Testing (and, statistically* The report concluded that "reason- — replace/cut

~~able gains could be made on S.A.T.'s through relatively~~ — cut

~~small amounts of coaching."~~ The average improvement — cut

after a coaching course is 15 points on the verbal section —

and 20 points on the mathematics section. ~~The word~~ — cut

~~average~~ infers that some students *of courses have* ~~may make~~ considerably — replace

higher *gains* ~~scores;~~ *others improved* some less. One ~~student,~~ *senior* Donna Sukenik of — replace

Shaker Heights, Ohio, ~~complains~~ *reported* that *she thought* ~~her verbal score~~ — replace

~~actually was lower after a coaching course.~~ *coaching courses* "I think they — replace/cut

can be very helpful in math, where ~~you can refresh your~~ *they help* — replace

~~memory about formulas and things like that,"~~ *students review formulas.* she said. — replace/cut

"But I needed help in verbal—and my verbal score went

down," *she complained* According to ~~the~~ *an* Educational Testing Service — add/reorder/replace

study, ~~it would take~~ 40 hours of class time and ~~a lot of~~ *S.A.T. preparation course many more* — cut/add/replace

~~extra~~ homework *hours of* *might help a student* *additional* to answer two or three questions cor- — replace/add

rectly in each section for an average gain of 13 points on *the* — add

verbal *section* and 21 points on *the section* math. — add

The following chart shows how the revision techniques (adding, cutting, replacing, and reordering) can be combined with the evaluation guidelines to solve writing problems. The other composition chapters contain charts that apply the four revision techniques to each specific form or type of writing.

REVISING A DRAFT		
PROBLEM	**TECHNIQUE**	**REVISION**
Content The ideas and details do not help to explain, describe, persuade, or tell the story.	Add/Cut	Add explanations, supporting arguments, descriptive details, or narrative details. Cut information unrelated to the purpose of the composition.
The reader will not be interested.	Add/Replace	Add interesting examples, anecdotes, dialogue, or more narrative details. Replace details unrelated to the audience's interests or background.
Unfamiliar terms are not explained.	Add/Replace	Add a definition or explanation to the composition. Replace any unfamiliar terms with more familiar ones.
The information is insufficient for the audience to understand the topic.	Add	Add details, facts, examples, etc., to support the topic.
Some information does not support the topic and may confuse or distract the reader.	Cut	Cut the information (sentences or parts of sentences) that does not relate directly to the topic and purpose.

PROBLEM	TECHNIQUE	REVISION
Organization The reader cannot follow the ideas.	Reorder	Check the order set in the informal plan. Move the draft's ideas or details to clarify meaning.
Connections between ideas are not clear.	Add	Add transitional words to link sentences: *this, when, then, first, in addition, as a result,* etc. Add missing information.
Style The tone is unsuitable for audience and purpose.	Replace	Create a lighter tone by replacing formal words with less formal ones (slang, contractions, etc.). Create a more serious tone by replacing slang and contractions with standard vocabulary.
The tone does not convey the writer's intended attitude.	Add/Replace	Add words or details consistent with the attitude (angry, approving, comic, etc.), or replace inconsistent ones.
The sentences are monotonous.	Add/Replace/ Reorder	Combine sentences by joining them with *and, but, for,* or *or;* by making one subordinate to another; or by making one a modifying phrase. Change word order to begin sentences in different ways.
The words are dull or vague. Meaning is not clear.	Replace	Replace general terms with precise, exact words. Replace uninteresting descriptions with vivid, sensory details.

EXERCISE 21. Revising a First Draft. Using the evaluation you completed for Exercise 19, revise the excerpted paragraphs. For each problem that you found, identify a technique to correct it (add, cut, reorder, or replace). Then make the necessary improvements, referring to the preceding revision chart.

EXAMPLE

Evaluation Unnecessary information is included.
  Technique Cut part of the sentence.
    Revision One of the advantages to living in a cave, if you are a troglodyte, is that the weather poses no threat.

REVIEW EXERCISE B. Revising a First Draft. Using the evaluation from Exercise 20, revise your first draft.

PROOFREADING

When you have finished revising, you turn to the next stage in the writing process, proofreading: finding and correcting errors in grammar, usage, and mechanics.

PROOFREADING YOUR WRITING

1I. Proofread your revised version.

Proofreading your own writing requires particularly keen attention. Some techniques will help you focus on this task.

> *Techniques for Proofreading.* To improve your accuracy in proofreading, use the following techniques:
>
> - Put your paper aside for a while. You will see errors more quickly.
> - Cover the lines below the one you are proofreading. You will not read ahead and pass over an error.
> - Read the paper twice: once sentence-by-sentence and once letter-by-letter. You will catch errors in usage and grammar as well as in mechanics.

CRITICAL THINKING:
Applying the Standards of Written English

The purpose of proofreading is to apply the standards of written English to your writing. These standards, summarized in the Guidelines for Proofreading that follow, are the rules generally used in books, magazines, and newspapers. Writers follow these standards to prevent readers from being confused because of inaccurate writing or distracted by mistakes.

GUIDELINES FOR PROOFREADING

1. Is every sentence complete? (pages 339–42)
2. Does every sentence end with a punctuation mark? Are all punctuation marks correct? (pages 637–78)
3. Does every sentence begin with a capital letter? Are all proper nouns and appropriate proper adjectives capitalized? (pages 620–36)
4. Does every verb agree in number with its subject? (pages 510–23)
5. Are verb forms and tenses correct? (pages 548–58)
6. Are subject and object forms of personal pronouns correct? (pages 530–43)
7. Does every pronoun agree with its antecedent in number and in gender? Are pronoun references clear? (pages 356–61, 523–26)
8. Are frequently confused words (such as *lie* and *lay, fewer* and *less*) used correctly? (pages 559–64, 597–615)
9. Are all words spelled correctly? (pages 679–96)
10. Is the paper neat and free from obvious crossed-out words and erasures? (pages 31–32)

EXERCISE 22. Applying the Standards of Written English. In each sentence, find and correct the error in grammar, usage, or mechanics. If you cannot correct an error, you may use other sections of this book for reference. Then make the correction.

1. One of the girls know the answer. (subject-verb agreement with indefinite pronouns)
2. Please give me the loaf of bread, that is on the bottom of the front row. (punctuating restrictive adjective clauses)
3. Between you and I, we've just run out of time. (using the objective case of pronouns for the object of a preposition)
4. Where did you put the tickets. (punctuating questions)

5. Whenever I don't get enough sleep or feel really tense and nervous. (sentence fragments)
6. I wish you wouldn't be so late, you know how I like to get to places on time. (run-ons)
7. The boat had sank to the bottom of the lake. (forming the past participles of irregular verbs)
8. She felt badly when she lost the tennis match. (using adjectives and adverbs correctly)
9. She had lain the box on the kitchen table, but it disappeared. (correct use of *lie* and *lay*)
10. Elaine goes to John F. Kennedy junior high school in North Miami Beach. (capitalizing names of specific buildings)

EXERCISE 23. Proofreading a Revised Draft.   Proofread the draft you revised for Review Exercise B or another revised paper. Use the preceding Guidelines for Proofreading and the Revising and Proofreading Symbols (page 34).

WRITING THE FINAL VERSION

CORRECT MANUSCRIPT FORM

The last step in the writing process is to prepare a final, clean copy of your revised and proofread paper. Although there is no single correct way to prepare a manuscript, the Guidelines for Correct Manuscript Form that follow are widely accepted standards. Your final recopying of the paper is also the time to correct common errors in abbreviations, number usage, and word divisions.

1m. Write the final version in correct manuscript form.

GUIDELINES FOR CORRECT MANUSCRIPT FORM

1. Use lined composition paper or, if you type, $8\frac{1}{2}$ x 11-inch white paper.
2. Write on only one side of the paper.
3. Write in blue or black ink, or typewrite using double-spacing.
4. Leave margins of about one inch at the top, sides, and the bottom of a page.

The left-hand margin must be straight; the right-hand margin should be as straight as possible.

5. Indent the first line of each paragraph about one-half inch.
6. Follow your teacher's instructions for placing your name, the class, the date, and the title on the manuscript.
7. Number all pages. Place the number in the upper right-hand corner, about one-half inch from the top.
8. Write legibly and neatly. If you are typing, do not strike over letters or cross out words. If you must erase, do it neatly.
9. Before handing in your final version, proofread it carefully to make certain that your recopying has been accurate.

Abbreviations

(1) Use only customary, accepted abbreviations.

In most writing, you should spell out words rather than abbreviate them. Some abbreviations, however, are acceptable.

The abbreviations *Mr., Mrs., Ms., Dr., Jr., Sr., Rev.,* and *St.* are used with names. Spell them out in other uses. The college degrees, *B.S., Ph.D.,* etc., may be used with or without a name.

EXAMPLES   I called **Dr.** Lee for the junior varsity player.
The pastor of **St.** John's Church is **Rev.** E. W. Miller, **Jr.,** who holds an **M.A.** in history as well as a **Ph.D.** in theology.

The abbreviations *A.D., B.C., A.M.,* and *P.M.* are acceptable when used with numbers (**30 B.C., A.D. 642, 1:30 P.M.**). Abbreviations for organizations are acceptable if they are generally known (**EPA, Y.W.C.A., UN**). Note that periods are usually omitted in abbreviations of governmental agencies.

Numbers

(2) Follow the rules for writing numbers.

The general rule for number usage is to spell out numbers that can be expressed in one or two words and to use numerals for others (**five million, $1.99, the forty-first yardline, 342, 1987**). Numbers in writing, however, do not easily conform to a single rule, and common usage requires several exceptions. A number beginning a sentence is spelled out. Days of the month and page numbers are written as numerals. A mixture of numbers—some one or two words, some longer—should all be written in the same way, either as words or as numerals. Statistical and technical writing generally expresses all measurements as numerals.

EXAMPLES **One hundred ninety** people died in the crash on **April 3** (either April 3 or the third of April, not April 3rd).

How could a team of **5** researchers discover what an association of **250** scientists could not?

In the experiment, **74 percent** of the subjects could not convert **3 liters** into a nonmetric measurement.

Hyphenation

(3) Divide words correctly at the ends of lines.

When you must divide a word at the end of a line, hyphenate it between syllables. Use the following general rules, but consult a dictionary if you are unsure of a word's syllables.

Do not divide a one-syllable word. Divide a word with double consonants between the consonants. Hyphenate words with prefixes and suffixes between the root and the prefix or suffix. In addition, avoid dividing words so that a single letter ends a line or only two letters begin a line. In these instances, a slightly uneven margin is preferable to an awkward hyphenation.

EXAMPLES   laughed (not laugh-ed); com-mitment; trans-mission; fall-ing (not fal-ling; *ing* is a suffix); evac-uate (not e-vacuate); acces-sory (not accesso-ry)

EXERCISE 24. Writing the Final Version.   Write the final version of the paper you proofread for Exercise 23. Follow the rules for correct manuscript form or your teacher's instructions. Be sure to proofread your recopying carefully.

CHAPTER 1 WRITING REVIEW

Applying the Writing Process.   Write a paragraph or brief composition on a topic of your choice. Complete each step of the prewriting stage. Then write a first draft, evaluate it, and revise it. Finally, proofread your final revision and recopy the paper in correct manuscript form.

REVISING AND PROOFREADING SYMBOLS

Symbol	Example	Meaning of Symbol
☰	Maple High school	Capitalize a lowercase letter.
/	the First person	Lowercase a capital letter.
∧	the first May *(of)*	Insert a missing word, letter, or punctuation mark.
∧	sep*a*rate	Change a letter.
⌐	*during* after the dance	Replace a word.
ℛ	Tell me the the plan	Leave out a word, letter, or punctuation mark.
ꙅ	an unus*g*ual idea	Leave out and close up.
⌒	a water fall	Close up space.
N	rec*ie*ve	Change the order of the letters.
(tr.)	the last Saturday of September (in the month)	Transfer the circled words. (Write (tr.) in nearby margin.)
¶	¶"Help!" someone cried	Begin a new paragraph.
⊙	Please don't go ⊙	Add a period.
⋀	Well what's new?	Add a comma.
#	bird#cage	Add a space.
(:)	the following ideas (:)	Add a colon.
⋀⋁	Houston, Texas; St. Louis, Missouri; and Albany, New York	Add a semicolon.
=	two teen=agers	Add a hyphen.
⋁	Sally's new job	Add an apostrophe.
(stet)	An extremely urgent message	Keep the crossed-out material. (Write (stet) in nearby margin.)

CHAPTER 2

Writing Paragraphs

STRUCTURE, DEVELOPMENT, PURPOSES

As a unit of thought, a paragraph may be complete in itself or part of a longer piece of writing. In this chapter you will review the structure of the paragraph and learn to apply the stages of the writing process to the paragraph form. You will also learn methods of developing paragraphs for different purposes.

THE STRUCTURE OF A PARAGRAPH

THE MAIN IDEA

2a. A paragraph is a series of sentences that presents and develops one main idea about a topic.

An effective paragraph introduces one main idea and develops it clearly by presenting additional, more specific information. The ideas are arranged in a logical order and smoothly connected. In the following paragraph the writer, a native American, develops one main idea by giving specific examples.

> **The widespread use of cloth brought on many new variations to women's dresses.** One popular style used a cape, decorated with beadwork and shells, which could be worn over any plain calico dress. Some capes were actually the

decorated remnants of worn-out cloth dresses. Some cloth dresses were decorated with buckskin additions that were fringed. Some dresses were made of velvet, with decorations of ribbons and metal sequins. The most valuable dresses had their tops covered with elk teeth or cowrie shells.

BEVERLY HUNGRY WOLF

THE TOPIC SENTENCE

2b. The topic sentence states the one main idea of a paragraph.

In most paragraphs, like the one above by Beverly Hungry Wolf, the main idea is expressed in a single sentence. This *topic sentence* controls the content of the other sentences by focusing on one particular aspect of the topic.

Often, the topic sentence is the first sentence of the paragraph. Placing the topic sentence at the beginning helps readers by giving them a clear idea of what is going to be discussed in the paragraph. Stating the main idea at the beginning also helps writers keep clearly in mind the main idea they are going to develop.

The topic sentence may appear elsewhere in the paragraph. In the following paragraph, for example, the writer concludes with a topic sentence that summarizes the details presented.

Convinced that he had identified "the African," about whom his grandmother had spoken, [Alex] Haley searched through shipping records in London and Annapolis to trace Kunta Kinte's arrival in America in 1767 and his sale to the Waller family of Spotsylvania County, Virginia. After that line was established, his job was largely a matter of working through census records to trace the family's migrations from Virginia to North Carolina and, after emancipation, to Tennessee. *Roots* **is Haley's account of his family, from Africa to America, from freedom to slavery and on to freedom again.**

DAVID HERBERT DONALD

The Implied Main Idea

In your reading you will find that not every paragraph has a topic sentence. In some paragraphs, particularly narrative and descriptive ones, the main idea is implied, or suggested, rather than stated directly. The details themselves answer the question "What happened?" or create a main impression or mood.

The main idea of the following paragraph describing Sylvia Beach, who was a patron of many writers during the 1920s, is implied rather than stated directly. What is the paragraph's main idea?

> When I first saw her, in the early spring of 1932, her hair was still the color of roasted chestnut shells, her light golden brown eyes with greenish glints in them were marvelously benign, acutely attentive, and they sparkled upon one rather than beamed, as gentle eyes are supposed to do. She was not pretty, never had been, never had tried to be; she was attractive, a center of interest, a delightful presence not accountable to any of the familiar attributes of charm. Her power was in the unconscious, natural radiation of her intense energy and concentration upon those beings and arts she loved.
>
> KATHERINE ANNE PORTER

The implied main idea of this paragraph is that Sylvia Beach's attractiveness had more to do with her intelligence and personality than with her appearance.

For most of the paragraphs you will write in this chapter, you will be asked to state your main idea in a topic sentence. Learning to write effective topic sentences provides valuable practice in determining your main idea and expressing it clearly.

Topic and Restriction Sentences

Sometimes two sentences work together to express the main idea of a paragraph. The first sentence introduces a general idea; the second one restricts or limits that idea by focusing on one particular aspect of it. These two sentences are called *topic and restriction sentences.*

> [TOPIC] **Crisp is a splendid word, blessed with a great etymological pedigree that runs parallel to its onomatopoeia: the word's sound helps evoke its meaning.** [RESTRICTION] **Crispy is an itsypooism.** It's O.K. to say *crunchy,* because the imitative noun, *crunch,* needs a *y* to turn it into an adjective, but *crisp* is an adjective that later was used by English potato-chip makers as a noun. One of the senses of *crisp* is *short;* surely this adjective needs no lengthening. Stick with *crisp;* resist itsypooisms.
>
> WILLIAM SAFIRE

SUPPORTING SENTENCES

2c. Other sentences in the paragraph provide specific information that supports the main idea.

The other sentences in the paragraph must give enough details to make the main idea clear. In general, three or more details (facts, examples, reasons, etc.) are needed to develop a main idea adequately.

The supporting sentences should present additional, more specific information, not just repeat the main idea in different words. Compare the following two versions of a paragraph.

WEAK **Every student can benefit from engaging in some extracurricular activity.** A student needs experience in such activities. No student should leave school every day when the final bell rings, having no definite interest to follow in after-school hours. Everyone can benefit from extracurricular work. No one should think of school as solely a place to study.

IMPROVED **Every student can benefit from engaging in some extracurricular activity.** Through extracurricular activities you learn to work and play harmoniously, to give and take, to win and lose. When, as a member of a club, you are given a job to do, you learn to assume responsibility and to work unselfishly for the good of the group. In a radio or photography club, you can acquire practical skills that may prove useful in the long run. Similarly, if you work hard in dramatics or in musical organizations, you will develop talents that will be satisfying to you all your life. Finally, extracurricular activities can broaden your perspective by expanding your circle of friends.

EXERCISE 1. Revising Weak Paragraphs. Each of the following paragraphs is weak because it does not contain enough information to develop the main idea clearly and specifically. Revise each paragraph, adding more supporting information. (You may need to do some research to find the information.) You may also revise the topic sentence.

1. Learning to handle a checking account is one of the uncelebrated milestones on the way to becoming an adult. It is important to pay bills promptly. You need to be able to figure out how much money is in the checking account. Bouncing checks is not good.
(*Hint:* Tell why it is important to pay bills promptly and what the disadvantages are of bouncing a check. Give other reasons that explain why handling a checking account is a sign of maturity.)

2. Psychologists and interior decorators know that colors can influence people's moods. Yellow is supposed to stimulate mental activity. Blue is restful and relaxing.
(*Hint:* Tell about other colors, and give more information about each color's effects.)

3. If you could watch every single television show broadcast, you would probably find that TV programs can be categorized. There is the situation comedy. There are dramas. There are soap operas and news or educational programs.

(*Hint:* Vary the sentence structure, and give examples or more specific information about each type of program. Consider whether there are other categories of TV programs, and if there are, mention them also.)

THE CLINCHER SENTENCE

2d. A paragraph may end with a clincher sentence.

A **clincher,** or **concluding, sentence** may restate the paragraph's main idea. It may also summarize the paragraph's main points, reveal an insight the writer has gained, or suggest a course of action. In the following paragraph, the writer restates the main idea expressed in the topic and restriction sentences.

> **The interpretation of words is a never-ending task for any citizen in modern society. We now have, as the result of modern means of communication, hundreds of thousands of words flung at us daily.** We are constantly being talked at, by teachers, preachers, salesmen, public officials, and moving-picture sound tracks. The cries of the hawkers of soft drinks, soap chips, and laxatives pursue us into our very homes, thanks to the radio —and in some houses the radio is never turned off from morning to night. Daily the newsboy brings us, in large cities, from thirty to fifty enormous pages of print, and almost three times that amount on Sundays. The mailman brings magazines and direct-mail advertising. We go out and get more words at bookstores and libraries. Billboards confront us on the highways, and we even take portable radios with us to the seashore. **Words fill our lives.**
>
> S. I. HAYAKAWA

Not every paragraph needs a clincher sentence. Avoid weak concluding sentences such as "Now you know why baseball is my favorite sport," and do not simply tack a clincher sentence on to a paragraph that is effective without it.

EXERCISE 2. Writing Clincher Sentences.   For each of the following paragraphs, try writing several different versions of a clincher sentence. Choose the version that you think is most effective.

1. If your vision needs correcting and you prefer not to wear eyeglasses, you can choose from at least four different types of contact lenses. Hard contacts, which are made of Plexiglas, are the oldest type and probably the least popular. The softer gas-permeable lenses allow oxygen to reach the eye, which makes them more comfortable to wear. Soft contact lenses are cellophane-thin, flexible, porous pieces of plastic. The latest development in contact lenses, extended-wear lenses, may be left in the eyes up to thirty days.

2. College students have many opportunities to participate in short-term overseas study programs. Organizations such as Experiment in International Living offer students a chance to attend seminars and travel around countries doing research and writing about their observations. Some organizations, such as the American-Scandinavian Foundation, sponsor overseas programs that enable students to work at a wide variety of jobs. Earthwatch, which sponsors museum work and anthropological research, matches interested students with research projects. Other overseas programs are sponsored by the Future Farmers of America, the President's International Youth Exchange Initiative, and the International Association for the Exchange of Students for Technical Experience.

THE DEVELOPMENT OF A PARAGRAPH

The writing process, with its many writing and thinking steps, can be used to develop a paragraph.

PREWRITING

CHOOSING AND LIMITING A SUBJECT

2e. Choose a subject and limit it to a topic that is suitable for a paragraph.

Although paragraphs vary in length, most are only about 150 to 200 words long. To find a topic that you can develop adequately in such a restricted space, you must limit a broad subject considerably. (See pages 9–11 for more on choosing and limiting subjects.)

EXERCISE 3. **Choosing and Limiting a Subject.** Choose one of the following subjects or another subject that interests you. Limit it to find at least three suitable topics for a paragraph, and choose one topic to write about.

1. Electronics
2. The American Revolution
3. Musical notation
4. The Super Bowl
5. Pollution

CONSIDERING PURPOSE, AUDIENCE, AND TONE

2f. Determine your purpose for writing, identify your audience, and consider your attitude toward your topic.

A paragraph may contain elements of more than one of the four basic types of writing (exposition, persuasion, narration, and description). Usually, however, a writer has one main purpose. An expository paragraph may include an incident, for example, but its primary purpose is to inform or to explain. Determining what your primary purpose is helps you gather appropriate details and select an effective pattern of organization.

Considering the needs and interests of your audience also helps you plan your paragraph. Although you cannot predict precisely how your readers will respond to your writing, you can adapt your writing to their reading and comprehension skills. For example, if you are aware of the specific backgrounds and interests of your audience, you are able to select language and examples or details that the audience will understand and appreciate. When you know your readers, you know what terms you should define, and you know what they will find offensive or pleasing.

Considering your attitude, or point of view, toward your topic is also important as you plan your paragraph. This attitude is expressed in the tone of your writing and is conveyed through the language and details you choose to write about your topic. The tone of a paragraph, as with other writing, can be serious or humorous, positive or negative, formal or informal.

(Review the information on pages 4–9 and 11–12 on how purpose, audience, and tone affect writing.)

Techniques for Prewriting. To consider how your purpose, your audience, and your attitude toward your topic will affect your writing, ask yourself:

- Is my primary purpose to explain or to inform, to persuade, to tell a story, or to describe?
- What topic will most interest my audience?
- What background information will they need to understand my ideas? What language will best convey my ideas to this audience?
- What is my attitude toward my topic, and how will I express this through the tone of my writing?

EXERCISE 4. Identifying Purpose, Audience, and Tone. Bring to class three paragraphs from newspapers or magazines. Be prepared to identify the primary purpose, the intended audience, and the tone of each paragraph.

GATHERING INFORMATION

2g. Gather information on your limited topic.

Use one or more of the information-gathering techniques (see pages 12–18) to collect details on your topic. Be sure to take detailed notes, and remember to keep your audience and purpose in mind.

EXERCISE 5. Gathering Information. Gather information on the topic you chose for Exercise 3 or on another suitably limited topic. Save your paper for later use.

DEVELOPING A PARAGRAPH PLAN

2h. Develop a paragraph plan: write a topic sentence; select supporting details and arrange them in a logical order.

Writing Effective Topic Sentences

An effective topic sentence meets the following three requirements:

(1) A topic sentence should be neither too limited nor too broad.

The main idea in a topic sentence must be one that can be developed by the other sentences in the paragraph. For this reason, a single fact is usually too limited to serve as a topic sentence. On the other hand, a statement that cannot be developed clearly and precisely in a single paragraph is too broad for a topic sentence.

TOO LIMITED Milk is a good source of Vitamin D.

TOO BROAD Vitamins are good for you.

SUITABLE Vitamin D, one of the vitamins essential for healthy bones, can be found in many foods.

(2) A topic sentence should state the paragraph's main idea precisely.

An effective topic sentence is neither vague nor wordy. Replace vague words with precise ones, and eliminate unnecessary phrases such as "This paragraph is about. . . ."

VAGUE There are some new devices to help deaf people.

WORDY A new device recently invented helps hearing-impaired people to "hear" when they are using the telephone because the telephone tones are changed from tones to print that they can read.

PRECISE A new device for hearing-impaired persons converts a telephone's touch tones into printed messages.

VAGUE Some people are really annoying.

WORDY I am going to talk about those annoying people who always like to give advice on what should have been done or what might have been done long *after* something has already happened.

PRECISE A "Monday-morning quarterback" is someone who criticizes others' decisions about past events.

(3) A topic sentence should arouse the reader's interest.

Try to catch the attention of the reader by including a vivid detail or by addressing the reader directly.

WEAK Money can be many things.

IMPROVED A remarkable variety of items other than bills and coins—from stones to dried fish—have served as money.

WEAK Everybody should know how to do the Heimlich maneuver.

IMPROVED If you have ever choked on a piece of food, you have some idea of how important the Heimlich maneuver can be.

Techniques for Prewriting. To evaluate your topic sentence, ask yourself:

- Is it neither too broad nor too limited?
- Does it express my main idea directly and precisely?
- Will it catch the interest of my audience?

EXERCISE 6. Revising Topic Sentences.   Revise each of the following topic sentences, adding any information you need to make it more effective.

1. Some people work too hard.
2. I'd like to tell you something about what it was like, according to my grandmother, growing up in the days before television.
3. An hourglass measures time.
4. Most birds fly, but not the ostrich.
5. There are four basic blood types: A, B, AB, and O.
6. I'm going to tell you some interesting information about penguins.
7. The human ear is very complicated.
8. A great many people are extremely afraid of every snake that they ever see, but everyone should be made aware of the fact that most snakes are beneficial to people.
9. Have you ever tried to use a potter's wheel?
10. The sitar is a stringed instrument of India.

EXERCISE 7. Writing Topic Sentences.   For each of the following lists of details, write an effective topic sentence. You will not necessarily use all of the details in a paragraph.

1. *Details:*
   a. Israeli scientists using inexpensive technique for measuring air pollution
   b. Using vegetable plants sensitive to different kinds of air pollution
   c. Alfalfa plants sensitive to sulfur dioxide
   d. Eggplant sensitive to ozone and nitrates
   e. Tomato, lettuce, and cucumber plants measuring amounts of nitrates in the air
   f. Research scientists at Technion Institute in Haifa and Hebrew University in Jerusalem
   g. Damage to plants grown at various distances from industrial sites reflects relative air quality

2. *Details:*
   a. Survey results: less leisure time for Americans in 1983 than in 1973
   b. Average leisure time per week 26.2 hours in 1973, 18.1 hours in 1983
   c. Average work week 47.3 hours in 1983, 40.6 hours in 1973
   d. Leisure time activities: watching TV, attending sports events, exercising, eating out, attending concerts and movies
   e. Women average 23 percent less leisure time per week than men: women 15.6 hours, men 20.3

3. *Details:*
   a. Vitamin D necessary for body to absorb calcium and to maintain strong, healthy bones
   b. Vitamin D in skin activated by exposure to sunlight; approximately 15 minutes in midsummer for young, light-skinned people; more time for elderly or dark-skinned people and for people using sunscreens
   c. Increased need for Vitamin D during winter, when sunlight weaker and less time spent outdoors
   d. Doctors suggest that people, especially elderly persons, get outside during winter for half-hour walk or "sunbath"
   e. Recent discovery that some types of depression triggered by lack of sunlight in winter

Selecting and Arranging Details

Analyze the information you have gathered, making sure that each detail is directly related to your main idea as you have stated it in your topic sentence. Remove any details that do not support your main idea, and arrange the remaining material in a logical order (see pages 48–54).

Techniques for Prewriting. To determine whether a detail is directly related to your main idea, ask yourself:

- Does the detail provide strong support for my main idea?
- Will it help my audience understand the main idea rather than confuse or distract them?
- How does the detail function within the paragraph—is it a fact? An example? A reason? A concrete or sensory detail?

REVIEW EXERCISE A. **Developing a Paragraph Plan.** Write a topic sentence for the limited topic on which you gathered information for Exercise 5. Then decide which details most effectively support your main idea, and arrange them in a logical order. Save your paper.

WRITING

UNITY

2i. Every sentence in a paragraph should be directly related to the main idea.

A *unified* paragraph is one in which all of the sentences are directly related to the main idea as it is stated in the topic sentence. Any sentences that do not help develop that idea should be removed. As you read the following paragraph, identify the two sentences that destroy its unity.

> Because in most cities and towns all the water we need gushes forth at the mere touch of a faucet and because water is cheap, we Americans use it lavishly. New York City alone consumes one and a half billion gallons a day. Every day each of us uses about eighty-three gallons: twenty-four for flushing; thirty-two for bathing, laundry, and dishwashing; twenty-five for other uses, such as swimming pools, watering lawns, etc.; and the mere two gallons we use for drinking and cooking. These figures are surprising enough, but they do not cover the much greater daily consumption of water in agriculture and industry. In 75 percent of the world, cities and towns lack any municipal supply of pure water. Citizens are forced to draw water from wells and streams, which are often contaminated. These facts about our consumption of water should make us wonder how long our supply will last if we continue to drain it so recklessly.

EXERCISE 8. **Identifying Sentences That Destroy Unity.** Identify the sentence(s) not directly related to the main idea in each of the following paragraphs. Copy them onto your paper, and be ready to explain how they destroy the paragraph's unity.

1. **A dishonest newspaper may warp the day's news either by hiding a story or by slanting headlines.** A paper with a strong political bias may hide a story favorable to the opposing party by placing it in an inconspicuous

position. On the other hand, it may give large headlines and a front-page position to news favorable to its own party. Newspapers may also change the total effect of a story by giving it a headline that is deliberately misleading or slanted. Headline writing is highly demanding work. Once considered the drudges of the newspaper office, headline writers have in recent years been accorded greater respect, as reflected in shorter hours and higher pay. MAYOR JONES CRACKS DOWN ON CRITICS, for example, gives quite a different impression from MAYOR JONES REPLIES TO CRITICS.

2. **The popularity of first names changes, with certain names in fashion for a generation or so.** For example, in 1928 the ten top names for girls were Mary, Marie, Anne, Margaret, Catherine, Gloria, Helen, Teresa, Jean, and Barbara. None of these names made the top-ten list for girls in 1983. That year the ten most popular girls' names were Jennifer, Jessica, Melissa, Nicole, Stephanie, Christina, Tiffany, Michelle, Elizabeth, and Lauren. Unusual-sounding names can cause problems for children. One California lawyer, for example, named his son Shelter because he wanted him to have a unique first name. The most popular boys' names have changed also. John, William, Joseph, James, Richard, Edward, Robert, Thomas, George, and Louis were the most popular boys' names in 1928. In 1983, however, the ten top boys' names were Michael, Christopher, Jason, David, Daniel, Anthony, Joseph, John, Robert, and Jonathan.

3. **Seminole Indians in Florida are pursuing a new venture to reduce the 47 percent unemployment rate on the Big Cypress reservation deep in the Everglades.** With the help of an electronics company, thirteen Seminoles are receiving training in electronics in preparation for the opening of Seminole Electronics, Inc., on the reservation, which is thirty to forty miles from the nearest town. Typical of the trainees is Josephine North, 31. North, until recently a part-time artist, will earn about $7.00 an hour as an employee of Seminole Electronics, Inc. The Seminoles are a 1,600-member tribe governed by a five-member tribal council. In the early eighteenth century, the Seminoles separated themselves (the name *Seminole* actually means "separatist") from the Creek Indians and later fled to Florida to escape capture by U.S. troops. The training program, funded by a government grant, is being supervised by Pocon, Inc., an electronics company in Pompano Beach.

COHERENCE

2j. The ideas in a paragraph should be arranged in a logical order and clearly connected.

A *coherent* paragraph is one in which the ideas flow smoothly from one sentence to the next, and the relationships between the ideas are clear. One way to achieve coherence is to arrange the ideas in a logical order. A second way is to provide clear transitions between the ideas.

Logical Order

Five ways to arrange the ideas in a paragraph are in chronological order, in spatial order, in order of importance, in an order that reveals comparison or contrast, and in an order that reveals an analogy.

Chronological Order

(1) Ideas may be arranged in chronological order.

Chronological order is used in narrative paragraphs to relate a series of events. In expository paragraphs it is used to explain the steps in a process. The following paragraph, for example, explains a simple process: an experiment to prove that sound waves travel through air. Each step in the experiment is described in the order in which it must be done.

> Light a candle. Put a tin can on its side with the open end of the can about two inches from the lighted candle. The flame should be near the center of the open end of the can. Hold the can firmly and tap it hard on the bottom. Notice what happens to the flame each time the bottom of the can is struck. The bottom of the can vibrates and sets the air in the can to vibrating. The vibrating air causes the flame to flicker or go out.
>
> ILLA PODENDORF

EXERCISE 9. Writing a Paragraph Using Chronological Order. Using the following information, write a paragraph in which the ideas are arranged in chronological order. You may combine or reword the sentences in any way you choose.

Topic sentence: The night of the Great Blackout turned out to be a lot of fun for our family.

a. We were all home by 7:00 P.M., when the power went off.
b. Dad had driven home from the plant by 6:00 P.M., and Mom had just come in from work when the lights went out.
c. We cooked hamburgers on a charcoal grill outdoors and made a big salad for dinner.

d. Since the telephones weren't working either, the house was quiet.
e. Jim found a transistor radio, and we listened to the news of the blackout.
f. People were trapped for hours in elevators and crowded subways; we were lucky to be home.
g. After dinner all five of us played a long game of Scrabble.
h. By 10:00 P.M. all of us were sitting around the fireplace telling funny stories about things we did when we were little.
i. The first thing we did was scramble to find candles and flashlights.
j. During the game, Dad and Jim got a fire going in the fireplace.

EXERCISE 10. Writing a Paragraph Explaining a Process. Write a paragraph telling how to do one of the following processes or a process of your own. Choose a process familiar to you, one which can be explained in a single paragraph. Give all the steps in the process in their correct order, and include any necessary equipment or supplies in your explanation. Define any terms unfamiliar to your audience.

1. How to study for a final exam
2. How to ask someone for a date
3. How to fly a kite (or a paper airplane)
4. How to hit a home run
5. How to see a movie

Spatial Order

(2) Ideas may be arranged in spatial order.

Descriptive writing usually uses *spatial order,* which shows where items are in relation to one another. The writer directs the reader's attention from one part of the scene to the next in an orderly, consistent way. In describing the Van Tassel farmhouse, for example, Washington Irving presents the house as a visitor would see it. Notice how the boldfaced transitional expressions clarify the positions of the objects.

It was one of those spacious farmhouses with high-ridged but low-sloping roofs, built in the style handed down from the first Dutch settlers, the low projecting eaves forming a piazza **along the front** capable of being closed up in bad weather. **Under this** were hung flails, harness, various utensils of husbandry, and nets for fishing in the neighboring river. Benches were built **along the sides** for summer use, and a great spinningwheel **at one end** and a churn **at the other** showed the various uses to which this important porch might be devoted. **From this piazza** the wondering Ichabod entered the hall, which formed the center of the mansion and the place of usual residence. **Here** rows of resplendent pewter, ranged **on a long dresser,** dazzled his eyes. **In one corner** stood a huge bag of wool ready to be spun; **in another** a quantity of linsey-woolsey just from the loom; ears of Indian corn and strings of dried apples and peaches hung in gay festoons **along the walls,** mingled with the gaud of red peppers; and a door left ajar gave him a peep **into the best parlor, where** the clawfooted chairs and dark mahogany tables shone like mirrors; andirons, with their accompanying shovel and tongs, glistened **from their covert of asparagus tops;** mock-oranges and conch-shells decorated the mantelpiece; strings of various colored birds' eggs were suspended **above it;** a great ostrich egg was hung **from the center of the room,** and a corner cupboard, knowingly left open, displayed immense treasures of old silver and well-mended china.

WASHINGTON IRVING

EXERCISE 11. Writing a Paragraph Using Spatial Order. Using the following information, write a paragraph in which the details are arranged in spatial order. You may add specific information (colors, types, etc.) and combine or reword sentences in any way you choose.

a. Small table beside the bed—clock radio, pile of magazines, box of tissues, red metal lamp
b. Bed against the wall—blue bedspread, newspaper and jacket on bed
c. Socks on floor; dirty laundry overflowing from wicker hamper
d. Three posters on the wall
e. Concert ticket stubs on dark cork bulletin board
f. Desk covered with books, papers, dirty clothes
g. Blue director's chair
h. Wooden dresser; trophies and books on shelves above dresser
i. Stereo and two speakers; record collection in orange-crate
j. Collection of caps and hats

Order of Importance

(3) Ideas may be arranged in order of importance.

Using order of importance in an expository or persuasive paragraph enables you to emphasize those reasons that provide stronger support for your main idea. Usually, the reasons are arranged with the most important one placed last, where it will linger in the reader's mind. When one reason is far more important than the others, however, the writer may begin with it. In the following paragraph, the actress Helen Hayes gives three reasons to explain why elderly people should write an autobiography. Identify the three reasons and the order in which she has arranged them.

> I also like to see older folks write an "autobiography." Writing is very therapeutic. In fact, experts say it promotes self esteem and personal integration. Personally, I think it also clears away the cobwebs and stimulates a fresh way of thinking and looking back at your life. Most important, perhaps, it leaves a private history of yourself and your family. Don't you wish your grandmother and her grandmother before her had done that?
>
> HELEN HAYES

EXERCISE 12. Writing a Paragraph Using Order of Importance. Choose one of the following topic sentences (*should* or *should not*). Then decide which of the reasons given support that topic sentence, list them in order from least important to most important, and write a paragraph. You may add information and combine or reword sentences in any way you choose.

Topic sentence: Employees (should, should not) be required to retire at seventy.

Reasons:
a. People who have been working all of their lives deserve to spend the last years of their lives relaxing.
b. Some people over seventy no longer have the necessary physical stamina.
c. People who work past seventy are taking jobs away from younger workers.
d. People over seventy have valuable experience unmatched by that of younger workers.
e. People who are willing and able to work past seventy should have the freedom to do so.
f. Many people over seventy need to earn money to survive.
g. People who derive their only satisfaction from their work feel unwanted when they retire.
h. Some people over seventy no longer have the necessary mental alertness.
i. People who develop outside interests earlier in life keep busy after they retire.

Comparison and Contrast

(4) Ideas may be arranged in an order that reveals comparison or contrast.

A *comparison* shows how two or more aspects of a topic are alike; a *contrast* shows how they are different. These patterns of organization may appear in any of the four types of writing. Facts, incidents, sensory or concrete details, and examples may be used to point out similarities or differences between two topics.

A paragraph of comparison or contrast may be arranged according to the *block method,* in which all of the ideas about one aspect of the topic are presented first, followed by all of the ideas about the next aspect of the topic. The following paragraph uses the block method.

If you travel over regions where the buildings were made in earlier times, you will notice great differences from North to South. In the North the roofs are steep to shed the snow, the windows small to keep out the cold, the building materials often easily worked soft woods provided by the abundant nearby forests. The ceilings are low to conserve heat, the chimneys numerous or large, the doors and windows arranged to baffle chilling drafts, and the hearth is the focus of the dwelling. As you move south, the roofs flatten, the windows grow larger, the ceilings rise, so that houses on the steamy James River, in Virginia, for example, have very high ceilings and also a through hall to permit easy cooling of the rooms. As you near the tropics, the woods become harder to work and more vulnerable to dampness and insects. The roofs may get still flatter unless the rainfall is torrential, in which case they steepen again as in Celebes. The patio usually replaces the hearth, and the walls of adobe or stone become thicker in order to preserve coolness; now the windows are small and deeply recessed to keep the hot sun from penetrating the interiors. All these practical arrangements were worked out empirically long ago.

topic sentence

buildings in the North

buildings farther south

buildings in the tropics

JOHN BURCHARD

The ideas in a paragraph of comparison or contrast may instead follow the *alternating,* or *point-by-point, method,* in which each feature of the topic is discussed one at a time, as in the following paragraph. The boldfaced transitional expressions signal the introduction of a new point.

In several respects, living in an apartment building is easier than living in a house. **For one thing,** there is no outside work to do in an apartment building. Apartment dwellers can forget those chores that keep homeowners busy, like mowing the lawn and repairing the porch. A **second advantage** to living in an apartment building is that the responsibility for maintenance falls on the building superintendent, not on the occupants. When a sink is stopped up or a short develops in an electrical circuit, homeowners must either solve the problem themselves or pay a plumber or an electrician. **Finally,** since an apartment is usually smaller and has fewer rooms, it is easier to clean than a house.

contrast 1

contrast 2

contrast 3

EXERCISE 13. Writing Paragraphs of Comparison or Contrast.
Select two of the following numbered items or two other sets of topics. Write two paragraphs, one of comparison and the other of contrast. Use the block method for one paragraph and the point-by-point method for the other one.

1. A novel you have read and its movie or television version
2. Two types of cooking
3. Two heroes (or heroines) in a novel or movie
4. Going to the dentist and going to the doctor
5. Getting ready for a job interview and getting ready for a date

Analogy

(5) Ideas may be arranged in an order that reveals an analogy.

An *analogy* is an extended comparison, one that draws parallels between two basically dissimilar topics. It explores the nature of an unfamiliar topic by relating it to another, more familiar topic. In the following paragraph, for example, Eudora Welty discusses the points of correspondence between her fiction and the family trips of her childhood.

> I think now, in looking back on these summer trips—this one and a number later, made in the car and on the train—that another element in them must have been influencing my mind. The trips were wholes unto themselves. They were stories. Not only in form, but in their taking on direction, movement, development, change. They changed something in my life: each trip made its particular revelation, though I could not have found words for it. But with the passage of time, I could look back on them and see them bringing me news, discoveries, premonitions, promises—I still can; they still do. When I did begin to write, the short story was a shape that had already formed itself and stood waiting in the back of my mind. Nor is it surprising to me that when I made my first attempt at a novel, I entered its world—that of the mysterious Yazoo-Mississippi Delta—as a child riding there on a train: "From the warm windowsill the endless fields glowed like a hearth in firelight, and Laura, looking out, leaning on her elbows with her head between her hands, felt what an arriver in a land feels—that slow hard pounding in the breast."
>
> EUDORA WELTY

An effective analogy is neither self-evident nor strained. It is more effective to elaborate on only a few points of correspondence than to try to draw parallels where none exist.

EXERCISE 14. Writing a Paragraph of Analogy. Write a paragraph of analogy using one of the following topics or one of your own.

1. Friends
2. Writing
3. Dreams
4. The future
5. Homes

REVIEW EXERCISE B. Choosing a Logical Order for Arranging Ideas. For each of the following topics, tell which kind of order you would use: chronological, spatial, order of importance, comparison and contrast, or analogy. (For some topics, more than one order is possible.) Be prepared to discuss your choices.

1. Why people should eat a balanced diet
2. An accident that you were involved in
3. A savings account and a checking account
4. Advertisements on television and advertisements in print media (newspapers and magazines)

5. The place where you would most like to live
6. Important safety tips for automobile drivers (or for pedestrians or for bicyclists)
7. Your earliest memory
8. Why people watch horror movies
9. A promise that was broken
10. Your room

Relationships Between Ideas

Direct references and transitional expressions clarify how ideas within and between sentences are related.

Direct References

(6) Connect ideas in a paragraph with pronouns, synonyms, or repeated words and phrases.

Direct references weave sentences together by reminding the reader of ideas mentioned earlier. These references may be pronouns, synonyms, or repeated words and phrases.

As you read the following paragraph, notice how the direct references (in boldfaced type) help the writer develop the main idea by *adding* specific information, not just repeating the same idea in different words.

> One final effect of radio and TV on the language must be noted. There is no doubt that **these great media of information** have cut down considerably the time that used to be devoted to reading, both of newspapers and of books. **This** means in turn that while **radio and TV** may enhance the **spoken language** (if indeed **they** do), **they** also tend to make of us a nation of functional illiterates, absorbing our **language** through the ear rather than the eye. Some may view **this** as a return to **language** in **its** original form and function; others may consider **it** a reversal, pure and simple, to the semi-**literate** Middle Ages.
>
> MARIO PEI

Transitional Expressions

(7) Keep the thought of a paragraph flowing smoothly from sentence to sentence by using transitional expressions.

Transitional expressions (sometimes called *linking expressions* or *connectives*) are words and phrases that indicate the relationships between ideas. Notice in the following paragraph how the boldfaced transitional expressions tie the ideas together and help make the writer's line of thought easy to follow.

> Much is said and written about the number of deer reputedly slaughtered by wolves. Very little is said about the actual numbers of wolves slaughtered by men. **In one case** a general falsehood is widely and officially disseminated; **in the other** the truth seems to be suppressed. **Yet** one trapper operating along the boundary between Manitoba and Keewatin, in the winter of the first year of my study, collected bounty on a hundred and eighteen wolves of which one hundred and seven were young ones born the previous spring. According to law he should have killed those wolves by trapping or shooting them. **In fact** he did what everyone else was doing —and still does in the Far North, with the covert permission of Governments: he spread strychnine so indiscriminately over an immense area that almost the entire population of foxes, wolverines, and many lesser flesh-eaters was wiped out. That did not matter **since** foxes fetched no price that year. Wolves were worth twenty dollars each for bounty.
>
> FARLEY MOWAT

Transitional expressions can be grouped according to the kind of relationship they indicate.

Transitional Expressions

To link similar ideas or add an idea

again	equally important	likewise
also	further	moreover
and	furthermore	similarly
another	in addition	then
besides	in the same way	too

To limit or contradict an idea

although	however	on the contrary
and yet	in spite of	on the other hand
but	instead	otherwise
conversely	nevertheless	still
even if	nor	yet

To indicate cause, purpose, or result

as	for	so
as a result	for this reason	then
because	hence	therefore
consequently	since	thus

To indicate time or position

above	beyond	nearby
across	eventually	next
afterward	finally	now
around	first (second, etc.)	opposite to
at once	here	thereafter
before	meanwhile	thereupon

To indicate an example, a summary, or a conclusion

as a result	in any event	in short
consequently	in brief	on the whole
for example	in conclusion	therefore
for instance	in fact	thus
in any case	in other words	to sum up

REVIEW EXERCISE C. Analyzing a Paragraph for Coherence.
In the following paragraph, identify the direct references and transitional expressions that give the paragraph coherence. Be prepared to discuss your answers in class.

A crow's morning greeting is something that has to be experienced to be believed. I don't know whether it corresponds to some timeless ritual of the species, but it was always the same, and it was so strikingly, so emphatically a demonstration of pleasure at seeing us, that today, still, decades later, I smile inwardly when I think of it. I see him again, standing on the windowsill, the blue-black of his feathers glistening in the soft morning light, beginning to bow. With slow dignity he lowered his head, and the bluish eyelids came down over his bright little eyes. At the same time he spread his wings out and down, fanlike, until the long feathers touched the windowsill. When he was fully into his *revérence,* he cooed in a gentle burble that was more like dove than crow. Two or three coos like this, raising and lowering the head with each one, and then it was time to get down to business again: inspection of the room, shoplifting, grabbing bits of food, disciplining us with a sharp blow of his beak if we got in his way.

RUDOLPH CHELMINSKI

WRITING A FIRST DRAFT

2k. Write the first draft of your paragraph.

In shaping your ideas into your first draft, write freely, keeping in mind your purpose and audience. Remember that you will have time later to review and improve your writing.

Techniques for Writing. In drafting your paragraph,

- use your paragraph plan as a guide.
- keep your purpose and audience in mind.
- write freely, expressing your ideas as clearly as possible.
- add related details as you think of them.
- choose language that reflects the appropriate tone.

EXERCISE 15. Writing a First Draft. Using the paragraph plan you prepared for Review Exercise A (page 46), write the first draft of your paragraph.

EVALUATING

EVALUATING YOUR PARAGRAPH

2l. Evaluate the content, organization, and style of your draft.

As you evaluate your draft, use the following general guidelines. You will find guidelines for evaluating specific types of paragraphs in the section "Four Types of Paragraphs" on pages 64–84.

GUIDELINES FOR EVALUATING PARAGRAPHS

Main Idea	1. Is one main idea about a suitably limited topic either stated directly in a topic sentence or clearly implied?
Topic Development	2. Is enough specific information provided to develop the main idea clearly and precisely?
Unity	3. Is every sentence directly related to the main idea?
Concluding Sentence	4. Does the clincher sentence, if there is one, provide a strong conclusion for the paragraph?
Order of Ideas	5. Are the ideas arranged in a logical order that is appropriate for the purpose?
Relationships Between Ideas	6. Do the ideas flow smoothly from one sentence to the next? Are direct references and appropriate transitional expressions used to link the ideas?

Word Choice	7. Is the language specific and vivid? Is it appropriate for the audience? Are technical terms and difficult words defined or explained?
Sentence Variety	8. Are the sentences appropriately varied in structure and length?
Tone	9. Is the tone suitable for the purpose and the audience? Is it consistent?

EXERCISE 16. Evaluating a First Draft. Use the guidelines above to evaluate the following first draft. Answer each question from the guidelines, in writing, keying your answers to the numbers of the guidelines. Save your paper.

> Restaurant work, the kind of work teen-agers can get at a summer resort, has some good things going for it. It doesn't pay very much, though. If you work the evening shift, you can goof off all day. You can make lots of friends, in addition. And you get free food and a place to stay. Sharing a room is not my idea of fun, but my cousin Ramona met her future sister-in-law when she shared a room with her the summer they worked in the Poconos. In conclusion, it has certain advantages. And it gets you away from home.

EXERCISE 17. Evaluating Your Paragraph. Using the guidelines above, evaluate the draft you wrote for Exercise 15. You may also want to use the appropriate guidelines from the section "Four Types of Paragraphs" (pages 64–84). Save your paper for later use in this chapter.

REVISING

REVISING YOUR PARAGRAPH

2m. Revise your first draft.

Once you have identified which aspects of your paragraph need to be improved, you can use four basic techniques to revise your writing: *adding, cutting, reordering,* and *replacing.* The chart on the following page shows how these four revising techniques can be applied to the paragraph form.

REVISING PARAGRAPHS

PROBLEM	TECHNIQUE	REVISION
The main idea is not clear.	Add/Replace	Add a topic sentence. Add or replace details that imply the main idea.
The topic sentence is too broad.	Cut/Add	Remove words, phrases, or clauses that do not focus on one main idea. Add words, phrases, or clauses that qualify, and thus restrict, the topic sentence.
The topic sentence is too narrow.	Add	Add words, a phrase, or a clause that expands the scope of the main idea.
The topic sentence is dull.	Add/Replace	Add vivid details. Add an unusual comparison or a startling fact. Replace general words with specific ones. Address the audience directly.
One or more sentences do not directly relate to the main idea.	Cut	Remove the sentence(s).
The main idea is not developed.	Add/Replace	Add facts, statistics, examples, causes, effects, reasons, concrete or sensory details, or an incident. Replace vague statements with precise ones.
The paragraph trails off or ends abruptly.	Add	Add a clincher sentence: restate the main idea, summarize the information, emphasize an important point, or suggest a course of action.

PROBLEM	TECHNIQUE	REVISION
The ideas are not easy to follow.	Reorder	Rearrange the ideas in a logical order that the reader can follow easily.
The ideas do not flow smoothly.	Add/Replace	Add direct references and transitional expressions. Substitute more appropriate transitional expressions to connect ideas.
The language is dull.	Add/Replace	Add vivid nouns, verbs, adjectives, and adverbs. Replace general words with specific ones.
The language is too difficult.	Add/Replace	Add definitions and explanations. Substitute easier words and shorter, simpler sentences.
The sentences are monotonous.	Add/Replace	Combine sentences. Vary sentence beginnings. Vary sentence length.
The tone is inappropriate or inconsistent.	Replace	Substitute more formal/informal, humorous/serious, etc., terms.

The following example shows the changes one writer made in revising a first draft.

~~Many people concerned with education~~ are begin-   replace
Educators

ning to ~~think about~~ whether ~~or not~~ computers are   replace/cut
question

being used ~~right~~ in the schools. In high schools,   replace
properly

computer literacy courses take up 64% of students'

time according to a recent study. ~~They~~ spend another   add/replace
of 1,082 schools made at Johns Hopkins University. Students

of their computer time

18% in drill and practice. Another 6% in recreational   add/replace

games. Many teachers complain that drill and practice on   add

the computer, for most students, is a waste of time. The   reorder

computer is nothing more than a workbook page, and it   cut/replace

is cheaper and easier to use a workbook. One way in   replace

which computers are being used well is in word process-

ing, teaching students how to write and revise their   replace

writing on the computer. And teachers of learning dis-   cut

abled and handicapped students are crazy about the   replace

computer. But computer programs do not utilize the   replace

computer's unique powers except rarely. In one software   cut

program, students can dissect a frog and then put it back   replace/add

together again. When the parts are put back in the right   replace

place, the frog jumps up and off the screen. Another   replace/add/cut

teacher uses a computer hooked up to a piano to teach   replace

students to compose their own music.   cut

    add

EXERCISE 18. Revising a First Draft. Using your answers for Exercise 16, revise the first draft in that exercise. First, copy the paragraph as it is printed; then use the chart above to improve it by adding, cutting, reordering and replacing. Copy the revised paragraph on a separate sheet of paper.

REVIEW EXERCISE D. Revising Your Paragraph. Using your answers for Exercise 17 and the Revising Chart on pages 60–61, revise the draft of the paragraph you wrote for Exercise 15. Save your paper for later use.

PROOFREADING AND PREPARING A FINAL COPY

PROOFREADING YOUR PARAGRAPH AND PREPARING A FINAL COPY

2n. Proofread your paragraph, make a final copy, and proofread again.

Proofread your revised draft carefully, using the Guidelines for Proof-reading on page 30. Then recopy the paragraph, following correct manuscript form or your teacher's instructions (see pages 31–33), and proofread it again.

EXERCISE 19. Proofreading Your Paragraph. Referring to the Guidelines for Proofreading on page 30, proofread and correct your paragraph. Remember to proofread your paragraph again after you make a final copy.

REVIEW EXERCISE E. Writing Paragraphs. Choose four topics from Review Exercise B (page 54) or four other topics. Write a paragraph on each topic, using a different order for each one: chrono-logical order, spatial order, order of importance, analogy, and compari-son or contrast.

PREWRITING First, make sure that the topic is limited enough for a paragraph; if not, limit it further. Next, determine your purpose, identify your audience, and consider your attitude toward the topic. Then gather information, select and arrange the details you plan to use, and write a topic sentence.

WRITING As you draft each paragraph, keep your purpose and audience in mind. Express your ideas clearly and make sure that the tone is appropriate and consistent.

EVALUATING, REVISING, AND PROOFREADING Use the Guidelines for Evaluating Paragraphs (pages 58–59) and the appropriate guidelines from page 23 to evaluate your writing. You may also ask a classmate to read and evaluate your paragraph. Then use the paragraph revision chart (pages 60–61) to revise it. Refer to the Guidelines for Proofread-ing (page 30) as you correct your revised draft and your recopied final version.

FOUR TYPES OF PARAGRAPHS

Most paragraphs can be classified into four types, depending on the writer's primary purpose:

1. An *expository paragraph* informs or explains.
2. A *persuasive paragraph* attempts to convince the reader to agree with an opinion and, sometimes, to perform a specific action.
3. A *descriptive paragraph* describes a person, place, or object.
4. A *narrative paragraph* relates a series of events.

Many paragraphs contain elements of more than one purpose. Description, for example, is often combined with narration. Usually, however, one purpose largely determines the content and the language.

THE EXPOSITORY PARAGRAPH

An expository paragraph may inform, explain, or define. It may be developed with facts and statistics, with examples, by means of cause and effect, by definition, or by a combination of these methods. It should be direct and unemotional in tone, avoiding vague words and emotional appeals, and it should be objective rather than subjective— the writer's personality should not intrude.

SUBJECTIVE   When I lost my book bag full of schoolbooks and notes, I learned the hard way that people have got to have identification on their luggage, book bags, and other important stuff.

OBJECTIVE   To ensure that luggage, book bags, and other valuables can be properly identified and returned if they are lost, tag all such valuables with your name, address, and telephone number.

Developing with Facts and Statistics

2o. Develop an expository paragraph with facts and statistics.

A *fact* is a statement that can be proved to be true; a *statistic* is a numerical fact that summarizes large quantities of data. The following paragraph, which gives information, uses facts to support the main idea.

Basic to all the Greek achievement was freedom. The Athenians were the only free people in the world. In the great empires of antiquity—Egypt, Babylon, Assyria, Persia—splendid though they were, with riches beyond reckoning and immense power, freedom was unknown. The idea of it never dawned in any of them. It was born in Greece, a poor little country, but with it able to remain unconquered no matter what manpower and what wealth were arrayed against her.

EDITH HAMILTON

The following paragraph uses facts to explain the formation of condensation trails.

Condensation trails, usually called contrails or vapor trails, are artificial clouds of water droplets or ice crystals that form in the wake of an airplane. They form because the water in the engines' exhaust condenses in the cold air. For a contrail to form, the air around the plane must be colder than $-60°$ C. If the air is warmer, the warmth will prevent condensation of the moisture coming from the engines, and no contrail will form. Jets, which fly in the very cold upper layers of the atmosphere, are the planes most likely to produce contrails.

CRITICAL THINKING:
Distinguishing Between Facts and Opinions

To write effective expository and persuasive paragraphs, you must be able to distinguish between facts and opinions. A *fact* is information that can be proved to be true. It is a fact, for example, that the capital of Utah is Salt Lake City. An *opinion,* on the other hand, states a judgment or a belief; it can be explained, but cannot be proved. As a reader and a listener, you must be able to determine whether statements are accurate and verifiable or simply someone's opinion. Opinions often use words that indicate some kind of judgment, such as *most, should, should not, greatest, best.*

FACT   Twenty-three students in this class have bought a particular brand of pocket calculator.
OPINION   This is the best brand of pocket calculator.

FACT   Public schools in this city close for two months during the summer.
OPINION   Public schools should be open eleven months a year.

EXERCISE 20. Distinguishing Facts from Opinions. Some of the following statements are facts; some are opinions. Write *F* for each fact and *O* for each opinion. (Assume that statements that are written as facts are true.)

1. The number of corporate mergers has increased during the past fifteen years.

2. There should be more women executives in industry.
3. Local department stores reported record-setting sales in December of this year.
4. Men and women should wait until they are at least twenty-one years old to marry.
5. Cup for cup, tea contains less caffeine than coffee.
6. Anne McCaffrey is the best writer of fantasy.
7. For many years automobile companies in several nations have been researching the possible use of air bags as a safety device in automobiles.
8. A bibliography is an alphabetical list of the sources used for a research paper.
9. Every high-school student should be required to take two years of a foreign language.
10. Driver's licenses are renewable every four years; learner's permits must be renewed yearly.

EXERCISE 21. Writing Paragraphs Using Facts and Statistics.
Write a paragraph based on the information given in each of the following numbered items. Refer to the material that follows Item 2 on page 67 as you plan, write, evaluate, and revise each paragraph.

1

Survey Question: Here is a list of things that people sometimes say are problems in professional sports. For each, tell me what kind of problem you think it is.

	BIG PROBLEM	SMALL PROBLEM	NO PROBLEM
Drug abuse	74%	24%	2%
High player salaries	55%	27%	18%
High ticket prices	54%	34%	12%
Alcohol abuse	52%	38%	10%
Unnecessary violence	41%	50%	9%
Team owners who meddle	34%	46%	20%
Too much TV pro sports	27%	25%	48%
Poor sportsmanship	24%	56%	20%
Fixed games	24%	35%	41%
Incompetent officials	23%	47%	30%
Too many pro teams	17%	27%	56%
Racial discrimination	11%	26%	63%

THE MIAMI HERALD

2

a. 1.8 million adults in United States enrolled in basic education courses
b. Federal government spending $75 million a year to support these programs; state and local governments spend about the same
c. Averages two dollars per year for each adult who is functionally illiterate (can't read or write)
d. Not enough space in programs for adults who want to learn basic reading and writing skills
e. More than 26 million Americans functionally illiterate—cannot read a notice, address an envelope, or write a check
f. Lisette Quinones, age 20, waiting for two years to begin a basic education course at LaGuardia Community College in New York
g. Critics: to eliminate long waiting periods, much more money needs to be spent for basic education courses for adults

PREWRITING Do not try to use all of the statistics or facts given in the numbered items; you do not want to overwhelm or confuse your audience. For each paragraph, decide first which four or five pieces of information will best suit the needs and interests of your audience. Arrange the material in an order that will be easy to follow, and write a topic sentence that expresses your main idea. Make sure that the information you have chosen effectively supports that idea.

WRITING Concentrate on expressing your ideas clearly in fairly formal language. Be sure to define or explain any terms your audience may find difficult or unfamiliar.

EVALUATING AND REVISING Ask yourself: Have I included neither too much information nor too little? Have I arranged the material in a logical order? You may also ask someone else to read your draft and tell you whether it is easy to understand. Then use the Guidelines for Evaluating Expository Paragraphs on page 72 to judge your writing, and refer to the paragraph revision chart on pages 60–61 as you improve it.

PROOFREADING AND MAKING A FINAL COPY Use the Guidelines for Proofreading on page 30 to proofread your paragraph. Remember to proofread again after you make your final copy.

Developing with Examples

2p. Develop an expository paragraph with examples.

An *example* is an item or instance that represents others of the same kind. Using examples helps you illustrate a general point concisely. In the following paragraph, the writer uses several examples to illustrate the point in the topic sentence.

> **Victoria was considerably more cultivated than some of her biographers allowed.** She spoke perfect German, excellent French, and adequate Italian; she was well-read in literature and history; she sketched charmingly, and she had a trained ear for music. Because as queen she was uncomfortable in the company of scientists of whose fields she was ignorant, it is sometimes assumed that she was less well-educated than she was. But few men of her era, let alone women, received any training at all in the sciences. Victoria was almost a bluestocking by modern standards.
>
> LOUIS AUCHINCLOSS

EXERCISE 22. Writing a Paragraph Using Examples. Write an expository paragraph developed with examples. You may use one of the following topics or one or your own.

1. American colonies founded on religious freedom
2. Popular musical groups whose fame results from a single recording
3. Gemstones associated with months of the year ("birthstones")
4. Outstanding dishes Italian cooking has contributed to the United States
5. Accomplishments of the U.S. space program

PREWRITING Begin by listing three or more examples and noting other details that will help you clarify the examples. (You may need to do some research.) Arrange the examples and supporting information in an easy-to-follow order, and write a topic sentence stating the main idea the examples illustrate. Then review your notes again, and remove any details that do not provide strong support for your main idea.

WRITING As you write your first draft, keep your purpose and audience in mind. Be sure to include enough supporting information to make each example clear.

EVALUATING AND REVISING Ask yourself: Have I included enough examples to make my main idea clear? Does each one truly illustrate my main idea? Then use the Guidelines for Evaluating Expository Paragraphs (page 72) and the paragraph revision chart (pages 60–61) to improve your paragraph.

PROOFREADING AND MAKING A FINAL COPY Proofread your paragraph carefully, using the guidelines on page 30. Then make a final copy and proofread it.

Developing by Means of Cause and Effect

2q. Develop an expository paragraph by analyzing cause and effect.

A *cause* is an event or situation that produces a result; an *effect* is anything brought about by a cause. Basically, there are two types of cause-effect paragraphs. In one type, you begin by stating an effect and then discuss the cause or causes. Such a paragraph answers the question "Why?" In the following paragraph, Barbara Tuchman explains why the combatants in World War I refused to accept U.S. President Woodrow Wilson's proposal to end the war without proclaiming either side the victor.

> Wilson's offer of December 1916 to bring together the belligerents for negotiation of a "peace without victory" was rejected by both sides. Neither was prepared to accept a settlement without some gain to justify its suffering and sacrifice in lives, and to pay for the war. Germany was not fighting for the status quo but for German hegemony of Europe and a greater empire overseas. She wanted not a mediated but a dictated peace and had no wish, as the Foreign Minister, Arthur Zimmermann, wrote to Bernstorff, "to risk being cheated of what we hope to gain from war" by a neutral mediator. Any settlement requiring renunciations and indemnities by Germany—the only settlement the Allies would accept—would mean the end of the Hohenzollerns and the governing class. They also had to make someone pay for the war or go bankrupt. A peace without victory would not only terminate dreams of mastery but require enormous taxes to pay for years of fighting that had grown profitless. It would mean revolution. To the throne, the military caste, the landowners, industrialists and barons of business, only a war of gain offered any hope of their survival in power.
>
> BARBARA TUCHMAN

The second type of cause-effect paragraph does not answer the question "Why?" Rather, it shows the effects, or results, of a cause. In the following paragraph, the writer discusses several different causes and their effects.

Strong gases and toxic fumes from such things   cause 1
as paint solvents and industrial chemicals may be
absorbed in the soft-contact-lens plastic, causing   effect 1
eye irritation if the concentration is strong enough.
Cosmetics, lotions, soaps and creams, hair sprays,   cause 2
or any aerosol discharges that come in contact with

the lenses may also stick. Eye irritation may result,   effect 2
and the lenses may get coated to a point where they
have to be replaced. Chemicals such as iron in   cause 3
ordinary tap water can also damage soft lenses.   effect 3
Hands should be washed and rinsed thoroughly,
and dried on a lint-free towel, before soft lenses are
handled.

DR. JOHN A. DYER

EXERCISE 23. Writing a Cause-and-Effect Paragraph. Write an expository paragraph developed by means of cause and effect. You may use one of the following topics or one of your own.

1. Causes of shyness
2. Effects of a cold virus
3. Effects of high interest rates
4. Causes of the War of 1812
5. Effects of being left-handed in a "right-handed world"
6. Causes of low voter turnout in national elections

PREWRITING Begin listing at least three related causes or effects for the topic you have chosen. Review your list carefully to make sure that the items do not contradict one another, and, if necessary, gather additional information. Then arrange the material in order: You may find that presenting causes in order from most to least important is effective, while using the opposite order works well for effects. Finally, write a topic sentence that states your main idea clearly.

WRITING As you write, try to express your ideas as clearly as possible. Consider using transitional expressions such as *as a result, because, consequently,* and *since* to help your audience follow your line of thought.

EVALUATING AND REVISING Ask yourself: If my supporting sentences present causes, do they clearly explain why an effect came about? If they are effects, do they clearly show the consequences of a cause? Then use the Guidelines for Evaluating Expository Paragraphs (page 72) and the paragraph revision chart (pages 60–61) to evaluate and revise your paragraph.

PROOFREADING AND MAKING A FINAL COPY Refer to the guidelines on page 30 as you proofread your paragraph. Remember to proofread again after you make a final copy.

Developing by Definition

2r. Develop an expository paragraph by definition.

The definition of an object or idea first identifies, usually in the topic sentence, the general class to which the item belongs. The supporting sentences provide details that show how the item is different from all other members of that class. This two-stage method—general class and distinguishing characteristics—is also used to define abstract terms, such as *love, happiness,* or *success.* Since an abstract term does not have physical features, examples, incidents, and quotations from authorities are often used to clarify what the term means to the writer. In the following example the writers first define romantic fiction in a general way. Then they give many facts and examples to clarify the phrase "escape from reality."

> **Romantic fiction is primarily the kind which offers the reader an escape from reality.** It often deals with distant lands and times. The things that happen in it are more exciting or mysterious or adventurous or strange than the things that happen in real life. Often it deals with such things as tournaments and besieged castles and perilous journeys through hostile country. Sometimes its characters have long journeys to go alone through forests, . . . are besieged in lonely old houses, or are shut up on islands in the midst of faraway lakes, or lie in hushed hiding while a mortal foe treads close by. Sometimes there are pirates, hidden treasures, shipwrecks, thrilling flights from a close-pursuing enemy, last-minute rescues, ominous prophecies, missing heirs, disguised princes, intrigue, murder, breathless suspense. Again, romance is often pervaded by an atmosphere of strange things about to be revealed; often it deals with places and people now changed or forgotten or long since passed away. In short, romance shows life not just as it is, but as we like to imagine it to be.
>
> RALPH P. BOAS and EDWIN SMITH

EXERCISE 24. Writing an Extended Definition.   Write an expository paragraph developed by definition. You may use one of the following terms or choose another term. Identify the general class to which the term belongs and include its distinguishing characteristics.

1. The Renaissance
2. Success
3. Bald eagle
4. Democracy
5. Lyric poetry

Techniques for Prewriting. As you prepare to write an expository paragraph,

- choose a method of development (or combination of methods): facts and statistics, examples, cause and effect, or definition.
- arrange the information you have gathered in a logical order that will be easy for your audience to follow.
- write a topic sentence that states your main idea clearly and directly.

Evaluating and Revising Expository Paragraphs

You can use the following guidelines for evaluating the expository paragraphs you write. Once you have determined which aspects of your paragraph need to be improved, refer to the paragraph revision chart on pages 60–61 for revision techniques.

GUIDELINES FOR EVALUATING EXPOSITORY PARAGRAPHS

Topic Sentence	1. Does the topic sentence identify a suitably limited topic and suggest that the purpose of the paragraph is to explain or inform?
Topic Development	2. Is the method of development (or combination of methods) appropriate for the main idea and for the audience? Are enough details given to make the main idea clear? Is the information clear, complete, and accurate?
Unity	3. Is each sentence directly related to the main idea as it is expressed in the topic sentence?
Conclusion	4. Does the clincher sentence, if there is one, provide a strong conclusion?
Order of Ideas	5. Are the ideas arranged in a logical, easy-to-follow order?
Relationships Between Ideas	6. Do the ideas flow smoothly from one sentence to the next? Are they linked with direct references and appropriate transitional expressions (*for example, because,* etc.)?
Word Choice	7. Is the language specific? Is it appropriate for the audience? Are technical terms and difficult words defined or explained?
Tone	8. Does the paragraph have an objective tone?

EXERCISE 25. Evaluating and Revising Expository Paragraphs.
Using the guidelines above, evaluate the following paragraphs. Then revise them on a separate sheet of paper, using the paragraph revision chart on pages 60–61.

1. One reason for the high dropout rate among high-school students in some schools is that students are tired of going to school. Another reason is that many students want or need to work, and some decide to work full time at part-time jobs they already have.

2. Americans move a lot. The average American moves ten times in his or her lifetime, and about 16 percent of the American population moves each year. This means that children change schools a lot. They have to keep making new friends. Adults find new jobs and are separated from their families sometimes.

REVIEW EXERCISE F. Writing an Expository Paragraph. Write an expository paragraph on one of the following topics or a topic of your own. Begin by planning your paragraph: Determine your specific purpose (to explain, to inform, or to define) and identify your audience; gather information; choose a method of development; arrange the information in a logical order; and write a topic sentence. Then write a first draft, and use the guidelines on page 72 to evaluate it and the paragraph revision chart on pages 60–61 to revise it. Proofread your revised draft, using the guidelines on page 30. Then make a final copy and proofread again.

1. The significance of *honor* in modern life
2. What a person's body language reveals
3. The benefits of having a part-time job
4. The effects of peer pressure on teen-agers
5. How to identify poison ivy or poison oak

THE PERSUASIVE PARAGRAPH

A persuasive paragraph attempts to convince the reader to agree with an opinion or to follow a course of action.

Developing with Reasons

2s. Develop a persuasive paragraph with reasons.

The topic of a persuasive paragraph should be a serious, debatable issue, one that has significance beyond that of a personal preference.

NOT APPROPRIATE   Basketball is the best high-school sport.
NOT APPROPRIATE   Rye bread is better than white bread.
APPROPRIATE   One hour should be added to the school day.
APPROPRIATE   Every high-school student should be required to take a one-year computer course.

The topic sentence, or *position statement,* should state the writer's opinion clearly and concisely. It should not be so brief that it is uninteresting, however.

The position statement should be supported by at least three *reasons*—statements that explain why the writer holds the opinion. Reasons are most convincing when they are supported by evidence in the form of facts, statistics, or examples. Together, the reasons and supporting evidence make up the writer's *argument.*

The United States' electoral college system is position statement outmoded and ineffective, and it should be abolished; the President should be elected instead by direct popular vote. Three times in United States reason 1 history (1824, 1876, 1888) the loser in popular votes was actually sworn in as President. Under the present system, the candidate who takes a plurality reason 2 of votes in a state takes all of the state's electoral college votes. Thus, millions of voters are in effect disenfranchised. Although 1.8 million Texans voted for Jimmy Carter in 1980, for example, Carter received none of Texas' electoral college votes. Currently, the weight of any person's vote depends reason 3 on the population of the state in which the person resides. In Alaska, for example, 95,000 voters cast 3 electoral votes, while in Texas, a single electoral vote requires 372,000 voters. Write to your Congressional representative, urging him or her to call to action work to replace the electoral college system with a system by which the President and Vice-President are elected by popular vote.

One type of reason that you may use to support an opinion is a quotation by an *authority,* an expert in the field being discussed. In the following paragraph, a knowledgeable and experienced political science professor is cited (quoted) in support of the opinion that the electoral college should be abolished.

> Dr. Elizabeth McElderry, political science professor at State University, supports the movement for direct popular election of the President. "Why should the Presidency and Vice-Presidency be the only national offices that are not elected by direct popular vote? Surely each citizen of the United States should have an equal vote and a vote that, somehow, should be effective—not lost in the electoral college system."

If you were writing to support an opposing viewpoint—that the electoral college system should be retained—you could doubtless find an authority who agrees with you. That is what makes persuasive writing so challenging; you can create an argument in support of an opinion, and you can also create an equally effective argument in support of the opposite opinion.

Reasons in a persuasive paragraph are usually arranged in order of importance, with the most important reason last; this ends the paragraph forcefully. A paragraph that gives the most important reason first may also be effective. In either case, the reader should be able to distinguish important from less important reasons.

The clincher, or concluding, sentence in a persuasive paragraph may reemphasize the writer's opinion, summarize the argument, or specify a course of action. Such a sentence provides an effective ending by giving the paragraph a sense of completeness.

The tone of a persuasive paragraph should be serious and unemotional to convey that you have researched the issue thoroughly and that your argument is fair and reasonable. Avoid name-calling and using words with negative connotations. Be specific, accurate, clear, and forceful in presenting your ideas.

Techniques for Prewriting. In preparing to write a persuasive paragraph,

- evaluate your topic to make sure that it is a serious, debatable issue, not just a personal preference.
- express your opinion clearly and concisely in a position statement.
- gather at least three reasons that explain your opinion and evidence to support each reason.
- arrange the material in order of importance.

Evaluating and Revising Persuasive Paragraphs

You can use the following guidelines to evaluate the persuasive paragraphs you write. The paragraph revision chart on pages 60–61 will help you revise those aspects that need to be improved.

GUIDELINES FOR EVALUATING PERSUASIVE PARAGRAPHS

Topic Sentence	1. Does the position statement express an opinion on a serious, debatable issue? Is it clear, concise, and interesting?
Topic Development	2. Are at least three reasons given to explain the opinion? Is each reason supported by accurate evidence (facts, examples, quotations from authorities, etc.)?
Unity	3. Is each sentence directly related to the opinion in the position statement?
Conclusion	4. Does the clincher sentence, if there is one, provide a strong conclusion for the paragraph?
Order of Ideas	5. Are the reasons arranged in order of importance? Are the less important and more important reasons readily distinguished?
Relationships Between Ideas	6. Is the line of reasoning easy to follow? Are direct references and appropriate transitional expressions (*most important, finally,* etc.) used to link ideas?
Word Choice	7. Have name-calling and words with negative connotations been avoided?
Tone	8. Is the tone consistently serious and unemotional?

EXERCISE 26. Evaluating and Revising a Persuasive Paragraph.
Using the guidelines above, evaluate the following paragraph. Then revise the paragraph, using the paragraph revision chart on pages 60–61. Write your revised version on a separate sheet of paper.

> Just because they're still in high school, seniors shouldn't have to have a curfew. If you work, sometimes the only time you get to see your friends is late at night. And even if you don't work, the weekends are too short for all the things young people want to do before they graduate. For example, many students enjoy going to parties, shopping, and, my favorite pastime, playing in a band.

REVIEW EXERCISE G. **Writing a Persuasive Paragraph.** Write a persuasive paragraph supporting one of the following opinions or an opinion of your own.

1. Presidential elections should (should not) be held during a twenty-four-hour period so that the polls in all four time zones open and close at the same time.
2. Restaurants should (should not) be required to have non-smoking sections.
3. Students who are caught cheating on a final examination should (should not) automatically fail the course.
4. One member of the school board should (should not) be a high-school student.
5. High-school students should (should not) be required to pass a series of competency exams to graduate.

PREWRITING Once you have decided which position you will take, list all the reasons you can think of to support that position. Review your list, and select the three or four reasons your audience will find most convincing. Then gather evidence to support each reason, and arrange the material in order of importance. You may also reword the position statement to make it clearer or more interesting.

WRITING As you draft your paragraph, remember to avoid using words with negative connotations. If you decide to include a clincher sentence, decide what specific purpose you want it to perform—to reemphasize your opinion, to summarize your reasons, or to suggest a course of action.

EVALUATING AND REVISING Ask yourself: Is my argument logical and convincing? Have I established and maintained a serious, unemotional tone? You may also have someone else read your paragraph and comment on it. Then use the Guidelines for Evaluating Persuasive Paragraphs (page 76) and the paragraph revision chart (pages 60–61) to judge and revise your writing.

PROOFREADING AND MAKING A FINAL COPY Read your revised draft carefully, using the Guidelines for Proofreading (page 30). Remember to proofread again after you make a final copy.

THE DESCRIPTIVE PARAGRAPH

Descriptive writing creates images in the reader's mind by using language that appeals to the senses. Passages of description are usually woven into other writing. Most paragraph-length descriptions focus on one person, place, event, or object.

Developing with Concrete and Sensory Details

2t. Develop a descriptive paragraph with concrete and sensory details.

In the following paragraph, the writer describes part of a German city. Notice in this paragraph two important elements of description: (1) the use of many carefully selected concrete and sensory details and (2) the use of figurative language (in boldfaced type).

> Closer to the center of town a few dusty trees break the linear bleakness. Then on a boulevard, divided in the middle by a row of trees that meet overhead with trees on either curb to form two leafy tunnels, the traffic begins to swirl, dragging you mercilessly on, past a park into the unfinished glass and chrome and concrete world of the city. **Modest skyscrapers act as bookends** for lower structures, furniture showrooms and stores of electronic equipment. Vast windowless walls of concrete, some studded, some **quilted** for texture, loom over garages, amusement arcades, record shops, restaurants, and **potbellied trucks dribbling** their premixed concrete near the **hoardings** of a would-be skyscraper. At the end of a short street, drab with two-story buildings, rooming houses, and **dejected shops, squats** a miniature station, its newly painted **gingerbread eyebrows** giving it a **sullen expression. Half-defiant, half-apologetic,** a remnant of the past, it looks out on the wrong century.
>
> ANN CORNELISEN

The details in a descriptive paragraph may be given in either spatial or chronological order. Ann Cornelisen organizes her description spatially. In the following example, which combines narration with description, N. Scott Momaday uses chronological order; the details are given in the order in which the woman senses or imagines them.

> She went out into the soft yellow light that fell from the windows and that lay upon the ground and the pile of wood. She knelt down and picked up the cold, hard lengths of wood and laid them in the crook of her arm. They were sharp and seamed at the ends where the axe had shaped them like pencil points, and they smelled of resin. When again she stood, she inadvertently touched the handle of the axe; it was stiff and immovable in the block, and cold. She felt with the soles of her feet the chips of wood which lay all about on the ground, among the dark stones and weeds. The long black rim of the canyon wall lay sheer on the dark, silent sky. She stood, remembering the sacramental violence which had touched the wood. One of the low plateaus, now invisible above her, had been gutted

long ago by fire, and in the day she had seen how the black spines of the dead trees stood out. She imagined the fire which had run upon them, burning out their sweet amber gum. Then they were flayed by the fire and their deep fibrous flesh cracked open, and among the cracks the wood was burned into charcoal and ash, and in the sun each facet of the dead wood shone low like velvet and felt like velvet to the touch, and left the soft death of itself on the hands that touched it.

N. SCOTT MOMADAY

Often, as in these two models, the main idea of a descriptive paragraph—an impression or a mood—is implied rather than stated directly in a topic sentence. In the preceding paragraph, for example, the details and the writer's style create a silent, somber mood.

Techniques for Prewriting. As you prepare to write a descriptive paragraph,

- gather precise concrete and sensory details.
- select those details that will most effectively create a dominant mood or main impression, and arrange them in spatial or chronological order.
- decide whether you will state your main idea directly or imply it.

Evaluating and Revising Descriptive Paragraphs

You will find the following guidelines useful for evaluating the descriptive paragraphs you write. The paragraph revision chart on pages 60–61 will help you revise your writing.

GUIDELINES FOR EVALUATING DESCRIPTIVE PARAGRAPHS

Purpose	1. Does the paragraph focus on a single person, place, object, or event? Does it clearly state or imply a single main idea?
Topic Development	2. Are enough concrete and sensory details presented to enable the reader to visualize or otherwise mentally experience the topic?

Unity	3. Is every sentence directly related to the main idea?
Order of Ideas	4. Are the details arranged in spatial or chronological order?
Relationships Between Ideas	5. Do the ideas flow smoothly? Are direct references and appropriate transitional expressions (*over, past,* etc.) used to show where the details are in relation to one another?
Word Choice	6. Is the language specific rather than general? If figurative language is used, is it appropriate and effective?

EXERCISE 27. Evaluating and Revising a Descriptive Paragraph.
Using the guidelines above, evaluate the following paragraph. Then revise the paragraph, using the paragraph revision chart on pages 60–61. Write your revised version on a separate sheet of paper.

> The sunset was beautiful. The light seemed to change every moment. A lot of colors lit up the clouds, and the different colors changed. Finally, it was dark.

REVIEW EXERCISE H. Writing a Descriptive Paragraph. Write a paragraph describing one of the following topics or a topic of your own.

1. A football scrimmage
2. A stranger seen on a bus or a subway
3. The inside of a telephone booth
4. An alley
5. A garden

PREWRITING Begin by observing (or recalling) your topic. Take detailed notes on the sights, sounds, tastes, textures, and smells you experience (or remember). Then review your notes carefully, determine what mood or main impression you want to create, and decide whether you will state your main idea directly or imply it. Eliminate from your list any details that do not directly support that idea, and arrange the remaining details in an order that will help reinforce your main idea. If you plan to state your main idea directly, write a topic sentence.

WRITING Write your first draft freely, concentrating on using specific language. If other related details occur to you as you write, include them.

EVALUATING AND REVISING   Ask yourself: Have I included enough concrete and sensory details? Do all of the details contribute to my main idea? You may also ask someone else to read and comment on your paragraph. Then use the Guidelines for Evaluating Descriptive Paragraphs (pages 79–80) and the paragraph revision chart (pages 60–61) to judge and revise your draft.

PROOFREADING AND MAKING A FINAL COPY   Read your revised draft carefully, using the Guidelines for Proofreading (page 30). Proofread again after you make a final copy.

THE NARRATIVE PARAGRAPH

A narrative paragraph tells a story or relates a series of events. Most narrative paragraphs appear as parts of longer works, such as personal narratives, novels, or short stories. A one-paragraph narrative based on an experience that occurs within a short period of time may be complete in itself.

Developing with an Incident

2u. Develop a narrative paragraph with an incident or an anecdote.

In some narrative paragraphs, the topic sentence makes a point that is developed by the incident related.

> **Luck is sometimes the deciding factor in a game.** In the eighth inning of the deciding game of the World Series of 1924, the Giants were leading the Senators by the fairly comfortable margin of 3–1. A hard-hit ground ball struck a pebble and bounded over the head of third baseman Fred Lindstrom, and two runs came in, tying the game and sending the contest into extra innings. In the last of the twelfth, the Giant catcher, about to dash for a pop fly behind the plate, caught his foot in his mask and missed an easy out. The batter, given another chance, then doubled. The next man up hit another grounder toward third base. The ball again struck a pebble, soaring over the third baseman, and the Senators won the series.

Instead of a topic sentence that states the main idea directly, many narrative paragraphs have an introductory or concluding sentence that summarizes the action, tells how it came about, or comments on its significance.

Occasionally, narrative writing is combined with other kinds of writing. Narration and description are often combined, and sometimes an incident is used in an expository paragraph. In the following paragraph, which illustrates the combination of narration with description and exposition, the first two sentences summarize what the writer learned from the incident she relates.

In my sensory education I include my physical awareness of the *word*. Of a certain word, that is; the connection it has with what it stands for. At around age six, perhaps, I was standing by myself in our front yard waiting for supper, just at that hour in a late summer day when the sun is already below the horizon and the risen full moon in the visible sky stops being chalky and begins to take on light. There comes the moment, and I saw it then, when the moon goes from flat to round. For the first time it met my eyes as a globe. The word *moon* came into my mouth as though fed to me out of a silver spoon. Held in my mouth, the moon became a word. It had the roundness of a Concord grape Grandpa took off his vine and gave me to suck out of its skin and swallow whole, in Ohio.

EUDORA WELTY

Most narrative paragraphs are arranged in chronological order, which enables the reader to understand how one event leads to another. In longer narratives you may encounter *flashbacks,* sections that show what happened before the events of the main story. Such flashbacks are themselves generally organized chronologically too.

Techniques for Prewriting. In preparing to write a narrative paragraph,

- use the *5 W-How?* questions to gather details of the incident.
- arrange the ideas in chronological order.
- consider writing a topic sentence that makes a general point or an introductory or concluding sentence that summarizes the action, tells how it came about, or comments on its significance.

Evaluating and Revising Narrative Paragraphs

You will find the following guidelines useful for evaluating the narrative paragraphs you write. The paragraph revision chart on pages 60–61 will help you revise your writing.

GUIDELINES FOR EVALUATING NARRATIVE PARAGRAPHS

Purpose	1. Does a topic sentence make a general point, or does an introductory or concluding sentence summarize the action, tell how it came about, or comment on its significance?
Topic Development	2. Are enough details included so that the reader can understand what happened?
Unity	3. Have repetitive and unrelated details been left out?
Order of Ideas	4. Are the events arranged in the order in which they occurred?
Relationships Between Ideas	5. Do the ideas flow smoothly? Are direct references and appropriate transitional expressions (*later, before, in the meantime,* etc.) used to link ideas?
Word Choice	6. Are precise nouns, verbs, and modifiers used to help the reader picture the action? Is the language appropriate for the audience?

EXERCISE 28. Evaluating and Revising a Narrative Paragraph.
Using the guidelines above, evaluate the following paragraph. Then use
the paragraph revision chart on pages 60–61 to revise it, and write your
revised version on a separate sheet of paper.

> Some kinds of fun can be a lot of work. Last weekend my friends Al and
> Rosie invited me and Terry to go with them to a workshop on contra
> dancing, which is dancing in two lines with the partners lined up facing each
> other. I really thought I'd have a good time because I always enjoy watching
> dancing in old movies on TV. Unfortunately, the caller seemed to think that
> everyone in the group was already an expert. And most of the other
> people—including Terry, Al, and Rosie—caught on right away. But not
> me!

REVIEW EXERCISE I. Writing a Narrative Paragraph.   Write a
narrative paragraph using an incident to illustrate one of the following
ideas or an idea of your own.

1. A simple misunderstanding can have long-lasting consequences.
2. A week without television can give you an extremely new perspective
   on life.
3. Setting a goal and working hard to achieve your goal is enormously
   satisfying.

4. Volunteers often receive more than they give.
5. What appears to be a bargain may turn out to be extremely costly.

PREWRITING Use the *5 W-How?* questions to make a list of details that the reader will need to know to understand the incident. Then arrange the actions of the incident in chronological order, and write an introductory or concluding sentence that makes a general statement which the incident illustrates. (If you are using one of the ideas suggested above, you may reword the sentence in any way you choose.)

WRITING With your notes in front of you, write your first draft freely, concentrating on trying to express your ideas clearly. Add related details as you think of them, but remember that your incident should keep to the point you are trying to make.

EVALUATING AND REVISING Ask yourself: Have I included enough details to make the incident clear and interesting? Have I left out unnecessary or repetitive details? Then use the Guidelines for Evaluating Narrative Paragraphs (page 83) and the paragraph revision chart (pages 60–61) to judge and improve your writing.

PROOFREADING AND MAKING A FINAL COPY Read your paragraph carefully, using the Guidelines for Proofreading on page 30. Proofread again after you make a final copy.

CHAPTER 2 WRITING REVIEW

Writing Paragraphs for Different Purposes. Write four paragraphs, one for each of the types of writing. You may use the same subject as a starting point for all four paragraphs, or you may use two or more different subjects. Remember to keep your audience and purpose in mind as you limit the subject for each paragraph. Gather information on your limited topic; arrange it in a logical order; and write a topic sentence that states your main idea. (For the descriptive and narrative paragraphs, you may instead imply your main idea.) Then write a first draft, and use the appropriate guidelines to evaluate your writing. Refer to the paragraph revision chart (pages 60–61) as you improve your paragraphs and to the Guidelines for Proofreading (page 30) as you correct them. Proofread again after you make your final copies.

CHAPTER 3

Writing Expository Compositions

THE WHOLE COMPOSITION

To compose means "to form by putting together." A composition is a piece of writing that takes form as you put together the ideas you have on a subject. To write a composition you must first have a number of specific ideas on the subject about which you plan to write. You must then be able to put those ideas together in such a way that they will form an effective whole composition.

Like the paragraphs you studied in earlier chapters, a composition has a controlling idea that must be supported by specific ideas and details. A composition is made up of several paragraphs that are usually arranged into an introduction, a body, and a conclusion.

As the title indicates, the emphasis in this chapter will be on expository writing. Keep in mind, however, that the four modes —exposition, persuasion, narration, and description—often overlap. An expository composition, for example, often contains elements of persuasion, narration, and description.

PREWRITING

SEARCHING FOR SUBJECTS

3a. Search for subjects for your expository composition.

Unless your teacher specifies what you are to write about, your first step in writing is to search for possible subjects. Two sources to draw from in your search are (1) your own experiences and (2) the experiences of others.

Your Own Experiences

Your first thought may be that you have no experiences, knowledge, or interests that other people would want to read about. All writers, however, start with what they know. Like other writers, you live in a family, a community, and a nation. You have formed ideas about people, places, and things. You have read books and watched television. You have participated in group activities. In other words, you have obtained from your own experiences information that may interest other people. Two of the most useful techniques for drawing on this information for composition subjects are the writer's journal and brainstorming.

If you keep a writer's journal, a notebook of your thoughts and feelings recorded on a daily or an occasional basis, you have a ready source of information about your own experiences. You can read through that journal in search of subjects for your writing. Since your purpose in expository writing is to inform or explain, you will look in your journal only for those subjects that will lend themselves to that purpose. For example, you might find a note about your frustrations with an incompleted biology experiment. That note might lead to the following subjects suitable for an expository composition: science courses in high schools, the benefits of studying biology, choosing a college major, and prizewinning biologists.

When brainstorming a subject you allow your mind to flow freely from one thought to the next, generating as many ideas as possible without stopping to evaluate them. You can begin brainstorming with a question such as "What have I done this week?" or with a word or a phrase such as "television" or "leisure time." If you begin brainstorming with the word *television,* for example, you might develop the following list of subjects:

> television viewing habits
> selecting a new television
> using television wisely
> the effects of television on children
> watching football on television
> playing video games
> computer technology
> computers in school

Techniques for Prewriting. To draw on your own experiences for a possible subject for an expository composition, ask yourself:

- What am I interested in? Why?
- What do I know how to do well?
- What do I know a great deal about?
- What unusual experiences have I had?
- Which of my interests or experiences lend themselves to the purpose of an expository composition—to inform or explain?

EXERCISE 1. Drawing on Your Own Experiences for Subjects. Using your writer's journal or brainstorming, develop a list of at least fifteen possible subjects for an expository composition.

The Experiences of Others

To actively search for subjects outside your own firsthand experience, observe closely. Keep a notebook and pencil with you as you walk through your neighborhood, down your street, or through a crowded shopping area. Look for subjects of interest to other people: a new collection in the local museum, the activities sponsored by the parks and recreation department, the ins and outs of the city bus system.

You can also search for subjects as you read or watch TV. Keep a notebook nearby as you read your daily newspaper or watch a favorite program. Perhaps a newspaper article about a local politician will suggest an idea about voter registration. A televised consumer update on best-selling audio tapes might give you an idea about the care and handling of tapes and tape players.

EXERCISE 2. Drawing on Outside Experiences for Subjects. For two days, keep a notebook of your observations and of ideas suggested by your reading and TV viewing. Keep in mind the purpose of expository writing: to inform or explain. List at least fifteen possible subjects for expository writing.

SELECTING AND LIMITING SUBJECTS

3b. Select and limit a subject for your expository composition.

Drawing on your own experiences and the experiences of others, you have identified possible subjects for your composition. You are now ready to select one subject and limit it to a manageable topic.

Selecting a Subject

To write an effective expository composition, your interest in and knowledge of your subject must be deep enough to enable you to develop several paragraphs about that subject. It is therefore important that you carefully analyze the subjects you have identified.

Techniques for Prewriting.   To analyze the subjects you have identified, ask yourself:

- Is this subject more interesting to me than the other subjects I have identified?
- Do I know enough about this subject to explain it clearly or to be effectively informative about it?
- Is my experience with this subject wide enough to enable me to explain it to someone else?

By using these questions to analyze the subjects you have identified, you should be able to select one subject that you can handle better than the others. For example, in analyzing the brainstorming list on page 86, you might discover that although you are interested in the subject "computer technology," you have neither the knowledge nor the experience to explain it or to inform others about it. On the other hand, you might discover that you really enjoy your computer classes and that your observation of how computers are used in the different classrooms in your high school has made you both knowledgeable about and interested in the subject "computers in school." This subject would, therefore, be a good choice for you to write about.

EXERCISE 3. **Selecting a Subject for Your Expository Composition.**   Analyze the subjects you developed for Exercises 1 and 2. Use the Techniques for Prewriting above to make your analysis. Then select one subject for an expository composition.

Limiting a Subject

The *subject* of your composition is the broad area of content: "dieting" or "physical fitness." The *topic* is the more focused or specific content:

"how to stop dieting and stay thin" or "investing twenty minutes a day in physical fitness."

The topic not only provides a focus for the broader subject, it also limits the subject to a manageable size. A subject should be limited so that you will be able to cover it adequately in the space at your disposal. Most in-school expository compositions, for example, are about five pages or 500 words long. Study the following examples of how a subject may be limited:

Broad Subject	Energy
Slightly Limited Topic	The energy problem today
More Limited Topic	Renewable sources of energy
Further Limitations	How a solar-energy cell works
	Growing trees for fuel
	Building a backyard windmill

Each additional limitation narrows the previous subject or topic by focusing on specific parts or aspects. The first two limitations might be covered adequately in a book or a long report. The last three topics are suitable for shorter compositions.

Techniques for Prewriting.   To limit a topic, ask yourself:

- What are some aspects, or specific parts, of the subject?
- Which of these aspects are limited enough in focus to cover adequately in the space at my disposal?
- Which of these aspects clearly lend themselves to the purpose of exposition: to explain or inform?

Then to select one topic to write about, ask yourself:

- Which of these limited topics best suits my interests, knowledge, and experience?

EXERCISE 4. **Limiting Your Subject.**   Using the subject you selected in Exercise 3, list at least ten limited topics related to that subject.

CONSIDERING PURPOSE, AUDIENCE, AND TONE

3c. Evaluate your topic: consider purpose, audience, and tone.

The purpose, audience, and tone of an expository composition are usually dictated by the writing assignment. Nevertheless, you must consider purpose, audience, and tone throughout the writing process— beginning with your initial choice of subject and continuing through the last revision of your final draft.

Considering Purpose

Since your purpose in writing an expository composition is to inform or explain, you need to consider whether the topic you have chosen clearly lends itself to that purpose. A topic such as "why the United States should provide food to developing nations" will lead the writer into a persuasive argument rather than into a straightforward presentation of information. A more appropriate topic for an expository composition would be "current efforts of the United States to provide food to developing nations." The latter topic clearly calls for information: What are the current efforts? How are they being implemented?

> *Techniques for Prewriting.* When considering a topic in terms of purpose, ask yourself:
>
> ● Does the topic clearly meet the expository purpose of my composition: to explain the topic or to convey information about it?
> ● Is the topic limited enough to enable me to explain it adequately or to convey information about it in the space at my disposal?

EXERCISE 5. **Rewriting Topics According to Purpose.**   Some of the topics below are appropriate for an expository purpose and some are not. Identify the topics that are inappropriate, and rewrite them as necessary to make them appropriate for an expository composition. Be prepared to explain your decisions.

1. How to create a square-foot garden
2. Why we need a student council
3. The importance of voting
4. How women won the right to vote
5. The use of standardized tests in secondary schools

Considering Audience

The audience for your expository composition may be your teacher, other members of your class, readers of a school magazine or newspaper, or a group of parents. Since different audiences will have different backgrounds and interests, you must study the needs of your audience to determine how to develop your topic.

Suppose, for example, that you plan to write a composition on a physical-fitness program. For a group of teen-agers, you would probably provide information on forms of exercise appropriate for physically active people. For a group of businesspeople, you would probably provide information on forms of exercise appropriate for people with busy schedules. For either of these groups, you would want to present the information in a nontechnical manner and define any specialized terms you use. On the other hand, if you are writing the paper for a group of physicians, you would provide a highly technical explanation of the fitness program and its physiological effects.

Techniques for Prewriting. To evaluate your topic in terms of a particular audience, ask yourself:

- For what audience am I writing?
- What is the background of my audience? What might they want to know or need to know about my topic? What do they already know?
- What attitude do they have toward my topic? How might that attitude affect what I have to say?
- What special help will this audience need to understand my topic or the technical terms I may use to explain it?

EXERCISE 6. **Evaluating Your Audience.** Select three of the topics you developed for Exercise 5, or any three topics of your choice. Then use the questions above in Techniques for Prewriting to evaluate the audience for your expository composition. Write your answers on a sheet of paper and be prepared to discuss them in class.

Considering Tone

The tone of a composition reflects the writer's attitude toward the topic and must be appropriate for the intended audience. For example, a mocking or satirical tone in a composition on the importance of political parties in America would be inappropriate for an audience made up of campaign workers for a particular political party. On the other hand, such an audience would probably be delighted with a composition that pokes fun at the weaknesses of the other political party. Remember that the purpose of an expository composition is to inform or explain; that purpose cannot be achieved if your audience stops reading because the tone of the composition is inappropriate.

More often than not, the tone of an expository composition will be serious. Other tones may be taken, however—admiring, critical, satirical, mocking, light, humorous—as long as the tone does not interfere with the writer's ability to convey information. Notice how Russell Baker uses a light and humorous tone to explain punctuation in the following model. Baker's tone adds to, rather than interferes with, the expository purpose.

> A colon is a tip-off to get ready for what's next: a list, a long quotation or an explanation. This article is riddled with colons. Too many, maybe, but the message is: "Stay on your toes; it's coming at you."
>
> RUSSELL BAKER

Tone is communicated primarily through *diction,* the words that a writer uses to explain or inform. The writer's diction may be *informal,* as in the above paragraph by Russell Baker, or it may be *formal.* Notice Baker's use of words: *tip-off, what's,* and *Stay on your toes.* The informal *tip-off,* as compared with more formal words such as *suggestion* or *intimation,* contributes to the light tone of the essay. The expression "Stay on your toes" is far more informal than "Scrutinize the forthcoming information." Contractions such as *what's* are also informal; they are conversational in tone and suggest that the writer is approaching the subject in a light, almost casual way. More formal diction, on the other hand, consists generally of more difficult or abstract vocabulary. A formal tone also avoids contractions and any suggestion of casualness.

Tone is also affected by the *point of view* the writer takes. If the writer writes in a first-person point of view, the tone is more friendly, more personal, than in a third-person point of view. The third-person point of view separates the reader from the writer, while the first-person point of view brings the reader and writer closer together. Notice the difference in tone between the following passages, the first written in first person and the second written in third person.

> Before I begin building a bookcase, I usually spend a few hours looking over the plans and making sure that I have all the equipment and materials I'll need.

Before amateur carpenters begin building bookcases, it is to their advantage to spend a few hours studying the plans to ensure that all needed equipment and materials are at hand.

When considering point of view for your own expository writing, you should keep in mind that contemporary formal writing is frequently in the first-person point of view. At one time the first-person point of view was considered embarrassingly familiar for most kinds of writing. Today, many writers consider the third-person point of view too artificial and avoid it whenever possible.

Techniques for Prewriting. To evaluate your attitude toward your topic, ask yourself:

- What is my attitude toward my topic—admiring or critical, satirical or straightforward, formal or informal, etc.?
- Is that attitude appropriate for my purpose and for my intended audience?
- How can my choice of words help reflect the tone I want to convey? For example, does the wording of my topic reflect an informal attitude ("Who says teens can't deal with responsibility?") or a formal attitude ("Most teen-agers act responsibly")?

EXERCISE 7. **Writing in a Formal Tone.** Using what you have learned about how diction and point of view reflect a writer's tone or attitude toward a subject, rewrite the paragraph by Russell Baker (page 92) in a formal tone.

EXERCISE 8. **Analyzing Tone for an Expository Composition.** For each of the three topics you selected for Exercise 6, identify your own attitude and the tone you would use in an expository composition. Be prepared to discuss why you chose the tone and how that tone will affect the writing of your composition.

REVIEW EXERCISE A. **Evaluating Your Own Topic for Purpose, Audience, and Tone.** Choose one of the three topics you analyzed in Exercise 8. Refer to the Techniques for Prewriting on pages 90 and 91 and above to evaluate that topic for purpose, audience, and tone.

CHOOSING A TITLE

3d. Choose a title that reflects your topic and purpose.

Once you have considered the purpose, audience, and tone of your composition, a title may occur to you. Keep in mind, however, that in addition to reflecting your topic and your purpose, a good title should catch the attention of your audience. Suppose, for example, that you are thinking about a title for an expository composition about "growing trees for fuel." You would begin with your purpose: to inform. Then you would consider how you might best catch the interest of your audience of energy-aware adults and at the same time suggest what the composition is about. Finally, you would consider your attitude toward the topic and how you might reveal your tone in the title. One result might be "Today's Seedlings—Tomorrow's Energy." The title attracts interest and reflects both purpose and topic.

EXERCISE 9. Writing Titles.   The following topics have been developed for expository compositions with a serious tone. An audience is specified for each of the five topics. For each topic, write a title that attracts attention and reflects the informative purpose and the topic.

1. Characteristics of a good student   Parents
2. How to win the game (any game)   Amateur players
3. Choosing the right shoes   Any sports enthusiast
4. Growing responsibilities of   General adult
    high-school students
5. Robots in the home   General adult

EXERCISE 10. Writing a Title for Your Expository Composition.
Write a title for each of the three topics you used in Exercise 8. Assume that you will eventually choose one of the three topics and corresponding titles for your own composition.

GATHERING INFORMATION

3e. Gather information on your topic.

If you have developed a topic that is familiar to you, you probably already have a great deal of information for your composition. Now that you have evaluated your limited topic and written a title, you are ready to add to that information.

There are several techniques you can use to gather additional information on your topic. If your topic developed from an idea you had jotted down in your journal, you may find information by reading through your journal again. For example, if an entry in your journal led you to the topic "preparing for the S.A.T.'s," you might go back to that entry and review everything you wrote about the experience..You might find a note about getting a good night's sleep before the test as well as one about the success rate of students who took the SAT review course offered by the school.

Certain questioning strategies are also helpful in the search for information. You can prod your own thinking process by asking yourself questions, and you can gather new information by asking other people questions. The *5 W-How?* questions, *Who? What? When? Where? Why?* and *How?*, are useful in gathering information for any kind of writing. The point-of-view questions can help you examine your topic from three different perspectives: What is it? How does it change or vary? What are its relationships? (See Chapter 1, pages 16–18, for a discussion of questioning strategies.)

Two techniques that work especially well when you are attempting to stimulate your own thinking about a topic are brainstorming and clustering. The purpose of brainstorming is to create a free, uninterrupted flow of thought, without stopping to judge the relative value of your ideas. Suppose, for example, that you have decided to write a composition on the topic "objections to TV commercials." After five minutes of brainstorming, you might arrive at the following list of ideas:

necessity for commercials	no commercials in some countries
interrupt programs too often	some good commercials
irritating ads	emphasize luxuries
too much repetition	no reasons given why product
singing commercials	is best
romantic touch	dramatic
sexist commercials	banks and finance companies
cure-all medicines	cold cereals
my favorite TV programs	detergents
meaningless terms	cosmetics
tiresome slogans	pretty women and handsome men
meaningless testimonials	keeping up with the Joneses
insulting ads	false scientific statements
dangerous ads	magazine ads
15-second ads	applies to radio, too
misleading	children (box tops, etc.)
false impressions of life	

Like brainstorming, the purpose of clustering is to generate ideas quickly. When clustering, however, you circle each idea on your list and connect it with lines to the ideas that precede and follow it. This technique lets you see the relationships among the ideas being developed. Another advantage of clustering is that the resulting visual picture of the connections and relationships among your ideas can give you a head start on organizing your composition. After a few minutes of clustering on the topic "objections to TV commercials," you might produce a diagram similar to the following one:

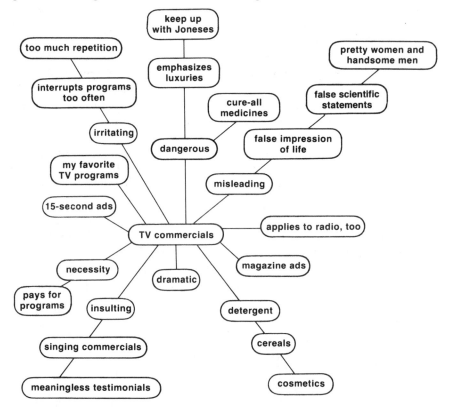

The techniques discussed above can be helpful as you gather ideas to develop your topic into a complete composition. Try your best to generate or gather as much information as possible so that you will have an abundance of details and ideas to use in your paper.

EXERCISE 11. Gathering Information on a Topic. Using the three topics you evaluated in Exercise 8, gather information for an expository composition. Use a different information-gathering technique—journal review, *5 W-How?* questions, or clustering—for each of the three topics. Be prepared to discuss which of the three techniques seemed most useful.

CLASSIFYING AND ARRANGING IDEAS

3f. Classify and arrange your ideas.

The next step in writing a composition is to classify and arrange the ideas you have gathered. Begin by analyzing the information to determine the major ideas under which it should be organized. Give each major idea a heading, and then you will be able to group the other ideas in lists under the appropriate heading. For the topic "objections to TV commercials," you might classify your ideas according to your major objections to TV advertising. The groupings that result might look something like those shown below.

Major Heading	*Details/Examples*
why some commercials are insulting	meaningless testimonials
	singing commercials
why some commercials are dangerous	keeping up with Joneses
	emphasize luxuries
	cure-all medicines
why some commercials are irritating	interrupt programs too often
	too much repetition

Notice how similar these groupings are to the clusters that were formed on page 96. Notice also that some of the ideas that were generated earlier cannot be classified under any of the three major headings. Additional supporting details for one or more of the major headings will probably have to be found.

After you have identified the major ideas and classified the supporting details, the next step is to think about how to arrange those ideas and details. Usually this organization becomes obvious as you think about your topic and the main ideas. Since background information is often necessary to help the reader understand what you have to say, you would give that information and define technical terms first. Then you would arrange your ideas. If you were explaining how to win the game of *Scrabble,* for example, you might list your ideas chronologically (what you should do first, next, and last) or you might list them in order of importance. In the example on TV commercials, you would want to proceed from the least to the most important objections. Consequently, the headings would be rearranged in the following order: (1) why some commercials are irritating, (2) why some commercials are insulting, and (3) why some commercials are dangerous.

As you begin classifying and arranging ideas for your own composition, do not hesitate to experiment. Try more than one kind of order and keep moving the details and examples around until you find the arrangement that seems most logical. Keep in mind that your list of major headings and supporting details and ideas may change during this process. You will find that some of the original material should be eliminated altogether, that some of it should be rephrased or revised slightly, and that some of it should be combined.

EXERCISE 12. Classifying and Arranging Ideas and Details. In Exercise 11 you gathered information on three different topics. For each of those three topics, classify and arrange the ideas and details you gathered. Remember that you may find it necessary to rephrase, combine, or eliminate some of the material you have gathered.

Developing a Topic Outline

When you classified and arranged your ideas in Exercise 12, you developed an informal plan, or outline, for your expository composition. This plan can be further developed as a topic outline. In a topic outline, each item—a main topic or a subtopic—is written as a single word or as a phrase. The example below is a topic outline of the first part of a composition on objections to TV commercials.

    I. Why commercials are necessary
       A. To pay costs of a TV program
       B. To sell sponsors' products
   II. Why some commercials are irritating
       A. Too repetitious
       B. Too frequent

Developing a Sentence Outline

For some assignments, however, you may prefer to use a sentence outline. A sentence outline is preferable when you want to communicate to someone else the full meaning of the shorter headings in a topic outline. A comparison of the sentence outline below with the topic outline above will indicate this advantage of the sentence form.

  I. Commercials are necessary.
     A. The money a sponsor pays to a station to air commercials during a TV program pays for the production costs of that program.
     B. It is the commercials, not the program, that sell the sponsors' products.
 II. Some commercials are irritating.
     A. The constant repetition is irritating.
     B. The too-frequent interruption of programs is irritating.

Rules for Outlining

When making either a topic outline or a sentence outline for your own expository composition, observe the following rules:

1. Place the title above the outline. It is not part of the outline and should not be numbered.

2. Place a statement of purpose before the first main head in the outline. This statement will help you keep your purpose in mind as you write your composition.

3. The terms *Introduction, Body,* and *Conclusion* should not be included in the outline. They are not topics; they are merely organizational units in the writer's mind.

4. Use Roman numerals for main topics. For subtopics use alternating letters and numbers as shown below.

Correct Use of Numbers and Letters

  I. Main topic
     A. ⎫
        ⎬ Subtopics of I
     B. ⎭
         1. ⎫
            ⎬ Subtopics of B
         2. ⎭
             a. ⎫
                ⎬ Subtopics of 2
             b. ⎭
                 (1) ⎫
                     ⎬ Subtopics of b
                 (2) ⎭
                     (a) ⎫
                         ⎬ Subtopics of 2
                     (b) ⎭
 II. Main topic
     A. Etc.

5. Indent subtopics so that all letters or numbers of the same kind will come directly under one another in a vertical line.

6. Begin each topic and subtopic with a capital letter; otherwise, capitalize only proper nouns and proper adjectives.

7. In a topic outline do not follow topics with a period. In a sentence outline, each sentence is followed by a period.

8. Since a topic cannot be divided unless there are at least two parts, a topic must have two subtopics—or none at all.

9. In a topic outline, main topics should be parallel in form, and subtopics under the same topic should be parallel in form. If, for example, the first topic in a list of topics is a noun, the others should also be nouns. If the first topic is a phrase, the other topics should be similar phrases. However, subtopics need not be parallel with main topics. In a sentence outline, of course, each main topic and each subtopic is written as a complete sentence. Note the faulty parallelism of the subtopics in the following example:

   IV.   Dangerous commercials
       A.   Create demand for luxuries
           1.   Dissatisfied family [adjective and noun]
           2.   Parents in debt [noun and phrase]

10. For each number or letter in an outline there must be a separate topic. Never, for example, write *IA* or *A1* in an outline.

The complete outline for the composition on TV commercials is given below. Compare this outline with the original list of ideas and details in the brainstorming example on page 95, the clustered ideas and details on page 96, and the classification and arrangement of ideas on page 97. Notice that in this final outline the topic "why commercials are necessary" has been added. This additional topic acknowledges the reasons for commercials while raising objections to them. Notice also that some of the supporting ideas have been rephrased to make the outline clear and consistent in form.

TV Commercials: A High Price for a Favorite Program
Purpose: To explain that, while necessary, television commercials can be irritating, insulting, and dangerous.

    I.   Why commercials are necessary
       A.   To pay costs of a TV program
       B.   To sell sponsors' products

   II.   Why some commercials are irritating
       A.   Too repetitious
       B.   Too frequent

III. Why some commercials are insulting
    A. Unexplained virtues of the product
    B. Meaningless testimonials to the product
IV. Why some commercials are dangerous
    A. Create demand for luxuries
        1. Dissatisfied families
        2. Debt-ridden parents
    B. Promote phony cure-alls

EXERCISE 13. Developing a Topic Outline. Arrange the items in the following list into a topic outline. Begin by placing the title, which is included in the list, at the top of your paper. Then group related topics and find a main topic for each group. The topics are correctly phrased so that if properly grouped they will be parallel. Finally, place and letter the subtopics correctly and copy the outline neatly in perfect arrangement.

Counselor at summer camp	Shelf stocker in a supermarket
Indoor work	Requires an interest in children
From tips	Waiter at a summer hotel
The right summer job for you	Confines one to camp
Heavy work	From baby-sitting for guests
Assures an outdoor life	Enjoying hotel's social life
Making extra money	Close to home

EXERCISE 14. Writing Your Own Topic Outlines. For Exercise 12 you classified and arranged ideas and details for three different topics. Create a topic outline for each of the three topics.

WRITING A THESIS STATEMENT

3g. Write a thesis statement for your expository composition.

After classifying and arranging your information and creating a topic outline, you are ready to write a thesis statement for your composition. A thesis statement is the controlling idea of the composition. It states what you will write about in your composition; it reflects your purpose; and it suggests the tone of your composition. Like the topic sentence of a paragraph, the thesis statement focuses your attention and that of your audience on the direction your composition will take.

    The thesis statement is usually included in the introductory section or the introductory paragraph of the composition. Some writers will wait until the end of the paper to state the thesis; others strongly suggest the thesis without ever making a complete statement. You will find, however, that using the thesis statement at the beginning of your paper will serve as a helpful guide as you write the paper.

To develop a thesis statement, start with your topic and expand it to create a precise statement of what you will write about in your composition. Make your thesis statement so direct that it can apply only to one paper, so direct that only one composition could be written to support it. Compare the following two thesis statements for the composition on objections to TV commercials. The first one is vague and undirected while the second one provides an exact, clear direction for the paper.

1. TV commercials are objectionable in many ways.
2. Although TV commercials are necessary, most of them are irritating, insulting, or dangerous.

EXERCISE 15. Writing Thesis Statements.   Write a thesis statement for each of the three topic outlines you developed in Exercise 14.

WRITING

WRITING THE FIRST DRAFT

3h. Write the first draft of your composition.

If you have effectively completed the prewriting stage, you will have already solved many of the problems involved in the actual writing of an expository composition. You have selected and limited a topic and have developed an outline. You have carefully considered your purpose, your audience, and your tone. Using the thesis statement you have developed as the controlling idea of your composition, you are now ready to write.

Writing the Introduction

(1) The introduction makes clear the purpose of the composition and arouses the interest of the audience.

In a short composition, the introduction might be a single sentence. In a long composition, it might be one paragraph or more. Whatever its length, a good introduction should make the purpose of the composition clear. In most cases the introduction should contain the thesis statement or suggest the thesis of the paper. The introduction should also arouse the interest of the readers so that they will want to read further. Four ways to attract the audience's attention are (a) by beginning with a story, (b) by beginning with a startling statement, (c) by beginning with a question, and (d) by beginning with an example.

Beginning with a Story

The paragraphs that follow introduce an article entitled "Clothes Make the Eskimo" that explains how we can learn from the Eskimo the secret of dressing warmly in cold weather. Notice how the story about an Eskimo woman arouses interest because it chronicles intriguing events using vivid images.

> During the winter of 1909, an elderly woman of Flaxman Island, northern Alaska, went out to gather driftwood half a mile from her house. She was wearing only one coat or shirt, hair side turned in. With a sudden onslaught rare in the Flaxman country, a gale descended. She could not find her way home; she had to wait the storm out.
>
> Most Eskimos would have built themselves some sort of a shelter in such a blizzard, but our aged woman thought it too much bother. In the blinding storm, she felt around with her feet until she discovered a tiny knoll. Taking off her mittens, she placed them on the hillock and sat down, using them as insulation to keep her body heat from melting the snow beneath her. Like all good Eskimo garments, her jacket was so designed that she could slip her bare arms out of the sleeves to cross them within the coat upon her bare breast, thus warming them and using them as added radiators to warm the inside of her shirt. With her back to the wind, she settled herself to wait the gale out, leaning slightly forward with elbows on knees so as not to topple over when she fell asleep. Every now and then, stiffened from sitting, she would pick up her mittens and walk around in a small circle. When tired of this, she would sit down again on them and try to sleep. The gale lasted till late afternoon the next day.
>
> When the weather cleared, the old lady came home. She was not very hungry, because she had slept or rested most of the time. It was during the first day that she had been most hungry. No one thought anything of her experience, except that some argued that she should have taken the trouble to build a shelter.
>
> Had she known she was going to be caught out, she would have worn two coats, the entire costume weighing about ten pounds. What she wore weighed six or seven. A Minneapolis businessman going to his office in January would wear from twenty to thirty pounds, and he wouldn't be planning to sit out a two-day blizzard. The difference in their clothing

systems explains largely why the average Minnesotan is more eager to move to California than the average Eskimo. In our time, the Eskimo has been the sole possessor of a clothing system adequate in the sense that it permits in January a degree of mobility, efficiency, and comfort similar to that of July. We have taken a long time to understand how it works, and we are still a long way from making full use of its principles.

VILHJALMUR STEFANSSON—"Clothes Make the Eskimo"

Beginning with a Startling Statement

The following sentences are the opening sentences of five articles in which each writer attracts the attention of the reader by stating a startling fact or opinion.

1. What we have to do, what at any rate it is our duty to do, is to revive this old art of lying.—OSCAR WILDE

2. In one comic book story, out of fifty-one pictures, no less than forty-five are scenes of violence and brutality.—FREDERIC WERTHAM

3. The past fifty years of what we call civilization have utterly ruined childhood.—PHILIP WYLIE

4. Europeans have made a cliché of saying that nothing is so sad as the sight of Americans having a good time.—BERNARD DE VOTO

5. Never was there a stranger purpose than that which brought us together that June night in Euston Railway Station.—VIRGINIA WOOLF

Beginning with a Question

Asking a question at the beginning of a composition has two advantages. First, it is a simple way to clarify what the composition is about since the reader will assume that the writer will answer the question. Second, a question forces the reader to think about the subject—to wonder how the question will be answered. Here are examples of how two writers effectively use questions to introduce their articles.

What is a tropical jungle like, not from distant generalities or sweeping surveys, but as seen by an ordinary human on a very usual walk?

WILLIAM BEEBE

What do college grades predict? Can you forecast from the record of a young man graduating from college now how successful he's likely to be a few decades from now?

SYLVIA PORTER

Beginning with an Example

Beginning an introduction with an example calls direct attention to evidence in support of the writer's thesis. It is a vivid and colorful way of attracting attention while leading the reader directly to the purpose of the essay. Notice, for example, how the introductory paragraph of the composition on TV commercials begins with examples of typical slogans from TV commercials.

> Restore happiness to your household by using Fluff-O fabric softener. Your family will love you for it. End those lonely Saturday nights—use Breatheen mouthwash. Only Aloha Airways will fly you to Hawaii with leg room to spare! Thus the barrage of TV commercials continues day and night in almost every American home. I think most of the commercials are irritating or insulting or dangerous. I believe they should be improved so that they will be not only less offensive to the public but also more effective as advertisements.

EXERCISE 16. Identifying Good Introductions.   Leaf through several magazines looking at the opening paragraphs of articles. Try to find an example of each of the four kinds of beginnings mentioned in this chapter. If you discover any other methods writers use to attract the reader's attention, note them as well. Copy the introductions and be prepared to discuss them in class.

EXERCISE 17. Writing Introductions for Your Own Composition. Select one of the three topic outlines and thesis statements you developed for Exercises 14 and 15. Choose the one you find most interesting and feel most comfortable writing about. Assume you are going to use this outline and thesis statement to write a complete composition; write three different introductions using three of the techniques discussed above. After you have finished writing, select the introduction that you feel is most effective and save it for your composition.

Writing the Body

(2) The body develops the main ideas in the outline.

Using Paragraphs Effectively

As you write, you must decide at what point a new paragraph begins. Keep in mind that when you begin a paragraph, you signal the reader that you are taking up another phase of your subject. Moreover, the amount of space you devote to an idea is an indication of the emphasis you want that idea to have. In a brief composition, therefore, you may find it advisable to devote one paragraph to each of the major (Roman numeral) topics in your outline. For example, if you have listed three main topics, you will have three main paragraphs. Add to these an introductory paragraph and a concluding paragraph and you will have a five-paragraph composition. In the sample composition on pages 110–13, which is written from an outline with four major topics, there are eight paragraphs. Two of these are the introductory paragraph and the concluding paragraph. The six other paragraphs are necessary because two of the four major topics require two paragraphs each for proper development and emphasis.

Most, but not all, of the paragraphs in your expository composition will be developed by using one of the methods recommended for expository paragraphs (pages 64–71). In expository writing, however, the other modes often overlap. Refer to Chapter 2 for suggested methods for developing effective narrative, descriptive, and persuasive paragraphs. For example, including description in an expository composition may help clarify an example or an idea.

Achieving Coherence

When you arranged the topics and subtopics in your outline, you were designing a plan to achieve coherence. Now you must consider how you can achieve coherence by arranging in logical order the paragraphs that make up the body of your composition. The order you choose will depend on your topic. A composition that explains an opinion is frequently arranged in order of importance. In a composition that explains how to do or to make something, chronological or spatial order may be the most appropriate method of arranging ideas. For many topics, some ideas need to be presented first because they help to explain later ideas. See pages 47–54 of Chapter 2 for a more thorough discussion of arranging ideas to achieve coherence.

The beginning of a paragraph signals a shift to another phase of your topic. You should therefore make your train of thought clear to the reader by showing the relationship between the new phase and the phase discussed in the preceding paragraph. There are several devices for accomplishing this transition between paragraphs:

> *Pronouns.* Use pronouns to refer to a person or idea mentioned in the preceding paragraph.

Repetition. Repeat in the first sentence of a paragraph a key word or term used in the preceding paragraph.

Direct Reference. Refer directly to a preceding idea, perhaps by means of a summarizing phrase.

Connectives. Use transitional expressions such as *accordingly, for example, similarly,* and *thus.*

You can use all four of these devices to keep thoughts flowing smoothly from paragraph to paragraph in the same way that linking words and connectives keep the thought flowing from sentence to sentence. For a more thorough discussion of transitions, see pages 55–57 of Chapter 2.

Sometimes, especially in a long paper, you may want to let your reader know that you have completed your discussion of one phase of the subject and are now about to take up another. A brief paragraph will easily accomplish this purpose. Such a paragraph, like the following example, is called a transitional paragraph.

> So much, then, by way of proof that the method of establishing laws in science is exactly the same as that pursued in common life. Let us now turn to another matter (though really it is but another phase of the same question), and that is, the method by which, from the relations of certain phenomena, we prove that some stand in the position of causes toward the others.
>
> THOMAS HENRY HUXLEY

Notice how Huxley uses the first sentence of the paragraph to summarize the preceding discussion. In the second sentence of the paragraph, he suggests the content of the discussion that is to follow. Such paragraphs are especially useful whenever there is a major shift in the content of your essay or composition.

EXERCISE 18. Identifying Transitional Expressions. Examine a daily newspaper or a current magazine to find examples of transitional devices used by professional writers. Copy five paragraph openings that contain such devices. Underline the transitional expressions and be prepared to discuss how they are used.

EXERCISE 19. Writing the Body of Your Own Composition. Using the thesis statement and outline for which you wrote an introductory paragraph in Exercise 17, write the body of your composition.

Writing the Conclusion

(3) The conclusion summarizes or reemphasizes the main points of the composition.

Once you have completed the body of your composition, you are ready to write the conclusion. The conclusion should bring the composition to a satisfactory close for the reader. Sometimes a conclusion summarizes the main points made in the composition; at other times a conclusion suggests or predicts changes that may occur in the future. When you write your own conclusion, remember that you should create a definite closing and not leave your readers feeling that you simply ran out of things to say. Experienced writers use many different techniques to create a satisfactory conclusion. Notice the variety in the following examples:

1

But as Mr. Backster and all other scientists know, his hypothesis could be wrong. The hypothesis will have to be tested by other scientists in other laboratories.

Suggests future course of action

EDWIN STEINKAMP

2

You have now made a basic trout-fly. Tell someone to go catch a fish with it.

J. A. MAXTONE GRAHAM

Summarizes process explained in essay and concludes with light, catchy suggestion

3

Then, Sir, from these six capital sources—of descent, of form of government, of religion in the Northern Provinces, of manners in the Southern, of education, of the remoteness of situation from the first mover of government—from all these causes a fierce spirit of liberty has grown up. It has grown with the growth of the people in your Colonies, and increased with the increase of their wealth; a spirit that unhappily meeting with an exercise of power in England which, however lawful, is not reconcilable to any ideas of liberty,

Summarizes main points of the composition: there are six sources of disobedience in the colonies

much less with theirs, has kindled this flame that is ready to consume us.

EDMUND BURKE

4

In the case of some cities, no given advantage can be found to "explain" their existence in a specious way. All that Birmingham seems to have had, to begin with, was a good supply of drinking water—no novelty in Renaissance England. Alcaeus made the point in 600 B.C. when he wrote of the other given cities of Greece, "Not houses finely roofed nor the stones of walls well built nor canals nor dockyards make the city, but men able to use their opportunity."

Uses quotation to restate thesis that "cities simply cannot be 'explained' by their locations or other given resources"

JANE JACOBS

Conclusions vary in length as well as in technique. They may be as brief as one or two sentences or as long as two or three paragraphs. The brief, one- or two-sentence conclusion may be in a separate final paragraph or it may be included as the end of the final paragraph in the body of the paper.

EXERCISE 20. Analyzing Conclusions.   Using newspapers or magazines, analyze the conclusions of three different articles.

EXERCISE 21. Writing a Conclusion for Your Own Composition. Write a conclusion for the composition you began in Exercises 17 and 19. Be sure the conclusion is a definite signal to the reader that the composition has been completed.

STUDYING A SAMPLE COMPOSITION

The following composition is a model developed from the outline you studied on pages 100–101. Read the composition and examine its organization. Notice how the introduction captures the audience's interest and states what the composition will be about. Also notice how the body develops the headings in the sample outline and how the conclusion brings the composition to a satisfactory close for the reader.

TV COMMERCIALS:
A HIGH PRICE FOR A FAVORITE PROGRAM

Restore happiness to your household by using Fluff-O fabric softener. Your family will love you for it. End those lonely Saturday nights—use Breatheen mouthwash. Only Aloha Airways will fly you to Hawaii with leg room to spare! Thus the barrage of TV commercials continues day and night in almost every American home. Although TV commercials are necessary, most of them are irritating or insulting or dangerous. I believe they can be improved so that they will be not only less offensive to the public but also more effective as advertisements.

Even while I am registering my objections to commercials, I recognize that commercials are necessary. Without them we would have no television programs, for it is the sponsor who pays the bill. Since the money that pays for a TV program comes from the sale of the sponsor's products, the sponsor must have air-time in which to advertise. Americans must put up with the hourly brainwashing, and they must buy the sponsor's products if they want to enjoy television. They should not, however, have to endure the kind of advertising that accompanies most of the programs.

This advertising is objectionable, first, because it is irritating. The two sources of irritation are the endless repetition of the same commercial and the too-frequent interruption of programs. I suppose that once advertisers have a slogan that has proved effective, they are reluctant to give it up. If they realized, however, that the familiar words become meaningless after a thousand repetitions, they might discover that an occasional change would be effective. My parents say that some of the phrases commonly heard today—for example, "a combination of medically proved and tested ingredi-

title

introduction

uses examples to create interest

thesis statement

transition—key words
topic sentence

(compare outline: I, A and B)

transition—direct reference
topic sentence

transitional word

(compare outline: II, A)

ents"—were used in radio advertising in the forties. The truth is that no one pays any attention to the worn-out slogans, and everyone is irritated rather than interested when the familiar lines begin.

I think, too, that advertisers lose more than they gain when they insist on interrupting a program every ten minutes to plug their product. Irritating the viewer-buyer is surely not the way to sell anything. Just as the bad guys are about to destroy the good guys, a program is cut off, and we are taken into a sparkling kitchen to observe the wonders of a floor wax or a detergent or a hand lotion—wonders we have heard proclaimed night after night. As we are poised on the brink of disaster in an adventure film or carried away by the immortal lines of Shakespeare, the illusion is shattered by the shouted advice that only by banking at National can we become millionaires. If sponsors would all agree to confine commercials to the beginning and end of programs, the public's appreciation would be reflected in its buying. If they would realize how weary we get of the same old commercials, they might find an occasional change to be surprisingly effective.

(transitional word)
(topic sentence)

(compare outline: II, B)

Another kind of objectionable commercial is the kind that insults our mentality with its meaningless claims. When we analyze the claims made by many TV commercials, we find ourselves asking, quite logically, "Well, so what?" In our simpleminded way, however, we are expected to accept blindly the word of a cowpuncher or a water-skier as sure proof of the quality of a soft drink. Every Little Leaguer knows that a .360 batting average is not the result of eating a particular breakfast food. Similarly, parents know that not all family problems will be solved by swallowing a couple of headache pills. Even shy and desperate

(transitional expression)
(topic sentence)

(transitional word)

(compare outline: III, A and B)
(transitional word)

Danny doubts that a change in deodorant, shaving lotion, or mouthwash will make him irresistible to the prettiest models on TV. Claims that are completely without reason are insulting to thinking people. The writers of commercials should give the viewer credit for some intelligence.

Finally, TV commercials can be dangerous. They can endanger the finances of the American family. The goal of advertisers is to create a demand if none exists. Everyone should have the latest dishwasher, the newest electric hair dryer, a second car, and such status symbols as a backyard swimming pool and a winter vacation. To listen to the honeyed pleas of the handsome, suntanned, obviously happy announcers, one wonders how any of us can possibly live another minute without all the luxuries of a millionaire. But, then, the solution is so easy. Just apply for a personal loan—fast, courteous, no questions asked—and let the Easy Loan Finance Company pay all your bills at once. "We'll even write the checks." This lure could be irresistible to a young breadwinner trying to keep up with the standard of living fostered by the commercials the family watches every night as they try to see a favorite program in between.

transitional word
topic sentence

(compare outline: IV, A, 1 and 2)

Commercials endanger our health as well as our budgets. Although the writers are careful to advise us to see our doctors "if the pain persists," they do strongly suggest that we ailing viewers can get the relief we want just as well by following the do-it-yourself patent-medicine approach. We are presented with a sure cure for every ailment. We can fill our medicine cabinets until they are bursting with cure-alls, fill our objecting stomachs with pills, and cover ourselves with creams and ointments. Certainly the daily bombardment leads many people into a way of living that is dangerous to both their pocketbooks and their health.

transition—direct reference
topic sentence

(compare outline: IV, B)

The irritations, insults, and dangerous misrepresentations in TV commercials have been accepted as inevitable for far too long. Perhaps in the near future the broadcasting industry will recognize its mistakes and make changes to accommodate the needs and intelligence of the viewers.

> conclusion—
> summarizes main
> points and suggests
> direction for the
> future

EXERCISE 22. Studying an Expository Composition. Refer to the composition above as you answer the following questions. Be prepared to explain your answers. You may find it helpful to refer to page 94 and pages 103–109.

1. How effective is the introduction in arousing interest and stating the main idea of the composition?
2. Review the organization of the body. Is the supporting information presented in a logical order?
3. Study the paragraphs in the body. What other details, if any, do you think the writer could have added to support each topic sentence more effectively? Have any details been included that should be omitted? If so, what are they?
4. How effective is the conclusion? Does it bring the composition to a close in a satisfactory manner?
5. How might you rewrite the title to make it more interesting or more indicative of the content of the composition?

CRITICAL THINKING:
Synthesizing Ideas

Synthesis is the critical thinking skill that involves the bringing together of a number of parts or elements to create a whole. To write an expository composition, you must use the critical thinking skill of synthesis. When you synthesize you bring together the thesis statement, the outline, the supportive details you have generated, and your knowledge of organization to create a whole—the complete composition.

REVIEW EXERCISE B. Synthesizing Ideas for an Expository Composition. Select a topic that is appropriate for an expository composition. You may, if you wish, choose a topic developed in previous exercises. Gather information for your topic, develop a thesis statement and an outline, and write the first draft of an expository composition. Use the Guidelines for Writing Expository Compositions on pages 120–21 as an aid in the writing process.

EVALUATING

EVALUATING EXPOSITORY COMPOSITIONS

3i. Evaluate your first draft for content, organization, and style.

At earlier stages in the writing process, you were asked to evaluate your own writing and the writing of others. You will find, also, that evaluation is very effective when you have completed your first draft. Problems that might have slowed down your creativity if you had stopped to solve them earlier can be dealt with more efficiently at this stage in the writing process.

When you have finished the first draft of your paper, you must, in a sense, stop being the writer and become the reader, the editor, the critic. You must be able to distance yourself from your own words and evaluate what you have written.

When you evaluate you must consider three aspects of your draft: (1) content (what you have said), (2) organization (how you have arranged your ideas), and (3) style (how you have used words and sentences to express your ideas). The guidelines that follow provide a convenient checklist for evaluating the first draft of an expository composition.

GUIDELINES FOR EVALUATING EXPOSITORY COMPOSITIONS

Introduction	1. Does the introduction include a statement of the thesis and attract the attention of the reader?
Topic Unity	2. Does each paragraph relate to and support the thesis of the composition?
Paragraph Unity	3. Does each paragraph discuss only one main idea?
Topic Development	4. Is the thesis adequately developed; that is, are enough details included to support the thesis stated in the introduction?

Conclusion	5. Does the conclusion bring the composition to a satisfactory close for the reader?
Coherence	6. Are the paragraphs in the body of the composition arranged in an order that is clear to the reader?
	7. Are transitional devices used to link ideas within paragraphs and to show the relationships among ideas in different paragraphs?
Audience	8. Are the paragraphs of a length that will be easy for the reader to follow?
Emphasis	9. Is the amount of space devoted to any given topic in proportion to the importance of that topic?
Tone	10. Is the language appropriate for the intended audience and for the expository purpose of the composition?

EXERCISE 23. Applying the Guidelines for Evaluating Expository Compositions.   Below is an early draft of the fifth paragraph in the sample composition on pages 110–13. As you read the draft, apply the Guidelines for Evaluating Expository Compositions. Then answer the questions that follow the draft. Be prepared to give reasons for your answers.

There is also the kind that insults our mentality with its meaningless claims. If one studies the claims, one will find himself or herself asking, quite logically, "Well, so what?" In a simple-minded way, people are expected to accept blindly someone else's word as sure proof of the quality of a soft drink. Every kid knows that a .360 batting average is not the result of eating breakfast cereal. Parents know that not all family problems will be solved by downing headache pills. Claims that are completely without reason are insulting to thinking people. Even shy and desperate Danny doubts that a change in deodorant, shaving lotion, or mouthwash will make him irresistible to the prettiest models on TV.

1. Does the paragraph flow smoothly from the paragraph that precedes it?
2. Are transitions needed to connect any of the ideas in the paragraph?
3. In which, if any, instances should the wording be changed to make the tone more appropriate or to make the meaning clearer?
4. Which, if any, of the details that support the writer's main idea seem to be out of order?
5. Does the paragraph come to a satisfactory end, or should something be added to clinch the writer's main idea?

6. What specific changes to the paragraph do you think the writer should make? Be prepared to give a reason for each suggested change.

EXERCISE 24. Evaluating Your Own Draft. Evaluate the first draft you wrote for Review Exercise B by applying the Guidelines for Evaluating Expository Compositions. Mark places in your draft where changes should be made and keep the marked draft for later use. You may also find it helpful to exchange papers with a classmate and evaluate one another's work.

REVISING

REVISING A FIRST DRAFT

3j. Revise your first draft, making any changes needed to improve the content, organization, and style.

Most of the changes needed to improve the content, organization, and style of your first draft can be made by using one of four techniques: cutting, adding, reordering, or replacing. The following chart for revising expository compositions shows how you can use these techniques to improve the draft you evaluated for Exercise 24.

REVISING EXPOSITORY COMPOSITIONS

PROBLEM	TECHNIQUE	REVISION
The introduction lacks interest.	Add	Begin with an interesting story, a startling statement, a question, or an example.
The introduction does not make clear the thesis statement, or what the composition will be about.	Add	Include the thesis statement or a sentence that suggests the thesis.

PROBLEM	TECHNIQUE	REVISION
Some of the paragraphs are too long.	Cut/Add	Remove details that are not directly related to one idea. Develop a new paragraph with these ideas or add them to an existing, shorter paragraph on the same idea.
The relationship between paragraphs is not clear.	Add	Use a transitional device (pronoun reference, connectives) that will help the reader follow the train of thought and clarify the relationships between the paragraphs.
The order of ideas is difficult to follow.	Reorder	Identify the sentence or paragraph that is out of order. Move it so that the order of ideas is easy to follow.
It is not clear which ideas are the most important.	Add	Identify the most important ideas and emphasize them by adding details related to those ideas.
The ending is not forceful.	Add	Add details to the ending that summarize or reemphasize the main ideas in the composition. If appropriate, end with a suggestion for future action or with a catchy phrase.
Some of the language is not appropriate for the intended tone.	Replace	To make the tone more serious, replace slang, contractions, and informal expressions with more formal language. To make the tone lighter, replace more formal language with slang and contractions.

The revision below shows the changes made by the writer in the draft in Exercise 23. As you study the revisions, refer to the notes in the margin. They indicate the revision strategies used by the writer. The lines have been numbered for easy reference in Exercise 25.

Another kind of objectionable commercial is

1   ~~There is also~~ the kind that insults our mentality   replace

When we analyze

2   with its meaningless claims. ~~If one studies~~ the   replace

made by many TV commercials, we   ourselves

3   claims, ~~one~~ will find ~~himself or herself~~ asking, quite   add/replace

our

4   logically, "Well, so what?" In a simple-minded way,   replace

however, we   the

5   ~~people~~ are expected to accept blindly ~~someone else's~~   replace

of a cow-puncher or a water-skier

6   word as sure proof of the quality of a soft drink.   add

Little Leaguer

7   Every kid knows that a .360 batting average is not   replace

a particular food Similarly, parents

8   the result of eating breakfast ~~cereal~~. ~~Parents~~ know   add/replace/add

9   that not all family problems will be solved by

swallowing a couple of

10   ~~downing~~ headache pills. (Claims that are completely   replace/reorder

11   without reason are insulting to thinking people.)

12   Even shy and desperate Danny doubts that a change

13   in deodorant, shaving lotion, or mouthwash will

14   make him irresistible to the prettiest models on TV.   add

*The writers of commercials should give the viewer
credit for some intelligence.*

EXERCISE 25. Evaluating a Revised Paragraph.   Answer each of the following questions by referring to the preceding revised paragraph.

1. Why do you think the writer revised the beginning of the first sentence? (Before answering this question, read the paragraph in the sample composition, pages 110–13, that precedes the revised paragraph.)
2. In line 2, why do you think the writer added the phrase "made by many TV commercials"?
3. How does the change in pronouns in lines 2 and 3 add to the consistency of the paragraph?

4. How does the change in line 6 add interest to the paragraph?
5. Why do you think the writer moved the sentence in lines 10–11?
6. Why do you suppose the writer added a sentence to the paragraph?
7. Does changing *kid* to *Little Leaguer* (line 7) and *downing* to *swallowing* (line 10) make the tone of the paragraph more formal or less formal?
8. Where in the paragraph did the writer add transitions? How do these transitions make the ideas easier to follow?

EXERCISE 26. Revising Your Own Composition.   Revise the first draft of the expository composition you evaluated for Exercise 24 on page 116. Use the chart on pages 116–17 for revising expository compositions to decide what techniques you should use in your revision. Then make the necessary changes.

PROOFREADING

PROOFREADING EXPOSITORY COMPOSITIONS

3k. Proofread your expository composition for errors in spelling, grammar, usage, and mechanics.

If it is to meet its purpose, to inform or explain, expository writing must be clear and precise. Errors in spelling, punctuation, capitalization, grammar, or usage may confuse or irritate your audience and thus interfere with your attempt to convey information. By proofreading carefully, you will be able to identify and correct any errors that might have slipped by unnoticed in the revision process.

EXERCISE 27. Proofreading Your Expository Composition. Proofread the expository composition you revised for Exercise 26. Read your paper several times, each time concentrating on a separate aspect: spelling, punctuation, capitalization, grammar, or usage. Make notations on your paper indicating the corrections that should be made on your final copy. Refer to the Guidelines for Proofreading on page 30 and to the Symbols for Proofreading and Revising on page 34.

WRITING THE FINAL VERSION

PREPARING THE FINAL DRAFT OF YOUR EXPOSITORY COMPOSITION

3l. Prepare the final copy of your composition.

After you have proofread your revised draft, you are ready for the final stage of the writing process: preparing a final copy of your composition. Your main concern at this stage is to implement the revisions you have made in various drafts and the corrections you have made in the proofreading stage. You need to create a neat, attractive final copy that will reflect the thought and care you have devoted to the whole process. Follow correct manuscript form (see Chapter 1) or your teacher's specific instructions for this assignment. After writing the final version, proofread again to identify any inadvertent errors that might have occurred in the retyping or rewriting of your composition.

EXERCISE 28. Preparing Your Final Version. Prepare a final version of the expository composition you proofread for Exercise 27.

CHAPTER 3 WRITING REVIEW

Writing an Expository Composition. Write a three- to five-page expository composition on a topic of your choice. Keep in mind that the purpose of an expository composition is to inform or explain. Refer to the guidelines below and to the specific Techniques discussed throughout this chapter.

GUIDELINES FOR WRITING EXPOSITORY COMPOSITIONS

Prewriting

1. Choose a topic you understand well. If you do not understand the topic, you will have difficulty explaining it to others.
2. Limit your topic so that it is manageable in a relatively short composition.
3. Take time to gather ample information to support your topic. Depending on your topic and audience, gather facts, statistics, specific details, examples, or incidents.

4. Keep your audience in mind. Determine whether any technical terms or unusual vocabulary will have to be defined in your composition.

5. Organize the information in a logical order. Use an informal plan or an outline to establish the basic organization for your paper.

Writing

6. Write an interesting introduction that clearly indicates what the composition is about.

7. Use your informal plan or topic outline as a guide when you draft the body of your composition. If your composition is to be brief, write one paragraph for each main topic. If your composition is to be longer than a couple of pages, consider devoting one paragraph to each subtopic in your outline. (See the sample composition on pages 110–13 as a model for paragraphing.) Remember that a topic or subtopic may be emphasized by the space devoted to it in the composition. Use transitions (expressions and paragraphs) to show how ideas are related to one another.

8. Consider the tone you want to convey and try to choose words and create sentence structures that are appropriate to that tone. Remember also that the language you choose should be appropriate for your audience.

9. When you write your concluding paragraph, attempt to bring a satisfying end to the thoughts in your composition. You may want to restate your thesis, summarize your main points, or project future possibilities.

Evaluating, Revising, and Proofreading

10. Check to see if you have included appropriate and sufficient information for your audience and your purpose. Study your organization to determine whether it is logical and appropriate for your content. Reevaluate your choice of words by considering how appropriate your language is for your audience and the tone you wish to convey.

11. Revise, making changes to improve the problems you discovered by evaluating.

12. Proofread carefully and make any needed changes in grammar, mechanics, and usage.

CHAPTER 4

Writing Expository Compositions

SPECIFIC EXPOSITORY WRITING ASSIGNMENTS

The general principles of writing exposition apply to most of the writing you will do in school. Nevertheless, certain kinds of expository writing come up often enough to merit special treatment. These types include exposition that informs, exposition that explains, informal (personal) essays, explaining cause and effect, essays of classification, essays of definition, critical reviews, and essays of literary analysis.

EXPOSITION THAT INFORMS

A common purpose of expository writing is to inform. The essay questions that you answer on an examination and the reports that you write for your teachers are two examples of informational writing.

When you write a paper whose purpose is to inform, you take a subject and open it up to your audience. Your purpose is not to argue or to persuade but to convey information clearly and accurately.

Prewriting Hints for Exposition That Informs

1. *Select a subject on which you either have or can find adequate information.* When you write about something known to you, you will not be at a loss for ideas.

2. *Identify the audience for whom you are writing.* Consider

the kind of audience you are writing for as you determine the complexity of ideas and the language you will use in your explanation.

3. *Limit your subject by analyzing its categories or logical divisions.* Arrive at a manageable topic by taking a careful look at your subject to determine exactly what it consists of. If your subject is "pets," you could focus on unusual indoor pets, the responsibilities of caring for pets, etc.

4. *Gather information on your topic.* Using the techniques on pages 12–18, collect information on your topic.

5. *Explain your purpose in a thesis statement.* In a paper on "pets as therapy," the following thesis statement will indicate the direction of your paper: "Researchers are learning how pets can help cheer the depressed, reform delinquents, and even lower blood pressure."

6. *Organize your information in an informal outline.* Write your thesis statement at the top of a sheet of paper. Then list the facts that you have gathered about your subject. Review your list, looking for main ideas and for specific details that support each main idea. Arrange these in the most logical order for your particular topic. Add any details related to the topic. Discard details that do not support a main idea.

Writing Exposition That Informs

In the following informational composition about skiing, note that the first sentence in the introduction states what direction the exposition will take: the beginnings of the sport. The body provides information that focuses on the development of skiing as a sport. In the conclusion, the audience is left with a sense of the present-day popularity of skiing as a sport.

SKIING—THEN AND NOW

We can't be sure just where skiing began. *introduction*
However, there is no doubt about how it began. In *thesis statement*
northern Europe and Asia, deep snow blanketed
the land most of the year. Ancient peoples moving
from place to place are known to have experimented with crude footwear for easier going in the
snow. Those primitive efforts probably resulted in
history's first snowshoe. This was a help, but not
the answer.

We can guess that one day someone walking *body*

down a steep, icy hill started to slide. Amazingly, the trip to the bottom was accomplished in record time. And it was much easier than legging it one step at a time through the snow.

main idea: probable circumstances of invention

History's first skier was probably quite pleased with the discovery and set about to improve his or her sliding shoes. Smooth wooden slats attached to the shoes were the result. We know this because the word *ski* comes from a northern European word meaning "a splinter cut from a log."

How old is skiing? Well, a pair of skis in a Swedish museum is thought to be at least five thousand years old. Stone carvings in a Norwegian cave, said to date back at least four thousand years, show skiing. And by the seventh century A.D. the Chinese were writing about it.

details
main idea: chronology

Skis helped people travel and hunt in the frigid Scandinavian countries for centuries before anyone thought about using them for sport. Then, in the eighteenth century, Norwegian soldiers on skis took part in a sporting contest in what is now the city of Oslo. Zigzagging between bushes and trees on their way down the slope, they accidentally hit on the idea of the slalom. The slalom today is one of skiing's most popular and demanding events.

details
main idea: early uses

In the 1850s, the Norwegians began holding annual competitions in the valley of Telemark. They developed a means of holding the heel in place on the ski, thereby making the first ski jump possible, which took place on Norway's Huseby Hill, in 1879. In 1883, two main kinds of skiing— cross-country racing and jumping—were separated out for competition purposes.

details
main idea: beginnings of annual competition

During the next few decades, the new and exciting sport from Norway spread to almost every country that had snow, including England. It was in England that standards and rules for the modern slalom were officially set down, even though slalom

details
main idea: spread of skiing

is a Scandinavian word (*sla* means "slope" and *lom* means "track left in the snow").

Skiing has grown extremely popular in the United States. The first U.S. ski club was organized in 1867 in, believe it or not, Laporte, California!

Today, wherever you can find a mountain and some snow, you are likely to see cars with ski racks on their roofs heading for the slopes and bumpers on the cars displaying stickers saying, "Think snow!"

details

conclusion

DON SMITH with DR. ANNE MARIE MUESER

GUIDELINES FOR EVALUATING EXPOSITION THAT INFORMS

Topic	1. Is the subject limited to a manageable topic?
Thesis Development	2. Does the thesis statement tell the audience the direction the paper will take?
Topic Development	3. Is each main idea supported with specific details? Is adequate information included to inform the audience about the topic?

EXERCISE 1. Writing Exposition That Informs. Using the following suggestions, write an informational exposition.

1. Select a subject on which you can write an informational paper. Analyze the subject and divide it into a number of logical divisions or main topics that can be developed in no more than seven paragraphs. As you write your first draft, refer to the Prewriting Hints for Exposition That Informs on pages 122–23 and to the model.
2. Use the Guidelines for Evaluating Exposition That Informs and the Guidelines for Evaluating Expository Compositions (pages 114–15) to identify any problems in your draft.
3. Referring to the chart on pages 27–28, revise your first draft.
4. Use the Guidelines for Proofreading (page 30) to proofread your revised draft for accurate spelling, punctuation, grammar, and usage.
5. As you write the final draft, follow correct manuscript form (pages 31–33) or your teacher's instructions for this assignment. Proofread your final draft for any recopying or retyping inaccuracies.

EXPOSITION THAT EXPLAINS

The kind of exposition that you use most often is exposition that explains. You may frequently find yourself telling someone (1) how to get somewhere, (2) how to make or do something, or (3) how something works. When you explain a process, it is especially important to arrange your ideas in logical order so that your explanation is clear to your audience.

Prewriting Hints for Exposition That Explains

1. *Select a subject that can be explained within the limits of your composition.* In a seven-paragraph paper on "how to study," the subject might be one aspect of studying: conditions, for example.

2. *Identify your audience.* Consider your audience when you decide on the complexity of the ideas and the language in your explanation.

3. *Gather information on your subject.* Determine exactly which steps you must describe in the process you are explaining. Then list the ideas you might include in your explanation. (For help in finding information on a subject that requires library research and taking notes, see pages 255–68.)

4. *Organize your information.* Break down the steps of the process that you are explaining into those details that support each step. For example, if one of the steps toward the establishment of successful study habits is assembling proper equipment, include details related to that step (suitable chair, adequate lighting, etc.). An informal plan or a topic outline (pages 98–101) will help you organize your list.

5. *Arrange the steps in the process in an order that will be easy for your audience to follow.* In a process explanation, the most natural order is chronological order—the sequence in which each step is taken.

6. *Determine beforehand which parts of the process require thorough explanation.* Keep the needs of your audience in mind. Be prepared to define technical terms in words that the audience will understand. If necessary, include a simple diagram to make a complicated step in a process easier to comprehend. If the process involves amounts, measurements, or distances, be as precise as possible.

Writing Exposition That Explains

As you read the following explanation, note how the process being described has been broken down into three main steps with a series of supporting details (or in this instance, substeps). Note also that the writer includes a diagram (not shown) and makes use of definitions, examples, and transitional words. (This example is an excerpt from a longer explanation and, consequently, has no conclusion.)

MAKING ELECTRICITY FROM A MOUNTAIN STREAM

If you live in a mountainous area and a brook flows swiftly through your property, you can tap its energy with the miniature equivalent of a hydroelectric power station. A relatively small and simple system based on a water-driven turbine and a small electric generator can supplement current from your local utility. With a larger turbine and generator, you can free yourself from commercial power sources altogether. Large systems are costly, but where utility-supplied power is not available and the only alternative is a gasoline- or diesel-powered generator, a home system can prove competitive.

The ability of a stream to produce electric power depends on two factors: flow, the technical term for the volume of water the stream carries; and head, the drop in elevation along the portion of the watercourse where the system will be built. Where little head is available—as in a river flowing through flatlands—an expensive, complex dam is essential to back up the stream and create an artificial difference in water level. A mountain stream, on the other hand, often supplies sufficient head for a home hydroelectric system and needs only to be dammed with a few boulders or logs to channel sufficient flow into the system's inlet pipe, called the penstock.

Before planning a water-powered generating system, you must calculate both the head and the flow available from your stream. (Remember, however, that even streams running through private property are subject to laws regarding conservation and water rights; check with the local water resources agency before undertaking a hydroelectric project.) The easiest way to measure the

[margin annotations:]
introduction
thesis statement

body
definition of technical term
definition of technical term

definition of technical term

transition
first step

detail supporting step 1

flow of a stream no more than 7 feet wide is to interrupt it with a temporary plywood weir (*opposite*). The flow of a larger stream may be listed at a local U.S. Geological Survey office or, in Canada, at the municipal or district office responsible for natural resources. If not, you can hire a civil engineer to take flow readings. In any case, you will need monthly flow figures for an entire year to be sure that the water level does not drop too low for the generating purposes during the dry season. Also check to see that the stream is not subject to destructive flooding.

To measure the head that your stream can provide, you will need a long measuring pole marked off in 6-inch increments, a second pole exactly 5 feet long, a 50-foot steel tape, a hand-held sighting level and a helper. In general, you will need at least 50 feet of head to make home electrical generating practical.

Once you have exact figures for the flow and the head, a simple formula allows you to calculate the amount of power available in the stream. Multiply the head measurement, in feet, by the flow, in cubic feet per minute; then divide the result by 708 to get the theoretical yield, in kilowatts of electric power. Because no system, no matter how efficient, will enable you to tap completely the theoretical potential of a stream, the calculated yield should be at least twice the number of kilowatts you need for your household.

You will need the head and flow figures—as well as your kilowatt requirements and a detailed description of the topography surrounding your stream—when you begin shopping for a turbine and generator. Turbine manufacturers—most of them small firms in the western United States —generally sell their equipment in complete systems, each tailored to the customer's site and

reference to diagram of weir (not shown here)

detail supporting step 1

detail supporting step 1

detail supporting step 1

materials needed and exact measurements

transition

second step

detail supporting step 2

transition

detail supporting step 2

transition; third step

needs. The system will include the turbine and either an alternating- or a direct-current generator. For systems that are to be interconnected with public utility lines, the supplier will also include hardware and electric-safety devices to ensure that the electricity produced is compatible with that delivered by the utility.

From *Home Repair and Improvement*/ENERGY ALTERNATIVES. © 1982 by Time-Life Books Inc. Reprinted by permission of Time-Life Books Inc.

GUIDELINES FOR EVALUATING EXPOSITION THAT EXPLAINS

Topic	1. Is the topic limited so that it can be adequately explained in the space allowed?
Audience	2. Are the ideas developed in language appropriate to the audience?
	3. Are any terms that might be unfamiliar to the audience explained?
Order	4. Are ideas arranged in chronological order?
Topic Development	5. Are examples, comparisons, specific measurements, and other explanatory details used as needed?

EXERCISE 2. Writing Exposition That Explains.   Using the following suggestions, write an exposition that explains.

1. Plan and write a composition that explains how to do something or how something works. Limit the subject to one that can be developed in no more than seven paragraphs. As you write your first draft, refer to the Prewriting Hints for Exposition That Explains.
2. Use the Guidelines for Evaluating Exposition That Explains and the Guidelines for Evaluating Expository Compositions (pages 114–15) to mark places where you should change your draft.
3. Using the Revising Chart on pages 27–28, decide what strategies you will use to revise your draft. Then, make the necessary changes.
4. Use the Guidelines for Proofreading (page 30) to proofread for any inaccuracies in spelling, punctuation, grammar, and usage.
5. As you write the final draft, follow correct manuscript form (pages 31–33) or your teacher's instructions for this assignment.
6. Proofread your final draft for any recopying or retyping inaccuracies.

INFORMAL (PERSONAL) ESSAYS

The informal essay presents the writer's personal view(s) on a subject. Almost any subject is suitable, as long as the writer develops it in a discussion that holds the audience's interest. The writer creates and sustains this interest by taking a fresh, unique approach and developing the subject in an entertaining and enlightening discussion.

The informal essay may appear to be more loosely organized than the formal essay. However, like all effective compositions, the informal essay develops one main idea (the thesis) according to a systematic plan worked out during the prewriting stage.

Prewriting Hints for Informal Essays

1. *Select and limit your subject.* Choose a subject that you know well and have strong feelings about. Jot down ideas about it. Then, look over your list. Which ideas suggest a new slant on your subject that will interest your audience? State this idea in a single sentence, which will become your thesis.

2. *Gather sufficient information on your topic.* List specific facts, examples, and details about your topic. Under the topic "how you enjoy job interviews," for example, you might list your discomfort before going to your first interview, your experiences at the interview, and your various reasons for enjoying interviews now. Let your ideas flow and gather as much information as you can.

3. *Organize your information in a logical plan.* Identify the main ideas that you will use to develop your thesis. Order your ideas in a sequence that will catch and hold your audience's attention. You could introduce your thesis in the first paragraph with an amusing anecdote, a question, a surprising statement, or some other engaging opening. You could then go on to develop your topic with supporting facts, specific details, or examples. Generally, you will want to present your most striking information at the beginning and at the end of your essay to attract your audience's attention and to leave the audience with a memorable idea or instance.

4. *Decide upon an appropriate tone and use it consistently.* Humor, irony, fear, sorrow, and other emotional points of view are often well suited to the tone of an informal essay. Since most subjects can be approached from several points of view, identify your tone early in your planning so that you can maintain it consistently. Handle your tone carefully so that it neither overpowers nor weakens your essay. Concentrate instead on expressing your ideas with words and details that carry, not broadcast, your tone.

5. *Strive to keep your audience interested.* Your personal views and interests may bore your audience unless you express your ideas in an interesting and informative way. Therefore, concentrate on providing enough information so that your audience can first understand your feelings. Then focus on keeping them interested with vivid, entertaining details and examples. Examine your plan and keep changing it until you are confident that your essay will attract and hold your audience's interest.

Writing Informal Essays

In the following informal essay, the author, William Safire, gives his view on automobile telephones. The first paragraph begins the essay with an amusing anecdote, which is followed by four paragraphs of specific information about mobile telephones and their growing acceptance in society. The writer then asserts his differing position on mobile telephones and in the sixth paragraph states his thesis: that "the invasion" of mobile phones "is an abomination and a horror show." The rest of the essay goes on to detail several of the writer's personal reasons for not wanting a telephone in his car.

Notice how the author attracts and holds his audience's interest by (1) using specific, vivid words and examples; (2) supporting his views with specific, personal incidents that his audience can relate to; and (3) creating a humorous tone by overstating some examples.

In reading the essay, notice that these three techniques overlap. Analyze the essay carefully, noting where you can use similar techniques in your essay.

CALLING ALL CARS

A generation ago, working on a story for the *New York Herald Tribune* about the radio pioneer David Sarnoff, I was told that I could reach him on the telephone in his car. That sounded exciting. As instructed, I dialed zero and asked for the mobile operator—and wound up connected to a woman in Mobile, Ala., who thought I had <u>gone bananas</u>.

specific, personal incident used to introduce subject

use of vivid language to set tone

That would not happen in today's era of the cellular mobile phone. In an editorial, the *New York Times* gave warm support this week to a proposal to auction channels on the radio spectrum to car-phone companies.

That idea was first propounded on another subject by the conservative economist Milton Friedman, whose notion—much derided by liberals 20 years ago—was to get the Federal Communications Commission to stop giving away licenses to use the public airwaves for broadcasting, and instead to sell those licenses to the highest bidders, letting the free market rather than the regulators decide who gets to be heard.

transition

It is gratifying to see *The Times* embrace the Friedman no-free-lunch philosophy, but one sentence in that editorial cries out for rebuttal.

summary of introduction leading up to statement of thesis

"For example," went this encomium to the pace of change in communications technology, "everyone agrees that cellular mobile telephones are a boon."

Hold on. I'm part of "everyone," and I think the invasion of the sanctity of the personal automobile by the most intrusive instrument yet invented is an abomination and a horror show.

thesis

Why? Because I am one of the millions who drive to work alone.

supporting reason begins here

That makes me an elitist in the eyes of social engineers who want all worker-ants to march onto mass transportation, ride together in a delivery-efficient mode, and march to their jobs in an uncongested stream.

use of overstatement to create a humorous tone

That makes me a perpetrator of a highway-clogging "single-occupant vehicle" to traffic planners who reserve fast lanes to bureaucratically acceptable "high-occupancy vehicles."

use of specific jargon to poke fun at traffic planners

But I enjoy driving to and from work alone. That half-hour each way is the only time I am unreachable by telephone.

Oh, lots of times at work I rev up my word-processing terminal and say imperiously to my assistant, "I cannot be reached," but she knows that if the President calls, I can be reached. Or the

specific examples

Vice President. Or the publisher. Or "Mr. Good-fellow," the White House speaker.

My house number is unlisted, like the Beverly Hills Fire Department, to give me a chance to think—but the office is open late and on weekends and has the home number, so I'm reachable. I take a great many messages on my home phone for my daughter, who has worked out her own way to be unreachable to some guys and I'm it.

That leaves my blessed "drive time." My car is a 1969 Cougar, and its violent trembling when in neutral soothes my back better than any lounge chair with built-in vibrator-massager now being featured in the catalogues. A modern cassette stereo radio sits in the dashboard, playing the old Sinatra-Garland-Jolson songs that—if I tried playing them at work or home—would make my colleagues and family members sick. (My "Prince" remains Machiavelli.)

I am all alone, not by the telephone, and I can sing along with Frank or daydream about the budget deficit without having to account, even subconsciously, for the time. I'm driving; I'm getting someplace; I'll be right there; not guilty.

Comes the telephone in the car, and all that freedom is finished. We will all become always-reachables, under the tyranny of the telephone in the dominion of the dialed. Why do you think they call the mobile phones "cellular"? Because each geographical area is considered a cell, a word previously most often associated with prisoners and Communists.

Ah, the cellmasters say, it's all voluntary. You don't want a telephone in your car, you don't have to have one.

That's what they said about bathtubs. And telephones, and color television sets, and video-corders, and boiling-water faucets. You don't have

---

use of overstatement

use of personal examples to present information and establish identity with audience

specific words and images that make the discussion of a drive to work vivid and humorous

reference to one of the "old songs" author enjoys

transition linking information about mobile phones with personal information examining the key term

transition from previous paragraph

to have them, but if you don't, you're a pariah. The day is coming when your boss will say "Whaddya mean, he's in his car—get him on the cellular phone!" And you better be there in your cell.

"Everyone agrees," says the editorialist, "that cellular mobile telephones are a boon." Some boon. When Reachability Day closes in on you, call him with your complaints; I'll be out of touch.

author's conclusion

WILLIAM SAFIRE

GUIDELINES FOR EVALUATING INFORMAL ESSAYS

Thesis	1. Is the essay's purpose stated or clearly implied within the first few paragraphs?
Unity	2. Are all the paragraphs related to the thesis statement?
Tone	3. Is the tone established within the first few paragraphs of the essay, and is the tone consistent throughout the essay?
	4. Is the tone appropriate for the content under discussion? Is the tone properly proportioned so that it does not dominate the essay?
Order	5. Are the ideas presented in an order that keeps the audience interested?
Topic Development	6. Is enough information given so that the audience can easily understand the writer's views on the topic?
	7. Are vivid incidents, anecdotes, and examples used to discuss and illustrate the general ideas?
	8. Can any examples, incidents, and other supporting details be changed or replaced to make them more informative or interesting?

EXERCISE 3. Writing an Informal Essay. Refer to the following suggestions to prepare an informal essay.

1. Choose a subject of your own and develop it into an informal essay. Before you begin writing, review the Prewriting Hints for Informal Essays and the model on pages 130–34. Also, your teacher may want to approve the topic you select before you begin.
2. Use the Guidelines for Evaluating Informal Essays and the Guidelines for Evaluating Expository Compositions (pages 114–15) to locate

problems or items you should change in your first draft. Ask a friend, relative, or classmate to read your draft and evaluate its content, organization, and style.
3. Use the four revising strategies and the Revising Chart on pages 27–28 to improve your draft.
4. Refer to the Guidelines for Proofreading (page 30) to proofread your revised draft for inaccuracies in spelling, punctuation, grammar, or usage.
5. Adhere to correct manuscript form (pages 31–33) or your teacher's specific instructions to prepare your final draft.
6. Before submitting your final draft to your audience, proofread it one last time to catch any recopying errors.

EXPLAINING CAUSE AND EFFECT

You have already learned how to write a process explanation, which focuses on *how* something is done or *how* something happens. To explain *why* something happens, you write an essay of causal analysis, which explains cause and effect. Causal analysis is useful for research papers in which you begin with an effect and investigate its causes or in which you support your thesis statement by investigating a series of cause-effect relationships. Causal analysis is also useful in less formal writing in which you explain the "why" of such topics as losing friends or winning arguments. The hints, models, and guidelines that follow will help you use causal analysis in both kinds of assignments.

Prewriting Hints for Cause-Effect Explanations

1. *Select and limit your subject.* Choose a subject and limit it to a topic that you can explain in the assigned space. In a research paper, for example, you could explain the causes of environmental pollution. In a seven-paragraph explanation, however, it would be better to limit your topic to the causes of only a single kind of pollution.

2. *Identify the audience for whom you are writing.* Consider your audience when you decide on the complexity of the ideas and of the language that you will use in your explanation.

3. *Make a list of cause-effect relationships related to your topic.* Then decide which would make the most effective cause-effect explanation.

4. *Further limit your topic by writing a one-sentence cause-effect statement.* For example, *Convenience packaging has led to extensive land pollution.*

5. *Develop a detailed list of causes that are directly related to your cause-effect statement.* Arrange your list in two columns, showing the likely causes that bring about a specified effect.

Cause ⟶
Cause ⟶ Effect: Land pollution
Cause ⟶ brought about by convenience
Cause ⟶ packaging

*For a research paper on environmental pollution, your list could include the causes related to several kinds of pollution. Each set of causes should be grouped so that they show a specific effect. For example, list likely causes related to land pollution; then list likely causes related to air pollution, and so on.

6. *Review your list carefully.* Omit causes that are unrelated to your statement. Add causes that should have been included.

*Study your list of causes to determine if any are related to one another. If *sewage* and *increased temperature*—two major causes of air pollution—appear on your list, check for other listed causes related to sewage (*organic wastes*, for example) and to increased temperature (*industrial use of water as a coolant*, for example).

7. *Organize your list in a logical way.* Write your cause-effect statement at the top of a sheet of paper. Then write the causes in a sensible order. The causes in a cause-effect explanation may be arranged in either of two ways: in chronological order (pages 48–49) or in the order of importance (pages 50–51). In the latter arrangement, it is usually more effective to begin with the least important or least significant cause and to end with the most important or most significant cause. *Refer to Chapter 7 for specific suggestions on gathering information for a research paper, organizing a research paper, and developing a formal outline from note cards.

Note: The starred hints will be of special interest to you if you are planning to write a cause-effect research paper.

Writing Cause-Effect Explanations

The following model has been excerpted from a research paper in which the writer has used causal analysis to develop her thesis statement. (Note: For purposes of this excerpt, footnotes have been omitted.)

Although it generates fewer headlines than a   introduction
flood or an earthquake, the pollution of the environment is potentially one of the greatest dangers

to human life. An understanding of what has
caused the poisons being pumped into our air,
water, and land may lead to measures that will
guarantee a habitable world in the next several
decades.

thesis statement
signals cause-effect
relationships to be
traced in paper

The paper goes on to define three different types of environmental
pollution (air, land, and water). The three paragraphs that follow
discuss the two different kinds of pollutants found in the air (solids and
gases). Note how the writer uses words and expressions such as *is due to,
may be caused by,* and *is created by* to signal cause-effect relationships.
Note also that the writer at times deals with a cause-effect chain, in
which the effect of one cause becomes the cause of other effects.

Solid pollutants are called "particulates." The
three major particulates found suspended in air are
soot, dust (from soil), and plant pollens. The
presence of soot in the air is due mainly to the
smoke from oil-burning and coal-burning furnaces
in power plants, factories, and homes. Additional
soot may be caused by the burning of garbage in
incinerators located in municipal dumps and in
apartment houses as well as by the burning of
leaves and trash. Someone has said that attempts to
get rid of waste by burning have resulted in changing one kind of garbage into another—air
pollution.

cause of soot
signals cause-effect

signals cause-effect
cause of soot

cause of soot

Most of the dust that appears in homes is a
mixture of soot and of dust that is blown into the
air from the soil. Because soot is greasy and
smudges easily, it is by far a more annoying pollu-
tant than dust. However, both dust and plant
pollens, the third major particulate, are disturbing
to people who suffer from allergies.

cause of dust

The principal gas pollutants in the air are sulfur
dioxide, carbon monoxide, oxides of nitrogen and
hydrocarbons. Sulfur dioxide is created mainly by
the burning of coal and of fuel oil. Sulfur dioxide is
a poisonous gas that can produce irritants in the
nose and throat. When combined with droplets of

cause of
sulfur-dioxide

signals cause-effect

water in the air, it forms corrosive acids that attack human lungs. The remaining gas pollutants <u>result mainly from</u> the burning of gasoline in automobile engines. All of the gasoline exhaust gases are poisonous; in a closed space, they can cause death. The nitrogen oxides and the hydrocarbon gases cause smog and are largely responsible for the recurrent smog in Los Angeles.

> cause-effect chain reaction
>
> signals cause-effect
>
> cause of carbon monoxide, oxides of nitrogen, and hydrocarbons
>
> cause-effect chain reaction

The paper goes on to discuss why water and land have become polluted and how knowing the causes can lead to a partial cure.

The following composition is an example of a less formal cause-effect explanation. In it the writer gives several causes for the loss of friendships. Note that the writer has arranged the causes in order of importance. Note also that the causes are not merely named; they have been fleshed out with examples and illustrations.

WHY FRIENDSHIPS ARE LOST

Some of us make friends easily enough but find that keeping them is another matter. If you have difficulty holding on to your friendships, it may be time to look at yourself as a friend in order to discover the <u>reasons</u> for your <u>inability to retain friends.</u>

> introduction
>
> thesis statement: signals cause-effect explanation

You may be losing friends <u>because</u> of a need always to be right; therefore, anyone who disagrees with you is wrong. Without being aware of it, you may be suggesting to your friends that you are better informed than they are. Thus in your need to be right, you may be sabotaging your friendships by coming across as a know-it-all.

> first cause
>
> effect: inability to retain friends

<u>Another cause</u> of sabotaged friendships is neglect. Instead of occasionally initiating suggestions for spending time together, perhaps you regularly wait for your friends to call you and to plan activities. Consequently, you give the appearance of expecting your friends to do all the giving while you sit back and do all the taking.

> transition
>
> second cause
>
> illustrations

<u>In a somewhat different way</u>, you may not be as sharing with your friends as they are with you. If,

> transition
>
> third cause

for example, you refuse to share your feelings with them while expecting them to share their feelings with you, they may assume that you do not want them as friends.

examples

Not too surprisingly, <u>a major cause</u> of lost friendships is disloyalty. At times you may have criticized a friend in order to build up your own ego, or you may have allowed someone else to attack a friend unjustly without coming to your friend's defense. The ultimate disloyalty— dropping a friend at the first sign of trouble— does not bode well for present or future friend- ships.

fourth cause

illustrations

A hard look at yourself as a friend and at certain actions and attitudes that may have caused you to lose friends in the past may help you to keep friends in the future. As Emerson put it, "The only way to have a friend is to be one."

conclusion

GUIDELINES FOR EVALUATING CAUSE-EFFECT EXPLANATIONS

Topic	1. Is the topic limited to a cause-effect relationship that can be explained adequately in the space allowed?
Thesis Development	2. Does the thesis clearly state the cause-effect relation- ship(s) that the explanation will trace?
Order	3. Are the causes explained either in order of importance or in chronological order?
Transition	4. Is the relationship between each cause and effect indi- cated by using such words and expressions as *cause, result, create, the reason for,* etc.?
Topic Development	5. Are the cause-effect explanations fleshed out with illustra- tions and examples that are appropriate to the audience?

EXERCISE 4. Writing a Cause-Effect Explanation.   Use the follow- ing suggestions to prepare a cause-effect explanation.

1. Choose a topic that is appropriate for a cause-effect explanation. As you write your first draft, refer to the Prewriting Hints for Cause-Effect Explanations on pages 135–36 and to the models.

2. Using the Guidelines for Evaluating Cause-Effect Explanations and the Guidelines for Evaluating Expository Compositions (pages 114–15), identify any areas of your first draft that need changing. If you developed a research paper, refer also to the Guidelines for Evaluating Research Papers (pages 278–79).
3. Revise your draft, using the four revising strategies and the Revising Chart on pages 27–28.
4. Referring to the Guidelines for Proofreading (page 30), proofread your revised draft for any inaccuracies in spelling, punctuation, grammar, and usage.
5. As you write the final draft of your cause-effect explanation, follow correct manuscript form (pages 31–33) or your teacher's specific instructions for this assignment. If you wrote a research paper, refer also to the appropriate sections in Chapter 7.

ESSAYS OF CLASSIFICATION

Dividing information into classes is a way of organizing ideas. Items placed in each class must share common characteristics. For example, many colleges divide applicants into classes, or categories, according to high-school grades, standardized test scores, and the quality of recommendations. Students in Class A might be those with the highest ratings in each of the areas, students in Class B with the next highest, and so on.

Classification is more than simply dividing information into groups, however. It is also a way of understanding and using the information. For example, most colleges believe that students in Class A described above will perform better in college than students in the other groups, that students in Class B will be next highest in performance, and so on. Many colleges, therefore, use this information as the basis for admitting and counseling students.

In papers that explain classifications, a limited topic is divided into classes. The writer defines each class and sometimes divides the classes into subclasses. The writer describes in some detail the classes and subclasses and provides examples. In addition, relationships among the classes are analyzed. (Does the student in Class A really succeed better in college than the student in Class B?)

Prewriting Hints for Essays of Classification

1. *Select a subject that suits your purpose and audience.* Consider your audience in selecting your subject. If your audience is a general

one, for example, avoid subjects whose classes are too technical or too removed from the knowledge and interests of your readers.

2. *Limit the subject to a suitable topic.* Limit your subject to a topic with no more than three to five main groups, which can each be thoroughly developed in your essay. Remember that you want to define, describe, and give examples of each class involved.

3. *Gather information about your topic.* Clustering is one highly effective way to generate information about classes. Write your limited topic in the middle of a sheet of paper. Then, around the topic, write the names of its major classes. (Circle each class and draw connecting lines.) Continue dividing into classes and subclasses as appropriate.

EXAMPLE

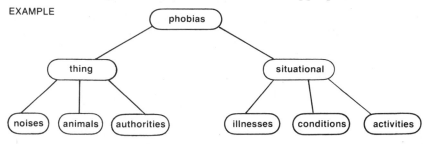

To gather additional detail about the classes and subclasses, use any of the methods for gathering information described on pages 12–18.

4. *Organize your information in a logical way.* Use an informal outline (pages 98–101) to organize your material. List each major class as a heading and subclasses as subheadings. (If you divide a class or subclass, remember to divide it into at least two parts.) Depending upon the length of your outline, you might also include details describing classes and subclasses.

EXAMPLE

Understanding Phobias
Natural fears versus phobias
Thing phobias
   Categories
      Noises
      Animals
      Authorities
   Cause
Situational phobias
   Categories
      Illnesses
      Conditions
      Activities
   Cause

In a classification paper, major classes are equally important; therefore, do not use importance as a rationale for organization. In the sample paper on pages 142–45, "thing" phobias are described first because they are the easier of the two major classes of phobias to understand. Once a class is defined and described, its subclasses are usually discussed before the next major class is introduced.

Writing Essays of Classification

The following example, "Understanding Phobias," illustrates the classification explanation paper. The writer explains phobias by dividing them into two large classes. Each class is defined and then broken into three subclasses as a further explanation. For each class the writer provides examples, traces a possible cause, and describes treatment.

UNDERSTANDING PHOBIAS

Everyone has fears. Young children are often terrified of being left alone in the dark, trembling in their beds at night. With a slightly queasy stomach, a passenger momentarily grips the seat arms as the huge jet lumbers up the runway for a takeoff. A high-school student faced with a three-minute speech in front of classmates feels weak-kneed and dry-mouthed as the moment approaches. These fears are normal; everyone has them, or fears like them, at some time. For most people, however, the moment passes and so do the fear and its accompanying physical reactions. The child grows older and becomes less afraid of the dark; the traveler continues to fly; the student survives the speech.

first paragraph of introduction; introduces topic and captures audience's interest

For some people, however, the fears do not leave. The fears remain, so severely sometimes that lives are permanently affected. These people —almost ten percent of the population of the United States—with what might be called permanent fears are phobics. The fears they have are called phobias. Unlike normal fears, phobias defy logic and are long lasting.

second paragraph of introduction; defines phobia by distinguishing from normal fear

Generally, phobias can be divided into two

thesis statement;

large categories: fears of things and fears of situations. Most phobics in the first category have a specific fear of one or two things—things that can be seen, touched, smelled, tasted, or heard. Thing phobias may themselves be divided into smaller groups. The largest and best known of these subgroups are noises (thunder, fireworks, wind, and so on), animals (especially rats, mice, worms, snakes, spiders, dogs, and cats), and people in authority (including police and fire officers, teachers, doctors, and nurses). Not all thing phobias, however, can be so easily classified. The list, in fact, is almost endless. There are scientific names for fears of the northern lights, details, mushrooms, money, fish, numbers (especially the number thirteen), taxis, almost any existing color, and any number of other items.

Many psychologists believe that most thing phobias begin in childhood with a frightening experience, followed by a slowly developing behavior pattern. A child, for example, may be frightened by an unexpected encounter with a large snake. Upon seeing the next snake (of any size), the child gives it a wide berth until, gradually over the years, a phobia about snakes develops. Even forgetting the early physical experience, the phobic may learn to tremble at the sight of a snake in a magazine or on television or even at the mention of the word "snake."

The second large category of phobias—fears of situations—is perhaps the more complex of the two. Rather than fearing a specific object such as a cat or dog, a situational phobic fears any number of situations or conditions, often in combinations called "clusters." This type of phobic, for example, might live in terror at the thought of performing an activity (or activities) in public—such as eating,

Margin annotations:

gives topic and purpose

statement and definition of first class; subclasses of first class

details

discussion of origins of phobias in first class

details

statement and definition of second class

analysis of relationship between two major classes

drinking, speaking, writing, or even being looked at by others.

Common types of situational phobias include fears of illnesses (such as cancer, diabetes, heart attack), fears of conditions (being in enclosed spaces or at heights, for example), and fears of activities (including riding a bicycle, flying on an airplane, or driving a car). What is perhaps the most common phobia of all in the United States, agoraphobia, belongs in the class of situational phobias. Agoraphobics fear being in public places. When the phobia is severe enough, agoraphobics may refuse even to step outside the house. Some therapists, in fact, specialize in home visits for the treatment of agoraphobia.

subclasses of second class

details

Like thing phobias, the class of situational phobias includes some rather bizarre examples. There are situational phobics, for example, who fear walking, being happy, thinking, having objects placed on their left, fear itself, and, quite simply, everything. Because of the famous Edgar Allan Poe stories, one of the better known unusual situational phobias is taphephobia—the fear of being buried alive.

examples

Although their origins seem more complex than those of thing phobias, some situational phobias also <u>begin</u>, psychologists believe, <u>with early experiences.</u> The famous movie director Alfred Hitchcock, for example, had an irrational fear of being put into jail. Hitchcock once explained that when he was a child, his father had him placed in a cell for a few minutes to frighten him into good behavior.

discussion of origins of phobias in second class

details

For both classes of phobics, treatment can help them overcome their phobias. For situational phobias, however, treatment can be long and costly. Fortunately, the future looks brighter. Results of recent research about the brain's role in the emo-

conclusion

tion of fear might soon make the lives of phobics easier. Also, the public is gradually learning that victims of these dreadful fears are more than immature cowards. Finally, phobics may get the treatment and understanding they so desperately need.

GUIDELINES FOR EVALUATING ESSAYS OF CLASSIFICATION

Topic	1. Is the subject limited to a topic with few enough classes for a short paper?
Organization	2. Is the topic divided into two or more classes (and possibly subclasses)?
	3. Do the items in each class and subclass share common characteristics?
Order	4. Is the information about classes and subclasses organized in a logical way?
Topic Development	5. Are details and examples of each class and subclass provided?
	6. Are relationships among the classes explained?

EXERCISE 5. Writing an Essay of Classification. Use the following suggestions to write an essay of classification.

1. Choose a topic of your own that is suitable for a classification paper. In writing your first draft, refer to the Prewriting Hints for Essays of Classification on pages 140–42 of this chapter and to the sample paper on pages 142–45. Refer also to the Guidelines for Writing Expository Compositions on pages 120–21.
2. Before you begin, review the above guidelines and those on page 23 to evaluate your first draft. Mark any areas that need revising.
3. Cut, add, reorder, or replace to revise your draft. Use the chart on pages 27–28 to help you.
4. Following the Guidelines for Proofreading on page 30, proofread your paper for inaccuracies in usage, spelling, grammar, and mechanics.
5. As your teacher directs, recopy your paper for submission, incorporating proofreading changes. Before submitting the paper, proofread it once again. If your teacher approves, make neat and clear corrections on this final copy.

ESSAYS OF DEFINITION

The essay of definition develops a topic by answering the question "What is it?" To arrive at a specific definition, a two-step process is used. The first step is classification, in which the subject being defined is assigned to a larger class, or category; for example, *tiger* can be assigned to the larger category of "cat." The second step is differentiation, in which specific features of the subject are presented to show how the subject differs from other members of the larger category; for example, a tiger is a *large Asian* cat *having a tawny coat with black stripes.*

The definition of *tiger* given above is a *limited* definition (sometimes called a *dictionary* definition), which presents a brief statement of the characteristic features of the subject being defined. An *extended* definition goes into greater detail about the subject by describing and explaining key characteristics that define the subject. Extended definitions are often useful when dealing with complex terms, such as *happiness, life, democracy,* and other subjects that have many meanings. Extended definitions are also well suited to detailed discussions of subjects that have many features, such as a gasoline engine, Great Britain, or the American Revolution.

In addition to the two-step process of classification-differentiation, other methods are used to write an extended definition. Comparison-contrast can define a subject by showing how it is similar to or different from other things the audience knows well. A tiger, for example, can be compared and contrasted to a housecat. Another method is to identify the use(s) of the subject; for example, a tiger is a large cat that plays an important role in maintaining the ecological balance of Asian jungles. In some cases, discussing how a subject develops can help define it; for example, a tiger is a large cat that can become a threat to native villagers when it is injured or becomes old and must seek easier prey than wild game. Other methods of exposition, such as narration, description, and analysis, can also help to define.

Prewriting Hints for Essays of Definition

1. *Select and limit your subject.* Limit your subject to a topic that can be categorized and then differentiated within the length and time limits of your essay. Generally, you will do this by focusing on the particular features of your subject that you want to develop. For example, rather than try to define fully what a tiger is, you could focus on particular characteristic features.

2. *Consider the interests and knowledge of your audience.* Determine

what your audience needs and wants to know about your subject. Do not choose features that will either bore or confuse them. For example, your classmates may be bored with an essay that simply defines the physical characteristics of a tiger. They might be more interested in a definition that focuses on the tiger's hunting skills.

Define terms and ideas that your audience is not likely to know, and do not include information they already know. However, in many cases, you will still want to present at least part of the basic specific definition of your subject. If you were discussing tigers, you could probably assume that your audience knows that a tiger is a large Asian cat with tawny, black-striped fur. Nevertheless, you would probably present one or more of these characteristic features to relate additional information about your subject that will interest your audience.

3. *Gather and organize information about your subject.* Look at the defining features you have chosen to discuss. List as many details and facts as possible about each feature. Use the *5 W-How?* questions (page 16) to generate ideas.

To organize your information, use several of its distinctive features to classify it within at least one category. Next, differentiate your topic from other members of the category by discussing specific features that it does not share with them. Conclude with a further insight about your topic, perhaps an advantage, use, or ability, or a disadvantage, misuse, or inability revealed in your definition.

To help your audience progress smoothly through your paragraphs, begin with commonly known ideas and details and use transitional words and phrases to introduce less familiar information.

4. *Make sure that your definition is useful.* Avoid common fallacies that will weaken your definition. One such fallacy is making the definition circular, which means using the topic of the definition within the definition itself, as in defining *freedom* as "the state of being free." A circular definition obviously contributes nothing to your audience's knowledge of the topic.

A second fallacy is making the definition too broad or vague so that the definition does not specify the topic. For example, a definition that states only that "a tiger is a large cat that sometimes attacks humans" is so broad that it could also apply to lions and panthers.

On the other hand, avoid the fallacy of defining the topic too narrowly, so that important features of it are not included. An example of a definition that is too narrow would be "a tiger is a large cat that lives in India." This definition is correct as far as it goes, but it may mislead the audience into believing that tigers only live in India, which is false.

5. *Make your definition both precise and interesting.* Use enough concrete, vivid details to make it clear what your topic is or means. Examples, comparisons, and contrasts will also help clarify your definition in an interesting, lively way.

Writing Essays of Definition

In the following essay, "The Wood Stove," the author defines wood-burning stoves by using a variety of methods to describe their characteristic features.

Immediately following the thesis statement, similarities between wood stoves and fireplaces are discussed. In the third paragraph, several physical similarities between wood stoves and fireplaces are given; then, in the fourth paragraph, the author begins to present characteristic features that distinguish wood stoves.

Detailed descriptions of the wood stove's specific features are accompanied by discussions of how these features are used. This allows the audience to see both what a wood stove looks like and how it works. Because the main purpose of a wood stove is to cook food, detailed discussion of this key feature provides a clear picture of a wood stove. Be alert for the most important features of your topic so that you can explore these key features in detail through additional methods of definition.

The author concludes with three paragraphs that offer insights into the advantages and disadvantages of using wood stoves. This discussion makes the definition practical and useful for the audience. Although informal usage is generally out of place in a composition, the colloquial quotation given in the closing paragraphs helps to leave the audience with a folksy impression that is well suited to a discussion of a rustic topic like a wood stove.

THE WOOD STOVE

    Wood stoves were considered to be an improvement over fireplaces for cooking, but they still required a lot of attention. As with the fireplace, dry kindling and green wood had to be cut to fit the firebox and kept on hand, and the fire had to be watched so that it didn't go out or get too hot.

    The fire was built in the firebox located on the left-hand side of the stove right under the cooking surface. To save time, people often used coals right

title

introduction
thesis statement
specific features
that classify wood
stoves with fireplaces

body

from the fireplace to start the fire.

At the bottom of the firebox is a coarse iron grate through which the ashes fall into the ash box. The soot which rises into the flue later falls back down into the soot tray which is directly underneath the oven. Both the ash box and soot tray are drawers that must be cleaned out once a week if the stove is used regularly.

The cooking surface of a wood stove usually has six eyes (round openings with iron lids). Sometimes they are all the same size, sometimes of varying sizes. The one at the center in the back of the stove is the hottest, the two over the woodbox are middling, and the other three are the cooler ones. The heat under the eyes cannot be regulated individually, so pots have to be moved from one to the other according to how much heat is required. Sometimes, when people wanted to heat something in a hurry, they would remove an eye and place the pot directly over the flames in the firebox.

Most of the stoves were fairly simple, though some of them got quite elaborate. One larger variety even had a flat griddle on top for frying things like pancakes, eggs, and bacon.

The oven is usually located on the right-hand side of the stove and is heated from the left and top by the circulation of heat from the firebox. The heat flows from the firebox through a four-inch high air space directly under the cooking surface to the other side. It heats more evenly than one might imagine, but if something tends to cook more on one side than the other, it has to be turned around at regular intervals. The main problem with the oven is that it is difficult to keep the temperature constant. Many varieties have a temperature gauge on the door, but this acts as a warning signal rather than as a regulator. If the oven gets too cool, more wood has to be added; and if it gets too hot, the only thing that can be done is to open the door

specific description that relates wood stoves to fireplaces

specific features that differentiate wood stoves from fireplaces

note that discussion of how wood stoves are used aids in specifying characteristic features

description of additional special features

discussion of characteristic feature of wood stoves—again, note that discussion of how oven works adds defining details slightly or put a pan of cold water on one of the racks. For something that takes an hour to bake, the fire has to be tended three or four times to maintain the temperature.

When cooking biscuits and cornbread, early cooks often started them on the lower rack of the oven to brown the bottom and then placed them on the higher rack to brown the top. Cakes, pies and roasts were usually kept on the bottom rack all the time. When broiling meat or toasting bread, the top rack was used.

specific details on cooking aid in identifying characteristic feature of oven

About two feet above the cooking surface, most wood stoves have two warming closets. These are metal boxes about six inches deep with a door on each, and they are used to keep food warm until it is ready to be served. The stoves also have a damper that seals off the right side of the firebox and greatly cuts the circulation of heat. It doesn't put out the fire, but it cools the rest of the stove so that it can be left unattended fairly safely. When the damper is closed, the coals will remain hot for several hours. It has to be left open when the stove is in use.

characteristic feature of wood stoves and details about its use

characteristic feature of wood stoves and details about its use

We asked Margaret Norton, a real chef on a wood stove, what some of the advantages and disadvantages of using one are. Here's what she told us—"I've always used a wood stove because we live up here in the woods and there's always plenty of wood. They're good in the wintertime because they sure do warm up the kitchen. In the summer it gets uncomfortable hot in here; 'course we can go out on the porch every few minutes. But we're used to it. With this you have to build a fire and wait till it's ready, but by the time you make up your cornbread or peel your potatoes, it's hot.

conclusion

advantage and disadvantage of wood stoves

"Sometimes wind'll blow down the pipe hard and smoke the house, and the soot flies out all over the place and you have to wipe off everything. And

additional disadvantages of wood stoves

you have to clean it out every so often and watch that sparks don't fall out on the floor.

"And of course you have to gather your wood, and that's a disadvantage when you're out of it. But if the electricity goes off or the gas gives out, you're all right if you've got wood."

another disadvantage, followed by an advantage of wood stoves

ELIOT WIGGINTON

GUIDELINES FOR EVALUATING ESSAYS OF DEFINITION

Topic	1. Is the subject limited to a topic that can be adequately defined in the essay?
Topic Development	2. Has the topic been classified and differentiated?
	3. Is the definition specific enough so that it could not also fit another topic? Are all key features of the topic discussed?
	4. Is each characteristic feature described in enough detail? Has unnecessary or repetitive information been omitted?
Audience	5. Will the audience find the definition interesting? Have unfamiliar terms been defined and has information already known to the audience been omitted?
Language	6. Have precise terms been used to specify the elements of the definition?
Conclusion	7. Does the conclusion suggest further insights or implications about the topic?

EXERCISE 6. Writing an Essay of Definition. Use the following suggestions to prepare a final draft of your essay of definition.

1. Select a subject and develop it into an essay-length extended definition. Begin by using the two-step classification-differentiation method to create a specific definition; then, review the Prewriting Hints for Essays of Definition and the model.
2. Using the Guidelines for Evaluating Essays of Definition and the Guidelines for Evaluating Expository Compositions (pages 114–15), identify weaknesses in your first draft that need changing.
3. Revise your first draft, using the Revising Chart on pages 27–28 to guide you.
4. Referring to the Guidelines for Proofreading (page 30), proofread

your revised draft for inaccuracies in spelling, punctuation, grammar, and usage.

5. Follow correct manuscript form (pages 31–33) or your teacher's instructions to write the final draft of your essay of definition.

6. Before submitting your final version to your audience, proofread it one more time to catch any inaccuracies in recopying.

CRITICAL REVIEWS

The critical review examines the content and evaluates the effectiveness of a creative work (such as a book, film, painting, or recording) so that the review's audience can determine whether the work would appeal to them. The critical review provides (1) a summary of the work's subject and main theme or story line, (2) a discussion of major points and elements in the work, and (3) the reviewer's assessment of the work's strengths and weaknesses. The critical review may either praise or find fault with a work; usually, a mixed evaluation is given, citing strengths in some areas and weaknesses in others.

Prewriting Hints for Critical Reviews

1. *Identify and limit your subject.* Identify the work you are reviewing by classifying it according to various categories, such as *subject matter* (fiction, nonfiction, opera), *medium* (novel, film, record album), *genre* (science fiction, documentary, still life), or *audience* (teen-agers, tennis players, farmers). Next, in one or two sentences state the work's subject and unifying idea—its theme, thesis, or main story line. Under this statement note the work's main sections or scenes that present the unifying idea. You will use these notes in composing your summary, which should take up not more than a third of your review.

2. *Gather sufficient information on your topic.* Thoroughly know the work that you are reviewing. If it is a film, see it more than once. If it is a recording, listen to it a number of times. As you repeatedly experience the work, note specific quotes, incidents, background scenery or melodies, and other details that you can use to illustrate important characteristics of the work. Gain further knowledge by reading reviews and discussions about the work, about its creator, about its sources, or about other aspects of it. Identify major points and elements of the work. To recognize what is important in a work, look for elements that (1) are repeated, (2) are given the most space or time, (3) are emphasized by the characters or the creator of the work, (4) are

necessary to present the work's unifying idea, and (5) are necessary to an appreciation of the work.

3. *Organize your information in a logical plan.* Organize the information in your summary using the same pattern or order in which it appears in the work. Next, examine the work's major points or elements according to their order of importance, their order of appearance, their relationships to one another, or according to one of the other organizational methods discussed in Chapter 2. Using the objective information in your summary and your examination of major elements, evaluate the strengths and weaknesses of the work. Discuss how the parts, singly and in combination, affect the work's overall effectiveness or your enjoyment of the work. To gain insight into the work for your evaluation, ask yourself:

    a. Has experiencing this work made me aware of something I did not know or feel before?

    b. Have any of the arguments, dramatizations, or other elements in this work changed or confirmed my views?

    c. What can an audience expect or hope to gain from this work?

    d. To whom would I recommend or not recommend this work?

Make sure that your views and evaluations are supported by specific details from the work, so that the audience can judge whether your opinions are well-founded.

4. *Give your audience an accurate representation of the work.* Make sure that you cover all important elements of the work and that you give them proper emphasis so that you do not misrepresent the work's content, style, or theme. The surest ways to make your review accurate are to maintain an objective approach and to use specific details and quotations from the work to present information and to express your opinions.

5. *Describe any special features of the work.* Special features and distinctive methods of presentation can enhance or diminish a work. For example, a book might have an interesting variety of typefaces or especially large type for those with poor eyesight, or it might have uncomfortably small type, which could also be blurred or in some other way difficult to read. Illustrations, maps, photographs, indexes, footnotes, and other special features can be helpful or intrusive, depending upon the context and characteristics of the particular work. Be sure to let your readers know of any special or distinctive features that play a significant role in the work you are reviewing.

6. *Give your individual response to the work.* Do not merely claim

that a work is "good" or "bad" or that you liked or disliked it. Give specific reasons and examples, explaining why the work was or was not enjoyable or worthwhile. Your response to the work is prompted by specific elements within it. Determine which elements led you to respond favorably or unfavorably; then, explain in your review why or how these elements influenced your opinion. Avoid overstatements, snide comments, and other inappropriate evaluations.

Writing Critical Reviews

Following are three critical reviews: the first of a novel, the second of a film, and the third of a recording. There is no set form for the heading of critical reviews. In many cases the review, like an essay, is titled, and the name of the work being reviewed, its creator, and other information about it are given in the discussion or in a listing below the title. In other cases, the review is titled by the name of the work being reviewed. The reviewer's name is given either below the review's title or at the end of the review. Sometimes, only the reviewer's initials appear at the end of the review, and the reviewer's name is listed elsewhere, usually in the masthead of a magazine or index in an anthology.

In the following review of *Heretics of Dune,* the reviewer begins with his favorable evaluation of the book and its author and relates this book to its predecessors in the *Dune* series.

HERETICS OF DUNE

By: Frank Herbert. G.P.
Putnam's Sons. $16.95

Despite occasional disappointments, the *Dune* series remains one of science fiction's landmark achievements. The writer's complex canvas of cultural, social and political analysis, combined with his incisive understanding of character, rivals the best works in the so-called mainstream. This fifth volume of the series, taking place many centuries after the events of the last book (*God Emperor of Dune*), shows the slowly evolving plan of the Bene Gesserit Sisterhood nearing its completion.

reviewer's evaluation

points out special feature of book as part of series

Modeled after Catholicism's Jesuits, the Bene Gesserit make use of special social, physical and mental techniques to pursue a plan known in detail

summary of the story line

only to the innermost circle of its leaders. To help bring it to fruition, the Sisterhood calls one of its best military people out of retirement. Miles Teg must protect and see to the education of a special protege—Duncan Idaho. Idaho made his appearance in the first book of this series, as swordmaster and teacher to the revered mystic and leader Paul Atreides. Killed in battle protecting Paul, he returns again and again as *ghola,* a genetic replica of the original. Miles must use not only his military skills, but also those special skills that make him a *mentat,* a human computer, to protect Idaho from enemies both within and without the Sisterhood. Slowly he begins to understand his true role in the Sisterhood's plan, a plan that involves all of the major groups from earlier groups, a new group returning from a centuries-long exile in deep space, and a young girl capable of commanding the giant sandworms of Rakis, once called Arrakis, or Dune.

discussion of important characters

specific terms from work used to present information

Herbert has few equals in his ability to tell a tale at once complex and suspenseful. The interplay of ideas merges gracefully with the plot, and even newcomers to the series should have no trouble following the book's various threads.

reviewer's evaluation and advice to audience

N.C. [NEIL K. CITRIN]

reviewer's initials

The next review deals with the film *Dune.* The introductory paragraph states the reviewer's evaluative thesis. As in the book review above, take note of how the reviewer uses specific details from the work to support his opinions and evaluations.

'DUNE' PLOT LOSES OUT TO WEIRDNESS
By Jay Boyar

Entertainment, as we ordinarily understand the word, is only an incidental consideration in the movies of David Lynch.

introductory statement of reviewer's thesis

His first feature, an outrageous cult film called

background of director

Eraserhead, is an avant-garde masterpiece but only marginally enjoyable. And although *The Elephant Man,* his next movie, is a terrific horror picture, the considerable amusement it provides seems to emerge almost accidentally.

Now along comes *Dune,* which Lynch wrote and directed, making it quite clear that all this time he has been less the showman than the *freak* showman. Lynch is mainly interested in discovering weirdness. His attitude appears to be that if what he's exploring happens to interest moviegoers, fine. If not, fine too.

reviewer's opinion supporting reference to previous films

I'll be surprised if his latest film catches on big with audiences; it's sophisticated in ways that turn in on themselves and risk shutting the viewer out. Like a freak show, *Dune* is fascinating without actually being engrossing.

David Lynch was an odd choice to adapt Frank Herbert's popular 1965 science-fiction novel. What's best about the book is the intricacy of Herbert's plotting. The multi-layered narrative pulls you in completely, and you're delighted to remain in Herbert's world for as long as he will have you.

discussion of book upon which film is based

But Lynch, who was trained as a painter and sculptor, seems to have little interest in—or talent for—storytelling. Perverse pageantry is more his style.

People who loved the book might like the movie for the striking visualizations it offers of characters and settings. (Herbert himself is said to have enjoyed the film.) But considered on its own merits, the movie seems only partially formed. And if you are new to the *Dune* mythos, you won't be confused by the film as much as you'll feel a bit

more of reviewer's opinion and evaluation

stranded. Lynch's stripped-down plot seems to lack a crucial dimension.

Much of the story is set on Dune, a world where water is so scarce that its inhabitants wear outfits called stillsuits that trap and recycle the moisture of their bodies. This parched planet is important because it's the only place in the known universe where a miraculous spice known as melange is found. The spice is in great demand because it expands life and consciousness. Opposing superpowers—the good Atreides and the evil Harkonnens—battle for control of Dune.

summary of story line

At the center of the story is a handsome young man named Paul Atreides (Kyle MacLachlan), who may or may not be Dune's messiah. The chief villain is the disgusting Baron Vladimir Harkonnen (Kenneth McMillan). Many characters drift in and out of the saga, most of whom speak in the measured tones common to science-fiction epics. (To me, such characters have always sounded like Tonto with a Ph.D., but it's a convention of the form you can learn to live with.) In the cast are many well-known actors, including Sting, the rock star, who, despite the hype about his appearance in the movie, gets only about five minutes of screen time.

discussion and evaluation of leading characters

reviewer's response to minor characters

David Lynch doesn't approach moviemaking like any other director, so it follows that when he makes a film with special effects, those effects are really special. In the sword fight scenes, the participants seem to become panes of plexiglas to do battle. And a Rube Goldberg contraption that Paul uses to test his reflexes may remind you of a videogame with the dangers made real and three-dimensional.

discussion of special effects

One reason the effects seem so original is that Lynch has manufactured arresting sounds to accompany the images. This is particularly true when it comes to the giant sandworms of *Dune*. Their 1,000-foot bodies are commanding creations in themselves, but the thunder they make as they race across the planet's surface and their bleak, raspy cries further the illusion. In fact, Lynch's use of sound and music (by Toto and Brian Eno) throughout the film is experimental and uncommonly expressive.

discussion of soundtrack

reviewer's evaluation of special features

Dune doesn't hold together, but it's not negligible either. Watching the film, the overall impression is of seeing an underwater parade. The floats seem really to float and everything appears to move in slow motion. Some of what's on view is startling, possibly unique. But always there's the risk that an unforeseen current will sweep across the screen, carrying everything away.

reviewer's evaluation and personal response

The final example is a review of Bruce Springsteen's record album *Born in the U.S.A.*

RETURN OF THE ROCK HEROES

[Bruce] Springsteen has aspired to be a rock-and-roll hero—an ambition that has sometimes seemed a curse. In the past he has strained to give his songs a mythic stature by writing about romantic stereotypes—"tramps like us"—and then by singing the lyrics as if he were trying to belt each word out of the ballpark.

introduction and discussion of work's creator

In the better part of "Born in the U.S.A.," however—and in the album's anthem, "Dancing in the Dark"—his writing and singing have a welcome air of restraint. The single exists in two radically different versions. The original version

transition and statement of reviewer's thesis

specific supporting example

(which is also in the album) is relatively una-
dorned; but this week Columbia will issue an
exciting dance remix created by Arthur Baker, who
recasts the song as a rock-and-roll symphony in the
spirit of "Born to Run." In either version, it's a
breathtaking record. Keyed to a synthesizer line
that sounds like a French horn, the music is sunny
and spacious. The relentless, battering beat recalls
Martha and the Vandellas' "Dancing in the
Street." The record celebrates the romance of
rock, but it's also about the claustrophobia and
despair behind that romance. When Springsteen
sings "I'm just tired and bored with myself," he
captures in a line the listlessness and lack of
self-esteem that has led more than one lonely
teen-ager to lose himself in the vicarious excitement of rock and roll.

discussion of distinct special feature

discussion of work's theme

specific supporting example

further development of reviewer's thesis-specific reference

Springsteen's newfound austerity first became
apparent two years ago on "Nebraska," an album
of downbeat songs he recorded solo, recasting rock
in the image of Woody Guthrie's dust-bowl ballads.
But this time he evokes the American dream
running on empty through music that is brash,
clotted, electrifyingly direct. There has never been
an Eddie Cochran-style rave-up quite like "Working on the Highway," with its chain-gang lyrics
cutting against its good-times jangle. And when
Springsteen's voice arches into a falsetto at the
close of "I'm on Fire," his eeriest new song, it's
one of the purest, most affecting moments on
record this year. It will be interesting to see whether Springsteen, in his long-awaited tour that starts
June 29, can bring moments like this to life in the
context of the larger arenas he will be playing.

analogy to other recording artists

specific reference

reviewer's evaluation

JIM MILLER

GUIDELINES FOR EVALUATING CRITICAL REVIEWS

Summary	1. Does the summary of the work's subject and thesis, theme, or story line accurately tell what the work is about?
Topic Development	2. Do specific citations from the work express and support the summary, examinations of elements, and evaluations?
	3. Does the review discuss strong and weak elements or features of the work?
	4. Does the reviewer evaluate the work's parts and its overall effectiveness with examples from the work?
Identifying Details	5. Is enough accurate information given so that the audience can determine whether the work will be of interest?
Document Citation	6. Does the review contain the work's title, creator's name, and other information that the audience would need to identify or locate the work?
Special Features	7. Are any distinctive features of the work, such as illustrations or typeface variations in a book, or background music and costuming in dramatic productions, covered in the review?

EXERCISE 7. Writing a Critical Review. Use the following suggestions to prepare a critical review.

1. Write a critical review on any work of your choice. You might want to choose a work you are familiar with, or you might want to take this opportunity to experience a new work. Remember that your teacher may want to approve your topic. Before you begin writing your review, closely reexamine the Prewriting Hints for Critical Reviews on pages 152–54 and the three models.

2. Reread your draft several times, marking areas that need changes. For help in recognizing problem areas, consult the Guidelines for Evaluating Critical Reviews and the Guidelines for Evaluating Expository Compositions (page 114–15).

3. Revise your draft, making changes until you are satisfied that your review gives your audience a complete, well-organized discussion and evaluation of the work being reviewed.

4. Refer to the Guidelines for Proofreading (page 30) while you check your revised draft for inaccuracies in spelling, punctuation, grammar, and usage. Pay special attention to the rules concerning quotation marks and to the use of other marks of punctuation with quotation marks.

5. Adhere to correct manuscript form (pages 31–33) or to your teacher's specific instructions when you write your final draft.
6. Before you submit your review to your audience, carefully proofread your final draft one last time to eliminate any possible recopying inaccuracies.

ESSAYS OF LITERARY ANALYSIS

Through the process of analyzing a literary work, you will discover much about its composition and meaning. When you organize your findings into an essay of literary analysis, you pass along a portion of your knowledge to your audience. In this way, both you and your audience can enjoy a greater appreciation of the work by gaining insight into its sources, themes, allusions, and other aspects that add dimension to it.

To conduct an analysis of a literary work, you must be familiar with the terms and concepts used to identify major elements within that genre of literature. Such elements include plot, setting, and dialogue in fiction (short stories, dramas, and novels), while the major elements of poems and songs include rhyme scheme, meter, and scansion. Several major elements—for example, symbolism, allusion, point of view, and imagery—are found in most literary works and should be examined in any literary analysis.

When you write your essay of literary analysis, remember to adhere to the rules and conventions that apply to any expository composition (see Chapter 3).

Prewriting Hints for Essays of Literary Analysis

1. *Identify and limit your subject.* Limit the literary work you are analyzing to a suitable topic by examining categories that apply to the work. Begin with categories of literary elements. If you were analyzing a drama, you could examine its characters, theme, dialogue, or setting, for example. Approach each category with questions. For a drama, you could ask: Are the characters realistic or stereotyped? Does the drama's main theme provide a unique insight into human nature or a reaffirmation of common knowledge? Further specify your topic by applying categories from other fields of knowledge, such as history, psychology, law, or physics. For example, from psychology you could ask: Does a character's speech or behavior provide any significant insight(s) into

human motivation, learning, personality, or other psychological behavior? By asking questions from more than one category, you can quickly arrive at a specific topic. For instance, you could examine how a dramatic protagonist's main conflict (two literary categories) is against an unjust law (legal category) that existed during a particular era (historical category). Specific topics are sometimes suggested by problems, such as those you encounter yourself while reading the work, or those presented in class discussions or exercises and study guides in your text(s).

2. *Gather sufficient information on your topic.* Reread the work that you will be analyzing. If it is a lengthy work, such as a novel, skim through it, spending extra time closely reading sections that particularly apply to your topic. As you read, study the work's characters, plot, theme(s), imagery, rhyme scheme, and other literary elements related to your topic. Make notes—write down all ideas, quotations, and details that you can use to develop your analysis. If you have a long passage to cite, jot down key ideas, images, or phrases, along with the page number of the passage. Keep in mind that you probably are not finished gathering information. Later, as you are developing your analysis, you may discover that you need additional details. If you do not find enough information, refocus your topic or choose another one.

3. *Organize your information in a logical plan.* Use the defining features of your topic as headings for organizing your information. For example, if you were to analyze a dramatic protagonist's opposition to an injustice during a particular historical era, you would group your information under *the protagonist's opposition, the injustice,* and *the particular historical era.* Some details and quotations may fall under more than one heading, and others may not seem to fit anywhere. Star those that belong in more than one group; they may provide a good transition point between paragraphs later when you write your essay. Do not discard any information that does not fit into your groupings, because you may change your plan later and have a use for it. Examine your groupings of information to identify relationships between items within each group and between groups. One relationship that is commonly found in literary and other analyses is comparison-contrast. (For discussion of comparison-contrast, see Chapter 2, pages 51–53). Additional relationships that you could analyze include cause and effect, chronological order, and order of importance. As you analyze your information, ask yourself: What do the relationships between my topic and information reveal about the work that will enhance a reader's knowledge and appreciation of the work? Try to state your answer in

one sentence. Keep formulating an answer until you have a statement that analyzes some aspect of the work and does not merely summarize it. This statement will be your thesis. If necessary, reexamine your topic or reorganize your information until you develop a suitable thesis. For the sample headings discussed above, your analysis might lead to the following thesis: "In this drama the protagonist's conflict against the injustice of his times reflects the growing unrest of the populace, which eventually brought this era of history to an end." You would then use the groupings of information as the main points and supporting details to develop your thesis.

4. *Consider your audience's familiarity with the work.* If your audience is familiar with your work, avoid summarizing it. Simply refer to specific passages and details at appropriate points in your discussion. If your audience is not familiar with the work, summarize its main elements, such as plot, theme, imagery, or dialogue in a short paragraph in the introduction or immediately following it. Whether your audience is familiar with the work or not, include short bits of summary at specific points in your essay to clarify the ideas or information you are discussing. Nevertheless, minimize summary information and devote the majority of your essay to your analysis.

5. *Support your analysis with specific information from the work.* Use specific details and quotations to support the ideas that you present in your analysis. Make sure that all direct quotations are given exactly as they appear in the work and are enclosed in quotation marks. Clearly show the connections between ideas and supporting information by linking them with transitions, relative pronouns, and other devices that specify how they are related. Fit all quotations smoothly and correctly into your discussion.

Writing Essays of Literary Analysis

Read the following poems:

OTHERS, I AM NOT THE FIRST

Others, I am not the first,
Have willed more mischief than they durst:
If in the breathless night I too
Shiver now, 'tis nothing new.

More than I, if truth were told,
Have stood and sweated hot and cold,
And through their reins in ice and fire
Fear contended with desire.

Agued once like me were they,
But I like them shall win my way
Lastly to the bed of mould
Where there's neither heat nor cold.

But from my grave across my brow
Plays no wind of healing now.
And fire and ice within me fight
Beneath the suffocating night.

A. E. HOUSMAN

FIRE AND ICE

Some say the world will end in fire,
Some say in ice.
From what I've tasted of desire
I hold with those who favor fire.
But if it had to perish twice,
I think I know enough of hate
To say that for destruction ice
Is also great
And would suffice.

ROBERT FROST

Look over the poems again. Read them, silently and aloud, several times. Your repeated readings of the poems may lead you to see similarities and differences between them. For example, both authors deal with harmful human emotions, and the words *fire* and *ice* appear as metaphors in both poems. You could relate these points of likeness and difference and develop them into a comparison-contrast between the two works.

Begin your examination by looking up the meanings of unfamiliar words, such as *reins* and *agued* in "Others, I Am Not the First." *Reins* refers to the region of the loins and kidneys, once believed to be the seat of the affections and emotions. *Ague* is an attack of fever and recurring chills; therefore, to be *agued* means to be subject to fits of fever and shivering. To organize your examination of the likenesses and differences between the two poems, you might find it helpful to devise a chart of significant elements of the poem and your thoughts about them, perhaps this way:

Points of Comparison and Contrast Between "Others, I Am Not the First" and "Fire and Ice"

"Others, I Am Not the First"	"Fire and Ice"
The words "fire" and "ice" appear in lines 7 and 15. In both stanzas there is	The words "fire" and "ice" have literal meanings.

the idea of strong conflict.

Some predict "the world will end in fire" (line 1); others predict "in ice" (line 2).

Fire is associated with desire, ice with fear (lines 7–8).

The words "fire" and "ice" take on symbolic meaning.

The speaker's desire calls for "more mischief" than he dares. He is restrained by fear (lines 2, 8, 15).

Fire (line 4) stands for unbridled desire.

Ice (line 7) stands for hate.

The contest between the two emotions affects him physically. He is "agued" (line 9).

These forces are not antagonists, but alternatives.

He shivers although it is a calm ("breathless") night (lines 3–4).

He sweats "hot and cold" (lines 3, 6).

He relates his suffering to the suffering of others (lines 1, 5–8, 9).

There is no relief for his suffering (lines 13–14).

He has known first-hand the destructive nature of fire and ice. He has "tasted of desire" and knows "enough of hate" to imagine their potential for destruction.

The conflict within him will be resolved only in death (lines 10–12).

Housman emphasizes the personal suffering caused by conflicting emotions

Frost emphasizes the danger of destructive emotions.

You might conclude from this set of notes that Housman uses the words "fire" and "ice" to create a metaphor for personal emotional conflict, while Frost uses the words both literally and figuratively to project a vision of the world's destruction. This could become the thesis of your essay, and you could gather supporting ideas, details, and quotations under the defining features of this thesis.

The main ideas that would be developed in each section of your essay could be outlined this way:

INTRODUCTION

Paragraph 1   *Thesis:* Housman uses the words "fire" and "ice" to create a metaphor for the personal conflict between desire and fear, while Frost uses the words both literally and figuratively to present twin visions of the world's destruction.

BODY

Paragraph 2   In Housman's poem "fire" stands for intense desire and "ice" for the paralyzing fear that frustrates desire, thereby causing physical and emotional anguish.

Paragraph 3   In Frost's poem "fire" and "ice" are not antagonists but alternatives, either of which can annihilate the earth.

CONCLUSION

Paragraph 4   Housman explores a conflict of warring emotions; Frost, the danger of destructive emotions.

You could relate the specific ideas in your chart to each main idea or paragraph topic. Then, using the resulting outline, you could write an essay, such as the one that follows:

THE EMOTIONS OF "FIRE" AND "ICE" IN A. E.   title
HOUSMAN'S "OTHERS, I AM NOT THE FIRST" AND
ROBERT FROST'S "FIRE AND ICE"

A. E. Housman, in "Others, I Am Not the   introduction
First," and Robert Frost, in "Fire and Ice," explore different dimensions of harmful human emotions. Despite the differences in their investigations, both poets use the terms *fire* and *ice* to identify emotional states. Housman uses the words   thesis statement to create a metaphor for the personal conflict between desire and fear, while Frost uses the words both literally and figuratively to present twin visions of the world's destruction.

In Housman's poem, fire stands for intense   topic sentence desire and ice for the paralyzing fear that frustrates desire, thereby causing physical and emotional   body anguish. The speaker in the poem states that his desire calls for "more mischief" than he is willing   specific quotations to dare because he is restrained by fear, which   and details used to makes him "shiver." As this physical reaction   analyze key words indicates, the contest between desire and fear affects him bodily. He suffers both heat and cold (line 6) and describes himself as "agued." Although the night is "breathless" and oppressively hot, he shivers as well as sweats, experiencing both chills and fever. There is no consolation, "no wind of healing," in the knowledge that he does not suffer alone and that many others have "sweated hot and cold." The conflict between desire ("fire") and fear ("ice") will have its resolution only in death—"the bed of mould."

In Frost's poem, fire and ice are not antagonists but alternatives, either of which can annihilate the earth. In the opening lines of the poem, the speaker alludes to predictions that "the world will end in fire" or "in ice." The speaker reflects that these physical forms may not be the only kinds of "fire" and "ice" that could bring the earth to a cataclysmic end. Like Housman's speaker, he associates fire with desire. Based on what he has "tasted of desire," he agrees "with those who favor fire" as the force that will destroy the world. On the other hand, he states that he knows "enough of hate" to believe that ice "would suffice" as an equally devastating form of destruction. Through the images of "fire" and "ice," the poem suggests that emotional extremes of desire and hatred could bring about the destruction of the world.

Both Housman and Frost deal with harmful human emotions. Housman explores a conflict of warring emotions; Frost, the danger of destructive emotions. In Housman's poem, fire and ice are opposing forces in human nature, burdening the speaker with desires that he is afraid to pursue. In Frost's poem, fire and ice are not opposites but options in human nature, both equally powerful and destructive. The "fire" and "ice" discussed in these two poems can represent a number of specific destructive forces, but all of them share one quality, which may be the key to their harmfulness— they are all extremes.

Margin annotations:

topic sentence

specific details and quotations used to analyze key words

analysis of poem's meaning

conclusion

topic sentence

summary of thesis and analysis

suggestions of further meaning in the poem

GUIDELINES FOR EVALUATING ESSAYS OF LITERARY ANALYSIS

Thesis	1. Is the thesis of the essay stated clearly in the introduction? Does the introduction also give the title and author of the work being analyzed?
Thesis Development	2. Is the thesis developed by convincing main points and analysis within the body of the essay?
	3. Do enough details and quotations from the work support each point of the analysis?
	4. Is enough summary and explanatory information given to help the audience follow the points made in the literary analysis?
Quotations	5. Have all quotations been given verbatim as they appear in the work and been enclosed in quotation marks?
Conclusion	6. Does the conclusion summarize the main result(s) of the analysis and suggest additional meanings or implications of these results?

EXERCISE 8. Writing a Literary Analysis. Use the following suggestions as you prepare an essay of literary analysis.

1. Write an essay of literary analysis on a novel, short story, drama, or poem of your choice. Remember that your teacher may want to approve of your selection before you begin writing. Also, before you begin, review the Prewriting Hints for the Essay of Literary Analysis on pages 161–63 and the model.

2. As you evaluate your draft, consult the Guidelines for Evaluating Essays of Literary Analysis and the general guidelines for evaluation discussed in Chapter 1 on page 23.

3. Use the Revising Chart on pages 27–28 to revise your first draft.

4. Refer to the Guidelines for Proofreading (page 30) as you review the spelling, punctuation, grammar, and usage in your draft.

5. Follow correct manuscript form (pages 31–33) or your teacher's specific instructions when you write the final draft of your essay of literary analysis.

6. Be sure to give your essay one final proofreading to correct any inaccuracies you may have made in recopying it. Reread it more than once, and if possible, try to have someone else read it before you submit your essay to your audience.

CHAPTER 5

Writing Persuasive Compositions

LANGUAGE AND LOGIC

Argument is a feature of your daily conversation. The word *argument* in this sense means "a debate or discussion," not "an angry disagreement." Any time you express an opinion or belief and give your reasons for it, you are engaging in argument. Essay-type examination questions often ask your opinion and expect you to support it with knowledge. People in all kinds of work—scientists, teachers, sales representatives, lawyers—know the importance of being able to argue convincingly.

In argumentative, or persuasive, writing your purpose is to convince the reader to accept your views on a debatable subject. In its simplest form, persuasive writing states an opinion backed up by reasons and evidence. In its more elaborate form, persuasive writing uses skillful planning and tight reasoning, not only to convince an audience of a certain opinion but also to persuade the audience to take a specific action.

DEVELOPING A PERSUASIVE COMPOSITION

Perhaps more than with any other type of writing, the prewriting steps are of crucial importance in persuasive writing. Argument is a highly structured form of composition, and it is before you begin writing that you plan the logical presentation of your opinion, reasons, and evidence.

PREWRITING

CONSIDERING FORM AND AUDIENCE

In this chapter you will study two forms of persuasive writing: the letter to the editor and the persuasive composition. For both forms you must develop a sound argument, although the brief form of a letter requires you to be concise, while the longer composition form allows you more space for supporting evidence.

A *letter to the editor* is a brief essay that appears on the editorial page of a newspaper or magazine. The audience for a letter to the editor will be the readers of the newspaper or magazine. A *persuasive composition* has at least five paragraphs (an introduction, three or more paragraphs in the body, and a conclusion), but it is often much longer. Persuasive compositions may also be written for a specific audience, both in and out of school.

For both the letter and the composition, it is important to identify your audience. You must consider how familiar your readers are with your topic. Will they need to have important terms defined, to know what the current situation is, what the history of the problem is? You must also consider their biases, or opinions and ideas for or against a topic, as you prepare your argument. For example, an essay about selecting jury members may be directed to lawyers or to persons accused of crimes. Lawyers might want to keep the process of jury selection the same, while persons accused of crimes might want to change the process so that juries reflect the population of the community. If your audience has a bias against your opinion, you will have to provide additional evidence to convince them. If, however, your audience agrees wholeheartedly with your views, you might choose a more challenging topic on which there is some likelihood of disagreement.

Techniques for Prewriting. To consider your audience, ask yourself:

- Will this audience have an interest in the topic?
- What background information or explanations of terms will they need?
- What biases, if any, does the audience hold on the issue?

EXERCISE 1. Identifying Audience Attitudes.   Decide what attitude each of the following audiences is likely to have about the expressed opinion: strongly oppose it, moderately oppose, neutral (no particular bias), moderately favor, or strongly favor. Be prepared to explain your answers.

1. *Opinion:* As a graduation requirement, all high-school students should work two hours weekly for a community service project.
   a. High-school seniors
   b. Parents of high-school students
   c. Directors of community service projects
2. *Opinion:* People should not be able to obtain driver's licenses (even learner's permits) until they are 21 years old.
   a. Insurance company executives
   b. Eighteen-year-olds with full-time jobs
   c. Police officers
3. *Opinion:* High-school students should be able to make decisions about course offerings and graduation requirements.
   a. High-school principals and teachers
   b. School-board members
   c. A group of parents of high-school students

CHOOSING A TOPIC

5a. Choose a limited topic that is debatable and serious.

Choose a debatable issue as a topic for a persuasive composition, one for which arguments can be made pro (for) and con (against). The topic must also state an opinion and not a fact, because facts are not debatable. By definition, a *fact* is a statement that can be proved to be true. An *opinion,* on the other hand, is a judgment or belief that may be debated.

NOT SUITABLE   Polls on the East Coast close three hours before polls on the West Coast. (Fact)

SUITABLE   Polls should be open for a 24-hour period and close at the same time all over the United States. (Opinion)

NOT SUITABLE   Special-interest groups often hire lobbyists who try to influence the voting behavior of members of Congress. (Fact)

SUITABLE   Conversations between lobbyists and members of Congress should be made public so the public can see how lobbyists try to influence politicians. (Opinion)

A persuasive composition must also be about a significant and serious issue. Like verifiable facts, personal tastes are unsuitable topics for persuasive writing. A statement of personal preference is an expression of opinion, but it is not an arguable proposition because matters of taste cannot be resolved by presenting evidence. To be sure, you could write a composition to support your taste, but no argument will ever prove a personal preference to be true or false.

NOT SUITABLE   Roses are the most beautiful flowers.
NOT SUITABLE   Tennis is more fun than golf.

EXERCISE 2. Choosing Suitable Topics for Persuasive Writing. Indicate which of the following statements are suitable topics for persuasive writing. Write *S* for those that are suitable and *NS* for those that are not. Be prepared to explain your answers.

1. In 1973 Rosemary Casals won the Family Circle tennis tournament.
2. The school year should be extended to eleven months.
3. Engineering is a more interesting field of study than literature.
4. The federal government should spend more money funding research for the cure of cancer.
5. Marian Anderson received the Presidential Medal of Freedom in 1963.

WRITING A POSITION STATEMENT

5b. Express your opinion clearly in a single sentence.

Once you choose a topic, you should express your opinion about it in a declarative sentence called the *position statement*. Also called a *thesis statement* or *proposition*, the position statement often contains the words *should* or *should not*.

EXAMPLES   My client is innocent and should be acquitted.
           Money being spent on space exploration should be spent instead on solving domestic problems.

Sometimes issues that interest you are so complicated that you may not be sure what your opinion is. If so, take time to research the issue: read current magazine and newspaper articles, or discuss the issue with people whose opinions you respect. By trying to understand different viewpoints, you can decide on your own opinion.

Techniques for Prewriting. To determine your opinion on an issue, ask yourself:

- What different conclusions can be drawn about the issue?
- Which conclusion do I favor?
- What action do I think should be taken?

CRITICAL THINKING:
Making Position Statements Specific

A position statement should be worded so that its meaning is definite and its terms are not ambiguous. Even a specific position statement may require explanation or definition of terms, which can be given in the introduction of the composition. The position statement should also state a plan for solving a problem. Which of the following is the most specific?

a. This community should do something about teen-age recreational facilities.
b. Recreational facilities for teen-agers need to be improved.
c. The city should sponsor a supervised recreation center for teen-agers in the old McDonald Center.

Of these statements, the third is the most specific. It tells what should be done, who should do it, and where the recreation center should be. Both statements *a* and *b* are too vague.

EXERCISE 3. Making Position Statements Specific. The following statements are too vague or general to serve as position statements. Rewrite each statement so that it is specific enough to be a position statement. Remember that position statements often use the words *should* or *should not.*

1. We have to find a way to keep students from dropping out of high school.
2. There are too many highway accidents caused by drunk drivers.
3. What can we do about people who have no homes in the winter?
4. Vandalism on school property is a problem.
5. There are too many advertisements on television programs for young children.

EXERCISE 4. Writing Position Statements. Read the following news items carefully. Decide what your opinion is on each issue, and write a clear position statement for a letter to the editor. Remember that, whenever possible, a position statement should also suggest a specific course of action.

1. Dr. Robert E. Gould, a New York psychiatrist, believes that television sports are brutal. Watching sports on TV, he says, "instills viewers with a love of brutality. They hunger for blood." Other psychiatrists at an annual convention of the American Academy of Psychoanalysis speculate that television sports harm children by teaching them the brutality of intimidation and "winning at any cost."

2. A heart operation in which a baboon heart was transplanted into the body of a human infant has been widely criticized. Some critics say the doctors involved did not try hard enough to find a human heart because they were eager to experiment with an animal-to-human heart transplant. Other people criticize the whole procedure because they claim the baboon was killed solely to obtain its heart for the transplant. These critics believe it is wrong to take the life of an innocent animal in an attempt to save a human life.

3. WASHINGTON, D.C—The National Council of Teachers of Mathematics has recommended that calculators be available in classrooms from kindergarten through fourth grade. The Council suggests that teachers in elementary schools reconsider their emphasis on teaching students fractions, decimals, and percentages. According to the report, "Since computers and calculators can perform such operations more quickly and accurately . . . the traditional goals of elementary school mathematics must be re-examined." The report suggests that students be allowed to use calculators, even during tests.

BUILDING AN ARGUMENT

You now need to outline a logical argument which supports your position statement. That is, you must present believable reasons and sound evidence in a clear, orderly manner.

Choosing Reasons

5c. Support your position statement with reasons and evidence.

Reasons are statements that explain why you hold your opinion and why the reader should also hold your opinion. A reason may be a fact, a statistic, an example, or an incident—anything that strongly supports your opinion.

The following outline for an argument gives three reasons to support the opinion in the position statement.

Position Statement: High-school seniors should be excused from final exams in courses in which they have maintained a B average.

Reasons: a. Students with a B average have already demonstrated their knowledge.
b. Students will work harder to maintain a B average if they know this will excuse them from final exams.
c. Except in borderline cases, the final examination is not weighted heavily enough to affect the final grade.

CRITICAL THINKING:
Evaluating Reasons

Consider the preceding argument. Are you convinced that seniors with B averages should be excused from final exams? The forcefulness of an argument—how convincing it is—depends almost entirely on the reasons given to support the position statement. They should be *sufficient, distinct,* and *relevant.* To have sufficient reasons, a persuasive composition should contain at least three. The more sound reasons you have to support your opinion, the more convincing your argument will be.

The reasons given in an argument must be distinct, or clearly different from each other. They should not repeat or rephrase a previously stated reason.

WEAK   *Position statement:* This state should pass a mandatory seat belt law.
   Reason 1: If you are in an automobile accident, your chances of being seriously injured are less if you are wearing a seat belt.
   Reason 2: People who wear seat belts are safer than people who don't wear seat belts.
   Reason 3: A mandatory seat belt law would protect drivers and their passengers.

This outline looks as if it has three reasons, but they are not distinct reasons. All three repeat or rephrase the same idea: that wearing a seat belt protects people in automobiles. Of the three reasons, only Reason 1 is clearly stated; both Reasons 2 and 3 are vague and repeat Reason 1. The argument, therefore, is weak.

IMPROVED *Reason 1*: If you are in an automobile accident, your chances of being seriously injured are less if you are wearing a seat belt.

Reason 2: Statistics show that few automobile drivers and passengers regularly use seat belts when it is their decision whether to wear them.

Reason 3: Statistics from states with mandatory seat belt laws show that the number of automobile drivers and passengers using seat belts dramatically rises under a mandatory seat belt law.

Notice that this argument outlines three entirely different, or distinct, points which present a logical argument. If you accept the truth of the three reasons, then there is only one logical conclusion: that a mandatory seat belt law should be passed (the statement made in the position statement).

A *relevant* reason is one that directly relates to the position statement. Just as a paragraph must be unified, all the reasons in an argument must directly support the position statement. Adding irrelevant reasons only indirectly related to the position statement will weaken your argument and confuse your reader.

IRRELEVANT *Reason:* Automobile manufacturers and legislators have long discussed mandatory air bags in automobiles.

IRRELEVANT *Reason:* Some automobiles have shoulder belts that automatically lock into place.

These are true statements, but they are not reasons that are relevant to the argument about a mandatory seat belt law; they should be omitted from the argument.

EXERCISE 5. Evaluating Reasons. Read the position statement, and carefully consider the reasons that follow. Choose the reasons that you think would make the strongest case to support the position. Be prepared to explain your choices.

Position statement: High-school students should only be allowed to work on weekends and during vacations—not during the school week.

  a. Students who work during the school week are too tired to devote their energies to school work.

  b. Students who work during the school week do not have time to do homework assignments or study for tests. They cannot possibly keep up good grades.

c. More than half of the senior class has after-school jobs.
d. Many students need the money that they earn in after-school jobs.
e. Students who have after-school jobs and also try to keep up with their school work and social activities endanger their health by not getting enough sleep.
f. Schools do not have the right to infringe on students' freedom by preventing them from working after school.
g. Too many freshmen and sophomores who begin with after-school jobs end up by dropping out of high school before they graduate.
h. School is a student's work and should be the prime focus of a student's attention.

EXERCISE 6. Choosing Reasons. Choose one of the position statements that you wrote for Exercises 3 or 4, or write another one. Then list as many reasons as you can think of to support your opinion. Evaluate the reasons on your list; look carefully for those that are not distinct and relevant. Eliminate any reason that merely repeats the position statement or another reason. Delete also any information that, although true, is only indirectly related to the argument. On your paper, write the position statement you have chosen, followed by all the reasons you have created that strongly support your opinion.

Refuting the Opposing Viewpoint

5d. Prepare to refute arguments that support the opposing viewpoint.

The topic of persuasive writing must be debatable, with other people holding views completely opposite from yours. Thus, your success may depend largely on how well you refute the opposing arguments. To plan a persuasive composition, then, take time to consider opposing arguments and to prepare a strong reply.

For example, review the argument on page 175 for excusing seniors with a B average from final exams. If you were trying to support this position statement, you would have to consider the opposing arguments, which might include these reasons:

Reason 1: Taking final examinations reinforces learning by forcing students to review forgotten material.
Reason 2: Taking final examinations assures better learning by prompting the student to review the course material.
Reason 3: If students with B averages are excused from final examinations, they will not want to do any work as the course ends.

How would you refute these reasons? You might do so by stating the opposing reason and then by telling why you believe it is false. In effect, you are telling the reader, "This is what my opponent says, but it is not true, which I will prove to you." You might, for example, refute Reason 3 in this way:

> People who believe that all students should be required to take all final exams claim that even successful students (those with B averages and higher) would not study if they did not have to take exams. In a survey of thirty-two experienced teachers in our school, more than 90 percent said that they did not believe that this would happen. "Students who do well throughout a semester," said Mrs. Abrams, chair of the math department, "are students who care about learning. They will study no matter what —even if they do not have to take a final."

You might make your refutation even stronger by citing a survey of students whose grades are B and above. If they say that they will continue to study and complete all assignments and projects even if they are excused from a final, you have additional evidence to refute an opposing reason. In effect, you are telling the reader, "This is what my opponent says, but it is not true, and I will prove it to you."

EXERCISE 7. Analyzing the Pros and Cons. Reasons supporting an opinion are the pro (reasons for) position, while opposing reasons are called the con (reasons against) position. Carefully study the following list of pros and cons for a particular issue; then answer the questions that follow it.

Position statement: Federal air- and water-pollution controls for industries are too strict and should be drastically reduced.

PRO

Reason 1: The high costs of meeting federal requirements must necessarily be passed on to the consumer when the industry prices its product. Lowering pollution standards would decrease the cost of products.

Reason 2: With the costs of meeting pollution requirements so high, many industries have gone out of business and jobs have been lost.

Reason 3: Local communities should have the right to decide how much air and water pollution is acceptable without federal interference.

CON

Reason 1: Since air and water pollution have far-reaching effects, the federal government must control setting and enforcing pollution standards. We cannot leave these matters up to individual communities or states.

Reason 2: Meeting pollution standards is an integral part of manufacturing the product, so increases in a product's cost must be borne by the consumer.

Reason 3: We cannot jeopardize the nation's health simply to keep manufacturers in business. If businesses fail and jobs are lost because of the cost of meeting pollution standards, that is the fault of management for not making operations efficient.

1. Which position do you agree with? Why?
2. For the side you have chosen, what is the strongest reason? The weakest? List at least three additional reasons to support this side.
3. Among the opposing arguments, what is the strongest reason? The weakest? List at least three additional reasons to support this viewpoint.
4. How would you refute the reasons given for the opposing viewpoint?
5. Reason 3 in the *pro* argument and Reason 1 in the *con* argument directly contradict each other. How can you tell which one is true? Explain your answer.

EXERCISE 8. Refuting Opposing Arguments.   Using your position statement from Exercise 6, or another one, list all the opposing arguments you can think of. Then write a paragraph refuting each opposing reason. (You may need to do some research by reading or by discussing the issue with people who hold opposing opinions.)

Choosing and Gathering Evidence

With a position statement and reasons to support it, you should gather the evidence which supports each reason. *Evidence* is the specific factual information that backs up a reason. Pieces of evidence are often facts such as statistics. You can also use examples, incidents, and quotations from experts. Whenever possible, each reason in an argument should be supported by some kind of evidence.

5e. Gather sufficient evidence to support each reason and to refute opposing reasons.

The evidence which supports your reasons should come from a reliable source or should be the result of many personal observations. Facts and statistics offer strong support for a reason because they can be verified, or proved to be true. When *pro* and *con* statements are directly contradictory, you might expect that one statement is probably true and the other necessarily false. Facts, statistics, and examples will show which one is true. Another valuable type of evidence is the opinion of an authority or expert in the field. Although an expert's opinion is not verifiable as facts are, an unbiased opinion from a respected expert can lend powerful support to an argument.

Techniques for Prewriting. To gather evidence:

- Use the *Readers' Guide* and recent almanacs to locate current facts and statistics.
- Refer to articles in encyclopedias, newspapers, magazines, or specialized journals and to recent books.
- Cite, or quote, an authority's opinion on an issue.
- Use observation, interviews, or surveying for familiar topics.

CRITICAL THINKING:
Evaluating Evidence

Any evidence given to support a reason must be *relevant* to that reason—that is, it must directly and logically relate to the reason. Any irrelevant piece of evidence should be eliminated from the argument. Effective persuasive writing is tightly knit and logical; irrelevant information will weaken the argument and confuse the reader. In the following example, which evidence is relevant, and which is irrelevant?

> *Reason*: Since air and water pollution have far-reaching effects, the federal government must control setting and enforcing pollution standards. We cannot leave these matters up to individual communities or states.
> *Evidence*: a. Airborne pollutants from factories in industrial states are carried by winds, combine with rain, and dump acid rain in faraway communities that have not caused the pollution.
> b. Most communities and states already have regulations on tolerable levels of air and water pollution.

The first piece of evidence is relevant: it gives an example of the far-reaching effect of pollution. The second piece of evidence, while it is true and related to the topic, is not directly related to the reason. It does not offer any information about the federal government's responsibility to maintain pollution standards.

As you construct a persuasive argument, develop reasons relevant to the position statement and evidence relevant to each reason. Evaluating relevance is a skill that can be improved with practice.

EXERCISE 9. Selecting Relevant Evidence. Choose the items of evidence that are relevant to the reason given. Be prepared to explain your answers.

Reason: Industrial air pollution is a threat to the health of plants, animals, and humans.
Possible Evidence:
   a. Results of a four-year study on the causes and effects of acid rain on plants and animals
   b. Quotation from a lung specialist on the effects of industrial air pollution on the lungs of animals and humans
   c. Quotation from a factory owner on the amount of money spent to install safety devices
   d. A case study of an accident within a nuclear energy plant; no wastes were released into the air outside the plant
   e. A quotation from the President of the United States on the need for increased cooperation between industry and government

EXERCISE 10. Choosing and Gathering Relevant Evidence. List the kinds of evidence you would look for to support each reason for your argument from Exercise 6. Then gather the evidence, using the resources listed on page 180. (If you cannot think of or locate evidence to support a reason, change the reason to one you can support.)

Outlining the Argument

5f. Outline your argument as an effective writing plan.

The final prewriting step in developing a persuasive composition is to outline your argument, which consists of your position statement, the supporting reasons, and the evidence. If you wish to end with a "call to action," that, too, should be included in the outline. The outline should be written in clear sentences, following this format:

Position statement
   Reason 1
      Evidence
      Evidence
   Reason 2, *etc.*
Call to action

The number of reasons and the amount of evidence will vary. In general, a persuasive composition should have at least three reasons, with each supported by evidence. The more specific, factual evidence you can offer to support each reason, the more convincing your argument will be.

As you develop your outline you should also decide upon an order for listing your reasons. For persuasive writing, order of importance— moving from the least important reason to the most important—is effective. Decide which of your reasons is most important; then outline your argument so that you build up to the most important reason.

EXERCISE 11. Outlining Your Argument. Outline your argument, using the position statement, reasons, and evidence you have developed in previous exercises. Follow the outline format on page 181, and arrange your reasons in the most effective order.

CRITICAL THINKING:
Evaluating an Argument

Use the following guidelines to evaluate your argument for a persuasive composition. (You may also apply these questions to persuasive writing that you read or to persuasive speeches that you hear.)

GUIDELINES FOR EVALUATING A PERSUASIVE ARGUMENT

1. Is a specific position clearly stated?
2. Do at least three reasons support the position?
3. Is each reason relevant to the position?
4. Is each reason distinct from other reasons and from the position statement?
5. Is each reason backed up by relevant, reliable evidence?

EXERCISE 12. Evaluating a Persuasive Argument. Use the preceding guidelines to evaluate the argument you outlined for Exercise 11, or develop and evaluate another argument on a debatable topic. Make any necessary changes to strengthen your argument.

REVIEW EXERCISE. Collecting and Analyzing Letters to the Editor. Clip two letters to the editor from recent magazines or from local or school newspapers. Analyze each letter by answering the following questions:

1. What is the specific topic of the letter to the editor?
2. What is the writer's opinion about the topic? Is the opinion stated in a position statement? If so, what is it?
3. Outline the argument in the letter: the reasons and evidence the writer gives to support the opinion. Are the reasons and evidence arranged in the most effective order? Explain your answer.
4. Does the writer include a specific call to action? What is it?

WRITING

WRITING THE FIRST DRAFT

5g. Write the first draft of your persuasive composition.

Use the outline of your argument as a working plan for your first draft.

The Introduction

Your composition should begin with an *introduction* that presents the topic and includes your position statement, often the last sentence of the paragraph. The introduction should also arouse the reader's interest and provide background information.

Sometimes an introduction is more than one paragraph, as in the following example from an essay by Tom Wicker entitled "Tambora's Lesson."

> On July 4, 1816, thick layers of ice formed in New England, New York, and Pennsylvania. In June, snow had fallen from 7 to 10 inches deep in Massachusetts, Vermont, and New York. But the worst was yet to come; in August, according to one account, "ice formed nearly an inch in thickness and killed every green thing in the United States."
>
> In Virginia, Thomas Jefferson applied for an emergency bank loan to tide him over his crop failures. Europe, too, was hard hit by the unseasonable cold and 1816 became known in England as "the year without a summer." Henry and Elizabeth Stommel argue in *Volcano Weather*, their book about the phenomenon, that a typhus epidemic that killed more than 65,000 people in the British Isles in 1816 was related to cold-induced famine.

The cause of this global misery was the eruption of Mount Tambora, a volcano in the Dutch East Indies. In probably the most powerful volcanic outburst in 10,000 years, Tambora spewed 25 cubic miles of debris into the upper atmosphere. The heavier particles fell into the Pacific Ocean, forming a slush of pumice two feet thick; the lighter debris stayed aloft for months, circled the globe, and blanketed the skies over most of the Northern Hemisphere.

But the eruption of Tambora was minor compared with the blast effect of a full-scale nuclear exchange between the United States and the Soviet Union; and "the year without a summer" was mild and brief compared to the "nuclear winter" that would descend upon the Northern Hemisphere after a Soviet-American holocaust.

EXERCISE 13. Analyzing an Introduction. Refer to the introduction of "Tambora's Lesson" to answer the following questions.

1. When is the specific topic of the essay made clear? What is the specific topic?
2. What do you think the writer's opinion is? Is it stated in a position statement? If not, write one.
3. What specific details has the writer included about "the year without a summer"—1816?
4. Why does the writer include the information about the effects of the 1816 eruption of Mount Tambora?
5. How effective is the introduction? Do you want to read further? Explain your answer.

The Body

The paragraphs between the introduction and the conclusion constitute the *body* of the persuasive composition. In the body, each reason and its supporting evidence (as outlined in prewriting) should be developed in a separate paragraph. You may treat your refutation of the opposing viewpoint as one reason, and you may present this refutation either before or after your other reasons.

As you read the body of Mr. Wicker's essay "Tambora's Lesson," notice the amount of evidence and the sources that he cites for this evidence.

The theory that such a disastrous man-made winter—postulated in 1983 by a group of scientists working outside the Government—would follow nuclear war has now been given legitimacy by the National Academy of Scientists, in a study commissioned by the Department of Defense. The study was conducted by a committee headed by George F. Carrier of

Harvard, who termed its results "quite consistent" with earlier nuclear-winter studies.

The committee of specialists from Government laboratories, private industry, and academia found that exploding only about half the world's nuclear arsenals, equivalent to 6,500 megatons of TNT, together with the resulting fires, would propel at least 15 million tons of dust and 180 million tons of smoke into the atmosphere. That would blacken the skies for 6 to 20 weeks; and if it happened in spring or summer, temperatures throughout Eurasia and North America would drop by 18 to 55 degrees.

Within days, the pall of smoke and dust would block 99 percent of the sunlight normally falling on the Northern Hemisphere. Temperatures would drop catastrophically, destroying agriculture for at least a year, and many forests. The consequences—while not calculated by the academy study—are estimated in a new book, *The Cold and the Dark,* by four of the original nuclear-winter theorists, Paul Ehrlich, Carl Sagan, Donald Kennedy, and Walter Orr Roberts.

Together with crops, most farm animals would freeze and die, and plant photosynthesis and thus new crop growth would be all but impossible; famine would be an inevitable consequence. In the Arctic darkness of nuclear winter, blast survivors—many without shelter—would suffer from pollution, radiation, sub-freezing temperatures, hunger, the resulting disease, and hopelessly inadequate medical care and relief facilities. Resistant species such as rats and roaches, with their natural predators killed off, would proliferate to torment humans.

The academy committee did not estimate precisely how long the nuclear winter would last, since the rainfall that might wash the dust and soot back to earth could also be disrupted by the accumulation of the sun's heat in the upper atmosphere. But the authors of *The Cold and the Dark* suggest that even returning sunlight would bring a new danger—lethal ultraviolet radiation—because much of the upper atmosphere's protective ozone layer would have been burned away.

Taken with the incalculable destruction and loss of life that would be caused by nuclear blast, nuclear winter raises at least the possibility of human extinction following a Soviet-U.S. war. It certainly means that after such a war anything remotely like civilization would cease to exist in the Northern Hemisphere.

EXERCISE 14. Analyzing the Body of a Persuasive Essay. Refer to the preceding paragraphs and to the essay's introduction on pages 183–84 to answer the following questions.

1. The writer mentions a committee as the source of the information about nuclear winter. Who was on the committee, and who commissioned their work?

2. What exactly did the committee say would happen if there were an explosion of about half the world's nuclear arsenals?
3. The writer cites four authors of a book entitled *The Cold and the Dark*. According to these authors, what would happen to human life if the weather changed in the way that the committee predicted?
4. There is no way to test the truth of what the committee and the authors say will happen, so whether you believe the information in this essay depends on the credibility of the sources of information. How believable is the committee commissioned by the Department of Defense? How believable are the authors of *The Cold and the Dark*? Explain your answers.

The Conclusion

The *conclusion*, usually one paragraph, may restate the writer's opinion or summarize the argument (the reasons supporting the position statement). Sometimes a conclusion also asks the reader to perform a specific action, such as making a contribution or writing a letter to an elected official. Occasionally, the concluding paragraph will state the writer's conclusion based on the evidence and reasons presented in the rest of the paper. In the following example, Mr. Wicker states the conclusion he has reached based on the assumption that all the information he has related is true.

> Therefore, the Academy of Sciences report can only speed the world's growing understanding that nuclear weapons *can never be used* except suicidally, and have no military or political value except to deter their use by others. That knowledge inevitably points toward fewer, not more nuclear weapons—a conclusion that even Moscow and Washington must someday begin to act upon as well as talk about.

EXERCISE 15. Analyzing a Writer's Argument.   Refer to the introduction (pages 183–84), body (pages 184–85), and conclusion of Tom Wicker's article to answer the following questions:

1. In your own words, what does the writer's conclusion state?
2. Do you think this is a logical conclusion if the facts stated in the rest of the essay are true?
3. Outline the reasons and the evidence that might be used to support the opposing viewpoint.
4. How is the introductory information about the eruption of Mount Tambora related to the writer's argument? What exactly is Tambora's lesson?

5. Mr. Wicker supports his opinion about nuclear weapons with facts about the eruption of Mount Tambora, information stated by a scientific committee, and information stated by four scientist-authors. How believable do you think his argument is? Explain your answer.

EXERCISE 16. Writing a First Draft. Use the argument you have developed earlier in the chapter, or outline another argument on a topic of your choice. Write a persuasive composition. Include a precisely worded position statement in the introduction. If you have a call to action, be sure to include it in the conclusion.

EVALUATING

EVALUATING A FIRST DRAFT

5h. Evaluate the content, organization, and style of your first draft.

In order to decide what changes would improve your draft, you must become an objective reader of your own writing, judging how well you have presented your argument to your audience. Use the following guidelines to discover what changes you should make to achieve your persuasive purpose: to present reasons and evidence clearly so the reader follows and accepts the logic of your argument.

GUIDELINES FOR EVALUATING PERSUASIVE COMPOSITIONS

Position Statement 1. Does a position statement clearly express a specific opinion on a serious, debatable topic?

Introduction 2. Does the introduction catch the reader's interest? Does it include the position statement?

Reasons 3. Is the opinion supported by at least three relevant and distinct reasons? Is each reason developed in a separate paragraph?

Evidence 4. Is each reason supported by relevant, reliable evidence?

Audience 5. Is audience background and attitude considered? Has an opposing viewpoint been acknowledged and refuted?

Conclusion	6. Does the conclusion state the writer's opinion, summarize the argument, or include a "call to action"?
Coherence	7. Are the reasons arranged in an effective order? Do transitional expressions (*first, finally, therefore,* etc.) make the logic of the argument clear?
Tone	8. Is a serious, formal tone used in the paper?
Fallacies	9. Does the paper avoid emotional appeals and fallacies in logic (see pages 203–206)?

EXERCISE 17. Evaluating a First Draft. Use the preceding guidelines to evaluate the draft you wrote in Exercise 16. You may want to exchange papers with a classmate to evaluate each other's work.

REVISING AND PROOFREADING

REVISING A FIRST DRAFT

5i. Revise your first draft.

To revise your persuasive composition, use the four basic revising techniques: adding words or ideas; cutting words, phrases, or sentences; reordering, or rearranging, words, sentences, or paragraphs; and replacing words or ideas. The following chart suggests how you can use these techniques based on your evaluation of a first draft.

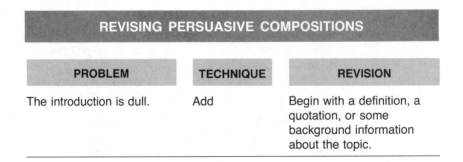

REVISING PERSUASIVE COMPOSITIONS		
PROBLEM	**TECHNIQUE**	**REVISION**
The introduction is dull.	Add	Begin with a definition, a quotation, or some background information about the topic.

PROBLEM	TECHNIQUE	REVISION
The writer's opinion is not clear.	Replace/Add	Make sure you have clearly stated whether you are pro or con. Add a sentence that states a specific position on the issue. Add a suggested action to your opinion in the conclusion.
A reason supports or repeats another reason, or repeats the position statement.	Replace/ Reorder	Replace the weak reason with a distinct reason. Consider using the weak reason as evidence, or discard it.
A reason or some evidence does not fit the argument.	Cut/Replace	Remove any irrelevant ideas. Make sure you still have sufficient reasons and evidence to support your argument. Do additional research if necessary.
The argument does not respond to a known audience bias or opposing argument.	Add	Add ideas that clearly refute opposing views. Make sure you have considered and clearly addressed audience background, attitude, and knowledge.
The argument is not built in order of importance.	Reorder/Add	Move the strongest reasons and evidence toward the end. Add or reorder ideas in the last paragraph to emphasize the logic of the argument.
It is hard to follow the argument.	Add/Replace	Add transitional words, such as *first* and *also* to connect ideas. Add background information to help clarify ideas. Replace long expressions with more concise wording.

PROBLEM	TECHNIQUE	REVISION
A paragraph discusses more than one reason.	Cut/Reorder	Cut the additional reason or make a new paragraph for it and the supporting evidence.
The composition does not end obviously and strongly.	Add	Add a summary of your argument, a restatement of your opinion, or a specific call to action.
The tone is either too informal or too emotional.	Replace/Cut	Replace slang, colloquialisms, contractions, and other informal expressions with formal wording. Omit unacceptable emotional wording, or replace it with serious, reasonable language.
The essay includes emotional appeals and/or fallacies in logic.	Cut/Replace	Omit emotional appeals, or replace them with logical reasons and evidence. Replace fallacies with logical reasons and sound evidence.

The following paragraph shows part of a composition on student involvement in designing a curriculum. Notice how the writer has used the revising techniques.

It seems to me that students will be more interested   cut
are consulted

in their classes and more likely to learn if they have some   replace
about   *and if they are involved in making the school work. They may*

say over what courses are offered. They'll also be less   cut/add/replace

likely to drop out of school maybe. It seems to me that all   cut

of the fuss about making school harder and having   cut

students meet minimum requirements is OK. But you've   cut

need

got to remember that students have to feel that what   cut/replace *they are   in school*   *When students are*

~~they're~~ learning is important in their life. ~~I heard about a~~   add/replace

self-motivated they achieve more. For example, in

~~school called~~ Middle College High School in New York   replace

City, ~~It has a program that really gets students involved.~~   cut

Peer counselors, ~~who are~~ trained by the faculty, help   cut

students with problems. ~~And~~ a peer-faculty committee   cut

and

decides on disciplinary problems. Another group of   add

s

students ~~help to~~ tutor other students who are having   cut/add

peer

trouble in school. All of this ~~type of~~ involvement ~~by~~   replace/cut

~~students~~ has resulted in ~~the consequence of a~~ daily   cut

attendance of more than 85 percent ~~of the students.~~   cut

nonexistent   *more than 80 percent*

Behavior problems are almost ~~not around~~, and ~~most~~ of   replace

the students go on to college.

EXERCISE 18. Revising a Persuasive Composition. Revise the composition you evaluated for Exercise 17. Refer to the preceding revising chart and to the chart on pages 27–28.

PROOFREADING AND MAKING A FINAL COPY

5j. Proofread your revised composition and prepare a final copy.

The most effective way to proofread is to reread the revised version several times, focusing each time on a separate task. Use the Guidelines for Proofreading on page 30 to check the important aspects of mechanics and usage. Errors in grammar, usage, and mechanics may distract your readers or prompt them to question your careful thinking.

After you have proofread, write the final version. Follow correct manuscript form (see pages 31–33) or your teacher's instructions. Be sure to proofread the final version again to catch any recopying mistakes.

EXERCISE 19. Proofreading and Making a Final Copy. Proofread the composition you revised in Exercise 18. Then write the final version of your composition, and proofread it once again.

LOGICAL THINKING

Logic, sometimes called clear thinking, is at the heart of persuasive writing. Learning to think more logically will help you become a more effective writer, speaker, and listener. In this section you will study and practice two basic types of logical thinking: inductive reasoning and deductive reasoning. You will also learn to identify ten common fallacies so that you can avoid these errors in reasoning in your persuasive writing.

INDUCTIVE REASONING

5k. Use inductive reasoning to make a generalization based on specific observations or evidence.

Inductive reasoning begins with a series of specific, concrete experiences or evidence. After carefully studying this evidence, you reach a conclusion based on the information you have gathered. This conclusion is often a *generalization,* a statement that explains all of the specific evidence and goes even further to make a general statement about a whole class of experiences.

Gathering Evidence

Suppose, for example, that you were investigating why students drop out of high school. You might begin by asking students who have left school what their reasons were.

EVIDENCE   Joe left school because he needed to earn money.
Sarita left school because she got a good job.
Tony dropped out of school to look for work.
Dina left school for a full-time job.

Making a Generalization

On the basis of this evidence, you might reach the following conclusion:

GENERALIZATION   Students drop out of high school to work.

You have made this generalization about all students on the basis of four pieces of evidence: your interviews with four students. Your *sampling* (the number of specific instances you studied) is far too small to make this a valid conclusion. The word *valid* means that you have correctly followed the rules of reasoning. In order to reach a valid conclusion about why students drop out of high school, you would need to sample many, many more specific cases. Perhaps you would have to interview hundreds of students, perhaps thousands. Probably you would find that students drop out of high school for many reasons.

Even if you interviewed several thousand drop-outs, you would still have to make what is known as "the inductive leap" in order to reach a conclusion. You know that there is no possible way for you to interview every student who has dropped out of school during the past sixty or so years. Your generalization is based not on *all* of the evidence, but on a *sampling* of all of the evidence.

You may recognize inductive reasoning as the method that scientists use when they make conclusions based on a series of experiments and measurements. The three basic steps in inductive reasoning may be summarized as follows:

1. Gather many specific pieces of evidence. Record your observations.
2. Study the evidence to try to explain it.
3. Make a generalization (conclusion) based on the evidence.

To make a sound (valid) generalization, you must follow three rules for gathering evidence and wording your conclusion.

(1) A generalization must be based on sufficient evidence.

One, two, or three pieces of evidence cannot lead to a sound conclusion. A generalization based on only a few pieces of evidence is, in fact, a fallacy called a *hasty generalization*. (See pages 203–204.) In an inductive argument, the evidence cannot *prove* that the generalization is true; rather, the evidence *supports* the generalization. The more evidence there is, the more likely it is that the generalization will be sound and believable.

(2) The evidence must be drawn from a random sampling of the population being studied.

Your evidence will be more reliable if it comes from a random sampling of the *population* (group) being studied. For example, suppose that you are trying once again to make some conclusions about why students drop out of high school. The answers you get from students that you interview are more likely to represent the whole population of drop-outs if you interview students at different schools across the country than if you interview only four friends at your school.

(3) The generalization must explain all of the evidence.

Because generalizations are such broad statements, it is often a good idea to add a qualifying or limiting word or phrase, such as one of the following: *some, many, most, sometimes, often, usually, are likely to, probably, occasionally, may, among those studied*, etc. The generalization about high-school drop-outs and work would be more likely to be true if a limiting word were added. In the following examples, notice that the generalization no longer makes a statement about all high-school students who drop out of school.

EXAMPLES   Some high-school students drop out of school to work.
                Many high-school students drop out of school to work.
                One of the reasons why some high-school students drop out of school is to find work.

EXERCISE 20. Making a Generalization.   For the two items below, write a sound generalization based on the evidence presented. (More than one generalization may be possible and correct.)

1. The following figures show the median annual earnings for year-round full-time workers.

	WOMEN	MEN
1960	$3,293	$5,417
1970	$5,323	$8,966
1980	$11,197	$18,612
1983	$15,082	$25,584

2. Cholesterol, a fatty substance found in varying amounts in human blood, is thought to be a cause of heart disease. Each person's cholesterol level can be tested with a simple blood test. The resulting figures measure the milligrams of cholesterol per 100 millimeters of blood serum. The National Institute of Health has issued the following figures, which rate the risk of certain levels of cholesterol by the age of the person being tested.

AGE	MODERATE RISK	HIGH RISK
2–19	Greater than 170	Greater than 185
20–29	Greater than 200	Greater than 220
30–39	Greater than 220	Greater than 240
40–plus	Greater than 240	Greater than 260

Using Inductive Reasoning in Persuasive Writing

Whenever you begin an argument by presenting your evidence and end by making a logical conclusion based on the evidence, you are using inductive reasoning. Your logical conclusion must be true if all of your evidence is true.

For example, look at the argument outlined on page 176 for passing a mandatory seat belt law. The three reasons given are equivalent to the evidence in an inductive argument. Each reason can be proved to be true by means of facts, statistics, and examples. Now, assuming that you accept as true the three reasons and their supporting evidence, only one logical conclusion is possible: This state should pass a mandatory seat belt law.

Also consider Tom Wicker's essay "Tambora's Lesson" on pages 183–86. Mr. Wicker builds to a conclusion by presenting three pieces of evidence: (1) facts about the effects of the 1816 eruption of Mount Tambora, (2) predictions made by a scientific committee commissioned by the Department of Defense, and (3) predictions made by four scientist-authors. If you accept these three pieces of evidence as true, then Mr. Wicker's conclusion (see page 186) is a logical one.

EXERCISE 21. Outlining an Inductive Argument.   For each generalization below, indicate what evidence would support the generalization. If you disagree with the generalization, reword it to your satisfaction.

1. Students should eat a nutritious breakfast to learn well.
2. Every person can learn to read.
3. Students who know how to use computers are more likely to find jobs than students who do not know how to use computers.
4. Movies are better than they ever were.
5. Male drivers under twenty-five are involved in more automobile accidents than female drivers under twenty-five.
6. Poor communication can cause serious misunderstandings.

CRITICAL THINKING:
Evaluating an Inductive Argument

When you are writing or reading a persuasive paper, you may recognize that the argument is inductive. Use the following guidelines to evaluate an inductive argument:

GUIDELINES FOR EVALUATING AN INDUCTIVE ARGUMENT

1. What is the conclusion?
2. What is the evidence on which the conclusion is based?
3. Is there enough evidence to warrant the conclusion?
4. What is the source of the evidence? Is the source reliable?
5. Does the generalization explain all of the evidence, or is it contradicted by some of the evidence?
6. Does the generalization make a universal statement?
7. Does the argument contain any fallacies? (See pages 203–206.)

EXERCISE 22. Analyzing an Argument. The following paragraphs are from an article entitled "Studies Weigh Hazard of Legal Drugs and Driving." Read the paragraphs; then answer the questions that follow.

While numerous studies have been done to establish exactly how alcohol affects drivers and how many crashes can be blamed on drinks, similar data do not exist about [legal] drugs and driving. The Food and Drug Administration requires warnings to drivers on all sedatives, but the requirement is based on an assumption that such drugs as tranquilizers, pain-killers and antihistamines affect driving skills, not on actual tests.

The information that does exist indicates that the problem of [legal] drugs and driving is far-reaching. Simulated road tests at the Southern California Research Institute showed that the drug diazepam, more commonly known as Valium, impaired drivers' abilities to stay in their lane, maintain an even speed and determine exits, and increased the time and distance needed to stop the car.

One study found that psychiatric patients taking one or more medications have two to three times as many accidents as psychiatric patients who are not taking drugs. Another determined that allergy sufferers have 50 to 100 percent more accidents and time lost from work because of accidents than nonallergy sufferers.

A study of accident victims admitted to Oslo hospitals indicated that 20 percent showed Valium in their blood. Eleven percent of those showed evidence of Valium alone, the rest showed a mixture of Valium and alcohol. A similar study in Dallas found Valium in the blood of 10 percent of drivers killed in car crashes.

"The weight of the circumstantial evidence in this case builds to an irrefutable conclusion," said J. F. O'Hanlon, a professor at the Traffic Research Center in the Netherlands.

LISA BELKIN

1. The paragraphs do not state the "irrefutable conclusion" J. F. O'Hanlon refers to in the last paragraph. Using the evidence given, state that generalization in your own words.
2. How much evidence does the writer cite? What are the sources?
3. How reliable is this evidence? Explain your answer.
4. What kind of evidence would you need to prove the conclusion you stated for Question 1?
5. What do you think can be done to prevent car accidents that result from drivers having taken legal drugs?

DEDUCTIVE REASONING

5I. Use deductive reasoning to reach a logical conclusion based on a generalization.

Deductive reasoning begins with a generalization, applies that generalization to a particular example, and arrives at a conclusion. Inductive reasoning moves from the particular to the general; deductive reasoning, on the other hand, moves from the general to the particular.

GENERALIZATION	All animals need water.
SPECIFIC EXAMPLE	Camels are animals.
CONCLUSION	Camels need water.

The Syllogism

A three-part deductive argument is called a *syllogism.* The first part is a generalization, sometimes called the *major premise.* The second part, called the *minor premise,* applies that generalization to a particular example, leading to the third part of the syllogism: the conclusion.

GENERALIZATION	All human beings need oxygen to live.
SPECIFIC EXAMPLE	You are a human being.
CONCLUSION	You need oxygen to live.

Syllogisms do not have to deal only with facts. When deductive reasoning is used in persuasive writing, the generalization often states an opinion.

GENERALIZATION	It is the duty of every American citizen eighteen and older to vote in every election.
SPECIFIC EXAMPLE	Juan Rivera is an eighteen-year-old American citizen.
CONCLUSION	It is Juan Rivera's duty to vote in every election.

Deductive reasoning is tricky, for sometimes the reasoning seems to be logical, but the conclusion is false. A *valid* (logical) and true conclusion meets three criteria for deductive reasoning.

(1) Both premises in a syllogism must be true.

The conclusion cannot be true if either the major or the minor premise is false. Consider the following examples.

> All two-legged animals are human beings. (false major premise)
> An ostrich is a two-legged animal.
> An ostrich is a human being.

In the example above, the major premise is false: there are many two-legged animals that are not human beings. The conclusion, therefore, is false even though the syllogism follows the correct rules of reasoning.

> All ostriches have feathers.
> A poodle is an ostrich. (false minor premise)
> A poodle has feathers.

In the second example, the minor premise is false. A poodle is not an ostrich. Because the minor premise is false, the conclusion is false.

(2) The generalization in a syllogism must make a universal statement.

A universal statement is one that applies to *all* instances of the population being discussed. Universal statements contain or imply the word *All* or *Every*. A statement that contains a limiting word (such as *several, many, most, some, few*) is not a universal statement.

UNIVERSAL STATEMENT	All butterflies are insects.
	Butterflies are insects.
	Every butterfly is an insect.
LIMITED STATEMENT	Some seniors have applied to colleges.
	Many seniors have applied to colleges.
	Several seniors have applied to colleges.

If you try to use a limited statement as either the major or minor premise in a syllogism, you cannot make a valid conclusion.

EXAMPLE Some seniors have applied to colleges.
Jana is a senior.

No conclusion is possible because you have no way of knowing if Jana is one of those "some seniors" who have applied to colleges.

(3) The minor premise must be a specific example of the group identified in the major premise.

This requirement in a syllogism is a little trickier than the other two requirements. You can understand it best by looking at two examples of a false syllogism.

FALSE SYLLOGISM   Communists believe in government ownership of natural resources.
Mrs. Doe believes in government ownership of the coal mines.
(Therefore,) Mrs. Doe is a Communist.

FALSE SYLLOGISM   All people need love.
Rover, our dog, needs love.
Rover is a person.

In both syllogisms, the premises are true but the conclusions do not follow. In the first syllogism, the premise does not state that all people who believe in government ownership of coal mines are necessarily Communists. "Mrs. Doe" is not identified as an example of the group—"Communists"—named in the major premise.

In the second syllogism "Rover" is not a specific example of the population—"people"—named in the first premise. If the second premise were an example of the first, you could reach a valid and true conclusion.

EXAMPLE   All people need love.
Donald is a person.
Donald needs love.

Using Deductive Reasoning in Persuasive Writing

If you begin an argument with a generalization that you assume to be true and then consider a specific case of that generalization, you are probably using deductive reasoning. Of course, you do not include actual syllogisms in your composition, but sometimes the argument that you build is a development of ideas that could be stated in the form of a syllogism.

Consider, for example, the issue of day care for preschool children. One way to summarize an argument against such day care might be as follows:

SYLLOGISM   Preschool children who are not cared for at home by their parents suffer from the emotional trauma of separation.

Preschool children who are sent to day-care centers are not being cared for at home by their parents.

Therefore, the preschool children who are sent to day-care centers are suffering from the emotional trauma of separation.

CRITICAL THINKING:
Evaluating a Deductive Argument

As you write persuasive compositions and listen to persuasive arguments, ask yourself whether the statements and conclusions are true. Use the following guidelines to evaluate a deductive argument:

GUIDELINES FOR EVALUATING A DEDUCTIVE ARGUMENT

1. What are the writer's premises? (Sometimes the premises are not clearly stated, but are assumed.)
2. Are the premises true? How can you tell if they are true?
3. Does the generalization make a universal statement?
4. What is the writer's conclusion?
5. Does the conclusion follow logically from the premises? Is the conclusion true?
6. Does the argument contain any fallacies? (See pages 203–206.)

EXERCISE 23. Analyzing a Letter to the Editor.   Read the following letter to the editor, and answer the questions below. The writer is referring to an $800 million surplus in New York State funds and to a proposed $800 million tax cut.

To the Editor:

I disagree with those who think an $800 million tax cut for New York State is a good idea.

Present tax rates were not established frivolously simply to "spend." They are required to bring in the money to pay for public services, which all of us benefit from. Public schools, streets and highways, police protection, libraries, shelters for the homeless, hospitals, fire protection, all require tax dollars to exist.

Is there a presumption that these and other public services in New York State, and in its cities and towns, are in such great shape that no improvement is necessary?

We have overcrowded classrooms in our schools, mentally ill people wandering the streets confused and penniless, understaffed police forces in our cities, decent families paying 40 percent of their income for indecent housing, and citizens who would like to attend public college part-time but who can't afford the tuition. One might think of other problems. Why the big rush for a tax cut?

If we have a surplus in the state budget, after these years of austerity, let's use it to begin to address the many inadequacies in public services that New Yorkers have endured and are enduring.

And should we reach the level of adequacy, would it spoil some universal plan if we strove for excellence?

The public services that we purchase through our government are as much a part of the quality of our lives as the things we purchase individually.

We New Yorkers should stop apologizing for taxing ourselves to improve the society we commonly share.

EDWARD C. SULLIVAN
Assemblyman, 69th District

1. What would you say are the writer's premises? Are they true?
2. What do you think is the writer's conclusion? Is this conclusion logical? Explain your answer.
3. State the writer's argument as a syllogism.

EXERCISE 24. Identifying Inductive and Deductive Reasoning. Number your paper 1–5. After studying each item, tell whether the reasoning is inductive (I) or deductive (D). Also be prepared to discuss whether the conclusion is true.

1. Only Caribou Airlines flies nonstop between here and Atlanta. Carl said he was coming from Atlanta on a nonstop flight, so he must be flying on Caribou Airlines.
2. Based on the number of new cars in college parking lots, and the number of college students who spend their winter vacations at ski resorts and their summers abroad, I'd say that college students these days must be wealthy.
3. The per-pupil cost of education is greater in high school than in elementary school. In the future a greater proportion of pupils will be in high school. The total cost of education, therefore, is sure to increase.
4. Statistics show that there has been an increase in muggings and violent crimes in the subways in the past two years. In a random survey of 1,600 subway riders, all complain that they feel unsafe on the subways. To protect riders, each subway train should have at least three police officers patrolling the cars.

5. Based on hundreds of tests with each make and model of automobile, government officials have concluded that small compact cars get more miles per gallon of gas than large, heavy cars.

EXERCISE 25. Creating Syllogisms. Write five original syllogisms. Test them by exchanging papers with your classmates. You might give them your premises alone and see what conclusions they reach.

ARGUMENT BY ANALOGY

5m. Develop an analogy to clarify and strengthen an argument.

A person may sometimes use an analogy to clarify a point. An *analogy* is a comparison. To be effective, the two things or situations being compared must have many points in common. If there are too many dissimilarities, the analogy is weak and will not be convincing.

WEAK ANALOGY   Being a student in school is like being a soldier in an army. Students must obey hall monitors, just as soldiers must obey their officers, so that the school can function effectively.

By drawing this analogy, the writer hopes to persuade readers to be more cooperative and obedient. However, the analogy is weak, even though both an army and a school must have discipline. Is military discipline appropriate for a school? Is the job of an army officer like that of a hall monitor? Is winning a battle much like furthering an educational program? This analogy appears weaker as you study it.

Remember that an analogy can never *prove* anything. Nevertheless, analogies have their place in argument because of their clarifying effect. Almost invariably, analogies are interesting to an audience and will help them to understand an argument better.

EXERCISE 26. Analyzing an Analogy. Read the following letter, and then answer the questions that follow it.

Imagine you were playing a game of checkers—playing to win.

Someone leans over your shoulder, puts a thumb on one checker and says, "Go ahead and play—just don't move this checker." Then someone else leans over your other shoulder and puts a thumb on another checker. Then a third person immobilizes still another checker, then another, then another . . . Soon all thumbs; no moves.

Could you ever expect to win a game like that?

Of course not!

Yet . . . most Americans expect their Senators and Congressmen in Washington to solve the monumental problems of recession, inflation, devastating unemployment, and a dangerous energy crisis while working under the same insurmountable conditions.

In the struggle to find solutions to these grave problems, the restricting thumbs are the high-pressure demands of special-interest groups—they do not really want to paralyze the nation's problem-solving efforts. Each just wants to immobilize one checker. Each is simply looking after its own special interest—making sure that their financial gains are not affected, insuring that certain tax advantages are not disturbed, guaranteeing that subsidies are maintained, etc. Collectively, they prevent *any* solution.

And in real life you can't see whose thumbs are coming down on the checkerboard. You don't know what forces are making the game impossible to win. That's why we the citizens must step in and say, "THUMBS OFF!"

JOHN GARDNER

1. What situations are compared in this analogy?
2. How effective do you think the analogy is?
3. What do you think the writer wants the reader to do?
4. What important difference is pointed out in the last paragraph?

EXERCISE 27. Developing an Analogy.   Choose a persuasive topic, perhaps one from a previous exercise. Develop at least one analogy for a persuasive composition on the topic. Then write a paragraph presenting the analogy as part of an argument to support your opinion.

AVOIDING ERRORS IN REASONING

5n. Learn to recognize fallacies, and avoid them in your writing.

An error in reasoning is called a *fallacy*. Arguments that contain fallacies are not logical arguments, so their conclusions are necessarily false. Learning to recognize common fallacies should enable you to build better arguments and to detect errors in logic when you read or listen to others' attempts to persuade you.

CRITICAL THINKING:
Recognizing Fallacies

Hasty Generalization

A generalization based on insufficient evidence is called a *hasty generalization*. A generalization must be based on a great deal of evidence or on many personal observations—not just one or two experiences.

FAULTY   A month ago, I was forced off the highway by a car driven by a high-school student who insisted on passing, even though there was not enough room to pass. To avoid being sideswiped, I drove into the ditch. It is obvious to me that teen-age drivers are a menace and that the driving age in this state should be raised to twenty-one.

Stereotype

A *stereotype* is a belief that all members of a particular group share certain characteristics just because they are members of the group. Stereotypes lead to prejudice—prejudging individuals on their group identities rather than on their individual merits.

FAULTY   Foreigners can't be trusted.
          Englishmen have no sense of humor.

Cause-and-Effect Fallacy

The *cause-and-effect fallacy* mistakenly assumes that just because one event preceded another, the first event caused the second event. The Latin name for this fallacy is *post hoc, ergo propter hoc,* which means "After this, because of this."

FAULTY   The school's basketball team played in the state championship and had to travel a whole day to reach the city where the game would be played. They played the game the same day they traveled and lost badly. Obviously they lost because they were tired from traveling. Championship games should not be played on the same day that a team travels.

Just because the team traveled before the game does not mean the traveling caused them to lose. The team may have been tired from traveling, but they may have lost for a number of other reasons as well. Maybe they lost because the team that defeated them was a better team with greater depth.

Only Cause Fallacy

The example for the cause-effect fallacy also illustrates the only cause fallacy. In the *only cause fallacy* a complex situation is seen as the result of a single cause. Usually, a situation has many causes—not just one.

Being open-minded allows you to see that more than one cause is possible and that, similarly, more than one solution is possible to a problem.

FAULTY 1. We can stop traffic fatalities if we make every instance of drunk driving punishable with a twenty-year prison sentence.
2. The drop-out rate for high-school students would decrease to almost nothing if classes were smaller.

False Analogy

You know that an analogy is a comparison used to clarify a point. A *false analogy* is a weak or far-fetched comparison. The items being compared are so dissimilar that the comparison is not effective.

FAULTY Like the manager of a wild animal circus, the principal of a high school is engaged in the business of training animals. There is always the strain of having to keep the animals under control. A school can no more permit students complete freedom than a circus can release its wild animals. In both instances, the public would protest vigorously.

Attacking the Person

When you attempt to discredit an opponent's views by *attacking the opponent's character* or circumstances, you are guilty of the *ad hominem fallacy,* which means "to the person." In responding to an opponent's arguments, deal with the argument directly rather than with the person.

FAULTY Lee Ann has proposed a series of reforms in the way the student government is run. Everyone knows that Lee Ann is never serious about anything. She is always joking and fooling around, so we shouldn't waste our time considering the reforms she has proposed. I'm sure it's all a big joke to her.

Either-Or Fallacy

Thinking of a problem or a solution as having only two possible extremes (causes, courses of action, etc.) is *either-or* thinking. A person guilty of the *either-or fallacy* sees situations as either good or bad, right or wrong, black or white, and ignores all possibilities between these extremes.

FAULTY 1. Either we will have to sell more tickets, or we will have to cancel the play completely.
2. If we don't reelect Governor X, the state government will be ruined.

Non Sequitur

Non sequitur means "It does not follow" in Latin. When a conclusion does not logically follow from a premise (or premises), the writer has committed a *non sequitur fallacy.*

FAULTY   More than two thirds of the students participate in some extracurricular activity. Because 100 percent of the student body does not participate in these activities, all of these activities should be canceled.

Circular Reasoning

Circular reasoning occurs when you give no distinct reasons to support your opinion, instead just restating and rephrasing the position statement.

FAULTY   My candidate is the best qualified of all. In character, experience, education, and intellectual ability, she is superior to everyone else who is running for this office. No one even remotely approaches her qualifications for the position. She stands head and shoulders above the other candidates. Therefore, she deserves your vote.

Begging the Question

If you assume that a judgment or an opinion is true and accepted by your reader, you may be committing the fallacy of *begging the question.*

FAULTY   Everyone agrees that this is an unfair tax.
          We all know that the senator's statement is ridiculous.

EXERCISE 28. Illustrating Fallacies.   Make up one example of each of the ten fallacies discussed on pages 203–206. See if other students in the class can identify the fallacies.

EXERCISE 29. Detecting Fallacies in Writing.   Read the editorials, letters to the editor, and advertisements in several issues of a daily newspaper. Bring to class at least three examples of fallacies in reasoning.

PROPAGANDA: APPEALS TO EMOTION

5o. Learn to recognize and evaluate propaganda techniques.

When an organized group (government, institution, business) sets out to win over the public, the ideas and arguments it uses in its favor are called *propaganda*. The purpose of propaganda is to convince and persuade to action. Not all propaganda is bad, although the word has negative connotations. Most people would agree that a physician who tries to persuade an audience to stop smoking cigarettes is using "good propaganda."

In your persuasive writing, you will probably not use many appeals to the emotions. As you have learned, persuasive writing should be an appeal to logic and clear thinking. However, you may occasionally use some of these emotional appeals, just as you should learn to recognize them in others' attempts to influence your actions or thinking.

Loaded Words

Loaded words are words with strong emotional associations—whether positive or negative. *Love* and *peace* are positively loaded words, for example; *cheat* and *war* have negative connotations. (See pages 323–25 for more about loaded words and connotations.)

Glittering Generalities

The loaded words in the *glittering generality* are so strongly positive in emotional content that they make you feel good just by hearing them.

EXAMPLE   A group of *clean-cut, all-American* volunteers will dance at the Inaugural Ball.

Propagandists often use slogans, another form of glittering generality, to oversimplify arguments and reduce them to a few words.

EXAMPLE   The right is more precious than the peace.
          All that counts is liberty, equality, fraternity.

The Bandwagon

The *bandwagon appeal* asserts that you should do something because "everyone else" is doing it, thus appealing to the human need not to feel left out.

EXAMPLE   Don't be the last person to buy a yearbook. Almost five sixths of the senior class have already reserved their copies. Hurry—before the copies are all gone.

Plain-Folks Appeal

The *plain-folks appeal,* often found in advertisements, uses average, ordinary, everyday people to make you want to do what they are doing. If you see the "common man" or "average woman" using a product, you will supposedly be tempted to use it, too.

EXAMPLE   Ordinary working people are giving their support to Candidate X because he knows what their problems are and will work to help them.

Snob Appeal

Snob appeal is the opposite of the plain-folks appeal. Advertisers portray "beautiful people," the "jet set," wealthy, privileged, and sophisticated men and women to help sell a product. The implied message is that if you use this product, your life will be more glamorous, interesting, and exciting. Sometimes, the snob appeal approach tells you that you are unique, special, and extraordinary and should, therefore, use a certain product.

EXAMPLE   Only the elite wear Ultralovely watches—the timepiece of a select society.

Testimonial

You have seen that to cite an authority, an expert in the field, is acceptable evidence in an argument. However, the *testimonial* device uses a famous person to recommend a product or candidate for office. When that person is not an expert in the field, his or her preference or opinion is simply an appeal to the emotions. If you like the person presenting the product or candidate, you will supposedly like that person's preference as well.

EXAMPLES   Kandy Kane, the beautiful singer, urges you to vote for Candidate X for state senator.

Frank R., an actor who plays a doctor in a television series, recommends this brand of cereal because he says it is the most nutritious.

EXERCISE 30. Identifying Emotional Appeals. Make up an example of each of the six emotional appeals on pages 207–208. See if other members of the class can identify the technique you have used.

CHAPTER 5 WRITING REVIEW 1

Writing a Persuasive Composition. Select a limited topic on a debatable issue for an essay or a letter to the editor. Write a persuasive composition based on your position (*pro* or *con*) and the reasons you choose to support the position statement. Provide evidence to support each reason. Research as necessary to locate the appropriate evidence. Evaluate your paper with the guidelines on pages 187–90. Then revise, proofread, and prepare a final copy.

CHAPTER 5 WRITING REVIEW 2

Identifying Fallacies and Emotional Appeals. You experience persuasive writing most often in advertising, as advertisers use pictures, music, and words to influence you to buy or use their products. Look through several magazines and listen critically to television and radio advertisements. Bring to class at least five examples of advertisements using fallacies in logic and emotional appeals.

Also bring to class at least three examples of "good propaganda"— ones that try to convince you to perform a beneficial action, such as advertisements from the American Heart Association. Also be prepared to discuss the emotional appeals and fallacies in logic of these examples.

CHAPTER 6

Imaginative and Expressive Writing

PERSONAL NARRATIVES, STORIES AND PLAYS, AND POETRY

Imaginative writing grows out of the writer's creativity and imagination. Expressive writing may also be imaginative, but it has the additional characteristic of revealing the writer's own thoughts and feelings. In this chapter, you will learn to write imaginatively and expressively through personal narratives, short stories, plays, and poetry.

In a personal narrative, the writer relates a true story about an experience or event that is personally significant. In a short story or a play, the writer creates imaginary characters with an imaginary conflict. The story and the play are fiction and do not necessarily express the writer's own feelings or thoughts. Since poetry is both imaginative and expressive, the poet may transport the reader to imaginary places and times or express deep personal feelings through movement, sound, and images.

WRITING A PERSONAL NARRATIVE

When you write a personal narrative, you share your feelings about how an experience affected you or taught you something significant. This first-person account may include elements of suspense and action, vivid description, and dialogue.

PREWRITING

CHOOSING A PERSONAL EXPERIENCE

6a. Choose a personal experience that is interesting or unusual.

People enjoy reading about experiences that help them recall or appreciate similar personal experiences. They also enjoy reading about experiences that are unlike any they have had, that give them new insights or satisfy their curiosity about the lives of others. Use the questions below to discover some experience of your own that others will enjoy reading.

Techniques for Prewriting. To find an experience for a personal narrative you would be willing to share, ask yourself:

- What event in my life has been exceptionally exciting, instructive, humorous, or moving?
- Has there been a wonderful (or a disastrous) first time for doing something?
- What memorable conflict or struggle have I experienced?
- Have I had a once-in-a-lifetime experience, such as meeting a famous person?
- Has there been a "turning point" in my life?

Read your journal for descriptions of interesting experiences and select one that you would like to share. You may also use the technique of clustering. To use clustering, begin by writing and circling one of the five categories in the center of a blank piece of paper. Focus on the category and write whatever experiences come to mind. As you write each idea, circle it and connect it with a line to the circle in the center or to other ideas. Do not judge what you are writing; make the connections freely, without being critical. Continue to write ideas, circling and connecting them to the ideas already on your paper. When you have finished, analyze what you have written and select the experience you think is most interesting or unusual.

EXAMPLE

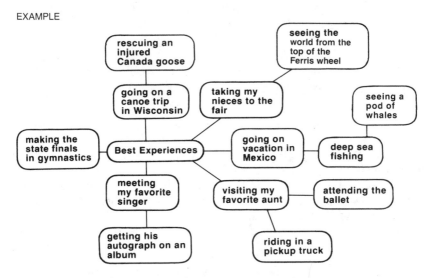

EXERCISE 1. Choosing a Personal Experience. Search for and select one interesting or unusual experience suitable for a personal narrative. You may use the questions on page 211, your writer's journal, or clustering to search for subjects.

IDENTIFYING AUDIENCE AND TONE

6b. Identify your audience and choose an appropriate tone.

Once you have selected a subject, think about the people with whom you will be sharing it. Depending on your audience, you may need to include background information or explanations of terms. You also must consider how to write about your experience to interest people of different ages and backgrounds.

After you identify your audience, you must choose a tone. Your own attitude toward the experience and how you would like your audience to respond to it will determine the tone you want to use. Later, when you write your narrative, the details you include and the language you use will reflect this tone.

EXERCISE 2. Considering Audience and Tone. Choose an appropriate tone for each audience given with the following subjects. First select an appropriate tone for audience *a,* and then choose one for audience *b.* Be prepared to explain your answers.

EXAMPLE 1. *Subject:* A practical joke that backfired
            Audience: a. Close friends; b. Young children
         1. *Tone: a. Humorous; b. Serious*

1. *Subject:*   The time I learned to swim
   Audience: a. Classmates; b. Readers of a sports magazine
2. *Subject:*   The night I was lost in the woods
   Audience: a. Readers of the school newspaper; b. Young children
3. *Subject:*   Meeting a famous movie star
   Audience: a. Readers of movie magazines; b. Community members
4. *Subject:*   The day I learned how to lose gracefully
   Audience: a. Close friends; b. General audience
5. *Subject:*   The most frightening moment of my life
   Audience: a. General audience; b. Young children

EXERCISE 3. Identifying Audience and Tone for a Personal Narrative. Identify your audience and an appropriate tone for the subject you selected in Exercise 1. Decide if your audience will need any background information; also decide if the tone you intend to use is appropriate for your audience and subject. (You may decide to change your subject, the tone, or both.)

GATHERING INFORMATION AND PLANNING YOUR PERSONAL NARRATIVE

6c. Gather information and plan your personal narrative.

Gathering information for your narrative depends on retrieving memories. This process can be aided by reading your journal for an account of an event. Brainstorming and clustering are also effective methods of recalling details, actions, and emotions.

To *brainstorm,* you concentrate on one subject, such as "my canoe trip," and list words and phrases ("life jackets," "white-water rapids," and "leaky tent") that come to mind. Without pausing to evaluate, write everything that occurs to you. Then as you review your list, select the most important details about your subject, filling in related descriptions and events.

Clustering, the technique discussed on pages 15–16, helps you concentrate on making connections between your subject and specific details and actions (page 15). For example, as you concentrate on the canoe trip, the memory of the white-water rapids might lead you to the memory of a friend falling out of the canoe. After using this technique, decide which of these related memories to use in your narrative.

Once you have gathered sufficient information, plan your narrative by organizing the events in a logical order. The most frequently used order is *chronological,* the sequence in which events occur. You may use an informal format in your plan:

First: Three friends and I went to the Wolf River . . .
Then: We set up camp and . . .
Then: We climbed into the two canoes and . . .
Then: (and so forth)
Finally: We learned how resourceful we could be . . .

Make sure your plan does not include events that fail to contribute to developing the experience. For example, if you are planning a personal narrative about playing basketball, include details about going to a game only if they have direct bearing on your experience. You should also indicate where you feel it is most appropriate to include a personal summary or commentary on the experience.

In his book *Growing Up,* Russell Baker describes the change from childhood to adolescence, marked by his first pair of long pants. Notice the organization and the tone of the narrative.

The changeover from knickers to long pants was the ritual recognition that a boy had reached adolescence, or "the awkward age," as everybody called it. The "teenager," like the atomic bomb, was still uninvented, and there were few concessions to adolescence, but the change to long pants was a ritual of recognition. There was no ceremony about it. You were taken downtown one day and your escort—my mother in my case—casually said to the suit salesman, "Let's see what you've got in long pants."

For me the ritual was performed in the glossy, mirrored splendor of Bond's clothing store on Liberty Street. She had taken me for a Sunday suit and, having decided I looked too gawky in knickers, said, "Let's see what you've got in long pants." My physique at this time was described by relatives and friends with such irritating words as "beanpole," "skinny," and "all bones." My mother, seeing me through eyes that loved, chose to call me "a tall man."

The suit salesman displayed a dazzling assortment of garments. Suit designers made no concessions to youth; suits for boys were just like suits for men, only smaller. My mother expressed a preference for something with the double-breasted cut. "A tall man looks good in a double-breasted suit," she said.

The salesman agreed. Gary Cooper, he said, looked especially good in double-breasted suits. He produced one. I tried it on. It was a hard fabric, built to endure. The color was green, not the green of new grass in spring, but the green of copper patina on old statues. The green was relieved by thin, light gray stripes, as though the designer had started to create cloth for a bunco artist,[1] then changed his mind and decided to appeal to bankers.

"Well, I just don't know," my mother said.

Her taste in clothes was sound rather than flamboyant, but I considered the suit smashing, and would have nothing else. The price was $20, which was expensive even though it came with two pairs of pants, and upon hearing it I said, "We can't afford it."

"That's what you think, mister," she said to me. "It's worth a little money to have the man of the house look like a gentleman."

In conference with the salesman, it was agreed that she would pay three dollars down and three dollars a month until the cost was amortized. On my attenuated physique, this magnificent, striped, green, double-breasted suit hung like window drapes on a scarecrow. My mother could imagine Gary Cooper's shoulders gradually filling out the jacket, but she insisted that Bond's do something about the voluminous excesses of the pants, which in the seat area could have accommodated both me and a watermelon. The salesman assured her that Bond's famous tailors would adjust the trousers without difficulty. They did so. When finally I had the suit home and put it on for its first trip to church, so much fabric had been removed from the seat that the two hip pockets were located with seams kissing right over my spine.

My mother was dazzled. With visions of a budding Gary Cooper under her wing, she said, "Now you look like somebody I can be proud of," and off to church we went.

RUSSELL BAKER

Why do you think Baker placed the commentary at the beginning rather than at the end? In what order does he relate events? What comes first, second, and so forth? Why might a reader find this particular experience interesting? What words, phrases, and details reveal Baker's humorous tone?

EXERCISE 4. Gathering Information for Your Personal Narrative. Using the experience you identified in Exercise 1, or a different one, gather information for your narrative by reviewing your journal, brainstorming, or clustering.

EXERCISE 5. Planning Your Personal Narrative. Plan your narrative by arranging details relevant to your experience and your personal commentary or reaction in a logical order.

---

[1] *Bunco artist:* a swindler, in particular one who works as one of a group of swindlers in a card game or lottery.

WRITING

WRITING THE FIRST DRAFT

6d. Write a first draft of your personal narrative.

In a first draft, you will put your thoughts down on paper. Although you will have a plan to follow for your personal narrative, you may alter it as you write.

> *Techniques for Writing.* To write the first draft of your personal narrative,
>
> - refer to your informal plan and any other notes.
> - write in the first person. (Use the pronoun *I*.)
> - keep in mind your audience and tone as you select details and language.
> - capture the interest of your audience and establish a tone in the opening paragraph.
> - fill in important background information, sensory details, essential actions, and any needed dialogue.
> - include a personal summary or commentary at the beginning or at the end.

EXERCISE 6. Write a Draft of Your Personal Narrative. Reviewing the suggestions above, write the first draft of your personal narrative. Use the plan you developed in Exercise 5.

EVALUATING, REVISING, AND PROOFREADING

EVALUATING, REVISING, AND PROOFREADING YOUR NARRATIVE

6e. Evaluate, revise, and proofread your personal narrative.

Evaluating

You can evaluate and revise your draft more objectively if you set it aside for two or three days and clear your mind before you begin. Read it several times, each time focusing on something different.

CRITICAL THINKING:
Evaluation

When you judge the effectiveness of a piece of writing, you are *evaluating* it. This critical thinking skill enables you to apply criteria, or standards, to assess your own writing and the writing of others. As you evaluate, you determine how well the writer has achieved his or her purpose through organization, content, and style.

GUIDELINES FOR EVALUATING PERSONAL NARRATIVES

Beginning	1. Does the beginning of the narrative arouse the interest of the audience and clearly establish the tone?
Coherence	2. Is the organizational pattern appropriate and easy to follow?
Point of View	3. Is the first-person point of view consistently maintained throughout the narrative?
Topic Development	4. Do the details contribute to the audience's understanding of the personal experience?
Tone	5. Are personal feelings or attitudes about the experience conveyed through tone?
Personal Commentary	6. Is a personal commentary or summary included?

Revising and Proofreading

After you evaluate your draft, revise it by adding, cutting, replacing, or reordering. The chart below provides suggestions for revising specific problems in your draft. After you revise your draft, proofread it to catch errors in grammar, usage, and mechanics. Refer to the Guidelines for Proofreading on page 30. Proofread again after you prepare a final copy.

REVISING PERSONAL NARRATIVES

PROBLEM	TECHNIQUE	REVISION
The beginning fails to create interest.	Cut/Replace	Cut the opening so it quickly captures the audience's interest. Replace the opening with one that includes vivid details and descriptions or a surprising statement.
The tone is not clear.	Add	Add words or details that reflect the tone, or attitude toward the experience, you want to convey.
The organization is confusing.	Cut/Reorder	Cut material that is confusing and unnecessary. Reorder out-of-place events.
The first-person point of view is not used consistently.	Cut/Replace	Cut errors or inconsistencies in point of view. Replace with first-person pronouns.
The details do not contribute to the audience's understanding of the personal experience.	Cut/Replace	Cut details that are confusing or merely irrelevant, and replace them with appropriate details that support your purpose and tone.
The tone does not reflect personal feelings.	Add	Add words or ideas that reflect your attitude toward the experience.
A personal commentary or summary is missing.	Add	Add a summary of the experience, an explanation of what you learned from this experience or why it is significant to you.

The following example shows one writer's evaluation and revision. How do the changes strengthen the narrative, make the tone consistent, and correct inaccuracies?

By the time I reached the turn-off for Chicago, it was starting to get dark;

all I could see were endless pairs of red lights stringing ahead of me and

endless pairs of yellow lights behind. I felt like ~~a bead on~~ a multicolored, *the movie astronauts caught in* *streaked corridor of hyperspace with no exit. Where was Mission Control when* ~~necklace that glowed in the dark.~~ *you needed them?* Should I stay in the center lane or move to

the right? If I moved to the right, could I stop in time in case a driver merged

too fast, or was the road too slippery? Would I be caught in the world's

longest chain collision on a Chicago highway? Why aren't these cars *"Come in, Mission Control!"* following the rules they taught us in driver's education? Every time I tried to

allow enough space between me and the car ahead of me. someone cut in.

Again, ~~I felt~~ my fingers cramping. The small of my back ~~began to~~ ache *-ed and* *-d*

because I was sitting bolt upright, as stiff as a steel rod. We never had this

much traffic in Lansing. */*

As you analyze the writer's revisions, consider what has been added, deleted, or moved. Why do you think the writer changed the second sentence in the paragraph? Why did the writer change the position of one sentence in the paragraph? How do the revisions improve this personal narrative?

EXERCISE 7. Evaluating the Writing of Others. Exchange drafts with a classmate or find an example of a personal narrative in a magazine or book. Evaluate the narrative, using the Guidelines for Evaluating Personal Narratives (page 217). Answer each question, pointing out strengths as well as weaknesses and providing specific examples to support your evaluation.

EXERCISE 8. Evaluate, Revise, and Proofread Your Personal Narrative. Evaluate and revise the personal narrative you wrote for Exercise 6. Refer to the proofreading guidelines on page 30 and make a final, clean copy of your draft.

WRITING STORIES AND PLAYS

In writing both short stories and plays, you create a compact world of fiction that is shaped from your imagination and experience. Although they differ in format, stories and plays share common elements: conflict (a problem or struggle), plot (the development and outcome of the action), character (the people who participate), dialogue (the characters' spoken words), and setting (the time and place of the action).

PREWRITING

CHOOSING A SITUATION AND CONFLICT

6f. Choose a situation and conflict suitable for a story or a play.

The subject for a story or a play must contain a situation and a problem in which a struggle occurs. Although this struggle or conflict suggests the clash of opposing forces, it does not mean violence. A character may be in conflict with the rules of authority or society, with the forces of nature, or with another character. A character may even experience the conflict of internal forces, such as honesty conflicting with loyalty. The ideas for a situation and conflict may come from outside sources, but your imagination converts them into interesting subjects.

Techniques for Prewriting.   To find a situation and conflict for a short story or play,

- interview friends, community members, or family members, especially older relatives.
- scan the news for human interest stories.
- review your writer's journal.
- closely observe the actions and lives of people around you.
- decide what situations and conflicts can be limited to a short period of time—a day or, at the most, a few weeks.

EXERCISE 9. Choosing a Situation and Conflict.   Referring to the suggestions above, write one or more possible conflicts for each situation listed below. Then, select a situation and a conflict to develop in a short story or a play.

EXAMPLE 1. *Situation:* A new video game is installed at a neighborhood store.
     1. *Conflict:* *A community group tries to force the store owner to remove the video game.*
        Conflict: *A high-school student worries that her brother is becoming obsessed with the video game.*

1. A student must earn money to replace a broken window before a cranky neighbor discovers the damage.
2. The worst tornado in history hits a small town.
3. The city council rules that high-school students must observe a 9:00 P.M. curfew.
4. A person witnesses a friend's dishonesty.
5. A student is accused of cheating on a scholarship test.

CONSIDERING A THEME

6g. Consider the theme of your story or play.

The theme of a story or play is an implied or stated insight about life or human nature. Rather than actually state the theme, many writers allow the interaction of the characters, action, and conflict to reveal a universal truth. Most memorable stories and plays embody some statement about life that readers or viewers can relate to their own experience.

Techniques for Prewriting. To consider a theme for your short story or play, ask yourself:

- In memorable stories or plays I've read or seen, how were the themes developed?
- What theme might emerge naturally from the situation and conflict I've selected?
- Is this theme a universal truth about life?
- Is this theme the particular insight about life or human nature that I want my audience to have after reading my story or play?
- Can I project this theme through the interaction of characters, actions, and conflict in my story or play?

EXERCISE 10. **Considering a Theme.**   Using the questions above, identify one or more themes that might grow out of the conflict you chose in Exercise 9.

EXAMPLE   *Conflict:*   A town is threatened by a flood, and the people must work together to save their homes.

Possible Themes: 1. *In times of trouble, people display their best or worst qualities.*
   2. *Some people discover what they really value in life only through a crisis.*

CONSIDERING PURPOSE, AUDIENCE, AND TONE

6h. Consider the purpose, audience, and tone of your story or play.

The *general purpose* of a short story or play is to entertain, but the *specific purpose* may be to evoke certain feelings (joy, fear, amusement, grief). That specific purpose reflects your own attitude toward the conflict; for example, you want your audience to be moved to tears because you feel that the situation your characters face is sad.

You reveal your attitude, or the *tone* of the story or play, through the details and language that you select. For example, to convey horror, you describe the pitch-black night and the creaking sound of the floorboard just outside the door.

You should also consider what effect the backgrounds and interests of your audience will have on your story or play. If, for example, your audience is made up of students from a large city, how will you make them understand a teen-ager's conflict between helping to harvest the tomatoes before frost and marching with the band in the homecoming parade? The members of the audience must understand the plot and the characters to enter imaginatively into the conflict.

Techniques for Prewriting.   To analyze purpose, audience, and tone for your short story or play, ask yourself:

- What is the specific purpose of this story or play?
- What is my attitude toward this conflict and the characters involved in it?
- What details and language can I use to convey that tone?
- What are the backgrounds and interests of my audience?
- What will I need to do to capture and hold my audience's interest in this story or play?

EXERCISE 11. **Analyzing Purpose, Audience, and Tone.** Review the situation and conflict you identified in Exercise 9 or any other situation and conflict. Analyze your purpose, audience, and tone by writing your answers to the questions above.

SELECTING A POINT OF VIEW

6i. Select a point of view appropriate for your story.

You may use either first-person or third-person point of view for a story. In first-person point of view, the story is told from the point of view of one person who either participates in or witnesses the conflict. The story is narrated in the first person, *I*, which closely involves the audience, but only the narrator's thoughts and observations are expressed. Everything the reader learns is through the perceptions of one character.

In the third-person, or omniscient, point of view, the story is narrated by someone *outside* the story who knows all and can express each character's thoughts and actions. This gives the writer freedom to reveal what any character thinks or does. Because of the distance created by this viewpoint, however, readers do not feel as close to the action.

Once you select a point of view, you must use it consistently throughout the story. Note the differences among the three points of view in the following examples:

> *First-person, directly involved in the conflict.* Dreading this moment, I swallowed hard as I entered the manager's office.

> *First-person, a witness to the conflict.* As Anita entered the office, I could tell she was nervous, despite her determined look. Ms. Whiting also looked determined—like a general about to order an attack.

> *Third-person, omniscient.* Anita squared her shoulders and tried to recall what she had planned to say. But Ms. Whiting stared at her menacingly, waiting for her to make that first little mistake.

EXERCISE 12. **Writing from Different Points of View.** Read the following situation and write a few sentences from each of the three points of view. Also explain which point of view, in your opinion, would be most appropriate for a story based on this situation.

Situation: Two friends, walking through the park, find a wallet in the grass. When they open it, they discover one thousand dollars.

GATHERING INFORMATION AND
PLANNING A SHORT STORY OR A PLAY

6j. Gather information and develop a plot outline for your story or play.

You cannot begin planning a story or a play until you have gathered information. For these kinds of imaginative writing, you will probably be inventing or creating information, as well as gathering it. Use any of the typical information-gathering techniques—brainstorming, clustering, consulting your journal, questioning, and so forth—until you have a thorough understanding of the action, the characters, the setting, and the conflict in your story or play.

When you have enough information, you are ready to develop a plan or outline of the *plot* (the series of actions that builds to a climax after which the conflict is resolved).

A basic plan for a story or play has a beginning, middle, and end. Study the following excerpts from a story by Hector Hugh Munro to see how he crafted each of these parts. The outline on the right shows how a plan might have been developed for this story.

"THE SCHARTZ-METTERKLUME METHOD"

Beginning:

Lady Carlotta stepped out onto the platform of the small wayside station and took a turn or two up and down its uninteresting length to kill time till the train should be pleased to proceed on its way. Then, in the roadway beyond, she saw a horse struggling with a more than ample load, and a carter of the sort that seems to bear a sullen hatred against the animal that helps him to earn a living. Lady Carlotta promptly betook her to the roadway, and put rather a different complexion on the struggle. Certain of her acquaintances were wont to give her plentiful admonition as to the undesirability of interfering on behalf of a distressed animal, such interference being "none of her business." Only once had she put the doctrine of noninterference into practice, when one of its most eloquent exponents had been besieged for nearly three hours in a small and extremely uncomfort-

Typical Plot Outline

Beginning: Introduce Lady Carlotta, a woman who takes what people say literally. Establish ironic tone. Suggest beginning of plot and conflict, Lady Carlotta's pretense of being the governess.

able may tree by an angry boar-pig, while Lady Carlotta, on the other side of the fence, had proceeded with the water-color sketch she was engaged on, and refused to interfere between the boar and his prisoner. It is to be feared that she lost the friendship of the ultimately rescued lady. On this occasion she merely lost the train, which gave way to the first sign of impatience it had shown throughout the journey, and steamed off without her. She bore the desertion with philosophical indifference; her friends and relations were thoroughly well used to the fact of her luggage arriving without her. She wired a vague noncommittal message to her destination to say that she was coming "by another train." Before she had time to think what her next move might be, she was confronted by an imposingly attired lady, who seemed to be taking a prolonged mental inventory of her clothes and looks.

"You must be Miss Hope, the governess I've come to meet," said the apparition, in a tone that admitted of very little argument.

"Very well, if I must I must," said Lady Carlotta to herself with dangerous meekness.

. . .

Summary of Middle:
[Several paragraphs have been omitted in which Lady Carlotta goes to the Quabarl mansion, shocks Mrs. Quabarl with her frank discussion of other people for whom she has worked, and takes Mr. and Mrs. Quabarl literally when they say she should make history come to life when she instructs the children.]

Middle: Show how Lady Carlotta shocks Mrs. Quabarl. Lead toward climax— Quabarls recommend making history come to life; Carlotta has children acting out the parts of Romulus and the she-wolf.

. . .

End:
"Wilfrid! Claude! Let those children go at once. Miss Hope, what on earth is the meaning of this scene?"

End: Build to climax when Mrs. Quabarl fires Lady Carlotta,

"Early Roman history; the Sabine women, don't you know? It's the Schartz-Metterklume method to make children understand history by acting it themselves; fixes it in their memory, you know. Of course, if, thanks to your interference, your boys go through life thinking that the Sabine women ultimately escaped, I really cannot be held responsible."

"You may be very clever and modern, Miss Hope," said Mrs. Quabarl firmly, "but I should like you to leave here by the next train. Your luggage will be sent after you as soon as it arrives."

"I'm not certain exactly where I shall be for the next few days," said the dismissed instructress of youth; "you might keep my luggage till I wire my address. There are only a couple of trunks and some golf clubs and a leopard cub."

"A leopard cub!" gasped Mrs. Quabarl. Even in her departure this extraordinary person seemed destined to leave a trail of embarrassment behind her.

"Well, it's rather left off being a cub; it's more than half grown, you know. A fowl every day and a rabbit on Sundays is what it usually gets. Raw beef makes it too excitable. Don't trouble about getting the car for me, I'm rather inclined for a walk."

And Lady Carlotta strode out of the Quabarl horizon.

The advent of the genuine Miss Hope, who had made a mistake as to the day on which she was due to arrive, caused a turmoil which that good lady was quite unused to inspiring. Obviously the Quabarl family had been woefully befooled, but a certain amount of relief came with the knowledge.

"How tiresome for you, dear Carlotta," said her hostess, when the overdue guest ultimately arrived; "how very tiresome losing your train and having to stop overnight in a strange place."

and Lady Carlotta makes up an outrageous story about the contents of her luggage. End with real governess arriving at Quabarl mansion and Lady Carlotta arriving at her original destination.

"Oh, dear, no," said Lady Carlotta; "not at all tiresome—for me."

SAKI (H. H. MUNRO)

Techniques for Prewriting. To develop a plot outline for a short story or play, ask yourself:

- Beginning: How will I present the characters, establish the tone, introduce the conflict, and create interest?
- Middle: How will I arrange a series of actions that will build to a climax, or point of greatest intensity?
- End: How will the conflict be resolved?

EXERCISE 13. Gathering Information. Using one of the information-gathering techniques (see pages 12–18), gather information about the situation and conflict you selected in Exercise 9 or any other situation and conflict of your choice.

EXERCISE 14. Developing a Plot Outline. Develop a plot outline based on the information you gathered in Exercise 13. Arrange the information into a beginning, a middle, and an end.

WRITING

MAKING WRITING INTERESTING

6k. Make your story or play interesting by using specific language and vivid images.

Interesting Writing Is Specific

Specific writing contains precise details and examples, whereas vague or general writing does not. Compare the expressions below:

VAGUE   a beautiful day
SPECIFIC   mountainous white clouds in a pale blue sky
VAGUE   She bore a great burden.
SPECIFIC   After their mother's death, Sylvia helped raise her younger sisters and brothers.

In the following three accounts, note how additional details produce more specific writing:

1. Some of the children on the outing seemed to be more interested than others in the planned activities.

2. The younger children at the Firefighter's Picnic could hardly wait for the games and races to begin. The older children, apparently indifferent toward sack races, the broad jump, and softball, stood around talking and watching the adults.

3. The younger children at the Firefighter's Picnic besieged Chief Barnard, jumping up and down, clamoring for the games and races to begin. The older children, apparently indifferent toward sack races, the broad jump, and softball, stood in a group by themselves, talking and watching the adults prepare lunch.

How is the second example more specific than the first? What specific details have been added in the third?

In specific writing, every general statement or abstraction is followed by an example that clarifies what the writer means. In the following excerpt from her short story "Tears, Idle Tears," Elizabeth Bowen includes specific examples to clarify Mrs. Dickinson's behavior.

Everybody had noticed how much courage she had; they said: "How plucky Mrs. Dickinson is." It [*general statement*] was five years since her tragedy and she had not remarried, so that her gallantness kept on coming into play. She helped a friend with a little hat shop called *Isobel* near where they lived in Surrey, bred [*specific example*] puppies for sale and gave the rest of her time to making a man of Frederick. She smiled nicely and carried her head high. Those two days while Toppy [*specific example*] had lain dying she had hardly turned a hair, for his sake: no one knew when he might come conscious again. When she was not by his bed she was waiting about the hospital. The chaplain hanging about her and the doctor had given thanks that there were [*specific example*] women like this; another officer's wife who had been her friend had said she was braver than could be good for anyone. When Toppy finally died the other woman had put the unflinching widow into a taxi and driven back with her to the Dickinsons' bungalow. She kept saying: "Cry, dear, cry: you'd feel better." She made tea and clattered about, repeating: "Don't mind me, darling: just have a big cry." The strain became so great that tears streamed down her own face. Mrs. Dickinson looked past her palely, with a polite smile.

specific example

ELIZABETH BOWEN

Interesting Writing Is Rich in Images

An image is usually a word picture. A police officer is an image, whereas "the law" is an abstraction. "Democracy" is an abstraction; a voter casting a ballot is an image. You cannot see the law or democracy, but you can see a police officer and you can see a voter casting a ballot. Abstract terms are necessary, but the interesting writer frequently strives to give them specific equivalents.

A specific image is usually more effective. "A police officer" is less specific than "a heavy-set police captain wearing a glistening gold badge."

Although adjectives create specific images, they are specific in varying degrees. The vague phrase "pretty girl" produces an almost meaningless image. "A slender redhead with startling blue eyes," however, is more vivid.

Evaluate the images in the following descriptions of the same scene.

1. From our vantage point on the mountainside, we could see several small towns scattered about the valley.

2. From our narrow rock ledge high on the snowy mountainside, we could see the white church spires of five tiny villages scattered across the green valley.

Specific, active verbs also contribute to more interesting writing. The colorless verb *be* (*am, is, are, was, were, be, being, been*) does nothing to enliven style, and verbs like *walk, act,* and *move* produce only vague images. If they are specific enough, verbs do not need modifiers. "The players *trotted* toward the sidelines" describes the action so exactly that adverbs such as *mechanically* and *dutifully* are unnecessary.

EXERCISE 15. Using Specific Language and Vivid Images. Read the following account of a boy and his father leaving their farmhouse early on a winter morning. List at least ten examples of the writer's use of specific details and images.

With a faint rending noise the tires came loose from the frozen earth of the barn ramp. The resistance of the car's weight diminished; sluggishly we were gliding downhill. We both hopped in, the doors slammed, and the car picked up speed on the gravel road that turned and dipped sharply around the barn. The stones crackled like slowly breaking ice under our tires. With a dignified acceleration the car swallowed the steepest part of the incline, my father let the clutch in, the chassis jerked, the motor coughed. Caught, *caught,* and we were aloft, winging along the pink straightaway between a pale green meadow and a fallow flat field. Our road was so little travelled that in the center it had a mane of weeds. My father's grim lips half-relaxed. He poured shivering gasoline into the hungry motor. If we stalled now, we would be out of luck, for we were on the level and there would be no more coasting. He pushed the choke halfway in. Our motor purred in a higher key. Through the clear margins of the sheet of frost on our windshield I could see forward; we were approaching the edge of our land. Our meadow ended where the land lifted. Our gallant black hood sailed in the sharp little rise of road, gulped it down, stones and all, and spat it out behind us.

JOHN UPDIKE

DEVELOPING INTERESTING, BELIEVABLE CHARACTERS

6l. Develop interesting, believable characters for your story or play.

To generate interest or concern, fictional characters must be interesting and believable. Engaged in a conflict, the main character (*protagonist*) is usually opposed by another character (*antagonist*). Other secondary characters may also be included.

In developing characters for a short story or play, remember that believable characters are consistent in their behavior. Show a logical reason, a motivation, for any change in behavior. For example, if you created a character who suddenly stops being kind and generous and starts being cruel and heartless, you must explain why.

You should also avoid stereotypes—the crotchety elderly person or the unintelligent beauty—in your story or play. Such characters are one-sided, trite, and predictable.

Using Description

In a play, the stage directions usually include a description of the characters. These directions aid the director in casting the part and the actor or actress in playing the part. Occasionally, one character describes another in dialogue, a technique that should not be used often. In a story, however, you attempt to *show* rather than *tell about* the character. Select vivid, specific language (see pages 227–30) to create word pictures of the character's appearance, personality, and behavior.

In the following excerpt from "Tears, Idle Tears," the narrator describes a woman whose son has just created a scene in the park. Notice how the writer combines vivid physical description with descriptions of the woman's actions and thoughts to create a specific impression.

> Once she had got so far as taking her pen up to write to the Mother's Advice Column of a helpful woman's weekly about them. She began: "I am a widow; young, good-tempered, and my friends all tell me that I have great control. But my little boy—" She intended to sign herself "Mrs. D., Surrey." But then she had stopped and thought no, no: after all, he is Toppy's son . . . She was a gallant-looking, correct woman, wearing today in London a coat and skirt, a silver fox, white gloves and a dark-blue toque put on exactly right—not the sort of woman you ought to see in a park with a great blubbering boy belonging to her. She looked a mother of sons, but not of a son of this kind, and should more properly, really, have been walking a dog. "Come on!" she said, as though the bridge, the poplars, the people staring were to be borne no longer. She began to walk on quickly, along the edge of the lake, parallel with the park's girdle of trees and the dark, haughty windows of Cornwall Terrace looking at her over the red may. They had meant to go to the Zoo, but now she had changed her mind: Frederick did not deserve the Zoo.
>
> ELIZABETH BOWEN

What are the woman's physical characteristics? How do her actions and thoughts contribute to a specific impression of her character? What is that impression?

The following excerpt is from the stage directions for the play *You Can't Take It with You*. Notice how these descriptive notes include physical description as well as a description of the character as the play opens.

> PENELOPE VANDERHOF SYCAMORE is a round little woman in her early fifties, comfortable looking, gentle, homey. One would not suspect that under that placid exterior there surges the Divine Urge—but it does, it does.
>
> After a moment her fingers lag on the keys; a thoughtful expression comes over her face. Abstractedly she takes a piece of candy out of the skull, pops it into her mouth. As always, it furnishes the needed inspiration —with a furious burst of speed she finishes a page and whips it out of the machine. Quite mechanically, she picks up one of the kittens, adds the sheet of paper to the pile underneath, replaces the kitten.
>
> MOSS HART and GEORGE S. KAUFMAN

Techniques for Writing. To develop a character for a short story or play,

- avoid stereotypes.
- use actions and dialogue to reveal character and personality.
- provide motivation for changes in behavior.
- use vivid, specific language.
- in stage directions, include a detailed physical description and a description of the character's behavior as the play opens if he or she is on stage.
- in a short story, include a detailed physical description if it is relevant to your purpose.

EXERCISE 16. Writing a Description of a Character for a Short Story or a Play. Using a character from your notes and plot outline (Exercises 13 and 14) or another character of your choice, gather or invent information about the person's physical appearance, actions, and personality traits. Then write a one- or two-paragraph description for a short story or for the stage directions in a play.

Using Dialogue

A character's words and how they are spoken can reveal significant clues about the character's background, personality, and motivations. In a short story or a play, therefore, effective dialogue is important.

In the following exchange between Tony and his father (Kirby) in *You Can't Take It with You,* what does the dialogue reveal about Tony's motivations and his attitude toward his father?

KIRBY (*quietly*): That's enough, Tony. We'll discuss this later.
TONY: No. I want to talk about it *now.* I think Mr. Vanderhof is right—dead right. I'm never going back to that office. I've always hated it, and I'm not going on with it. And I'll tell you something else. (ED *starts down the stairs and crosses to* PENNY.) I didn't make a mistake last night. I knew it was the wrong night. I brought you here on purpose.
ALICE: Tony!
PENNY: Well, for heaven's—
TONY: Because I wanted to wake you up. I wanted you to see a real family—as they really *were.* A family that loved and understood each other. You don't understand *me.* You've never had time. Well, I'm not going to make *your* mistake. I'm clearing out.

KIRBY: Clearing out? What do you mean?

TONY: I mean I'm not going to be pushed into the business just because I'm your son. I'm getting out while there's still time.

KIRBY: But, Tony, what are you going to do?

TONY: I don't know. Maybe I'll be a bricklayer, but at least I'll be doing something *I want to do.* (*Doorbell.*)

MOSS HART and GEORGE S. KAUFMAN

The dialogue reveals that Tony is desperate to get out from under his father's domination. His father, on the other hand, does not seem to understand his son's needs. What does the first line spoken by Kirby tell the audience about Kirby's personality? What part of the dialogue shows the audience that Tony is voicing feelings he has never admitted before? What other personality traits and background information do we learn from this dialogue?

When writing dialogue for a short story, keep in mind that you will need to include explanatory details that let your audience know who is speaking and how he or she is speaking. In a short story, for example, part of the dialogue in the excerpt from *You Can't Take It with You* might be written as follows:

Tony stopped in the middle of the stairway and glared at his father. "Because I wanted to wake you up. I wanted you to see a real family—as they really *were*. A family that loved and understood each other. You don't understand *me*. You've never had time. Well, I'm not going to make *your* mistake. I'm clearing out."

Puzzled by Tony's behavior, Kirby approached his son. "Clearing out? What do you mean?"

"I mean I'm not going to be pushed into the business just because I'm your son. I'm getting out while there's still time."

Techniques for Writing. In writing dialogue for a short story, keep in mind that:

- A character's words should reveal his or her personality, background, and motivations. (If a character is very shy, halting, quiet speech will reveal that trait.)
- Speeches do not have to be long; in real conversations, people usually use short sentences or phrases.
- Explanatory details must accompany dialogue for a short story (who is speaking, how the character is speaking, etc.).

EXERCISE 17. Revealing Character Through Dialogue. Using the character you described in Exercise 16, create a situation and write dialogue. Include at least one other character who talks with the main character.

CREATING A SETTING

6m. Create a setting that is appropriate for your story or play.

Using Stage Directions in a Play

The scenery and the lighting in a play help create the setting (the year, time of day, or location of the actions). This information is included in stage directions at the beginning of the script.

In addition to creating a physical place in which the characters live, the setting establishes a tone for the play. Notice how the first paragraph of the stage directions for *You Can't Take It with You* establishes a mood of friendly chaos. In the second paragraph of the directions, note how the character Penny interacts with the setting.

> The home of MARTIN VANDERHOF—just around the corner from Columbia University, but don't go looking for it. The room we see is what is customarily described as a living room, but in this house the term is something of an understatement. The every-man-for-himself room would be more like it. For here meals are eaten, plays are written, snakes collected, ballet steps practiced, xylophones played, printing presses operated—if there were room enough there would probably be ice skating. In short, the brood presided over by MARTIN VANDER-HOF goes on about the business of living in the fullest sense of the word. From GRANDPA VANDERHOF down, they are individualists. This is a house where you do as you like, and no questions asked.
>
> At the moment, GRANDPA VANDERHOF's daughter, MRS. PENELOPE SYCAMORE, is doing what she likes more than anything else in the world. She is writing a play—her eleventh. Comfortably ensconced in what is affectionately known as Mother's Corner, she is pounding away on a typewriter perched precariously on a rickety card table. Also on the table is one of those plaster of Paris skulls ordinarily used as an ash tray, but which serves PENELOPE as a candy jar. And, because PENNY likes companionship, there are two kittens on the table, busily lapping at a saucer of milk.
>
> MOSS HART and GEORGE S. KAUFMAN

Techniques for Writing. In writing stage directions, consider:

- *Location:* Is the setting indoors, in a specific room, or outdoors, in a forest, desert, cave?
- *Time:* Does the conflict occur in the past, present, or future? Is it morning, afternoon, or night? How can you show this in the setting?
- *Tone:* What details of setting would establish the mood of your play? What objects on the stage might contribute to the tone?
- *Characters:* If a character is present as the curtain rises, what is he or she doing?

EXERCISE 18. Writing Stage Directions. Using the above questions, write stage directions for the situation, conflict, and characters you developed in previous exercises.

Using Description in a Short Story

A reader's mental picture of a setting is inspired by vivid, specific, descriptive details. This description is often interwoven with character descriptions, actions, and dialogue to create a total effect—an active, fictional world.

In the following excerpt from "Tears, Idle Tears," note how the setting relates to the action and character development.

> Frederick burst into tears in the middle of Regent's Park. His mother, seeing what was about to happen, had cried: "Frederick, you *can't*—in the middle of Regent's Park!" Really, this was a corner, one of those lively corners just inside a big gate, where two walks meet and a bridge starts across the pretty winding lake. People were passing quickly; the bridge rang with feet. Poplars stood up like delicate green brooms; diaphanous willows whose weeping was not shocking quivered over the lake. May sun spattered gold through the breezy trees; the tulips though falling open were still gay; three girls in a long boat shot under the bridge. Frederick, knees trembling, butted towards his mother a crimson convulsed face, as though he had the idea of burying himself in her. She whipped out a handkerchief and dabbed at him with it under his gray felt hat, exclaiming meanwhile in fearful mortification: "You really haven't got to be such a *baby!*" Her tone attracted the notice of several people, who might otherwise have thought he was having something taken out of his eye.
>
> ELIZABETH BOWEN

In this paragraph Elizabeth Bowen has combined vivid, colorful images of the setting with the development of character and action. Where is this scene taking place? In what way does the setting relate to the action that is taking place? What are some examples of the vivid and colorful language Bowen has used to describe the setting?

Techniques for Writing. In writing the description of setting for a short story, provide:

- Details that contribute significantly to the tone and the mood.
- Sensory details (sounds, smells, colors, etc.).
- Images that are brief but vivid and colorful.
- Characters and action that interact with the setting.

EXERCISE 19. Writing a Description of Setting for a Story. Select an appropriate setting for a scene in the plot outline in Exercise 14. Using the suggestions above, write one or two paragraphs in which you weave the setting and characters together to create a mood.

WRITING A FIRST DRAFT

6n. Write a first draft of your short story or play.

To begin your first draft, review your plot outline and notes on character development, setting, conflict, and action. As you write, focus on a beginning that will capture your audience's attention; then concentrate on developing a sequence of actions that builds in intensity, creating suspense that explodes in the climax. Finally, unite all the elements in your story in the outcome by resolving the conflict. Remember, too, that you will have the opportunity to revise later.

EXERCISE 20. Writing a Draft of Your Short Story. Write a short story based on your plot outline (Exercise 14) or on a new conflict. If you choose a new conflict, be sure to gather information, think about characters and setting, and plan the plot and action.

EXERCISE 21. Writing a Draft of Your Play. Write the first draft of your play using your plot outline (Exercise 14) or a new situation and conflict. For a new situation and conflict, gather information on characters and setting and make a plot outline. Prepare your stage directions, and write your draft in play format (see pages 231–34).

EVALUATING, REVISING, AND PROOFREADING

EVALUATING, REVISING, AND PROOFREADING YOUR STORY OR PLAY

6o. Evaluate, revise, and proofread your story or play.

Evaluating

Allow time between finishing your draft and beginning your evaluation so that you can read more objectively. First, consider your work as a whole and judge whether all the actions contribute to the story line, move it along, or make it believable. Use the following guidelines to locate specific problems in successive readings. Then you may do what many professional writers do at this point—ask someone else to evaluate the draft, to point out flaws and to reinforce strong points.

GUIDELINES FOR EVALUATING STORIES

Beginning	1. Does the beginning of the story capture the audience's interest, establish the tone, and suggest the conflict?
Conflict	2. Is the conflict appropriately limited for a short story?
Suspense	3. Do the actions of the story flow logically and build suspense?
Resolution	4. Is the outcome—resolution of the conflict and possible change in the main character—believable and satisfying?
Point of View	5. Is the point of view consistent throughout the story?
Characters	6. Are the characters believable and interesting? Is the main character developed convincingly through description, dialogue, and actions?
Dialogue	7. Does the dialogue sound natural?
Setting	8. Is the setting described in vivid, precise language? Does it contribute to the mood, tone, and story line?

GUIDELINES FOR EVALUATING PLAYS

Stage Directions	1. Do the stage directions establish the setting, mood, and tone of the play?
	2. Do they describe the first actions of the characters as the curtain rises?
Dialogue and Characters	3. Are directions for characters' actions and reactions included with the dialogue?
	4. Does the dialogue sound natural?
	5. Does it reveal the personality, background, and feelings of the main character?
Conflict	6. Is the conflict developed clearly?
	7. Is the setting appropriate for the conflict?
Outcome	8. Is the outcome convincing and satisfying?

Revising and Proofreading

After you evaluate your short story or play, you are ready to revise. You can revise by adding, cutting, replacing, or reordering. The following chart suggests techniques for revising specific problems in a draft of a short story or play. After you revise, proofread your story or play for accurate spelling, grammar, and punctuation, referring to the Guidelines for Proofreading on page 30. Make a final copy and proofread once again to catch any copying errors.

REVISING SHORT STORIES AND PLAYS

PROBLEM	TECHNIQUE	REVISION
Short Stories The beginning does not capture the audience's interest, establish the tone, and suggest the conflict.	Replace	Write a new beginning including details, description, or dialogue that suggest the conflict in a provocative way; select words carefully to establish the tone you want to convey to your audience.

PROBLEM	TECHNIQUE	REVISION
The conflict is too broad for a short story.	Cut	Cut the dimensions of the conflict by focusing on a particular problem in the short story.
The action does not flow logically, nor does it build suspense.	Add/Reorder	Add explanatory details and details to build suspense. Reorder events so the plot sequence is clear and logical.
The outcome does not seem believable	Replace	Develop a resolution that is the logical outcome of the characters and the action in the story.
The point of view is not consistent.	Replace	Replace inconsistent pronouns. (Use either first- or third-person pronouns, and take into account the limitations of each point of view.)
The characters are neither interesting nor believable.	Add	Add details about the characters' mannerisms, habits, and eccentricities to make them more interesting and believable.
The main character is not developed convincingly.	Add	Add dialogue, description, and actions which reveal the character's dominant trait. (Avoid making the character one-sided: in reality, most people are too complex to be all good or all bad.)
The setting does not contribute to the mood, tone, and story line.	Replace	Use sensory details to help the reader visualize the setting; choose words that establish the mood and convey the appropriate tone.

PROBLEM	TECHNIQUE	REVISION
The dialogue does not sound natural.	Replace	Substitute words, phrases, short sentences, colloquialisms, and informal expressions that real people would use.
Plays The stage directions do not clearly establish the setting, mood, and tone.	Add	Add details that establish the setting, mood, and tone.
The stage directions do not describe the characters' actions as the curtain rises.	Add	Add descriptions of the characters' actions. (Visualize the stage and the action taking place as the curtain rises.)
The dialogue does not include directions for the characters' actions and reactions.	Add	Add details that present the characters' actions and reactions.
The dialogue does not sound natural.	Replace	Replace unnatural dialogue with short sentences, phrases, colloquialisms, and informal or formal language appropriate for the characters.
The dialogue does not reflect the personality, background, and feelings of the main character.	Add	Add dialogue that reveals the main character's dominant traits, feelings, and background.
The conflict is not clearly developed.	Add/Reorder	Add details that will clarify the main conflict. Rearrange events that are out of sequence.
The setting is not appropriate for the conflict.	Replace	Substitute a setting in the stage directions that supports the main conflict of the play.

PROBLEM	TECHNIQUE	REVISION
The outcome does not seem convincing or satisfying.	Replace	Substitute a resolution that grows naturally out of the conflict, actions, and characters. (Remember: a convincing outcome is believable, and a satisfying resolution is not necessarily a "happy ending.")

EXERCISE 22. Evaluating, Revising, and Proofreading Your Story.
Evaluate and revise your first draft from Exercise 20. Proofread your revised story, referring to the guidelines on page 30. Prepare a final copy, proofreading again to catch any errors.

EXERCISE 23. Evaluating, Revising, and Proofreading Your Play.
Evaluate and revise the first draft you wrote in Exercise 21. Proofread your play (see the guidelines on page 30) and make a final copy. Follow the play format used in the excerpts in the text (pages 231–34).

WRITING POETRY

Poetry has long been part of human expression, since before the development of written language. A poem may express feelings, share an experience, or simply recapture an unusual image—with or without patterns of meter and rhyme. This section will present some techniques to help you write poetry.

PREWRITING

SELECTING A SUBJECT AND DEVELOPING IDEAS FOR POETRY

6p. Select an appropriate subject and develop ideas for your poem.

Your experience and imagination are unlimited sources for poetic subjects. As you select and develop your subject, however, be certain you will feel comfortable sharing your poem with others.

An essential part of the poetic process is concentration. You must focus your full attention on the subject, becoming aware of all related images, impressions, and emotions. Exercises 24 and 25 suggest methods for selecting a subject and for exploring it by concentrating on its possibilities.

Techniques for Prewriting. To draw on your experience and imagination for poetry, concentrate on:

- Selecting a subject
  —a significant person in your life
  —a place you recollect with strong emotion
  —an object that you value, hate, or fear
- Gathering ideas
  —review your writer's journal for subjects or events you have discussed with feeling or intensity
  —recall memorable conversations about subjects or ideas
  —talk with family or friends about shared experiences

EXERCISE 24. Selecting a Subject for Poetry. One way to select a subject for a poem is to list things about which you feel strongly: seasons, time of day, places, possessions, holidays, animals, music, food, activities, people, etc. Use a chart like the one below to identify the extremes of your feelings. Then evaluate your list by determining why you feel strongly about each item. Identify your most significant subjects by placing an *X* next to them.

	MOST FAVORITE (I like, love . . .)	LEAST FAVORITE (I dislike, hate . . .)
Season	*spring*	*winter*
Place		
Music, etc.		

EXERCISE 25. Developing Ideas for Poetry. Brainstorm about one of your subjects from Exercise 24, as in the following example:

Spring: melting snow   lilacs
blossoms on the trees   soft rain
children playing, laughing   lonely walks
mud splashing on my legs   robins chirping
perfumed flowers   new clothes
cats meowing at night   wind blowing

After you brainstorm, place an *X* beside the impressions or associations that most strongly reflect your feelings. Then, concentrating on those words, write specific sensory details and descriptions for each, as in the following example:

> *lilacs:* light lavender; deep, royal purple; fragile petals clustered together; soft, sweet scent . . .

WRITING

USING RHYTHM AND REPEATED SOUNDS TO DEVELOP MEANING

6q. Use rhythm and repeated sounds to develop the meaning of your poem.

Poets communicate their feelings not only through the meaning of the words they choose, but also through rhythms and repeated sounds.

Rhythm

Rhythm, or meter, conveys meaning and tone. The skillful poet combines words to take advantage of their natural accents, using the meter to stress certain words and create movement. These efforts can effectively enhance the poem's meaning. Notice how the alternating stressed and unstressed syllables contribute to meaning in the following lines. Both Donne and Longfellow control the meter, emphasizing the syllables that convey the meaning. Read the lines aloud if possible.

> I lóng / to tálk / with sóme / old ló / ver's ghóst
> Who díed / befóre / the gód / of lóve / was bórn.
> JOHN DONNE

> Téll me / nót, in / móurnful / númbers,
> Lífe is / but an / émpty / dréam.
> HENRY WADSWORTH LONGFELLOW

The poet uses meter to control the poem's movement. For instance, a series of unstressed syllables, each followed by a stressed syllable, suggests a walking movement. The rhythm should be appropriate to the subject of your poem. For example, a drumbeat meter would be inappropriate for a poem about a fragile spring lilac.

Most poetry written before the nineteenth century (and some written in this century) has a regular rhythmic pattern. The rhythm may be consistent in every line; or it may change from one line to another, remaining consistent within the whole poem (for example, three accents in the first, second, and third lines, followed by four accents in the fourth). Read the following stanzas from a seventeenth-century poem. The rhythm changes in the fourth line of each stanza but remains constant from one stanza to the next. What relationship do the accented syllables have to the poem's meaning?

> Sweet day, so cool, so calm, so bright,
> The bridal of the earth and sky;
> The dew shall weep thy fall tonight,
>   For thou must die.
>
> Sweet rose, whose hue angry and brave
> Bids the rash gazer wipe his eye;
> Thy root is ever in its grave,
>   And thou must die.
>   GEORGE HERBERT

The preceding poem by George Herbert is an example of *formal poetry,* sometimes called traditional poetry because it was the established way of writing for hundreds of years. *Free verse,* poetry that does not have a regular rhythm or rhyme, is frequently used by contemporary writers.

Free verse does not use a regular meter. Its rhythm is a natural rhythm, like the sounds of speech. Just as accented syllables of words stress meaning in everyday speech, as in "Ĭ wánt tŏ gó," the accented and unaccented syllables in free verse reinforce the meaning. Read the following stanza from *Song of Myself,* and then compare its natural rhythms to the regular ones in Herbert's poem.

> I believe a leaf of grass is no less than the journey-work of the stars,
> And the pismire is equally perfect, and a grain of sand, and the egg of the wren.
> And the tree toad is a chef d'oeuvre for the highest,
> And the running blackberry would adorn the parlors of heaven,
> And the narrowest hinge in my hand puts to scorn all machinery.
> And the cow crunching with depressed head surpasses any statue,
> And a mouse is miracle enough to stagger sextillions of infidels. . . .
>   WALT WHITMAN

How does the natural rhythm work to convey Whitman's meaning? Do you think you would have enjoyed this poem more if it had been written in regular meter?

Repeated Sounds

Patterns of repeated sounds help convey a poem's meaning in much the same way rhythm does. The repeated sounds may be regular or random, exact or inexact. They may occur at the beginning, middle, or end of lines. The following repeated sounds are used to evoke an emotional response and convey meaning:

1. bring / sling / thing / fling
2. I climb sky high
3. hear the roar of snarling cars
4. the weary woman wondered why

Each group of words represents a pattern of sound. The first group shares a common vowel sound and a common sound at the end. These are called exact, or perfect, *rhymes.* The second group repeats a vowel sound, the long *i.* This kind of repeated sound is called *assonance.* The third group repeats the consonant sound of *r* within or at the end of words; this is called *consonance.* The fourth group of words repeats identical or similar sounds at the beginning of words; this is called *alliteration.*

Formal poetry contains regular rhyme as well as regular rhythm. In Christina Rossetti's poem, notice the regular pattern of exact rhyme at the ends of the lines.

Remember me when I am gone away,	a
Gone far away into the silent land;	b
When you can no more hold me by the hand,	b
Nor I half turn to go, yet turning stay.	a
Remember me when no more day by day	a
You tell me of our future that you plann'd:	b
Only remember me; you understand	b
It will be late to counsel then or pray.	a
Yet if you should forget me for a while	c
And afterwards remember, do not grieve:	d
For if the darkness and corruption leave	d
A vestige of the thoughts that once I had,	e
Better by far you should forget and smile	c
Than that you should remember and be sad.	e

CHRISTINA GEORGINA ROSSETTI

The first eight lines of the poem (a sonnet) have the rhyme scheme *abbaabba*; the next six lines have the rhyme scheme *cddece*.

In a poem, rhyme has three purposes: (1) it gives the audience the pleasure of hearing repeated sounds, usually at regular intervals; (2) it sets off the lines; and (3) it helps hold the poem together. As in music, rhyme in poetry can also be an emotional stimulus. In the following lines from a sonnet, notice how the rhyme contributes to the poet's feelings about his love:

> For thy sweet love remember'd such wealth brings
> That then I scorn to change my state with kings.
> WILLIAM SHAKESPEARE

To better understand the purpose of rhyme, compare your response to these lines to your response when the feeling is expressed without the rhyme: When I remember your love, I know I would not change places with kings.

Techniques for Writing. To write a poem with regular rhyme and rhythm:

- Concentrate on the impression you want to convey (threatening, lighthearted, fearful, etc.).
- Develop a regular rhythm and rhyme scheme that reflects the meaning.
- Rhyme important words with words that support the meaning.
- Use any of the repeated sound patterns: exact rhyme, assonance, consonance, and alliteration.
- Avoid producing a monotonous or mechanical effect.

In free verse, the repeated sounds are much more likely to be irregular and inexact, unlike the perfect rhyme used by Christina Rossetti. Notice the lack of regularly repeated sounds in the following excerpt from "The Horses"[1] by Edwin Muir.

> And then, that evening
> Late in the summer the strange horses came.
> We heard a distant tapping on the road,
> A deepening drumming; it stopped, went on again
> And at the corner changed to hollow thunder.
> We saw the heads
> Like a wild wave charging and were afraid.

[1] In this poem, the world has been devastated by atomic war, and tractors can no longer be used to till the soil.

We had sold our horses in our fathers' time
To buy new tractors. Now they were strange to us
As fabulous steeds set on an ancient shield
Or illustrations in a book of knights.
We did not dare go near them. Yet they waited,
Stubborn and shy, as if they had been sent
By an old command to find our whereabouts
And that long-lost archaic companionship.
In the first moment we had never a thought
That they were creatures to be owned and used.
Among them were some half-a-dozen colts
Dropped in some wilderness of the broken world,
Yet new as if they had come from their own Eden.
Since then they have pulled our ploughs and borne our loads.
But that free servitude still can pierce our hearts.
Our life is changed; their coming our beginning.

                                          EDWIN MUIR

Techniques for Writing.   To write a free-verse poem:

- Concentrate on significant words that express your ideas, and put them in a meaningful order.
- Listen to the natural rhythmic patterns the important words create.
- Decide how you will use repeated sounds (exact rhyme, assonance, consonance, and alliteration) to reinforce meaning.

EXERCISE 26. Writing a Poem with Regular Rhyme and Rhythm.
Using the ideas you developed in Exercise 25, or another set of ideas, write a poem of at least eight lines that uses a regular rhythm and rhyme scheme.

EXERCISE 27. Writing a Free-Verse Poem.   Using the ideas you developed in Exercise 25, or another set of ideas, write a free-verse poem of at least twelve lines.

USING SENSORY DETAILS AND VIVID LANGUAGE

6r. Use sensory details and vivid language in your poem.

Everything you experience through your senses may be recalled in descriptive images. Recall of sensory perceptions, evoked by memory or words, is known as *imagery*. As you read the following poem, concentrate on its imagery; try to experience the poem's sights, sounds, smells, and physical sensations. (Sensory details are underlined.)

MEETING AT NIGHT

The gray sea and the long black land;
And the yellow half-moon large and low;
And the startled little waves that leap
In fiery ringlets from their sleep,
As I gain the cove with pushing prow,
And quench its speed i' the slushy sand.

Then a mile of warm sea-scented beach;
Three fields to cross till a farm appears;
A tap at the pane, the quick sharp scratch
And blue spurt of a lighted match,
And a voice less loud, thro' its joys and fears,
Than the two hearts beating each to each!

ROBERT BROWNING

Notice the poet's use of *vivid language*—specific words that identify or describe the sensory details that he wishes his readers to experience. In line 1, for example, the adjectives *gray, long,* and *black* help us picture the sea and the coast. Note also the effective use of specific verbs, such as *leap* (line 3) and *quench* (line 6), and of specific nouns, such as *tap, scratch* (line 9), and *spurt* (line 10).

EXERCISE 28. Writing a Poem with Sensory Details and Vivid Language. Use a subject from Exercise 24 or another subject of your choice to write a poem that includes sensory details and vivid language describing them. You may also give your poem a title.

USING FIGURATIVE LANGUAGE

6s. Use figurative language in your poetry.

In addition to using sensory details and vivid language, poets use *figurative language*. Those *figures of speech* used most frequently in poetic expression are the simile, the metaphor, and personification.

A *simile* is a direct comparison of two things that are usually unlike. The comparison is introduced by *like* or *as* or by a similar word (*seem, appear,* for example). Read these examples of similes:

1. I am still as an autumn tree. —ANNE MORROW LINDBERGH
2. We have tomorrow
   Bright before us
   Like a flame. —LANGSTON HUGHES

Notice the structure of the simile: (1) something is mentioned (*I* in example 1); (2) then a word such as *like* or *as* is used; (3) then something else is mentioned (*autumn tree* in example 1).

A *metaphor* is an indirect comparison that implies a likeness between two unlike things without using *like* or *as*. Read these examples of metaphors:

1. Love is a clock and the works wear out. —CARL SANDBURG
2. Tears
   The crystal rags
   Viscous tatters
   of a worn-through soul. —MAYA ANGELOU

In example 2, instead of saying that "Tears are *like* crystal rags," Maya Angelou implies that tears *are* crystal rags.

Personification is a metaphor in which human qualities are given to nonliving things, abstractions, or animals. Notice how *morning* is personified in the following metaphor.

But look, the morn, in russet mantle clad,
Walks o'er the dew of yon high eastward hill.
            WILLIAM SHAKESPEARE

Techniques for Writing.   To use figurative language in a poem:

- Concentrate on fresh, vivid comparisons. Avoid clichés such as *gentle as a lamb* and *roared like a lion.*
- Consider using an "extended metaphor," in which you develop one comparison throughout an entire poem.
- Evaluate your simile or metaphor before you develop your poem around it; make sure the two things being compared are fundamentally and interestingly different.
- Search for vivid, precise, and unusual verbs in using personification.

EXERCISE 29. Using Figurative Language. Make an unusual or a fresh comparison by completing each item below.

1. A thunderstorm is like . . .
2. I'm as frustrated as . . .
3. The night is . . .
4. The river roams . . .
5. Friends are like . . .
6. My hands . . .
7. A speck of dust . . .
8. The taxicab . . .

EXERCISE 30. Writing a Poem with Figurative Language. Write a poem in which you use simile, metaphor, or personification. Use a subject that you identified in Exercise 24 or another of your choice. You may also want to title your poem.

EVALUATING, REVISING, AND PROOFREADING

EVALUATING, REVISING, AND PROOFREADING YOUR POEMS

6t. Evaluate, revise, and proofread your poetry.

Evaluating

Set your poem aside for a while, so that when you evaluate it, you can experience its sensory details and picture its images freshly—as your readers might. Since poetry should please the ear as well as the eye, one of the best ways to evaluate is to read your poem aloud several times. Use the following guidelines to evaluate your poetry. You may also want to exchange poems with your classmates to evaluate one another's work.

Note that each line of a poem usually begins with a capital letter. Some poets, however, use capitalization, or the lack of it, to reflect their meaning; for instance, by writing everything in lower case, a poet could make important ideas seem trivial. Punctuation in poetry affects the rhythm—commas indicate slight pauses, colons and end punctuation indicate longer pauses.

GUIDELINES FOR EVALUATING POETRY

| Rhyme | 1. Does the rhyme enhance the meaning and imagery of the poem? Does it sound natural, or is it forced and repetitive? |

Repeated Sounds	2.	Do assonance, consonance, or alliteration contribute to the meaning and imagery of the poem?
Meter	3.	Does the meter, or rhythm, accurately control the desired movement of the poem?
Imagery	4.	Does the poem include sensory details and vivid language that evoke the desired imagery?
Figurative Language	5.	Is the figurative language clear and fresh?
Punctuation & Capitalization	6.	Are the punctuation marks and capital letters appropriate for the meaning, rhythm, and poetic form?

Revising and Proofreading

After you evaluate the first draft of a poem, use the chart below to revise it. It suggests techniques for solving the specific problems you discovered as you evaluated. As you revise your poetry, do not be too easily satisfied; some poets often spend hours, even days, revising a single line. After you revise, proofread your poem, using the guidelines on page 30. Then make a final copy, proofreading once again to catch any errors.

REVISING POETRY

PROBLEM	TECHNIQUE	REVISION
The rhyme sounds monotonous and mechanical.	Replace/ Reorder	Replace words that are repetitive or that overpower the meaning and the imagery. Rearrange words until the rhyme sounds more natural, calling less attention to itself.
The rhyme does not enhance the meaning and imagery.	Replace/ Reorder	Replace words that do not carry the intended meaning and imagery. Reorder words to achieve the desired rhyme scheme.

PROBLEM	TECHNIQUE	REVISION
Repeated sounds do not contribute to the meaning and imagery.	Cut/Replace	Cut or replace alliteration, assonance, or consonance that distracts the reader's attention.
The meter does not control the movement of the poem.	Replace/ Reorder	Experiment with replacing and reordering words; you may also try free verse or another meter.
The poem does not use sensory details.	Add	Add details that evoke definite sensory memories in the reader.
The poem does not use vivid language to evoke images.	Add	Add words that create a picture your reader can easily visualize.
The figurative language is trite and dull.	Replace	Replace trite or ineffective figures with ones that are clear and fresh. (Remember: Originality is vital.)
The punctuation and capitalization distort the meaining and form.	Replace/Cut/ Add	Replace punctuation that slows or alters the rhythm of the poem. Cut or add capital letters to focus on key ideas.

EXERCISE 31. Evaluating, Revising, and Proofreading Your Poetry. Evaluate, revise, and proofread the poems you wrote in this chapter. When you make a final copy, be sure to give each poem a title.

CHAPTER 6 WRITING REVIEW 1

Writing About Conflict and Theme. Write a short story or play about a character's internal conflict over two possible actions. Consider the conflict and then determine the theme. For example:

CONFLICT   A young woman is about to go away to college. She is excited, but she has been having nightmares about failing. Her fears have grown so strong, she is tempted to stay home.

THEME   People fear the unknown.

PREWRITING   Review your writer's journal, find human-interest features, brainstorm, cluster, or talk to people to gather ideas and information on a conflict and theme. Plan descriptions, dialogue, and actions that will reveal the main character's personality and background. Consider the setting and how it can reflect your tone and the character's struggle. Write a plot outline, specifying the beginning, middle (actions and climax), and outcome.

WRITING   Create an interesting beginning and then build suspense toward the climax. Show how the resolution causes a believable change in the main character. Use interesting, specific language. For a story, maintain one point of view. For a play, include stage directions.

EVALUATING, REVISING, AND PROOFREADING   Put aside your first draft before you evaluate and revise. Then read your draft as a whole, evaluating its content, organization, and effectiveness. Use either the Guidelines for Evaluating Stories (page 237) or the Guidelines for Evaluating Plays (page 238) and the revising chart on pages 238–41. Proofread your revised version, using the guidelines on page 30, and make a final copy.

CHAPTER 6 WRITING REVIEW 2

Writing a Sonnet.   Write a sonnet about something that has affected you deeply. Use a rhythm that suits the meaning of your poem, and choose one of the following rhyme schemes: *abbaabbacddcee* or *ababcdcdefefgg*.

PREWRITING   Read your journal entries, observe people and events around you, brainstorm, or cluster to identify a subject. Collect the sensory impressions, vivid words, and fresh comparisons your subject evokes. Determine how you want readers to respond and select a tone to evoke that response. Consider how rhyme and meter can enhance your subject.

WRITING   Begin with a line and build your poem. Vary the rhythm occasionally to avoid a singsong meter. Use alliteration, assonance, and consonance as alternatives to exact rhymes. Include sensory details and figurative language to heighten the effect of your poem. Choose a title.

EVALUATING, REVISING, AND PROOFREADING Wait a day or two before you begin your evaluation and revision. Use the Guidelines for Evaluating Poetry (pages 250–251) and the revising chart on pages 251–52.

After you revise, proofread, using the guidelines on page 30, and prepare a final copy of your sonnet. Be sure to title your poem.

CHAPTER 7

Writing a Research Paper

RESEARCH, WRITING, DOCUMENTATION

A research paper is an extended expository composition based on information gathered from a variety of sources to support the writer's ideas. In this chapter you will learn to use the writing process to prepare a research paper. You will also learn certain special procedures that apply primarily to papers based on research.

PREWRITING

SELECTING A SUBJECT

7a. Select a subject that interests you and that can be researched in the sources available to you.

In a way, the research paper requires you to become an authority on a subject. Thus, you should choose a subject that will hold your interest and that will lend itself to research in the available sources. For this reason, avoid subjects about which very little has been published, such as highly technical or recently developed subjects. No matter how interested you are in a subject, it will not be usable unless you have access to source material on it. Also, be certain that the subject you select can be presented objectively, or impartially. The purpose of a research paper is to explain or inform; you should therefore avoid controversial subjects that would be more appropriate for a persuasive paper.

Techniques for Prewriting. Consider the following suggestions to choose a subject for a research paper:

- To gather subject ideas, thumb through the subject cards in the library card catalog, skim articles in current magazines and newspapers, look at articles and pamphlets in the library's vertical file, or use techniques to search your own experiences (such as reviewing a writer's journal, brainstorming, or clustering).
- Avoid straight biography. If the subject is already famous, such a report would simply be a narrative, summarizing one or more biographies; if the subject is not well known, information would probably be difficult to locate.
- Check the library to be sure ample, up-to-date sources about the subject are available.

EXERCISE 1. Selecting a Subject. Using the preceding suggestions, list at least five subjects to research. Evaluate the suitability of the subjects and choose one to research. Save your work for later use.

GETTING AN OVERVIEW

7b. Do some preliminary reading to gain an overview, or general understanding, of your subject.

Begin your research by reading general articles in encyclopedias and scanning books to develop an overview, or broad understanding, of your subject. This overview will guide you as you limit the subject to a topic and determine the basic questions your research will answer. It will also be invaluable later as you begin to read and take notes. With a basic understanding of your subject, you will be more likely to use your time efficiently and less likely to take notes on unimportant or irrelevant information.

Techniques for Prewriting. To get an overview of your subject:

- Find two or more general articles about your subject in encyclopedias or specialized reference books (see pages 710–20). Note headings and subheadings in each article as possible ways to limit the subject. Then, begin a list of possible limited topics and basic questions about your subject.
- Look up your subject in the *Readers' Guide to Periodical Literature* (see pages 706–7) and read the titles of articles listed there.
- Using the subject cards in the card catalog, locate two or more books on your subject. Examine both the table of contents and major headings in the index and add to your list of possible topics and basic questions.
- Look for your subject in the library vertical file, skim available articles or pamphlets, and add any new ideas to your list of topics and questions.

EXERCISE 2. Getting an Overview. Use the preceding suggestions to get an overview of the subject you selected in Exercise 1. Save your notes for later use.

LIMITING YOUR SUBJECT

7c. Limit your subject to a topic that you can cover adequately within the assigned length of the paper.

If you try to write a research paper on a broad subject, you will either spend far too much time on the paper and exceed the assigned length or simply skim the surface of the subject. Taking the time to limit the scope of the subject now will save you time and energy later and result in a better paper. At the same time be careful not to develop a topic that is too limited; too little information might be available for you to meet the assignment's requirements.

Limiting a subject involves analyzing the subject to determine its logical divisions. (See pages 9–11.) For example, the writer of the sample paper on page 284 began with the general subject "parapsychology" and limited the subject as follows.

1. Parapsychology
2. Extrasensory perception (a specific branch of parapsychology)

3. Clairvoyance (a specific type of extrasensory perception)
4. Scientific studies of clairvoyance (a specific aspect of clairvoyance)

EXERCISE 3. Recognizing Suitable Topics. Indicate which of the following topics are suitable for research papers and which are too broad, too limited, or otherwise unsuitable (not expository). Then suggest how each unsuitable topic might be improved.

1. Why nuclear arms should be banned
2. Careers in the arts
3. The renovation of the Statue of Liberty
4. The contributions of Hispanics
5. The life of Sacajawea
6. The European Communities
7. Solar energy for industrial power
8. The Ferraro-Bush vice-presidential debate
9. Anthropomorphism in children's literature
10. Brain cell abnormalities in victims of Alzheimer's disease

EXERCISE 4. Limiting Your Subject. Analyze the subject you selected in Exercise 1 or another subject to develop at least five topics suitable for a research paper. Save your work.

CONSIDERING PURPOSE, AUDIENCE, AND TONE

7d. Evaluate your topic in terms of purpose, audience, and tone.

Before you begin your research, consider your limited topic in terms of the purpose, audience, and tone of a research paper.

CRITICAL THINKING:
Evaluating Your Topic

Evaluating involves using criteria, or standards, to judge an idea or practice. The criteria for evaluating the topic of a research paper have long been established.

Begin by determining if your topic meets the expository purpose of a research paper: A topic such as "the special effects in the original *Star Wars* movie" might result in a good descriptive composition, but it is not appropriate for a research paper. Evaluate your topic to make sure that it will result in exposition. If not, limit your subject again to arrive at an expository topic.

Assume that the audience for your research paper is a general one: educated people of many different backgrounds who are interested in almost any topic that has some significance and that is developed with fresh and specific information. A general audience might be interested in reading a nontechnical explanation of the glacial formation of the Great Lakes. However, this topic would not be suitable for an audience of professional geographers, for it would offer them no new information. On the other hand, keep in mind that your audience is a general one and avoid highly technical topics appropriate for specialists.

The research paper requires a serious tone. Therefore, your topic should reflect a tone that is formal and impersonal. For example, the topic "my reactions to women's outlandish threads in the old days" is inappropriate; it uses the first-person pronoun *my*, and "outlandish" and "threads" are informal expressions. Recasting the topic as "women's fashions in the post-World War II era" instead conveys a serious attitude.

EXERCISE 5. **Evaluating Topics.** Indicate which of the following topics for research papers are appropriate in terms of purpose, audience, and tone. Then, rewrite those that are unsuitable.

1. Errors of calculation in Beethoven's symphonic orchestration
2. Hispanic voting patterns in the 1986 U.S. Senate elections
3. My super trip to a whale of a cave in Kentucky
4. Ethnic distribution of visitors to the 1984 New Orleans World Fair
5. Philosophical issues in the art of M. C. Escher

REVIEW EXERCISE A. **Evaluating Your Topic.** Evaluate the five topics you developed in Exercise 4 in terms of purpose, audience, and tone. Select one topic for your paper and, if necessary, revise it so that it is appropriate. (Your teacher may want to approve your topic before you begin your research.)

PREPARING A WORKING BIBLIOGRAPHY

7e. Prepare a working bibliography.

The first step in researching your topic is to compile a working bibliography of potential sources of information.

Research Aids

To find sources of information on your topic, you will use a number of the library research aids (card catalog, *Readers' Guide,* and reference works). These research aids are explained in Chapters 33 and 34. You might review those chapters before you continue your research to make sure that you are thoroughly familiar with the information in them. As you use the card catalog, in particular, do not confine your search to materials filed under your specific topic. If your topic is "clairvoyance," for example, you will probably find useful materials under more general headings, such as "Parapsychology" and "Extrasensory Perception." As you use library sources, note the titles listed at the end of general articles in encyclopedias and look for these sources. Then, when you find one source, check its bibliography to identify other possible sources. Also, always examine both the index and table of contents in a book to find out the extent of the information the source has about your topic.

Remember, however, that the library is not the sole source of information. Think creatively about what other possible sources may be. Bookstores carry many excellent books in paperback; government publications, personal interviews and correspondence can also be good sources. For a paper on your community's history, you might interview a local historian and examine records and documents at a local museum. If you plan to write for information, do so early enough to allow time for a response.

Scholarly journals can also be excellent sources. Like magazines, journals are published periodically (once a month, four times a year, etc.) However, unlike magazines, these journals are written for readers with specialized knowledge of a particular field. The *New England Journal of Medicine,* for example, publishes medical news for physicians and health professionals. These scholarly journals are not included in the *Readers' Guide,* but you can find articles by checking a specialized index for your area of interest. In large libraries, the reference librarians will be able to direct you to appropriate specialized indexes.

Evaluating Sources

Simply locating adequate sources will not insure that your research will result in an outstanding paper. Not all sources are equally valuable or reliable. Whenever you encounter a new source, take time to evaluate, or judge, its usefulness for your purposes.

Techniques for Prewriting. Ask the following questions to evaluate potential sources:

- Does the author appear to be an authority on the subject? Authors with several books and articles on a subject or those cited in other sources or bibliographies are usually reliable.
- Can the source be relied on for objective, impartial information? A book about a President's foreign policy written by a member of his staff may not be an objective source.
- For what audience was the work intended? Works written for younger readers often simplify topics or lack specific facts, while books for specialists may be too technical.
- How current is the information? A 1969 study of hazardous wastes is probably out-of-date and, therefore, unreliable. Even for topics about the past (post-Civil War reconstruction), recent articles may reveal previously undiscovered facts or new theories.
- Does an article appear in a scholarly journal, a special-interest magazine, or a general-interest magazine like those found on most newsstands? Does the periodical have a reputation for accurate, knowledgeable treatment of a topic?

EXERCISE 6. Evaluating Sources. Locate at least five potential sources of information about your topic. Evaluate each source by asking yourself the preceding questions. Replace any unreliable sources with more suitable ones.

Bibliography Cards

To compile your working bibliography, record each source on a separate card. Include *all* the information listed below; you will need it later, when you prepare your final bibliography. For books, you can obtain this information from the library catalog; for articles, from the *Readers' Guide.* For pamphlets and newspapers, you must check each source to find the necessary information.

BOOKS

1. Call number in upper right-hand corner of the card
2. Author's (or editor's) full name, last name first, for alphabetizing later (Indicate editor by placing *ed.* after the name.) If a book has two or more authors, only the name of the first author is written last name first; the names

⑦ 133.8
Koe

Koestler, Arthur. *The Roots of Coincidence*. New York: Random House, 1972. — book

② Cherry, Lawrence. "Physicists Explain E.S.P." *Science Digest* Sept.-Oct. 1980: 84-87. — signed magazine article

⑮ "A Stepchild of Science Starts to Win Friends". *U.S. News and World Report* 31 July 1978: 41, 42 — unsigned magazine article

⑥ Hebb, D.O. "The Role of Neurological Ideas in Psychology." *Journal of Personality* 20, 1951: 40-52 — scholarly journal

source number — ④ 032 — call number
Enc

Eysenck, H.J. "Theories of Parapsychological Phenomena." *Encyclopaedia Britannica Micropaedia* 1979 ed. — encyclopedia article

Cards in a Working Bibliography

of the others are written first name first. For three or more authors, write only the first author's name and add *et al.*, a Latin expression meaning *and others* (Rhine, J. B., et al.).

3. Title and subtitle, underlined (and editions, if second or later; and number of volumes, if more than one). Pamphlets only: series and number, if any
4. City of publication
5. Publisher's name (shortened, if clear)
6. Most recent copyright year (or date, for some pamphlets)

MAGAZINE, SCHOLARLY JOURNAL, NEWSPAPER, AND ENCYCLOPEDIA ARTICLES

1. Author's full name (unless article is unsigned)
2. Title of article, in quotation marks
3. Name of magazine, journal, newspaper, or encyclopedia, underlined
4. For popular press magazines: date and page numbers. For newspapers: date, edition, section, page numbers. For scholarly journals: volume, year of publication (in parentheses), page numbers. For encyclopedias arranged alphabetically: edition (if given) and year of publication.

For a book, the card catalog will list information needed for a working bibliography card, although it will not reveal much about the book's contents. To examine potentially useful books, go to the shelf in the library where sources are located according to call numbers. Nonfiction books are classified by subject, so by locating a source you will also find other books the library has on the subject on the neighboring shelves. A glance at the table of contents and the index in these books will tell you how useful each book might be. If the table of contents does not reveal information on your subject, look in the index to see whether the book includes information on your subject and, if so, how extensive the information is.

Assign each card in your working bibliography a number, and write it clearly in the upper left corner. Later you will use this number to identify the source on your note cards. Notice the arrangement and punctuation of the information on the previous sample cards.

EXERCISE 7. Preparing Bibliography Cards. Prepare bibliography cards for the items below. Add underlining and quotation marks where necessary.

1. A book entitled The Soul of a New Machine by Tracy Kidder, published in Boston in 1981 by Atlantic-Little.
2. An unsigned article entitled Personal Computers, published in the December 1983 issue of Consumer Reports on pages 73 through 88.

3. An article written by Michael Rogers, entitled Computer Culture Made Easy, published in the November 19, 1984, issue of Newsweek on page 102.
4. A book entitled Whole Earth Software Catalog, edited by Stewart Brand, published in New York in 1984 by Doubleday.
5. A book entitled Digital Deli, edited by Steve Ditlea, published in New York in 1984 by Workman.

EXERCISE 8. Preparing Your Working Bibliography. Prepare a working bibliography on your topic. (Your teacher may ask you to prepare a minimum number of bibliography cards.)

WRITING A PRELIMINARY THESIS STATEMENT

7f. State the preliminary thesis of your paper in one sentence.

To bring your topic into sharper focus before you research your potential sources, state the paper's thesis, or main idea, in one declarative sentence. This preliminary thesis statement further limits your topic and provides a guide for your research.

You may well revise this preliminary thesis several times as you continue your research and write and revise the paper. Expressing it as clearly as possible at this stage, however, will enable you to avoid gathering material that does not support your ideas. Be sure your thesis statement reflects an expository purpose and a serious tone.

The writer of the research paper on scientific studies of clairvoyance (pages 284–92) drew up the following *preliminary* thesis statement:

> According to the findings of some recent research, people with clairvoyance can "see" things without the use of the senses.

EXERCISE 9. Writing a Preliminary Thesis Statement. Keeping in mind the purpose, audience, and tone appropriate for a research paper, write a preliminary thesis statement for your paper.

PREPARING A PRELIMINARY OUTLINE

7g. Prepare a preliminary outline as a guide to your research.

Before you can take notes in an organized way, you must have some idea of the kinds of information you will be looking for. One way to do so is to formulate a series of *questions about the topic,* anticipating the questions your paper should answer. Your tentative answers to these questions can then become the headings and subheadings of a preliminary outline.

At this point, you do not need to concern yourself with matters of style or with the final organization of the headings. As you read and take notes, you may decide that some headings are irrelevant or are not covered well enough in the available resources. In addition, you will undoubtedly find other information to include. Like the preliminary thesis statement, the preliminary outline may be revised several times before you complete the paper.

Follow these suggestions in drawing up your preliminary outline:

1. Put the title of your paper at the top of a sheet of paper.
2. Below the title, write the word *Thesis* and your thesis statement.
3. Do not make the preliminary outline too detailed; you will add to it as you read and take notes.

The writer of the paper on scientific studies of clairvoyance formulated the following questions about the topic.

What is clairvoyance?
How do researchers conduct experiments on clairvoyance?
What kinds of experiments into clairvoyance have been conducted?
Do all scientists agree on the existence of clairvoyance?
What lies ahead for clairvoyance studies?

Using these questions, the student drew up the following preliminary outline. (You may want to compare this with the final outline on page 285.)

Title: Scientific Studies of Clairvoyance
Thesis: According to the findings of some recent research, people with clairvoyance can "see" things without the use of the senses.

1. Definition of clairvoyance
2. Scientific approach to clairvoyance
3. Experiments with clairvoyance
   —studies by J. B. Rhine
   —studies by Rhine's followers
4. Objections to experiments
5. Future of clairvoyance studies

EXERCISE 10. Preparing a Preliminary Outline.   Develop questions about your topic and use them to draw up a preliminary outline.

GATHERING INFORMATION ON YOUR TOPIC

7h. Take notes on cards classified by the headings and subheadings on your preliminary outline.

Your working bibliography, preliminary thesis statement, and outline are a plan of action for your research. Always take notes *as you read;* your memory is not a reliable guide for detailed information and quotations. Without a complete, accurate record of your research, you will find it impossible to reconstruct information when you write the paper. With a package of 4 x 6-inch index cards, you are ready to read your sources. The note cards should be larger than working-bibliography cards for two reasons: First, the cards will accommodate longer notes; and second, you will be able to distinguish them from your smaller bibliography cards.

The following numbered items explain the entries on the sample card on page 267. Each explanation is numbered to correspond to the appropriate key number in the illustration. Be sure to use the same format on your note cards.

1. *The "slug."* In the upper left corner, write a point from your preliminary outline, called a "slug." Include only information related to that point on the note card. Some notes may not fall naturally under one of the headings or subheadings in your preliminary outline. If you find that your notes do not fit into your outline, revise the outline accordingly and enter the new slugs on cards. You also may delete points if you cannot find enough usable information on them. If you combine two headings, change your outline as well as the slugs on the appropriate cards. Be sure to put notes about different slugs on separate cards, even if the notes are from the same source.

2. *The bibliographical reference.* Enter the source number from your working bibliography in the upper right corner. This will save you from recopying the publication information onto the note cards. Several sources will often provide information on the same point; thus you will have several cards with the same slug, each representing a different source.

3. *The note.* To avoid taking unnecessary notes and to increase your overall understanding, start with a reliable, knowledgeable source that gives a detailed treatment of your topic. If other sources give the same information, you will not need to record it again. Then write most of your notes in your own words so that your research paper is not just a string of quotations. Also avoid a *derived* style, one that sounds like the

style of your sources rather than like your own style. Think carefully about the kind of note you want to take: *summarize* to record an author's main ideas; *paraphrase,* or restate in your own words, to record specific facts or details; *quote,* enclosing an author's exact words in quotation marks, to indicate when an author's language is as important as his or her ideas.

Whether you summarize, paraphrase, or quote, you must credit your sources. *Plagiarism*—the use of another person's words or ideas without acknowledging the source—is a serious, punishable offense, one you must always avoid.

When you take notes in your own words, save time by (1) using abbreviations for as many words as you can without affecting the clarity of your notes, (2) using symbols for short words (& for *and*), and (3) writing phrases rather than sentences. Always write legibly, and include all the information you will need to understand the note later.

4. *The page reference.* At the end of each note, write the page or pages on which you found the information. You may need to return to the specific page later to clarify a point, and you must include page numbers when you prepare citations for your paper. If information runs over from one page to the next, place a slash mark in the note to show where the page break occurs.

1. slug—from preliminary outline   2. number of working bibliography card

> *Studies by J. B. Rhine*   ①
>
> *Rhine used Zener cards:*
>
> *5 symbols - circle, cross, square, star,*
>
>   *wavy line*
>
> *1 symbol per card*
>
> *25 cards per deck. p. 31*

3. note   4. page reference

Sample Note Card

EXERCISE 11. Gathering Information on Your Topic. Read and take notes on your topic, following the preliminary outline you prepared in Exercise 10. Revise your preliminary outline as you find additional points to include or as you delete others.

CLASSIFYING AND ORGANIZING INFORMATION

7i. Classify and organize your notes, and prepare a revised outline.

Your preliminary outline was based only on a general understanding of your topic. Through research you probably have encountered new ideas and information. You may also have discovered that some points in your preliminary outline are not as significant as you originally thought. Now you should organize the notes you have gathered.

Taking time now to prepare a well-organized formal outline will give you a sound plan to follow as you write your first draft. Usually, the material for a research paper can be organized under six or fewer main headings. If you have more than six, review the organization of the material and the material itself to make sure that you have not included too much information or mistaken minor points for major ones. Also, your teacher may ask you to submit your revised outline with your completed research paper.

Techniques for Prewriting. To prepare a revised outline,

- Put all cards with the same slug (heading) in one group.
- Review each group of cards separately. Does each group adequately explain a point or should you gather additional information? Do any cards contain unrelated information? Does each group relate to your thesis, or should any be omitted?
- Compare each group of cards with the headings in your preliminary outline. What headings or subheadings should be added, omitted or revised?
- Think carefully about organization. Are headings and sub-headings arranged in a clear and logical order? Is each subheading a logical divison of that particular heading? Should you move any groups to another place in the outline? Should you rearrange the order of notes within a group?
- Prepare a formal outline, correctly using Roman numerals, capital letters, and Arabic numerals. (See pages 98–101.)

REVIEW EXERCISE B. Preparing a Revised Outline. Classify and organize your note cards, revise your thesis statement if necessary, and prepare a revised outline. (Your teacher may want to check your note cards, thesis, and outline before you begin writing.)

WRITING

WRITING THE FIRST DRAFT

7j. Write the first draft from your revised outline.

With your revised outline, your notes, and your bibliography cards nearby, you are ready to write your first draft. Remember that the first draft is for your use only. You may start wherever you want; the important thing is to put your ideas in a form you can follow when you revise the paper. As you write, note two important mechanical considerations: to indicate you are omitting words from a direct quotation, use an ellipsis (. . .); to quote more than four lines (an extended quotation), set the quotation off from the text by indenting each line ten spaces.

CRITICAL THINKING:
Synthesizing

The first draft of any composition is a synthesis, or putting together, of separate elements to form a new whole. Writing the first draft of a research paper is particularly complex because you must bring together information from many sources, digest it thoroughly, acknowledge your sources appropriately, and present your findings in a unified, coherent fashion.

As you write, keep in mind your purpose, audience, and tone. Use the information on your note cards to support your thesis clearly and effectively, and credit your sources for both ideas and quotations, using one of the methods explained below. Remember that ideas that become familiar to you during your research may not be as well known to your readers, who will be relying on transitions, definitions of technical terms, and logical sentence and paragraph structure to understand your paper.

Documentation

Three methods of documenting sources are used for research papers: parenthetical citations, footnotes, and endnotes. Your teacher may prefer that you use a particular method. No matter which method you use, remembering that your audience is a general one will help you decide which information to document, or credit.

> **Techniques for Writing.** Use the following guidelines for documenting information from sources in your research paper.
>
> - Always document the source of a direct quotation.
> - Document the source of specific surveys, scientific experiments, public polls, and research studies.
> - Document a new or unusual theory or opinion, or one held by a particular author, even if you present the author's ideas in your own words.
> - Document rare, unusual, or questionable facts or statistics, especially if they appear in only one source. Usually it is not necessary to document facts or ideas that appear in several sources. Do not document facts widely available in reference books (Cleopatra was a queen of Egypt) or commonly accepted theories (comets are composed of frozen gases).
> - Never assume too much knowledge on the part of your audience. If you do not know whether a particular fact is general or specialized knowledge, give its source.
> - When possible, introduce source material with the name of the author or title of the work, so that source material will be clearly distinguished from your own ideas, and the paper will read more smoothly.

Footnotes

Footnotes are numbered notes which give information about a source: the author's name, the title, the publishing information, and a page reference. To indicate a footnote, write or type a number slightly above and to the right of the final punctuation mark at the end of a quotation or idea taken from a source. This number refers the reader to the footnote, which appears at the bottom of the page. You must plan each page so that there will be enough space at the bottom for the footnotes for that page. Number the footnotes consecutively, unless your teacher directs otherwise. Remember that you must document all quotations and all summarized or paraphrased information from your sources.

Use the following guidelines to prepare footnotes for your research paper. As you study the examples (taken from several research papers), notice the punctuation. Also note that months—except May, June, and July—are abbreviated, and that the first line of the footnote is indented.

1. The footnote for a book or pamphlet gives the name of the author (first name first); the title (underlined); the city of publication, the publisher, and the copyright date; and the page number(s).

EXAMPLES

[1]Doris Lessing, A Small Personal Voice: Essays, Reviews, Interviews (New York: Knopf, 1974) 47. [book by one author]

[2]Cleanth Brooks and Robert Penn Warren, Modern Rhetoric, 4th ed. (New York: Harcourt Brace Jovanovich, 1979) 179. [book by two authors]

2. The footnote for a magazine or newspaper article gives the author (unless the article is anonymous); the title (in quotation marks); the name of the publication (underlined); the volume number, if any (for scholarly journals only); the date; and the page number(s).

EXAMPLES

[3]Timothy Ferris, "Einstein's Wonderful Year," Science 84 Nov. 1984: 61–63. [article in a monthly popular press magazine]

[4]Carol Beckwith, "Niger's Wodaabe: 'People of the Taboo,'" National Geographic 164 (1983): 502. [article in a magazine that numbers its pages continuously throughout each volume year]

[5]"Navahos Upheld on Land Claims," New York Times, 30 June 1970, late ed.: A20. [unsigned newspaper article]

3. Different kinds of sources follow different footnote formats.

EXAMPLES

[1]Virginia Woolf, The Diary of Virginia Woolf, 5 vols. (New York: Harcourt Brace Jovanovich, 1979–84) 2: 115. [one volume in a multivolume work in which all have the same title]

[2]Robert Coles, Eskimos, Chicanos, Indians, vol. 4 of Children of Crisis (Boston: Atlantic–Little, 1978) 12. [one volume in multivolume work with different titles]

[3]Virgil, Aeneid, trans. Allen Mandelbaum (Berkeley: U of California P, 1971) 92. [translation; U stands for *University*, P for *Press*]

[4]Maxwell Perkins, "Thomas Wolfe," Thomas Wolfe: A Collection of Critical Essays, ed. Louis Rubin, Jr. (Englewood Cliffs: Prentice, 1973) 80. [one article in a collection of articles by different authors]

[5]Louis C. Faron, "American Indians," Encyclopedia Americana, 1984 ed. [signed article in an alphabetized encyclopedia]

· [6]Florence Wright, personal interview, 4 May 1984. [interview]

[7]"Music in the Age of Shakespeare," PBS, WGBH, Boston, 17 Sept. 1980. [television program]

[8]MacWrite, computer software, Apple Computer, 1984.

[9]Frederic McDowell, "Recent British Fiction: Some Established Writers," Contemporary Literature 2 (Summer 1970): 108 qtd. in Paul Schlueter, The Novels of Doris Lessing (Carbondale: Southern Illinois U P, 1973) 75–76. [a quotation or an idea the author of a source has, in turn, taken from another author]

4. Once you have provided complete documentation for a source the first time you refer to it, you may use a shortened form for later references to the same source. The author's last name and the page number are usually sufficient.

EXAMPLES

[1]Doris Lessing, A Small Personal Voice: Essays, Reviews, Interviews (New York: Knopf, 1974) 47.

[2]Lessing 52.

5. If you use two or more sources by the same author, however, you must include a shortened form of the specific title each time you cite either source.

EXAMPLES

[4]Lessing, Voice 70

[5]Lessing, Stories 116.

6. If you mention the title of the specific work in your paper, you do not need to include the title in the footnote. Similarly, if you include the author's name in your paper, you may omit it from the footnote.

EXAMPLES

> [8]Lessing, Voice 64. [neither name nor title mentioned in text]

> [8]Lessing 64. [title mentioned in text]

> [8]Voice 64. [name mentioned in text]

EXERCISE 12. **Preparing Footnotes.** Assign footnote numbers and write footnotes for the following five items, in the order given. Assume that neither the authors' names nor the titles are mentioned in the text. Add underlining and quotation marks where necessary.

Footnotes on page 1 of text:
a. An article entitled Psychic Research, by W. Stuckey, published in Science Digest volume 80, October 1976. Reference to page 32.
b. The same article as above, same page.
c. A book by C.E.M. Hansel entitled ESP and Parapsychology: A Critical Reexamination, published in Buffalo in 1980 by Prometheus Books. Reference to page 280.

Footnotes on page 2 of text:
d. An unsigned article in Discover volume 5, February 1984. Reference to page 8. Title of article: A PSI Gap.
e. An article entitled Clairvoyance, by Rex Stanford, in Psychic Exploration: A Challenge for Science, edited by John White and published in 1974 in New York by G. P. Putnam's Sons. Reference to pages 133–134.

Endnotes

Endnotes appear at the end of a research paper, rather than at the bottoms of the pages. They contain the same information as footnotes and follow the same format, but they are collected on a separate page headed "Notes," just before the bibliography. Endnotes should always be numbered consecutively within the manuscript.

Parenthetical Citations

Since 1984, the highly respected Modern Language Association (MLA) has recommended a simplified form of documenting sources. This form, called *parenthetical citation,* identifies sources in parentheses placed as close as possible to the borrowed words or ideas. Just enough information is given to refer the reader to the source in the bibliography. Usually, this information consists only of an author's last name and the page number or numbers from which the material is taken: (Smith 22). If the author's name is mentioned nearby in the text of the paper, even the name is not necessary: (22). When no author is given for a source in the bibliography—the entry is alphabetized by title—then a shortened form of the title and the page number or numbers are placed in parentheses: ("Navaho Claims" 84). If the title is mentioned nearby in the paper, then the title need not be used either: (84).

To use parenthetical citations to document sources for a research paper, follow these MLA guidelines:

1. In most instances you need only include in the parentheses the author's last name and the page number(s) from which the author's words or ideas have come. There is no punctuation between the author's name and the page number(s), only a space. Notice also that the words *page* or *pages* or their abbreviations do not appear in the citation. Place the citation as close as possible to the quotation or to the author's ideas. Usually, the parenthetical citation is placed at the end of a sentence before the final punctuation. If the material is quoted, close quotation marks, insert the parenthetical citation, and then place the closing punctuation mark.

EXAMPLES   Clairvoyance, say scientists, is one of four categories of extrasensory perception: (1) telepathy—reading the thoughts of another, (2) precognition—sensing future events, (3) psychokinesis—affecting objects by thinking about them, and (4) clairvoyance—perceiving objects or events that are impossible to perceive by the normal senses (Cherry 84).

Remarks D. O. Hebb, professor of psychology at McGill University,"I do not accept ESP for a moment, because it does not make sense" (45).

The bibliography at the end of the sample research paper on pages 290–91 indicates that the information in the first example above was taken from page 84 of an article by Laurence Cherry titled "Physicists Explain ESP," appearing in the Sept./Oct. 1980 issue of *Science Digest.*

The second example above includes a direct quotation, so the citation appears after the closing quotation marks and before the final punctuation of the sentence. Only the page number from which the quote is taken appears in parentheses. The author's name is not necessary because it appears nearby in the paper.

2. If the bibliography lists two or more works by the same author, then use both the author's last name and a shortened form of the title in

the citation. In this case, a comma comes between the author's name and the title.

EXAMPLES   (Stuart, The Thread 32)
           (Stuart, The Land 134)

These references are to two novels by Jesse Stuart: The Thread That Runs So True, page 32, and The Land Beyond the River, page 134.

3. If your bibliography has two or more authors with the same last names, use both the first and last names.

EXAMPLES   (John Smith 105)
           (Mary Smith 134)

4. If the work has more than one author, you may use all the last names, separated by *and* and followed by the page number(s). You may also use only the last name of the first author, followed by *et al.* (and others) and the page number(s).

EXAMPLES   (Johnson and Leiberman 53)
           (Vasquez et al. 22)

The following examples show additional types of citations. Study also the citations that appear in the sample research paper on pages 284–92.

(Durant and Durant, Lessons 32)   [two authors; more than one work by these authors in bibliography; the complete title is Lessons of History]

(J. B. Rhine et al., Extrasensory 108–110)   [more than two authors; a work by another author with the same last name is included in the bibliography; the complete title is Extrasensory Perception]

(Woolf 2: 115–118)   [the source is a multivolume work]

(McAllister)   [the entire work, rather than a specific page, is cited]

(Bernstein 100; Strunk and White 81)   [two sources are cited for the same information]

(qtd. in Bell 91)   [original source not available; material quoted from an indirect source]

(2.1. 48–53)   [quoted from Act 2, Scene 1, lines 48–53 of a play]

The Bibliography

Sometimes labeled "Works Cited," the bibliography provides the support for your research paper. It should include only those materials that you actually quote or paraphrase in the paper, not all of those you compiled for your working bibliography.

The following guidelines will help you arrange and style the bibliography entries.

1. Alphabetize the entries according to the last names of the authors (for an anonymous work, use the first important word in the title instead). Do not number the entries.

2. If you cite more than one work by the same author, do not repeat the author's name. Instead, alphabetize the works by title, and use three hyphens in place of the name for each work after the first one.

3. Indent all lines after the first line of an entry.

4. Place a period at the end of each entry.

The following examples are not in alphabetical order because most of them are drawn from different bibliographies. For a complete bibliography in alphabetical order, see page 292.

Lessing, Doris. A Small Personal Voice: Essays, Reviews, Interviews. New York: Knopf, 1974. [book with one author]

———. Stories. New York: Knopf, 1978. [book by the author of the previous entry]

Brooks, Cleanth, and Robert Penn Warren. Modern Rhetoric. 4th ed. New York: Harcourt Brace Jovanovich, 1979. [book with two authors; also the book's fourth edition]

Woolf, Virginia. The Diary of Virginia Woolf. 5 vols. New York: Harcourt Brace Jovanovich, 1978–84. Vol. 2. [one volume of a multivolume work used; reference to specific volume number appears in the text]

Coles, Robert. Eskimos, Chicanos, Indians. Vol. 4 of Children of Crisis. 5 vols. Boston: Atlantic–Little, 1978. [only one volume in multivolume work with different titles used]

Virgil. Aeneid. Trans. Allen Mandelbaum. Berkeley: U of California P, 1971. [translation; *U* stands for *University* and *P* for *Press*]

Perkins, Maxwell. "Thomas Wolfe." Thomas Wolfe: A Collection of Critical Essays. Ed. Louis Rubin, Jr. Englewood Cliffs: Prentice, 1973. 87–102. [one article in a collection of articles by different authors]

Ferris, Timothy. "Einstein's Wonderful Year." <u>Science 84</u> Nov. 1984: 61–63. [article in a monthly popular press magazine]

Beckwith, Carol. "Niger's Wodaabe: 'People of the Taboo.'" <u>National Geographic</u> 164 (1983): 483–509. [article, continuous pagination magazine or scholarly journal]

"Navahos Upheld on Land Claims." <u>New York Times</u> 30 June 1970, late ed.: A20. [unsigned newspaper article]

Faron, Louis C. "American Indian." <u>Encyclopedia Americana</u>. 1984 ed. [signed encyclopedia article]

Wright, Florence. Personal interview. 4 May 1984. [interview]

"Music in the Age of Shakespeare." PBS. WGBH, Boston. 17 Sept. 1980. [television program]

EXERCISE 13. Preparing a Bibliography. Prepare bibliography entries for the following items. Add underlining and quotation marks where needed, and alphabetize the entries.

1. A magazine article by Charles Tart entitled Psychic Lessons in Human Behavior, volume 7, February 1978, page 51.
2. An unsigned magazine article entitled Science, the Media, and the Paranormal in Science News, volume 112, August 20, 1977, page 118.
3. A book entitled The ESP Experience: A Psychiatric Validation by Jan Ehrenwald, published by Basic Books, in New York, in 1978.
4. A book by Naomi Hintze and J. Gaither Pratt, entitled The Psychic Realm: What Can You Believe?, published by Harper & Row, in New York, in 1975.
5. A book of articles edited by Patrick Grim, entitled Philosophy of Science and the Occult, published by the State University of New York Press in Albany in 1982.

Charts, Diagrams, and Illustrations

Charts and diagrams may be included in your paper where they are of real value. For each one that is not your own, give the source from which you copied it. Never cut illustrations from library sources.

REVIEW EXERCISE C. Writing the First Draft. Write your first draft, incorporating your research findings and crediting your sources.

EVALUATING AND REVISING

EVALUATING YOUR RESEARCH PAPER

7k. Evaluate the content, organization, and style of your research paper.

Evaluation and revision are different, but closely related, activities. Evaluation involves careful examination of a piece of writing to determine where it succeeds and where it needs improvement. Revision involves making changes to eliminate weaknesses and to strengthen a piece of writing. It may be easier to combine evaluation and revision by examining and then improving one aspect of your research paper at a time.

Once you have prepared a rough draft of your paper, reread it critically, rethinking the scope of your ideas and looking for irrelevant material, unclear transitions, illogical arrangement of information, and unsupported assertions. Remember that your objective is to support your thesis, not simply to discuss or illustrate it.

CRITICAL THINKING:
Evaluating a Draft of a Research Paper

In order to evaluate a draft of a research paper, you need a set of criteria. The following Guidelines for Evaluating Research Papers provide standards against which you can judge your work. (You may also want to review the Guidelines for Evaluating Expository Compositions on pages 114–15.) Ask yourself the questions in the guidelines each time you evaluate the paper. It may be helpful to exchange papers with a classmate and to evaluate each other's papers. Evaluate your own paper as objectively as possible, since it will in turn be evaluated by your teacher with these or similar criteria.

GUIDELINES FOR EVALUATING RESEARCH PAPERS

Introduction 1. Does the introduction include a thesis statement that clearly states the purpose of the paper and reveals the writer's attitude? Does it catch the audience's attention?

Topic Development	2. Does each paragraph in the body develop one idea about the topic? Does each paragraph include specific details and examples from the writer's research?
	3. Is there enough information for readers to follow the line of reasoning? Is there any unrelated or irrelevant information? Are quotations and ideas from sources incorporated into the text to achieve the paper's purpose?
Conclusion	4. Does the end of the paper obviously conclude the presentation? Does it reinforce the thesis statement?
Coherence	5. Are ideas about the topic presented in a logical order, both in paragraphs and in sentences within each paragraph? Are there clear and logical transitions, or connections, between paragraphs and between major sections in the paper?
Emphasis	6. Is the emphasis on various ideas clear by means of the wording, placement, or amount of text devoted to them?
Word Choice	7. Is the language appropriate for a general audience? Are technical terms and unusual vocabulary defined or explained? Does the language reveal the serious tone appropriate for a research paper? Does the title clearly indicate the paper's topic?
Format	8. Are sources documented in the text, correctly using the MLA format (parenthetical notes) or some other acceptable format? Are short quotations incorporated into the text? Are longer quotations set off from the text? Are correct form and alphabetical order used in the bibliography?

EXERCISE 14. Evaluating Your First Draft. Evaluate the first draft of your research paper using the guidelines above and the Guidelines for Evaluating Expository Compositions on pages 114–15. Keep notes on your draft about items you need to improve. You may also want to exchange papers with a classmate to evaluate each other's papers.

REVISING YOUR FIRST DRAFT

7l. Revise your first draft to improve content, organization, and style.

After identifying parts of your paper that need to be improved, you are ready to make revisions, or changes, to strengthen your writing.

Revision involves analyzing, carefully breaking down and examining your writing to determine how to eliminate or correct weaknesses in it. To make changes, you should use the same basic techniques (adding, cutting, reordering, and replacing) you use to revise other forms of exposition. The particular technique you use will depend on the nature of the weakness you want to correct. Remember, as you make changes in the text of your paper, that you may also need to revise the outline, citations, and the bibliography. Use the revision chart on pages 27–28 to revise your research paper.

EXERCISE 15. **Revising Your Research Paper.** Revise your research paper, using the revising chart on pages 27–28. Be sure to check each revision against the chart. Your teacher may ask you to save your first draft to submit along with the revised paper.

PROOFREADING

PROOFREADING YOUR RESEARCH PAPER

7m. Proofread your research paper for grammar, usage, and mechanics.

When your research paper represents your best effort, proofread it carefully to check for and correct errors in grammar, usage, and mechanics. Remember that you want your audience to focus on the ideas and information in your paper, not on proofreading errors. (Review the Guidelines for Proofreading on page 30.)

EXERCISE 16. **Proofreading Your Revised Draft.** Proofread your paper carefully to correct the grammar, usage, and mechanics.

PREPARING A FINAL VERSION

PREPARING THE FINAL VERSION OF YOUR RESEARCH PAPER

7n. Prepare a final version of your research paper, following correct manuscript form.

Your final step is to prepare a clean copy of your revised and proofread draft. To make sure that you have copied correctly, proofread this version as well. Then assemble the parts of the paper, using the following MLA guidelines or your teacher's instructions.

1. Type or write your paper neatly and legibly on one side of acceptable paper.
2. Leave one-inch margins at the top, bottom, and sides of your page.
3. Double-space throughout, including title, quotations, and bibliography. (Long quotations are an exception; see note on page 668.)

You will also need to assemble the parts of the paper in the following order or the order your teacher requires:

1. *The cover.* Using staples, metal clasps, or other fasteners, bind your paper in a stiff cover. Give the title of the paper on the outside; make the cover simple but attractive.

2. *The title page.* Use a separate page as a title page. Place your name, information about your class (name and number of the course), and the date one inch from the top of the first page, even with the left margin. Double-space between these lines. The title is centered, with double-spacing between the information described above and the title. Do not put quotation marks around your title.

3. *The final outline.* Insert your revised outline directly after the title page. In this position, the outline serves as a kind of table of contents for your audience.

4. *The paper itself.* Begin the page numbering with the first page. Number consecutively all the pages of the paper, including the bibliography and those pages containing only charts or diagrams. Place page numbers in the upper right corner of each page, one-half inch below the top of the page and fairly close to the right margin. Use a number with or without the words *page, pages,* or their abbreviations. Write your title at the top of the first page, and quadruple-space between the title and the first line of your paper.

5. *The list of works cited.* Use as many pages as you need for the bibliography, allowing the same margins as those on the pages of the paper itself.

REVIEW EXERCISE D. Preparing the Final Version of Your Research Paper. Prepare the final version of your paper, and proofread it carefully. Then assemble the parts of your paper, following your teacher's directions.

CHAPTER 7 WRITING REVIEW 1

Writing a Research Paper Based on Personal Observation. Select a subject and analyze it to develop a topic that you can research in your own community through personal observation, such as site visits and interviews. Prepare a research paper based on your findings.

CHAPTER 7 WRITING REVIEW 2

Improving a Research Paper from Another Subject. Select a research paper you have written in one of your other content-area subjects. Evaluate this paper by applying the guidelines on pages 114–15. Then revise the paper, using the chart on pages 27–28, and proofread it, referring to the guidelines on page 30. Be prepared to explain specific improvements you have made.

ABBREVIATIONS USED IN SOURCES

The following list explains a number of scholarly abbreviations you may encounter in your research. For the most part, you should avoid using these abbreviations in your own paper; exceptions are those shown in the examples in this chapter, such as *ed.* and *trans.*

c *or* © *copyright*; used before a date (©1965) to indicate when copyright was obtained. (The circled *c* is the international copyright symbol.)

c., ca. *about* (from the Latin *circa, circum*); used with dates—"c." or "ca. 1732" means "about 1732."

cf. *compare* (from the Latin *confer*); "cf. the Atlantic Treaty" means "compare with the Atlantic Treaty."

ed. *editor, edited, edition*

e.g. *for example* (from the Latin *exempli gratia*)

et al. *and others* (from the Latin *et alii*); also, *and elsewhere* (from the Latin *et alibi*)

f., ff. *following page, pages;* "p. 25f." means "page 25 and the following page"; "p. 25ff." means "page 25 and the following pages."

ibid. *in the same place* (from the Latin *ibidem*); no longer recommended by the MLA.

id. *the same* (from the Latin *idem*)

i.e. *that is* (from the Latin *id est*)

l., ll. *line, lines*

loc. cit. *in the place previously cited* (from the Latin *loco citato*)

ms., mss. *manuscript, manuscripts*

N.B. *note well* (from the Latin *nota bene*)

n.d. *no date*; publication date not given in book

op. cit. *in the work previously cited* (from the Latin *opere citato*); no longer recommended by the MLA.

p., pp. *page, pages*

q.v. *which see, whom see* (from the Latin *quod vide* or *quem vide*)

sic *thus* (from the Latin); used (in brackets) after an error in a passage, to make clear that the original was copied accurately

vide *see* (from the Latin)

Michael Davis

Psychology

April 8, 1988

CLAIRVOYANCE: INVESTIGATING A "SIXTH SENSE"

[The following sample pages are from a high-school student's research paper. Use them as a model in preparing your own paper.]

OUTLINE

Thesis: For many years, clairvoyance, the ability to "see" objects or events without the use of the senses, was not considered a suitable subject for scientific study; more recently, however, scientific studies have been conducted that attempt to prove the existence of this "sixth sense."

   I. Definition of clairvoyance

       A. Comparison with other types of extrasensory perception

       B. Examples of clairvoyant ability

  II. Scientific approach to clairvoyance

       A. Need for valid evidence

       B. Need for extensive evidence

 III. Experiments with clairvoyance

       A. Studies by J. B. Rhine

          1. Method of card-guessing

          2. Interpretation of data

          3. Favorable results of studies

       B. Studies by Rhine's followers

          1. Use of separate rooms

          2. Use of categories for subjects

          3. Use of random-number generator

          4. Use of remote locations

          5. Use of hypnosis

  IV. Objections to experiments

       A. Possibility of fraud

       B. Lower scores from tighter controls

       C. Variable results from repeated efforts

   V. Future of clairvoyance studies

Clairvoyance: Investigating a "Sixth Sense"

One night a young woman was driving home with her husband. They came to a roadblock, where a police officer told them about an accident a half—mile ahead. After they had made a detour and had continued driving for a few minutes, the woman began to tremble and cry. She told her husband that her sister was lying dead on the road they had just left! Forty—five minutes after they had arrived home, the phone rang. The caller, a local doctor, told the woman that her sister was dead. She had been killed instantly in a car accident, the same accident the couple had heard of an hour before (Louisa E. Rhine, "Psychological Processes" 95—96).

Was this woman's experience simply a strange coincidence? Have you ever had a hunch or made a wild guess that proved correct? Such sudden insights, some scientists claim, may have been a form of extrasensory perception called clairvoyance. For many years, clairvoyance, the ability to "see" objects or events without the use of the senses, was not considered a suitable subject for scientific study; more recently, however, scientific studies have been conducted that attempt to prove the existence of this "sixth sense." [thesis]

Clairvoyance, say scientists, is one of four categories of extrasensory perception: (1) telepathy--reading the thoughts of another, (2) precognition--sensing future events, (3) psychokinesis--affecting objects by thinking about them, and (4) clairvoyance--perceiving objects or events that are impossible to perceive by the normal senses (Cherry 84). The category of clairvoyance includes such acts as guessing the unknown contents of a sealed envelope or describing the location of a lost child.

Was the woman's sudden knowledge about her sister's death an example of clairvoyance? Montague Ullman, a leading researcher of extrasensory perception, warns, "Scientifically, of course, such cases don't prove anything, because they can be called coincidence, unconscious self-deception, or deliberate hoaxes" (47). [direct quotation]

Ullman and other investigators insist that clairvoyance exists; yet in order to prove their claim, they recognize the need for reliable data. Accordingly, clairvoyance has been the focus of experiments based upon careful controls. Following the scientific method, scientists gather evidence from these experiments and use the evidence as the basis of proof.

During experiments, subjects may guess at hidden cards, locations, numbers, or a variety of other items. If enough of these
guesses are correct, then scientists can be certain that more
than mere luck is at work. However, as an added precaution
against lucky guesses, scientists require extensive evidence,
drawn from thousands of experiments. They may even repeat a
particular experiment with one person hundreds of times before
accepting its results.

This experimental research is relatively new. It began during the 1930's, when Dr. J. B. Rhine conducted experiments for
all four categories of extrasensory perception (Bowles and Hynds
27). In his earliest attempts, he found clairvoyance the most
suitable for research. He stated:

> Clairvoyance experiments are the easiest of all to conduct.
> . . . Not only is it easier to control against the more
> common experimental errors, but it is also easier to elimi-
> nate any alternative hypothesis that might be applied to
> the data (Rhine and Pratt 53). [extended quotation]

Enthusiastically, Dr. Rhine performed hundreds of experiments, testing the clairvoyant powers of ordinary people. His
method was surprisingly simple; in fact, with patience and accurate record keeping, anyone can imitate it.

Rhine used a pack of cards called Zener cards, which contained five symbols: a star, a circle, a cross, a square, and a wavy line. One of these symbols was printed on each card. In the deck there were twenty-five cards, five of each symbol.

After shuffling the cards, the experimenter placed the deck on a table. Behind an opaque screen, which concealed the experimenter and the cards at all times, the subject either wrote down or called out in order the symbols in the deck (Bowles and Hynds 31). By pure chance, one would expect five correct guesses out of twenty-five in a single run-through of cards. Any scoring consistently higher than five correct guesses, Rhine concluded, was evidence of clairvoyance (Cohen 76).

[*The paper goes on to discuss Dr. Rhine's interpretation of his data, the favorable results of his studies, and the experiments of Dr. Rhine's followers. The following paragraphs make a transition from this section of the paper to the objections against clairvoyance experiments.*]

7

One recent development in clairvoyance research involves hypnosis. In tests, two groups of people perform Dr. Rhine's card-guessing experiment. One group is awake, while the other group is under hypnosis. The group under hypnosis has scored a significantly greater number of correct guesses than the other group. Although researchers find these results encouraging, they are performing further tests to measure the effect of hypnosis (Sargent).

As research into clairvoyance continues, however, opponents refuse to accept the findings. According to Bowles and Hynds, the unfavorable publicity the Rhines' work received may still be influencing the general public's attitudes toward psychical research (27). Critics cite three overwhelming problems in the studies: first, that researchers do not guard enough against fraud; second, that they get lower scores as they improve their testing methods; and third, that they cannot get the same results every time they repeat an experiment. [transitional paragraph]

[*The next section of the paper discusses each objection. The paper concludes as follows:*]

10

Defenders, meanwhile, claim that scientific standards, such as requiring similar results each time an experiment is repeated, need not apply to research into the human mind. Arthur Koestler writes, "[The standard of] repeatability [is] valid in the physical sciences, but less so in the frontiers of medicine and even less in those branches of psychology which involve unconscious processes . . ." (29).

Although Koestler and others claim that clairvoyance "is a hard reality" (23), many disagree, and the future of clairvoyance studies is uncertain. Philip H. Abelson, editor of the authoritative journal Science, sums up the controversy when he states that "these extraordinary claims require extraordinary evidence. Findings that question the basic laws of nature must be subjected to rigorous scientific scrutiny" ("A Stepchild of

Science" 42). Many, like Abelson, believe that statistical evidence charting an unknown power at work gives insufficient reason for abandoning assumptions about the way the mind works. Remarks D. O. Hebb, professor of psychology at McGill University, "I do not accept ESP for a moment, because it does not make sense" (45).

Skeptics like Abelson and Hebb may be unfairly dismissing the positive results of clairvoyance studies, which, compared with many other fields, are still very new. By demanding "extraordinary evidence" that extrasensory perception exists, they may be overlooking much of the evidence this paper has discussed.

On the other hand, scientists who claim that clairvoyance is a fact of life are exaggerating, for many questions remain. H. J. Eysenck, professor at the University of London, calmly states the crux of the issue:

> . . . very intriguing demonstrations have been given that suggest the existence of something outside the purview of physics and psychology, but no one has yet succeeded in bringing this something under adequate experimental control (1004).

Until scientists can present a reasonable explanation for clairvoyance, Eysenck contends, "it would be unwise to claim any more" (1004).

WORKS CITED

Bowles, Norma, and Fran Hynds. PsiSearch. New York: Harper, 1978.

Cherry, Laurence. "Physicists Explain ESP." Science Digest Sept./Oct. 1980: 84–87.

Cohen, Daniel. ESP: The Search Beyond the Senses. New York: Harcourt Brace Jovanovich, 1973.

Eysenck, H. J. "Theories of Parapsychological Phenonomena." Encyclopaedia Britannica: Macropaedia. 1979 ed.

Hansel, C. E. M. ESP: A Scientific Evaluation. New York: Scribner's, 1966.

Hebb, D. O. "The Role of Neurological Ideas in Psychology." Journal of Personality 20 (1951): 40–52.

Koestler, Arthur. The Roots of Coincidence. New York: Random House, 1972.

Palmer, John. "Progressive Skepticism: A Critical Approach to the Psi Controversy." Journal of Parapsychology 50 (1986): 29–42.

Puthoff, Harold E., and Russell Targ. "Remote Viewing: New Research Frontier." The Signet Handbook of Parapsychology. Ed. Martin Ebon. New York: New American Library, 1978. 78–90.

Rhine, J. B. The Reach of the Mind. New York: Smith, 1972.

Rhine, J. B., et al. Extrasensory Perception After Sixty Years: A Critical Appraisal of the Research in Extrasensory Perception. Boston: Humphries, 1966.

Rhine, J.B., and J. G. Pratt. Parapsychology: Frontier Science of the Mind. Springfield: Thomas, 1972.

Rhine, Louisa E. Hidden Channels of the Mind. New York: Sloane, 1961.

---. "Psychological Processes in ESP Experiences: Part 1, Waking Experiences." Journal of Parapsychology 26 (1962): 88–111.

Sargent, Carl L. "Hypnosis as a Psi–Conducive State." Journal of Parapsychology 42 (1978): 264–67.

"A Stepchild of Science Starts to Win Friends." U.S. News and World Report 31 July 1978: 41,42.

Taylor, John. Science and the Supernatural. New York: Dutton, 1980.

Ullman, Montague. "Can You Communicate with Others in Your Dreams?" The Psychic Scene. Ed. John White. New York: New American Library, 1974. 47–52.

CHAPTER 8

Writing Business Letters and Completing Forms

STANDARD PRACTICE IN BUSINESS CORRESPONDENCE

The practical skills of writing business letters and completing forms are important to everyone. This chapter will give you instruction and practice in communicating the required information efficiently and clearly.

PREWRITING

FORM IN BUSINESS LETTERS

Business letters are always written according to a standard form.

8a. Observe standard practice in the writing of business letters.

(1) Use appropriate stationery.

Standard business stationery is plain white paper that is $8\frac{1}{2}$ x 11 inches; a smaller size, $5\frac{1}{2}$ x $8\frac{1}{2}$ inches, may be used for very brief letters.

(2) Make an attractive "letter picture."

FertiGlobe, Inc
855 Third Avenue
New York, New York 10017
Telephone 212-588-0338

Telex WUI-999628 FER ULU
Telex WUO-645475 FER GLO
TWX 7108615213
Cable FERTIGLOBE

FertiGlobe

March 22, 1988

Mr. Paul Bruno
Sales Manager
Balzac Bag Company
555 South Monroe Street
Baltimore, Maryland 21224

Dear Mr. Bruno:

   Thank you for your letter of February 4, 1988, and enclosed pricelist. We
would like to order the following items:

1.	5,000 woven polypropylene bags with poly- ethylene liners, 22½" x 35", delivered to Tampa latest April 20th, and marked "DAP - M/V Catherine P", @ $0.55 per bag:	$2,750.00
2.	4,500 woven polypropylene bags with poly- ethylene liners, 23" x 39", delivered to Tampa latest May 10th, and marked "URA - M/V Miss Calvi", @ $0.62 per bag:	$2,790.00
	Total:	$5,540.00

   All bags should be delivered to the warehouses of Manley Stevedoring, Inc.,
710 Kings Road, Port Authority Complex, Tampa, Florida.

   As always, it is a pleasure to do business with Balzac.

                                        Yours truly,

                                        Jeanette Hudson

                                        Jeanette Hudson
                                        Operations

CABLE ADDRESS "ELMER"   (212) 888-4400

JOHN M. RIEHLE & CO.
INCORPORATED
Complete Insurance Service
SINCE 1886
757 THIRD AVENUE
NEW YORK N Y 10017

February 4, 1988

Miss Margaret Scanlon
651 East 78th Street
New York, NY 10089

Re: Homeowner's Insurance
     Plymouth Insurance Company
     Policy No. 88HO4297721

Dear Miss Scanlon:

Enclosed please find your Homeowner's Insurance policy No. 88HO4297721
issued by Plymouth Insurance Company for the period March 1, 1988
through March 1, 1989.

The annual premium, as indicated on the enclosed invoice, is $150.00.

Please return payment at your earliest convenience. A self-addressed
envelope has been provided. If you have any questions, please do not
hesitate to call.

Sincerely,

M. A. Roberts

M. A. Roberts
Account Executive

MAR/dq

Enclosures

MT. KISCO, NEW YORK   •   NEW CANAAN, CONNECTICUT   •   MASSAPEQUA, NEW YORK

The "letter picture" is the overall picture a letter presents to the reader at first glance. To frame the picture attractively, you must center the letter on the page, leaving equal margins on the sides, top, and bottom. Consistently follow a standard pattern of indentation and punctuation, and make the letter absolutely free of strikeovers, erasures, and other marks of carelessness.

On page 294 two business letters appear in miniature. Two popular styles are represented: the block style, without paragraph indentations, and the semiblock style, with paragraph indentations. Note that the text of each letter is placed attractively in relation to the letterhead.

(3) Follow standard practice in continuing a letter on a second page.

A business letter should be as short as possible without being abrupt or confusing. If a letter must be continued on a second page, use a second sheet and write at least three lines on it; never write on the reverse side of a page. The first line of the second page on $8\frac{1}{2}$ x 11-inch stationery should be about two inches from the top. The page number should be centered about four lines above the first line of writing.

PARTS OF A BUSINESS LETTER

(4) Make the six parts of the letter conform to standard practice.

While you are studying the following description of the six parts of a business letter, refer frequently to the model letter on page 297.

The Heading

When you use stationery bearing a letterhead, you need to supply only the date in the heading. When you have no letterhead, you must give a complete heading: your street address on the first line; city, state, and ZIP code on the second line, with a comma between the city and state; date on the third line, with a comma between the day and the year. If you use abbreviations, use them consistently.

The Inside Address

The inside address must give the name of the person or the firm (or both) to whom you are writing and the address. This is because businesses often file letters under the name of the person or firm to which they are written. The inside address is placed four typewriter spaces below the date and flush with the left-hand margin. You may give the person's title after the name on the same line or, if the title is too long, on a separate line below. In an address, always use a title with a person's name. Permissible abbreviations are *Mr., Messrs., Mrs., Ms., Dr., Hon.* Others should be spelled out: *Professor* Grace Tamura, *Reverend* Thomas E. Haupt. Some businesses use the two-letter code recommended by the postal service for states.

EXAMPLES   Mrs. Lucinda Green   Mr. James Moore, Principal
               Plant Supervisor   Westbend High School
               King Products, Inc.   Westbend, Iowa 50597
               1420 Havens Blvd.
               Chicago, IL 60637

The Salutation

The salutation, or greeting, is placed below the inside address (two spaces on the typewriter) and flush with the left-hand margin. It is always followed by a colon. The salutation varies with the nature of the inside address.

If you are writing to a company or a department, not to a specific individual, the traditional salutation is *Gentlemen:* (which assumes that the group contains both men and women). Some people, however, prefer other forms of salutation.

EXAMPLES   Soundcraft Corporation
            10 East 52nd Street
            New York, New York 10022

            Dear Sir or Madam: Dear Personnel Department:
            Dear Soundcraft Corporation: Dear Editors:

If you are writing to a specific person, but know only the person's title, not the name, you may use *Dear Sir or Madam:*. An impersonal salutation is also acceptable.

EXAMPLE   Personnel Manager
           Airborne Instruments Laboratories, Inc.
           160 Old Country Road
           Mineola, New York 11501

           Dear Personnel Manager:

If you are writing to a man and have included his name in the inside address, the proper salutation is *Dear Mr. ——:*

EXAMPLE   Mr. D. H. White, Manager
Eastern Oil Company
60 East 42nd Street
New York, New York 10017
Dear Mr. White:

When writing to a woman who does not identify herself as *Miss* or *Mrs.*, you may use *Ms.* in the salutation. You may also use both the first and last names of a man or woman in the salutation.

EXAMPLES   Dear Ms. Alvarez: Dear Mr. Wright:
             Dear Jane Alvarez: Dear Philip Wright:

High-ranking government officials may be addressed as follows:

THE PRESIDENT

The President
The White House
Washington, D.C. 20015

Dear Mr. President:

SENATOR, REPRESENTATIVE, GOVERNOR, MAYOR

The Honorable Nancy Landon Kassebaum
United States Senate
Washington, D.C. 20015

Dear Senator Kassebaum:

The Body

It is important to use simple, courteous language, clearly and directly phrased. Avoid trite phrases such as *please be advised that* and *thanking you in advance*. For discussion of the contents of particular kinds of letters, see pages 300–305.

The first line of the body of a business letter is placed two typewriter spaces below the salutation. In semiblock style, it may be indented either the usual five spaces of a typed manuscript or as far as the length of the salutation. Subsequent paragraph indentations will be uniform with the first one (see the letter pictures on page 294). In block style, indentations are not used: paragraphs are distinguished by extra spacing between them.

The Closing

The standard form for the closing, or leave-taking, is *Yours truly* or *Very truly yours*. Less formal but frequently used is *Sincerely yours*. In writing to high-ranking government and church officials, you may use *Respectfully yours*.

The closing is begun just to the right of the middle of the page if you have used paragraph indentations or flush with the left margin if you have not used paragraph indentations. It is followed by a comma. Note that only the first word is capitalized.

```
                        188 Fernwood Terrace         ⎤
                        Westtown, New York 10998     ⎬ ──── heading
                        June 20, 1988                ⎦


    The Honorable John Knowles        ⎤
    City Hall                         ⎬ ──── inside
    Westtown, New York 10998          ⎦        address

    Dear Mayor Knowles:  ──────────────────────────── salutation

        The four acres north of the Palisades Avenue play-   ⎤
    ground will go on the market next week. Unless the village│
    buys this land to enlarge the playground, the land will  │
    undoubtedly be acquired by a real estate developer. On be-│
    half of the West End Association, I am writing to ask you to│
    urge the Village Council to buy the four acres for a play-│
    ground and public park.                                  │
                                                             │
        The present playground is so inadequate that many    ⎬ ──── body
    youngsters who should be using it are staying away because│
    of the crowded conditions. This situation will be made much│
    worse if children from a new twenty-five home development │
    should want to play there.                               │
                                                             │
        It seems to the two hundred families in the West End │
    that an enlarged play area for our children would be a sound│
    investment for the future of Westtown.                   ⎦

                        Very truly yours,  ──────────── closing

                        𝒜𝓁𝓁𝑒𝓃 𝒞. 𝐵𝒶𝓇𝓃𝑒𝓈  ──────── signature

                        Allan C. Barnes
                        Secretary, West End
                        Association
```

Model Business Letter

The Signature

The signature is written in ink immediately below the closing and flush
with it. The writer's name should be typewritten directly below the
signature and may be accompanied by his or her official position.

EXAMPLE   Very truly yours,
          James MacPherson
          James MacPherson
          President

A woman may choose to place *Miss, Mrs.,* or *Ms.* in parentheses before
her signature.

EXAMPLES   Very truly yours,   Very truly yours,
           (Miss) Virginia Shaw   *(Mrs.) Elizabeth Blake*

In general, however, do not put a title before a signature.

EXAMPLES   Very truly yours,   Very truly yours,
            Thomas Strong   *Sally Blake*

The Envelope

(5) Make the envelope conform to standard practice.

The addresses on the envelope should conform with the addresses used in the letter itself. Your own name and address are placed in the upper left-hand corner of the envelope. The recipient's name and address are placed just below the middle of the envelope and slightly to the right. If a particularly long line is necessary, use a second line and indent it a few spaces from the left margin of the address. The name of the person you are addressing should be preceded by the proper title (*Mr., Dr., Ms.,* etc.). Always include the initial or the first name: *Ms. Georgia V. Bryce,* or *Ms. G. V. Bryce,* not *Georgia Bryce* or *Ms. Bryce.* Your own name in the return address need not be accompanied by a title (see page 300).

(6) Fold the letter according to standard practice.

If a letter written on standard $8\frac{1}{2}$ x 11-inch stationery is to be placed in a long envelope, the letter is folded twice: up from the bottom about a third of the way, then down from the top; when unfolded, it will be right side up. If it is to be placed in a small envelope, the letter should be folded up from the bottom to within a quarter of an inch of the top; then the right side is folded over a third of the way and the left side folded over that fold. Insert the letter in the envelope with the fold at the bottom of the envelope (see below).

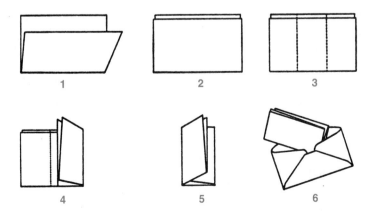

```
John Davis
1649 Muir Drive
Port Huron, MI 48060




              Ms. Stephanie Kinnery, President
              Kinnery Leathercraft, Inc.
              325 South Ames Street
              Marian, IN 46952
```

The Envelope

WRITING

KINDS OF BUSINESS LETTERS

8b. Learn the requirements for various types of business letters.

From time to time, you will almost certainly need to write the four types of business letters described on the following pages: the order letter, the letter of inquiry or request, the letter of adjustment or complaint, and the letter of application.

The Order Letter

When you do not have printed order forms, you need to write order letters. An effective order letter will meet the requirements that follow.

1. Include a list of the items you are ordering; type the list in a column.

2. Include all appropriate details as to quantity, catalog number, size, style, and price. The symbol @ means *each* or *apiece:* 3 boxes @ $1.25 = $3.75. Specify the magazine or paper in which you saw the items advertised.

3. Indicate how you are paying for the order: by check, money order, C.O.D., or charge account. Never send cash through the mail.

21 Cranberry Road
Harmon, Illinois 61042
November 20, 1988

New Fashions Shop
187 Main Street
Castleton, Illinois 61426

Gentlemen:

Please send me the following articles advertised in
the *Journal* for November 19.

1 Heatherland tweed skirt, size 24 waist	$29.95
2 prs. Slimfit slacks, gray, size 10 long @ $22.95	45.90
1 Hemper blouse, white, Style A, size 34	19.95
Total	$95.80

I am enclosing a money order for $97.35 to cover the
order and parcel post charges of $1.55.

Very truly yours,

Judy Abbott

Judy Abbott

345 Graham Road
Bellmore, New York 11710
October 10, 1988

Box Office
Majestic Theater
245 West Forty—fourth Street
New York, New York 10018

Gentlemen:

Please send me three tickets @ $16.00 for the
matinee performance of Hamlet on Saturday, November 28.
Acceptable alternate dates are November 21 and December
5.

I am enclosing a check for $48.00 and a self—
addressed, stamped envelope.

Very truly yours,

Albert Armstrong

Albert Armstrong

Model Order Letters

4. If you want the merchandise sent to an address different from the address in the heading, give the address clearly in the body of the letter.

5. Make a copy of the letter and the form of payment you have enclosed. Keep the copy until your order has been filled.

The Letter of Inquiry or Request

Occasionally you may require information that can be obtained only by writing a letter. Common situations of this kind include writing for material to use in a research paper, for facts about travel in a certain locality, or for a college catalog. Be brief and direct, but courteous. Remember that you are asking someone to take time to do something for you.

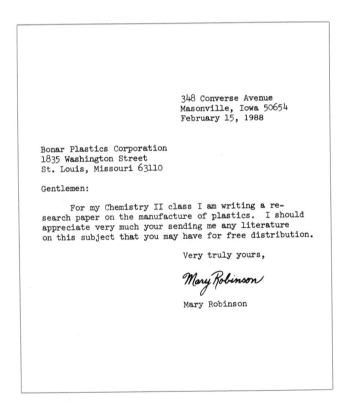

```
                                    348 Converse Avenue
                                    Masonville, Iowa 50654
                                    February 15, 1988


     Bonar Plastics Corporation
     1835 Washington Street
     St. Louis, Missouri 63110

     Gentlemen:

          For my Chemistry II class I am writing a re-
     search paper on the manufacture of plastics.  I should
     appreciate very much your sending me any literature
     on this subject that you may have for free distribution.

                         Very truly yours,

                         Mary Robinson

                         Mary Robinson
```

Model Letter of Inquiry

```
                              118 Mountain Road
                              Kingston, New York 12401
                              April 17, 1988

     School of Agriculture
     Cornell University
     Ithaca, New York 14850

     Gentlemen:

          Please send me your general catalogue and any
     additional literature you have on admission to the
     School of Agriculture and courses in dairy farming.

                              Very truly yours,

                              Walter Owen

                              Walter Owen
```

Model Letter of Request

The Letter of Adjustment or Complaint

When you write to a business firm to ask for correction of an error or to register a complaint of any kind, you will get better results if you restrain your annoyance and adopt a courteous tone. This is true also when you write to a government official complaining about poor service being given by municipal, state, or government employees. No one in business deliberately antagonizes customers by errors in service.

In a letter of adjustment or complaint, go as far into the history of the transaction as you need to in order to explain the error. Also, never write a letter of complaint without indicating clearly the way in which you would like the error corrected. If you do not know the best method of making the adjustment, say so, and tell the recipient of your letter that you will wait for suggestions.

```
                                      14 Oklahoma Avenue
                                      Tulsa, Oklahoma  74106
                                      May 24, 1988


      Guerber's Sports Company
      85 Court Street
      Maysville, Oklahoma  73057

      Gentlemen:

            On May 14 I sent you an order which included two
      white T-shirts, No. 86, size 36, @ $3.00.  When the
      shipment arrived, I found that you had neglected to send
      the shirts.  I assume that this was merely an oversight
      in packing and will appreciate your sending me the
      shirts.

                                      Very truly yours,


                                      Ralph Gray


                                      Ralph Gray
```

Model Adjustment Letter

The Letter of Application

You must make sure that your letter of application is correct in every detail and sufficiently convincing to make the reader consider your application further. It should, if possible, be typewritten.

You should follow these steps for writing an effective application.

1. Begin by naming the position for which you are applying. Mention how you learned about it.

2. State your age, education, experience.

3. Indicate that you are familiar with the requirements of the position, and explain why you believe you can meet them.

```
                                        321 Fifth Street
                                        Riverside, Missouri 64168
                                        March 2, 1988


Personnel Director
Central Insurance Company
41 Bank Street
Riverside, Missouri 64168

Dear Sir:

        Please consider me an applicant for the secretarial posi-
tion advertised in Sunday's Herald.

        I am eighteen years old and graduated last June from
Riverside High School.  Since then I have completed a six-
months' course in secretarial training at the Clarkson Business
Institute.  In high school I completed two years of courses in
shorthand and typing and worked as a student assistant for two
years in the office.  At Clarkson I studied office practice, busi-
ness machines, business English, and bookkeeping.

        For the past two summers I was employed as a fill-in
stenographer by the Moore Trucking Company, where I did
filing and billing as well as regular stenographic work.  I feel
at home in a business office and enjoy being given extra duties
and responsibilities.

        The following people have given me permission to use
their names as references:

        Miss Catherine Greenberg
        Head of the Commercial Department
        Riverside High School

        Mr. Stanley Williams
        Moore Trucking Company
        Riverside, Missouri 64168

        I shall be glad to come for a personal interview at your
convenience.  My telephone number is 592-3107.

                                Very truly yours,

                                Jane Parkman

                                Jane Parkman
```

Model Letter of Application

4. Give references (three, if possible) with addresses and telephone numbers. If you have held other jobs, be sure to include one of your former employers. Include also a teacher who knows you well. Before giving someone's name as a reference, ask permission.

5. Request an interview at the employer's convenience.

6. Be especially careful with all the details of letter form, neatness, spelling, and grammar. Be sure that your letter is perfect—to make the best possible impression.

EXERCISE 1. Making the Letter Picture. Using the models on pages 294 and 298, arrange on a piece of typing paper a business letter. Use neatly drawn lines for the body of the letter and your own address and the present date in the heading. Make up an inside address. Be sure that the salutation is proper and that the closing and signature are correct.

EXERCISE 2. Revising the Inside Address and Salutation. Rewrite the following inside addresses in correct form. Beneath each, write the proper salutation.

1. Fred Emerson, a professor at Columbia University, West 116th Street, New York City 10027
2. Miami University, Dean of Admissions, Oxford, Ohio 45056
3. 10 East 53rd Street, Harper & Row, New York City 10022
4. Representative from your congressional district in the House of Representatives in Washington, D.C. 20015
5. Personnel Director of the Bradley Company, Cass City, 82–84 South Avenue, Illinois 61016, Carol T. Brooks

EXERCISE 3. Writing Order Letters. Write to any firm you wish, ordering at least three different articles advertised in a magazine or newspaper. Order more than one of some of the articles. Refer to the models on page 301.

EXERCISE 4. Writing a Request Letter. Write a letter to the Dean of Admissions of any college or university. State that you wish to apply for admission at a certain date and request an application blank and other necessary forms. Refer to the models on pages 302–303.

EXERCISE 5. Writing an Adjustment Letter. Write a letter to a business firm asking why you have received a bill for an order for which you have already paid C.O.D. Give all of the important details. Refer to the model on page 304.

EXERCISE 6. Writing Letters of Application. Write each letter described below, referring to the model on page 305.

1. From your local newspaper, select a help-wanted advertisement and answer it with a letter of application. Clip the advertisement to your letter when you hand it in.

2. Whether or not you are going to work immediately upon graduation from high school, you probably have in mind the kind of ideal position you eventually would like to apply for. Write an imaginary letter of application for such a position.

KINDS OF FORMS

8c. Learn the requirements for various types of forms.

You will often be asked to provide specific information on preprinted forms. To fill out forms correctly, remember the following points:

1. Read the directions carefully. Read through the entire form (including the fine print) before you fill in any of the blanks.

2. Use a typewriter or print in blue or black ink. Do not use a pencil unless the form requires it.

3. Be sure that you answer each question on the correct line. If a question does not apply to you, write *N/A* (Not Applicable) unless the form asks you to do otherwise.

4. Read through the entire form before you sign it. Make sure you have not omitted a question. Remember that you may be held legally responsible for the information you have provided on the form.

Job application forms and college admission application forms are especially important as you consider what you will do after you graduate from high school. Study the completed forms on pages 308–10. When you apply for jobs or fill out applications for colleges, you will be asked to complete forms that are similar to these.

The Employment Application

Study the employment application on page 308. Notice that it is divided into five general parts. The items on this application are numbered, but some job applications will not have numbered items. In either case, it is important to work from left to right, making sure that you do not omit any of the questions. Notice that you do *not* write below the line near the bottom of the page.

If the form asks you to name the position you are applying for (see item 2), write the job title that was advertised. "Dependents" (item 8) are people who depend on you for financial support. If you are looking for full-time employment, your career goal (item 10) should be related to the work that the company does.

EMPLOYMENT APPLICATION

1. Date _12/8/88_
2. Position Desired _Cook's helper_
3. Social Security No. _579-24-1852_

PERSONAL

4. Name _Antonio Vaamonde._   5. Phone No. _859-2670_
6. Address _86 Center Street Belmont, California. 94812_
7. Years at this address _16_   8. Dependents (List names and relationship) _none_

9. Check one: 10. Career goal _Restaurant Chef_
   U.S. citizen _✓_   11. Relatives employed by this company _none._
   Reg. Alien _____
12. How did you hear about this position? _San Jose Mercury advertisement_

EMPLOYMENT HISTORY

13. Are you currently employed? _Yes_   14. If so, where? _Burger Town Inc._
15. May we contact your present employer? _Yes_   16. Salary desired _$6.00 hr_
17. Former employers (List last one first.)

Dates	Name and Address	Title	Salary	Why did you leave?
6-88 to Now	James Santos BurgerTown 601 Oak St. Belmont	Clerk	$4.50 hr	Opportunity to advance
9-84 to 5-88	William Green, 58 Rey Rd. Belmont.	Gardener	$4.50 hr	Graduated from High School

EDUCATION

18. Schools attended

Dates	Name and Address	Date Graduated	Average Grade
9-84, 6-88	Belmont High, Belmont, Ca	6/88	B-
9-81 to 6-84	Willard Jr. High, Belmont Ca	6/84	C

19. What classes have you taken that may help you do the job applied for?
Cooking classes at Belmont H.S. and Willard J.H.
20. Honors, prizes _My cake recipe won second prize in S.F. Chronicle's Junior Class Contest_
21. Languages you can speak fluently _Spanish_

REFERENCES

22. List three references other than former employers

Name	Address	Phone Number
Mrs. Ellen Goodman	79 Stanton Rd, Richmond, CA 94804	(415) 232-9365
Lamar Polk	2058 Linden St, San Leandro CA 94578	(415) 471-0917
Tim Barnheart	87 Evergreen Rd, Apt 5, Belmont, CA 94802	(415) 849-3706

OTHER

23. Have you ever been convicted of a crime? _No_   24. If yes, give details
_N/A_
24. Hobbies and interests _Cooking, Soccer, Oakland Big Brothers Inc._
25. Willing to relocate? _Yes_

I AUTHORIZE THIS COMPANY TO MAKE INVESTIGATIONS THAT WILL VERIFY ANY STATEMENT THAT I HAVE MADE HERE.
Date _12/18/88_   Signature _Antonio Vaamonde._

DO NOT WRITE BELOW THIS LINE

COMMENTS _____   Interviewed by _____
                                        Date

Employment Application

Since you usually complete this type of application at the company's personnel office, you might bring with you information, such as addresses and phone numbers, that you will need to complete some items. Be sure to ask people if you may list them as a reference (item 22); a company will usually call at least one of the people you have listed.

Answer all of the questions truthfully. If you have been convicted of a crime (not just arrested), write yes for item 23, but also write *I will discuss this at my interview* for item 24. Be sure that you date and sign the application. Your signature at the end should be the only handwriting on the application. All of the other items should be carefully printed—in ink unless you are asked to use pencil. If you have had to cross out answers, ask for another application so that you can make a clean copy.

The College Admission Application

The application for college entrance (see page 310) is usually more involved than an application for employment. Some college applications are several pages long. One important advantage that you will have in completing this type of application is that you will be able to do it at home. This means that you can think about the answers and can practice filling it out. After you receive the blank form, make several photocopies of it; work on them before you draft your final copy. Unless you can print very clearly and neatly, type your answers.

Notice that the model college application is also organized into five general sections. It asks some of the same questions seen on the employment application but emphasizes academic achievements and extracurricular activities. You may be asked some questions about your parents' financial situation that you consider highly personal. Be assured that the admissions office has good reasons for asking each question and that your answers will be confidential.

If you need more space to answer a question, attach a separate sheet and note that there is additional material for this item. "Siblings" (item 8) are brothers and sisters. (Look up the meaning of any word that you don't know on the application.) For item 13, if you are in the top 20 or so in a large senior class, you may want to write *15th in a class of 1026*, for instance. Otherwise you may write something like *top 20% in the class, second highest in math.* Sound as if you are the type of student this institution seeks, but tell the truth. The application will be just one of the ways the college evaluates you.

APPLICATION FOR ADMISSION

PERSONAL INFORMATION
1. Last name _Yee_ First _Elizabeth_ Middle _Lillian_ 2. Phone _(617)995-6929_
3. Female _X_ Male _N/A_ 4. Weight _100 lbs._ 5. Height _5'2"_ 6. Birthdate _7/10/70_
7. Address _812 Ashland Drive, Bedford, Massachusetts, 01730_

8. Siblings Name   Age   Current Occupation
   Robert Yee   12   Student

9. Father's occupation _Teacher (4th Grade)_ 10. Mother's occupation _Teacher (Piano)_
11. Will you apply for financial aid? _Yes_

ACADEMIC INFORMATION
12. List schools attended (Grades 7–12)

Name	City, State, ZIP	Dates	Principal/Head
Bedford High School	Bedford, MA 01730	9/83–Now	Dr. Albert Souza
Altamonte Jr. High	Boston, MA 02108	9/80–6/83	Mrs. Susan Yamoto

13. Prizes, honors, awards _Math Prize Medallist, '85, '86;_
14. Rank in high school graduating class _4th in class of 586_
15. If you have been out of high school for more than one year, describe your activities, employment, classes and colleges attended _N/A_

16. Possible major _Mathematics_ 17. Career goal _Computer Scientist_

EXTRACURRICULAR ACTIVITIES
18. List school, community, and church activities

Activity	Achievements
Piano Accompanist for school	Accompanied choir for 4 years; toured New England, Feb. '85
Volunteer Coordinator at	Coordinated student volunteers at placement home for
Elmwood Children's Home	children waiting for foster care

19. Other activities, hobbies, interests _Reading; Music (piano lessons for 11 years); Computers and computer programming; Hiking; Pets; Babysitting_
20. Which three books that you read during the past year most impressed you?
    List title and author. _Foundation by Isaac Asimov; Cosmos by Carl Sagan; In Search of Schrodinger's Cat by John Gribbin_

EMPLOYMENT EXPERIENCE
21. List jobs held, including part-time work

Employer	Type of Work	Hours Weekly	Dates
Newton Public Lib.	Library Aide	10 (approx.)	Summers '85–'86
Mrs. Carla Perez	Babysitting	6	Every Saturday, '86

RECOMMENDATIONS
22. List the names and addresses of three people (including one teacher and one employer)
    Ms. Alice Jones, Head, Math Dept. Bedford H.S., Bedford, MA 01730
    Mr. Robert Ryan, Supervisor, Children's Room, Newton Public Library, Newton, MA 02175
    Mr. Sylvia Brown 5960 Arlington St. Boston, Ma 02116

THE INFORMATION ON THIS APPLICATION IS TRUE AND COMPLETE

Date _12/1/88_ Signature _Elizabeth M. Yee_

College Application

Some colleges also require a personal essay or writing sample, often based on a specific question that can be answered in four or five paragraphs. Follow the steps in the writing process to prepare your essay; be creative, but try not to sound "clever" or boastful. Attach the essay to your application.

Be sure that you make a copy of the completed application (and any attachments) before you send it in. Before your interview, review your application. The interviewer may question you about your application or may want to discuss your answers.

EXERCISE 7. Completing Forms. If your teacher provides the forms, fill out either an employment application or a college admission application. Refer to the models on pages 308 and 310.

EVALUATING

EVALUATING YOUR BUSINESS LETTERS AND FORMS

8d. Evaluate the drafts for your business letters and forms.

Since your letter or application form represents you to people you have not met, it is important that it represent you favorably. As you evaluate your rough draft, look for problems in accuracy, clarity, and effective expression.

GUIDELINES FOR EVALUATING BUSINESS LETTERS AND FORMS

Appearance	1. Does the letter follow standard practice? Is the stationery an appropriate size? Is the letter centered on the page and neatly handwritten or typed with consistent paragraph indentations? Is each part of the letter correctly placed?
Conventions	2. Does the letter follow standard conventions for punctuation and capitalization?
Purpose	3. Will the reader know immediately why the letter was written? Does the letter contain all of the necessary information?

Tone   4. Is the letter brief, yet courteous? Is the language clear and directly phrased?

Envelope   5. Are the return address and the recipient's address accurate and correctly placed? Is the letter folded correctly?

Clarity   6. Are all questions on the form correctly answered on the proper lines? Are the answers neatly and clearly written?

EXERCISE 8. Evaluating Your Business Letters. Evaluate the business letters you wrote for Exercises 1–6, using the preceding Guidelines for Evaluating Business Letters and Forms. Mark places on your draft that need to be changed; keep your draft for later use. You may want to exchange letters with a classmate to evaluate each other's work.

EXERCISE 9. Evaluating Your Forms. Review the application you completed in Exercise 7. Evaluate it with question 6 of the preceding guidelines. Mark places where you need to make changes. You may want to exchange applications with a classmate, taking the role of Personnel Director or Dean of Admissions, to evaluate each other's work.

REVISING

REVISING YOUR WRITING

8e. Revise your draft, making changes that will improve your letter or form.

After you have located where you need to change your draft, you should revise your letter or form, making changes that will improve it. You may want to review the techniques for revising your work on pages 27–28. The following chart suggests how you can use the techniques of cutting, adding, reordering, and replacing to revise and improve your letter or form.

REVISING BUSINESS LETTERS AND FORMS

PROBLEM	TECHNIQUE	REVISION
The first paragraph is indented, but the next two paragraphs are flush with the left-hand margin.	Replace	Make the letter consistently block or semiblock style, with all paragraphs flush with the left-hand margin or consistently indented.
The parts of the heading are out of order.	Reorder	Rearrange the lines according to correct business letter form.
The salutation or closing is inappropriate.	Replace	Substitute proper forms for those that are unsuitable.
The purpose of the letter is unclear.	Add	Add a topic sentence or supporting details that indicate why you are writing the letter.
The letter sounds discourteous.	Replace	Replace impolite words or expressions with courteous ones.
On the envelope, both the two-letter code for the state and the name of the state appear in the recipient's address.	Cut	Cut the name of the state from the recipient's address.
The line after several of the questions on a form has been left blank.	Add	Answer the questions that have been omitted, or write N/A if they do not apply to you.

EXERCISE 10. Revising and Proofreading Your Letter or Form.
Use the preceding revising chart to improve your letter or application form. For additional help on revising, refer to Chapter 1. Make the necessary changes. You may want to exchange your letter or form with a

classmate. After you have revised your work, proofread it carefully by referring to the Guidelines for Proofreading on page 30. Then make a final copy, proofreading once again.

CHAPTER 8 WRITING REVIEW

Writing a Business Letter or Form. Choose one of the following items and follow the directions. Prepare the assignment clearly, neatly, and accurately. Also prepare an envelope for that item, following the correct format.

1. Write a letter in which you order several items advertised in a newspaper.
2. Write a letter to the editor of your local newspaper complaining about the school board's decision to eliminate extracurricular activities.
3. Write a letter to a local bookstore requesting book donations for your school library.
4. Write a letter of application for a summer job that would solve your financial problems for a year.
5. Fill out an application form for a job or for college admission.

☞ NOTE   The United States Postal Service recommends the use of two-letter codes for states, the District of Columbia, and Puerto Rico. The Service also recommends the use of nine-digit ZIP codes. The two-letter code is in capital letters and is never followed by a period. The following is a list of two-letter codes. When you use two-letter codes for states and nine-digit ZIP codes, the address on business correspondence should look like this:

EXAMPLE   Ms. Ann Washington
405 Vera Park Drive
Orlando, FL 32804-4335

Alabama	AL	California	CA
Alaska	AK	Colorado	CO
Arizona	AZ	Connecticut	CT
Arkansas	AR	Delaware	DE

District of Columbia   DC
Florida   FL
Georgia   GA
Hawaii   HI
Idaho   ID
Illinois   IL
Indiana   IN
Iowa   IA
Kansas   KS
Kentucky   KY
Louisiana   LA
Maine   ME
Maryland   MD
Massachusetts   MA
Michigan   MI
Minnesota   MN
Mississippi   MS
Missouri   MO
Montana   MT
Nebraska   NE
Nevada   NV
New Hampshire   NH

New Jersey   NJ
New Mexico   NM
New York   NY
North Carolina   NC
North Dakota   ND
Ohio   OH
Oklahoma   OK
Oregon   OR
Pennsylvania   PA
Puerto Rico   PR
Rhode Island   RI
South Carolina   SC
South Dakota   SD
Tennessee   TN
Texas   TX
Utah   UT
Vermont   VT
Virginia   VA
Washington   WA
West Virginia   WV
Wisconsin   WI
Wyoming   WY

CHAPTER 9

Effective Diction

APPROPRIATE CHOICE OF WORDS

USING EFFECTIVE DICTION

The word *diction* comes from the Latin *dicere,* meaning "to point out in words." Knowing that, you will not be surprised to learn that diction means two things—the words a speaker or writer selects and the specific ways in which the words are put to use. Diction may be either *formal* or *informal,* depending on its purpose.

If you are writing a report on the Civil War or on DNA, you will use formal diction. If you are writing a letter to a friend, you will use informal diction—probably with some informal expressions and slang, if slang is part of your personal "voice." If you write a profile of your neighborhood for a newspaper, you most likely will use formal diction, possibly with a few informal expressions but without slang. If you accept a young-adult magazine's invitation to write a book review of Isaac Asimov's *Foundation* series, you will choose diction that the young subscribers understand. Of course, if you write the same sort of review for an adult magazine, you will be free to use more complex words and discuss more complicated ideas.

Whatever the audience, your choice of words can make all the difference between a vigorous, clear writing style and a weak or ambiguous one. In each of the following pairs the first passage is vague and uninteresting; the second is detailed and vivid.

a. About half way between West Egg and New York the motor road goes alongside the railroad to avoid an ash dump.

b. About half way between West Egg and New York the motor road hastily joins the railroad and runs beside it for a quarter of a mile, so as to shrink away from a certain desolate area of land. This is a valley of ashes—a fantastic farm where ashes grow like wheat into ridges and hills and grotesque gardens. . . .

F. SCOTT FITZGERALD

a. The San Bernardino Valley is very different from the moist coast of California because it is subject to the hot winds from the Mojave Desert.

b. The San Bernardino Valley . . . is in certain ways an alien place; not the coastal California of the subtropical twilights and the soft westerlies off the Pacific but a harsher California, haunted by the Mojave just beyond the mountains, devastated by the hot dry Santa Ana wind that comes down through the passage at 100 miles an hour and whines through the eucalyptus windbreaks and works on the nerves.

JOAN DIDION

a. You don't know me unless you have read a book entitled *The Adventures of Tom Sawyer,* but that doesn't make any difference. That book was written by Mark Twain. He chiefly told the truth in that book, but I never knew anyone who told the truth all of the time.

b. You don't know about me without you have read a book by the name of *The Adventures of Tom Sawyer;* but that ain't no matter. That book was made by Mr. Mark Twain, and he told the truth, mainly. There was things which he stretched, but mainly he told the truth. That is nothing. I never seen anybody but lied one time or another, without it was Aunt Polly. . . .

MARK TWAIN

Notice that the professional writers are much more specific in their diction. Instead of vaguely relating that "the road goes alongside" the railroad, Fitzgerald tells us "it hastily joins" the railroad. Instead of writing that the road "avoids" the dump, he makes it "shrink away" from it. The professional writers often use figures of speech, comparing one thing to something else that seems quite different. Fitzgerald compares the valley of ashes to a farm that grows grotesque gardens—a figure of speech that ironically reminds us ashes cannot grow anything.

The professionals also use sensory words to help us experience what they are describing. Didion tells us that the Santa Ana wind is "hot" and "dry" and that it "whines." The westerlies, on the other hand, are "soft." In addition to concrete words, Fitzgerald and Didion both draw on words with strong emotional effects: "desolate," "fantastic," "alien," "haunted," "devastated."

Mark Twain's diction would not be appropriate in a report to the chairman of the board, but the genius of his novel *Huckleberry Finn* is that Twain decided to use the conversational diction of his late-nineteenth-century hero, not the standard English of an impersonal narrator. Through this language, his hero comes alive.

In this chapter we will look at diction—first at correct word choice, then at how different types of diction can affect your writing.

EXACT MEANINGS OF WORDS

9a. Know the exact meanings of words.

Some fine distinctions among word meanings are interesting chiefly to purists. The following verse depends for its humor on the thin difference between the alligator and the crocodile:

THE PURIST

I give you now Professor Twist,
A conscientious scientist.
Trustees exclaimed, "He never bungles!"
And sent him off to distant jungles.
Camped on a tropic riverside,
One day he missed his loving bride.
She had, the guide informed him later,
Been eaten by an alligator.
Professor Twist could not but smile.
"You mean," he said, "a crocodile."

OGDEN NASH

We laugh at Professor Twist, who is more concerned with diction than with the fate of his wife. Despite Nash's mockery of the pedantic professor, however, we are obligated to be certain we are using the correct word in our speaking and writing.

Many words are spelled so much alike that they are easily confused —*dessert* and *desert*, for example. Other words have such subtle distinctions in meaning that a writer often carelessly chooses the wrong one—or really intends the sense of another, as in choosing *uninterested* when *disinterested* might be the proper choice.

EXERCISE 1. Choosing the Correct Words. Look up the words in parentheses below. Choose the word that best completes each sentence. Be prepared to give the meanings of the incorrect words.

1. Denise makes a big point of (flouting, flaunting) the lunchroom rules.
2. "Scrambled" is a more (livid, vivid) verb than "went."
3. The old man looked at his first Christmas tree in (childish, childlike) wonder.
4. The spy received (oral, verbal) directions, rather than written ones.
5. Pulver (inferred, implied) that he would give up watching soap operas.
6. Cicero's name was on the (prescribed, proscribed) list, which meant he was a criminal who could be killed by anyone.
7. The Puritans believed that God was (immanent, imminent) in all of the natural world.
8. Ellsworth will (persecute, prosecute) his case against the fast-food chain.
9. Nora told yet another (anecdote, antidote) about her trip to Pikes Peak.
10. Which European leaders (capitalized, capitulated) to the Nazis?

MIXED IDIOMS AND METAPHORS

9b. Avoid mixed idioms and metaphors.

At times writers use not only the wrong words but also the wrong idioms or metaphors.

An *idiom* is an expression that is peculiar to a certain language and cannot be taken literally. We can say one thing when we mean another—for example, "lose your head"—and get away with it because everyone else knows the meaning we intend. We could not translate "make believe" and "fall for" literally and expect those idioms to make any sense. "Stephanie fell for Carl" does not mean that Carl was supposed to fall but Stephanie agreed to do it for him.

A *metaphor* is a comparison that shows a likeness between two otherwise dissimilar things. The "roof of the mouth," the "arm of the chair," the "foot of the table," the "nose of the plane" are all metaphors. William Shakespeare's "All the world's a stage," Psalm 23's "The Lord is my shepherd," and Emily Dickinson's "Hope is the thing with feathers" also are metaphors.

Sometimes people mix idioms or metaphors, often giving us absurd or humorous mental images as a result. If you said that "The ship of state went into a tailspin," you'd be mixing two metaphors and calling up just such an image. A ship, of course, cannot go into a tailspin.

EXERCISE 2. Identifying Mixed Idioms or Metaphors. Tell what idioms or metaphors the writer is mixing in the following sentences. Then write a sentence explaining what each statement means.

1. In 1969 the moon became another place where "the hand of man had set foot."
2. A senator speaking about the American spirit: "It's vital to find out whether we will keep that spirit bright or let the light dim to keep the boat from rocking."
3. A memo from a corporate executive: "The President is sitting on a time bomb and he's running out of gas."
4. A legislator reports after a visit to constituents: "I've been keeping my ear to the grindstone."
5. An agency warns: "We're steamrolling our way down the drain."

USING SPECIFIC WORDS

9c. Make the descriptions in your writing specific.

Our language is full of general nouns and verbs. The word *house* is a general noun that could refer to any number of specific dwellings: a brick row house, an apartment house, a split level, a prefab, an adobe hut, a Cape Cod, a mobile home, a farmhouse. Suppose you say you went to a *store.* Are you referring to a 5 & 10, a hardware store, a grocery, a deli, a boutique? You could even be more specific with the verb *went.* How did you go to the store? Did you *walk, run, dash, meander, fly?* Maybe you rode the streetcar or drove.

If professional writers agree on anything, it is that word choice in effective writing is particular rather than general. Homer, Shakespeare, Tolstoy, Twain—all wrote in terms of the particular. Thus, Shakespeare did not have a character declare, in *Julius Caesar,* that ghosts were talking in the streets. The character reported that "ghosts did *shriek* and *squeal* about the streets."

EXERCISE 3. Supplying Specific Nouns and Verbs. For each generalized noun or verb listed below, supply at least three specific words or phrases and use them in sentences.

1. dog	5. shoes	9. move
2. desert	6. run	10. use
3. chair	7. go	
4. lunch	8. talk	

AVOIDING WEAK WORDS

9d. Substitute strong, precise words for weak ones in your writing.

Many beginning writers tend to overuse certain vague, "weak" words such as *say, go, have, do, nice, great, neat.* These words are perfectly legitimate, but they provide little substance for your composition. When you find your writing is overloaded with such words, look for precise substitutes. Brainstorming can help. Eventually, you will think of a word or phrase for each need that will be vivid and expressive. In fact, this is how professional writers work. A good writer might spend as much time staring at the paper, trying to think of "a better word," as in fashioning the actual composition.

A thesaurus will help you find synonyms. Here, for example, are some of the synonyms Roget's *International Thesaurus* lists for the verb *say:*

> utter, articulate, enunciate, pronounce, whisper, express, formulate, pour forth, chorus, chime, affirm, allege, proclaim, blurt, exclaim, murmur, mutter, mumble, sigh, yell, growl, snap, roar (and more)

Suppose you describe a story as "nice." Think for a moment and list all the adjectives or adjective phrases you could substitute for *nice.* Which one articulates your true feeling? *Exciting, sad, enjoyable, satisfying, puzzling, warm-hearted, true-to-life?* Perhaps in calling the story "nice," you really are giving it a negative appraisal. Do you really mean the story was *mediocre, so-so, easy to read but not memorable, unconvincing, lackluster?* Be precise. Find the words that express your thoughts adequately.

EXERCISE 4. Using Precise Words. The imprecise words in the following sentences are in italics. For each imprecise word, suggest at least three specific substitutes (words or phrases) and write sentences using them.

1. The mountain is *nice.*
2. Hilda is a *nice* girl.
3. That is a *great* boat.
4. *The Glass Menagerie* is a *great* play.
5. Lilly *said* goodnight to Antoine.
6. "Who's there?" *said* the person behind the door.
7. The dog *went* down the walk.
8. The car *went* down Route 1.

9. The hiker *went* into the woods.
10. Lucille *goes* to Philadelphia every Wednesday.

USING VIVID WORDS

9e. Use vivid words in your writing.

The three passages labeled (b) below are from Edward Abbey's essay "The First Morning," which is about his job as a park ranger in Utah. Each passage by Abbey is preceded by a passage that basically says the same thing but uses vague, imprecise diction:

    a. It was snowing when I went to the park.
    b. "Snow was swirling through the air when I crossed the unfenced line and passed the boundary marker of the park."
    a. Some birds are near the rock, making noises.
    b. "Three ravens are wheeling near the balanced rock, squawking at each other and at the dawn."
    a. The birds call and flap their wings. I smell breakfast cooking.
    b. "The ravens cry out in husky voices, blue-black wings flapping against the golden sky. Over my shoulder comes the sizzle and smell of frying bacon."

You might have noticed by now that precise language is often language that creates mental pictures or evokes sensations. "It was snowing" does not create a very specific picture of what is going on with the weather, but "Snow was swirling" in effect gives vigor to our own imagination. To relate that the birds were "making noises" does not help us hear them, but "The ravens were squawking" gives us a specific auditory image. To tell the reader that you "smell breakfast" does not supply the reader any specific sensory images, but to write that over your shoulder "comes the sizzle and smell of frying bacon" creates two specific sensory images, of sound and odor.

EXERCISE 5. Using Precise and Vivid Words.   Rewrite each of the following sentences so that it expresses its idea in more precise and vivid language. Use as many sentences as you want in your new version.

1. Mickey's car is full of stuff.
2. I smelled breakfast cooking.
3. The weather was pretty bad.
4. A lot of noises came in the open windows.
5. We did lots of things on the eve of the holiday.

CONNOTATIONS AND LOADED WORDS

9f. Learn to recognize connotations and loaded words.

Semantics is the study of the meanings of words, changes in those meanings, and the *connotations* of words. When you are selecting the right words, you must be aware of their connotations. Connotations are the various emotions and associations that a word may suggest. A connotation is distinct from a word's *denotation,* which is the word's strict dictionary definition. Not all words have connotations. *Pen, paper, set, off,* and *listen,* as examples, suggest no particular emotions or associations. But such words as *skinny, slender, green, gray, intellectual,* and *egghead* do.

Connotations become attached to words through usage and common experience. The words *log cabin,* for example, refer literally to a dwelling made of logs. Suppose several people are looking at such a structure. One might think of it in terms of simplicity, strength, our pioneer past, and Abraham Lincoln. Another might describe it as a shack, associating it with poverty and unpleasantness. Yet another person might describe the dwelling as a "lodge," a word we associate with country retreats and hunting. Still another might see it as a "chalet," which suggests Switzerland and perhaps a ski resort.

Suppose you want to write about someone who is not working. You might refer to that person as "unemployed," "out of work," "at leisure," "at loose ends," or "between jobs." None of those terms have strongly negative connotations. If you described the person as a "freeloader" or a "moocher," however, your word choice would load your readers' feelings against the person.

The story is told that, during the Boer War, the Boers were described in the British press as "sneaking and skulking behind rocks and bushes." The British forces, when they finally learned from the Boers how to employ tactics suitable to veldt warfare, were described as "cleverly taking advantage of cover."

EXERCISE 6. **Recognizing Connotations.** The words in the following pairs have similar denotations, or dictionary definitions. Their connotations are different. Some differences in meaning are subtle; some are obvious. Which word in each pair has a positive connotation? Which suggests negative feelings? In a sentence, explain the distinctions between the words in the pair. In your sentence (or sentences), tell what emotions or associations are suggested by each word.

1. cautious / timorous
2. courageous / foolhardy
3. optimist / Pollyanna
4. hopeful / presumptive
5. lie / equivocate

6. concise / laconic
7. solemn / grim
8. guidance / manipulation
9. curious / nosy
10. freedom / license

EXERCISE 7. Defining Connotations. The names of animals frequently carry strong connotations, depending on the characteristics we
associate with them, whether or not those associations are based on
scientific evidence. Tell whether each of the following names would
have positive or negative connotations if applied to a person. What
mannerisms or habits of each animal account for the name's emotional
effect?

1. snake	3. swine	5. worm	7. bat	9. skunk
2. owl	4. lamb	6. toad	8. whale	10. cat

Loaded Words

Words or phrases that are heavily connotative are often referred to as
loaded words. Because such words can be used to "slant" writing, they
are often regarded with suspicion. Loaded words are often used in
commercials and advertisements, where the intelligent consumer recog-
nizes them as attempts to manipulate.

Connotation is an important element in our use of language,
particularly when we want to express our own attitude toward a subject
and possibly influence the attitude of our audience. Here, for example,
are reports on a trial from two newspapers with different points of view
about the defendant. Their biases are clearly shown in the way they
"slant" their descriptions of one day's testimony. The first newspaper's
account:

> Deathly silence prevailed this morning in the courtroom when in a
> monotone Halevy described in detail what he saw. The jurors listened
> transfixed to Halevy's story and the feeling among observers was that this
> was David Halevy's day.

This is the other newspaper's description:

> The atmosphere in the court was one of exhaustion when *Time*
> correspondent Halevy continued giving evidence and described the period
> of heavy bombing of Beirut. Three of the ten members of the jury fell asleep
> and even the judge, Abraham Sofaer, yawned just before the noon break.

EXERCISE 8. Recognizing Loaded Words. The sentences in each of the following pairs have more or less the same denotative meaning yet suggest different feelings toward the subject. Which words load the sentences positively? Which words load the sentence negatively? Can you explain the emotions or associations attached to the "loaded" words in each sentence?

1. Lenahan dines every evening at 7.
2. Lenahan eats every night at 7.
3. The President has been obstinate as a negotiator.
4. The President has been firm as a negotiator.
5. Armand is fastidious about commas.
6. Armand is a nitpicker about commas.
7. The Nets squandered their ten-point lead.
8. The Nets lost their ten-point lead.
9. The subway was filled with the aroma of perfume.
10. The subway was filled with the stench of perfume.

EXERCISE 9. Using Connotative Meanings. Write two descriptions of a room, a meal, or a game. In one paragraph, use words that give your sentences positive emotional weight. In the other, use words that will give your readers negative feelings about the subject.

COLLOQUIALISMS

9g. Avoid colloquialisms in formal writing.

A colloquial writing style is the most informal style. It uses *colloquialisms*—words, idioms, and expressions that are characteristic of spoken English but not acceptable in formal written English. Dictionaries usually label colloquial usage (Colloq.). This label does not indicate that the usage is nonstandard or slang. Many colloquialisms have acquired enough permanence in the language to be accepted in informal writing. Writers of short stories, dramas, personal essays, plays, and even poems often use colloquialisms to create realistic dialogue and a convincing "voice." The following extracts use colloquialisms effectively.

> The most useful thing I could do before this meeting today is to keel over. On the other hand, artists are keeling over by the thousands every day and nobody seems to pay the least attention.
>
> KURT VONNEGUT

> In the boondocks, we didn't wear shoes unless it was an absolute necessity.
>
> GEORGE GRIZZARD

> There were lots and lots of houses available. We heard this from a lady named Mrs. Black. . . . She took us to visit a house which would have been perfect for us and our books and our children, if there had been any plumbing.
>
> SHIRLEY JACKSON

> I used to get all revved up.
>
> PHILIP BOOTH—THE NEW YORKER

These writers have deliberately used colloquial language to give their language a contemporary informal tone or add humor. But if you were writing a report for your history teacher, you would not say that "President Lincoln *keeled over* after John Wilkes Booth fired his shot." You would say he "collapsed" or "slumped over."

If you were writing a report for a corporation, you would not propose expanding its business "into the *boondocks.*" Notice in this case how imprecise the colloquialism is. This is a characteristic of colloquial language and is one of the reasons it is not acceptable in formal writing. In your corporate report, you would have to say exactly where you were proposing the expansion. By "boondocks," do you mean the suburbs, the small towns nearby, or the farming area?

If you were writing a report on *The Glass Menagerie,* you would not say that Laura has "*lots and lots* of insecurities." You would say she has "several insecurities," or "many," or "two main insecurities."

If you were writing a letter to a prospective employer, you would not say you were "*all revved up* about this *big deal* job." You would say you were "very excited about this important job."

In formal writing, then—in reports for school, in business letters, in office memos—you should avoid colloquial language. In your own informal writing, colloquialisms are acceptable as long as they express your meaning precisely.

EXERCISE 10. Replacing Colloquialisms with Formal Diction. Rewrite each of the following sentences, replacing each colloquial expression with precise formal diction. If you have any questions about which words or phrases are colloquial, check the dictionary.

1. Lillian has gobs of energy.
2. Ernesto says he has the stuff to be class president.
3. The *News* has pegged McNaughton as a man of action.

4. As an actress, Tina can deliver the goods.
5. Ellsworth fell for the guy's phony sales pitch.
6. The famous miser Silas Marner salted away his money for years.
7. The plan to make Madeline a beauty didn't pan out.
8. The salesman racked up a large bonus.
9. At 10:00 P.M. the boss called it a day.
10. Fred wore a stupid hat to the movie.

SLANG

9h. Avoid slang in formal writing.

Slang consists of new words, or old words in new uses, that are vivid and colorful. High-school and college students enjoy adopting the latest slang. Most slang is short-lived. It enjoys a brief popularity and then is forgotten. For that reason, it is difficult to compile an illustrative list of slang terms that will be meaningful even a year later. The expressions in the following list were current a short while ago. How many of them do you recognize? Are any of them still in use?

SLANG

cool it	it's not my bag
groovy	heavy
uptight	nuts (crazy)
it's a drag	oddball
goof off	square
dig it	far out
cop out	bummer
off the wall	hang-up
bug off	weirdo
lousy	awesome

Occasionally a slang expression makes its way up the usage ladder and becomes acceptable even in formal writing, whereupon, of course, it is no longer slang. Slang should rarely be used in writing, and then only for a special purpose, as to reproduce dialogue. Although dictionaries label words *informal* or *slang,* you cannot rely on their arbitrarily drawn distinctions as a means of deciding whether a word is appropriate to your composition. A word that does not fit the general *tone* of your composition should not be used, regardless of its dictionary label.

The following sentences were taken from formal compositions. Note how inappropriate the italicized words are.

In any eighth-grade classroom where *kids* of the same chronological age are grouped together, we expect to find a physiological age range of six or seven years.

There is a grave danger that we may expose far too many students of only medium ability to the long course of professional study in our universities. The employment situation in some professional areas, we must admit, is *not so hot.*

Dickens' *bag* was to reveal the social evils of the day so that they could be destroyed one by one.

EXERCISE 11. Identifying Slang or Informal Language. Point out the words and expressions in the following passage that are slang or so informal as to be inappropriate to the general tone.

While it is true that the students in the top ten percent of any grade are capable of doing good work in the grade above them, to undertake a general upward transfer of these students would produce more socially maladjusted kids than you could shake a stick at. Efforts to meet the problem by cutting out the arbitrary division of a school into grades have been successful in small schools, where the need to classify and control has not been great and where parents couldn't care less what grade their children are in. Today the schools that allow children to go at their own speed, with a child doing sixth-grade work in one subject and third- or fourth-grade work in another, are considered pretty far out. Eventually this method of school organization may become general practice.

CLICHÉS

9i. Avoid clichés in formal writing.

A *cliché* is an expression so overused that it has become dull and nearly meaningless. The term comes from a French word for a plate used in printing. The same plate is used to make hundreds or thousands of impressions, all of them, of course, exactly alike. In the same sense, clichés are expressions used over and over again, lacking originality.

There are thousands of clichés in the English language. Many of them are figures of speech—metaphors, similes, or personifications. Many are hyperboles—exaggerations used for special effect. The expressions may have been considered original and forceful or amusing at one time, but overuse has dulled their effect. Here are three clichés based on figurative language:

cold as ice
fly off the handle
miss the boat

To say someone "flies off the handle" was once an original way of describing an erratic temper. The person with the temper might lose control and cause an uproar, just as an axe-head might cause a disturbance if it comes loose and flies off the handle when the tool is swung. To say someone "missed the boat" was once an original way of describing a person who missed out on a rewarding event or opportunity, just as a person who actually missed a boat would be deprived of a cruise.

Some clichés come to us so naturally that we use them without thinking. That is the point. They offer handy, ready-made comparisons and expressions. They help us avoid having to be original. In fact, clichés are so handy that it is often difficult to find fresh terms to replace them. We should try, nonetheless.

EXERCISE 12. Recognizing Clichés.   The following interview with a cliché expert mocks our overuse of clichés. Read it and answer the questions that follow.

Q: You mean you get a handsome salary?

A: I prefer to call it a princely stipend. You know what kind of coin I'm paid in?

Q: No. What?

A: Coin of the realm. Not that I give a hoot for money. You know how I refer to money?

Q: As the root of all evil?

A: No, but you have a talking point there. I call it lucre—filthy lucre.

Q: On the whole, you seem to have a pretty good time, Mr. Arbuthnot.

A: Oh, I'm not complaining. I'm as snug as a bug in a rug. I'm clear as crystal—when I'm not dull as dishwater. I'm cool as a cucumber, quick as a flash, fresh as a daisy, pleased as Punch, good as my word, regular as clockwork, and I suppose at the end of my declining years, when I'm gathered to my ancestors, I'll be dead as a doornail.

Q: *Eh bien! C'est la vie!*

A: *Mais oui, mon vieux.* I manage, I'm the glass of fashion and the mold of form. I have a finger in every pie, all except this finger. I use it for pointing with scorn. When I go in for malice, it is always malice aforethought. My nods are significant. My offers are standing. I am at cross-purposes and in dire straits. My motives are ulterior, my circles are vicious, my retainers are faithful, and my hopefuls are young. My suspicions are sneaking, my glee is fiendish, my stories are likely. I am drunk.

Q: Drunk?
A: Yes, with power. . .

FRANK SULLIVAN

1. Identify at least five clichés in the interview that are based on figures of speech.
2. Rewrite a portion of the interview, replacing the clichés. Is it always clear what the cliché expert is saying?
3. Answer one of the interviewer's questions with a litany of clichés of your own.

EXERCISE 13. Replacing Clichés with Fresh Comparisons or Descriptions. Each of the following sentences contains a cliché based on a figure of speech. Eliminate the cliché and replace it with a fresh comparison or description of your own. (The directions in parentheses might help.)

1. Mildred is as straight as an arrow. (Describe Mildred's character without the cliché.)
2. The typist is as busy as a bee. (Describe the typist's movements without the cliché.)
3. Uncle Morty is as old as the hills. (Describe Uncle Morty so the reader gets a visual sense of his age without the cliché.)
4. The goalie is as tough as nails. (Describe the goalie's abilities and character, suggesting toughness, without the cliché.)
5. Uriah's hand feels as cold as ice. (Describe Uriah's handshake without the cliché.)

JARGON

9j. Avoid jargon in formal writing.

Jargon can have two meanings. First, it can refer to the specialized language of a particular group of people who do the same work or who have the same interests. Military personnel, computer users, editors, truck drivers, doctors, astronauts, and baseball players all have their own jargon. A waiter uses jargon when he calls into the kitchen, "Two eggs, wreck 'em!" An actress uses theater jargon when she says to a colleague going on stage, "Break a leg!" (In theater, this means "Good luck!") A sportswriter uses jargon in writing, "Carl Furillo popped out to shortstop."

In all these cases, jargon is perfectly acceptable. But jargon in a second sense is not acceptable in any kind of writing. That's when it consists of language that is incoherent and cumbersome, obscuring meaning rather than clarifying. This kind of jargon uses unnecessarily long and complicated words, often of Latin origin, as well as too many words to express a thought. Thus, this kind of jargon always delivers much less meaning than it seems to promise.

Here is a famous little proverb restated in jargon:

> A plethora of culinary specialists has a deleterious effect upon the quality of purees, consommés, and other soluble pabula.

In plain English this says:

> Too many cooks spoil the broth.

Can you translate the following jargon into the plain English of the original proverb?

> A mobile section of petrified matter agglomerates no bryophytes.

At times, a writer or speaker will use jargon deliberately to obscure an unpleasant meaning. He or she replaces a truth with a euphemism. Thus, people who steal computer programs are not called robbers or cheats but "pirates." Government bureaucrats refer to increased taxes as "revenue enhancement." A nuclear power plant official speaks of an "energetic disassembly" instead of an explosion, "rapid oxidation" instead of a fire, and of a "normal aberration" instead of a reactor accident. One state no longer has a Death Row; it has a "capital sentences unit." A large corporation recently circulated a memo that referred to "eliminating redundancies in the human resource area," instead of referring to layoffs or firing people.

Such pompous language is often called *gobbledygook,* a word coined by a United States Representative who had heard enough of such "official talk" in Congress. The origin of the word *jargon* also points to the emptiness of such use of language. The word is ultimately of "echoic" origin, meaning it reproduces a particular sound in nature. *Jargon* comes from a Middle French word meaning "a chattering of birds."

EXERCISE 14. Identifying Examples of Poor Diction.   The following speech is a parody of the kind of speech a modern government official might write, if he or she were composing the Gettysburg Address today. That address, of course, is one of the greatest of all American speeches. It was delivered by President Abraham Lincoln at the dedication of the Soldiers' National Cemetery on November 19, 1863. The parodist's intent is not to mock the Gettysburg Address, but to contrast Lincoln's effective, eloquent diction with the kind of empty talk used by many politicians. Find the parody's examples of the misuses of diction that have been pointed out in this chapter—imprecise words, mixed idioms and metaphors, colloquialisms that are out of place in a formal speech, clichés, and jargon. Next to each example, write the simple, eloquent words used by Lincoln.

I haven't checked these figures but 87 years ago, I think it was, a number of individuals organized a governmental set-up here in this country, I believe it covered certain Eastern areas, with this idea they were following up based on a sort of national independence arrangement and the program that every individual is just as good as every other individual. Well, now, of course, we are dealing with this big difference of opinion, civil disturbance you might say, although I don't like to appear to take sides or name any individuals, and the point is naturally to check up, by actual experience in the field, to see whether any governmental set-up with a basis like the one I was mentioning has any validity and find out whether that dedication by those early individuals will pay off in lasting values and things of that kind.

Well, here we are, at the scene where one of these disturbances between different sides got going. We want to pay our tribute to those loved ones, those departed individuals who made the supreme sacrifice here on the basis of their opinions about how this thing ought to be handled. And I would say this. It is absolutely in order to do this.

But if you look at the over-all picture of this, we can't pay any tribute—we can't sanctify this area, you might say—we can't hallow according to whatever individual creeds or faiths or sort of religious outlooks are involved like I said about this particular area. It was those individuals themselves, including the enlisted men, very brave individuals, who have given this religious character to the area. The way I see it, the rest of the world will not remember any statements issued here but it will never forget how these men put their shoulders to the wheel and carried this idea down the fairway.

Now frankly, our job, the living individuals' job here, is to pick up the burden and sink the putt they made these big efforts here for. It is our job to get on with the assignment—and from these deceased fine individuals to take extra inspiration, you could call it, for the same theories about the set-up for which they made such a big contribution. We have to make up our minds right here and now, as I see it, that they didn't put out all that blood, perspiration and—well—that they didn't just make a dry run here, and that all of us here, under God, that is, the God of our choice, shall beef up this idea about freedom and liberty and those kind of arrangements, and that government of all individuals, by all individuals and for the individuals, shall not pass out of the world-picture.

OLIVER JENSEN

PURPOSE, TONE, MOOD, AND DICTION

9k. Adjust your diction to control purpose, tone, and mood.

Writers choose diction not only to suit their audiences but also to suit their purposes. The most common purpose of writing is probably to give information (Chapter 3). Other purposes may be descriptive or narrative (Chapter 2) or persuasive (Chapter 5). Revealing a particular tone or mood may also be part of a writer's purpose.

Tone and Mood

Tone refers to the attitude the writer takes toward his subject. It can always be described by an adjective: *formal, informal, critical, approving, sarcastic, ironic, nostalgic, sad, angry, sentimental, bitter, strident, tongue-in-cheek, mocking, tender, horrific,* and so on. Mood is the atmosphere the writer creates. Mood is also described by adjectives.

Tone or Mood of Horror

Suppose you are telling about a particular setting and wish to convey a tone of horror. Paul Theroux does just that in this passage describing a tree in Malaysia called "The Midnight Horror." (The corolla are the petals of the tree's flowers.)

> During the day the tree looked comic, a tall simple pole like an enormous coatrack, with big leaves that looked like branches—but there were very few of them. It was covered with knobs, stark black things; and around the base of the trunk there were always fragments of leaves that looked like shattered bones, but not human bones.
>
> At night the tree was different, not comic at all. It was Ladysmith who showed me the underlined passage in his copy of Professor Corner's *Wayside Trees of Malaya.* Below the entry for *Oroxylum indicum* it read, "Botanically, it is the sole representative of its kind; aesthetically, it is monstrous. . . . The corolla begins to open about 10 P.M., when the tumid, wrinkled lips part and the harsh odor escapes from them. By midnight, the lurid mouth gapes widely and is filled with stink. . . . The flowers are pollinated by bats which are attracted by the smell and, holding to the fleshy corolla with the claws on their wings, thrust their noses into its throat; scratches, as of bats, can be seen on the fallen leaves the next morning. . . ."
>
> PAUL THEROUX

Note the specific words that communicate a sense of horror: stark black things; leaves that look like nonhuman bones; monstrous; tumid, wrinkled lips; harsh odor; lurid mouth; stink; bats. This paragraph is from the opening of a horror story and it does, in fact, set the tone for the rest of the story's events.

EXERCISE 15. Using Diction to Control Tone. Write a paragraph describing Theroux's tree, but change the diction so that your tone is different. In your own paragraph, describe the tree in words that make it seem beautiful and mysterious, not disgusting. You can change any detail you wish. Do not worry about being scientifically accurate.

Tone or Mood of Nostalgia

If you wanted to suggest a tone of nostalgia, you would choose words that suggest a fondness for things past. Eudora Welty does that in this passage describing a store she remembers from her childhood. Notice that she uses sensory diction, as Theroux does, but she uses words that evoke *pleasant* sensations.

> Running in out of the sun, you met what seemed total obscurity inside. There were almost tangible smells—licorice recently sucked in a child's cheek, dill-pickle brine that had leaked through a paper sack in a fresh trail across the wooden floor, ammonia-loaded ice that had been hoisted from wet croker sacks and slammed into the icebox with its sweet butter at the door, and perhaps the smell of still-untrapped mice.
>
> Then through the motes of cracker dust, cornmeal dust, the Gold Dust of the Gold Dust Twins that the floor had been swept out with, the realities emerged. Shelves climbed to high reach all the way around, set out with not too much of any one thing but a lot of things—lard, molasses, vinegar, starch, matches, kerosene, Octagon soap (about a year's worth of octagon-shaped coupons cut out and saved brought a signet ring addressed to you in the mail. Furthermore, when the postman arrived at your door, he blew a whistle). It was up to you to remember what you came for, while your eye traveled from cans of sardines to ice cream salt to harmonicas to flypaper (over your head, batting around on a thread beneath the blades of the ceiling fan, stuck with its testimonial catch).
>
> Its confusion may have been in the eye of its beholder. Enchantment is cast upon you by all those things you weren't supposed to have need for, it lures you close to wooden tops you'd outgrown, boy's marbles and agates in little net pouches, small rubber balls that wouldn't bounce straight, frazzly kite-string, clay bubble-pipes that would snap off in your teeth, the stiffest scissors. You could contemplate those long narrow boxes of sparklers gathering dust while you waited for it to be the Fourth of July or Christmas, and noisemakers in the shape of tin frogs for somebody's birthday party you hadn't been invited to yet, and see that they were all marvelous.
>
> EUDORA WELTY

EXERCISE 16. Using Diction to Control Tone. Write a paragraph describing Welty's little store, but change the diction so that your tone is not nostalgic, but frightened and uneasy.

Conveying Different Tones

Here are two writers, both of whom are writing about explorers. One uses an ironic, even sarcastic, tone to make us laugh at the incredible hardships explorers seem to bring on themselves. The other is serious and admiring. Which is which? Find words that help convey each writer's tone.

> Above all others, the perseverance of La Salle in his search for the mouth of the Mississippi was unsurpassed. While preparing in Quebec, he mastered eight Indian languages. From then on he suffered accidents, betrayals, desertions, losses of men and provisions, fever and snow blindness, the hostility and intrigues of rivals who incited the Indians against him and plotted to ambush or poison him. He was truly pursued, as Francis Parkman wrote, by "a demon of havoc." Paddling through heavy waves in a storm over Lake Ontario, he waded through freezing surf to beach the canoes each night, and lost guns and baggage when a canoe was swamped and sank. To lay the foundations of a fort above Niagara, frozen ground had to be thawed by boiling water. When the fort was at last built, La Salle christened it Crèvecoeur—that is, Heartbreak. It earned the name when in his absence it was plundered and deserted by its half-starved mutinous garrison. Farther on, a friendly Indian village, intended as a destination, was found laid waste by the Iroquois with only charred stakes stuck with skulls standing among the ashes, while wolves and buzzards prowled through the remains.
>
> When at last, after four months' hazardous journey down the Great River, La Salle reached the sea, he formally took possession in the name of Louis XIV of all the country from the river's mouth to its source and of its tributaries—that is, of the vast basin of the Mississippi from the Rockies to the Appalachians—and named it Louisiana. The validity of the claim, which seems so hollow to us (though successful in its own time), is not the point. What counts is the conquest of fearful adversity by one man's extraordinary exertions and inflexible will.
>
> BARBARA TUCHMAN

> Cherry-Garrard insists that one morning when he peeped out of the tent his clothing froze instantly, trapping his head in that position. He claims that for the next several hours he had to pull the sledge with his head screwed around at an angle. Now this is ridiculous. This is the sort of thing you see in a Hollywood cartoon, but our Oxford egg-collector is no humorist. Presumably it happened.

At last they got to the penguin rookery and after zoologist Wilson had completed his research they stole five eggs and started home. En route Cherry-Garrard broke two of these precious eggs. He was carrying them inside his mittens and he explains simply that they "burst." Maybe. Maybe it happened. But eggs seldom break unless they have been rudely handled. Nevertheless, he tells us without further clarification, his eggs "burst." All right, let it go. He emptied one mitten but kept the broken egg in the other because he thought that when they stopped to eat he would pour it into the cooker. For some reason he neglected to do this, "but on the return journey I had my mitts far more easily thawed out . . . and I believe the grease in the egg did them good." . . .

Two days after the tea vanished the weather improved enough for them to prepare a meal—tea and pemmican flavored with burnt seal blubber, penguin feathers, and hair from the sleeping bags. . . .

Three of the five eggs at last reached the Natural History Museum in London where they were accepted and studied with no particular excitement. The value of this trip, therefore, depends on your interpretation. One biographer commented that it had drawn Cherry-Garrard and his companions together in permanent spiritual bondage—which makes it sound almost worthwhile. Another said that few men ever have absorbed so much punishment for the sake of adding such an insignificant brick to the edifice of knowledge. In other words the rookery had as much meaning, or as little, as the Pole itself.

EVAN CONNELL

EXERCISE 17. Changing Diction to Change Tone. Rewrite Connell's account of the explorers at the Pole who were searching for the penguin eggs. This time, make the account admiring in tone.

CHAPTER 9 WRITING REVIEW

Using Effective Diction. This assignment requires you to express yourself on one of the following statements—in two different ways. First, write a paragraph using formal diction and a serious, formal tone. Then write a paragraph using informal diction and an informal tone —sarcastic, angry, mocking, light-hearted, comic, relaxed.

1. Education involves unlearning more than learning.
2. Discipline and creativity do not go hand in hand.
3. It is much easier to destroy something than to create it.

PICTURE ᵀ ᴴ ᴱ POSSIBILITIES:

IDEAS FOR WRITING

Pictures have the power to prompt the memory, stir the emotions, and spark the imagination. In this section you will learn how to use pictures as a powerful source of ideas for writing.

Probing the Picture

You could use this picture, which shows one of the eight staircases in the recently restored Old Executive Office Building in Washington, D.C., to write an objective **description.** Focusing on the composition of the picture, you could ask questions such as *Which element of the picture do I notice first? In which direction do my eyes then move? What lines, shapes, and patterns dominate the picture? How are these diverse elements unified by the angle from which the picture was taken?*

Another possibility would be to use the picture as a source of ideas for a **persuasive** composition incorporating **exposition.** To find possible debatable issues, you could think about the restoration of a historic building in your own city, county, or state, asking questions such as *Should the building be restored? Should it be demolished? Should the government pay for the restoration? Should the people who live in the area contribute to a fund established to pay for the restoration?* You could then use exposition to build your argument, gathering reasons and evidence by observing, by reading newspaper and historical-society archives, and by interviewing local architects and engineers.

Writing Activities

Using the steps of the writing process, complete one of the following activities.

- Write an objective description of the picture.
- Write a persuasive composition on one of the issues suggested above or on another issue the picture suggests, using exposition to build your argument.

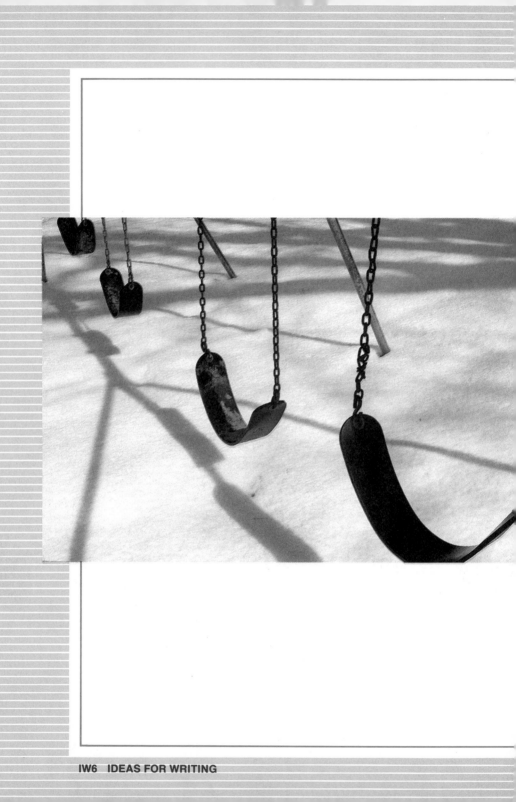

Probing the Picture

This picture could serve as the starting point for a personal **narrative.** On your own or with a group of your classmates, you could brainstorm to identify events you recall as you think about the picture. Once you had selected an experience that you felt comfortable sharing with your classmates, you could use brainstorming or clustering to gather narrative and descriptive details that would answer questions such as *Who took part in or witnessed the event? When and where did the event take place? Why did the experience make a lasting impression on me? What did I learn from it? How did I feel about it at the time? How do I feel about it now?*

Another approach would be to write a **poem** about a subject the scene suggests. You could begin by brainstorming on the first word or phrase that comes to mind when you look at the picture. Using the associations you discover, you could then generate sensory details and vivid images by asking questions such as *What sounds do I hear as I approach the playground? As I swing high into the air? As I slow the swing and jump off? How do my hands feel as I grip the chains of the swing? What sensation does riding on the swing create? What do the long shadows cast by the swings make me think of? With what significant event in my life could I compare the deserted playground?*

Writing Activities

Using the steps of the writing process, complete one of the following activities.

- Use the picture to write a personal narrative.
- Write a free-verse poem on a subject the picture suggests.

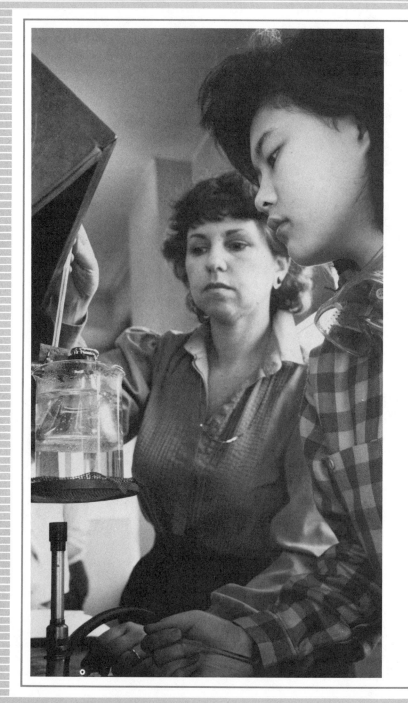

Probing the Picture

One way to use this picture of a laboratory experiment would be to analyze the subject "chemistry" in order to find topics for an **expository** composition. Using the *point-of-view questions* would then help you research the topic you choose. For example, for the topic "career opportunities in chemistry" you might develop questions such as *How much education is required to become a chemist? Where are chemists employed? What kinds of work do chemists do in industry? In government? In education? In the armed services?* Suppose the experiment in the picture deals with radon. For the topic "radon" you might ask *What is radon? What are its properties? How is it similar to and different from the other inert gases? How is it used? What health hazards does it pose?*

You could instead use the picture to generate ideas for a **persuasive** composition. Thinking about the relationship between the people and the setting, you could brainstorm to develop debatable issues such as *Should more women pursue careers in science? Should high school students be required to take four years of science? Should physics be a prerequisite for chemistry? Should the school board allocate additional money for improving the chemistry lab at your school?*

Writing Activities

Using the steps of the writing process, complete one of the following activities.
- Write an expository composition on a topic you find by limiting the subject "chemistry."
- Write a persuasive composition on one of the issues suggested above or on another issue the picture suggests.

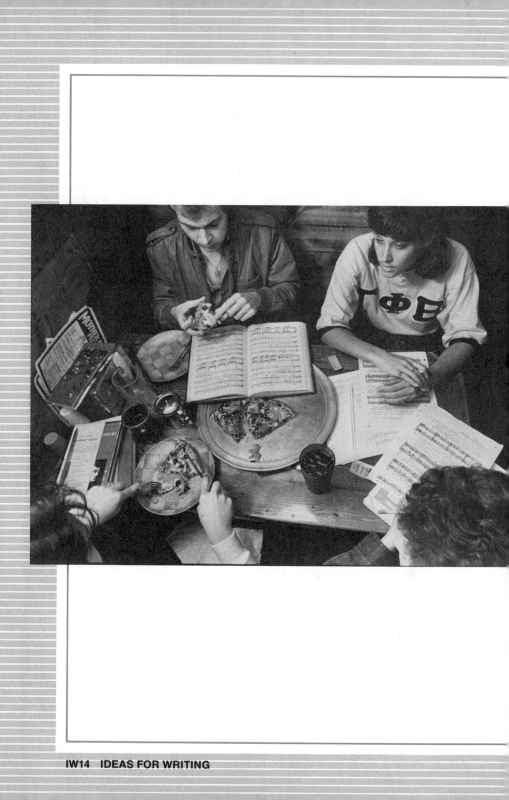

Probing Pictures to Discover Writing Ideas

The following questions will help you use any picture to discover ideas for writing.

1. What do I find most interesting in this picture? What specific idea does it suggest?
2. For what purpose could I use this idea?
3. What elements dominate the picture? What do those elements have in common? How has the photographer unified them?
4. Would using the 5 *W-How?* questions help me gather information to use?
5. What might have happened just before or just after the picture was taken? What might the person(s) have said?
6. What main impression does the picture create?
7. What concrete and sensory details do I observe in the picture? What details do I imagine when I think of myself as being in the scene or in a similar scene I remember?
8. Could I explain how to make or do what the picture shows?
9. Could I give information about what the picture shows by defining it, tracing its history, or showing how it is related to others of its kind?
10. What debatable issues does the combination of elements in the picture suggest?

On Your Own

Using any picture you have not written about, write a paper for your classmates. You may choose the form in which you will write and the purpose you want to achieve. Follow the steps of the writing process.

PART TWO

COMPOSITION:
Writing and Revising Sentences

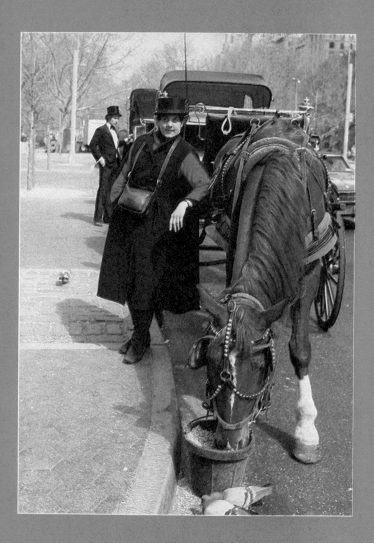

CHAPTER 10

Sentence Completeness

FRAGMENTS AND RUN-ON SENTENCES

Two kinds of sentence errors are all too common: fragments and run-on sentences. The first is the writing of only part of a sentence, a *fragment*, as though it were a whole sentence, with a capital letter and a period. The second is the writing of two or more sentences as though they were one sentence. The writer mistakenly uses a comma, or no punctuation at all, between the sentences. You may think of these two sentence errors as opposites. The fragment is not complete; the run-on sentence is more than complete.

SENTENCE FRAGMENTS

A group of words is a complete sentence when it has a subject and a verb and expresses a complete thought.

COMPLETE   After the flood the barn roof lay in the yard.
INCOMPLETE   After the flood the barn roof in the yard
INCOMPLETE   After the flood the barn roof lying in the yard

Because they lack a verb, the last two examples do not express a complete thought. Words ending in *-ing*, like *lying*, are not verbs when they are used alone. To serve as the verb in a sentence, such words need a *helping verb* to form a verb phrase (see page 421).

NO VERB   After the flood the barn roof lying in the yard

VERB PHRASE   After the flood the barn roof **was lying** in the yard.

10a. A *sentence fragment* is a group of words that does not express a complete thought. Since it is part of a sentence, it should not be allowed to stand by itself.

The Phrase Fragment

A phrase is a group of words acting as a single part of speech and not containing a verb and its subject.

There are many kinds of phrases (participial, gerund, appositive, prepositional, infinitive), but regardless of their kind, they all have one important characteristic—they are parts of a sentence and must never be separated from the sentence in which they belong. When a phrase is incorrectly allowed to stand by itself, it is a fragment.

Study the ways in which the unattached phrase fragments in the following examples are corrected.

FRAGMENT   Last Saturday I saw Gloria. Riding her new ten-speed bicycle. [This participial phrase fragment modifies the word *Gloria.* It should be included in the sentence with the word it modifies.]

FRAGMENT CORRECTED   Last Saturday I saw Gloria **riding her new ten-speed bicycle.**

FRAGMENT   We pitched our tent on the north side of the lake. At the edge of a grove of pine trees. [This prepositional phrase fragment modifies the verb *pitched* and belongs in the sentence.]

FRAGMENT CORRECTED   We pitched our tent on the north side of the lake **at the edge of a grove of pine trees.**

FRAGMENT   My parents finally gave me permission. To go with Gail to the game at West Point. [Here, an infinitive phrase fragment has been separated from the word *permission,* which it explains.]

FRAGMENT CORRECTED   My parents finally gave me permission **to go with Gail to the game at West Point.**

FRAGMENT   Aunt Deborah came bearing gifts. A wristwatch for Jean and a ring for me. [This appositive phrase fragment belongs in the sentence preceding it, separated by a comma from *gifts,* the word to which it refers.]

FRAGMENT CORRECTED   Aunt Deborah came bearing gifts, **a wristwatch for Jean and a ring for me.**

The Subordinate Clause Fragment

Another type of fragment is the subordinate clause that is incorrectly separated from the sentence in which it belongs. A clause is a group of words containing a subject and predicate and used as a part of a sentence. A subordinate clause does not express a complete thought and should not stand alone.

FRAGMENT   The orchestra played "A Night in the Tropics." Which Louis Gottschalk wrote in 1859.

FRAGMENT CORRECTED   The orchestra played "A Night in the Tropics," which Louis Gottschalk wrote in 1859.

10b. Do not separate a phrase or a subordinate clause from the sentence of which it is a part.

EXERCISE 1. Revising to Eliminate Fragments. Some of the items in this exercise consist of one or two completed sentences; others contain sentence fragments. Number your paper 1–10. If all the parts of an item are complete sentences, write *C*. If an item contains a fragment, revise it to include the fragment in the sentence.

1. Elizabeth Blackwell was born in 1821. And died in 1910.
2. When, in 1832, her parents could no longer tolerate the social and political situation in Bristol, England. They immigrated with their eight children to New York.
3. A few years later Elizabeth established a school for girls. Feeling depressed by the economic plight of her family.
4. A woman friend, dying of cancer, suggested that Elizabeth, who loved to study, become a doctor. At first, Elizabeth totally rejected this suggestion.
5. In spite of herself, the idea of being a doctor plagued Elizabeth. Leading her to inquire into the possibility of a woman studying medicine.
6. When told that it would be impossible for a woman to become a doctor, she became determined to follow her friend's advice. Not certain how she should proceed against the forces of prejudice.

7. Finally, in 1847 and after many rejections, the Medical Institution of Geneva College in northern New York State accepted Elizabeth Blackwell. Now known as Hobart College.

8. She graduated in 1849 at the head of her class. A young woman convinced that she was right and determined to change ideas about education.

9. She was not content with being the first woman in the United States to gain an M.D. degree from a medical school. Elizabeth Blackwell spent the next two years of her life doing graduate work in Europe.

10. In 1857 Elizabeth Blackwell established the New York Infirmary for Indigent Women and Children, a hospital staffed by women. She decided to open the hospital on May 12, the birthday of her friend Florence Nightingale.

RUN-ON SENTENCES

When a comma (instead of a period, a semicolon, or a conjunction) is used between two complete sentences, the result is a *run-on sentence*. One sentence is permitted to "run on" into the next.

Inexperienced writers make this type of sentence error more often than the fragment error. Usually it results from carelessness in punctuation rather than from lack of understanding. Because the error involves misusing a comma—to separate sentences—it is sometimes referred to as a "comma fault." A worse, but less common, kind of run-on sentence results from omitting all punctuation between sentences.

10c. Avoid the run-on sentence. Do not use a comma between sentences. Do not omit punctuation at the end of a sentence.

RUN-ON SENTENCE   Choosing a camera is difficult, there are many on the market.

These two sentences should be either separated by a period or joined into one sentence by a conjunction or a semicolon. There are four ways of correcting the error:

1. Choosing a camera is difficult. There are many on the market.
2. Choosing a camera is difficult, **for** there are many on the market.
3. Choosing a camera is difficult **because** there are many on the market.
4. Choosing a camera is difficult; there are many on the market.

☞ NOTE Do not be surprised, now that you know to avoid using sentence fragments and run-on sentences, if you occasionally find them in the best newspapers and magazines. To create a particular effect, professional writers do at times write fragments and use the comma between sentences. Leave this use of the comma and the fragment to the experienced judgment of the professional.

EXERCISE 2. Revising Run-on Sentences.   The items in this exercise are run-on sentences. Write the final word in the first sentence in each item and follow it with the first few words of the second sentence. Indicate how you would eliminate the faulty comma: for example, a semicolon, a conjunction, a period and a capital letter. Do not be satisfied with using a period and a capital letter in every case; to clarify the relationship between ideas, some of the items should be corrected in other ways.

EXAMPLE 1. Flo didn't hear about the party until Thursday, she had to change her plans.
1. *Thursday; therefore she had . . .*

1. In social studies this year we are studying about ways to solve our major national problems, so far we have covered poverty, unemployment, inflation, and pollution.
2. We have a pet lovebird at home, its call is as harsh and shrill as the screech of chalk on the chalkboard.
3. Lovebirds are comical creatures, they are always busy rearranging objects in their cage.
4. Ynes Mexia, the botanical explorer, discovered rare tropical plants on her expeditions to Mexico and South America, these discoveries were of great value to science.
5. Juan took an art elective and discovered he had talent, now he spends his afternoons in the art room.
6. At an advanced age she began to write the story of her colorful life, at least she thought her life had been colorful.
7. The astounding scientific developments of one generation are accepted commonplaces in the next generation, the computer and the cassette recorder, for instance, are taken for granted today.
8. A new club is being formed for the study of social behavior, instead of just reading, students will do research and conduct interviews.

9. A large suggestion box has been placed in the hall just outside the principal's office, students can, by this means, express their pet peeves about the school, they should not sign their names.
10. First try to do the work by yourself, if you can't do it, ask for help.

EXERCISE 3. Revising to Eliminate Sentence Fragments and Run-on Sentences. The following exercise contains sentence fragments and run-on sentences. Prepare to explain to the class how you would eliminate the sentence errors.

1. I have never known anyone who was a better worker than Paula. Who always did her homework in half the time I took, she usually had it done twice as well, too.
2. I asked Paula to help me with my math once. When I was particularly desperate, I hadn't been getting good grades for several weeks.
3. Mr. Rehman urges all musicians to continue to study their instruments in high school. Because he knows that as they get busier and busier, many students stop taking lessons, sports and other activities cut in on their practice time.
4. A mammoth crane was brought here to lift into place the steel girders. Huge orange-colored beams that were easily set into place. Almost as though they were matchsticks.
5. Everyone was asking me about Stacey. Where she was and what she was doing, wild rumors had been circulating.
6. The city's water supply has been threatened. Very little rain or snow having fallen during the past weeks.
7. I learned to like poetry when I read Kipling, his poems appealed to me. Because of their strong rhythm and their rhyme.
8. I have learned to recognize several kinds of customers. Especially the kind that likes to argue about the merchandise, when I see one of these coming, I duck out of sight.
9. Women's colleges were established in America in the nineteenth century. During the Victorian period. When girls were considered frail flowers to be kept safe and separate.
10. Audiences appeared to enjoy the play, the reviews in the papers, however, were unfavorable.

CHAPTER 11

Coordination and Subordination

RELATIONSHIPS BETWEEN IDEAS IN A SENTENCE

COORDINATE IDEAS

When a sentence contains more than one idea, the ideas may be equal in rank or unequal in rank. Ideas that are equal in rank are *coordinate*. (*Co-* means "equal"; *-ordinate* means "ordered" or "ranked.")

COORDINATE IDEAS   Mrs. Carter is an architect, **and** Mrs. Murphy is a lawyer.
We tried everything we could, **but** nothing worked.

The writer of the preceding sentences considered the two ideas in each sentence of equal rank; he gave them equal emphasis by expressing them in independent clauses. The clauses are coordinate clauses.

Clear Relationship Between Coordinate Ideas

The relationship between coordinate ideas is made clear by the word used to connect the two ideas. Different connectives express different relationships. The common kinds of relationship between coordinate clauses are *addition, contrast, choice,* and *result.*

Addition

The following connectives indicate that what follows is supplementary to what precedes.

EXAMPLES I wrote to her, **and** she wrote to me.

I like to get letters; **besides,** hers are amusing.

also	furthermore	besides	moreover
and	likewise	both . . . and	then

Contrast

The following connectives introduce an idea that in some way conflicts or contrasts with what has gone before.

EXAMPLES I wrote to her, **but** she did not write to me.

We are close friends; **nevertheless,** I am angry with her.

but	still	nevertheless
however	yet	

Choice

The following connectives introduce an alternate possibility.

EXAMPLES You write to her, **or** I will write to her.

You write to her; **otherwise,** I will not write to you.

either . . . or	or, nor
neither . . . nor	otherwise

Result

The following connectives state a result or consequence of the preceding statement.

EXAMPLE I wrote to her; **therefore** she wrote to me.

accordingly	hence
consequently	therefore

11a. Make clear the relationship between the ideas in coordinate clauses by using connectives that express the relationship exactly.

A good writer chooses connectives carefully, making certain that they will express exactly the relationship intended between the ideas in the sentence.

If the wrong connective is used, the relationship between the ideas will not be clear. The connectives in the following *not-clear* sentences were poorly chosen.

NOT CLEAR Mr. Bothwell took a vacation, and his health did not improve.

CLEAR Mr. Bothwell took a vacation, **but** his health did not improve.
[contrast]

NOT CLEAR The veterans spent a year in the hospital, but they emerged entirely well.

CLEAR The veterans spent a year in the hospital; **consequently,** they emerged entirely well. [result]

☞ NOTE When used to join coordinate clauses, the words *and, but, yet, or,* and *nor* are usually preceded by a comma.

When used to join coordinate clauses, the words *besides, likewise, furthermore, moreover, however, nevertheless, otherwise, consequently, therefore, hence,* and *accordingly* are usually preceded by a semicolon.

EXERCISE 1. Using Appropriate Connectives. Number your paper 1–10. Determine the logical relationship between the two clauses in each sentence, and write after the proper number what this relationship is: *addition, contrast, choice,* or *result.* Then write an appropriate connective from the preceding lists—the word which will make unmistakably clear the relationship between clauses. Give the correct punctuation mark with each connective.

EXAMPLE 1. The demand exceeded the supply   prices remained the same.
1. *contrast ; nevertheless*

1. The students were dismissed at one o'clock   nobody went home.
2. Bea was seriously injured in yesterday's practice   she will not be able to play in the game today.
3. Jimmy played right end   I played left end on the varsity.
4. Deliver the shipment by Friday   I will cancel my order!
5. Math is my hardest subject   I have never failed a math test.
6. In an auditorium of this size, you must speak louder   your audience will not be able to hear you.
7. This magazine publishes the best literary criticism   it is a financial failure.
8. The American economy has long depended on a high level of military spending   some people fear the economic consequences of ending the arms race.
9. The oil burner had stopped during the night   the house was cold when we awoke.
10. We had heard the assignment   we hadn't understood it.

SUBORDINATE IDEAS

When ideas in a sentence are unequal in rank, the ideas of lower rank are subordinate. (*Sub-* means "under" or "lower.") If the idea of lower rank is expressed in a clause, the clause is a *subordinate* clause.[1] The main idea of the sentence is expressed in an *independent* clause.

EXAMPLES The pilot, who was a veteran flyer, brought her crippled plane down safely. [Independent clause—greater emphasis: *The pilot brought her crippled plane down safely;* subordinate clause—lesser emphasis: *who was a veteran flyer.*]

Because each of them was politically ambitious, the council members rarely supported one another's proposals. [Independent clause—greater emphasis: *the council members rarely supported one another's proposals;* subordinate clause—lesser emphasis: *Because each of them was politically ambitious.*]

Adverb Clauses

11b. Make clear the relationship between subordinate adverb clauses and independent clauses by selecting subordinating conjunctions that express the relationship exactly.

The relationship between the idea in a subordinate adverb clause and the idea in an independent clause is made clear by the subordinating conjunction that introduces the subordinate clause. The common kinds of relationships between subordinate adverb clauses and independent clauses are *time, cause* or *reason, purpose* or *result,* and *condition.*

Some of the subordinating conjunctions can be used in more than one way and therefore appear in more than one list.

Time

The following subordinating conjunctions introduce clauses expressing a time relationship between the idea in the subordinate clause and the idea in the independent clause.

EXAMPLE Several guests arrived **before** *we were ready.*

after	before	until	whenever
as	since	when	while

---

[1] For a more detailed explanation of subordinate clauses see pages 464–76.

Cause or Reason

The following subordinating conjunctions introduce clauses expressing the cause or reason for the idea expressed in the independent clause. The subordinate clause tells *why*.

EXAMPLE   We stopped **because** *the light was red.*
          as   since   because   whereas

Purpose or Result

The following subordinating conjunctions introduce clauses expressing the purpose or the result of the idea in the independent clause.

EXAMPLES   Astronauts undergo the most rigorous training **so that** *they will be able to handle any emergency.* [The subordinate clause states the purpose of training described in the independent clause.]

Extreme differences of opinion developed in the committee **so that** *agreement seemed unlikely.* [The subordinate clause states a result of the committee's differences of opinion.]
        that   in order that   so that

Condition

The following subordinating conjunctions state the condition or conditions under which the idea in the independent clause is true. Think of *although, even though, though,* and *while* as meaning "in spite of the fact that." They introduce a condition in spite of which the idea in the independent clause is true.

EXAMPLES   **Although** (in spite of the fact that) *it was raining,* we went to the game. [The clause states the *condition* under which we went to the game.]

If *you pass the examination,* you will pass the course. [The clause states under what condition you will pass the course.]
        although   though   provided that   if
        even though   while   unless

EXERCISE 2. Using Appropriate Subordinating Conjunctions. Number your paper 1–10. From the preceding lists, choose a subordinating conjunction to fill the blank in each sentence, and write it after the proper number. Make sure the conjunction you choose fits the meaning of the sentence. After the conjunction, tell what relationship it expresses: *cause* or *reason, condition, purpose* or *result,* or *time.*

1. —— you buy a rare manuscript, make certain of its authenticity.
2. William Henry Ireland was one of the most successful forgers —— he was only a teen-ager at the height of his exploits.
3. Ireland began forging Shakespeare manuscripts —— his father had a keen interest in them.
4. —— he forged a document, Ireland had to do careful research on the proper details such a document would require.
5. Special blends of ink were required —— the age would be properly deceptive.
6. Ireland's father published a collection of his son's forgeries —— he considered his son worthy of complete confidence.
7. The skepticism of scholars increased enormously —— it became impossible to answer their objections.
8. Ireland published a confession —— the documents were proved to be fraudulent, and his father's health declined.
9. —— he tried to ease his father's disappointment, the older man died in disgrace at the height of the furor.
10. —— Ireland himself died in 1835, the art of forgery obviously did not die with him.

EXERCISE 3. Using Appropriate Subordinating Conjunctions.
Number your paper 1–10. From the lists on pages 348–49, choose an appropriate subordinating conjunction to fill the blank in each sentence. Notice that when an adverb clause begins a sentence, it is followed by a comma.

1. —— we had eaten, we sat by the fireplace and told ghost stories.
2. —— she had not slept well the night before, Melissa did not run as well as her coach had expected.
3. You will solve this problem —— you take one step at a time.
4. —— Van Gogh is now considered a great painter, his work was not appreciated in his lifetime.
5. I bandaged my cut —— it would not become infected.
6. —— you arrived so late, you will have to sit at the back.
7. —— I had ordered two pairs of gloves, the mail-order company sent me two pairs of pants instead.
8. —— the defense attorney made her final plea, the prisoner sat stiffly in a chair.
9. The doctor administered the new antibiotic —— no further complications would arise.

10. Many people fail to enjoy music —— they do not know how to listen properly.

EXERCISE 4. Revising Sentences by Inserting Subordinate Adverb Clauses. Revise each of the following sentences by adding a subordinate clause at the beginning or at the end of each sentence. Vary your choice of subordinating conjunctions.

EXAMPLE   1. The fans filed out of the stadium.
    1. *After the game was over, the fans filed out of the stadium.*

1. The heat became unbearable.
2. We started jogging in the afternoons.
3. Arturo agreed to come with us.
4. Lauren began clapping enthusiastically.
5. You will not have enough time to finish the composition.

Adjective Clauses

The subordinate clauses in the preceding exercises are *adverb* clauses. Subordinate *adjective* clauses are also helpful in clarifying the relationship between ideas because they permit a writer to emphasize one idea above another.[1] A writer may, for instance, wish to express the following ideas in one sentence: *Sacajawea acted as interpreter for explorers of the West. She was a Lemhi Indian.* To emphasize that Sacajawea acted as interpreter, the writer places this information in an independent clause and subordinates the other idea by placing it in an adjective clause.

> **Sacajawea,** who was a Lemhi Indian, **acted as interpreter for the explorers of the West.**

On the other hand, for a different purpose, the writer may wish to change emphasis by reversing the positions of the ideas.

> **Sacajawea,** who acted as interpreter for explorers of the West, **was a Lemhi Indian.**

11c. Make clear the relative emphasis to be given ideas in a complex sentence by placing the idea you wish to emphasize in the independent clause and by placing subordinate ideas in subordinate clauses.

EXERCISE 5. Revising Complex Sentences with Adjective Clauses. Change the emphasis in each of the following sentences by

[1] Adjective clauses may begin with *who, whom, whose, which, that* and *where.*

placing in the independent clause the idea that is now in the subordinate clause and by placing in the subordinate clause the idea that is now in the independent clause.

1. *Z,* which is a voiced palatal fricative, is the last letter of the English alphabet.

2. Dictionary listings, which end with words beginning with *z,* proceed alphabetically.

3. *Zeal,* which comes from an ancient Greek word meaning "jealousy," is one of the more familiar words found there.

4. Animal lovers, who may not welcome the name, can be called *zoophiles.*

5. *Zymurgy,* which means "the chemistry of fermentation," results in good wine and ends at least one dictionary.

CORRECTING FAULTY COORDINATION

Faulty coordination occurs when two unequal ideas are placed in coordinate clauses as though they deserved equal emphasis.

FAULTY COORDINATION   The Governor was a native of Ohio, and she was elected for a third term. [ideas of unequal rank]

The two ideas in this sentence are vastly different. It is unlikely that a writer would wish to give them equal rank. The faulty coordination can be corrected by placing one of the ideas in a subordinate position. Which idea the writer puts in the subordinate clause will depend on the purpose.

FAULTY COORDINATION CORRECTED   **The Governor,** who was a native of Ohio, **was elected for a third term.**

or   **The Governor,** who was elected for a third term, **was a native of Ohio.**

11d. Faulty coordination may be corrected by placing ideas of lesser emphasis in a subordinate position. An idea may be given less emphasis by being expressed in a subordinate clause or a modifying phrase or an appositive.[1]

(1) Subordination may be accomplished by a subordinate clause.

FAULTY COORDINATION   The books are on the new-book shelf, and they may be borrowed for a week.

CORRECTED BY AN ADJECTIVE CLAUSE   The books **that are on the new-book shelf** may be borrowed for a week.

---

[1] For the use of subordination in eliminating choppy sentences and in achieving sentence variety, see pages 386–94. For the use of subordination in correcting stringy sentences, see pages 399–400.

CORRECTED BY AN ADVERB CLAUSE   **If the books are on the new-book shelf,** they may be borrowed for a week.

EXERCISE 6. Revising Sentences by Correcting Faulty Coordination.

Clarify the relationship between ideas in the following examples of faulty coordination by placing one of the ideas in a subordinate clause, either an adverb clause or an adjective clause. Choose carefully the subordinating conjunctions that introduce your adverb clauses.

1. I am taking a course in bookkeeping this year, and I will have a better chance of getting an office job this summer.
2. Mr. and Mrs. Davis have donated a hundred books to our school's library, and they own a large bookstore in town.
3. Columbia College was originally named King's College, and it was established by King George III of England.
4. Mosquitoes and gnats buzzed around our heads, and we still had an enjoyable picnic in the park.
5. Nora and I heard that a course in photography would be given in the spring, and we signed up for it.

(2) Subordination may be accomplished by a modifying phrase.

FAULTY COORDINATION   The house is at the end of the street, and it is very modern in design.

CORRECTED BY A MODIFYING PHRASE   The house **at the end of the street** is very modern in design.

(3) Subordination may be accomplished by an appositive.

An appositive is a word, with or without modifiers, which follows a noun or pronoun and helps to explain it.

FAULTY COORDINATION   Ms. Fitch is the manager of the store, and she is tall and attractive.

CORRECTED BY AN APPOSITIVE   Ms. Fitch, **the manager of the store,** is tall and attractive.

EXERCISE 7. Revising Sentences by Correcting Faulty Coordination.

Revise the following sentences by correcting the faulty coordination in the ways prescribed.

Revise by inserting a modifying phrase:

1. The call was to abandon ship, and it came from the captain.
2. I need to find a recent magazine article, and it should be about the process of digital recording.
3. The woman was playing the accordion, and she had a repertoire of hundreds of folk songs.
4. Neal hit a line drive to left field, and it happened with two out and runners on first and third.
5. The bottle contained ammonia, and it fell onto the floor and spilled.

Revise by inserting an appositive:

6. Mr. Miller is the custodian of our building, and he came to this country only three years ago.
7. The new ruler is a woman of great experience in government, and she should be able to reconcile the factions in the country.
8. The violin was an instrument with a beautiful tone, and it belonged to my grandfather.
9. This passenger plane is the fastest one in the world, and it will take you to Europe in record time.
10. Her new book is a volume of poetry, and it got very good reviews.

SUMMARY

(1) Make clear the relationship between ideas in a sentence by using connectives that express the relationship exactly.

(2) Correct faulty coordination by placing ideas of lesser emphasis in a subordinate position. Use a subordinate clause or a modifying phrase or an appositive.

EXERCISE 8. Revising Sentences. The relationship between ideas in the following sentences is not clear: the conjunctions used are not exact, or the sentences contain faulty coordination. Revise the sentences. Some may be revised in more than one way.

1. The Bay Challenge Cup represents the highest achievement in sailing, and it was first put up for competition in 1903.
2. The principle that government employees shall not strike has been challenged, and it applies to both federal and state employees.

3. High school graduates are better educated today than ever before, and they have a hard time finding jobs.
4. The final chapters of this book outline a constructive program dealing with the problem, and they are the most important.
5. Every business has several ambitious competitors, and no business can afford to stand still.
6. The new regulations call for the opening of school at 7:30 every morning, and they are unpopular with both students and teachers.
7. Mr. Greenberg was a high-school coach for many years, and he is now coaching college teams in Ohio.
8. Representatives came from more than fifty countries, and they met in the United Nations Building in New York City.
9. The title of the book was interesting, and the book itself was dull.
10. The potato season was poor, and the potato farmers managed to avoid going into debt.
11. Miss Lang had not directed many plays, and she knew how to manage an inexperienced cast.
12. Helen may go to Wellesley next year, and she may go to Barnard.
13. Carl has taken piano lessons for only three years, and he is already a good pianist.
14. Mr. Stark has never paid back the money he borrowed, and he wants me to lend him more.
15. We waited on the corner for an hour, and the bus didn't come.
16. The Commercial High School is a large stone building on Market Street, and it is attended by students from all over the city.
17. Stewart Harrison was a famous detective, and he could not solve the arsenic murder case.
18. Miss Armstrong has been selling advertising for many years, and she has been made advertising director of the *Herald*.
19. I am going to the airport to meet a friend, and she is from Ohio.
20. Professor Drake had been head of the chemistry department for twenty years, and she died yesterday.

CHAPTER 12

Clear Reference

PRONOUNS AND ANTECEDENTS

The meaning of a pronoun is clear only when you know what it refers to. The word to which a pronoun refers is its *antecedent*. For example, the sentence "He was talking with them" has little meaning unless you know to whom the pronouns *he* and *them* refer.

In the following sentences, arrows connect the pronouns and their antecedents.

I asked Mr. Jordan for the answer, but he didn't know it.

The Potters have a new sailboat on which they intend to cruise.

Handing George the coat, the salesclerk said, "Try this on for size."

12a. A pronoun must refer clearly to the right antecedent. Avoid *ambiguous* **reference,** *general* **reference, and** *weak* **reference.**

Charlie is always thinking about cars. *It* [*cars?*] is his only interest. [The antecedent cannot be substituted; the reference is faulty.]

One simple way of testing pronoun reference is to substitute the antecedent for the pronoun.

Charlie is always thinking about cars. *They* [*cars*] are his only interest. [The antecedent fits.]

AMBIGUOUS REFERENCE

(1) Avoid *ambiguous reference*. **Ambiguous reference occurs when a pronoun refers confusingly to two antecedents so that the reader does not know at once which antecedent is meant.**

AMBIGUOUS The President appointed Senator Moore as chairman because he was convinced of the importance of the committee's work.

Here the pronoun *he* can refer to either the President or Senator Moore. The context in which such a sentence appears will ordinarily provide readers with the clues they need to identify the antecedent. Occasionally, however, the use of a pronoun that can refer to more than one antecedent causes momentary confusion. Such ambiguous reference can usually be avoided by rephrasing the sentence.

CLEAR The President, convinced of the importance of the committee's work, appointed Senator Moore as chairman.
CLEAR Because Senator Moore was convinced of the importance of the committee's work, the President appointed him as chairman.

Occasionally, the only way to avoid ambiguity is to replace the pronoun with the appropriate noun:

AMBIGUOUS The partnership between Jones and Potter ended when he drew the firm's money from the bank and flew to Brazil.
CLEAR The partnership between Jones and Potter ended when Jones drew the firm's money from the bank and flew to Brazil.

EXERCISE 1. **Revising Sentences by Correcting Ambiguous Pronouns.** Find the ambiguous pronoun in each of the following sentences. Make the sentence clear either by revising it or by replacing the pronoun with a noun.

1. Fay was arguing with Jane, and she looked unhappy.
2. One of the passengers told the bus driver that she didn't know the route very well.
3. Right after the accountant sent in a report to the treasurer, she became very much alarmed.
4. Raise the viewfinder to your eye, turning it slowly to the right until it is focused.
5. Our job was to remove the labels from the old bottles and wash them.

GENERAL REFERENCE

(2) Avoid *general reference*. **General reference occurs when a pronoun refers confusingly to a general idea that is only vaguely expressed.**

The pronouns *which, this, that,* and *it* are commonly used in a general way.

GENERAL The boys wore ski boots to their classes which the principal disapproved of.

In this sentence the pronoun *which* refers to the general idea, *the wearing of ski boots to class;* however, the pronoun is placed so that it appears to refer to *classes.*

CLEAR The principal disapproved of **the boys' wearing** ski boots to class.

In the next example, the pronoun *it* does not have a clear antecedent. A definite noun makes the meaning clear.

GENERAL Great ships were moving slowly up the harbor; tugs and ferryboats scurried in and out among them; here and there a white cabin cruiser sliced sharply through the blue water under the suspension bridge. It was thrilling to a young farmer.
CLEAR The **sight** was thrilling to a young farmer.

Although you can sometimes correct general reference by merely substituting a noun for the unclear pronoun, you will often find it necessary to revise the entire sentence.

GENERAL In her act Maria told jokes, did impersonations, and sang comic songs. This amused her audience.
CLEAR Maria amused her audience by telling jokes, doing impersonations, and singing comic songs.

EXERCISE 2. Revising Sentences by Correcting General References.   The following sentences contain examples of general, or vague, reference. Revise the sentences or replace the unclear pronouns with nouns.

1. The Chinese were bitter when Russia withdrew its technical assistance; they said it would harm the Chinese economy.
2. Macbeth's mind was constantly imagining horrible things, and that frightened him.
3. I enjoyed the author's style and the type of characters she wrote about. It made me want to read her other books.

4. Rabbi Meyer came to the house daily, from which a sturdy friendship grew.
5. A great deal of effort went into planning the expedition, hiring the right sort of men, and anticipating every emergency, which accounts for the success of the undertaking.

WEAK REFERENCE

(3) Avoid *weak reference*. Weak reference occurs when the antecedent has not been expressed but exists only in the writer's mind.

WEAK   We spent the day on a fishing boat, but we didn't catch a single one.

In this sentence there is no antecedent of the pronoun *one*. The adjective *fishing* is not the antecedent, since it is fish, not fishing, that *one* refers to. The writer meant the pronoun to stand for the noun *fish*.

CLEAR   We spent the day on a fishing boat, but we didn't catch a single **fish.**
CLEAR   We spent the day on a fishing boat trying to catch some **fish,** but we didn't catch a single **one.**

In other words, the antecedent of a pronoun should be a noun. When the antecedent is "hidden" in a modifier or a verb form, the reference is weak.

WEAK   The people want honest public servants, but that has not always been a virtue of politicians.

In this sentence the antecedent should be the noun *honesty,* but the noun is "hidden" in the adjective *honest.* Correct the sentence by replacing the weak pronoun with a noun.

CLEAR   The people want honest public servants, but **honesty** has not always been a virtue of politicians.

In the next sentence, the antecedent of *it* should be the noun *writing,* which is "hidden" in the verb *wrote.*

WEAK   Lois wrote whenever she could find the time, but none of it was ever published.
CLEAR   Lois wrote whenever she could find the time, but none of **her writing** was ever published.
CLEAR   Lois found time for her **writing** whenever she could, but none of **it** was ever published.

Correct weak references by replacing the weak pronoun with a noun or by giving the pronoun a clear antecedent.

EXERCISE 3. Revising Sentences by Correcting Weak References. The following sentences contain examples of weak references. Revise the sentences by correcting the weak references.

1. I take many pictures with my camera and consider it an enjoyable hobby.
2. Being neighborly is important because you may need their help someday in an emergency.
3. She was a virtuoso violinist, but she never owned a valuable one.
4. She is highly intelligent, but she hides it from people she doesn't know well.
5. Our guide said the Pueblo village was well worth seeing, but it would take three hours.

INDEFINITE USE OF PRONOUNS

12b. In writing, avoid indefinite use of the pronouns *it, they,* and *you*.

The indefinite use of *it, they,* and *you* occurs in ordinary conversation but is not acceptable in writing.

INDEFINITE   In the final chapter it implies that the hero died a martyr's death.
BETTER   **The final chapter** implies that the hero died a martyr's death.

INDEFINITE   On this flight to California, they serve meals without charge.
BETTER   On this flight to California, **meals** are served without charge.

INDEFINITE   In some countries, you don't dare express political views openly.
BETTER   In some countries, **the people** don't dare express political views openly.

☞ NOTE   The expressions *it is raining, it seems, it is late* are, of course, entirely correct.

EXERCISE 4. Revising Sentences by Correcting Faulty References. The sentences in this exercise contain examples of ambiguous, general, and weak references. There are some examples of the indefinite use of *it, they,* and *you*. Revise the sentences either by replacing a faulty pronoun with a noun, or by revising the entire sentence. Make the meaning unmistakably clear.

1. Golf wouldn't cost me so much if I didn't lose so many in the rough.
2. The radiator was leaking badly; it ran all over the garage floor.
3. In the cabin he checked the fuel. In those days this might mean the difference between life and death.
4. She overcame her hip injury which doctors had said was impossible.
5. Her spelling and sentence structure are not good, but most of it is due to carelessness.
6. Ruth saw Julie when she was in town last week.
7. In yesterday's editorial, it says the mayor has failed to live up to his campaign promises.
8. The witness testified that she had seen the accused when she was eating dinner in the dining car, which convinced the jury of her presence on the train.
9. The library does not have enough copies of some of the books in greatest demand by students writing research papers, which makes it hard for you.
10. In Washington they are skeptical about the success of the new farm program.

CHAPTER 13

Placement of Modifiers

MISPLACED AND DANGLING MODIFIERS

A modifier should clarify or make more definite the meaning of the word it modifies. If the modifier is placed too far from this word, the effect of the modifier may be either lost or diverted to some other word.

MISPLACED MODIFIERS

13a. Place phrase and clause modifiers as near as possible to the words they modify.

A misplaced modifier may mislead the reader or force him to reread the sentence in order to understand its meaning.

CONFUSING   Two meetings have been held to make arrangements for a return bout in the office of the State Athletic Commission.

Although most readers know that the return bout is not likely to be held *in the office of the State Athletic Commission*, they may be momentarily distracted by this interesting thought. Placing the phrase next to *held*, the word it modifies, makes the sentence clear.

CLEAR   Two meetings have been held in the office of the State Athletic Commission to make arrangements for a return bout.

CONFUSING   I bought a small computer for the accounting staff, which gave everyone a great deal of trouble.

The computer, not the staff, gave everyone trouble. The clause *which gave everyone a great deal of trouble* should be next to *computer*.

CLEAR   I bought the accounting staff a small computer, which gave everyone a great deal of trouble.

CONFUSING   The thief decided to make a run for it when he saw the police officer, abandoning the stolen car and dashing into the woods.

This sentence would be clearer if, on first reading, it did not give the impression that the police officer was abandoning the stolen car and dashing into the woods. Moving the adverb clause *when he saw the police officer* to the beginning of the sentence makes it clear that the thief, not the police officer, ran away.

CLEAR   When he saw the police officer, the thief decided to make a run for it, abandoning the stolen car and dashing into the woods.

The usual way to clarify a sentence containing a misplaced modifier is to move the modifier next to the word it modifies. In the sentence above, however, moving the participial phrases next to *thief* changes the meaning of the sentence: *The thief, abandoning the stolen car and dashing into the woods, decided to make a run for it when he saw the police officer.* Often, you can improve a sentence by moving an adverbial modifier (in this instance *when he saw the police officer*) to the beginning of the sentence.

The important factor in the placement of modifiers is that you make yourself clear at first reading. Do not try to hide behind the weak explanation, "You know what I mean."

EXERCISE 1. Revising Sentences by Correcting Misplaced Modifiers. The following sentences may be confusing on first reading because of a misplaced phrase or clause. Revise the sentences by placing modifiers near the words they modify. You may find that placing an adverbial modifier first often improves the sentence.

1. Commander Richardson was decorated for his action, but he was haunted by the memory of the men who had died in the battle.
2. The company now runs a late bus for skiers leaving at 6:15.
3. One of our observers sighted a plane through binoculars that she could not identify.

4. The causeway has a drawbridge to permit the passage of fishing boats from which all fishing is prohibited.
5. The community center was built by Mrs. Borden, who later became Mrs. Gruber, at a cost of $800,000.
6. At Tuesday's meeting, the mayor discussed the enormous cost of filling in the Buskill Swamp with city council members.
7. Father bought a gadget for his new car from a fast-talking salesclerk that was guaranteed to reduce gas consumption.
8. She wore a straw hat on the back of her head which was obviously too small.
9. Ms. Steinberg, the explorer, described her trips through the jungle in our social studies class.
10. Uncle Jim bought a new carriage for the baby that was named "Boodle Buggy."

DANGLING MODIFIERS

13b. A modifying phrase or clause must clearly and sensibly modify a word in the sentence. When there is no word that the phrase or clause can sensibly modify, the modifier is said to dangle.

DANGLING MODIFIER   Carrying a heavy pile of books, her foot caught on the step.

An introductory participial phrase (see pages 449–51) modifies the noun or pronoun following it. In this example, the phrase *carrying a heavy pile of books* appears to modify *foot*. Since a foot could not carry a pile of books, the phrase cannot modify it sensibly. The phrase, therefore, is a dangling modifier. You can correct the sentence in two ways:

1. By adding a word that the phrase can sensibly modify.

   Carrying a heavy pile of books, **she** caught her foot on the step.

2. By changing the phrase to an adverb clause.

   While she was carrying a heavy pile of books, her foot caught on the steps.

   Study the following examples of dangling modifiers and the ways in which they have been corrected.

DANGLING MODIFIER   Representing the conservative point of view, the liberals rebutted her.

CORRECTED   Representing the conservative point of view, she was rebutted by the liberals.

CORRECTED   Since she represented the conservative point of view, the liberals rebutted her.

DANGLING   To win the baseball championship this year, Luis and Oscar should
MODIFIER   join our team.

CORRECTED   If we are to win the baseball championship this year, Luis and Oscar should join our team.

CORRECTED   To win the baseball championship this year, we should get Luis and Oscar to join our team.

A few dangling modifiers are either so idiomatic as to be entirely acceptable or so clear that no possible confusion can result. The following examples are not objectionable:

> Relatively speaking, the cost of living has remained static for several years.
> To be perfectly frank, the rate of inflation is still too high.

EXERCISE 2. Revising Sentences by Correcting Dangling Modifiers.
Each of the following sentences contains a dangling modifier. Revise the sentences by correctly placing the modifiers.

1. Left alone in the house, the thunderstorm terrified him.
2. Enormous and architecturally striking, everyone is impressed by the new building.
3. When selecting a college, the social life seems to interest some students more than education.
4. While talking with friends, the topic of dentistry came up.
5. After flying in darkness for two hours, the moon rose, and navigation became less difficult.
6. To keep the guacamole dip from turning brown, its surface should be covered with a thin layer of mayonnaise.
7. After working in the fields all day, little strength was left for social activities.
8. To understand many of the allusions in modern literature, a knowledge of Greek and Roman myths is essential.
9. Having promised to be home by midnight, the family was annoyed when I came in at two o'clock.
10. Riding in the glass-bottomed boat, hundreds of beautiful tropical fish could be seen.

TWO-WAY MODIFIERS

A third way in which a careless writer sometimes causes confusion is by placing a modifier in such a way that it may be taken to modify two words. As a result, the reader cannot be sure which of the two possible meanings is intended. Such a modifier is called a *two-way*, or a *squinting*, modifier.

EXAMPLE Mary said *during the meeting* Jo acted like a fool.

Since the phrase *during the meeting* may be taken to modify either *said* or *acted*, this sentence is not clear. Did Mary say this during the meeting, or did Jo act like a fool during the meeting? The sentence should be revised to make it say one thing or the other.

CLEAR **During the meeting** Mary said Jo acted like a fool.

CLEAR Mary said Jo acted like a fool **during the meeting**.

Here is another example of a two-way modifier:

NOT CLEAR Tell Fred *when he comes home* I want to see him.

CLEAR **When he comes home**, tell Fred I want to see him.

CLEAR Tell Fred I want to see him **when he comes home**.

EXERCISE 3. Revising Sentences by Correcting Faulty Modifiers.
The sentences in this exercise contain misplaced, dangling, and squinting modifiers. Revise each sentence so that its meaning will be clear on first reading.

1. The Simpsons gave a toy robot to one of their children with a bullet-shaped glass head and flashing red eyes.
2. Pounding the piano keys with all her might, the chords of the prelude resounded through the concert hall.
3. We saw a herd of sheep on the way to our hotel.
4. To succeed in college, a great deal of time must be spent studying.
5. When only five years old, Dad took me to see my first baseball game.
6. Topped with yogurt, many people love fresh strawberries.
7. While trying to get ready for school, the doorbell suddenly rang.
8. Elaine told Joanne after the first act the drama gets more exciting.

9. By practicing a foreign language daily, great fluency can be gained.
10. A tarantula was shown to me by the museum's curator that had eight legs and a huge, hairy body.
11. Preferring the mountains to the seashore, the Great Smokies were chosen as our vacation spot.
12. After working in Washington for twenty years, the methods of lobbyists were familiar.
13. This bank approves loans to reliable individuals of any size.
14. Being completely untamed, Anita warned us that the animals were dangerous.
15. One can see more than a hundred lakes, flying at an altitude of several thousand feet.
16. Jack bought a book of shorthand lessons along with his new typewriter, which he read and studied diligently.
17. Living constantly under the eyes of the police, her nervousness increased.
18. Plans for a new road have finally been approved after three years of red tape to stretch across the valley.
19. Ramón wanted to know before the game began what the referees said to the two captains.
20. Rounding a sharp curve, a detour sign warned us of danger.

CHAPTER 14

Parallel Structure

STRUCTURES OF EQUAL RANK; FAULTY PARALLELISM

Parallelism in sentence structure exists when two or more sentence elements of equal rank are similarly expressed. Stating equal and closely related ideas in parallel constructions often adds clarity and smoothness to writing.

KINDS OF PARALLEL STRUCTURE

14a. Express parallel ideas in the same grammatical form.

There are three sentence elements which commonly require parallel treatment; coordinated ideas, compared and contrasted ideas; and correlative constructions.

Coordinate Ideas

Coordinate ideas are equal in rank. They are joined by coordinate connectives. The coordinate connectives most often used in parallel structure are *and*, *but*, *or*, and *nor*.

To express parallel ideas in the same grammatical form, pair one part of speech with the same part of speech, a verbal with the same kind of verbal, a phrase with a phrase, a clause with a clause. Do not pair unlike grammatical forms.

FAULTY   The committee studied all aspects of the problem—humane, political, and cost. [The adjectives *humane* and *political* are paired with the noun *cost*.]

PARALLEL   The committee studied all aspects of the problem—**humane, political**, and **financial**. [All three coordinate elements are adjectives.]

FAULTY   According to my teacher, my composition revealed exceptional creative ability but that I make too many spelling errors. [noun paired with clause]

PARALLEL   According to my teacher, my composition revealed exceptional creative **ability** but too many spelling **errors**. [noun paired with noun]

PARALLEL   According to my teacher, my composition revealed **that I have exceptional creative ability** but **that I make too many spelling errors**. [clause paired with clause]

Compared or Contrasted Ideas

FAULTY   Water-skiing no longer interests me as much as to go scuba diving. [gerund *water-skiing* paired with infinitive *to go*]

PARALLEL   **Water-skiing** no longer interests me as much as **scuba diving**. [gerund paired with gerund]

PARALLEL   **To water-ski** no longer interests me as much as **to scuba dive.** [infinitive paired with infinitive]

FAULTY   Her novel was praised more for its style than for what it had to say. [noun paired with clause]

PARALLEL   Her novel was praised more for its **style** than for its **ideas.** [noun paired with noun]

Correlative Constructions

Correlative constructions are formed with the correlative conjunctions *both . . . and, either . . . or, neither . . . nor, not only . . . but (also).*

FAULTY   At the gate they tried both persuasion and to force their way in. [noun paired with infinitive]

PARALLEL   At the gate they tried both **persuasion** and **force.** [noun paired with noun]

FAULTY   The new clerk soon proved herself to be not only capable but also a woman who could be trusted. [adjective paired with noun]

PARALLEL   The new clerk soon proved herself to be not only **capable** but also **trustworthy.** [adjective paired with adjective]

COMPLETED PARALLELISM

14b. Place correlative conjunctions immediately before the parallel terms.

NONSTANDARD Mrs. Sayers is not only president of the National Bank but also of the Chamber of Commerce. [*Not only* precedes a noun, *president,* whereas *but also* precedes a prepositional phrase, *of the Chamber of Commerce.*]

STANDARD Mrs. Sayers is president **not only** *of the National Bank* **but also** *of the Chamber of Commerce.*

NONSTANDARD The team both felt the satisfaction of victory and the disappointment of defeat.

STANDARD The team felt **both** *the satisfaction* of victory **and** *the disappointment* of defeat.

14c. In parallel constructions, repeat an article, a preposition, or a pronoun whenever necessary to make the meaning clear.

Note that the omission or inclusion of a word in the paired sentences below changes the meaning.

Before the meeting I talked with the secretary and treasurer. [The sentence may mean that I talked with one person who holds both offices.]
Before the meeting I talked with the secretary and **the** treasurer. [This sentence indicates that I talked with two persons.]

The weather was a greater handicap to the invading army than their enemy. [This sentence may mean that the invaders were handicapped more by the weather than by their enemy.]
The weather was a greater handicap to the invading army than **to** their enemy. [This sentence means that the invaders had the greater handicap.]

We feel certain that she is capable, she will succeed, and you will be proud of her. [In a series of parallel *that* clauses, the meaning is usually clearer if the introductory word is repeated in each clause.]
We feel certain **that** she is capable, **that** she will succeed, and **that** you will be proud of her.

EXERCISE 1. Revising Sentences by Correcting Faulty Parallelism. Revise the following sentences by putting parallel ideas into the same grammatical form. Correct any errors in the placement of correlative conjunctions and in the omission of necessary articles, prepositions, or pronouns.

1. Its large size, simple structure, and how readily available it is, make the common cockroach convenient to study.
2. Cockroaches have smooth, leathery skin; long, thin antennae; and they have a body that is thick and flat.
3. They are not only found in urban areas but in the tropics.
4. Cockroaches may be dark brown, pale brown, or of a green color that is delicate.
5. Cockroach eggs are laid in small cases, carried on the female body, and then they deposit them in hidden crevices.
6. A typical cockroach lives as a nymph for about a year, and as an adult its life lasts about half a year.
7. Cockroaches will eat anything, but they especially like sweet foods and foods that are starchy.
8. We might not only view the cockroach with disgust but also interest.
9. The cockroach both is the most primitive living winged insect and the most ancient fossil insect.
10. We have as much to learn from the cockroach's evolution as there is to gain from extinguishing it.

14d. Include in the second part of a parallel construction all words necessary to make the construction complete.

Occasionally you may fail to include in one part of a parallel construction all the words necessary to make the construction complete.

INCOMPLETE   Linda always chose topics that were more difficult than the other students.

COMPLETE   Linda always chose topics that were more difficult than **those of** the other students.

In the first of these sentences you feel that something has been omitted because the sentence compares *topics* with *students*.

EXERCISE 2. Revising Sentences by Using Correct Parallelism.
Correct the parallelism in each of the following sentences by inserting the words that have been omitted.

1. Ms. Connor's lectures are easier to comprehend than Ms. Moore.
2. A modern director's interpretation of *Hamlet* is very different from a nineteenth-century director.
3. A dog's ability to hear high-pitched sounds is much keener than humans.

4. How do your grades in English compare with science?
5. The biographical information in the encyclopedia is more detailed than the dictionary.
6. People have been more interested in reading the book than the movie version.
7. The view from the World Trade Center is even more spectacular than the Empire State Building.
8. The strength in my left hand is greater than my right hand.
9. Some birds like to eat fruit as much as insects.
10. This month the price of gold has risen more sharply than silver.

EXERCISE 3. Revising Sentences by Correcting Faulty Parallelism. The following sentences contain faulty parallelism. Rephrase the sentences so that the parallelism will be correctly and logically expressed.

1. One of the accident victims suffered a broken arm, several broken ribs, and one of her lungs was punctured.
2. She not only was industrious, but she could be depended on.
3. As we left the harbor, the radio weather report predicted gale-force winds, heavy rain, and that tides would be abnormally high.
4. A cloudy day is better for a game than sunshine.
5. She spoke about her experience in Australia and several predictions about the country's future.
6. To the unthinking person, war may be a romantic adventure, but a foolish and dirty business is the way the wise person regards it.
7. The unexpected cooperation of China was a greater surprise to Russia than the United States.
8. The skipper had a harsh voice, a weatherbeaten face, and was very stocky in build.
9. We were not sure that our request for a raise was fair or it would be granted.
10. The speech of cultivated Britishers is not so different as it used to be from Americans.
11. Attention has been centered on the need for more teachers, adequate classrooms, and there isn't enough new equipment.
12. This was a much harder assignment for me than Luis.
13. The ambassador did not know whether the President had sent for him or the Secretary of State.

14. Her friends not only were shocked by her failure but they felt a great disappointment.
15. The players were annoyed not so much by the decisions of the officials as the hostile crowd.
16. The company announced a bonus for all five-year employees and that deserving new employees would be given additional benefits.
17. The headmaster insisted that all of us return by ten o'clock and the housemasters must check us in.
18. High-school programs have been accused of being too closely tied in with college education and that they neglect the average teen-ager.
19. Pioneers came with hopes of being happy and free and to make their fortunes in the new world.
20. All delegates to the convention were advised that on their return they would both have to make a written and oral report.

CHAPTER 15

Unnecessary Shifts in Sentences

AWKWARD CHANGES IN SUBJECT AND VERB FORMS

Within a sentence a shift is a change from one subject to another or from one verb to another. Often shifts are acceptable because they are necessary to express the meaning the writer intends.

ACCEPTABLE SHIFT   The trials of peace are great, but the dangers of war are greater. [The shift in subject from *trials* to *dangers* is a natural one.]

The smoothness of a sentence is sometimes seriously affected, however, by an unnecessary and awkward shift.

AWKWARD   A student should choose books from the reading list so that you can be sure they are acceptable to the teacher. [The unnecessary shift from *student* to *you* is awkward and confusing.]

ACCEPTABLE   A **student** should choose books from the reading list so that **he or she** can be sure they are acceptable to the teacher.

AWKWARD   Pam did her math homework, and then her theme was written. [The shift from active to passive voice and the resulting shift in subject is unnecessary and awkward.]

ACCEPTABLE   Pam **did** her math homework, and then she **wrote** her theme.

15a. Avoid unnecessary shifts from one subject to another.

UNNECESSARY SHIFTS

Fishers from many states visit the Ontario lakes where *fish* are found in abundance and, in the cool, crisp air of the North woods, a welcome *relief* from summer heat is enjoyed. *Planes, trains,* or *automobiles* bring the fishers to the edge of the wilderness. From there *boats* are used to penetrate the remoter waters where *trout, bass, pickerel, perch,* and freshwater *salmon* are caught.

SHIFTS AVOIDED

Fishers from many states visit the Ontario lakes where *they* find fish in abundance and, in the cool, crisp air of the North woods, enjoy a welcome relief from summer heat. After coming by plane, train, or automobile to the edge of the wilderness, the *fishers* use boats to penetrate the remoter waters, where *they* catch trout, bass, pickerel, perch, and freshwater salmon.

15b. Avoid unnecessary shifts from one verb form to another within one sentence.

(1) Avoid unnecessary shifts in the voice of verbs.

Unnecessary shifts from one subject to another are often the result of a shift from active to passive voice.

When the subject of a verb is acting, the verb is in the *active voice.* When the subject of a verb is acted upon, the verb is in the *passive voice.*[1]

ACTIVE VOICE $S \longrightarrow V$ Jane **won** both events. [subject acting]

PASSIVE VOICE $S \longleftarrow V$ Both events **were won** by Jane. [subject acted upon]

Note that a shift in voice results in a shift in subject.

UNNECESSARY SHIFT   Volunteers made [active verb] the dangerous journey after dark, but no wolves were encountered [passive verb].

SHIFT AVOIDED   Volunteers **made** [active verb] the dangerous journey after dark but **encountered** [active verb] no wolves.

(2) Avoid unnecessary shifts in the tense of verbs.

Changing without reason from one tense to another within a sentence creates an awkward and confusing effect. Stick to the tense you start with unless there is an excellent reason for changing.

---

[1] A fuller treatment of voice will be found on pages 575–78.

UNNECESSARY   At this point the President reads [present tense] a prepared
SHIFT   statement but refused [past tense] to answer any questions.

SHIFT AVOIDED   At this point the President **read** [past tense] a prepared state-
                ment but **refused** [past tense] to answer any questions.

SHIFT AVOIDED   At this point the President **reads** [present tense] a prepared
                statement but **refuses** [present tense] to answer any questions.

In correcting unnecessary shifts in subject and verb, you will often find
the best method is to omit the second subject. This can usually be done
by using the second verb in the same voice as the first and making the
verb compound.

UNNECESSARY SHIFT   A good driver has complete control of the car at all times,
        and allowance is made for the carelessness of other drivers.

SHIFT AVOIDED   A good **driver has** complete control of the car at all times **and
        makes** allowances for the carelessness of other drivers. [The use of the
        compound active voice for both verbs corrects the awkward shift.]

EXERCISE 1. Revising Sentences to Eliminate Unnecessary Shifts in the Subject and in the Verb.

Most of the following sentences
contain unnecessary shifts from one subject to another or from one verb
form to another. By revising these sentences orally in class, show how
these shifts may be avoided. Two of the sentences are acceptable.
Identify them.

1. If one wants to try a delicious recipe from Puerto Rico, you should
   make rice with pigeon peas.
2. To start, sauté three tablespoons of diced salt pork until the fat has
   melted.
3. A chopped onion and two minced cloves of garlic should be added to
   the skillet, and then add two chopped green peppers.
4. After you have peeled two tomatoes, chopping them comes next.
5. The tomatoes, too, should be placed into the skillet, and you should
   cook the entire mixture for five minutes.
6. A tablespoon of capers goes in next, and you should follow this with
   a teaspoon of salt, two cups of uncooked long-grain rice, and three
   cups of water.
7. After you stir the rice, a pound of cooked pigeon peas needs to be
   added.
8. A tablespoon of achiote should not be forgotten to be included, since
   this spice imparts a lovely golden color to the food.

9. When the liquid comes to a boil, cover the skillet, the flame should be reduced, and simmer the mixture until the water has been absorbed.
10. Stir the mixture occasionally to keep the rice from sticking, and continue cooking until the rice is dry and fluffy.

EXERCISE 2. Revising Sentences to Eliminate Shifts in the Subject and in the Verb. The sentences in this exercise are awkward because of unnecessary shifts in the subject and in the verb. Revise the sentences to eliminate these shifts.

1. Adolescents naturally rebel against authority, but the authority of the law must be respected by them.
2. Lonely students might participate in an extracurricular activity so that new friendships can be made.
3. A senior must not only pass all courses and graduate, but also plans for your future must be made quickly.
4. My brother frequently procrastinates, and a tendency toward laziness is occasionally shown.
5. My father has some amusing peculiarities which are not recognized by him.
6. The union's demands were unacceptable even though some concessions were contained in them.
7. If a teacher wants to be liked, you must treat students impartially.
8. Coach Martin always insisted on long practice sessions and strict training, but her winning teams justify her methods.
9. The Vice-President flew to the Paris Conference, but few concrete results were accomplished by him.
10. A good student can win a college scholarship, and thus his parents are relieved of part of the cost of a college education.
11. When you buy a car, a person should be sure he can afford the upkeep.
12. In the end Robert stays with his mother, and the girl he loves is lost to him forever.
13. The cement and sand are first mixed thoroughly; then add the water.
14. The experienced boat operator is aware of the danger of fire, and when filling the gas tank, great precautions are taken not to spill gasoline in the bottom of the boat.

15. As a young district attorney he handled the Tammany Hall case, and the backing of the Republican Party was won.
16. As the bus careens toward the edge of the road, we thought our time had come, and we grab our seats in desperation.
17. Many doctors recognize the value of health insurance, but the kind we should have is something they could not agree on.
18. Searching for the right words, Livia composed her closing sentence, and another essay was brought to its logical conclusion.
19. Sammy had just finished his bitter denunciation of all teachers and of one chemistry teacher in particular, when he turns around and Ms. Lerner was seen in the laboratory doorway.
20. An explorer must study maps very carefully so that you will be able to plan your trip efficiently.

CHAPTER 16

Sentence Conciseness

AVOIDING WORDINESS
AND OVERWRITING

It is a mistake to believe that wordiness is a virtue. Most good writing is effective because it is not cluttered with unnecessary words.

Moreover, do not think that wordiness appears only in long compositions. A long piece of writing may contain no superfluous words, whereas a short piece may be full of them. Studying the principles and doing the exercises in this section will make you aware of wordiness in writing and help you to avoid it.

SUPERFLUOUS WORDS AND
UNNECESSARY REPETITION

The following example of wordiness was the opening paragraph of a high-school student's composition about an overnight hike. Lines have been drawn through the superfluous words.

> When ~~in the course of human events, when~~ a woman finds it necessary to rest her weary bones, she packs up and goes on what is inappropriately called a vacation. Last summer I had the good fortune to go ~~during the summer~~ to a mountain camp in ~~the mountains of~~ eastern Pennsylvania. On the day that I arrived, ~~when I got to camp~~ I found that the camp had been quarantined because of the measles that one of the younger campers had brought in, ~~and no one who was in the camp could leave.~~ After we had spent

a week in camp, the prospect of an overnight hike in the mountainous wilds looked especially good to us campers who had been so long confined ~~to camp by the quarantine~~.

16a. Avoid wordiness by eliminating superfluous words and the unnecessary repetition of ideas.

WORDY   The game is played with tiny, little round balls, which, in my opinion, I think, are made of steel.

BETTER   The game is played with tiny balls which, I think, are made of steel.

WORDY   After descending down to the edge of the river, we boarded a small raft that was floating there on the surface of the water.

BETTER   After descending to the edge of the river, we boarded a small raft.

EXERCISE 1. Revising Sentences to Eliminate Superfluous Words. Revise the following sentences, eliminating superfluous words.

1. We watched the big, massive black cloud rising up from the level prairie and covering up the sun.
2. Far away in the distance, as far as anything was visible to the eye, the small, diminutive shapes of the campers' tents were outlined in silhouette against the dark sky.
3. When what the speaker was saying was not audible to our ears, I asked her to repeat again what she had said.
4. During this year's current baseball season, all home games and many away games in other cities may be watched at home on your television screen as they are brought to you over station WPIX.
5. During the hours in the morning before noon, there is a variety of radio programs of different kinds to which you may listen to.
6. As you continue on in the book a little further, you will be surprised and amazed by the clever skill of the writer of the book in weaving in together the many previously unrelated threads of his story.
7. She was firmly determined to combine together both of the two divisions of the firm in order to achieve a stronger company eventually in the long run.
8. Circling around his adversary with a menacing look on his face, Broadhurst bided his time and waited for an opening through which he could connect up with his mighty right.
9. The President's struggle with Congress ended up in a victory for the

President when the public voted at the November election to reelect him again to the Presidency for another term of four years.

10. The final conclusion of the novel on which she had been working on for more than five years was disappointing to everyone who read the manuscript, and she decided to revise and change the story.

EXERCISE 2. Revising Sentences by Eliminating Unnecessary Words. Revise the following wordy paragraph. Eliminate all unnecessary words, but keep the ideas clear.

> When we were two hundred yards away from our objective, which was a small little grove of pine trees on the sloping side of a hill, we were confronted by a vast, wet swamp. I remembered that during the last two weeks we had had, out of fourteen days, ten days of rain, and decided in my own mind to send out a few scouts who might discover a way by means of which we could reach the grove without getting our feet wet. Then, when the scouts reported back that their efforts to try to find a dry path through the swamp had been unsuccessful, we gave up and resigned ourselves to sloshing knee-deep through the muddy water.

CONCISENESS THROUGH REDUCTION

The opposite of wordiness is conciseness. In your effort to write well, you will profit from studying some ways to make your writing more concise. Of course, there is a danger in being too economical in your use of words; writing that is too concise will not be clear and will not achieve its intended effect. Nevertheless, the following rule will call to your attention some helpful methods of avoiding wordiness.

16b. Avoid wordiness by reducing clauses to phrases, and phrases to single words. This process is known as *reduction.*

1. *Clauses reduced to participial, gerund, or infinitive phrases*

CLAUSE	**When they were trapped by a cave-in,** the miners waited for rescuers.
PARTICIPIAL PHRASE	**Trapped by a cave-in,** the miners waited for rescuers.
CLAUSE	**Because we had found no one home,** we left a note.
PARTICIPIAL PHRASE	**Having found no one home,** we left a note.
CLAUSE	**If you leave at noon,** you can get to Chicago at three o'clock.
GERUND PHRASE	**Leaving at noon** will get you to Chicago at three o'clock.

CLAUSE	We decided **that we would get an early start.**
INFINITIVE PHRASE	We decided **to get an early start.**

2. *Clauses reduced to prepositional phrases*

CLAUSE	The teams **that had come from Missouri** were not scheduled to play the first day of the tournament.
PHRASE	The teams **from Missouri** were not scheduled to play the first day of the tournament.
CLAUSE	**When the sun sets,** the streetlights come on.
PHRASE	**At sunset** the streetlights come on.

3. *Clauses reduced to appositives*

CLAUSE	Dr. Brown, **who is the chief surgeon,** will operate.
APPOSITIVE	Dr. Brown, **the chief surgeon,** will operate.
CLAUSE	Her two dogs, **one of which is a collie and the other a spaniel,** perform different duties on the farm.
APPOSITIVE	Her two dogs, **a collie and a spaniel,** perform different duties on the farm.

4. *Clauses and phrases reduced to single words*

CLAUSE	The dance classes **that have been canceled** will be rescheduled.
WORD	The **canceled** dance classes will be rescheduled.
CLAUSE	Laura is a runner **who never tires.**
WORD	Laura is a **tireless** runner.
PHRASE	Her career **in the movies** was brief.
WORD	Her **movie** career was brief.
PHRASE	She greeted everyone **in a cordial manner.**
WORD	She greeted everyone **cordially.**

Usually the time for reduction is during revision of your papers. Revising the sentences in the following exercises will give you practice in writing more concisely.

EXERCISE 3. Revising Sentences Through Reduction.   Revise the following sentences by reducing the italicized clauses to phrases or appositives or single words, and the italicized phrases to single words. Omit any unnecessary words, and, if needed, occasionally change the word order.

1. We decided to wait for the bus *in order that we might save money.*
2. After I had finished the assigned reading, I read three novels *that were written by Virginia Woolf.*

3. This small hotel, *which is situated in Connecticut,* is patronized mainly by *people from Boston.*
4. *After he lost a leg in an accident which occurred while he was hunting,* Monty Stratton, *who was a pitcher for the White Sox,* made a comeback in baseball *that was amazing.*
5. Our seats *in which we sat at the Michigan-Ohio State football game* were almost on the forty-yard line, *and they were at the top of the stadium.*
6. The poetry *of Blake* had an influence *that is notable* on the poetry *of Yeats.*
7. *While he was inspecting his new house, which is in the suburbs,* Mr. Doyle stumbled over a piece of flooring and fell down the stairs *leading to the cellar.*
8. Our days *that we spent in the north woods* last summer would have been perfect if it had not been for the mosquitoes *that were enormous and hungry.*
9. Inez, *who is an ambitious young actress,* found that the acting *that she did in a stock company in the summer* gave her the experience *that she needed.*
10. The most common complaint *that is made by students* is that every teacher chooses Friday *on which to give examinations.*

EXERCISE 4. Revising Sentences by Eliminating Unnecessary Words and by Using Reduction. Revise the following wordy paragraph. Eliminate all unnecessary words and reduce clauses to phrases or appositives or single words. You may change the word order, but you must keep the ideas clear.

Needless to say, I am not one of those who are members of the senior class who believe that the senior lounge should be closed during the week of exams. It goes without saying that seniors need a place that is quiet and relaxing in order for them to escape the pressures which accompany exam week. If the lounge is closed during this time, it would mean that seniors would be forced to use the cafeteria, which is crowded, or the auditorium, which is noisy, for the purpose of relaxation. Furthermore, the use of the senior lounge during exam week is by this time one of the few privileges that seniors are still able to enjoy here at East High; not long ago the right of seniors to park cars in the parking area reserved for members of the faculty was recently taken away by the Student-Teacher Council. If more privileges are taken away, the morale of seniors will weaken.

THE OVERWRITTEN STYLE

In their efforts to write impressively, high-school students sometimes produce writing that is so artificial, flowery, and cumbersome as to be absurd. Such a style results from the mistaken notion that big words, unusual words, and figures of speech, no matter how commonplace, are "literary." A mistake of this kind is made by trying too hard to sound like a great writer. The resulting style is said to be "overwritten."

16c. Avoid an overwritten style. Write naturally without straining after a "literary" effect.

Avoid the kind of overwriting exhibited by the following paragraphs.

HARBOR FOG

The fog slowly crept in and covered the metropolis with its sinister cloak of impressive quietude. An entire day of heavy rain had drenched the surrounding municipality, forming puddles in the thoroughfares which reflected the shimmering images of the gleaming street lights and the illumination emanating from multitudes of office windows.

As I stood on the magnificent span that arched above the swirling waters, the mournful warnings of the anchored ships pierced the dense fog. The constant beat of the harbor bell buoys and the gentle lapping of the murky water on the pilings of this bridge combined to permeate the night air with a mystic tenseness.

Although it was late, the never-ceasing rumble of activity from the nearby city could still be apprehended. The penetrating night air was heavy with moisture and with each soft puff of breeze the salt of the sea could be detected.

During World War II, Representative Maury Maverick of Texas became impatient with the overwritten style of some government writing and branded it "gobbledygook." Here is an example of the gobbledygook that troubled Mr. Maverick: "Illumination is required to be extinguished upon vacating these premises." You can see how much more effective "Turn out the lights when you leave" would be.

EXERCISE 5. Revising Sentences to Correct an Overwritten Style.
Each of the following sentences is an example of overwriting. Using simpler words, revise the idea that is here expressed in a forced and unnatural style.

1. In a vast explosion of frozen precipitation, Jan shot through the feathery drift, maintaining without apparent effort her equilibrium upon the fragile strips of ash strapped to the pedal extremities.

2. The bitterest irony of our fevered time is the oft-repeated concept that only by creating more magnificent and more deadly instruments of explosive destruction can human beings bring to this whirling planet the era of tranquility for which it has longed since the beginning of time.

3. Following our educational endeavors of the day, several of us conscientious seekers after knowledge relaxed our weary cerebrums by lending our ears to the latest discs at Kent's music emporium.

4. Bent upon a week's exploration of our nation's vast regions of tranquil pristine wilderness, I bade a fond farewell to my anxious mater and, with my earthly possessions ensconced in a commodious rucksack, embarked upon my great adventure via public omnibus.

5. Lifting the pigskin from the water-soaked gridiron with his trusty toe, Harvey booted it with mathematical precision directly between the white uprights silhouetted against the setting sun.

CHAPTER 17

Sentence Combining and Revising

VARIETY, INTEREST, EMPHASIS

SENTENCE COMBINING

Good writers avoid the choppy style caused by using too many short, subject-first sentences. Study how the following paragraph, written in a choppy style, has been revised to achieve a more fluent, more mature style. The revised version uses subordination, coordination, apposition, and other devices to indicate clearly the relationship between ideas.

The sinking of the *Titanic* was a great disaster. The *Titanic* weighed 42,000 metric tons. It was the largest ship of its time. It was the most luxurious ship of its time. The sinking was one of the worst maritime disasters in history. The *Titanic* was on its maiden voyage. The ship struck an iceberg off the Grand Banks of Newfoundland. The accident happened on the night of April 14, 1912. The night was clear and cold. The captain had received iceberg warnings. He had chosen to pass through a perilous ice field. The rate of speed was 42 kilometers per hour. He wished to reach New York ahead of schedule. The *Titanic*'s hull had sixteen watertight compartments. The iceberg punctured five compartments. The ship's designers thought no accident could puncture more than four compartments. The ship sank in less than three hours. Over 1,500 of the 2,220 passengers and crew drowned. Another ship, the *Californian*, lay stopped in the water. It was less than eighteen kilometers away. It did not respond to the distress signal. The radio operator was off duty. The *Carpathia* was ninety kilometers away. It reversed course. It sped through the ice floes. It picked up survivors. By the time it arrived, many lives had been lost. The *Titanic* disaster quickly led to the reform of maritime safety laws.

The sinking of the 42,000-metric-ton *Titanic*, the largest and most luxurious ship of its time, was one of the worst maritime disasters in history. On the clear, cold night of April 14, 1912, the ship, on its maiden voyage, struck an iceberg off the Grand Banks of Newfoundland. Although the captain had received iceberg warnings, he had chosen to pass through a perilous ice field at 42 kilometers per hour in order to reach New York ahead of schedule. The iceberg punctured five of sixteen watertight compartments in the ship's hull, one more than the ship's designers had thought possible in any accident, and the ship sank in less than three hours, with the loss of over 1,500 of the 2,220 passengers and crew. Another ship, the *Californian*, lay stopped in the water less than eighteen kilometers away, but it did not respond to the distress signal because its radio operator was off duty. The *Carpathia*, which was ninety kilometers away, sped through the ice floes and picked up the survivors, but by then many lives had been lost. The *Titanic* disaster led to the reform of maritime safety laws.

As you combine short, choppy sentences in the exercises that follow, you will be learning to achieve a more fluent style, richer in variety and interest.

17a. Combine short, related sentences by inserting adjectives, adverbs, and prepositional phrases.[1]

Note how the following three sentences have been rewritten as one sentence by eliminating unnecessary words.

THREE SENTENCES   The Prime Minister closed the session.
                 The Prime Minister felt weary.
                 He closed the session with the Cabinet.

ONE SENTENCE   The **weary** Prime Minister closed the session **with the Cabinet**.

There may be more than one correct way to combine short sentences.

THREE SENTENCES   The plane moved slowly.
                 The plane moved along the runway.
                 The plane moved toward the hangar.

ONE SENTENCE   The plane moved **slowly along the runway toward the hangar**.

                                    or

                 Along the runway, the plane moved **slowly toward the hangar**.

[1] See pages 445–48 for information on prepositional phrases.

There are other correct ways in which these sentences could have been combined. Although you often have some degree of choice in combining short, related sentences, you may find that some combinations do not read smoothly, such as, *Along the runway toward the hangar slowly the plane moved.* You should avoid these combinations as well as those that change the meaning of the original short sentences.

EXERCISE 1. Combining Sentences by Inserting Adjectives, Adverbs, or Prepositional Phrases. Combine each group of short, related sentences by inserting adjectives, adverbs, or prepositional phrases into the first sentence and by eliminating unnecessary words. Add commas and conjunctions where they are necessary.

EXAMPLE 1. Peregrine falcons soar.
  They soar gracefully.
  They soar near their nests.
  1. *Peregrine falcons soar gracefully near their nests.*

1. Peregrine falcons became scarce.
  They became scarce in the United States.
  They became scarce because of the pesticide DDT.
2. No breeding pairs remained.
  No pairs remained east of the Mississippi.
  No pairs remained by 1970.
  No pairs of falcons remained.
3. Scientists are reintroducing falcons.
  The scientists are from Cornell University.
  The falcons are wild.
  The scientists reintroduce falcons under controlled conditions.
  The scientists reintroduce falcons to the eastern United States.
4. The ban on DDT has helped the falcons.
  The ban was effective.
  The ban has helped considerably.
  The falcons have been endangered.
5. Peregrines are hatching eggs.
  These peregrines are in the Eastern wilderness.
  They are hatching eggs for the first time.
  It is the first time since the 1950's.

17b. Combine closely related sentences by using participial phrases.

Participial phrases—phrases containing a participle with its complements or modifiers—help you add concrete details to nouns and
pronouns. In the following example, the participial phrases describe the
subject of the sentence, the noun *ship*.

> **Badly damaged by high winds** and **deserted by half its crew**, the ship finally
> reached a safe harbor.

Participial phrases are a useful way to combine sentences.

TWO SENTENCES   The colors were orange, red, and blue.
                 The colors were painted on the ceiling.
ONE SENTENCE   The colors **painted on the ceiling** were orange, red, and blue.

The second sentence has been turned into a participial phrase, *painted
on the ceiling,* and inserted in the first sentence. Unnecessary words
have been deleted.

   A participle or participial phrase must always be close to the noun or
pronoun it modifies. Otherwise the sentence may be confusing.

MISPLACED   Wrapped in silver paper, the bride accepted the wedding present.
IMPROVED   The bride accepted the wedding present **wrapped in silver paper**.

EXERCISE 2. **Combining Sentences by Using Participial Phrases.**
Combine each of the following pairs of sentences into one sentence by
turning either the first sentence or the second sentence into a participial
phrase and inserting it into the remaining sentence. Punctuate the
combined sentences correctly.

EXAMPLE   1. The employee asked for a raise.
              The employee found out about the boss's temper.
           1. *Asking for a raise, the employee found out about the boss's temper.*

1. Tomb robbers searched inside a crypt.
   Tomb robbers found gold.
2. The pitcher concentrated on the batter.
   The pitcher forgot about the base runner.
3. The index in this book is very long.
   It contains every topic found on every page.
4. The student did not hand in her paper.
   The student realized that two pages were missing.
5. We held back our cheers.
   We waited for the speech to end.
6. The van failed to stop at the red light.
   It narrowly missed another car.

7. I left the bread in the oven too long.
   I burned the crust.
8. Our counselor was stung by a bee.
   Our counselor yelled angrily.
9. The teacher was pleased with the test results.
   The teacher congratulated the class.
10. The hurricane swept across the ocean.
    The hurricane demolished every boat in its path.

17c. Combine short, related sentences by using appositives or appositive phrases.

Appositives and appositive phrases add detail to nouns and pronouns by helping to identify or explain them. The appositive phrase in the following sentence helps identify the noun *captain.*

> The captain of the swim team, **holder of six school records,** won a full athletic scholarship.

Two sentences can often be combined through the use of an appositive or an appositive phrase.

TWO SENTENCES Many students in the school play lacrosse.
              Lacrosse is the national summer sport of Canada.
ONE SENTENCE Many students in the school play lacrosse, **the national summer sport of Canada.**

EXERCISE 3. Combining Sentences by Using Appositives or Appositive Phrases. Combine the following pairs of sentences by turning one of the sentences into an appositive or an appositive phrase. Punctuate the combined sentence correctly. Answers may vary.

EXAMPLE 1. Elizabeth Bowen was born in Ireland. She is one of the leading
            fiction writers in England since World War I.
         1. *Elizabeth Bowen, one of the leading fiction writers in England
            since World War I, was born in Ireland.*

1. In *The Death of the Heart* the protagonist is a sensitive person, ill at ease with the world.
   The Death of the Heart is one of Bowen's best-known novels.
2. Bowen was a nurse and an air-raid warden during World War II.
   Bowen wrote about the psychological effects of war on civilians.
3. In *Going Home*, Doris Lessing writes about a return visit to Rhodesia.

Going Home is an autobiographical narrative.
4. Doris Lessing is a sensitive observer of social and political struggles.
    She describes people attempting to find meaning in life.
5. Katherine Mansfield is a modern master of the short story.
    She died of tuberculosis at the age of thirty-four.

17d. Combine short, related sentences by using compound subjects or verbs or by writing a compound sentence.

Compound subjects and verbs, as well as compound sentences, are common. Writers, however, often overuse compound constructions by loosely stringing together ideas that belong in separate sentences (see pages 399–400). You should not only learn the appropriate function of various connectives but should also avoid the overuse of *and* or *so*.

Compound subjects and verbs are joined by coordinating conjunctions such as *and, but,* and *or* and by correlative conjunctions such as *either—or, neither—nor,* and *both—and.*

EXAMPLES   **Either** Mr. Sands **or** one of his students will bring the radio.
            We watched the game **and** cheered our team to victory.

Independent clauses are joined into a compound sentence by conjunctions such as *and, but,* and *for* or by other connectives such as *furthermore, yet, however, therefore, either—or*, and *neither—nor.* The relationship of the independent clauses determines which connective works best.

EXAMPLES   Two cats were stranded in the tree, **and** no one could rescue them.
            The police officer questioned him; **however**, he refused to answer.
            [Note the use of the semicolon.]

Ideas in separate sentences can be combined by using the appropriate connecting words. See pages 345–49 for a complete list of connecting words.

TWO SENTENCES   Rain had soaked the playing field.
                 Practice was not canceled.
ONE SENTENCE   **Although** rain had soaked the playing field, practice was not canceled.

EXERCISE 4. Combining Simple Sentences into a Compound Sentence. The following items consist of two closely related ideas. Combine these ideas into a single sentence, using the appropriate connectives.

EXAMPLE   1. The Congress will approve this bill.
          The President will veto it.
         1. *The Congress will approve this bill, but the President will veto it.*

1. The basketball team has played well all season.
   It will probably win the championship.
2. Frank worked hard on his homework.
   His friend had given him the wrong assignment.
3. America must learn to use less energy.
   There will be a more severe energy shortage in a few years.
4. The prospects are bleak for new gym equipment.
   The student council will recommend this important purchase.
5. School spirit sometimes wanes during the winter months.
   The seniors have organized a carnival in December.

17e. Combine short, related sentences into a complex sentence by putting one idea into a subordinate clause.

Subordination allows you to express the relationship between two unequal ideas within a single sentence. Methods for subordinating ideas include the use of an adjective clause, an adverb clause, and a noun clause. Mastering these methods of subordination will improve the variety and clarity of your writing.

(1) Use an adjective clause to combine sentences.

Adjective clauses, like adjectives, modify nouns or pronouns. In the following sentence, the adjective clause is printed in boldfaced type.

The detective **who solved the case** was a master at logical thinking.

To combine sentences by using an adjective clause, you must first decide which idea to emphasize (see page 351). Then you must choose the correct relative pronoun to join the sentences.

RELATIVE PRONOUNS   who, whom, whose, which, that

The adjective clause must always be placed close to the word or words it modifies.

TWO SENTENCES   The story has an intricate plot.
                 I found the plot hard to follow.
ONE SENTENCE   The story has an intricate plot **that I found hard to follow.**

EXERCISE 5. Using Adjective Clauses to Combine Sentences.

Combine the following pairs of sentences by subordinating one idea in an adjective clause. Punctuate your sentences correctly.

EXAMPLE   1. Martin Luther King, Jr., married Coretta Scott.
He met her while studying at Boston University.
1. *Martin Luther King, Jr., married Coretta Scott, whom he met while studying at Boston University.*

1. My uncle is an experienced traveler.
He has recently returned from the Grand Canyon.
2. Richard prefers trout fishing.
It requires more patience than deep-sea fishing.
3. Pedro drove the truck.
Pedro has just received his driver's license.
4. Melissa is about to begin her project.
You can reach her after eight this evening.
5. I forgot the notebook.
It was lying on the sofa.

(2) Use an adverb clause to combine sentences.

Adverb clauses can express a relationship of time, cause, purpose, or condition between two ideas within a single sentence.[1]

EXAMPLE   **Although you present a convincing argument,** I will not change my mind.

To combine sentences by using an adverb clause, you must first decide which idea should become subordinate. You must then decide which subordinating conjunction best expresses the relationship between the two ideas.

TWO SENTENCES   Elsie received the reply in the mail.
She tore open the envelope impatiently.
ONE SENTENCE   **When Elsie received the reply in the mail,** she tore open the envelope impatiently.

EXERCISE 6. Using Adverb Clauses to Combine Sentences.
Combine each pair of sentences by subordinating one idea in an adverb clause. Punctuate the combined sentences correctly.

EXAMPLE   1. Sally did her best.
She was unable to win the prize.
1. *Although Sally did her best, she was unable to win the prize.*

[1] See pages 348–49 for a list of common subordinating conjunctions.

1. The committee members could not agree.
   The whole matter was referred to the president.
2. The president took the responsibility.
   She wanted to settle the matter herself.
3. She decided to bring the issue before the entire club.
   Everyone could express an opinion.
4. There was a great deal of talk.
   Nothing was decided.
5. A decision is reached today.
   The donors will not give us the money.
6. The city council offered to give us money for a clubhouse.
   We would let the public use it.
7. We had never admitted the public to our meetings.
   We didn't want to admit them to our clubhouse.
8. We would not lose the chance for a new clubhouse.
   Some of us favored admitting the public.
9. I agreed with those in favor of admitting the public.
   I sympathized with the others.
10. No agreement was reached.
    The money went to another club.

(3) Use a noun clause to combine sentences.

A noun clause is a subordinate clause used as a noun. Read the following examples of noun clauses and note how they are used.

> **Whoever buys that car** will be sorry. [noun clause as subject]
> Yesterday we learned **what Napoleon had accomplished.** [noun clause as direct object]
> We can spend the money for **whatever we like**. [noun clause as object of preposition]

A noun clause can also be used as a predicate nominative and as an indirect object. Noun clauses are usually introduced by *that, what, whatever, why, whether, how, who, whom, whoever,* or *whomever.*

Noun clauses are sometimes used without the introductory word *that.*

EXAMPLE   My sister said the trip would take three days.

EXERCISE 7. Using Noun Clauses to Combine Sentences.
Combine each of the following pairs of sentences by turning the

italicized sentence into a noun clause. Use one of the introductory words listed above.

EXAMPLE 1. *They thought that they did not need help.*
This was a very foolish idea.
1. *That they did not need help was a very foolish idea.*

1. The new senator promised.
The state would get more aid.
2. *Could they endure the debate?*
That was uncertain.
3. *They might succeed.*
This was the incentive that kept them working.
4. The odor of smoke convinced the family.
They should call the fire department.
5. The attorney asked a question.
He asked how the defendant had found the money.

REVIEW EXERCISE A. Using Sentence-Combining Methods.
Using the sentence-combining methods you have practiced thus far, combine each group of sentences into one smooth, well-written sentence. You may omit unnecessary words and change the word order, but you may not change the meaning of the original sentences. Punctuate your combined sentences correctly.

EXAMPLE 1. Hugo Gernsback began publishing *Amazing Stories.*
He began in 1926.
Amazing Stories was the first science-fiction magazine.
1. *In 1926 Hugo Gernsback began publishing* Amazing Stories, *the first science-fiction magazine.*

1. Science fiction ranges from projection to speculation.
The projection is careful.
The speculation is outlandish.
Science fiction usually requires the appearance of credibility.
2. *Frankenstein* is an early example of science fiction.
Frankenstein is a novel by Mary Shelley.
Frankenstein describes the scientific creation of human life.
3. There is another early example of science fiction.
The example is H. G. Wells's *The Time Machine.*
The Time Machine entertains.
The Time Machine offers social criticism.
The Time Machine predicts the future.

4. Some critics did not accept science fiction as serious literature.
These critics did not accept it easily.
Writers often included science fiction in their works.
These writers were major twentieth-century authors.
5. Today science fiction has supporters.
Science fiction has many active supporters.
They hold annual conventions.
They present Hugo and Nebula awards.
These awards are for the year's best writing.

REVIEW EXERCISE B. Combining Sentences to Add Variety to a Paragraph. Combine the short, choppy sentences in the following paragraph into longer, smoother sentences. Be sure that the sentences you write add variety to the paragraph. Use correct punctuation.

Mount St. Helens erupted in May 1980. It is near Vancouver, Washington. The eruption was sudden. The force was over five hundred times that of an atomic bomb. The explosion was caused by pressure from gas and molten rock. It tore the top off the mountain. It threw ash high into the air. The explosion and subsequent mudslides caused many deaths. More than thirty people died. The destruction left many homeless. The force of the blast leveled huge trees. The area was wide. The mud killed hundreds of deer and elk. The mud turned Spirit Lake into a mudhole. The lake was formerly picturesque. Much of the ash fell to earth within a few days. A cloud of dust remained in the stratosphere. This cloud was over much of the Northern Hemisphere. People saw spectacular sunrises and sunsets. This continued for two years. The sunrises and sunsets were rose-colored. The sunsets were due to solar rays. They struck microscopic particles of ash. Scientists suspect that intermittent showers will continue. The showers will consist of volcanic ash. They will continue for the next two decades.

AVOIDING MONOTONY

17f. Experiment with the length and structure of your sentences to achieve greater interest and variety.

Sentences in English—both spoken and written—usually begin with the subject. Any piece of writing in which most of the sentences needlessly depart from this normal order will strike a reader as artificial. However, an unbroken sequence of subject-predicate sentences may result in another stylistic fault—monotony. Such a sequence of sentences is monotonous because it lacks the logical connections and special emphasis that variations in sentence structure can provide. For example, the following sentences are perfectly clear:

> The two friends quarreled violently over a matter of slight importance.
> They never spoke from that time on.

But a closer connection can be made between these two sentences by moving the adverb phrase, which refers to the quarrel, up to the beginning of the second sentence:

> The two friends quarreled violently over a matter of slight importance.
> **From that time on** they never spoke.

Similarly, an important idea expressed by a modifier can be emphasized:

> Sue was not impressive in the classroom.
> **On the tennis court,** however, she came into her own.

The contrast is less striking when the second sentence begins with its subject:

> Sue was not impressive in the classroom.
> She came into her own, however, on the tennis court.

The normal order of sentences should not be shunned merely for the sake of variety. However, beginning a sentence with an important modifier can increase the force and clarity of your thought as well as provide a pleasing variation.

The exercises that follow are intended to give you practice in using different kinds of sentence openers. Used sparingly, these devices will improve your writing.

(1) Begin some of your sentences with a transposed appositive or with one of these modifiers: single-word modifier, phrase modifier, clause modifier.

Appositives

> The human brain, an enormously complex mechanism, contains about ten billion nerve cells. [subject first]
> **An enormously complex mechanism,** the human brain contains about ten billion nerve cells. [transposed appositive first]

Single-Word Modifiers

> The book is long and badly written, and it failed to hold my interest. [subject first]

Long and badly written, the book failed to hold my interest. [single-word modifiers first]

A number of changes have been made recently. [subject first]

Recently, a number of changes have been made. [single-word modifier first]

Phrase Modifiers

She was almost unbeatable on the tennis court. [subject first]

On the tennis court, she was almost unbeatable. [prepositional phrase first]

Joe tired rapidly during the second set and decided to save his strength for the third set. [subject first]

Tiring rapidly during the second set, Joe decided to save his strength for the third set. [participial phrase first]

Kim worked late every night to win the essay prize. [subject first]

To win the essay prize, Kim worked late every night. [infinitive phrase first]

Clause Modifiers

Investigators of the cause of the crash had to depend on evidence found in the wreckage because there were no survivors or witnesses. [subject first]

Because there were no survivors or witnesses, investigators of the crash had to depend on evidence found in the wreckage. [clause first]

EXERCISE 8. **Revising Sentences by Varying Sentence Beginnings.** Revise each sentence so that it will begin with an appositive or a single-word, phrase, or clause modifier.

1. A bowling team was formed this winter for the first time in the history of the school.
2. A sinister figure stepped cautiously into the dark room.
3. Candidates for a driver's license must take a written examination to prove their knowledge of traffic regulations.
4. The children, when both parents are working, are cared for in nursery schools.
5. The audience, tired and hot, soon became impatient.
6. We were frightened by the explosion and dared not move.
7. More than half of the 90,000 acres under cultivation had been ruined by the recent drought.
8. Jim, a merchant sailor for ten years, knew every important port in the world.
9. The new houses, although they look exactly alike from the outside, have very different interiors.
10. A small boy, sobbing bitterly, ran toward me.

(2) Vary the structure of your sentences by means of subordination. Avoid the exclusive use of simple and compound sentences.[1] Skillful use of the complex sentence is an indication of maturity in style.

REVIEW EXERCISE C. **Using Subordination to Combine Sentences.** Using subordination, combine the short sentences in each group into one long, smooth sentence.

1. Amelia Earhart made her first solo crossing of the Atlantic in 1932.
   Five years later she attempted a round-the-world flight.
   She became a major figure of concern when her plane lost radio contact on the second of July.
2. Gwendolyn Brooks is a poet, the author of *A Street in Bronzeville*.
   She has won the Pulitzer Prize.
   She has taught poetry in several Chicago colleges.
3. Eleanor Roosevelt was both versatile and talented.
   She wrote some very important books.
   One of them was *On My Own*.
   She was twice a delegate to the United Nations.
4. The Shakespeare Memorial at Stratford-on-Avon houses a theater.
   Stratford-on-Avon is the birthplace of Shakespeare.
   The Memorial also contains a gallery and a library.
5. On March 10, 1876, Alexander Graham Bell spoke through the first electromagnetic telephone.
   He spoke to Watson, his assistant.
   He said, "Mr. Watson, come here; I want you."

AVOIDING "STRINGY" STYLE

17g. **Give variety to your writing by avoiding the "stringy" style which results from the overuse of *and* and *so*.**

In everyday conversation we tend to string our ideas out, one after another, by means of the simple conjunctions *and* and *so*. In writing, however, this sort of thing appears childish and monotonous.

(1) Correct a stringy sentence by subordination of ideas.

STRINGY   College admission standards continue to rise, *and* tension and
SENTENCE   anxiety build to a ridiculous point in college-preparatory seniors,
            and this spoils their final year in high school.

---

[1] For a review of subordination, see pages 348–54. For an explanation of the kinds of sentences, see pages 476–78.

IMPROVED   As college admission standards continue to rise, tension and anxiety build to a ridiculous point in college-preparatory seniors, spoiling their final year in high school. [One *and* has been removed by means of the beginning subordinate clause. The other has been removed by means of the participial phrase, *spoiling their final year in high school.*]

The use of *so* as a conjunction is considered poor form. Its use can usually be avoided by using a subordinate clause or a phrase expressing cause or reason.

POOR USE   Maria Martinez believed in tradition, *so* she experimented with
OF *SO*   ancient Pueblo pottery techniques.

IMPROVED   Believing in tradition, Maria Martinez experimented with ancient Pueblo pottery techniques. *or*
Because she believed in tradition, Maria Martinez experimented with ancient Pueblo pottery techniques.

STRINGY USE   We heard the static on the radio, *so* we were afraid of a
OF *SO*   thunderstorm, *so* we decided not to go out in the boat.

IMPROVED   Fearing a thunderstorm when we heard the static on the radio, we decided not to go out in the boat.

(2) Correct a stringy sentence by dividing it into two sentences.

STRINGY   I am very fond of foreign films, and so I go to the Celtic Theater
SENTENCE   more than to the other theaters, and we get only the best foreign films, so I not only learn a lot, but I see better pictures.

IMPROVED   Being very fond of foreign films, I go to the Celtic Theater more than to the other theaters. Since we get only the best foreign films, I not only learn a lot, but I see better pictures. [stringiness corrected by subordination and by division into two sentences]

EXERCISE 9. Revising Sentences. Revise the sentences by one or more of the following methods: subordination, division into more than one sentence, and reduction. Get rid of the monotonous use of *and* and *so*. You may add a few words of your own if the words will help you to improve the sentences.

1. Tom Sawyer made Becky Thatcher jealous by talking to Amy Lawrence, and then Becky became very upset, so she invited everyone except Tom and Amy to her picnic, and then spent recess with Alfred, and she pretended not to notice Tom.
2. Tom and Becky continued to be angry with each other for a while, and then eventually they made up, and Tom looked forward to going to Becky's picnic.

3. Mrs. Thatcher set the day for the picnic and Tom and Becky visited the cave called "McDougal's Cave" with the rest of the company, and played hide-and-seek after exploring the wonders of the cave.
4. They followed a little stream of water, and Tom played the role of a discoverer, and Becky thought that was fun and followed him.
5. They wound down through the cave this way and that and crept from cavern to cavern and found a spring-fed pool.
6. In one cavern the ceiling was completely lined with bats, and the bats swarmed down when Tom and Becky entered the cavern with their candles, and one of them almost snuffed Becky's candle out.
7. Soon the stillness of the caves dampened Tom and Becky's spirits, and they realized that they had gone some distance from the others, and suddenly they were afraid they might be unable to get back.
8. They started back, and indeed they had become lost, and there was no way Tom could remember which route they had followed, and they had only one piece of cake and a few candle-stumps.
9. After several false starts through the various tunnels their candles gave out, and they were left in total darkness, and Becky wept, and they both thought they were certain to die in the pitch-black cave.
10. Leaving Becky alone, Tom took a length of rope and traced his way through the tunnels looking for an exit and soon saw a candle, so he shouted at the top of his voice, and the next thing he knew a familiar face was there in front of him.

CHAPTER 18

Sentence Revision

PRACTICE EXERCISES

This chapter contains exercises only. The exercises will test your understanding of sentence correctness, clearness, and smoothness, and they will give you practice in revising faulty sentence structure.

REVISING SENTENCES BY CORRECTING ERRORS IN SENTENCE STRUCTURE

EXERCISE 1. Revising Sentences by Correcting Errors in Sentence Structure. You will find below a list of errors in sentence structure. Each faulty sentence in the exercise illustrates one of these errors. You are to do two things: (1) write *before* the number of the sentence the letter of the error illustrated, and (2) write *after* the number of the sentence a revision which eliminates the error. Make sure that your revision is correct, clear, and smooth. If the sentence is correct as it stands, write a + before its number.

A   Lack of agreement (subject and verb, or pronoun and antecedent)
B   Incorrect case of pronoun
C   Dangling modifier
D   Lack of parallelism or faulty parallelism
E   Unclear reference of pronoun (ambiguous, general, weak)

EXAMPLE   1. Do you know whom it was?
            B   1. *Do you know who it was?*

1. People may disapprove of laws, but that doesn't prove they are good or bad.

2. Human behavior is complicated and difficult, not only to analyze but for evaluation.
3. The law is society's tested system of behavior, and they would have even worse problems without it.
4. Unless two individuals observe the same laws, the more powerful can always take advantage of the weaker.
5. Any wise judge, as well as the more experienced citizens, can appreciate that.
6. The fundamental principle behind all laws are the same.
7. It is that the rights of others limit the rights of any individual.
8. The law has many arms touching all of us, and to prescribe the proper limits in all our different roles.
9. It governs you as a student and I as a writer.
10. Hoping for order in our social dealings with one another, the fact that legality requires judicial decision often makes us impatient.
11. The complexity of judicial decisions reflects how complex is law itself.
12. When a law is carelessly formulated or improperly applied, a judge can cut them down to size.
13. The presiding judge in an American court of law is a person whom scholars agree has no counterpart in other nations.
14. Making every effort to avoid the "tyranny" of politics, the Constitution was written by men who knew how the law can be twisted to the selfish interests of those in power.
15. In the Constitution, legislative and executive power is restricted more than they are in other national systems of government.
16. Facing one practical question after another, this restriction was less a matter of design than it was the result of many difficult decisions individually reached.
17. If the writers of the Constitution had not given the powers they did to the courts, they would have been subject to one of the other branches of government.
18. The mood of an executive and the whim of a legislator consequently does not determine one's fate in a court of law.
19. Instead, the acts of executives and the laws of legislatures all become subject, when necessary, to the judgment of a judge.
20. Abuse and violation of the existing law was the last resort of the colonists.

EXERCISE 2. Revising Sentences by Correcting Errors in Sentence Structure. Follow the directions for Exercise 1.

    A   Sentence fragment
    B   Run-on sentence
    C   Incorrect tense or verb form
    D   Misplaced modifier
    E   Unclear relationship between sentence ideas (lack of subordination, faulty coordination)

1. Our camp, which lays at the north end of the lake, is overshadowed by the cliffs that raise steeply above it.
2. Team teaching offers teachers at least one important advantage, it enables each teacher on the team to teach his specialty.
3. Since it has a full squad of seasoned players, this year's football team should win the championship.
4. The car was driven by a stunning girl with whitewall tires.
5. The band in its new uniforms and the high-stepping majorette with her twirling baton as well as the stirring music.
6. A compromise is a settlement of differences reached by mutual concessions between two parties.
7. Secret police with hidden cameras that were trying to take pictures at the meeting were physically ejected by angry students.
8. She had intended to have gone to the dance with her brother.
9. At home we suffer the constant interference of our parents, at college we will be free to make our own decisions.
10. Tickets for matinees will cost $3.50, and matinees will be given on Wednesdays and Saturdays.
11. These experiences will be valuable in my career as a social worker, and it is a career in which I shall work with all kinds of people.
12. At the beginning of my junior-level Spanish course, the teacher reviewed the material I had the year before.
13. During negotiations between labor and management, work in the factory continued as usual.
14. The five junior-high-school buildings will cost eight million dollars, and they were approved by the taxpayers in yesterday's balloting.
15. We found several of the students in the shop very busy. Learning how to take a motor apart and put it together again.
16. The senator denied the many charges that had been made against her briefly and categorically.

17. In high school I have been unable to take some courses I wanted and have been required to take others I did not want.
18. Twenty percent of the students said they were satisfied with their own study habits, fifty-four percent said they wished they knew how to study more effectively.
19. If you would have come earlier, you could have seen the first act.
20. The demand for good television material exceeds the supply, and some of the best material, important news events, is not being fully used, and the reason is that news telecasts are not profitable.

REVISING SENTENCES BY SELECTING THE BEST EXPRESSIONS

EXERCISE 3. Revising Sentences by Selecting the Best Expressions. Number your paper 1–20. The italicized part of each sentence below is revised in two ways. If you consider one of these revisions an improvement, write the letter of the better one (*a* or *b*). If you consider the sentence correct as it stands, write +.

1. Behind one of the doors waits a tiger, *and the other has a beautiful lady behind it.*
    a. . . . and behind the other waits a beautiful lady.
    b. . . . and a beautiful lady waits behind the other.
2. If you go on a trip, *it will give you an excellent chance to practice your camera technique.*
    a. . . . you will have an excellent chance to practice your camera technique.
    b. . . . an excellent chance to practice your camera technique will be yours.
3. When developing films, *a darkroom will be needed.*
    a. . . . one thing you will need is a darkroom.
    b. . . . you will need a darkroom.
4. A deep-sea fisher needs an outboard motor much larger *than a fisher who fishes in sheltered waters.*
    a. . . . than that used by a fisher in sheltered waters.
    b. . . . than one fishing in sheltered waters.
5. Although they listen to several news broadcasts each day, *most people continue to buy a daily paper.*
    a. . . . a daily paper continues to be bought by most people.

    b. . . . the buying of a daily paper by most people continues.

6. During the winter *Angela both developed her skill in skiing and ice-skating.*

    a. . . . Angela developed her skill in both skiing and ice-skating.

    b. . . . Angela developed both her skill in skiing and in ice-skating.

7. *Pat and him told Mike and I* the answers to the homework problems.

    a. . . . Pat and him told Mike and me . . .

    b. . . . Pat and he told Mike and me . . .

8. Ever since the accident, *driving past that spot*, the whole experience has returned.

    a. . . . while driving past that spot, . . .

    b. . . . as I have driven past that spot, . . .

9. *Was it he who* you thought stole the money?

    a. Was it he whom . . .

    b. Was it him whom . . .

10. When one of the girls *have completed their report, ask them* to bring it to me.

    a. . . . has completed their report, ask them . . .

    b. . . . has completed her report, ask her . . .

11. Don't expect *Jane and I to be as good as her* in English.

    a. . . . Jane and me to be as good as she . . .

    b. . . . Jane and I to be as good as she . . .

12. Plans for the P.T.A. party *include not only dancing but also* a floor show and a buffet supper.

    a. . . . not only include dancing but also . . .

    b. . . . include not only dancing, but also the guests will enjoy . . .

13. To my complete surprise the students *accepted the new type of examination which the teachers had prepared without a complaint.*

    a. . . . accepted the new type of examination without a complaint, which the teachers had prepared.

    b. . . . accepted without a complaint the new type of examination which the teachers had prepared.

14. The mayor's economy committee *has been investigating street-cleaning costs, and it has published a report on its findings.*

    a. . . . , which has been investigating street-cleaning costs, has published a report on its findings.

    b. . . . has been investigating street-cleaning costs, and a report has been published on its findings.

15. The two causes of "college neurosis" are trying to get into college *and then you try to stay there.*
    a. . . . and then to try to stay there.
    b. . . . and then trying to stay there.
16. *The students received the new yearbook,* which came out on the last day of school, *with enthusiasm.*
    a. The students received with enthusiasm the new yearbook . . .
    b. The students with enthusiasm received the new yearbook . . .
17. *The telegram reached me too late advising against going to Chicago.*
    a. Too late the telegram advising against going to Chicago reached me.
    b. The telegram advising against going to Chicago reached me too late.
18. *It is not the cost of a gift but its appropriateness that matters.*
    a. The cost of a gift does not matter, but the appropriateness of it does.
    b. It is not the cost that matters of a gift, but its appropriateness.
19. After being reprimanded twice, *the teacher, for further punishment, sent Ann to the principal.*
    a. . . . by the teacher, Ann was sent to the principal for further punishment.
    b. . . . the teacher sent Ann to the principal for further punishment.
20. *Driving through the mountains, we were impressed by the engineering achievements of road builders.*
    a. We were impressed by the engineering achievements of road-builders, driving through the mountains.
    b. We were impressed by the engineering achievements, driving through the mountains, of road builders.

REVISING AWKWARD SENTENCES

EXERCISE 4. Revising Awkward Sentences. This exercise is composed of awkward sentences which you are to revise in any way that will make them clearer and smoother. Your purpose is to express the same idea in a better way. Sentences may contain specific errors or they may be simply clumsy. You may add words or omit words wherever you wish, provided you do not alter the meaning. Each problem can be handled in a single sentence, but your teacher may allow you to divide some of the problems into two sentences.

1. She tried to find out the boy's name that she was to invite.
2. Featherbedding is one result of automation, which is the practice of keeping workers on the job, which is unnecessary, because the job has been made obsolete by machines.
3. The dean was more impressed by the candidate's scholastic record than his athletic record impressed him.
4. There are many persons who have jobs part of the year, and a job is not held by them the rest of the year, being among the unemployed.
5. There is a great deal of Franklin's philosophy which certainly everyone who reads it can benefit from in his *Autobiography*.
6. Soon families will have helicopters just like cars today and will be able to go from place to place much more easier than by car since there will be a direct route and the traffic will be much less.
7. Since we hadn't no tire repair kit, the motorcycle was pushed to the nearest gas station where we had a patch put on it.
8. Tammy was an optimist, easygoing, and nothing ever seemed to trouble her no matter what happened.
9. Opening the curtain, an empty stage was revealed, but the stage crew arrived a moment later and, busily working and talking, the set was soon up for the first act.
10. In a child a negative attitude may come from the natural desire for recognition and independence, but when an adult shows a negative attitude, it may be a symptom of neurosis.

PART THREE

TOOLS FOR WRITING AND REVISING:

Grammar ▪ Usage ▪ Mechanics

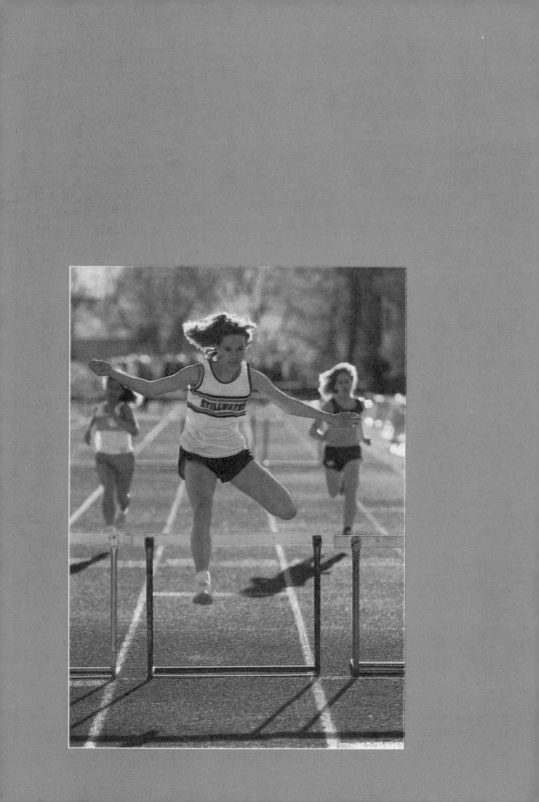

CHAPTER 19

The Parts of Speech

THEIR IDENTIFICATION AND FUNCTION

In your study of English, certain aspects will already be familiar from your English courses of previous years. Among these is grammar.

Grammar is important. It gives you the wherewithal to talk about language by providing a terminology and a system of classification. Also, by making you aware of the basic patterns of English sentences, it can help you develop a varied and interesting style in your speaking and writing. This is one of the main goals of the study of English.

The next few chapters will give you the opportunity to review and refine what you have learned in previous years. Chapter 19 deals with the parts of speech—the building blocks of language.

DIAGNOSTIC TEST

Identifying the Parts of Speech of Words. Number your paper 1–20. Write the numbered words from the following passage and the part of speech, using these abbreviations: *n.* (noun), *pron.* (pronoun), *adj.* (adjective), *v.* (verb), *adv.* (adverb), *conj.* (conjunction), *prep.* (preposition), *interj.* (interjection). Base your answers on the way each word is used in the sentence.

EXAMPLE   Writing can be (1) *inventive* and original.
     1. *inventive, adj.*

GRAMMAR

For less than five dollars (1) *you* can get to know yourself better! How can such a wonder be accomplished? Purchase a (2) *blank* notebook (3) *and* begin to keep a personal journal. Within a short time you will be amazed to see what you (4) *learn* (5) *about* yourself.

Keeping a journal is (6) *simple*. There is only one rule: date all entries. (7) *Usually* your mood will determine length. One type of entry is the (8) *daily* log, in which you record (9) *what* you did and how you felt on a particular day. Another is a (10) *record* of favorite songs and poetry. (11) *Most* important are those entries that have nothing to do with your "outer life," (12) *but* that (13) *record* your "inner life": your dreams, your thoughts, your questions, your goals, and especially your feelings. (14) *Because* the journal is a personal book, which no one else reads, it becomes a "free place" to say (15) *anything* you want. Most people find that writing four or five entries a week is a realistic goal. Rereading your entries (16) *later* will show you how you once were.

Does the journal really work? (17) *Wow!* You bet it does! One girl in (18) *Connecticut* wrote to her teacher that keeping a journal was "the closest I've come to knowing myself." The journal is an adventure (19) *in* self-awareness. (20) *Try* keeping one yourself.

THE NOUN

19a. A *noun* is a word used to name a person, place, thing, or idea.

Nouns may be classified in two ways: *proper* or *common* and *abstract* or *concrete*. A further classification for some nouns is *collective*.

A *proper noun* names a particular person, place, or thing and is capitalized: *Ann, New Mexico, Sears Tower*.

A *common noun* does not name a particular person, place, or thing. Common nouns are not capitalized: *woman, district, chair*.

An *abstract noun* names a quality, a characteristic, or an idea: *peace, civilization, honor, justice*.

A *concrete noun* names an object that can be perceived by the senses: *star, whisper, gravel, cinnamon*.

A *collective noun* names a group: *jury, band, family*.

> ☞ NOTE A *compound noun* is a noun composed of more than one word: *County Savings and Loan Association, roller coaster, weekend, forget-me-not*.

EXERCISE 1. Identifying and Classifying Nouns. After the proper number, write the nouns in the following sentences in order. After each noun, indicate its classification: proper or common.

1. Last summer our family drove to Chicago in our new van.
2. Because of their intelligence and athletic ability, Karen Cornell and Leonard Johnson were named "Scholar Athletes."
3. In one afternoon the crew repaired eleven helicopters.
4. We purchased tomatoes, lettuce, and corn grown by local farmers.
5. Congress debated the merits of a tax bill late into the night.
6. My goal is to visit every state in the United States.
7. When they saw the beauty of the snow-capped Rockies, the hikers paused and silently enjoyed the scene.
8. Her valuable experience as last year's class treasurer convinced a majority of the students to vote for her for class president.
9. Blunt honesty, quick wit, and fierce loyalty are the qualities I most admired in Huck Finn.
10. The crowd roared enthusiastically as Chip sank the winning basket just one second before time ran out.

WRITING APPLICATION A:
Defining Abstract Nouns

An abstract noun refers to something that cannot be pictured or heard or felt.

EXAMPLES   hope, freedom, awe, regret, success

Writing Assignment

Great writers usually focus on abstract ideas. For example, William Shakespeare explores *ambition* in *Macbeth* and *indecision* in *Hamlet.* Define an abstract noun in a clear, specific way and use an anecdote or a concrete illustration to make it meaningful for your readers.

THE PRONOUN

19b. A *pronoun* is a word used in place of a noun or of more than one noun.

EXAMPLE   The commuters complained to the mayor about the fare increase.
They said that **he** had not warned **them** about **it.**

In the preceding example, the pronouns *they* and *them* take the place of
the noun *commuters;* the pronoun *he* takes the place of the noun *mayor;*
and the pronoun *it* takes the place of the noun *increase.*

Sometimes a pronoun takes the place of another pronoun.

EXAMPLE   **One** of the film projectors is broken. **It** has been sent out for repair.
[The pronoun *it* takes the place of the pronoun *one.*]

The word to which a pronoun refers (whose place it takes) is the
antecedent of the pronoun. In the preceding example *one* is the
antecedent of *it.*

Pronouns are classified as *personal, reflexive, intensive, relative,
interrogative, demonstrative,* or *indefinite.*

Personal Pronouns

I, me	he, him	it	they, them
you	she, her	we, us	

Possessive Forms of Personal Pronouns

my, mine	his	its	their, theirs
your, yours	her, hers	our, ours	

Some of the possessive forms—*my, your, his, her, its, our, their*—are
used before a noun in the same way that adjectives are used to limit the
meaning of a noun: *my* parents, *your* home, *her* coat, etc. They are
possessive pronouns functioning as adjectives. In this book these words
are called pronouns. However, your teacher may prefer to have you call
them possessive adjectives.

Reflexive and Intensive Pronouns

myself	ourselves
yourself	yourselves
himself, herself, itself	themselves

Personal pronouns combined with *-self, -selves* may be used in two ways:

1. They may be used *reflexively.*

   Miranda explained **herself.**

2. They may be used *intensively* for emphasis.

   Miranda **herself** made the explanation.

Relative Pronouns

who	which	whose
whom	that	

Relative pronouns are used to introduce subordinate clauses (see Chapter 22, pages 466–68).

EXAMPLES   The college **that** I chose is in Texas.
Do you know the woman **whose** writing was mentioned?

Interrogative Pronouns

who	which	what
whom	whose	

Interrogative pronouns are used in questions.

EXAMPLES   **Who** borrowed my pen?
Which do you prefer?

Demonstrative Pronouns

this	these	that	those

Demonstrative pronouns are used to point out persons or things.

EXAMPLES   **That** is an excellent question.
This is the correct answer.

Most Commonly Used Indefinite Pronouns

all	everybody	no one
another	everyone	one
any	few	other
anybody	many	several
anyone	most	some
both	neither	somebody
each	nobody	someone
either	none	such

Pronouns that do not usually refer to a specific antecedent are called *indefinite pronouns*. Most indefinite pronouns express the idea of quantity: *all, few, none*.

EXAMPLES   **Most** of the members have voted.
Everyone favors a weekly meeting.

EXERCISE 2. Identifying Pronouns. Number your paper 1–10. After the proper number, write the pronouns in the order in which they occur in the sentence.

1. Last year our school gave two photography courses, neither of which had been offered before.
2. The course that I took dealt with the ways in which people perceive their environment.
3. Most of us block out our everyday surroundings.
4. You can prove to yourselves how blind all of us become to our surroundings.
5. Which of you, upon returning home from a trip, suddenly notices how different all of the rooms look to you?
6. Some of your possessions may look unfamiliar to you, and a few of them may seem totally alien.
7. Eventually your house takes on its familiar appearance again.
8. Each of us can regain the ability to see freshly if we make full use of our sense of sight.
9. We must see the objects themselves as shapes instead of thinking about their function.
10. Claude Monet, a French impressionist painter, stated that we must forget the names of the things that we are looking at.

THE ADJECTIVE

19c. An *adjective* is a word used to modify a noun or a pronoun.

To modify means "to limit," or "to make the meaning of a word more definite." Adjectives may modify nouns or pronouns in any one of three different ways:

1. By telling *what kind:* **green** apples, **small** car, **capable** student
2. By pointing out *which one:* **this** woman, **that** play
3. By telling *how many:* **some** birds, **two** squirrels

As the preceding examples show, the normal position of an adjective is directly before the word it modifies. Occasionally, for stylistic reasons, a writer may use adjectives after the word they modify.

EXAMPLE   The hikers, **tired** and **hungry,** straggled into camp.

A *predicate adjective* (see Chapter 20, page 440) is separated from the word it modifies by a verb.

EXAMPLES   Deborah is **practical.**
His stew tasted **delicious.**

GRAMMAR

Articles

The most frequently used adjectives are *a, an,* and *the*. These words are usually called *articles.*

A and *an* are indefinite articles; they refer to one of a general group.

EXAMPLES   **A** book fell down.
We worked **an** hour.

A is used before words beginning with a consonant sound; *an* is used before words beginning with a vowel sound. Notice in the second example above that *an* is used before *hour,* which begins with a consonant; that is because the *h* in *hour* is not pronounced. Remember that the *sound* of the noun, not the spelling, determines which indefinite article should be used.

The is the definite article. It indicates that a noun refers to someone or something in particular.

EXAMPLES   **The** book fell down.
Margaret ate **the** orange.
The hour passed quickly.

The Same Word as Adjective and Pronoun

A word may be used as more than one part of speech. This rule is especially true of the words in the list below, which may be used both as pronouns and as adjectives.

all	many	that
another	more	these
any	neither	this
both	one	those
each	other	what
either	several	which
few	some	

ADJECTIVE   **These** books are overdue. [*These* modifies the noun *books.*]
PRONOUN   **These** are overdue. [*These* takes the place of a noun previously mentioned.]

ADJECTIVE   We chose **neither** candidate. [*Neither* modifies the noun *candidate.*]
PRONOUN   We chose **neither.** [*Neither* takes the place of a noun previously mentioned.]

Nouns Used as Adjectives

Nouns are sometimes used as adjectives.

    sofa cushion   **hotel** lobby   **bread** pudding

When you are identifying parts of speech and you encounter a noun used as an adjective, label it as an adjective.

EXERCISE 3. Identifying Adjectives and the Words They Modify. Write the adjectives in the following sentences in order after the numbers of the sentences in which they appear. After each adjective, write the word(s) modified. Do not list articles (*a, an,* and *the*).

1. The first person to walk on the moon was Neil Armstrong, the American astronaut.
2. Young people admire the sleek look of a new car.
3. Nine players are needed to form a baseball team.
4. "That engine will work for many years," said Mr. Sanchez.
5. On a sultry July afternoon we enjoyed sitting under the branches of a beautiful willow tree.
6. The rich soil of Kansas accounts for the high agricultural yield of that state.
7. Eager fans waited for several hours to buy tickets for the rock concert.
8. Some regard Jim Thorpe, an Oklahoma Indian, as the greatest all-around athlete America has yet produced.
9. On an ordinary day the major television networks offer serious and comic programs.
10. Sharon made a narrow vase, a deep bowl, and a coffee mug in her pottery class; she was proud of these accomplishments.

EXERCISE 4. Identifying Nouns, Pronouns, and Adjectives. For each sentence below, write the italicized words in order in a column, numbering them as in the example. After each word, tell what part of speech it is. If a word is an adjective, write in parentheses the word that the adjective modifies. Do not list articles (*a, an,* and *the*).

EXAMPLE   1. *Everyone* in class is writing a poem about a *famous American.*
        1. *Everyone, pron.*
          famous, adj., (American)
          American, n.

1. *Some* students are writing *theirs* about well-known Presidents; *others* have chosen *military* heroes as *their* subjects.
2. *Most* of *us* are writing about *someone whom* we admire.
3. The *aviator* Amelia Earhart is a *popular* subject; *another* choice is Harriet Tubman, the *courageous* woman who led *many* people to *freedom* on the Underground Railroad.
4. *Both* of *these* women made lasting *impressions* in their time.
5. On Earhart's attempted around-the-world *flight, radio* contact aboard her plane was broken and never resumed.
6. *Speculation* about the *nature* of Earhart's flight continues; *many* believe that she was on an *intelligence* mission.
7. Tubman was *one* of *many* former slaves *who* devoted their lives to the *cause* of freedom and to the *advancement* of their people.
8. The *abolitionist* John Brown referred to her as *"General Tubman."*
9. Although she *herself* was *free,* she could not be happy while even *one* member of her family remained a *slave;* once she brought as many as *twenty-five* slaves to freedom in a *single* band.
10. *Nobody* in our class seems *unhappy* with his or her choice of *subject.*

WRITING APPLICATION B:
Replacing Drab Adjectives with Fresh, Lively Ones

You use adjectives to make nouns and pronouns more definite. Adjectives tell what kind, which one, or how many. Try to replace the old worn-out adjectives with fresh, even startling ones. For example, look at the fresh, vivid adjectives Gerard Manley Hopkins uses to describe a falcon in his poem "The Windhover": ". . . *dapple-dawn-drawn* Falcon . . . how he rung upon the rein of the *wimpling* wing. . . ."

Writing Assignment

Select a childhood experience that had particular meaning for you. As you describe this experience, try to use fresh, lively adjectives.

THE VERB

19d. A *verb* is a word that expresses action or otherwise helps to make a statement.

All verbs help to make a statement. Some help to make a statement by expressing action. The action expressed may be physical, as in *hit, play,* and *run,* or it may be mental, as in *think, imagine, believe.*

Transitive and Intransitive Verbs

Action verbs may or may not take an *object*—a noun or pronoun that completes the action by showing *who* or *what* is affected by the action. Verbs that have an object are called *transitive.* The verbs in the following examples are transitive:

EXAMPLES   The rain **lashed** the windows. [*Windows* is the object of *lashed.*]
My cousin **bought** a new car. [*Car* is the object of *bought.*]

Verbs that express action without objects are called *intransitive.*

EXAMPLES   The rain **fell.**
My cousin **drove.**

Some action verbs are transitive only (*ignore, complete*) and some intransitive only (*arrive, exist*). Most verbs in English can be either.

EXAMPLES   The chorus **sang** patriotic *songs.* [transitive]
The chorus **sang.** [intransitive]

☞ NOTE   Most dictionaries group the meanings of verbs according to whether they are transitive (*v.t.* in most dictionaries) or intransitive (*v.i.*).

Linking Verbs

Some verbs express a state or condition. These verbs link to the subject a noun, a pronoun, or an adjective that describes or identifies the subject. They are called *linking verbs.* These verbs are *intransitives.* The word that is linked to the subject is called a *subject complement.*

EXAMPLES   This **is** *she.* [*She* refers to the subject *this.*]
She **looks** *serious.* [*Serious* refers to the subject *she.*]

The subject complement always refers to the subject of the linking verb. It may identify the subject, as in the first example, or describe the subject, as in the second one.

The most common linking verb is the verb *be,*[1] which has the

---

[1] The verb *be* can also be followed by certain adverbs and adverb phrases: We were *there;* the men were *at work.* In this situation, *be* is not considered a linking verb.

following forms: *am, is, are, was, were, be, being, been* (and all verb phrases ending in *be, being,* or *been,* such as *can be, is being,* and *could have been*). Other common linking verbs are listed below.

Common Linking Verbs

appear	grow	seem	stay
become	look	smell	taste
feel	remain	sound	

Many of the verbs in the preceding list can also be used as action verbs—that is, without a subject complement.

LINKING   The singer **appeared** nervous.
ACTION   The singer **appeared** on television.

In general, a verb is a linking verb if you can substitute some form of the verb *seem* for it.

EXAMPLES   The audience **looked** [seemed] sympathetic.
The singer gradually **grew** [seemed] more relaxed.

The Helping Verb and the Verb Phrase

A *verb phrase* is made up of a main verb and one or more *helping verbs* (sometimes called *auxiliary verbs*). Helping verbs *help* the main verb to express action or make a statement. The helping verbs in the following phrases are printed in boldfaced type:

has played	**will be** coming
should have paid	**must have been** injured

In other words, a verb phrase is a verb of more than one word.

Common Helping Verbs

am	has	can (may) have
are	had	could (would, should) be
is	can	could (would, should) have
was	may	will (shall) have been
were	will (shall) be	might have
do	will (shall) have	might have been
did	has (had) been	must
have	can (may) be	must have
		must have been

The parts of a verb phrase may be separated from one another by words; i.e., the helping verb may be separated from the main verb.

EXAMPLES **Did** you **see** Lorraine Hansberry's play?
      We **have** not **seen** it yet.

EXERCISE 5. Identifying and Classifying Verbs and Verb Phrases.
Write in order the verbs and verb phrases in the following sentences. After each verb, tell whether it is transitive (*v.t.*), intransitive (*v.i.*), or linking (*l.v.*). List all the words in a verb phrase.

1. The Statue of Liberty, which has become a major American landmark, may well be the best-known structure in the world.
2. It possesses a twofold magic: it symbolizes human liberty, and it unfailingly awes the visitor by its sheer size.
3. Moreover, it has never fallen down and has survived everything that wind and weather can throw at it.
4. Although Frederic-Auguste Bartholdi designed the statue, the supporting framework came from the drawing board of Alexandre-Gustave Eiffel.
5. The copper statue has an intricate inner network that supports Liberty's somewhat awkward pose.
6. The statue itself was a gift from the people of France, but American contributions paid for the construction of the pedestal.
7. In newspaper editorials, Joseph Pulitzer persuaded the American people that they needed this statue.
8. They agreed, and in 1886 celebrated the dedication of the Statue of Liberty on what was then Bedloe's Island in New York Bay.
9. Bartholdi had borrowed his mother's features for Liberty's face.
10. Those features have remained symbols of quiet determination.

WRITING APPLICATION C:
Selecting Precise Verbs

The particular verb you choose can transform a vague idea into a highly specific one. Notice the shades of meaning suggested by the following verb changes: He *talked* (*negotiated, chattered*) for an hour.

Writing Assignment

An incident that on the surface seems unimportant may actually be quite significant. Write a journal entry describing such an event. Use fresh, specific verbs.

GRAMMAR

THE ADVERB

19e. An *adverb* is a word used to modify a verb, an adjective, or another adverb.

The adverb is used most commonly as the modifier of a verb. It may tell *how, when, where,* or *to what extent* (*how often* or *how much*) the action of the verb is done.

EXAMPLES   She reads **quickly.** [*Quickly* tells *how* she reads.]
She reads **early** and **late.** [*Early* and *late* tell *when* she reads.]
She reads **everywhere.** [*Everywhere* tells *where* she reads.]
She reads **thoroughly.** [*Thoroughly* tells *to what extent* she reads.]
She reads **frequently.** [*Frequently* tells *how often* she reads.]

Some adverbs, such as *really, actually, truly, indeed,* are used chiefly for emphasis. Classify these adverbs as adverbs of extent.

EXAMPLES   Rosa can **really** skate. [*Really* emphasizes the fine quality of Rosa's skating.]
She is **truly** a fine skater. [*Truly* emphasizes the fact that she is a fine skater.]
She can **actually** fly over the ice. [*Actually* emphasizes the fact that she can fly over the ice, which is apparently a surprise to the speaker.]

An adverb may modify an adjective.

EXAMPLE   She is a **really** intense competitor. [*Really* modifies the adjective *intense,* telling to what extent she is competitive.]

An adverb may modify another adverb.

EXAMPLE   She skated **very** well. [The adverb *very* modifies the adverb *well,* telling how well she skated.]

☞ NOTE   The word *not* is classified as an adverb; it tells *to what extent.*

Nouns Used as Adverbs

Some nouns may be used adverbially.

EXAMPLES   My parents left **yesterday.**
They will return **Saturday.**

In identifying parts of speech, label nouns used in this way as adverbs.

EXERCISE 6. Identifying Adverbs and the Words They Modify.
Write the adverbs in the following sentences in order after the proper number. After each adverb, write the word or words it modifies and state whether the adverb tells *how, when, where,* or *to what extent*.

1. Dr. Rosalyn Yalow is an American physicist who helped develop an extremely sensitive biological technique.
2. Radioimmunoassay is now used in laboratories here and abroad and can readily detect infinitesimal biological substances.
3. Dr. Yalow writes, "If you ever have a new idea, and it's really new, you have to expect that it will not be widely accepted immediately."
4. In other words, unlike Archimedes, scientists do not leap excitedly from the bath crying, "Eureka!"
5. Dr. Yalow and her colleague accidentally discovered radioimmuno-assay while observing two patients.
6. They then carefully interpreted their observations and arrived at their exciting discovery.
7. Although her collaborator was deceased, the Nobel Prize Committee promptly excepted its rule and awarded Dr. Yalow the undeniably prestigious Nobel Prize for Medicine.
8. Radioimmunoassay was an unquestionably important discovery; it soon became a scientifically basic tool for investigation in widely different areas of medicine.
9. According to Dr. Yalow, the technique was not quickly accepted because people ordinarily resist change.
10. She is convinced that progress cannot be obstructed forever and that eventually a highly original idea is accepted.

EXERCISE 7. Identifying the Parts of Speech of Words. Write the numbered, italicized words. After each word, tell what part of speech it is; then, after each adjective or adverb, tell what word or words it modifies.

Lizards may be sleek, slender, and (1) *graceful;* or they may be (2) *fantastically* ugly, with grotesque (3) *horns,* spines, and frilly collars. (4) *They* have startling habits. They may snap off (5) *their* tails when they are seized. (6) *Some* may rear up and run (7) *away* on their hind legs. (8) *Certainly*, there (9) *is* nothing (10) *commonplace* about lizards.

(11) *Warmer* portions of the earth (12) *have* the (13) *greatest* number and variety of lizards, but (14) *they* are (15) *also* found in temperate latitudes. There are about 125 (16) *different* kinds in the United States.

(17) *One* of the most familiar is the little chameleon, also called the anolis. (18) *It* (19) *belongs* to the iguana family and is (20) *quite* different from the (21) *true* chameleon family of Africa.

THE PREPOSITION

19f. A *preposition* is a word used to show the relation of a noun or pronoun to some other word in the sentence.

In the following sentences the prepositions are shown in boldfaced type. The words between which the prepositions show relationships are italicized.

> The first *speaker* **on** the *program* is my mother.
> Her cousin *will teach* **in** *San Diego* next year.
> The *two* **of** *us* edited the *article* **for** the *magazine*.

Object of a Preposition

A preposition appears at the beginning of a phrase (see Chapter 21, page 445). The noun or pronoun at the end of a prepositional phrase is the *object* of the preposition that begins the phrase.

EXAMPLES   before **lunch**   at the **game**

Commonly Used Prepositions

about	between	over
above	beyond	past
across	but (meaning "except")	since
after	by	through
against	concerning	throughout
along	down	to
amid	during	toward
among	except	under
around	for	underneath
at	from	until
before	in	unto
behind	into	up
below	like	upon
beneath	of	with
beside	off	within
besides	on	without

A group of words may act as a preposition: *on account of, in spite of.*

EXERCISE 8. Writing Sentences With Prepositions. Write five sentences, each containing a different one of the following prepositions. Underline each prepositional phrase and circle the object of each preposition.

1. against   2. below   3. during   4. into   5. until

THE CONJUNCTION

19g. A *conjunction* **is a word that joins words or groups of words.**

The conjunctions below are printed in boldfaced type; the words or groups of words that the conjunctions join are italicized.

> The bear *turned* **and** *lumbered* off into the woods.
> We can use a *pickup truck* **or** a *jeep.*
> She helped **both** *Carrie* **and** *me* with our applications.
> *The doctor will call back* **after** *he has studied the X-rays.*

There are three kinds of conjunctions: *coordinating* conjunctions, *correlative* conjunctions, and *subordinating* conjunctions.

Coordinating Conjunctions

and	but	or	nor	for	so	yet

Correlative Conjunctions

either . . . or	not only . . . but (also)
neither . . . nor	whether . . . or
both . . . and	

Correlative conjunctions are always used in pairs.

> These shirts are available **not only** in small sizes **but also** in outsizes.
> The speech was **neither** eloquent **nor** convincing.

Commonly Used Subordinating Conjunctions[1]

after	before	provided	unless
although	how	since	until
as	if	than	when
as much as	inasmuch as	that	where
because	in order that	though	while

---

[1] Some of these words may be used as prepositions: *after, before, since, until;* others may be used as adverbs: *how, when, where. That* is often used as a relative pronoun.

Subordinating conjunctions are used to begin subordinate clauses (see Chapter 22, pages 472–74), usually adverb clauses.

In the following sentences, the subordinate clauses are italicized, and the subordinating conjunctions are in boldfaced type.

This computer is even better **than** *we had anticipated.*
The sun had already set **when** *we reached Grand Canyon National Park.*

A subordinating conjunction does not always come between the sentence parts that it joins. It may come at the beginning of the sentence.

If the price is right, I will buy your bicycle.
Since you can't help me, I will do it myself.

EXERCISE 9. Identifying and Classifying Conjunctions. Number your paper 1–10. After each number, write the conjunction(s) in the sentence. Then classify the conjunction(s) as coordinating, correlative, or subordinating.

1. Our old car needs either a valve job or a new engine.
2. Before you write your paper, you must submit an outline.
3. I don't know whether I'll take physics or economics next year.
4. Taritha excels not only as a swimmer but also as a musician.
5. After I had read the novel *The Return of the Native,* I became a Thomas Hardy fan.
6. Workers here pay city, state, and federal income taxes.
7. Because the Tsang family had installed a smoke detector in their home, their lives were saved.
8. Both Mike and Sue work at the same supermarket.
9. Are you going to the movies or not?
10. When I looked in my wallet, I was amazed to find five dollars.

THE INTERJECTION

19h. An *interjection* is a word that expresses emotion and has no grammatical relation to other words in the sentence.

EXAMPLES   Oh!   My goodness!   Ah!   Ouch!

THE SAME WORD AS DIFFERENT PARTS OF SPEECH

Many words in English may be used as more than one part of speech. For example, *these* may be an adjective (*these books*) or a pronoun (*I want these*); *Tuesday* may be a noun (*Tuesday is my birthday*) or an adverb (*Come Tuesday*). Thousands of words like these can be classified by part of speech only when you see them in sentences.

EXAMPLES The **plant** was growing in a terrarium. [*Plant* names a living thing; it is a noun.]
We usually **plant** tomatoes in the spring. [*Plant* expresses action; it is a verb.]
Bacteria cause many **plant** diseases. [*Plant* modifies *diseases;* it is an adjective.]

REVIEW EXERCISE. Identifying the Parts of Speech of Words. In a column on your paper, write the italicized words in the following paragraphs. Determine the use of each word, and write its part of speech.

One summer (1) *night* (2) *several* years ago I was (3) *suddenly* awakened (4) *by* the noisy clatter of garbage cans. I quickly ran (5) *outside* (6) *where* I heard scratching noises from inside the large can (7) *that* held (8) *most* of our garbage. I cautiously (9) *removed* the lid and (10) *out* popped a family of raccoons.

Since then I have learned that a (11) *myth* about raccoons is (12) *untrue:* raccoons (13) *are* not (14) *fastidious*. True, they (15) *wash* their food before they eat (16) *it*. The purpose, however, is not improved hygiene (17) *but* improved taste. Moreover, raccoons will greedily eat (18) *everything* in sight. (19) *Among* their favorite dishes are berries, small birds, and, of course—(20) *ugh!*—garbage.

CHAPTER 19 REVIEW: POSTTEST 1

Identifying the Parts of Speech of Words. Number your paper 1–20. Each of the following sentences contains at least one word of the kind specified. Find those words and write them after the proper number. Base your answers on the way each word is used in the sentence.

EXAMPLES 1. I have an interesting job. (*noun*)
1. *job*

2. Did they hunt and fish yesterday? (*verb*)
2. *hunt, fish*

1. Dr. Samuel Johnson compiled the first dictionary in the English language. (*adjective*)
2. Did Elizabeth's parents want her to try out for the squad? (*pronoun*)
3. My keys were sitting on the table, but I was convinced that I had lost them in the yard. (*pronoun*)
4. Although she was blind and deaf, Helen Keller learned to communicate effectively with other people. (*noun*)
5. At the end of the game, neither the coach nor the team members could account for the lopsided score. (*conjunction*)
6. Drivers in the Indianapolis 500 must stay continuously alert and be extremely skillful. (*adverb*)
7. How can you best prepare yourself for an effective interview? (*noun*)
8. The ads for the movie *Summer Mystery* ironically promised that the film would be "a chilling thriller." (*adverb*)
9. We wanted to eat at the Russian Tea Room, but we couldn't afford the prices. (*conjunction*)
10. John Updike's novels have met with praise from critics and public alike. (*preposition*)
11. Mr. and Mrs. Lopez spent three snowy winters in Vermont. (*adjective*)
12. After her successful concert, Heidi said that the praise of her teacher, Ms. Hawkins, was her greatest reward. (*verb*)
13. The evening air felt rather cool as we opened the door of the densely packed gymnasium and stepped outside. (*adverb*)
14. A man with a full beard slipped a note to a sinister-looking character during the first intermission of the show. (*preposition*)
15. Oh, what a magnificent performance of *Faust*! (*interjection*)
16. The blurb on the jacket of the novel promised "the intense emotional experience of both sorrow and joy." (*noun*)
17. The detectives thought that there might have been a burglary when they noticed that the lock had scratch marks around it. (*verb*)
18. This antique clock chimes a soulful note every hour. (*adjective*)
19. When I had finished the test, I handed Ms. Martello my paper, returned to my seat, and became calmer. (*verb*)
20. At the start of the movie, I wondered about the sound effects that came toward me from all sides. (*preposition*)

CHAPTER 19 REVIEW: POSTTEST 2

Writing Sentences with Words Used as Specific Parts of Speech.
Write twenty sentences according to the following guidelines. Use the
dictionary for help.

1. Use *yesterday* as an adverb.
2. Use *when* as a subordinating conjunction.
3. Use *sound* as a noun.
4. Use *all* as a pronoun.
5. Use *fire* as a verb.
6. Use *leather* as an adjective.
7. Use *terrific* as an interjection.
8. Use *up* as a preposition.
9. Use *hard* as an adverb.
10. Use *both* as an adjective.

SUMMARY OF PARTS OF SPEECH

Rule	Part of Speech	Use	Examples
19a	noun	names	man, Iowa, corn, justice, cattle
19b	pronoun	takes the place of a noun	he, us, herself, mine, this, who
19c	adjective	modifies a noun or pronoun	red, large, two
19d	verb	shows action or helps to make a statement	is, does, have, wanted, seems
19e	adverb	modifies a verb, an adjective, or another adverb	rapidly, well, somewhat, too
19f	preposition	relates a noun or a pronoun to another word	into, below, from, of
19g	conjunction	joins words or groups of words	and, but, or, for, after, as, until
19h	interjection	shows strong feeling	Ow!

CHAPTER 20

The Parts of a Sentence

SUBJECTS, PREDICATES, COMPLEMENTS

With only two terms—*subject* and *predicate*—you could describe most English sentences. However, to achieve a fuller understanding of the structure of English sentences, you also need to know the name and function of some other important sentence elements: *object, predicate nominative,* and *predicate adjective,* to name only the most important. You have met all of these terms in previous English classes. Use the following diagnostic test to see which terms, if any, you need to review.

DIAGNOSTIC TEST

Identifying Subjects, Predicates, and Complements. Number your paper 1–20. For each sentence, identify the italicized word or words using these abbreviations: *s.*(subject), *v.*(verb), *d.o.* (direct object), *i.o.* (indirect object), *p.n.* (predicate nominative), and *p.a.* (predicate adjective).

EXAMPLE   1. Jim's *sarcasm* made him unpopular.
      1. *s.*

1. *Some* of your classmates will attend.
2. This experience taught me a valuable *lesson.*

3. Out of the darkness came a huge, lumbering *creature*.
4. To everyone's surprise, Jane and I *were* not late.
5. The water in the bay seemed very *cold*.
6. The only people in the water were the *children*.
7. This morning the mail carrier *left* this letter for you.
8. He gave *me* this one, too.
9. Lee Trevino is an excellent *golfer*.
10. Mechanics had just assembled and checked all *parts* of the motor.
11. Cheryl gave *me* her paper to proofread.
12. Yolanda is the *valedictorian* of her class.
13. Please put the *dishes* away.
14. Yesterday seemed rather *dreary*.
15. I *wrote* that essay in less than an hour.
16. Examples of religious music are *Gregorian chants, church hymns,* and *gospel singing*.
17. There are only fifteen *problems* for tonight's assignment.
18. Please do not omit any necessary *punctuation*.
19. Brian told *Arnie* some very funny stories.
20. In the middle of the road was a large *patch* of ice.

20a. A *sentence* is a group of words expressing a complete thought.

SENTENCE	The significance of the computer as a message carrier is often ignored.
NOT A SENTENCE	The significance of the computer as a message carrier
SENTENCE	A computer can instantly scan its entire library for documents of interest to the user.
NOT A SENTENCE	A computer instantly scanning its entire library for documents of interest to the user

SUBJECT AND PREDICATE

20b. A sentence consists of two parts: the *subject* and the *predicate*. The *subject* of the sentence is the part about which something is being said. The *predicate* is the part that says something about the subject.

SUBJECT	PREDICATE
Computers and electronic calculators	can solve problems quickly.

PREDICATE   SUBJECT
Ahead of us may lie   a universal computer language.

A subject or a predicate may consist of a single word or of many words. The whole subject is called the *complete subject;* the whole predicate, the *complete predicate.* However long a subject or predicate may be, it always has a core, or an essential part.

The Simple Subject

20c. The *simple subject* is the principal word or group of words in the subject.

EXAMPLES   The most distinguished participant at the ceremonies was the President. [subject: *The most distinguished participant at the ceremonies;* simple subject: *participant*]

The Memorial Coliseum in Los Angeles was filled to capacity. [subject: *The Memorial Coliseum in Los Angeles;* simple subject: *Memorial Coliseum*]

> ☞ NOTE   Throughout this book the term *subject,* when used in connection with the sentence, refers to the simple subject; the term *verb* refers to the simple predicate.

The Simple Predicate, or Verb

20d. The principal word or group of words in the predicate is called the *simple predicate,* or the *verb.*

EXAMPLE   The athletes were greeted with cheers. [predicate: *were greeted with cheers;* simple predicate: *were greeted*]

Compound Subjects and Verbs

20e. A *compound subject* consists of two or more subjects that are joined by a conjunction and have the same verb. The usual connecting words are *and* and *or*.

GRAMMAR

EXAMPLE   Jomo and Ahmed wore long, flowing robes. [compound subject: *Jomo . . . Ahmed*]

20f. A *compound verb* consists of two or more verbs that are joined by a conjunction and have the same subject.

EXAMPLE   Mary McLeod Bethune founded Bethune-Cookman College and served twice as its president. [compound verb: *founded . . . served*]

How to Find the Subject of a Sentence

To find the subject of a sentence, first find the verb (the simple predicate); then ask yourself the question "Who or what . . . ?" For instance, in the sentence "Outside the wall walked an armed guard," the verb is *walked.* Ask the question, "Who or what walked?" The answer is *guard walked. Guard* is the subject of the sentence.

In addition to this simple formula for locating the subject, here are some other facts you should keep in mind:

1. In sentences expressing a command or a request, the subject is always *you,* even though the word *you* may not appear in the sentence.

(You) Proofread your report after typing it.
(You) Please submit a cover sheet with your report.

2. The subject of a sentence is never in a prepositional phrase.

Neither of these books has an index. [verb: *has* What has? *Neither. Neither* is the subject. *Books* is not the subject. It is in the prepositional phrase *of these books.*]

The rules of punctuation are sometimes frustrating. [verb: *are* What are? *Rules. Rules* is the subject. *Punctuation* is the object of the preposition *of.*]

3. To find the subject in a question, turn the question into statement form.

QUESTION   What subject did you choose for your speech?
STATEMENT   You did choose what subject for your speech? [subject: *you;* verb: *did choose*]

4. *There* and *here* are not usually the subjects of a verb. Except in a statement like the previous sentence, *there* and *here* are either adverbs or expletives.

Here is your pencil. [verb: *is;* subject: *pencil* In this sentence the word *here* is an adverb telling where.]
There are several good points in your argument. [verb: *are;* subject: *points*]

In this last use, *there* is an *expletive,* a word used to get the sentence started. The word *it* may also be used as an expletive. *It is senseless to leave.*

EXERCISE 1. Identifying Subjects and Verbs. Number your paper 1–10. Write the subject and the verb of each sentence after the proper number. Underline subjects once and verbs twice. Include all parts of compound subjects and verbs, as well as all words in a verb phrase.

1. Researchers at Harvard and Stanford universities studied the exercise patterns of 17,000 subjects and reported the results.
2. Participants climbed stairs, walked, and engaged in sports.
3. High blood pressure and cardiovascular disease have been blamed on the lack of physical fitness.
4. However, until recently no scientific proof had been offered of the link between exercise and fitness.
5. Now scientists from Harvard and Stanford urge regular exercise.
6. Even brisk walks four times a week may prevent serious diseases.
7. The real discovery of this research is the presence of cardiovascular disease in sedentary people.
8. For years physicians have been aware of this connection but have not always succeeded in convincing their patients of it.
9. Carefully consider your own physical activities.
10. There could be changes in your approach to physical fitness.

COMPLEMENTS

Some sentences express a complete thought by means of a subject and verb only.

S   V   S   V
She won.   The spectators cheered.

Most sentences, however, have one word or more in the predicate that completes the meaning of the subject and verb. These completing words are called *complements.*

She won	the **race.**
Someone sent	**me** a **rose.**
She is	the **mayor** of our town.
The ripest ones are	**those.**
They seem	**industrious.**

GRAMMAR

He called	**me overconfident.**
Who made	**you boss?**

> ☞ NOTE An adverb modifying the verb is not a complement. Only nouns, pronouns, and adjectives function as complements.

Dr. Ames is **here.** [The adverb *here* modifies the verb *is.* It is not a complement.]
Dr. Ames is **brilliant.** [The adjective *brilliant* is a complement.]

Direct and Indirect Objects

Complements that receive, or are affected by, the action of the verb are called *objects.* There are two kinds: the *direct object* and the *indirect object.*

20g. The *direct object* of the verb receives the action of the verb or shows the result of the action. It answers the question *What?* or *Whom?* after an action verb.

We drove **Jim** to the train station. [We drove *whom?*]
He was carrying a large **suitcase.** [He was carrying *what?*]

Except when it ends in *-self* (*myself, himself*), the object of a verb never refers to the same person or thing as the subject.

> ☞ NOTE Sentence diagrams are "pictures" of the structure of a sentence. They are used in this book as aids so that the functions of words and word groups in a sentence can be more easily seen.

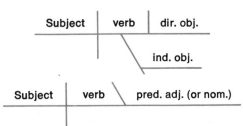

20h. The *indirect object* of the verb precedes the direct object and usually tells to whom or for whom the action of the verb is done.

If the word *to* or *for* is used, the noun or pronoun following it is part of a prepositional phrase; it is not an indirect object.

Mr. Bates promised me a job. [*Me* is an indirect object.]
Mr. Bates promised a job to me. [*Me* is part of the phrase *to me.*]

EXAMPLES   He gave **us** his permission. [gave *to* us]

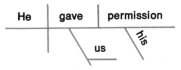

Bob made his **mother** a writing desk. [made *for* his mother]

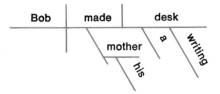

Objects of the verb may be compound.

Mrs. Spiers praised the stage **crew** and the **cast.**

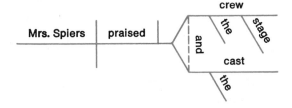

She gave **George** and **me** several suggestions.

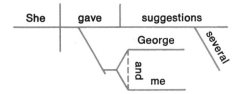

The Objective Complement

To complete their meaning, some action verbs require an additional complement following their objects. This additional complement is called an *objective complement* because it refers to the object; it may be a noun or an adjective.

> They elected Mary **chairwoman**. [The noun *chairwoman* refers to the direct object *Mary* and helps to complete the meaning of the verb *elected*. It is an objective complement.]

> You made her **angry**. [The adjective *angry* modifies the direct object *her* and helps to complete the meaning of the verb *made*. It is an objective complement.]

Only a few verbs take an objective complement. They usually mean "make" or "consider": *elect, appoint, name, choose, render, make, consider,* etc.

> The cat licked its paws **clean**. [*made* its paws clean]
> We painted my room **green**. [*made* my room green]
> I thought the joke **tasteless**. [*considered* the joke tasteless]

EXERCISE 2. Identifying Direct Objects, Indirect Objects, and Objective Complements.   Number your paper 1–10. After the proper

number, write the objects in the sentence. After each object, write *i.o.* for indirect object, *d.o.* for direct object, or *o.c.* for objective complement.

1. Computers may have created the automobile revolution of the 1980's.
2. A spokesperson for the industry showed reporters several examples of computerized cars.
3. One car has a computer display for its speedometer and its turn signals.
4. Another makes trips a pleasure with computerized information.
5. Some cars have seven computers on board.
6. A voice synthesizer in one car warns the driver of drowsiness.
7. According to engineers, computers can give us an amazing amount of detailed and accurate information about a car.
8. Car computers can make predictions about engine failure.
9. One computer even makes a car burglarproof.
10. On the negative side, some safety experts consider colorful computer panels a driving hazard.

Subject Complements

Complements that refer to (describe, explain, or identify) the subject are *subject complements*. There are two kinds: the *predicate nominative* and the *predicate adjective*.

Subject complements follow linking verbs only. The common linking verbs are the forms of the verb *be* (see page 421) and the following verbs: *become, seem, grow, appear, look, feel, smell, taste, remain, sound,* and *stay.*

20i. A *predicate nominative* is a noun or pronoun complement that refers to the same person or thing as the subject of the verb. It follows a linking verb.

New York is our largest **city.** [*City* refers to the subject *New York.*]

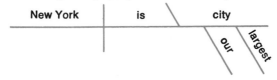

My favorite authors are **Austen** and **she.** [Compound predicate nominative: *Austen* and *she* refer to the same people as the subject *authors.*]

20j. A *predicate adjective* is an adjective complement that modifies the subject of the verb. It follows a linking verb.

This book is **dull.** [The predicate adjective *dull* modifies the subject *book.*]

His speech seemed **repetitious** and **tiresome.** [Compound predicate adjective modifying the subject *speech.*]

In the normal order of an English sentence, complements follow the verb. However, a complement may precede the verb.

This **song** he wrote in 1980. [*Song* is the direct object of the verb *wrote.*]

Fortunate are those who can learn from their mistakes. [*Fortunate* is a predicate adjective modifying the subject *those.*]

EXERCISE 3. Identifying Predicate Nominatives and Predicate Adjectives.

Number your paper 1–10. After the proper number, write any predicate nominatives or predicate adjectives in the sentence; identify each complement with the abbreviation *p.n.* or *p.a.* Some sentences contain more than one complement.

1. Her nominating speech was both effective and convincing.
2. In 1817, Monroe became the fourth President from Virginia.
3. Iago grew increasingly more ruthless and cunning.
4. The witness' account of the accident seems plausible.
5. The cats appeared nervous during the storm.
6. Pablo Casals was not only a famous cellist but also a respected conductor.
7. The spray tasted salty and the wind felt cold.
8. The rooms in the restored guardhouse smelled musty.
9. Those strawberries look ripe and delicious.
10. That reflector was once the most powerful telescope in the entire world.

REVIEW EXERCISE. **Identifying Subjects, Verbs, and Complements.** Number your paper 1–10. After the proper number, write the subject, the verb, and any complements in the sentence. After each complement, identify as follows: *d.o.* (direct object); *i.o.* (indirect object); *p.n.* (predicate nominative); *p.a.* (predicate adjective); or *o.c.* (objective complement).

1. "Mark Twain" is the pseudonym of the American writer Samuel Langhorne Clemens.
2. He became famous for his stories about the Mississippi.
3. Through his writings he has given us homespun pictures of America and tales of life in the mining camps of the West.
4. At his death in 1910, many critics considered him the most prominent American writer of his generation.
5. Twain had some curious notions about his life story.
6. Over the years those ideas became even more curious.
7. He told William Dean Howells the scheme of his autobiography.
8. That scheme was apparently a haphazard one.
9. The first published autobiographies were fragmentary and imperfect.
10. Charles Neider's edited version is, however, a magnificent document of value both as literature and as entertainment.

WRITING APPLICATION:
Using Complete Sentences in Your Writing
Add variety to your writing by experimenting with the placement of subjects and verbs.

EXAMPLE From out of the misty darkness, swaying and undulating around a steaming pot, appeared three filthy witches. [The verb *appeared* and the subject *witches* are at the end of the sentence.]

Writing Assignment

In literature, *an epiphany* is a sudden realization. Experiencing an epiphany is like turning a light on in a darkened room. Suddenly, you see what you didn't see before, perhaps about your own strengths and weaknesses. Write about an epiphany—your own, a friend's, or a fictional character's. At some point, vary subject and verb placement.

CHAPTER 20 REVIEW: POSTTEST 1

Identifying Subjects, Verbs, and Complements. Number your paper 1–20. For each sentence, identify the italicized word as follows: *s.* (subject), *v.* (verb), *d.o.* (direct object), *i.o.* (indirect object), *p.n.* (predicate nominative), *p.a.* (predicate adjective), or *o.c.* (object complement).

EXAMPLE   1. Studying the map carefully, we *decided* on the shortest route.
    1. *v.*

1. The gymnastics team elected Terry *captain.*
2. *Robert Frost* became famous as a poet.
3. The desk *was moved* to a corner of the room.
4. My little sister has an interesting coin *collection.*
5. The directions on the package were *clear.*
6. Rob gave *her* a smile.
7. The home economics class hosted a *luncheon* for their parents.
8. I *read* the newspaper for news of sales and bargains.
9. Margaret received a ten-speed *bicycle* for her birthday.
10. The factory owner gave his *employees* a raise in pay.
11. Each spring, millions of people *watch* the Academy Awards on television.
12. One of the most valuable experiences of my life was *scouting.*
13. Did you give *Ming Chin* directions to the beach?
14. My grandfather got a *part* in an amateur play.
15. After work, will *you* call me so that we can make plans?
16. I felt *energetic* after my exercise workout.
17. Alice Walker has become a well-known *writer.*
18. *Place* the disk in the disk drive first.
19. My mother is *taller* than any of her four sisters.
20. Without warning, out jumped a *mouse!*

CHAPTER 20 REVIEW: POSTTEST 2

Writing Sentences. Write your own sentences, one of each of the following kinds, and underline the subjects and verbs.

1. A sentence with a compound subject and a compound verb
2. A sentence with a direct object and an indirect object
3. A sentence with a direct object and an object complement
4. A sentence with a predicate nominative
5. A sentence with a predicate adjective

SUMMARY OF SENTENCE PATTERNS

You have learned that every sentence has two basic parts—subject and predicate. Within the subject there is a simple subject, commonly called the subject; within the predicate there is a simple predicate, commonly called the verb. The pattern of some sentences consists of subject and verb only.

```
            S          V
        Artists    paint.
```

Modifiers may be added to the subject and verb without changing the basic pattern of such a sentence.

```
            S                                 V
Several artists from the Senior Citizen Center paint in the mountains.
```

You have learned also that certain additions to the predicate, called complements, create other sentence patterns. These complete the meaning begun by the subject and verb. The different kinds of complements produce the different sentence patterns. These are the seven common sentence patterns:

```
      S        V
   Artists   paint.

      S        V        D.O.
   Artists   paint    landscapes.

      S     V      I.O.     D.O.
   She    gave    them    supplies.

      S      V          D.O.     OBJ.COMP.(ADJ.)
   These   made    the artists     happy.

      S      V        D.O.    OBJ.COMP.(NOUN)
   They    named     her     resident artist.

      S     V              P.N.
   She    is     their resident artist.

      S      V         P.A.
   She    seems    talented.
```

CHAPTER 21

The Phrase

KINDS OF PHRASES
AND THEIR FUNCTIONS

Words in a sentence act not only individually but also in groups. The grouped words act together as a unit that may function as a modifier, a subject, a verb, an object, or a predicate nominative. The most common group of related words is the phrase. In Chapter 19 you learned about the verb phrase, which is a verb of more than one word (*is coming, might have been*). This chapter provides a review of other kinds of phrases.

DIAGNOSTIC TEST

Identifying Phrases. Number your paper 1–20. Next to each number, identify the kind of phrase italicized in each sentence. Write *adj.* for a prepositional phrase used as an adjective, *adv.* for a prepositional phrase used as an adverb, *part.* for a participial phrase, *ger.* for a gerund phrase, *inf.* for an infinitive phrase, or *appos.* for an appositive phrase. Do not identify separately any phrases within a larger italicized phrase.

EXAMPLE   1. We had a tossed salad *with fresh tomatoes* at lunch.
　　　　　1. *adj.*

1. Marnie made an appointment *to audition for a part in the play.*
2. For a split second, the football sat balanced *on the goal-post bar.*

3. Dr. Martin, *the pediatrician,* has advertised for a receptionist.
4. *Sitting in the sun for three hours* gave Rebecca a headache.
5. *Smiling broadly,* the television commentator praised the work of the 4-H Club.
6. I saw the beautiful bouquet *of roses* on the table.
7. William Golding, *the British novelist,* was awarded the Nobel Prize for literature in 1983.
8. The biology class had mixed emotions about *dissecting the frog.*
9. Kai's ambition is *to drive a tractor-trailer truck.*
10. Shakespeare's plays are performed *in numerous languages* throughout the world.
11. *Moving their cars to the right,* the drivers let the ambulance pass.
12. Marianne and Fred intend *to run for class offices.*
13. *Filled with joy and happiness,* the bride and groom greeted their family and friends after the wedding ceremony.
14. Two clowns *from the circus* gave a benefit performance.
15. My friends *Alecca and Leon* sent me a postcard from Rome.
16. You can get help in an emergency by *dialing the operator.*
17. Donya wants to ride her bicycle from Washington, D.C., *to Seattle, Washington.*
18. The public library is a valuable resource for anyone who wants *to do research.*
19. My teacher recommended a book *about the Industrial Revolution.*
20. We watched three experts *discussing the economy* on television.

21a. A *phrase* is a group of words not containing a verb and its subject. A phrase is used as a single part of speech.

Five kinds of phrases are explained in the following pages: *prepositional phrases, participial phrases, gerund phrases, infinitive phrases,* and *appositive phrases.*

THE PREPOSITIONAL PHRASE

21b. A *prepositional phrase* is a group of words beginning with a preposition and ending with a noun or pronoun.

    for Lisa and you   **in** the park   **after** the game

The noun or pronoun that concludes the prepositional phrase is the object of the preposition that begins the phrase.

on the **way**   from **Angela** and **me**   with a **shout**

Prepositional phrases are usually used as modifiers—as adjectives or adverbs. Occasionally, a prepositional phrase is used as a noun:

Before lunch will be convenient. [The prepositional phrase is the subject of the sentence; it is used as a noun.]

The Adjective Phrase

21c. An *adjective phrase* is a prepositional phrase that modifies a noun or a pronoun.

Tucson has been the locale **of many Westerns.**

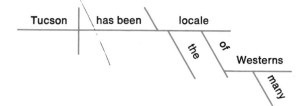

Tourists **from the East** visit the old frontier towns **in the West.**

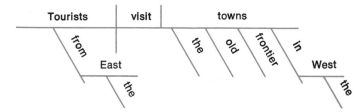

EXERCISE 1. Identifying Adjective Phrases and the Words They Modify. After each sentence number, list the adjective phrases in the sentence. Next to each phrase, write the noun modified.

1. The rivers of New Guinea are now popular areas for rafting enthusiasts.
2. A series of nearly continuous rapids crosses jungles of primeval beauty.

3. Twenty-eight major rapids on the Tua River make it a course for rafters with experience and courage.
4. There are butterflies with brilliant colors, and the metallic whine of cicadas almost drowns out the roar of the river.
5. The banks are a chaos of tumbled boulders and uprooted trees.

The Adverb Phrase

21d. An *adverb phrase* is a prepositional phrase that modifies a verb, an adjective, or another adverb.

The following sentences show the ways in which an adverb phrase can modify a verb.

> Tina exercises **with care.** [*how* Tina exercises]
> She exercises **before a meet.** [*when* she exercises]
> She exercises **in the gym.** [*where* she exercises]
> She exercises **to her capacity.** [*to what extent* she exercises]
> She exercises **for her health.** [*why* she exercises]

Note the following diagram.

In the following sentence, the adverb phrase modifies a predicate adjective.

> He was true **to his word.**

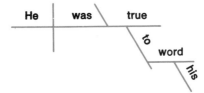

The following sentence illustrates the placement of an adverb phrase that modifies an adverb.

He threw the ball far **to the left.**

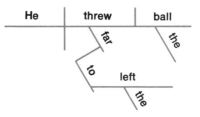

EXERCISE 2. Identifying Adverb Phrases and the Words They Modify.

Number your paper 1–10. After the proper number, list the adverb phrases in the sentence and the word(s) modified.

1. Nothing in Dutch memory compares with the flood of February 1953.
2. Some 50,000 houses were swept out to sea; 70,000 people were evacuated from their homes.
3. As a result of that deluge, engineers are erecting a massive coastal barrier.
4. Work on the barrier was not begun until 1978 but should be complete by 1990.
5. By that time this masterpiece of engineering will have cost Dutch taxpayers nearly three billion dollars.
6. From a distance the odd-looking structures resemble skyscrapers.
7. They are located near the Dutch town of Zierikzee and symbolize Holland's centuries-old struggle against the sea.
8. The barriers will be positioned between two islands and will reach from shore to shore.
9. These massive pillars were constructed in dry dock and will be moved into place by a special ship.
10. Holland may remain safe from the sea forever.

PHRASES CONTAINING VERBALS

Less common than the prepositional phrase but still very useful to a writer are verbal phrases: the *participial phrase*, the *gerund phrase,* and the *infinitive phrase*. These phrases are called verbal phrases because the most important word in them is a verbal. Verbals are formed from verbs; they may express action, have modifiers, and be followed by complements. However, verbals do not function as verbs in a sentence. They function as nouns, as adjectives, or as adverbs.

On the following pages you will find an explanation of each kind of verbal, followed by a discussion of the verbal as it is most commonly used—in a phrase.

The Participle and the Participial Phrase

21e. A *participle* is a verb form that can be used as an adjective.

> The rapidly **developing** storm kept small boats in port.
> **Developing** rapidly, the storm kept small boats in port.
> The storm, **developing** rapidly, kept small boats in port.

In these sentences, *developing,* which is formed from the verb *develop,* is used as an adjective modifying the noun *storm.*

In the following sentence the participle *crying* is used as an adjective modifying the pronoun *him.*

> I found him **crying.**

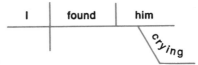

There are two basic kinds of participles: *present participles* and *past participles.* A present participle, like those in the preceding examples, ends in *-ing.* A past participle may end in *-ed, -d, -t, -en,* or *-n:* ask*ed,* sav*ed,* deal*t,* eat*en,* see*n.*

PRESENT PARTICIPLE   We watched the puppies **playing.**
PAST PARTICIPLE   The puppies, **exhausted,** collapsed in the grass.

Although participles are formed from verbs, they cannot be used by themselves as verbs. A participle may, however, be used with a helping verb to form a verb phrase.

PARTICIPLE   The **barking** dogs followed the colts into the barn. [*Barking* modifies *dogs.*]
VERB PHRASE   The dogs **were barking** excitedly. [The verb phrase *were barking* consists of the helping verb *were* plus the present participle *barking.*]

When participles are used in verb phrases, they are considered part of the verb and are not considered adjectives.

21f. A *participial phrase* is a phrase containing a participle and any complements or modifiers it may have.[1]

Removing his coat, Jack rushed to the river. [The participial phrase is made up of the participle *removing* and the complement *coat,* which is the direct object of *removing*. Like verbs, participles may take an object.]

Hesitating there for a moment, he quickly grasped the situation. [The participial phrase is made up of the participle *hesitating* plus its modifiers —the adverb *there* and the adverb phrase *for a moment.*]

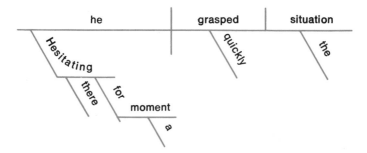

The participle usually introduces the phrase, and the entire phrase acts as an adjective to modify a noun or pronoun.

We saw Carl Lewis **receiving his first gold medal** in the 1984 Olympics.

Swaying rhythmically, the snake raised its head.

Spread with white linen, the table glowed in the candlelight.

EXERCISE 3. Identifying Participial Phrases and the Words They Modify.
Write on your paper the participial phrases in the following

---

[1] For work on the participial phrase as a sentence fragment, see pages 340–42. For exercises on the dangling participle, see pages 364–65.

sentences. Be sure to include all complements and modifiers. Before each phrase, write the number of the sentence in which it appears. After each phrase, write the word the phrase modifies.

1. High-school graduates replying to a questionnaire about their college courses often mention freshman English as the course giving them the most trouble.
2. Facing college standards, the graduates realize that they did not work hard enough on the themes assigned in high school.
3. Statistics reported by the National Education Association revealed that the vast majority of American colleges offer remedial English classes emphasizing composition.
4. Handicapped by their writing deficiencies, graduates seeking employment or advancement are often denied opportunities.
5. Recognizing the importance of practice, teachers of composition, imitating the athletic coach, conduct regular practice sessions.

WRITING APPLICATION A:
Using Participial Phrases in Your Writing

Participial phrases contribute to sentence variety while supplying pertinent information for the reader.

EXAMPLE *Reflecting a deep love of Ireland,* the poems of William Butler Yeats were awarded the Nobel Prize.

Writing Assignment

What does the word *heroic* mean to you? Are there still heroes? Does it have to be someone prominent, or can it be an ordinary person? Define what you think a hero is; then illustrate this definition with an example. Use at least three participial phrases. Underline these phrases.

REVIEW EXERCISE A. **Identifying Participial Phrases, Adjective Phrases, and Adverb Phrases.**   For each of the following sentences, write the italicized phrases in order on your paper. Place each phrase on a separate line. After each phrase, write the word it modifies and tell whether it is a *participial* phrase, an *adjective* prepositional phrase, or an *adverb* prepositional phrase. Include prepositional phrases within a larger italicized phrase with the larger phrase.

EXAMPLE 1. *Living far from the city,* I developed an interest *in nature at an early age.*

1. *Living far from the city,* I, participial

   in nature, interest, adjective

   at an early age, developed, adverb

1. *Having studied hard,* Karen walked rapidly *to school,* confident that she would do well on her test *in chemistry.*
2. *By next week* all of the students *trying out for the soccer team* will have heard *from the coach or his assistant.*
3. Today's newspaper, *printed last night,* made no mention *of this morning's traffic tie-up.*
4. Many *of the articles written for a newspaper* are based *on news-wire reports.*
5. *Annoyed by the mosquitoes,* Mr. Sims went *into his house for a while.*
6. *Rinsed with hot water,* the dishes were stacked up, *waiting to be washed.*
7. The gift *given to our principal, Mrs. Scott,* was a necklace *made of silver and turquoise.*
8. *Addressing her audience,* the principal spoke encouraging words.

The Gerund and Gerund Phrase

21g. A *gerund* is a verb form ending in *-ing* that is used as a noun.

Walking is healthful exercise. [*Walking* is formed from the verb *walk* and, as the subject of the sentence, is used as a noun.]

A gerund is a verbal noun. It may be used just as a noun may be used.

Good **writing** comes from much practice. [gerund used as subject]

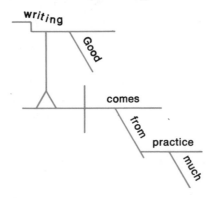

They do not appreciate my **singing.** [gerund used as object of verb]

By **studying** you can pass the course. [gerund used as object of a preposition]

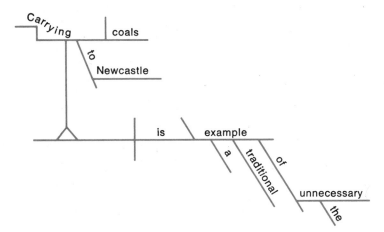

21h. A *gerund phrase* is a phrase consisting of a gerund and any complements or modifiers it may have.

Carrying coals to Newcastle is a traditional example of the unnecessary. [The gerund *Carrying* has *coals* as its direct object and is modified by the adverb phrase *to Newcastle.*]

Like the gerund alone, the gerund phrase may be used in any way that a noun may be used.

Writing that letter was a good idea. [gerund phrase as subject]
My cousin enjoys **working as a lifeguard.** [gerund phrase as direct object]
We were fined for **parking there.** [gerund phrase as object of preposition.]
Her most publicized achievement was **winning three gold medals.** [gerund phrase as predicate nominative]

EXERCISE 4. Identifying Gerund Phrases and Their Functions.
Number your paper 1–10. Identify the gerund phrase in each sentence.
Then identify as subject (*s.*), predicate nominative (*p.n.*), direct object
(*d.o.*), indirect object (*i.o.*), or object of a preposition (*obj. prep.*).

EXAMPLE   1. Learning to type is one of my most practical accomplishments.
      1. *Learning to type, s.*

1. Solving crossword puzzles is one of Geraldo's favorite pastimes.
2. Sylvia's method of making decisions reveals a great deal about her.
3. My grandparents enjoy walking briskly.
4. In making any changes, please notify our secretary, Ms. Erikson.
5. Producing a movie for Mr. Hisoka's cinematography course requires the ability to organize and communicate.
6. Ms. Sanapaw finished writing her paper.
7. Gaining the vote for women was Susan B. Anthony's mission.
8. One of the most interesting characteristics of bees is their dancing to communicate the location of distant food sources.
9. Hector earns money on the weekends by giving guitar lessons.
10. My brother's singing in the shower adds mirth and music to our morning routine.

WRITING APPLICATION B:
Using Gerund Phrases in Describing a Process

Gerund phrases are particularly useful in describing a process
because a process involves action.

EXAMPLE   You can improve your vocabulary by *keeping a notebook,*
listing new words, and making an effort to use these words.

Writing Assignment

Jot down the steps a person should follow to complete a process
(use one you are familiar with). Write down the process, using
gerund phrases. Underline them.

The Infinitive and the Infinitive Phrase

21i. An *infinitive* is a verb form, usually preceded by *to*, that can be used as a noun or a modifier.

to study   to write   to hope   to be

An infinitive is generally used as a noun, but it may also be used as an adjective or an adverb.

The infinitive used as a noun:

> **To leave** would be rude. [infinitive as subject]
> No one wants **to stay.** [infinitive as direct object]
> Her goal is **to win.** [infinitive as predicate nominative]

The infinitive used as an adjective:

> She is the candidate **to watch.** [The infinitive modifies *candidate.*]

The infinitive used as an adverb:

> We came **to cheer.** [The infinitive modifies the verb *came.*]

☞ NOTE Do not confuse the infinitive, a verbal of which *to* is a part, with a prepositional phrase beginning with *to,* which consists of *to* plus a noun or pronoun.

INFINITIVES	PREPOSITIONAL PHRASES
to go	to them
to sleep	to bed

The word *to,* called the sign of the infinitive, is sometimes omitted.

> The clowns made her [to] **laugh.**
> Help me [to] **clean** the car.

21j. An *infinitive phrase* consists of an infinitive and any complements or modifiers it may have.[1]

> They promised **to return soon.** [*Soon* is an adverb modifying the infinitive *to return.*]
> We have time **to walk to the concert.** [The prepositional phrase *to the concert* modifies the infinitive *to walk.*]
> I saved enough money **to buy a car.** [*Car* is the object of *to buy.*]

[1] For exercises on the use of the infinitive phrase to reduce wordiness, see pages 381–83.

Like infinitives alone, infinitive phrases can be used as nouns or as modifiers.

> We tried **to reason with her.** [The infinitive phrase *to reason with her* is the object of the verb *tried.*]
> There must be a way **to solve this problem.** [The infinitive phrase modifies the noun *way.*]
> His plan is **to go to college for two years.** [The infinitive phrase is a predicate nominative, referring back to *plan.*]

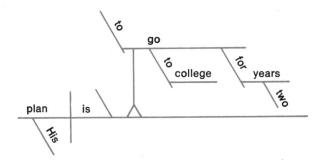

The Infinitive Clause

Unlike other verbals, an infinitive may have a subject as well as complements and modifiers.

> Everyone expected **Gina to win the nomination.** [*Gina* is the subject of the infinitive *to win.*]
> We asked **her to lead the discussion.** [*Her* is the subject of the infinitive *to lead.*]
> We believe **Andrew to be the winner.** [*Andrew* is the subject of the infinitive *to be; winner* is a predicate nominative referring to *Andrew.*]
> I found **it to be difficult.** [*It* is the subject of the infinitive *to be; difficult* is a predicate adjective referring back to *it.*]

When an infinitive has a subject, as in the preceding examples, the construction is called an *infinitive clause.* Notice that the subject of an infinitive is in the objective case.[1]

EXERCISE 5. Identifying Infinitive Phrases and Their Functions.

Number your paper 1–10. Identify the infinitive phrase in each sentence and indicate whether the phrase is used as a noun, an adjective, or an adverb. If it is used as a noun, identify it as the subject

---

[1] For rules concerning the use of the objective case, see pages 534–37.

(*s.*), direct object (*d.o.*), predicate nominative (*p.n.*), or object of a preposition (*obj. prep.*).

EXAMPLE 1. I like to compose music for the guitar.

1. *to compose music for the guitar, noun, d. o.*

1. To win an Olympic gold medal is the dream of every member of the women's ski team.
2. The candidate had the courage to speak on a controversial issue.
3. We went to Italy to see Michelangelo's statue, the *David*.
4. The Latin and French Clubs try to work together on projects.
5. Martin Luther King's dream was that all people should be free to exercise their rights as American citizens.
6. Louis Pasteur experimented for years to discover a method for preventing rabies.
7. The ability to speak distinctly is an advantage in job interviews.
8. To open the box required a hammer and a crowbar.
9. Alana's hobby is to spend hours each day developing original computer programs.
10. Marvella has always wanted to learn about horseback riding.

REVIEW EXERCISE B. Identifying Prepositional, Participial, Gerund, and Infinitive Phrases. Number your paper 1–20. In the following passage, most prepositional, participial, gerund, and infinitive phrases are numbered and italicized. Study the phrase, and after the corresponding number on your paper, write what kind of phrase it is. If it is a prepositional phrase, tell whether it is an adjective phrase or an adverb phrase. Include the prepositional phrase within a larger italicized phrase with the larger phrase.

(1) *Having read several poems by Robert Frost,* I suddenly saw the difference between (2) *enjoying prose and enjoying poetry.* (3) *Reading poetry* does not require the same kind (4) *of skill* as reading prose. Inexperienced readers (5) *of poetry* try (6) *to find* "messages." Many readers race (7) *through a poem* (8) *to seek that elusive nugget* (9) *of wisdom.* It is misleading (10) *to equate the enjoyment of a poem* with (11) *finding its central thought.* (12) *Enjoying a poem to its fullest* is somewhat like (13) *watching a baseball game.* (14) *During a game,* most fans are eager (15) *to participate vicariously in the pleasure* of

(16) *hitting a home run* or of (17) *making a double play.* (18) *Awaiting the outcome of a game,* the average fan also responds to the total experience of the game itself. (19) *To read a poem for meaning alone* can be compared to (20) *attending a baseball game and watching the scoreboard.*

THE APPOSITIVE[1]

21k. An *appositive* is a noun or pronoun—often with modifiers—set beside another noun or pronoun to explain or identify it.

> My cousin **Maria** is an accomplished violinist.
> Riboflavin, a **vitamin,** is found in leafy vegetables.

An *appositive phrase* is a phrase consisting of an appositive and its modifiers.

> My brother's car, **a sporty red hatchback with bucket seats,** is the envy of my friends.

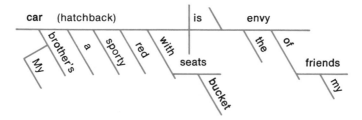

An appositive phrase usually follows the word it explains or identifies, but may precede it.

> Once a pagan **feast,** Valentine's Day is now celebrated as a day of love.

REVIEW EXERCISE C. Identifying Phrases. Number your paper 1–20. In the following passage, most of the phrases have been numbered and italicized. After the proper number, identify each phrase as prepositional, participial, gerund, infinitive, or appositive. In the case of a prepositional phrase, write whether it is an adjective phrase or an adverb phrase. Include prepositional phrases within a larger italicized phrase as part of the larger phrase.

---

[1] For rules on the punctuation of appositives, see page 650. For the use of the appositive in subordination of ideas, see page 353.

Altamont Pass, (1) *an area of grassy hills* (2) *surrounding San Francisco Bay,* is producing a new cash crop. Energy entrepreneurs are hurrying (3) *to lease wind rights on acreage* (4) *throughout the Altamont.* One rancher owns several hundred acres (5) *dotted with tall white wind machines.* (6) *Standing in rows on the windswept hills,* this crop is expected (7) *to produce electricity.* (8) *With any luck,* the wind-power industry may soon spread (9) *to other parts* of the country. The temperature differences (10) *between the cool coast and the hot valley* can create air surges (11) *funneling inland through natural gaps* (12) *like the Altamont.* According to some energy experts, there will be several hundred wind machines (13) *producing thirty million kilowatts per year,* the power (14) *used by 4,800 homes.* (15) *An economist and a trained engineer,* John Eckland has advocated (16) *generating electricity* by (17) *using these updated windmills.* Not until the oil shortages of the 1970's did a serious effort begin (18) *in the United States* (19) *to develop a wind industry.* Modern wind turbines may someday become as numerous (20) *in the United States* as windmills were in Holland.

CHAPTER 21 REVIEW: POSTTEST 1

Identifying Phrases.   Number your paper 1–20. For each sentence, write the italicized phrase. Then identify it as a prepositional, participial, gerund, infinitive, or appositive phrase. If it is a prepositional phrase, indicate whether it is used as an adjective or an adverb. Include phrases or verbals occurring within a longer italicized phrase as part of that phrase.

EXAMPLE:　1.　The sunlight shimmering *on the lake* was beautiful.
　　　　　　1.　*on the lake, prepositional, adverb*

1. Juanita likes *to take candid pictures of her friends.*
2. *Arriving late at school,* Bill stopped in the office to get a pass.
3. The sound *of the band* made everyone want to dance.
4. *Made in Ireland,* Waterford crystal is admired throughout the world.
5. By *inventing the telephone,* Alexander Graham Bell assured himself a place in history.
6. Try *to finish your work before dinner.*
7. Luciano Pavarotti, *the great Italian tenor,* received a standing

ovation at the end of his concert.

8. Ruth's secret ambition is *to do research in space.*
9. We stood on the deserted street *looking in vain for a taxi.*
10. Raul has the talent *to sculpt and design beautiful objects.*
11. Francine's hobby is *collecting earrings;* she has thirty pairs!
12. For great performers, *interpreting music* is an art as well as a skill.
13. *Having suffered through three days of a heat wave,* we decided to purchase an air conditioner.
14. In Cleveland, we visited our friend Barbara, *a prosecuting attorney.*
15. At the rodeo, I always enjoy *watching the courageous riders.*
16. "It is a pleasure to be with you today," remarked the mayor *at the beginning of her talk.*
17. Swaggering cowboys and daring sheriffs are stereotypes that appear *in many old western movies.*
18. Dr. Acevedo, *a noted cardiologist,* assured the patient's family that the operation had been successful.
19. Many pioneer women kept diaries and journals *of their experiences* settling the American wilderness.
20. *To speak freely on any issue* is a right guaranteed to all Americans.
21. *Speaking before a large audience,* the President delivered an important foreign policy speech.
22. We stood on the deserted street *looking in vain for a taxi.*
23. As Captain Williams stood *on the deck of the boat,* he scanned the horizon.
24. While the witness gave her testimony, the members *of the jury* listened carefully.
25. Karan went to the Upper Peninsula in Michigan *to swim in Lake Superior.*

CHAPTER 21 REVIEW: POSTTEST 2

Writing Sentences with Phrases. Write your own sentences according to the following guidelines:

1. Use *with patience* as an adverb phrase.
2. Use *for my friend Margaret* as an adverb phrase.
3. Use *from Chicago* as an adjective phrase.
4. Use *with vegetables* as an adjective phrase.

5. Use *looking from a distance* as a participial phrase.
6. Use *studying hard* as a gerund phrase that is the object of a preposition.
7. Use *writing letters* as a gerund phrase that is the subject.
8. Use *to dream* as an infinitive phrase that is the object of a verb.
9. Use *to study the piano* as an infinitive phrase that is the subject.
10. Use *our local newspaper* as an appositive phrase.

CHAPTER 22

The Clause

THE FUNCTION OF CLAUSES

By now you know that most sentences are made up not only of single words functioning as parts of speech but also of word groups functioning as single parts of speech. The phrase is one such word group; the clause is another. This chapter reviews the subordinate clause; your use of this word group will help you vary your sentences and so improve your writing.

DIAGNOSTIC TEST

A. Identifying Clauses. Identify each italicized group of words as an independent or a subordinate clause. If it is a subordinate clause, identify it as an adjective clause, an adverb clause, or a noun clause.

EXAMPLE 1. *As he cruised along the tranquil beach on his bicycle,* Warren could hear the waves beating on the rocky shore.
1. *subordinate clause—adverb clause*

1. Most Americans are not sufficiently familiar with American Indian culture; *yet it is rich and interesting.*
2. Why is it that I can never find a pencil *when I need one*?
3. As we walked along the road, *we saw the wheat waving in the wind.*
4. I don't care *what you think*!

462

5. Do you know *that Dr. Robert Goddard was the pioneer of the liquid-fuel rocket?*
6. I'm so happy *that I could dance and sing!*
7. *Because his art work received wide recognition,* Pablo Picasso became famous and wealthy.
8. I have concluded *that personal freedom involves both self-realization and service to others.*
9. *The pitcher read the catcher's signals* and then struck out the hitter with a fastball.
10. Please do not talk *while the test is in progress.*

B. Classifying Sentences.
Classify each sentence as simple, compound, complex, or compound-complex and then as declarative, interrogative, imperative, or exclamatory.

EXAMPLE 1. I can swim, but my sister can't, because she hasn't learned yet.
   1. *compound-complex—declarative*

11. On your way here, look for a group of strange people wearing space-age outfits.
12. Did the coach realize that she was looking at her strongest softball team in years?
13. As the lights dimmed in the theater, a hush fell over the audience, and the overture began.
14. "Mitosis" and "meiosis" are technical terms for most people, but they are merely everyday words for cellular biologists.
15. Set in the rural South, Flannery O'Connor's short stories present an assortment of odd characters.
16. Given to the United States by France in 1886, the Statue of Liberty stands in New York Harbor and is regarded as a symbol of American freedom.
17. Jerome has had a job as a chef for six months; he hopes to own his own restaurant in the future.
18. The realtor said the price of the house has been lowered by $100,000!
19. Is it true that Jack, who lives in Sacramento, California, works in San Francisco?
20. After the hurricane had destroyed many homes, the townspeople bravely began a difficult clean-up operation.

GRAMMAR

22a. A *clause* is a group of words containing a subject and a predicate and is used as part of a sentence.

Clauses are classified according to grammatical completeness. Those that can stand alone if removed from their sentences are called *independent clauses*. Those that do not express a complete thought and cannot stand alone are called *subordinate clauses*.

INDEPENDENT CLAUSES

When removed from its sentence, an independent clause[1] makes complete sense. Written with a capital at the beginning and a period at the end, it becomes a simple sentence. It is referred to as an independent *clause* only when combined with one or more additional clauses, independent or subordinate, into a larger sentence.

When two or more independent clauses are joined into a single sentence, the usual connecting words are *and, but, or, nor,* or *for.*

EXAMPLES   It was a hot, sunny weekend, **and** all the beaches were packed. [The conjunction *and* joins two independent clauses.]

The soup was delicious, **but** the main course tasted bland. [The independent clauses are joined by *but.*]

SUBORDINATE CLAUSES

Subordinate clauses,[2] which cannot stand alone as sentences, are used as nouns or modifiers in the same way as single words and phrases are. A subordinate clause is always combined in some way with an independent clause. The following examples are subordinate clauses.

whoever knows the song
which is my favorite song
as she has always insisted

Combined with an independent clause, each of these subordinate clauses plays its part in a sentence:

Whoever knows the song may join in.
We sang "Green Grow the Lilacs," **which is my favorite song.**
As she has always insisted, Mother will not sing at parties.

---

[1] Independent clauses are sometimes called *main* clauses.
[2] Subordinate clauses are sometimes called *dependent* clauses.

EXERCISE 1. Identifying Independent and Subordinate Clauses.
In each of the following sentences, a clause is printed in italics. If the italicized clause is an independent clause, place *I* after the proper number. If it is a subordinate clause, place *S*.

1. Egyptology is the branch of learning *that is concerned with the language and culture of ancient Egypt.*
2. *Until the Rosetta Stone was discovered in 1799,* the ancient Egyptian language was an enigma to scholars.
3. Boussard, *who was a captain under Napoleon,* found the stone in the trenches near Rosetta, a city near the mouth of the Nile.
4. Before the French had a chance to analyze its inscriptions, *the stone was captured by the British.*
5. Because the stone contained the same message in two kinds of Egyptian writing and in Greek script, *it provided the needed key for deciphering the Egyptian language.*
6. *When the Rosetta Stone was found,* part of the hieroglyphic portion was missing.
7. Scholars could easily read the Greek inscription, *which was nearly complete.*
8. *In 1818 Thomas Young succeeded in isolating a number of hieroglyphics* that he took to represent names.
9. *The message* that was written on the stone *was not very exciting.*
10. Since the priests of Egypt were grateful for benefits from the king, *they were formally thanking the king for his generosity.*

The Adjective Clause

Like a phrase, a subordinate clause acts as a single part of speech—as an adjective, an adverb, or a noun.

22b. An *adjective clause* is a subordinate clause that, like an adjective, modifies a noun or a pronoun.

EXAMPLES She is someone **who has shown remarkable courage.**

This book, **which I read for my history report,** is about Africa.

Since a subordinate clause, like a sentence, has a verb and a subject and may contain complements and modifiers, it is diagramed very much like a sentence. Adjective and adverb clauses are placed on a horizontal line below the main line. An adjective clause is joined to the word it modifies by a broken line drawn from the modified word to the relative pronoun at the beginning of the clause.

EXAMPLE   Students **whose work represents their second-best** are not real students. [The subordinate clause *whose work represents their second-best* modifies the noun *students*.]

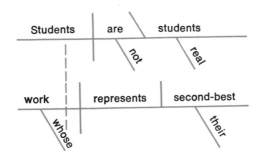

Relative Pronouns

Adjective clauses often begin with the pronouns *who, whom, whose, which,* or *that.* These pronouns refer to, or are *related* to, a noun or pronoun that has come before.

22c. A *relative pronoun* is a pronoun that begins a subordinate adjective clause and is related to a noun or a pronoun already mentioned or understood. The word to which the relative pronoun is related is its *antecedent.*

A relative pronoun does three things:

1. It refers to a preceding noun or pronoun:

   The amplifier was one **that we had seen** before.
   Let's listen to a weather forecaster **whom we can trust.**

2. It connects its clause with the rest of the sentence:

   Ms. Lopez is a counselor **who never betrays a confidence.** [The relative pronoun *who* joins the subordinate clause to the independent clause.]
   You should find a source **that is more up-to-date.** [The subordinate clause is joined to the independent clause by the relative pronoun *that.*]

3. It performs a function within its own clause by serving as the subject, object, etc., of the subordinate clause:

The principal appointed George, **who is a reliable student.** [*Who* is the subject of the verb *is* in the adjective clause *who is a reliable student.*]

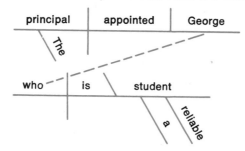

Show me the book **that you read.** [That is the object of the verb *read* (read what?).]

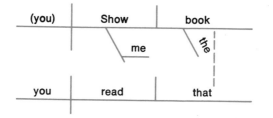

These are the assignments **for which you are responsible.** [*Which* is the object of the preposition *for.*][1]

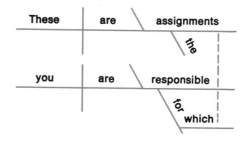

An adjective clause may also begin with the relative adjective *whose* or with the relative adverb *where* or *when.*

[1] In this sentence two words—*for* and *which*—begin the clause. Other two-word combinations of a preposition and a relative pronoun to begin a clause are *in which, by whom, for whom, from whom,* etc.

He is a coach **whose record has been amazing.** [*Whose,* the possessive form of the relative pronoun *who,* functions as an adjective modifying *record.*]

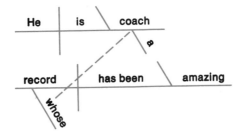

Do you remember the restaurant **where we ate lunch?** [*Where* acts as an adverb modifying *ate,* the verb in the clause. The antecedent is *restaurant.*]

EXERCISE 2. Identifying Adjective Clauses and the Words They Modify.

After the proper number, write in order the adjective clauses in the following sentences. After each clause, write the noun or pronoun that the clause modifies. Be prepared to state whether the relative pronoun or adverb is used as a subject, an object of a verb, an object of a preposition, or a modifier.

1. The Mars of the nonscientist is a planet of the imagination, where an ancient civilization has left its mark and where maps blossom with romantic place names like Utopia and Elysium.
2. "Earthlings," who were awed by the planet's red glow in the evening sky, looked on Mars as a home for creatures who might someday cross cosmic barriers and visit planet Earth.
3. Such thinking was encouraged by an Italian astronomer who observed the planet through a telescope and saw a series of fine lines that crisscrossed its surface.
4. He called the lines *canali,* which is Italian for "channels"; the word was erroneously translated into English as "canals."

5. A planet where there are canals must, of course, be inhabited by people who are capable of building not only canals but also the cities that presumably sprang up at their intersections.
6. Percival Lowell, the astronomer who founded the reputable Lowell Observatory in Flagstaff, Arizona, vitalized the Martian myths with nonscientific observations that most astronomers disputed.
7. Lowell reported a total of 437 canals, of which a large number were discovered by his own team of astronomers.
8. A writer whose interest was drawn to Mars was Edgar Rice Burroughs, whom we remember as the creator of Tarzan.
9. In his Martian books, Burroughs recounts the adventures of John Carter, who could get to Mars by standing in a field and wishing.
10. Burroughs' best-known literary successor is Ray Bradbury, who wrote *The Martian Chronicles,* published in 1950.

The Noun Clause

22d. A *noun clause* is a subordinate clause used as a noun.

In diagraming, a noun clause is pictured as a unit by placement at the top of a vertical line rising from the part of the diagram (subject, object, predicate nominative) to which the clause belongs.

EXAMPLE   **Whoever wins the election** will have many problems.

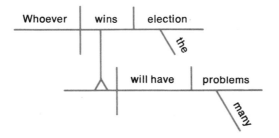

The entire noun clause *whoever wins the election* is the subject of the verb *will have.* Study the following pairs of sentences to see how a noun clause functioning in the same way that a noun functions may be a predicate nominative, an object of a verb, or an object of a preposition.

This is the **solution.** [*Solution* is a noun used as a predicate nominative after the linking verb *is.*]

This is **what we have been looking for.** [*What we have been looking for* is a noun clause used as a predicate nominative.]

We learned an interesting **fact.** [*Fact* is a noun used as the object of the verb *learned.*]

We learned **that she is a physicist.** [*That she is a physicist* is a noun clause used as the object of a verb.]

Here is a draft of my **proposal.** [*Proposal* is a noun used as the object of the preposition *of.*]

Here is a draft of **what I am proposing.** [*What I am proposing* is a noun clause used as the object of a preposition.]

A noun clause may begin with an indefinite relative pronoun—*that, what, whatever, who, which, whoever, whichever.* Unlike most relative pronouns, an indefinite relative pronoun does not have an antecedent in its sentence.

EXAMPLE He gave me **whatever I wanted.**

A noun clause may also begin with an indefinite relative adjective —*whose, which, whatever*—or an indefinite relative adverb—*where, when, how,* etc.

I know <u>whose car this is.</u>

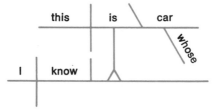

I know <u>where she went.</u>

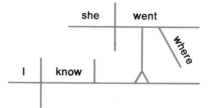

> ☞ NOTE   Adjective and noun clauses are sometimes used without an
> introductory word. Note that the introductory word is omitted in the
> second sentence in each of the following pairs:

I. M. Pei is an architect **whom most critics praise.**
I. M. Pei is an architect **most critics praise.**

She says **that James Earl Jones was once a pre-med student.**
She says **James Earl Jones was once a pre-med student.**

EXERCISE 3. Identifying Noun Clauses and Their Functions.   On
your paper, write the noun clauses in the following sentences. Before
each clause, write the number of the sentence in which it appears. After
each clause, write its function in the sentence: *subject, direct object,
predicate nominative, object of a preposition.*

EXAMPLE   1. I don't know what to think.
　　　　　1. *what to think—direct object*

1. The problem is that my finances don't quite allow me to live in style;
   in fact, I'm broke!
2. Do you know what the referee says to the opponents at the start of a
   boxing match?
3. What I like most about Harriet is that she never complains.
4. Scientists disagree about why dinosaurs died out.
5. Sometimes I am amused and sometimes I am amazed by what I read
   in the newspaper's advice column.
6. Through scientific research, psychologists have learned that everyone dreams during sleep.
7. What the dancers Agnes de Mille and Martha Graham did was to
   create a new form of American dance.
8. Can you tell me where the Museum of African Art is located?
9. Do you know whether Sakima has tried out for the track team?
10. I know how you are feeling, and I am happy for you.

EXERCISE 4. Identifying Adjective and Noun Clauses.   Each sen-
tence below contains at least one subordinate clause. List the clauses in
order after the proper number. After each clause, tell what kind it is:
adjective or noun. Be prepared to tell what word each adjective clause
modifies and how each noun clause is used in the sentence.

1. A person has found that toys are not meant only for children.
2. Athelstan Spilhaus, an oceanographer, admits he has sometimes been unable to distinguish between his work and his play.
3. Some of the toys he collects are simply to be admired; his favorites are those that can be put into action.
4. Some of his collectibles are put into intensive care, where he skillfully replaces parts that have been damaged or lost.
5. Dr. Spilhaus says that a toy is anything that enables us to tarry during the fast whip of ordinary life.
6. What is appealing about some toys is that they can make us laugh.
7. Someone once suggested that many physical principles began as playthings.
8. For example, the toy monkey that is activated by squeezing a rubber bulb uses the same principle as the jackhammer that digs up our streets.
9. Only those who have lost touch with childhood question what a toy is worth in dollars and cents.
10. Ask someone who knows toys what their enchantment is worth.

The Adverb Clause

22e. An *adverb clause* is a subordinate clause that, like an adverb, modifies a verb, an adjective, or an adverb.

In the following examples each adverb clause illustrates one of the typical adverbial functions of telling *how, how much, when, where, why, to what extent,* or *under what conditions.*

She practices **as though her life depended on it.** [*how* she practices]
She practices **whenever she has time.** [*when* she practices]
She practices **wherever the team travels.** [*where* she practices]
She practices **because she wants to win.** [*why* she practices]
She practices more **than anyone else does.** [*how much* more]
She practices on weekends **if her schedule permits.** [*under what conditions* she practices]

In diagraming, an adverb clause is written on a horizontal line below the main line of the diagram. The subordinating conjunction beginning the clause is written on a slanting broken line which links the verb of the clause to the word the clause modifies.

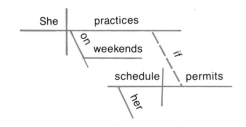

Adverb clauses may also modify adjectives and other adverbs.

> She is certain **that she will make the team.** [The adverb clause *that she will make the team* modifies the adjective *certain*.]
> He runs faster **than I do.** [The adverb clause *than I do* modifies the adverb *faster*.]

The Subordinating Conjunction

Adverb clauses often begin with a word like *after* or *because* that expresses the relationship between the clause and the rest of the sentence.

22f. A conjunction that begins an adverb clause is called a *subordinating conjunction*. It joins the clause to the rest of the sentence.

The following words are subordinating conjunctions. (Some may also be used as other parts of speech.)

Common Subordinating Conjunctions

after	because	so that	whenever
although	before	than	where
as	if	though	wherever
as if	in order that	unless	whether
as long as	provided that	until	while
as though	since	when	

The Elliptical (Incomplete) Clause

Sometimes we do not complete an adverb clause.

EXAMPLES   I am much taller **than you [are].**
            While [I was] running for the bus, I dropped my books.

In these adverb clauses the part of the clause given in brackets has been omitted. The missing part, however, could be readily provided by a reader or listener. Such incomplete clauses are said to be "elliptical."[1]

EXERCISE 5. Identifying Adverb Clauses. Write on your paper the adverb clauses in the following sentences. Before each clause, write the number of the sentence in which it appears. Draw a line under the subordinating conjunction that introduces the clause. After each clause, write what the clause tells: *how, how much, when, where, why, to what extent,* or *under what conditions.*

1. Because company was coming for dinner, Lola Gomez and her father prepared a special treat of Cuban-style black beans, one of their specialties.
2. After Lola had soaked a pound of black beans overnight, she drained them and covered them with fresh water; that makes the beans more easily digestible.
3. Before she lit the stove, she added chopped onion and green pepper, a bay leaf, coriander leaves, oregano, and salt pork to the beans.
4. While the mixture was simmering, Mr. Gomez prepared the sofrito, a necessary ingredient in many Latin American dishes.
5. Whenever a recipe calls for sofrito, you finely chop some onion, green pepper, and garlic.
6. Then you fry these vegetables in a little oil until they are tender, and add herbs such as basil, coriander, cumin, and black and white pepper.
7. As soon as the sofrito was ready, Mr. Gomez added it to the bean mixture.
8. He then crushed some of the beans against the side of the pot so that the bean mixture would become thicker.
9. When the mixture was thick, Lola put in some vinegar and sugar, which gives it that extra "tang."
10. Although this dish is usually served with rice, Lola and her father prepared a green salad instead.

---

[1] The definition of *ellipsis,* as applied to grammar, is an omission of one or more words obviously understood but necessary to make the expression grammatically complete. For the correct usage of pronouns in elliptical clauses, see page 542.

GRAMMAR

WRITING APPLICATION A:
Using the Adverb Clause to Express
Cause-and-Effect Relationships

One of the most important skills of reasoning is the ability to determine *why* something happens or *why* people act the way they do. Once the question has been answered, the answer usually includes an adverb clause. In addition to telling *why*, adverb clauses also tell *how, when, where, how much,* and *under what conditions*.

EXAMPLE   Frank Lloyd Wright's building was the only large building standing in Tokyo after the earthquake of 1923 *because he used steel and concrete and floated it on a sea of mud.* (In this cause-and-effect sentence, the cause is placed in a subordinate adverb clause.)

Writing Assignment

Think of a *why* question that you would like to answer. Either do the research or conduct interviews to find the answer. In your topic sentence, use an adverb clause to express this cause-and-effect relationship. Some ideas are the following:

1. Why are some scientists concerned about a "greenhouse effect"?
2. Why are high levels of cholesterol dangerous?
3. Why do students take Latin, which is called a "dead" language?
4. Why can't anything travel faster than the speed of light?

REVIEW EXERCISE A. Identifying Adjective, Noun, and Adverb Clauses. Each of the following sentences contains at least one subordinate clause. Write the clauses in order on your paper. Before each, write the number of the sentence in which it appears. After each, write what kind it is—adjective, noun, or adverb.

1. When a group of scholars first applied computer science to the study of literature, their colleagues expressed what can only be described as polite skepticism.
2. What, they asked, would the computer do?
3. Enraged scholars argued that measuring the length of Hemingway's sentences was dreary enough when it was done without computers.

4. Would precise mathematical profiles of style determine whether Thomas More wrote one of Shakespeare's plays?
5. Because initial studies were indeed made along these lines, they provided controversy when published.
6. Although such controversy raged for years, computers have won increasing support that has become more and more impressive.
7. Researchers use the computer whenever a project involves such mechanical tasks as compiling an index or a bibliography.
8. Since all of ancient Greek is now available on computer tape, scholars can make analyses that shed light on etymology.
9. There are certain elements in literary research that computers can pick up faster than readers can.
10. Many eminent scholars believe that the use of the computer as a literary tool has already produced results that are both significant and intelligible.

SENTENCES CLASSIFIED BY STRUCTURE

22g. Classified according to their structure, there are four kinds of sentences: *simple, compound, complex,* and *compound-complex.*

(1) A *simple sentence* is a sentence with one independent clause and no subordinate clauses.

Great literature stirs the imagination.

(2) A *compound sentence* is a sentence composed of two or more independent clauses but no subordinate clauses.[1]

Great literature stirs the imagination, and it challenges the intellect.
Great literature stirs the imagination; moreover, it challenges the intellect.

☞ NOTE Do not confuse the compound predicate of simple sentences with the two subjects and verbs of compound sentences.

---

[1] For rules concerning the punctuation of compound sentences, see pages 643–44 and 660–62.

Study the following diagrams.

Great literature **stirs** the imagination and **challenges** the intellect. [simple sentence with compound predicate]

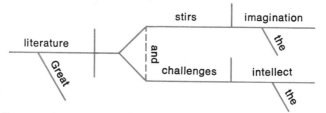

Great **literature stirs** the imagination, and **it challenges** the intellect. [compound sentence with two subjects and two verbs]

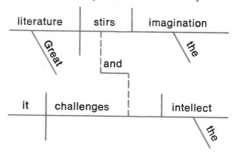

Independent clauses are joined by semicolons, coordinating conjunctions, or conjunctive adverbs.

Conjunctive Adverbs

also	furthermore	nevertheless	therefore
besides	however	otherwise	thus
consequently	moreover	then	still

(3) A *complex sentence* is a sentence that contains one independent clause and at least one subordinate clause.

Great literature, which stirs the imagination, also challenges the intellect.

(4) A *compound-complex sentence* is a sentence that contains two or more independent clauses and at least one subordinate clause.

Great literature, which challenges the intellect, is sometimes difficult, but it is also rewarding. [The independent clauses are *Great literature is sometimes difficult* and *it is also rewarding.* The subordinate clause is *which challenges the intellect.*]

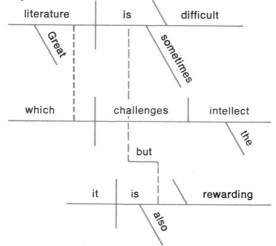

WRITING APPLICATION B:
Using a Variety of Sentence Structures in Your Writing

Notice in the following paragraph that the writer has used a variety of sentence structures to add vitality to his writing.

> When he was far up toward the top, he lay down and slept for a little while. [CX] The withered moon, shining on his face, awakened him. [S] He stood up and moved up the hill. [S] Fifty yards away he stopped and turned back, for he had forgotten his rifle. [CD] He walked heavily down and poked about in the brush, but he could not find his gun. [CD] At last he lay down to rest. [S] The pocket of pain in his armpit had grown more sharp. [S] His arm seemed to swell out and fall with every heartbeat. [S] There was no position lying down where the heavy arm did not press against his armpit. [CX]
>
> JOHN STEINBECK

Writing Assignment

Write a narrative paragraph of a memorable experience in your life. Use a variety of sentence structures to enliven your writing.

SENTENCES CLASSIFIED BY PURPOSE

22h. Classified according to their purpose, there are four kinds of sentences: *declarative, imperative, interrogative,* and *exclamatory.*

(1) A *declarative sentence* **is a sentence that makes a statement.**

Homes should be made safer for the elderly.

(2) An *imperative sentence* **is a sentence that gives a command or makes a request.**

Close that book and pay attention.
Please lower the volume.

(3) An *interrogative sentence* **is a sentence that asks a question.**

What was the name of that song?

(4) An *exclamatory sentence* **is a sentence that expresses strong feeling.**

How happy I am!

EXERCISE 6. Classifying Sentences According to Structure and Purpose. Number your paper 1–10. Classify each sentence in two ways: (1) according to its structure and (2) according to its purpose.

EXAMPLE   1. Look at this article I'm reading.
                1. *complex—imperative*

1. Are you aware that there is a worldwide demand for butterflies?
2. Millions are caught and sold each year to museums, entomologists, private collectors, and factories.
3. The plastic-encased butterflies that are used to decorate ornamental objects such as trays, tabletops, and screens are usually common varieties, most of which come from Taiwan, Korea, and Malaysia.
4. There is a difference, however, between what goes on there and what goes on in Papua.
5. Papua, which was administered by Australia until it gained its independence in 1975, is taking advantage of a growing interest in tropical butterflies.
6. Here butterfly ranchers gather, raise, and sell high-quality specimens that are accompanied by scientific data.

7. Because biologists have not yet detailed the life cycles of the Papuan butterflies, the villagers have become the experts; and as a result, butterfly ranching has improved the economy in many otherwise impoverished villages.
8. Some Papuan butterflies are quite small, but others are larger than an adult human hand.
9. As you examine these photographs, observe that a carefully stocked pasture of butterflies looks like a flower garden.
10. What rich, vibrant colors Papuan butterflies have!

REVIEW EXERCISE B. Classifying Sentences. Classify each sentence as simple, compound, complex, or compound-complex and then as declarative, interrogative, imperative, or exclamatory.

EXAMPLE   1. Whenever I need a piece of golfing equipment, I know that the To a Tee Shop is certain to have it in stock.
1. *complex—declarative*

1. Do you know that imaginative teachers who are enthusiastic about their work can make school pleasurable for their students?
2. Last year, when I took a social studies elective, Law and Order, I found myself looking forward to fourth period each day.
3. What our teacher, Ms. Schiavone, did to enrich our course was to bring the outside world into the classroom.
4. In addition to assigning reading, homework, and tests, she invited guest speakers to share their experiences with us throughout the school year.
5. By the end of three months, the class had met with a defense attorney, a prosecutor, and several local police officers; and we had interviewed the first FBI agent we had ever met.
6. In addition, Ms. Schiavone also arranged to have four prisoners, accompanied by police, tell us about how they were coping with prison life.
7. After we had listened to these men and women telling of their experiences, we all agreed that a career in crime is definitely not attractive!
8. In addition to bringing these people and experiences into the classroom, Ms. Schiavone set up a schedule of field trips, and she then took the classroom "into the world."

9. For example, on one day we visited the local jail; and on another, when we attended a session of a jury trial, we spoke personally with the judge.
10. I am glad that I was in Ms. Schiavone's class, and I was pleased when she was voted "Outstanding Educator of the Year."

CHAPTER 22 REVIEW: POSTTEST 1

A. Identifying Clauses. Identify each italicized group of words as an independent or a subordinate clause. If it is a subordinate clause, identify it as an adjective clause, an adverb clause, or a noun clause.

EXAMPLE 1. *While we were talking on the telephone,* our conversation was drowned out by noise on the line.
　　　　1. *subordinate—adverb*

1. *Tamara applied for the job last Monday,* and each day since then she has been waiting for a call from the company.
2. Do you think *that your parents will approve of your spending so much money for a stereo?*
3. *Please give me a break.*
4. Amelia Earhart, *who was the first woman to fly solo over the Atlantic and Pacific Oceans,* had great courage.
5. *Though he was a paraplegic because of injuries sustained in an auto accident,* Mr. Benoit was the best coach at Central High School.
6. As you wait for the signal, concentrate only on *what you have to do to win.*
7. Since last year Maureen and Jim have been rotating household tasks, and as a result, *each has become more understanding and more helpful.*
8. *If you study patterns of stock market transactions,* you will notice that prices often fall as interest rates rise.
9. How was I ever going to get the parts of the engine reassembled *before my father got home?*
10. *I won a soccer ball* when I was ten because I had raked more leaves than my brother and sister had in a "contest" devised by our clever parents.

11. Tired from a long day in the hot sun, the lifeguard reported *that there had been no accidents.*

12. In high school, Counsuelo Garcia set an all-city scoring record in basketball, *and she later went to college on a scholarship.*

13. Can you tell me *why there is still famine in parts of the world?*

14. After World War II, *President Harry Truman authorized the Marshall Plan, which was a massive program designed to speed economic recovery in Europe.*

15. The Vietnam memorial, a black granite wall engraved with the names of those *who died in the Vietnam War,* was designed by Maya Lin when she was a student at Yale University.

B. Classifying Sentences. Classify each sentence according to its structure (simple, compound, complex, or compound-complex) and according to its purpose (declarative, interrogative, imperative, or exclamatory).

EXAMPLE   1. How long have you been collecting old records?
                 1. *simple—interrogative*

16. Even though it has been years since his death, Elvis Presley's records still show good sales.

17. Where are you going in such a hurry that you have forgotten to put on your shoes?

18. Please proceed to the auditorium with your homeroom class and take the seats assigned to you.

19. President Lyndon Johnson, the thirty-sixth president, is credited with the passage of the Civil Rights Act of 1964, which is a landmark piece of legislation.

20. This morning the bank approved our loan, and this afternoon we began work on the new solar addition to our house.

21. As the molten lava moved down the mountain, residents who lived within a ten-mile radius were asked to evacuate their homes.

22. I am so relieved because the ordeal is over at last!

23. My friend Kaya likes to solve puzzles that are challenging; cryptograms are what he enjoys most.

24. When Bart says he will arrive at noon, I know I can expect him at any time between one o'clock and four.

25. Sometimes, on rainy Sunday afternoons, Carmen enjoys watching an old movie on television.

CHAPTER 22 REVIEW: POSTTEST 2

Writing Sentences. Write your own sentences, one of each of the following kinds:

1. A complex sentence with an adjective clause beginning with the relative adverb *where*
2. A complex sentence with a noun clause used as the subject of the sentence
3. A complex sentence with a noun clause used as the object of the main verb of the sentence
4. A complex sentence with an adjective clause beginning with the relative pronoun *who*
5. A complex sentence with an adverb clause beginning with the subordinating conjunction *because*
6. A complex sentence with an adverb clause beginning with the subordinating conjunction *while*
7. A compound-complex sentence
8. A complex sentence with an elliptical clause
9. An interrogative compound sentence
10. An imperative sentence

GRAMMAR

CHAPTER 23

The History and Development of English

ORIGINS AND VARIETIES OF THE LANGUAGE

English is a member of one of the largest and most widespread language families in the world. It is related to nearly all European languages and many of those spoken in South Asia, including Persian, Afghan, and several of India's principal tongues. This circumstance is the result of a long sequence of historical events. When we examine it, we become aware that language is a part of a people's culture and that languages, like societies, are in a constant state of change. We do not speak exactly like our parents. We speak even less like our grandparents. Over generations, as groups influence one another or break up and separate, small differences become significant ones. Finally the changes become so substantial that scattered descendants of the original speakers can no longer understand one another. So it is that thousands of years turn one language into a widespread family of languages.

This chapter will trace the history of English, beginning with the history of the language family to which English belongs. Then it will discuss the levels of usage in modern American English as they apply to your own listening, speaking, and writing.

INDO-EUROPEAN

About six thousand years ago a seminomadic people wandered in tribes, which even then were widely spread over eastern Europe and western Asia. We surmise from the vocabulary of their descendants that they herded flocks of sheep, kept horses and dogs, knew cold and snow. Their subsequent history suggests they were good travelers and fighters. A migration they began as early as 4000 B.C. ultimately spread forms of their language over half the globe. We have reconstructed that language from its descendant tongues, and we call it Proto- (first or earliest) Indo-European. The large language family that descends from it we call Indo-European.

Early Branchings

One of the tribes that split away from the parent group moved eastward, doubtless in successive waves, across western Asia and Asia Minor—by way of the Iranian plateau—to northern India. Today, in some of the modern languages and in surviving examples of the ancient literatures of India and Persia, we see the distinct yet closely related languages that developed from the dialects spoken by this people.

Another early migration moved southward or westward into Greece, the adjacent islands, and the coastal area of Asia Minor. A long series of invasions resulted in several varieties, or dialects, of the language in those areas, though modern Greek descends from only one of these, the dialect of Athens.

The following table gives the words for *ten* and *three* in some important Indo-European languages. Notice the similarities. Where differences exist, notice that the variations tend to be consistent within a single branch. Thus, in the word for *ten*, all Germanic languages have an initial *t* where the others have *d*. This kind of resemblance is a mark of close relationship within a branch of the language family.

Germanic	English	*ten*	*three*
	Saxon	*tehan*	*thrie*
	Old Norse	*tiu*	*thrir*
	Swedish	*tio*	*tre*
	Danish	*ti*	*tre*
	Norwegian	*tie*	*tre*
	Gothic	*taihun*	*thrija*
Italic	Spanish	*diez*	*tres*
	Italian	*dieci*	*tre*
	French	*dix*	*trois*

USAGE

Slavic	Old Slavonic	*desja*	*triye*
	Russian	*desyat*	*tri*
	Welsh	*deg*	*tri*
	Greek	*deka*	*treis*
	Sanskrit	*dasa*	*trayas*

Another westward migration carried a group of dialects into Italy. One of them was the ancestor of Latin. Centuries later, as a result of the Roman Empire conquests, dialects of Latin had spread over much of Europe. It is from these that the modern Romance languages, including French, Spanish, Italian, Portuguese, and Romanian, descend.

Two other important language groups that originated in the Indo-European homeland are Celtic and Balto-Slavic. After spreading over much of Europe and even into Asia Minor, the Celts were gradually conquered. Their language was largely displaced by dialects of Latin and Germanic. The most important surviving Celtic languages are Welsh, Breton, and Irish, with its Scottish dialect, Scots Gaelic. Balto-Slavic comprises two closely related groups of languages that include Lithuanian, Latvian, and the Slavic languages of the Balkans from Bulgaria to Poland, and the various dialects of Russian.

Germanic

One more language group of major importance descends from Proto-Indo-European. It is Germanic, one of whose most important members is English. The great expansion of Germanic peoples began in the first centuries of our era. It moved northward to the Scandinavian countries, on to Iceland, eastward into the Baltic territory, westward into what is now France, Spain, and England, and even southward to North Africa. The modern Germanic languages include many, though not all, of the languages of these areas. In addition to English, the best known are German in its various forms, Dutch, Norwegian, Danish, and Swedish.

The migration of Germanic tribes to the British Isles marked the beginning of English as a separate language. In the fifth century the Roman colony of Britain was a relatively peaceful and civilized community. The principal languages were varieties of Celtic, though many important persons also spoke Latin. Then waves of Germanic invaders began to storm ashore. They came from lands along the North Sea coast of modern Germany, Denmark, and the Low Countries. During more than a century of fighting, these relatively primitive newcomers drove

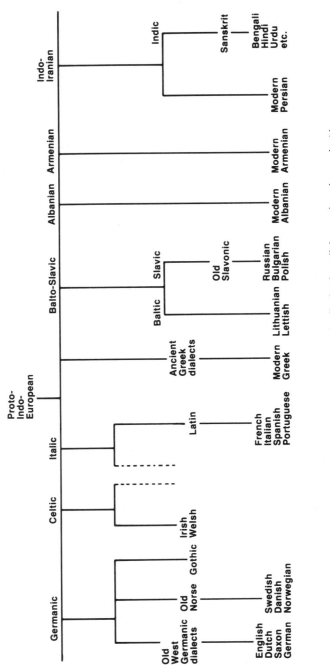

This chart shows the branches of the Indo-European family that have living modern descendant languages. In some instances, important ancient languages also appear. The two empty sub-branches under Celtic and Italic indicate ancient languages that have no important descendants.

USAGE

the Britons back until only a small part of their country was left to them—chiefly the western and northern mountainous areas. Thus, the Celtic of the Britons gave way to the Germanic speech of the conquerors. This language and the new country which the invaders had founded soon came to be called *Englisc* and *Engla land*, or "land of the Angles," after the largest of the invading tribes.

EXERCISE 1. Plotting the Migration of Indo-European Languages.
Find in a dictionary or encyclopedia a detailed chart of the Indo-European family of languages. (There is a good one in *Webster's Third New International Dictionary* at the entry "Indo-European languages.") With the help of the chart and the material in this chapter, plot the migration of the various IE languages on an outline map of Europe and Asia. Begin at a point somewhere east of the Black Sea and north of the Caspian Sea and draw in the movements, east and south to Iran and India, west and south to Greece, and so on. Be sure to include the Romance languages and, above all, the movement of peoples that resulted in the establishment of a Germanic language in England.

THE DEVELOPMENT OF ENGLISH

English was the first modern European language to reach the status of a literary language. We have documents containing written English from as early as the seventh century, and a considerable body of literature has survived from the eighth century. But great changes have taken place in English during the 1,300 years of its recorded existence. To study these changes, we will divide the language into three periods: Old English (or Anglo-Saxon), from the arrival of the Jutes, Angles, and Saxons in Britain to about A.D. 1100; Middle English, from 1100 to about 1450; and Modern English, from 1450 to the present. The languages of the respective periods differ considerably in sounds of speech, in grammar, and in vocabulary—the three features by which languages are usually described.

Old English

During the long Old English period, many changes took place in the language which clearly distinguished it from its parent western Germanic dialects. Yet, to the end, Old English held onto most characteristics of early Germanic. The most significant of them were grammatical. Like the other members of the Indo-European family, Old English was an inflected language. This means that the relationship between the words of a sentence was usually shown by endings added to the roots of words. Each noun in Old English had a set of endings that could identify the noun as subject, direct object, indirect object, a possessive, a singular, or a plural. Adjectives and articles, and such demonstratives as *the* and *this,* also had complete sets of endings. Modern English, in contrast, indicates relationships almost entirely by word order—and by otherwise meaningless signaling words such as articles and prepositions. The contrast may be seen in the following sentence from the Old English poem *Beowulf:*

> *Thone sithfaet him snotere ceorlas lythwon logon.*

Leaving each word in its place and translating literally, we get mostly confusion: "That journey him wise men not at all criticized." The confusion can be cleared up only if we know how to interpret the word endings. The *-ne* on *thone* marks the noun that follows it as a direct object. The *-m* on *him* is dative and is usually translated as "to him." The *-as* on *ceorlas* denotes a plural subject. The *-on* on *logon,* together with the form of the word's stem, shows this to be a past tense plural verb. Putting all these signals together, we see that the sentence means, "The wise men criticized that journey to him not at all."

Modern English delivers its signals almost entirely without the aid of inflectional endings. The subject is identified by its position before the verb and by the use of *the.* The verb, shown by its ending, is placed after the subject. *Journey* is identified as a noun by the presence of *that.* Its position immediately after the verb signals that it is a direct object. The sense of the old dative is indicated by the preposition *to* before *him.* Obviously, there is a vast difference between the older inflectional system and the new way of showing grammatical relationships.

A second grammatical feature in which Old English resembles the other members of the Indo-European family is possession of gender. Every noun in Old English is masculine, feminine, or neuter. The gender of a noun determines the correct ending for every word that modifies it. We can illustrate the point by using modern German, in which this is still true. *Der, die, and das* all mean "the," but *der* only modifies masculine nouns, *die* feminine nouns, and *das* neuter nouns. The Germans say *Der Knabe ist hier* (*"The boy is here"*) but *Die Frau ist hier* (*"The woman is here"*) and *Das Auto ist hier* (*"The car is here"*). Speakers of Old English referred to *seo hand* ("the hand") but *se fot* ("the foot") and *thaet eage* ("the eye").

USAGE

EXERCISE 2. Identifying Grammatical Features of Latin and English. Latin is one of the best-known languages with a fairly full set of inflections. In this respect it resembles Old English, as well as other early forms of Indo-European languages. In the following sentences *agricola* means "farmer" and *puella* means "girl." Identify the grammatical features that distinguish subject from direct object in the Latin. Do the same for the English translations.

Agricola puellam vocat. [The farmer calls the girl.]
Agricolam puella vocat. [The girl calls the farmer.]

EXERCISE 3. Understanding Grammatical Gender Features of Latin. You now know something about the subject and object forms of this class of nouns. Here is some other information you will need for the following exercise. In Latin, *agricola* is masculine and *puella* is feminine. The adjective *bon-* meaning "good" has one set of forms for use with masculine nouns and another for use with the feminine. Thus, for the subjective case the correct forms are *agricola bonus* but *puella bona*, and for the objective case *agricolam bonum* but *puellam bonam*. Notice that Latin adjectives usually come after the nouns they modify.

Try writing the following sentences in Latin. Since Latin does not use articles in the way that English does, simply ignore *the* whenever it occurs.

The good boy [*puer*, masc.] calls.
The good queen [*regina*, fem.] calls.
The good boy calls the good queen.

EXERCISE 4. Explaining Inflectional Features of Old English. In the following Old English sentence, *hund* ("dog") is masculine and *wylf* ("wolf") is feminine; *sliehth* means "kills." The remaining four words are forms of the demonstrative "the": *se* and *thone* are subject and object forms of the masculine, and *seo* and *tha* are subject and object forms of the feminine. Explain how the inflectional system signals the meaning in the two sentences.

Se hund tha wylfe sliehth.
Thone hund seo wylf sliehth.

You can better understand the nature of Old English vocabulary if you first consider how modern language vocabularies have been built. Modern English has picked up three-quarters of its words from other languages. We continue to do so with remarkable ease. For example, when we needed a word for the electronic system that brings us so much news and entertainment, we chose *television,* which in fact had been coined by the French. They had taken *tele* ("far") from Greek and *vision* from Latin. When we needed a word to describe the man who can "throw his voice" into the dummy on his knee, we borrowed the difficult word *ventriloquist* from Latin, which formed it from the words for "belly" and "speak."

In contrast, modern German forms most of its vocabulary simply by combining existing German words. In German, television is *Fernsehen,* from Fern ("far") and sehen ("to see"). The Norwegians, whose tongue also is Germanic, did not directly borrow the Latin word to name the voice-thrower. They chose to translate the Latin words for "belly" and "speak" into the Norwegian equivalents. They used *buk* ("belly") and *taler* ("speaker") to produce the new word *buktaler.*

This also is the way of Old English. Examples are *Laececraeft* ("the science of medicine") from *laece* ("physician") plus *craeft* ("art, skill, or craft"); *tungolcraeftiga* ("astrologer, magician") from *tongol* ("star") plus *craeftiga* ("one skilled in a craft"). Almost the only non-Germanic words in Old English were a few borrowed from Latin. Typical of the Germanic method of translating a Latin word into a word of its own is the Old English word for the Trinity. Modern English, characteristically, borrows its word from the Latin *trinitas,* related to Latin *tres, tria* ("three"). Old English, however, like Norwegian in the example above, translated the Latin into English elements, producing *thrines,* from Old English *thri* ("three") plus *nes,* which is equal to Modern English *-ness,* meaning "state of being."

EXERCISE 5. Finding the Etymologies of Words.

Look up the etymology of the following words in a dictionary that traces each element to its ultimate origin. Which words are formed of native elements and which are borrowed from other languages? Some of these words are similar in meaning to one or more of the others, although their origins are different. Which ones are they?

canine	eyeglass	loony	pyromaniac
dogtooth	firebug	lunatic	retain
doomsday	foresee	nostril	withhold

Grammatical developments that began to appear toward the end of the Old English period greatly altered the nature of the language in later centuries. Historical events of the late Old English and early Middle English periods helped influence the change.

The first of these events was the Norman Conquest. The last king of the royal English line of Alfred the Great died in 1066, leaving three powerful claimants for the throne. By law, the task of naming a successor fell to the English council of state. The council chose the man who already had the reins pretty much in his grasp. He was Harold Godwinson, the most powerful of the late king's officers. The other claimants did not accept this choice gracefully. Harold soon had to defeat the forces of the second claimant, Harald, king of Norway. Before he could rebuild his strength, however, the third claimant arrived from France with a far superior force. He was William, Duke of Normandy—a coastal area just across the English channel. Harold and William met near the town of Hastings on October 14, 1066; Harold was defeated and killed. The throne of England thus passed to a line of foreign kings, a significant event in the development of the English language.

One of William's first decisions as English king was to give most of England's high offices and great estates to his followers. Thus the native English governing classes were replaced in a relatively short period by men whose language was French.

French was the predominant language among England's upper classes for the next 150 years. It probably was spoken by many of the merchant classes as well. This had begun to change by 1200, however. English was slowly regaining its place among the aristocrats. By the fourteenth century, the English were learning French only from schoolbooks. English was again the language of literature, of the law courts, of the schools, and of business.

Middle English

It should be emphasized that whatever England's governing classes were speaking during all these generations after the Norman Conquest, the great majority of people went right on speaking English. They kept the familiar processes of language change at work upon the language during this period when Middle English was evolving. Changes occurred in pronunciation, in grammar, and, above all, in vocabulary. The dialects of the various parts of England, already different in Old English, continued to evolve differently, each in its relative isolation. There has probably been no equivalent period in the history of English when change was so great and so rapid.

Probably the most important contributing factor was the contact —we might almost say conflict—between the two languages, English and French. Middle English took from French virtually all the words and terms required for government, law, and education. Equivalent English words were gradually forgotten. Middle English borrowings in fact went much further than the fields just named. The vocabularies of religion and the church, of the arts and sciences, of military affairs, and especially of social life—clothes, manners, and food—all were heavily French. Among the many common words English borrowed from French after the Norman Conquest were *city, close, chair, catch, chase,* and *sure.*

It is interesting to observe that the division of the social classes of medieval England is reflected in French and English vocabulary for food items. Words for the animals of the field are commonly of English origin, for English was of course the language of the countryman: the peasant, the herdsman, and the small farmer. Thus *cow, calf, sheep,* and *swine* are English. But when the meat of these animals is brought to the table as food, it becomes of interest to the upper classes as well, and hence it appears in both Middle and Modern English as French derivatives: *beef, veal, mutton,* and *pork.*

EXERCISE 6. Finding the Etymologies of Words.

Look up the etymologies of the following words in a good dictionary. What do they tell you about the history of the English language and the roles of English and French?

authority	herb	paper	sermon
bacon	herdsman	peasant	servant
baron	holy	pen	sir
beauty	hound	pity	song
boil	house	plow	speak
castle	jail	poet	stomach
constable	judge	porch	story
court	manor	prayer	study
dinner	meal	private	tale
earl	medicine	public	taste
feast	music	roast	tower
grammar	noun	saint	write
gruel	pain	sausage	wound

We now consider another important cause of the significant changes in English that began at the end of the Old English period. It can be traced to a very early time in Germanic, before Germanic had begun to separate into different languages. It was the fixing of a strong stress accent on the first syllable of each word, with the exception of certain prefixes. The inevitable result of first syllable stress was the weakening of stress on the remaining syllables and, after many centuries, the complete loss of those syllables. The prehistoric Germanic word that might be written *findanan* turned up in Old English as *findan*, for example, and in late Middle English as *finde*. Today it is *find*, having been reduced from three syllables to one.

The grammatical endings of Old English were not stressed; since they were endings, they could not at the same time be first syllables. Most often, they were distinguished one from the other by differences of vowel. In late Old English, they were more weakly stressed and thus less clearly pronounced; the vowel differences that distinguished them gradually disappeared. For instance, in Old English the nominative plural case of many nouns ended in *-as*, and the genitive (or possessive) singular ended in *-es*. In the line from *Beowulf* on page 489, we see an example of the plural subject in *ceorlas*, or "men." The genitive singular of the noun would be *ceorles*, or "man's." By Middle English times the distinction between these endings had disappeared and both had become *-es*. This is, of course, still true in Modern English, where there is no distinction in sound between these forms of most nouns—as examples, *boys/boy's* and *churches/church's*.

The disappearance of the distinctions between the various grammatical forms of words was hastened by another force which operates in language evolution. It is called analogy, and it stems from our desire to make new or irregular words behave according to patterns already familiar to us. Children, knowing that for more than one cat we say *cats*, and hearing such other words as *roots, cans, pans, coats,* and so on, unconsciously reason that we add *-s* to form all plurals. Accordingly, when they want to describe more than one *foot* or *man* they form, by analogy, the plurals *foots* and *mans*. The children are incorrect, but this kind of logic is very important in languages generally. We see it operating in English today as we fit new words, easily and without any conscious application of "rules," into our grammatical system. When we create such new terms as *slimnastics* or *scuzzy,* or when we borrow *sputnik* from Russian, we never hesitate to choose easy plurals for these words. We ignore the Russian plural *sputniki* and say *sputniks,* for instance. This is analogy at work.

In the rather complex grammar of Old English, there were several different classes of nouns, adjectives, and verbs. Some nouns formed the nominative plural by adding *-a* or *-e* to the stem, like *aex* ("ax") and *wylf* ("wolf"), the plurals of which were *aexa* and *wylfa*. Some changed

-e to -u, like *spere/speru* ("spear"); some added -*n*, like *oxa/oxan* ("ox") and *blostma/blostman* ("blossom"); some added -*ru*, like *cild/cildru* ("child"); some changed the vowel of the stem, like *boc/bec* ("book"), *fot/fet* ("foot"), *toth/teth* ("tooth"), and *cu/cy* ("cow"); and some added nothing, like *sceap/sceap* ("sheep"), *hors/hors* ("horse"), and *word/word* ("word"). But the largest class of all was that which added -*as*, like *stan/stanas* ("stone") and *giest/giestas* ("guest"). We see among these classes some words that in Modern English have kept their old nominative plural forms: *ox* still adds -*n* in the plural *oxen*, *foot* still becomes *feet*, *sheep* still adds nothing, and we add -*r* in *children*. But most nouns have changed classes to become like *stone* and *guest*. This is the result of analogy.

The most common way to form plurals was by the addition of -*as*, which by Middle English times had become -*es*. More and more, people began forming the plurals of nouns by this most familiar means, whether or not the plural of the particular word had been formed that way in the older language. The result is that by the end of Middle English times, only a small proportion of English nouns remained in the old special classes.

A similar development took place in the adjectives and verbs of Old English. Partly as a result of the reduction of unstressed syllables and partly as a result of analogy, the only surviving adjective ending in the Middle English period was a final -*e*. Even this completely disappeared by the end of the period. The verbs in Old English, as in Modern English, were divided into two large classes, strong verbs such as *singan* ("sing") and weak verbs such as *fyllan* ("fill"). These were distinguished then, as now, principally by the method of forming the past tense and past participle. The strong verbs formed these by means of a vowel change (*sing, sang, sung*) and the weak by the addition of -*d* or -*t* (*fill, filled, filled*). In Old English the weak verbs were very much the more numerous.

The principal development in Middle English was the change of considerable numbers of strong verbs into weak ones. This again was the process of analogy, the more common pattern attracting to itself numbers of words originally belonging to the less common one. This development continues to the present time, with a number of verbs still in the process of moving from one class to the other. The past and past participle forms of *crow*, for example, may be the strong forms *crew* and *crown* or the weak form *crowed*. The past participle of *swell* may be either *swelled* or *swollen* and that of *shave* either *shaved* or *shaven*.

USAGE

EXERCISE 7. Tracing the Development of Verb Forms. The following verbs are, and in many cases have long been, in the process of shifting from one class to the other. Both the past tense and the past participle are shifting for some of them—or at least have developed double forms. For others, only the past participle has changed, and in some cases the double forms of the participle have developed different meanings, one for the verbal use and one for the adjective.

Look up these words in a good dictionary—that is, one with full treatment of the principal parts. Determine exactly what development the past tense and past participle forms have undergone.

abide	dive	hide	shine
awake	forget	knit	show
bid	get	light	speed
bite	hang	mow	strike
chide	heave	plead	thrive
dig	hew	sew	work

Modern English

We have seen that the almost complete loss of grammatical endings in Middle and early Modern English had a very important effect on English grammar as a whole. We had noted earlier that Old English, like the other languages of the Indo-European family, showed the relationship between words of a sentence primarily by means of an elaborate set of inflectional endings. As these endings were lost, the language had to rely more upon some other means of showing the relationship between such sentence parts as adjective and noun, subject and verb, and verb and object. The means that developed was, of course, that of Modern English. The subject came to be indicated primarily by the verb; nouns began to be identified less frequently by their endings and more often by the noun-marking or signaling words that preceded them, such as *the, a, some,* and *his.* Prepositions increased in importance and took over more of the task of signaling relationships that formerly had been shown also by the cases of nouns.

A result of all this was the complete disappearance from English of grammatical gender. Gender had always depended on the endings of nouns and the masculine, feminine, and neuter forms of the accompanying adjectives and demonstratives. With the loss of these endings and the reduction of the demonstratives to a few forms (*the, that, those*), there were no longer any distinctions to mark genders. Except for the relation between the form of the personal pronoun and the sex of its antecedent, gender simply disappeared.

By the end of the Middle English period, then, English grammar essentially amounted to that of Modern English. In the modern period there have been additional developments in the grammar of verbs, particularly those with auxiliaries, such as the progressive tenses. Other minor changes also took place, among them loss of the second person singular personal pronouns *thou, thee, thy, thine.* The main grammatical developments, however, were complete in Middle English.

A short quotation from a work from the last quarter of the fourteenth century will illustrate how far the changes from Old English had gone. Except for the spelling and a few words that have changed slightly in meaning, the passage might almost be Modern English. No really significant difference of grammar or word order is involved.

> Myda hadde, under his longe heres,
> (Midas had, under his long hair,)
>
> Growynge upon his heed two asses eres,
> (Growing upon his head two ass's ears,)
>
> The whiche vice he hydde, as he best myghte,
> (Which deformity he hid, as best he might,)
>
> Full subtilly from every mannes sighte.
> (Most artfully from every man's sight.)

The most important changes after the Middle English period were in pronunciation. They were sweeping in their effect on the language but are much too complex to consider here in any detail. As a few examples, in Middle English the *i* of *nice* or *vice* was an "ee" sound, like the modern vowel of *teeth*. The *e* of *meet* or *see* was in Middle English an "ay" sound, like the modern vowel of *late*. The *a* of *name* or *late* was in Middle English an "ah" sound, like the modern vowel of *father*. The *oo* of *tooth* or *moon* was an "oh" sound, like the modern vowel of *coat*. The changes were so extensive that an oral reading of the foregoing passage in the pronunciation of Chaucer would be very difficult for us to understand, even though the vocabulary and grammar are relatively familiar.

Early in the Modern English period, extensive changes brought nearly all vowels of Middle English fairly close to the quality that they have at present. As we might expect, however, vowel changes differed considerably in the various English dialects. In some dialects, for example, *er* remained more or less as it had been in Middle English, eventually becoming the "urr" sound heard in the usual American English pronunciation of *servant*. In others, it changed to *ar,* as in

USAGE

Modern English *parsley*. As more or less standard pronunciation developed over time, a mixture of dialects resulted in some of these words having -*ar* and some -*er* sounds. We still find words of this group that are pronounced differently in various parts of the English-speaking world. Most, such as *far, carve, harbor, farm,* are consistently pronounced as *ar*. Many others have remained *er,* such as *perfect, perch, sermon, verse, verdict*. At least one, *sergeant,* is spelled with *er* but always pronounced *ar*. But a considerable number are (or have been until recently) pronounced differently in different dialect areas. *Learn, servant, serpent, virtue,* as examples, were in the last century commonly pronounced, in many areas, "larn," "sarvent," "sarpent," "vartue." The Modern English *varsity* survives as a shortened form of a similar pronunciation, "univarsity." In the standard dialect of England, the word *clerk* and the place names *Derby* and *Hertford* still are pronounced "clark," "Darby," and "Hartford." The spellings of the names *Clark* and *Hartford* are representations of this pronunciation, just as the names *Carr* and *Kerr* are dialect variants of the same personal name.

A great many other English words that differ in pronunciation from one dialect or region to another can be traced to the sound changes that took place in various dialects in the earlier centuries of the Modern English period. Some examples, with the variant pronunciation respelled in quotation marks, are *deaf*/"deef"; *head*/"haid"; *either*/"eyether"; *home*/"hum"; and *roof*/"ruf" (with a vowel like that of *foot*).

Many of the strange-looking rhymes in older poetry also represent dialect variants of the stages through which the pronunciation of English has gone. Samuel Pepys (1633–1703) rhymed *root/foot/dispute;* Alexander Pope (1688–1744) rhymed *head/paid/shade;* Philip Freneau (1752–1832) rhymed *deaf/relief*. Pope, John Milton (1608–1674), and Robert Herrick (1591–1674) regularly rhymed *home/come,* and rhymes of *home* with *from* and *some* were very common in the seventeenth and eighteenth centuries.

Variations in the pronunciation of both early and recent Modern English are, of course, part of the explanation for the inconsistency of English spelling. The period during which these various changes were taking place in the dialects of English was also the time when English spelling was beginning to be fixed in something like its present form. In many instances the modern spelling reflects a pronunciation that is no longer in ordinary use. A simple example is that the vowels of *meat, great,* and *dead* are all *ea,* yet all are differently pronounced. In Middle English the words belonged to a large class pronounced with an "eh" sound, equivalent to the lengthened vowel of Modern English *there*. In the late Middle English this vowel developed differently in various dialects that contributed to the standard language. As a result, the original turned up in early Modern English usually as a sound like the vowels of Modern English *meat.* In a few words the sound was like that of *great.* In a good number of words it was modified very slightly to the sound we use in *dead.* Thus these three words survive as representatives of all three developments.

The spelling and pronunciation of English, then, are a record of particular events in the history of our language. The other characteristic features of Modern English are, of course, also the product of the historical process, which often has been referred to as *grammatical simplification.* The accuracy of the term, however, is doubtful.

The Modern English inflectional system obviously is simpler than that of Old English. But this is not the same thing as saying that the total system of Modern English is simpler than one based on full grammatical inflection. We have only to consider the complexities of our system. As an example, the order of the various types of adverbs and adjectives in English is flexible, but only within definite limits. The order of the adjectives in "the little new red ranch-type house" and the adverbs in "slowly walks upstairs now" may be rearranged in certain ways, but we are not likely ever to see or hear such an order as "the ranch-type little red new house" or "upstairs walks slowly now."

In one of the most important language developments of the twentieth century, English has added new words related to advances in technology. Many of these words were created by borrowing from another language. For example, *cybernetics* was borrowed from the Greek *kybernētēs* (pilot), and *video* was borrowed from the Latin *videre* (to see). Some new words, such as *radar* (<u>ra</u>dio <u>d</u>etecting <u>a</u>nd <u>r</u>anging) and *laser* (<u>l</u>ight <u>a</u>mplification by <u>s</u>timulated <u>e</u>mission of <u>r</u>adiation), were created from acronyms.

Modern English must seem enormously complex and exceedingly inconsistent to speakers of other languages. It is, but so are all languages. Much of the interest of language study comes from our recognition that much within the apparent complexity can be ordered, rationalized, and explained. If we can know enough, each inconsistency and all the complexities become examples of the processes of language and the fascinating events of its history and evolution.

EXERCISE 8. Finding the Etymologies of Words. Look up the etymologies of the following words in a good dictionary. You may cooperate with several friends, each looking up one column, and pool

USAGE

your results. Arrange them in groups according to the language of origin. What do they tell you of the history of English?

agenda	comedy	orange	skirt
alarm	cyclotron	ouch	snoop
alcohol	devil	piano	spaghetti
alibi	dock	poodle	stampede
animal	dumb	pope	syrup
atomic	extra	posse	take
balcony	frankfurter	potato	tattoo
barbecue	freight	priest	tea
black hand	gingham	propaganda	they
boss	giraffe	pump	umbrella
bungalow	gorilla	sandal	veto
cafeteria	knife	Santa Claus	weiner
camel	macaroni	scream	yam
church	manual	semester	zero
clan	opera	shanty	zinc

EXERCISE 9. Writing About the English Language. Write a composition of about 500 words on the effect of historical forces on the English language. As this is a very large subject, it will be best to limit your discussion to a particular language feature, such as vocabulary, or to a particular period. Illustrate your more important points by using well-chosen examples drawn from this chapter, from the list of words in the foregoing exercise, or from your own reading or investigation.

THE VARIETIES OF ENGLISH

The English of today is a rich and complex language which exhibits great variety among its native speakers. In general, we can distinguish two broad categories of English usage: *standard* and *nonstandard*.

Standard English

Standard English, which has evolved over many centuries, is the form used most widely. It is the language of most educational, legal, governmental, and professional documents. It is used in newspapers, magazines, and books. It is the English we hear from radio and television announcers and persons making formal speeches.

Standard English can vary in different situations, but certain conventions or rules within it are fairly constant, and well-educated people deem them worthy of being observed. That is why we apply the name *standard* to this variety. If you want to succeed in the academic and business worlds, as well as in many other pursuits, you must master the conventions of standard English.

Nonstandard English

Standard and *nonstandard* English are not, of course, different languages. Some words appear only in one or the other form, but most words can appear in either. The main differences are in the use of pronouns and certain verb forms. A user of standard English would say *brought,* for instance, where a user of nonstandard English might say *brung.* Some other examples:

STANDARD	NONSTANDARD
He did it **himself**.	He did it **hisself.**
You and **she** fight all the time.	You and **her** fight all the time.
He **doesn't** trust me.	He **don't** trust me.
She **ran** right into me.	She **run** right into me.

Sentences like those in the right-hand column are used by perhaps millions of English speakers. Our fiction is full of characters who use recognizably nonstandard speech. Eudora Welty and William Faulkner are among writers admired for their ability to capture the special lilt of certain dialects of nonstandard English. Occasionally someone makes nonstandard English his trademark. Dizzy Dean, a famous pitcher for the St. Louis Cardinals and later a radio and television announcer, turned his nonstandard speech into an asset. The following excerpt is from a *New York Times* interview with Dean:

> And I reckon that's why that now I come up with *ain't* once in a while, and have the Missouri teachers all stirred up. They don't like it because I say that Marty Marion or Vern Stephens *slud* into second base. What do they want me to say—*slidded?*
>
> Me and Paul [Dizzy's brother, also a pitcher for the Cards] didn't have to worry about that sort of stuff when we were winning games for the old Gas House Gang. And I don't know why I should get a sweat up now.
>
> Paul, he'd win one game and I'd win the next.
>
> Didn't nobody come around after the game and ask whether we'd throwed or threw the ball in there to make a play.
>
> We won 'em, no questions asked.

USAGE

There are so many varieties of nonstandard English—as there are standard and nonstandard varieties of all living languages—that it seems best to describe that form as simply scattered sets of conventions that are recognizably different from those of the standard language. But the audience for each set is relatively small. In contrast, standard English is the medium of communication certain to reach the broadest audience of speakers of English and find a hearing. The more general the audience we are trying to reach, the more exclusively we must turn to the standard language.

TWO KINDS OF STANDARD ENGLISH

Standard English is used in so many different situations—ranging from casual telephone conversations to formal speeches—that it would be impossible to name a particular kind appropriate for each situation. But we can distinguish two domains of standard English: *formal* and *informal*. However, most standard usage tends to fall somewhere between these two varieties.

Formal English

For the most part, formal English, like formal dress and formal manners, is language for special occasions. Sometimes referred to as "literary" English, it is the language of serious writing. It is used in formal essays, essay answers to examination questions, formal reports, research papers, literary criticism, scholarly writings, and addresses on serious or solemn occasions.

Formal English is likely to include words that rarely come up in ordinary conversation. The sentences are likely to be more elaborately constructed and longer than those of ordinary writing. Contractions are rarely used. Formal English pays close attention to refinements in usage and avoids slang.

Note the long and carefully constructed sentences in the following example of formal English. Notice also the formal vocabulary:

> Formidable and grand on a hilltop in Picardy, the five-towered castle of Coucy dominated the approach to Paris from the north, but whether as guardian or as challenger of the monarchy in the capital was an open question. Thrusting up from the castle's center, a gigantic cylinder rose to twice the height of the four corner towers. This was the *donjon* or central citadel, the largest in Europe, the mightiest of its kind ever built in the Middle Ages or thereafter. Ninety feet in diameter, 180 feet high, capable of

USAGE

housing a thousand men in a siege, it dwarfed and protected the castle at its base, the clustered roofs of the town, the bell tower of the church, and the thirty turrets of the massive wall enclosing the whole complex on the hill. Travelers coming from any direction could see this colossus of baronial power from miles away and, on approaching it, feel the awe of the traveler in infidel lands at first sight of the pyramids.

Seized by grandeur, the builders had carried out the scale of the *donjon* in interior features of more than mortal size: risers of steps were fifteen to sixteen inches, window seats three and a half feet from the ground, as if for use by a race of titans. Stone lintels measuring two cubic yards were no less heroic. For more than four hundred years the dynasty reflected by these arrangements had exhibited the same quality of excess. Ambitious, dangerous, not infrequently ferocious, the Coucys had planted themselves on a promontory of land which was formed by nature for command.

BARBARA TUCHMAN

Informal English

Informal English is the language most of us use most of the time. It is the language of most magazines, newspapers, books, and talks intended for general audiences.

The conventions of informal English are less rigid than those of formal English. Sentences may be long or short, and they are likely to sound more like conversation than the stately rhythms of formal English. Contractions often appear in informal English, and sometimes a slang expression is used. Here is an example of written informal English:

One day General Littlefield picked our company out of the whole regiment and tried to get it mixed up by putting it through one movement after another as fast as we could execute them: squads right, squads left, squads on right into line, squads right about, squads left front into line, etc. In about three minutes one hundred and nine men were marching in one direction and I was marching away from them at an angle of forty-five degrees, all alone. "Company; halt!" shouted General Littlefield. "That man is the only man who has it right!" I was made a corporal for my achievement.

The next day General Littlefield summoned me to his office. He was swatting flies when I went in. I was silent and he was silent too, for a long time. I don't think he remembered me or why he had sent for me, but he didn't want to admit it. He swatted some more flies, keeping his eyes on them narrowly before he let go with the swatter. "Button up your coat" he snapped. Looking back on it now I can see that he meant me,

USAGE

although he was looking at a fly, but I just stood there. Another fly came to rest on a paper in front of the general and began rubbing its hind legs together. The general lifted the swatter cautiously. I moved restlessly and the fly flew away. "You startled him!" barked General Littlefield, looking at me severely. I said I was sorry. "That won't help the situation!" snapped the general, with cold military logic. I didn't see what I could do except offer to chase some more flies toward his desk, but I didn't say anything. He stared out the window at the faraway figures of co-eds crossing the campus toward the library. Finally, he told me I could go. So I went. He either didn't know which cadet I was or else he forgot what he wanted to see me about. It may have been that he wished to apologize for having called me the main trouble with the university; or maybe he had decided to compliment me on my brilliant drilling of the day before and then at the last minute decided not to. I don't know. I don't think about it much any more.

JAMES THURBER

EXERCISE 10. Distinguishing Different Kinds of English. Read each of the following passages carefully and identify the type of English to which it belongs—formal, informal, or nonstandard. Note the particular words and constructions that cause you to label the passage as you do.

1

In a few weeks, you will each receive a copy of the treasurer's report. Anyone who wants to gripe about the way we're spending the club's money will get a chance at next Saturday's business meeting.

2

If I'd of known they was goin' to let you feed the elephants, I'd of went with you.

3

Those actions of his former subordinates that the General was now powerless to oppose, he elected to support. In his eagerness to anticipate any new mischief that might occur to the junta, he promulgated a series of new laws, each more harshly repressive than the last, which even the most rabid of the young officers would not have dared to propose.

4

One thing is, she don't take long walks like she used to. Every morning we used to see her out there, takin' those brisk steps. Just as fast! You'd of thought there was something after her. And if you was to meet her, she'd never stop to say nothing to you. Just bob her head at you and go right on. Now that she ain't comin' by anymore, we sort of miss it. When you get used to something, you kind of want it to keep on.

5

I passed all the other courses that I took at my university, but I could never pass botany. This was because all botany students had to spend several hours a week in a laboratory looking through a microscope at plant cells, and I could never see through a microscope. I never once saw a cell through a microscope. This used to enrage my instructor. He would wander around the laboratory pleased with the progress all the students were making in drawing the involved and, so I am told, interesting structure of flower cells, until he came to me. I would just be standing there. "I can't see anything," I would say. He would begin patiently enough, explaining how anybody can see through a microscope, but he would always end up in a fury, claiming that I could *too* see through a microscope but just pretended that I couldn't. . . .[1]

EXERCISE 11. Revising Passages for Specific Circumstances.
Revise each of the following passages as directed.

1. *Change this nonstandard English, used in an oral summary of an article, into standard informal English.*
   The President finally got his dander up and told them Russians to get their stuff out of Cuba fast or else! He said the Navy would search ships headed for Cuba and if they didn't stop they'd be sorry.

2. *A student tells her friends of a conversation she has had with the school principal. Put her sentence into the language she would use in reporting the same conversation to her class.*
   Yeah, old Sherlock Holmes told me that any kids caught sneaking out of assembly would get kicked out of school.

3. *A youngster used this nonstandard English to tell about an incident. Change it into standard informal English.*
   When Mom and me come home, we seen right away they'd been somebody messing around with the car.

4. *A mayor made these informal comments to the City Commission. Rewrite them, using the kind of English the mayor probably would choose to explain the same thing to an audience of citizens.*
   In a couple of weeks you'll all receive the report recommending a new high school. You can bet that there'll be plenty of moaning from those people up on the Hill.

WRITING APPLICATION:
Acquiring Flexibility in Levels of Usage

Examine these two ways of conveying the same information:

EXAMPLES
1. In cinema, an extraordinary new genre called scientific fantasy has been developed. Using formality of language and vividness of imagery, this genre portrays the universal theme of benevolence pitted against malevolence. Through the heroic and often macabre intergalactic confrontations, the struggle is waged for the ultimate purpose of establishing moral equilibrium.

2. There's a new kind of movie called science fantasy. The characters use big, scientific words. Some of the scenes are incredible. The theme is usually good versus evil. There are a lot of bloody battles out in space. In the end, good wins out.

Writing Assignment

Now write two paragraphs of your own, using a subject of your own choosing, to illustrate your ability to use both informal and formal English. As in the example above, use formal English in the first paragraph and informal English in the second.

IMPROVING YOUR USAGE

While we can speak generally about three kinds of English—formal standard, informal standard, and nonstandard—the lines between them are not always easy to draw. One kind of usage shades into another. An expression we think of as being informal may turn up in a formal address. A slang word that originates in nonstandard English may become an acceptable part of the informal vocabulary; many words and constructions that we think of as belonging to standard speech may come into use among speakers of nonstandard English. The great majority of our words and our ways of putting them together are common to all three.

Sources of Usage Information

If your language conforms to the conventions of standard English, your main concern will be to vary your specific word choices to meet a particular need. The need will be determined by the nature of the audience, whether you are speaking or writing.

There will be times, of course, when you cannot be sure whether a particular word or expression is suitable for the occasion. You can get help with your decision by turning to a textbook like this one, by referring to a dictionary, or by consulting a special book on usage, such as one of those listed on page 508. Most important of all, you can pay closer attention to the preferences of people who speak the language with obvious care.

You will find the rules of grammar a useful but not invariably reliable guide to usage. Remember, grammar describes the system of a language; usage is concerned with appropriate forms of expression. The two are not always the same, for language is a living and growing thing, and life and growth are not always logical. The people who use a language are constantly changing it. Since the rules of grammar describe the way the language works, when the system changes, the rules change.

The Importance of Standard English

Effective speaking and writing goes beyond mere acceptance of the most appropriate grammatical rules. It embraces such qualities as clarity, forcefulness of expression, honesty, originality, freshness, and—often—brevity. Yet the conventions of standard English should never be underestimated as the essential foundation of good speaking and writing. If you deviate from the conventions of standard English, people will think more about how you are expressing yourself than about what you are saying.

Any language that calls attention to itself or strikes listeners as unsuitable to the situation gets in the way of communication. If you speak as casually with a prospective employer as you do when talking with close friends, you may ruin your chances of getting the job. If you jokingly use nonstandard language around strangers, they may get the impression that you do not know standard English. It is important to know the different forms of English and to make wise choices from them.

EXERCISE 12. **Solving Usage Problems.** The words and expressions listed below represent usage problems. Look them up in this and whatever other textbooks are available to you. Most of the problems will be listed in the index. You may also consult the usage books listed below.

1. *It's me.* [pronoun usage]
2. *shall* or *will*
3. *imply* or *infer*
4. double negatives
5. *between* or *among*
6. *(the) reason* is *because*
7. split infinitive
8. *due to*

Guides to Usage

The following books contain accurate information about English usage problems. (Other dictionaries are listed on page 722.) None of them can tell you exactly what to say or write, but they can help you make up your mind.

American Heritage Dictionary of the English Language: New College Edition, Boston, Houghton Mifflin Company, 1978.

Bernstein, Theodore M., *The Careful Writer: A Modern Guide to English Usage,* New York, Atheneum, 1979.

Bryant, Margaret M., *Current American Usage,* New York, Funk & Wagnalls, 1962.

Copperud, *The Consensus,* New York, Van Nostrand Reinhold, 1979.

Evans, Bergen and Cornelia, *A Dictionary of Contemporary American Usage,* New York, Random House, 1957.

USAGE

Agreement

SUBJECT AND VERB, PRONOUN AND ANTECEDENT

Some words in English have matching forms to show grammatical relationships. Forms that match in this way are said to *agree*. For example, a subject and verb agree if both are singular or both are plural. Pronouns also agree with their antecedents, which are the words the pronouns stand for.

DIAGNOSTIC TEST

Selecting Verbs That Agree with Their Subjects and Pronouns That Agree with Their Antecedents. Number your paper 1–20. After the proper number, write the word in parentheses that correctly completes the sentence. Follow the practices of formal usage.

EXAMPLE 1. Neither of the pitchers (was, were) able to stop the Seagulls from winning the baseball game.
1. *was*

1. Each of the air traffic controllers (was, were) communicating with departing and arriving pilots.
2. Both of your answers (is, are) correct.
3. A team with too many superstars (has, have) trouble working as a unit.
4. "(Is, Are) mumps contagious?" I asked when my sister got the disease two days before I was to star in our school play.

509

5. Laura is one of those students who always (takes, take) good notes.
6. Luis' greatest problem before a race (is, are) nerves.
7. Ms. Caplice, in addition to Mr. Ruiz and Ms. Rogers, (was, were) asked to attend the conference.
8. Many a financial investor (has, have) a headache on a day when the stock market drops.
9. An adventure novel, *The Three Musketeers* (has, have) been made into a movie many times.
10. Kathy (doesn't, don't) look like her sister Missy at all.
11. Each of the students had brought (his, their) notes to the meeting.
12. When we got to the picnic grounds, we discovered that neither Fred nor Bill had brought (his, their) radio.
13. The number of people seeking jobs in the computer industry (is, are) rising rapidly.
14. Jane or the twins (is, are) sure to be home when you call.
15. At the dance, some of the food served during the breaks (was, were) home cooked.
16. Our city is proud of (its, their) cultural activities.
17. My mother thought that twenty-five dollars (was, were) too much to pay for the designer T-shirt.
18. As I shaded my eyes from the bright orange, yellow, and green plaid material, Doug said, "(Here's, Here are) my new trousers. What do you think?"
19. One of the women hurt (her, their) foot in the race.
20. The twin towers of the World Trade Center in New York City (is, are) an awesome sight.

AGREEMENT OF SUBJECT AND VERB

24a. A word that refers to one person or thing is *singular* in number. A word that refers to more than one is *plural* in number.

SINGULAR	PLURAL
car	cars
ox	oxen
this	these
either	both
he, she, it	they

24b. A verb agrees with its subject in number.

(1) Singular subjects take singular verbs.

A young **woman lives** next door.
This bake **sale was sponsored** by the Pep Club.

(2) Plural subjects take plural verbs.

Young **women live** next door.
These bake **sales were sponsored** by the Pep Club.

Most verbs ending in a single *s* are present-tense singular forms: he *is,* she *has,* he *thinks,* she *works,* etc. Most present-tense verbs not ending in a single *s* are plural: They *are, have, think, work,* etc. The exceptions, which should cause little difficulty, are verbs used with *I* and singular *you:* I *think,* you *work,* etc.

Notice that all the verbs given as examples in the preceding paragraph are in the present tense. Past tense verbs have the same form in the singular and plural. The exception is the verb *be,* which has a special form *was* that is used with *I, he, she,* and *it,* and all singular nouns.

SINGULAR	PLURAL
I threw	they threw
he applied	we applied
I was	we were

If English is your native language, you probably have little trouble in making verbs agree with their subjects when they directly follow the subjects. You will encounter sentences, however, in which it is not so easy to identify the subject correctly or determine whether it is singular or plural. These constructions, which create most agreement problems, are taken up separately on the following pages.

Intervening Phrase

24c. The number of the subject is not changed by a phrase following the subject.

A phrase that comes between a singular subject and its verb can easily mislead you if it contains a plural word. Remember that the verb agrees with its subject, not with any modifiers the subject may have.

USAGE

EXAMPLES   The **counselor was** very helpful.
            The **counselor** for the senior students **was** very helpful. [*Counselor*, not *students*, is the subject of the sentence.]
            A **solution has been found.**
            A **solution** to these problems **has been found.** [*solution has*, not *problems have*]

In formal writing, singular subjects followed by phrases beginning with *together with, as well as, in addition to,* and *accompanied by* take singular verbs.

EXAMPLE   The **singer**, as well as the musicians, **was** pleased with the recording.

EXERCISE 1. Selecting Verbs That Agree with Their Subjects.

Number your paper 1–10. Write after the proper number the subject of the sentence. After the subject, write the verb in parentheses that agrees in number with the subject.

1. The theory of plate tectonics (has, have) explained causes of earthquake activity throughout the world.
2. Enormous plates of rock (is, are) moving constantly beneath the earth's surface.
3. The movements, in addition to the pressure of molten rock, (causes, cause) the plates to collide.
4. The pressure of colliding plates (forces, force) the rock to bend until it breaks.
5. A ridge of these breaks (is, are) called a fault.
6. The cause of most earthquakes (is, are) the release of stress along a fault.
7. The Richter scale, as well as other measurements, (has, have) been used to record the magnitude of earthquakes.
8. The tremors of the great San Francisco earthquake (was, were) estimated to have measured 8.3 on the Richter scale.
9. California, with the San Andreas and Garlock faults, (has, have) about ten times the world average of earthquake activity.
10. The scientific community, especially seismologists and geologists, (is, are) studying the effects of earthquakes.

Indefinite Pronouns as Subjects

Pronouns like *everybody, someone, everything, all,* and *none,* which are more or less indefinite in meaning, present special usage problems.

Some of them are always singular, some are always plural, and others may be singular or plural, depending on the meaning of the sentence. In addition, such pronouns are often followed by a phrase. Therefore, you must first determine the number of the pronoun and then remember the rule about phrases that come between subjects and verbs.

24d. The following common words are singular: *each, either, neither, one, no one, every one, anyone, someone, everyone, anybody, somebody, everybody.*

EXAMPLES   **Each does** his own cooking.
              Each of the boys **does** [not *do*] his own cooking.
              Everyone enjoys the summertime.
              Every one of the campers **enjoys** [not *enjoy*] the summertime.

24e. The following common words are plural: *several, few, both, many.*

EXAMPLES   **Several** of the students **were** transferred.
              Few on the committee **attend** meetings.
              Both of the teams **play** very well.
              Many were impressed by the guest speaker.

24f. The words *some, any, none, all,* and *most* may be singular or plural, depending on the meaning of the sentence.

Usually, when the words *some, any, none, all,* and *most* refer to a singular word, they are singular; when they refer to a plural word, they are plural.[1] Compare these examples:

Some of the show **was** hilarious. [*Some* is singular because it refers to *show*, which is singular.]

Some of the actors **were** hilarious. [*Some* is plural because it refers to *actors*, which is plural.]

All of the workout **seems** simple.
All of the exercises **seem** simple.

Most of the program **was** new to me. [the major part of one program]
Most of the programs **were** new to me. [a number of separate programs]

Is any of the salad left?
Are any of the shirts clean?

None of the story **makes** sense.
None of the movies **were** exciting. [see note on page 514]

[1] Since the word referred to appears in a phrase following the subject, this rule is an exception to rule 24c.

USAGE

> ☞ USAGE NOTE *Was* could have been used in the last example, but modern usage prefers a plural verb in this situation. If you want the subject to be singular in such a sentence, use *no one* or *not one* instead of *none*.

WRITING APPLICATION A:
Observing Agreement Rules in Recording Observations

Indefinite pronouns can be tricky. They can be singular, plural, or either, depending upon the meaning of the sentence. Words like *each* are singular; words like *several* are plural; and words like *some* may be singular or plural, depending on the sentence.

Writing Assignment

Think of yourself as eyewitness to an important event. It could be a disaster, an impressive ceremony, or any other striking situation. Record your observations, following agreement rules carefully. In your written account, include at least four indefinite pronouns (such as *each, all, several, both, many,* etc.) used as subjects.

EXERCISE 2. Selecting Verbs That Agree with Their Subjects. Number your paper 1–10. Write the subject of each sentence. After it, write the verb in parentheses which agrees in number with the subject.

1. Each of the pictures (was, were) in a silver frame.
2. One of my friends (play, plays) the tuba.
3. All of our belongings (is, are) still unpacked.
4. Some of these rare books (has, have) leather covers.
5. None of the people in the theater (was, were) pleased with the film.
6. Every one of these jeans (is, are) too small.
7. A few in my class (was, were) asked to help out.
8. The lack of funds (present, presents) a problem.
9. Everybody living in Lewis Heights (go, goes) to George Washington Carver High School.
10. A band with two trumpet players and thirty-five clarinetists (sound, sounds) terrible.

EXERCISE 3. Writing Verbs That Agree with Their Subjects.
Revise these ten sentences, following the instructions that appear in brackets after each of them. Sometimes the addition will affect agreement. Be sure to make the subject and verb of the new sentence agree. Underline each subject once and each verb twice.

EXAMPLE 1. Each of the contestants was confused by the question. [Change *Each* to *Several.*]

        1. *Several* of the contestants *were confused* by the question.

1. All of the fruit has spoiled. [Change *fruit* to *oranges.*]
2. Each of my friends was angry about the election. [Change *Each* to *Many.*]
3. Has anybody joined the choir? [Change *anybody* to *any of the new students.*]
4. The class leaves tomorrow on the field trip. [Add *accompanied by two chaperons* after *class*. Put a comma before and after the added phrase.]
5. Our team is going to Austin for the debate tournament. [Add *Three members of* before *Our team.*]
6. Most of the classrooms were equipped with new microcomputers. [Change *Most* to *None.*]
7. The pitcher was disappointed in the coach's decision. [Add *as well as the other players* after *pitcher*. Set off the addition with commas.]
8. Every one of the smoke detectors was broken. [Change *Every one* to *All but two.*]
9. Both of them usually expect the worst to happen. [Change *Both of them* to *Everyone.*]
10. Some of her plan has been approved. [Change *plan* to *suggestions.*]

EXERCISE 4. Determining Subject-Verb Agreement. Number your paper 1–10. Read each of the following sentences. If the verb in a sentence agrees with its subject, write a + after the proper number on your paper; if the verb does not agree, write the correct form of the verb.

1. The mayor, as well as her aides, were in the parade.
2. Neither of the groups follow parliamentary procedure.
3. Some of the essay wasn't coherent.
4. The cause of the recent fires are being investigated.

5. Each of the computers run a different program.
6. None of the students has disagreed with my suggestion.
7. Only a few on any committee do all the work.
8. Luckily every one of the students have passed the test.
9. Most of his lectures holds my interest.
10. Either of your ideas seems reasonable.

COMPOUND SUBJECTS

As you will recall from Chapter 20, two words or groups of words may be connected to form the subject of a verb. These words, usually joined by *and* or *or,* are called a *compound subject.* Compound subjects may take singular or plural verbs, depending on whether the words joined are singular or plural and what the connecting word is.

24g. Subjects joined by *and* take a plural verb.

EXAMPLES   A **horse and** an **elephant are** mammals.
           Hannah and Dot have been friends for years.

EXCEPTION When the parts of a compound subject are considered as a unit or when they refer to the same thing, a singular verb is used.

EXAMPLES   **Bread and butter comes** with every meal.
           Joe's **brother and** best **friend is going** to college in New Mexico.

24h. Singular subjects joined by *or* or *nor* take a singular verb.

EXAMPLES   A **jacket or** a **sweater is** warm enough at night.
           Neither the **coach nor** the **trainer was** sure of the starting time.

24i. When a singular and a plural subject are joined by *or* or *nor*, the verb agrees with the nearer subject.

ACCEPTABLE   Either the singer or the musicians are off-key.

It is usually possible to avoid this awkward construction altogether:

BETTER   Either the singer is off-key, or the musicians are.

Another reason for avoiding this construction is that the subjects may be different in person. If this is so, the verb must agree with the nearer subject in person as well as number. In the following example, the verb must not only be singular to agree with *I*, but it must also have the form (am) that matches *I* as a subject.

ACCEPTABLE   Neither my girl friends nor I am working part-time.
BETTER   My girl friends are not working part-time and neither am I.

☞ **USAGE NOTE**   The rules in this chapter are consistently followed in standard formal English but are often disregarded in informal speaking and writing. Formal usage requires a singular verb after a singular subject. Informal usage, however, often permits the use of a plural verb if the meaning is clearly plural.

FORMAL   Neither Ellen nor Lola has a video camera.
INFORMAL   Neither Ellen nor Lola have a video camera. [Although joined by *nor*, which strictly calls for a singular verb, the meaning of the sentence is essentially plural: both Ellen and Lola lack cameras.]

FORMAL   The conductor, as well as a soprano and many stagehands, was trapped in the theater fire.
INFORMAL   The conductor, as well as a soprano and many stagehands, were trapped in the theater fire. [Although the construction calls for a singular verb, the meaning is clearly plural—all of them were trapped, not just the conductor. It is usually wise to avoid constructions that set up a conflict. The example would be better if it were written as "The conductor, a soprano, and many stagehands were. . . ."]

In some of the exercise sentences in this chapter, you will encounter such differences between formal and informal usage. For the purposes of these exercises, follow the rules of formal usage.

EXERCISE 5. Determining Subject-Verb Agreement.   Number your paper 1–20. Read each of the following sentences. If the verb in a sentence agrees with its subject, write a + after the proper number. If the verb does not agree, write the correct form of the verb. Follow the practices of formal usage.

1. One of the most precious resources in the nation is water.
2. The abundance and use of water vary greatly among the regions of the United States.
3. The water supply for all the states come from either surface water or underground water.
4. Unfortunately, neither overuse nor contamination of water supplies has stopped completely.

USAGE

5. Not one of the water sources are free from pollution.
6. After years of study, pollution of lakes, rivers, and streams continue to be a serious problem.
7. Lake Erie, as well as the Potomac and Cuyahoga Rivers, have been saved by clean-up efforts.
8. The government, in addition to environmentalists, are also worried about the quality and abundance of ground water.
9. Aquifers, a source of ground water, is layers of rock, sand, and soil that hold water.
10. About 88 billion gallons of water is pumped out of the ground each day.
11. In some regions, the drinking water for hundreds of people come from aquifers.
12. Every one of the recent studies of aquifers has revealed contamination to some degree.
13. The causes of contamination are varied.
14. Salt for melting ice on city streets cause pollution.
15. The chemicals that sometimes leak out of a sewer system or waste dump contaminates aquifers.
16. Fertilizers used on a farm also add pollutants to the water.
17. The extent of the damages from contamination are not known.
18. Another problem, according to scientists, is uncontrolled use of water sources.
19. Ground water in some areas are being used faster than the supply can be renewed.
20. Each one of the fifty states have a stake in preserving sources of water.

Other Problems in Subject-Verb Agreement

24j. When the subject follows the verb, as in questions and in sentences beginning with *here* and *there*, be careful to determine the subject and make sure that the verb agrees with it.

NONSTANDARD   How's Al and Roberta feeling?
STANDARD   How **are Al and Roberta** feeling?
NONSTANDARD   There's seven vegetables in the salad.
STANDARD   There **are** seven **vegetables** in the salad.

24k. Collective nouns may be either singular or plural.

A collective noun names a group: *crowd, committee, jury, class*. A collective noun takes a plural verb when the speaker is thinking of the individual members of the group; it takes a singular verb when the speaker is thinking of the group as a unit.

> The **audience were entering** the theater. [The speaker is thinking of the individuals in the audience.]
> The **audience was** one of the best. [The speaker is thinking of the audience as a whole, a single unit.]
> The **team have voted** eighteen to three to buy new uniforms.
> The **team has won** the semifinals.

SOME COMMON COLLECTIVE WORDS

army	crowd	orchestra
audience	flock	public
class	group	swarm
club	herd	team
committee	jury	troop

24l. Expressions stating amount (time, money, measurement, weight, volume, fractions) are usually singular when the amount is considered as a unit.

EXAMPLES   **Five years has been** a long time to wait.
Twenty pounds seems a lot to gain in a month.
Two thirds of the day is spent in school.

However, when the amount is considered as a number of separate units, a plural verb is used.

EXAMPLES   The **last six miles were** the most scenic.
There **are thirteen days** left in the month.
Two thirds of the holidays fall on a Friday or a Monday.

24m. The title of a book or the name of an organization or country, even when plural in form, usually takes a singular verb.

EXAMPLES   *Lilies of the Field* is on the late show tonight.
Friends of the Earth has held a membership drive.
The United States was represented at the summit conference.

EXCEPTION   Some names of organizations (Veterans of Foreign Wars, New York Yankees, Chicago Bears, etc.) customarily take a plural verb when you are thinking of the members and a singular verb when you mean the organization.

The **Veterans of Foreign Wars attend** this meeting.
The **Veterans of Foreign Wars is** a large organization.

24n. A few nouns, such as *mumps, measles, civics, economics, mathematics, physics,* although plural in form, take a singular verb.

EXAMPLES   The **mumps** usually **lasts** three days.
Nuclear **physics is** a controversial branch of science.

The following similar words are more often plural than singular: *athletics, acoustics, gymnastics, tactics.* The word *politics* may be either singular or plural, and *scissors* and *trousers* are always plural.

For more information on the use of words ending in *-ics,* look up *-ics* in your dictionary.

24o. When the subject and the predicate nominative are different in number, the verb agrees with the subject, not with the predicate nominative.

ACCEPTABLE   The last **act** featured **was** the singers and dancers.
ACCEPTABLE   The **singers and dancers were** the last act featured.
BETTER   The **singers and dancers were** featured last.

Although the first two examples are acceptable, it is usually better to avoid writing sentences in which the subject and predicate nominative are different in number.

24p. *Every* or *many a* before a word or series of words is followed by a singular verb.

EXAMPLES   **Every waitress, busboy,** and **cashier was** pleased with the new schedule.
Many a young **runner finishes** the grueling race in less than five hours.

24q. *Don't* and *doesn't* must agree with their subjects.

With the subjects *I* and *you,* use *don't* (*do not*). With other subjects, use *doesn't* (*does not*) when the subject is singular and *don't* (*do not*) when the subject is plural.

EXAMPLES   **I don't** like her painting.
You don't talk too much.
It [He, She, This] doesn't work anymore.
They don't agree.

USAGE

By using *doesn't* after *it, he,* and *she*, you can eliminate most of the common errors in the use of *don't*.

24r. In formal English, verbs in clauses that follow *one of those* are almost always plural.

Even though informal usage often permits a singular verb in the clause following *one of those*, the plural verb is almost always correct. Use a singular verb only when *one of those* is preceded by *the only*.

EXAMPLES This is **one of those** assignments that **require** research in the library.
Naomi is **one of those** players who **are** good losers.
Ron is the **only one of those students** who **has** permission to leave.

24s. The word *number* when followed by the word *of* is singular when preceded by *the*; it is plural when preceded by *a*.

EXAMPLES **The number** of volunteers **is** surprising.
A number of volunteers **are** signing up right now.

USAGE

EXERCISE 6. Selecting Verbs That Agree with Their Subjects.
Number your paper 1–20. After the proper number, write the correct verb in parentheses.

1. Neither the knife nor the scissors (was, were) sharp enough.
2. Forty dollars (is, are) too much to pay for jeans.
3. (Where's, Where are) her coat and boots?
4. Many a gymnast (dreams, dream) of participating in the Olympic Games.
5. There (seems, seem) to be something for everyone.
6. Every one of her quilts (has, have) been sold.
7. The captain of the football team and the president of the senior class (represents, represent) the students.
8. Macaroni and cheese (is, are) on the menu again.
9. *A Tale of Two Cities* (was, were) made into a movie for television.
10. The Chicago Cubs is one of those teams that (rallies, rally) in the late innings.
11. Neither civics nor mathematics (is, are) his best subject.
12. Each of the packages (contains, contain) a surprise gift.
13. Every volunteer in the city's hospitals (is, are) being honored at the banquet.

14. One half of the receipts (was, were) found in a shoe box.
15. The Society of Procrastinators (has, have) postponed the annual meeting.
16. That was one of those jokes that (offends, offend) everyone.
17. None of the peaches (was, were) bruised in shipping.
18. The acoustics in the auditorium (has, have) been improved.
19. Not one of the accusations (was, were) ever proved in court.
20. Some short stories by O. Henry (is, are) Ken's favorite book.

REVIEW EXERCISE A. Determining Subject-Verb Agreement. Number your paper 1–10. If the verb in a sentence agrees with its subject, write + after the proper number. If the verb does not agree, write the correct form of the verb.

EXAMPLES 1. Here's two letters for you.
    1. *Here are*
    2. The display in the auto dealer's showrooms represents more than $150,000 worth of cars.
    2. +

1. Each year, a faculty member and a student talks to the student body during an assembly on the opening day of school.
2. In the United States, there are a wide variety of ethnic groups in the population.
3. Can you believe that Leo don't go anywhere without his pocket calculator?
4. My sister Latrice is one of those people who make guests feel at ease.
5. As employers demand more skills from employees, the importance of studies after high school are evident to most seniors.
6. Some of the criticism aimed at children's cartoons are perceptive and accurate.
7. From my experience with team sports, I know that when neither the coach nor the team members has the will to win, there is little chance of victory.
8. The number of serious accidents that happen at home is surprisingly large.
9. The musical *Cats* was based on a group of poems by T. S. Eliot.
10. Every morning during swim season, each of the girls on the team were at the pool by 6 A.M.

WRITING APPLICATION B:
Writing Sentences with Subject-Verb Agreement

Writers make "agreement errors" when they do not see the *true* subjects of their sentences. You should always analyze your sentences for the *true* subjects so that you can make the verbs agree with their subjects.

INCORRECT   The players, as well as the coach, was disappointed.
CORRECT   The players, as well as the coach, **were** disappointed. [*Players*, not *coach*, is the subject of the sentence.]

Writing Assignment

Write ten sentences, each beginning with a different one of the following groups of words. Make sure that the verbs agree with their subjects.

1. *Great Expectations*
2. Five dollars
3. Neither of the sofas
4. The critics' reviews
5. Many a doctor
6. The man talking to the children
7. My aunt and uncle
8. Some of the salespeople
9. Peanut butter and jelly
10. Everyone in the contests

USAGE

AGREEMENT OF PRONOUN AND ANTECEDENT

24t. A pronoun agrees with its antecedent in number and gender.[1]

The antecedent of a pronoun is the word to which the pronoun refers. In the following examples, the antecedents and the pronouns referring to them are in boldfaced type. As a rule the pronoun is singular when the antecedent is singular and plural when the antecedent is plural. The pronoun is masculine (*he, him, his*) when the antecedent is masculine; feminine (*she, her, hers*) when the antecedent is feminine; neuter (*it, its*) when the antecedent is neither masculine nor feminine. This kind of agreement is agreement in *gender*.

She should have done it **herself.**
Keith hit **his** first home run today.
The **Fishers** returned from **their** fishing trip.
The **company** advertises **its** products on television.

[1] Pronouns also agree with their antecedents in *person* (see page 532). Agreement in person rarely presents usage problems.

(1) The words *each, either, neither, one, everyone, everybody, no one, nobody, anyone, anybody, someone, somebody* **are referred to by a singular pronoun**—*he, him, his, she, her, hers, it, its.*

The use of a phrase after the antecedent does not change the number of the antecedent.

EXAMPLES   **Each** of the women designed **her** own pattern.
Neither of the men left **his** coat on the seat.
One of the girls took **her** umbrella with **her**.

☞ USAGE NOTE   Sometimes the antecedent may be either masculine or feminine; sometimes it may be both. Some writers use the masculine form of the personal pronoun to refer to such antecedents. Other writers prefer to use both the masculine and feminine forms in such cases.

EXAMPLES   Everyone has handed in **his** paper.
Everyone has handed in **his or her** paper.

You can often avoid the awkward *his or her* construction by rephrasing the sentence in the plural.

The **students** have handed in **their** papers.

In conversation, you may find it more convenient to use a plural personal pronoun when referring to singular antecedents that can be either masculine or feminine. This form is becoming increasingly popular in writing as well and may someday become acceptable as standard written English.

EXAMPLES   If **anyone** calls, tell **them** I'll call back.
Someone left **their** umbrella.

Strict adherence to the rule of pronoun-antecedent agreement may lead to a construction so absurd that no one would use it:

ABSURD   Did *everybody* leave early because *he* wasn't enjoying *himself*?

In instances of this kind, use the plural pronoun or recast the sentence to avoid the problem:

BETTER   Did **everybody** leave early because **they** weren't enjoying **themselves**?
or
Did the **guests** leave early because **they** weren't enjoying **themselves**?

(2) Two or more singular antecedents joined by *or* or *nor* should be referred to by a singular pronoun.

Neither **Sue nor Maria** left **her** books on **her** desk.

(3) Two or more antecedents joined by *and* should be referred to by a plural pronoun.

Sue and Maria presented **their** reports.

☞ NOTE Like some of the rules for agreement of subject and verb, the rules for agreement of pronoun and antecedent show variations between formal and informal usage. Standard informal usage follows meaning rather than strict grammatical agreement. The sentences below marked "informal" are acceptable in informal writing and speaking. In exercises, however, follow the practices of formal English.

USAGE

FORMAL **Neither** of the women carried **her** purse with **her**.
INFORMAL Neither of the women carried their purses with them.
FORMAL **Every one** of the contestants was instructed to place **his** scorecard on the table in front of **him**.
INFORMAL Every one of the contestants was instructed to place their scorecards on the table in front of them.

WRITING APPLICATION C:
Making Pronouns Agree with Their Antecedents

Writers often use pronouns to avoid repeating nouns. Always check to make sure that the pronouns agree with their antecedents. Use the rules on pages 523–24 and this page to help you.

Writing Assignment

Write a narration about a humorous or light-hearted incident in which you and a friend or relative were involved. Wherever appropriate, use pronouns to avoid repeating nouns. When you proofread, check to see that the pronouns agree with their antecedents.

EXERCISE 7. Determining Pronoun-Antecedent Agreement.

Number your paper 1–10. If a pronoun in a sentence does not agree with its antecedent, write the pronoun on your paper and next to it write the correct form. If a sentence is correct, write a + after the proper number. Follow the practices of formal usage.

EXAMPLES   1. Neither Elena nor Barbara made any errors on their test.
            1. *their—her*
            2. Neither Stan nor Len wanted to endanger themselves.
            2. *themselves—himself*

1. Each of the skiers waxed their skis before leaving the lodge.
2. All of the senior citizens enjoyed their trip to Boston, where they walked the Freedom Trail.
3. Every one of the reporters at the press conference asked their questions too quickly.
4. I believe that anybody should be free to express their opinion.
5. No one brought their camera to the party.
6. Neither of the male soloists pronounced their words very clearly.
7. Neither of the newborn kittens seemed very steady or secure on his feet.
8. If anyone loses their way while exploring Salt Lake City, they should use the special street maps available from the tour guide.
9. As far as I could see, neither of the women made a mistake while presenting their argument during the debate.
10. One of the interesting quirks of American history is that neither President Gerald Ford nor Vice-President Nelson Rockefeller was elected to his high office.

REVIEW EXERCISE B. Determining Subject-Verb Agreement and Pronoun-Antecedent Agreement.

Number your paper 1–20. If a sentence is correct, write a + after the proper number; if it is incorrect, write the correct form of the verb or pronoun.

1. The number of accidents have been startling.
2. Each one of the terrorists were captured in a daring rescue attempt.
3. How's the heat and the humidity in Florida?
4. Has either of the brothers traveled before?
5. This is one of those cars that has a fuel injection system.
6. Anyone who speaks a foreign language increases their chance for a high-paying job.

7. Neither of the restaurants serves customers who aren't wearing shoes.
8. The experience of sailing the Great Lakes builds character in the young women.
9. Every part-time employee at the store was thanked for their help with taking the inventory.
10. She is one of the engineers that is working on the new design for the space shuttle.
11. When the bank's computer breaks down, every one of the tellers holds their breath.
12. The increase in taxes have met resistance.
13. A person who admits his mistakes is respected by all.
14. Three fourths of the audience always stay until the last note is played.
15. Each student needs a chance to think for himself.
16. Is there film and batteries in the camera?
17. All but three games in the final round was held at the community center.
18. A large number of scientists is studying the 843 pounds of rock and soil from the moon.
19. When one of the teachers retire, the students give him an engraved plaque.
20. The factory of the future will have robots working on its assembly line.

REVIEW EXERCISE C. Writing Verbs That Agree with Their Subjects. Revise the following sentences according to the directions given for each. Be sure to make changes or additions in verb forms, pronouns, etc. if necessary.

1. Some famous sports stars have made television commercials. [Change *Some famous sports stars* to *Many a famous sports star.*]
2. Where's my book? [Add *and my pen* after *book.*]
3. Both of the candidates have promised to reduce taxes. [Change *Both* to *Neither.*]
4. She writes neatly. [Add *is one of those students who* after *She.*]
5. Our basketball team has won the championship. [Add *Neither our football team nor* at the beginning of the sentence.]
6. People need friends to confide in. [Change *People* to *A person.*]

7. An application blank is required by the state university. [After *blank* add *together with a recent photograph and an autobiographical essay.* Put a comma before *together* and after *essay.*]

8. The tigers are growling ferociously. [At the beginning of the sentence, add *Either the lion or.*]

9. The movie screen is hard to see. [At the beginning of the sentence, add *The captions on.*]

10. A day in the library is all the time I need to finish my research. [Change *A day* to *Two days.*]

CHAPTER 24 REVIEW: POSTTEST

Determining Subject-Verb Agreement and Pronoun-Antecedent Agreement. Number your paper 1–25. If a sentence is correct, write a + after the proper number; if it is incorrect, write the correct form of the verb or pronoun.

EXAMPLE: 1. In September, the new teacher was delighted because the class were enthusiastic and cooperative.
1. *was*

1. One of the South's great ecological treasures are the estuary and flatlands of Galveston Bay.

2. Twenty miles are too far for someone to walk unless he can stop and rest frequently.

3. Neither Melinda nor Greta answered their phone yesterday.

4. During the five hours of deliberation, the jury was often in disagreement.

5. Public relations and advertising is exciting but often stressful work.

6. Anyone earning such a low salary will have trouble paying their bills.

7. Everyone who was at the tennis championship saw Chris Evert Lloyd and Martina Navratilova play their best match ever.

8. Is there any milk and apple pie in the refrigerator?

9. A completed application, in addition to a full financial statement, are required of students seeking college scholarships.

10. Every file cabinet, bookcase, and desk drawer were crammed with books and papers.

11. Where there's people and excitement, you're sure to find the twins Kazuo and Yori.
12. Not one of those nature programs that were shown on television this year have dealt with walruses.
13. Some of the information found in reference books need to be updated every year.
14. You might be surprised to know that many a city dweller grows vegetables in their own small yard.
15. Is Dolores one of the cheerleaders who are receiving a school letter at the sports banquet?
16. Each of the boys got a bonus for their hard work.
17. The Murphy family has made plans to visit relatives in Iowa.
18. Did you know that the city of Savannah, Georgia, has their own spectacular parade on St. Patrick's Day?
19. "Neither of the movies seem to have much hope of making the millions the producers want," commented the film critic.
20. All of the battalion was transfered to Fort Bliss in Texas.
21. Are the Lesser Antilles near Puerto Rico?
22. None of the competitors knew what his own chances of winning were.
23. A gentle snowfall is one of those winter events that is guaranteed to put me into a peaceful mood.
24. The number of people investing in companies that manufacture robots is increasing.
25. One junior, as well as four seniors, have been invited to attend the Milford Youth Council each month.

USAGE

Correct Use of Pronouns

NOMINATIVE AND OBJECTIVE CASE; SPECIAL PROBLEMS

USAGE

DIAGNOSTIC TEST

Selecting Pronouns to Complete Sentences. Number your paper 1–20. From the parentheses, select the pronoun that correctly completes the sentence and write it after the proper number on your paper. Base your answer on formal standard usage.

EXAMPLE   1. Jose and (her, she) completed the math test first.
    1. *she*

1. Greg and (I, myself) got our driver's licenses on the same day.
2. My Uncle Bill, (who, whom) I greatly admire, worked in the Peace Corps for two years after he had finished college.
3. As we waited at the starting line, I knew in my heart that the race was really going to be between Ted and (I, me).
4. At the town meeting, Ellen McCarthy asked, "If (we, us) voters don't vote, how can we expect the situation to change?"
5. I thought Manuel was in Kansas City; so when he walked into the restaurant, I could hardly believe it was (he, him).
6. Even though we are twins, Julie has always been taller than (I, me).
7. Does anyone know (who, whom) was using the computer?
8. My parents have a low tolerance for (me, my) playing rock music.

9. "May I help you?" asked the receptionist. "(Who, Whom) do you wish to see?"

10. The bus driver always greeted (us, we) students with a smile.

11. Owen said that for the first time the soccer team had elected co-captains, Mario and (he, him).

12. When you get to the airport, give your ticket to the person (who, whom) is at the check-in counter.

13. I remember (us, our) exploring the rocky coast of Maine when I was fifteen, and I have wanted to return there ever since.

14. Many people, adults as well as teen-agers, waste time worrying about (who, whom) is more popular in their social group.

15. "Does anyone dance better than (she, her)?" I wondered, as I watched Twyla Tharpe on the stage.

16. "When you and Regina were young children," said my grandfather, "I used to enjoy watching you and (she, her) playing Monopoly."

17. Knowing Noel and Bruce, I thought it had to be (they, them) who had played the practical joke on me.

18. Do you know that Stacy and (me, I) applied for the same job?

19. The President-elect knew exactly (who, whom) he wanted to appoint as Secretary of State.

20. I was so happy to see the new car that I could only gasp to my friend Danielle, "These wheels were made for you and (I, me)!"

USAGE

The function of a pronoun in a sentence is shown by the case form of the pronoun. Different functions demand different forms. For instance, a pronoun that acts as a subject is in the *nominative case;* a pronoun that acts as an object is in the *objective case;* and a pronoun that shows possession is in the *possessive case.*

PRONOUN AS SUBJECT   **We** called the doctor.
PRONOUN AS OBJECT   The doctor called **us**.
POSSESSIVE PRONOUN   **Our** call was an emergency.

Observe that the pronoun has a different form (*we, us, our*) in each case.

> ☞ NOTE   Since they are used in the same ways that pronouns are used, nouns may also be said to have case. The following sentence illustrates the three cases of nouns.

The *sculptor's statue* won an *award.*

sculptor's   noun in the possessive case
    statue   noun in the nominative case—subject
    award   noun in the objective case—direct object

However, nouns have identical forms for the nominative and objective cases, and they form the possessive in a regular way. Thus, case presents no problems as far as nouns are concerned.

25a. Learn the case forms of pronouns and the uses of each form.

Personal pronouns are those pronouns that change form in the different persons. There are three persons—first, second, and third—which are distinguished as follows:

First person is the person speaking: *I* (*We*) work.
Second person is the person spoken to: *You* are working.
Third person is a person or thing other than the speaker or the one spoken to: *He* (*She, It, They*) will work.

Personal Pronouns

Singular	NOMINATIVE CASE	OBJECTIVE CASE	POSSESSIVE CASE
FIRST PERSON	I	me	my, mine
SECOND PERSON	you	you	your, yours
THIRD PERSON	he, she, it	him, her, it	his, her, hers, its

Plural	NOMINATIVE CASE	OBJECTIVE CASE	POSSESSIVE CASE
FIRST PERSON	we	us	our, ours
SECOND PERSON	you	you	your, yours
THIRD PERSON	they	them	their, theirs

Since *you* and *it* do not change their forms, ignore them. Memorize the following lists of nominative and objective forms.

NOMINATIVE CASE	OBJECTIVE CASE
I	me
he	him
she	her
we	us
they	them

USES OF NOMINATIVE FORMS

25b. The subject of a verb is in the nominative case.

This rule means that whenever you use a pronoun as a subject, you should use one of the pronouns from the left-hand column on page 532. Ordinarily, you do this without thinking about it. When the subject is compound, however, many persons do make mistakes in their selection of pronouns. Whereas they would never say "Me am seventeen years old," they will say "Myra and me are seventeen years old." Since the pronoun is used as a subject in both sentences, it should be in the nominative case in both: *"Myra and I* are seventeen years old."

(1) To determine the correct pronoun in a compound subject, try each subject separately with the verb, adapting the form as necessary. Your ear will tell you which form is correct.

NONSTANDARD   Her and me are teammates. [*Her* is a teammate? *Me* am a teammate?]

STANDARD   **She** and **I** are teammates. [*She* is a teammate. *I* am a teammate.]

NONSTANDARD   Either Joe or him was in the gym. [*Him* was in the gym?]

STANDARD   Either **Joe** or **he** was in the gym. [*He* was in the gym.]

(2) When the pronoun is used with a noun (*we girls, we seniors,* etc.), determine the correct form by reading the sentence without the noun.

EXAMPLE   **We girls** painted the house. [*We* (not *Us*) painted the house.]

25c. A predicate nominative is in the nominative case.

A predicate nominative is a noun or pronoun in the predicate that refers to the same thing as the subject of the sentence. For the present purpose, think of a predicate nominative as any pronoun that follows a form of the verb *be.*

COMMON FORMS OF *BE*		PREDICATE NOMINATIVE
am		I
is, are		he
was, were	are	she
may be, can be, will be, etc.	followed	we
may have been, etc.	by	you
must be, might be		they

USAGE

EXAMPLES   I am **she.**
            Can it be **he?**
            It might have been **they** in the store.

☞ USAGE NOTE   It is now perfectly acceptable to use *me* as a predicate nominative in informal usage: *It's me.* The plural form (*It's us*) is also generally accepted. However, using the objective case for the third person form of the pronoun (*It's him, It's them*) is still often frowned on in standard English. When you encounter any of these expressions in the exercises in this book or in the various tests you take, you will be wise to take a conservative attitude and use the nominative forms in all instances.

EXERCISE 1. Using Pronouns in the Nominative Case.   Number your paper 1–10. After the proper number, write the personal pronoun that can be substituted for each italicized expression. In those sentences calling for [1st person pron.], use the appropriate one of the following pronouns: *I, we.*

EXAMPLES   1. Carl and *Sue Ann* are always happy.
            1. *she*
            2. Terri and [1st person pron.] were at the picnic.
            2. *I*

1. Jorge and *Mike* are tied for third place.
2. *Donna* and her parents have moved to San Antonio.
3. [1st person pron.] seniors will take the exam.
4. Can it be *some choir members* in that picture?
5. Either Ellen or *Sally* will be in charge.
6. The team and *Mr. Knight* have chartered a bus.
7. [1st person pron.] varsity men earned our trophies.
8. Neither *Carolyn* nor Michele has change for the bus.
9. Did you know that Greg and [1st person pron.] are leaving?
10. I am sure it was *Ed* and you on the dance floor.

USES OF OBJECTIVE FORMS

25d. The object of a verb is in the objective case.

The object of a verb answers the question "What?" or "Whom?" after an action verb.

EXAMPLE   We thanked **her.** [Thanked whom? Answer: *her,* which is the object.]

As their name suggests, the objective forms (*me, him, her, us, them*) are used as objects.

EXAMPLES   I helped **him** with the report.
She surprised **us** last night.
Him I have always admired.

Since both direct and indirect objects are in the objective case, there is no point in distinguishing between them in applying this rule.

EXAMPLES   They hired **her.** [direct object]
They gave **her** a present. [indirect object]

Like the nominative forms of pronouns, the objective forms are troublesome principally when they are used in compounds. Although you would hardly make the mistake of saying, "I helped *he* with the report," you might say, "I helped *Rod and he* with the report." Trying each object separately with the verb will help you to choose the correct pronoun for compound objects: "I helped *him* with the report."

When a pronoun is used with a noun (*we girls, us girls*), determine the correct form by omitting the noun.

It annoys **us** runners. [It annoys *us,* not *we.*]

EXERCISE 2. Using Pronouns in the Objective Case.   Referring to the list of objective forms, supply the correct pronouns for the italicized words in the following sentences. In sentences calling for [1st person pron.], use the appropriate one of the following: *me, us.*

1. Did you tell the superintendent or *Ms. Marshal?*
2. Carla and *Dave* I would never doubt.
3. Leave [1st person pron.] girls alone for a while.
4. Michelle will be inviting both you and [1st person pron.] to her birthday party.
5. Did you see Lois or *Andy* today?
6. I sent the admissions director and *her assistant* a letter.
7. The coach chose Joan and *Carmen and me.*
8. The principal should have notified *Sven* and Gail about the schedule change.
9. Ron just passed Tina and [1st person pron.] in the hall.
10. Please don't ask [1st person pron.] athletes about last Saturday's game.

EXERCISE 3. Selecting Pronouns in the Nominative or Objective Case to Complete Sentences. This exercise covers the use of personal pronouns as subjects of verbs, predicate nominatives, and objects of verbs. Number your paper 1–20. Write the correct pronoun in parentheses in each sentence.

1. The guests thanked Rita and (she, her).
2. Gloria and (I, me) have matching outfits.
3. That's (he, him) standing on the corner.
4. (We, Us) girls are studying self-defense.
5. What were you telling Chuck and (we, us) earlier?
6. Of course, I remember Monica and (she, her).
7. We knew it was (he, him).
8. Did Jean and (he, him) sing in the musical?
9. Give (we, us) girls the message as soon as possible.
10. My grandparents took Donna and (I, me) to the symphony.
11. Who will tell Georgia and (I, me) the truth?
12. I didn't hear the teacher and (they, them) arrive.
13. Jana and (she, her) are active members.
14. It's either you or (he, him).
15. I will call Jody and (they, them) tomorrow.
16. The teacher gave her friend and (she, her) more homework.
17. We are glad it wasn't Edna and (she, her) in the accident.
18. The volunteers and (I, me) distributed the posters.
19. You and (he, him) have been practicing every day.
20. I thought it was (she, her) on the stage.

25e. The object of a preposition is in the objective case.

Prepositions, as well as verbs, take objects. The noun or pronoun at the end of a prepositional phrase is the object of the preposition that begins the phrase. In the following prepositional phrases the objects are printed in boldfaced type:

from **Los Angeles**   at the **bottom**   to **them**

Errors in the use of the pronoun as the object of a preposition usually occur when the object is compound. Since you would not say "I gave the ticket to *she*," you should not say "I gave the tickets to *Jenny and she.*" By omitting the first of the two objects in a compound object, you can usually tell what the correct pronoun should be.

NONSTANDARD   We got the keys from Len and he.
  STANDARD   We got the keys **from** Len and **him.** [from *him*]

NONSTANDARD   Dwayne sat behind Norman and I.
  STANDARD   Dwayne sat **behind** Norman and **me.** [behind *me*]

EXERCISE 4. Selecting Pronouns in the Objective Case to Complete Sentences.   Number your paper 1–10. Find the preposition in each sentence, and write it after the proper number on your paper. After the preposition, write the correct pronoun in parentheses. Remember to choose the objective form.

1. The chess team sent a challenge to Don and (he, him).
2. The slide show was presented by my sister and (I, me).
3. We are planning to leave with (they, them) and Alice.
4. I dedicated my poem to both Marcia and (she, her).
5. Frank arrived right after Juanita and (I, me).
6. The responsibility has fallen upon (we, us) students.
7. Were you sitting near Tony and (she, her)?
8. The matter is strictly between Ms. James and (they, them).
9. Consuelo has been asking about you and (she, her).
10. Would you draw a cartoon for the girls and (we, us)?

REVIEW EXERCISE A. Selecting Pronouns in the Nominative or Objective Case to Complete Sentences.   Number your paper 1–20. Select the correct pronoun in parentheses and write it on your paper. After each pronoun, write its use in the sentence, using these abbreviations: s. (subject of a verb), p.n. (predicate nominative), d.o. (direct object), i.o. (indirect object), and o.p. (object of a preposition).

EXAMPLE   1. Leave the pamphlets with Kim and (he, him).
        1. *him, o.p.*

1. The coach chose Darrell and (he, him).
2. Luckily, the Smiths and (we, us) missed the heavy traffic.
3. I haven't heard from Mark and (she, her) in ages.
4. Is it really (she, her) walking down the road?
5. Mr. Weaver chaperoned the boys and (we, us).
6. It could be (they, them) across the street.
7. Ms. Grant, the Dodges, and (she, her) went to the reunion.
8. During the busy season, the boss relies on (we, us) workers.
9. The mayor granted (she, her) an interview.

USAGE

10. (We, Us) science students did our experiment at the fair.
11. (She, Her) and Heather always sit in the last row.
12. Mrs. Lemon said that (we, us) girls inspired her.
13. Would you please stop bothering Marla and (I, me)?
14. Adele painted a picture for (they, them) and (we, us).
15. Who is running toward (he, him)?
16. Neither the Spartans nor (we, us) Cougars play today.
17. Flora visited (she, her) and (I, me) in the hospital.
18. I thought it was Rob and (they, them) in the center aisle.
19. The team and (they, them) work well together.
20. The referee gave Manny and (he, him) a warning.

USES OF *WHO* AND *WHOM*

Like the personal pronouns, the pronouns *who* and *whoever* have three different case forms:

NOMINATIVE	OBJECTIVE	POSSESSIVE
who	whom	whose
whoever	whomever	whosever

Who and *Whom* as Interrogative Pronouns

Who and *whom* are interrogative pronouns when they are used to ask a question. The four rules on pages 533–36 governing the case forms of the personal pronouns apply also to *who* and *whom.*

EXAMPLES **Who** broke his leg? [The nominative form is required because *who* is the subject of *broke.*]
Whom did Nora choose? [The objective form is required because *whom* is the object of *did choose.*]

You may find it helpful, at first, to substitute *he, she—him, her* for *who—whom,* respectively. If *he* or *she* (nominative) fits the sentence, then *who* (also nominative) will be correct. If *him* or *her* fits, then *whom* will be correct.

EXAMPLES *(Who, Whom)* broke his leg? [**He** broke his leg. Hence, **Who** broke his leg?]
(Who, Whom) did Nora choose? [Nora did choose **him.** Hence, Nora did choose *whom.* **Whom** did Nora choose?]

Interrogative pronouns appear in both direct and indirect questions. A direct question uses the exact words of the speaker and is followed by

a question mark. An indirect question does not use the exact words of
the speaker and is not followed by a question mark.

DIRECT QUESTION   **Who** washed the dishes?
INDIRECT QUESTION   Joni asked **who** washed the dishes.
DIRECT QUESTION   **Whom** did she see?
INDIRECT QUESTION   I asked **whom** she had seen.

When the interrogative pronoun is used immediately after a preposition, *whom* is always the correct form.

EXAMPLES   **On whom** does it depend?
  For whom did you bake the bread?

☞ USAGE NOTE   In informal usage, *whom* is not usually used as an
interrogative pronoun. *Who* is used regardless of the case. In formal
usage, however, the distinction between *who* and *whom* is still recognized.

INFORMAL

Who were you calling?
Who did the club elect?

FORMAL

Whom were you calling?
Whom did the club elect?

Who and *Whom* as Relative Pronouns

When *who* and *whom* (*whoever* and *whomever*) are used to begin a
subordinate clause, they are relative pronouns. Their case is governed
by the same rules that govern the case of a personal pronoun. Although
whom is becoming increasingly uncommon in spoken English, the
distinction between *who* and *whom* in subordinate clauses is usually
observed in writing.

**25f. The case of the pronoun beginning a subordinate clause is deter-
mined by its use in the clause. The case is not affected by any word
outside the clause.**

In order to analyze a *who—whom* problem, follow these steps:

1. Pick out the subordinate clause.
2. Determine how the pronoun is used in the clause—subject,
predicate nominative, object of a verb, object of a preposition—and
decide its case according to the rules.
3. Select the correct form of the pronoun.

PROBLEM   Harry Houdini, (who, whom) audiences adored, performed daring escape tricks.

Step 1   The subordinate clause is *(who, whom) audiences adored.*

Step 2   In the clause the subject is *audiences;* the verb is *adored;* and the pronoun is the object of the verb *adored.* As an object it is in the objective case.

Step 3   The objective form is *whom.*

SOLUTION   Harry Houdini, **whom** audiences adored, performed daring escape tricks.

PROBLEM   Do you remember (who, whom) the escape artist was?

Step 1   The subordinate clause is *(who, whom) the escape artist was.*

Step 2   In the clause, *artist* is the subject and *was* is the verb; the pronoun is a predicate nominative. As a predicate nominative it is in the nominative case.

Step 3   The nominative form is *who.*

SOLUTION   Do you remember **who** the escape artist was?

In writing the sentence above, one might tend to use *whom,* thinking it the object of the verb *remember,* but *remember* is outside the clause and cannot affect the case of a word in the clause. The object of the verb *remember* is the entire clause *who the escape artist was.*

☞ USAGE NOTE   In determining whether to use *who* or *whom,* do not be misled by a parenthetical expression like *I think, he said,* etc.

EXAMPLES   We are the only ones **who**, I think, are taking jazz dance. [*who* are taking jazz dance]

She is the student **who** Mr. Hines thinks should be a chemist. [*who* should be a chemist]

EXERCISE 5. Selecting the Correct Case Form of *Who* and *Whoever* to Complete Sentences.

Number your paper 1–20. Using the three steps described on pages 539–40, determine the pronoun's correct form for each of the following sentences.

1. The two people (who, whom) I liked most were Will and Angela.
2. Someone called last night, but I don't know (who, whom) she was.
3. The announcer said that (whoever, whomever) finishes in the top ten can compete in the final round.
4. We did not hear (who, whom) the principal had named.
5. Neither of the two pianists was the musician (who, whom) the audience cheered.

USAGE

6. Anybody (who, whom) orders now will receive a free gift.
7. She is the teacher (who, whom) Al thinks will be our substitute.
8. The science club wants to find an astronomer (who, whom) will be an exciting guest speaker.
9. They are curious about (who, whom) you talked to so angrily.
10. Harriet Tubman was a woman (who, whom) we should revere.
11. The pedestrian (who, whom) the car hit suffered only minor cuts.
12. The police have not caught (whoever, whomever) stole my bike.
13. Several of the women (who, whom) had served on committees were considered for the position.
14. Anyone (who, whom) she can corner will be treated to a lecture on buying a home computer.
15. Allen is the only person in school (who, whom), I believe, has lived in a foreign country.
16. I never found out (who, whom) the driver was.
17. It does not matter (who, whom) wins, as long as you do your best.
18. I cannot find the person to (who, whom) this package belongs.
19. The player's reaction was to shout at the referee (who, whom) charged him with the penalty.
20. Ralph Bunche was a man (who, whom) many people respected.

WRITING APPLICATION A:
Using *Who* and *Whom* Correctly in Subordinate Clauses

When you are writing about characters in fiction, you are usually using formal English. In formal English, the distinction is still made between *who* and *whom*. These pronouns often introduce subordinate clauses in complex sentences that discuss literary characters.

EXAMPLE   The character *whom* the people hate in *An Enemy of the People* is Dr. Thomas Stockmann.
The son *who* closely resembles Willy Loman in *Death of a Salesman* is Happy.

Writing Assignment

Select a short story, poem, play, or novel you have read and discuss one or more of its important characters. At some point, use *who* and *whom* correctly in subordinate clauses. Underline these pronouns.

USAGE

PRONOUNS IN INCOMPLETE CONSTRUCTIONS

An "incomplete construction" occurs when something is omitted after the word *than* or *as* in a comparison. To avoid repetition, we say "The tenor sang louder than he" (than he *sang*). "The crash hurt Tim as much as her" (as *it hurt* her).

The meaning of the sentence may actually depend on the form of the pronoun.

EXAMPLE   We trust Jane more than **she.** [than she trusts Jane]
We trust Jane more than **her.** [than we trust her]

25g. After *than* and *as* introducing an incomplete construction, use the form of the pronoun you would use if the construction were completed.

EXERCISE 6. Selecting Pronouns in Incomplete Constructions. Number your paper 1–10. Write the part of each sentence beginning with *than* or *as,* using the correct pronoun and completing the sentence to show that the pronoun is correct. In several sentences either pronoun may be correct, depending on how the sentence is completed; in those cases, write the sentences both ways.

EXAMPLE   1. Nolan has worked longer than (he, him).
1. *than he has worked*

1. Have you lived in this city as long as (they, them)?
2. I don't know Brenda as well as (she, her).
3. Eva is shorter than (I, me).
4. The senior class scored higher than (they, them).
5. The trip will benefit Roger more than (I, me).
6. Is she six months older than (I, me)?
7. The results show that I do better on essay tests than (he, him).
8. Can they hit safely as often as (we, us)?
9. I understand him better than (she, her).
10. Can Ms. Edwards tutor Paula as well as (I, me)?

REVIEW EXERCISE B. Identifying and Correcting Errors in Pronoun Usage. Number your paper 1–10. Each sentence contains one error in pronoun usage. Write the incorrectly used pronoun and next to it, write the correct form.

EXAMPLE   1. Do you know who they gave the money to?
          1. *who—whom*

1. The two students whom the committee nominated were Genevieve and me.
2. Geraldine announced to Joe and me that Cleon and her would do the inventory.
3. If you can't trust Ed and her, who can you trust?
4. "We kids are better than the kids on Central's team," Phil said. "So why aren't we doing better than them?"
5. Brenda sat between Sheryl and I.
6. The two people in this class whom you can always rely on are Dave and her.
7. Oscar, whom I believe is the smartest member of our family, shares the evening newspaper with Tammy and me.
8. When Ann and I were young, us kids used to love to ride the tractor with my father.
9. When Laura told Greg and I that Ms. Cohen was going to retire, all three of us seniors felt sad.
10. When Andy and I study together, nobody in our class does better than us.

MINOR PROBLEMS IN THE USE OF PRONOUNS

25h. In standard formal English the pronouns ending in *-self, -selves* are usually used only to refer to another word in the sentence or to emphasize another word.

EXAMPLES   **I** hurt **myself.** [*Myself* refers to *I*.]
           She planned the party **herself.** [*Herself* emphasizes *she*.]
           The **boys themselves** invented the game. [*Themselves* emphasizes *boys*.]

Avoid the use of pronouns ending in *-self, -selves* in place of other personal pronouns if the pronouns do not refer to or emphasize another word in the sentence.

EXAMPLES   Joanne and **I** [not *myself*] are club members.
           Ms. Markham gave skating lessons to Al and **me** [not *myself*].
           The tickets belong to them and **us** [not *ourselves*].

USAGE

25i. An appositive is in the same case as the word with which it is in apposition.

NONSTANDARD   Two seniors, Abe and her, made the best speeches.
STANDARD   Two seniors, **Abe and she,** made the best speeches.

Abe and *she* are in apposition with *seniors,* the subject of the sentence. Since the subject of a verb is nominative, the appositive is also nominative; hence, *she* is correct.

STANDARD   For the lead roles, the director chose two people, **Abe and her**.

In apposition with *people*, which is the object of *chose, Abe* and *her* are also in the objective case; hence, *her* is correct.

25j. Use the possessive case of a noun or a pronoun before a gerund.

This use of the possessive case will appear reasonable if you understand that a gerund is a noun form.

EXAMPLES   We were flattered by the **critic's praise.**
We were flattered by the **critic's giving** such praise.

Did you object to **my comments?**
Did you object to **my making** the comments?

Sometimes a participle ending in *-ing* may be confused with a gerund. Use the objective case before a participle.

EXAMPLES   I followed **him hiking** through the woods.
I hear **them talking** outside.

The use of the possessive *his* in the first sentence would change the meaning to a far less likely idea: *I followed his hiking through the woods.* The second sentence identifies *them,* not *talking; I hear their talking outside* is an unlikely emphasis.

Whether or not you should use the possessive form before a word ending in *-ing* often depends on which word you wish to emphasize. If you wish to emphasize the action in the *-ing* word, you use the possessive. If you wish to emphasize the preceding word (the noun or pronoun), you do not use the possessive.

What did they say about Mary's jogging? [In this sentence the emphasis is on the kind of jogging Mary does.]
Can they imagine Mary jogging? [In this sentence the emphasis is on Mary, who apparently is not a jogger.]

WRITING APPLICATION B:
Using the Possessive Form Before a Gerund

In both your speech and writing you often use gerunds, which are simply verb forms used as nouns. Gerunds end in -*ing*. Participles ending in -*ing* can therefore be confused with gerunds. You must decide whether the -*ing* word is a participle or a gerund in determining whether to use the possessive form in front of it. If you wish to emphasize the **action** in the -**ing** word, use the possessive form of the noun or pronoun that precedes it.

EXAMPLES   I saw *him* taking the ACT this morning. (The word emphasized is *him*, not *taking;* therefore, the possessive form is not used before the -*ing* word.)

There is some question about *his* taking the ACT again to improve his score. (The word emphasized is *taking;* therefore, the possessive form is used before the -*ing* word.)

Writing Assignment

An important characteristic of mature people is the ability to listen carefully to advice, to weigh its merits, and then to decide whether or not to follow it. Think of some advice you have been given. How did you feel about it? Did you follow it or not? What has been the result? Write a summary of this important incident. Illustrate the use of the possessive form before a gerund. Underline the possessive.

EXAMPLE   I resented *their* urging me to watch the football game every Sunday.

EXERCISE 7. Identifying and Correcting Errors in Pronoun Usage.
Some of the following sentences contain errors in pronoun usage. Number your paper 1–10. Write + after the proper number for each correct sentence; write 0 for each incorrect sentence. After each 0, write the correct form of the pronoun.

1. The store's being closed annoyed us.
2. Both Ruth and myself take piano lessons.
3. We all looked forward to their singing.
4. The coach tried to understand him striking out.
5. My close friends, Alicia and her, joined the choir.

USAGE

6. After him promising to drive us, his car broke down.
7. Someone, either Irene or he, talked to the doctor.
8. They had not been told about us staying overnight.
9. The reporters interviewed his uncle and himself.
10. Their dancing thrilled the audience.

CHAPTER 25 REVIEW: POSTTEST

Selecting Pronouns to Complete Sentences Correctly. Number your paper 1–25. From the words in parentheses, select the pronoun that correctly completes the sentence and write it after the proper number on your paper. Base your answer on formal standard usage.

EXAMPLE   1. After a pause, I heard Tara say into the phone, "Yes, this is (she, me)."
1. *she*

1. Last summer, my friend Megan and (I, me) worked in a factory that produces microchips for computers.
2. Before we began, we made a pact that (we, us) teen-agers would show the adults that we were responsible workers.
3. For the first two weeks, everything ran smoothly because our supervisor, Mr. Karas, was a person (who, whom) we thought was firm and just.
4. In fact, we were surprised by (him, his) showing interest in our progress and going out of his way to train us.
5. When Mr. Karas went on vacation, we doubted that his assistant, Ms. Sullivan, would be as firm as (he, him).
6. Our first mistake was in thinking that Mr. Karas and (she, her) would have different sets of standards.
7. Also, we thought wrongly that (she, her) sitting in for him would decrease our work load.
8. Well, I'm sure you can guess (who, whom) the situation taught a lesson to.
9. We started giving (us, ourselves) ten extra minutes during our morning break just a week after Ms. Sullivan took over.
10. One morning Ms. Sullivan walked up to us at our job stations and said, "Megan and Rick, until now I had thought you were workers (who, whom) took pride in your work."

11. "In fact, I received a post card from Mr. Karas this morning, and he asked if (his, him) being away has affected your work in any way."

12. "Between you and (I, me)," she said, "he'll never know you failed a test this morning by taking extra time during your morning break."

13. "If you're late again," Ms. Sullivan said calmly, "we, Mr. Karas and (I, me), will be looking for two other trainees for this station after he gets back."

14. It's funny how even an assistant supervisor can make her meaning clear to people like (us, ourselves) in just a few sentences.

15. For the rest of that morning, you couldn't find two other workers concentrating as well as Megan and (I, me).

16. (Who, Whom) do you think we talked about during our lunch break? Right!

17. We, Megan and (I, me), agreed that we had made not just one but several mistakes.

18. First, (us, our) deliberately taking extra time was wrong.

19. Second, we had let Mr. Karas down because it was (he, him) who had hired us, trained us, and trusted us.

20. Third, we had stereotyped Ms. Sullivan, thinking that because she was a woman she wouldn't do her job as well as (he, him).

21. Fourth, we had let (us, ourselves) down by failing to do our best.

22. (Who, Whom) had we been kidding when we had said that we wanted to prove to the adults that teen-agers were mature and responsible?

23. In the two weeks that followed, Megan and (I, me) did our work conscientiously and punctually, keeping our goal in mind.

24. We also watched how Ms. Sullivan did her job, and we soon saw that Mr. Karas and (she, her) shared many of the same strengths we had admired in Mr. Karas.

25. Shaking hands with Mr. Karas and Ms. Sullivan at the end of the summer, (we, us) two agreed that we had earned good money, but that we had also learned important lessons for life.

USAGE

Correct Form and Use of Verbs

PRINCIPAL PARTS; TENSE, VOICE, MOOD

DIAGNOSTIC TEST

A. Using Verbs Correctly. The sentences in this exercise contain problems with verbs which will be discussed in this chapter. Number your paper 1–15. After the proper number, write the correct form of the verb in parentheses.

EXAMPLE 1. In a hurry to go to work, I couldn't remember where I had (laid, lain) my keys.
    1. *laid*

1. During the political rally, several balloons filled with helium (burst, bursted) as they rose from the ground.
2. Whenever Joan sits down to watch television, her Samoyed puppy (lies, lays) down at her feet.
3. If I (was, were) President, I would make world peace my first priority.
4. Mary Ann (swam, swum) the hundred-meter race in record time.
5. If I (had, would have) told the truth in the first place, the situation would have been much easier to handle.
6. (Cooking, Having cooked) a delicious Thanksgiving meal together, the newlyweds received many compliments from their guests.

7. When the math team came in second, the team members were upset because they (hoped, had hoped) to take first place.
8. Because we did not add the proper amount of yeast, the loaves of bread failed to (raise, rise).
9. The tree died because it (was hit, had been hit) by lightning.
10. The five riders are pleased (to qualify, to have qualified) for the equestrian team.
11. After I had (wrote, written) my autobiographical essay for my college application, I heaved a sigh of relief.
12. I wished that there (was, were) a good movie playing in town.
13. Because he had starred in four high-school productions, David hoped (to pursue, to have pursued) an acting career.
14. (Lie, Lay) your work aside and relax for a few minutes.
15. In 1984, Joaquim Cruz, whose right leg is slightly shorter than his left leg, was happy when he (won, had won) Brazil's first gold medal in the 800-meter run.

B. Recognizing Incorrect Verbs in Sentences. Each sentence below has an incorrect or awkward verb form. Rewrite each sentence correctly.

16. After running six miles, Nick said he could have drank a gallon of water.
17. The calculator was put together by Kristi with almost no assistance.
18. I was born in this town, and I lived here all my life.
19. If Mrs. Wyn has twins, she will have four children in three years.
20. The trip was taken by Mr. Jenson because of his poor health.

A verb is a word that expresses action or otherwise helps to make a statement.

KINDS OF VERBS

All verbs help to make statements about their subjects. Those that do so by expressing action, either physical or mental, are called *action verbs.*

ACTION VERBS   Arthur **dashed** across the busy street.
               She **wondered** about their strange behavior.

Some verbs help to make statements by linking the subject with a word in the predicate. Such verbs are called *linking verbs*.

LINKING VERBS   Their future **looked** bright. [*Bright,* an adjective, modifies the subject *future.*]
Elsa **is** my friend. [*Friend,* a noun, identifies Elsa.]

Some verbs can be either action verbs or linking verbs:

ACTION VERB   They **felt** the snake's smooth, dry skin. [*Felt* expresses action.]
LINKING VERB   I **felt** tired today. [This time, *felt* links the subject, *I,* with a word that describes it, *tired.*]

There are many fewer linking verbs than action verbs. (You will find a list of the most common linking verbs on page 421.) The verb used most often as a linking verb is *be,* whose forms are *am, is, are, was, were,* and all verb phrases ending in *be, being,* or *been: may be, was being, has been,* etc.

In addition to functioning as a linking verb, *be* can also be followed by an adverb or adverb phrase:

Rachel was **here.**
The cottage is **in the north woods.**

Although it resembles an action verb in this use, *be* is not generally classified as one. Just remember that *be* is always a linking verb except when followed by an adverb.

THE PRINCIPAL PARTS OF A VERB

Every verb has four basic forms called principal parts: the *infinitive, present participle, past,* and *past participle.* All other forms are derived from these principal parts.

INFINITIVE	PRESENT PARTICIPLE	PAST	PAST PARTICIPLE
talk	(is) talking	talked	(have) talked

The words *is* and *have* are given with the present participle and past participle forms to remind you that these forms are used with a helping verb: *am, is, are, was, were, has been, will be, have, has, had,* etc.

Regular Verbs

A regular verb is one that forms its past and past participle by adding *-d* or *-ed* to the infinitive form.

INFINITIVE	PAST	PAST PARTICIPLE
care	care**d**	(have) care**d**
jump	jump**ed**	(have) jump**ed**

Irregular Verbs

An irregular verb is one that forms its past and past participle in some other way than by adding -*d* or -*ed*.

This "other way" may involve changing the spelling of the verb or making no change at all.

INFINITIVE	PAST	PAST PARTICIPLE
drive	drove	(have) dri**ven**
ring	rang	(have) r**ung**
set	set	(have) set

The major problem in the correct use of verbs is the choice of the correct past and past participle forms of irregular verbs. Since irregular past tenses and past participles are formed in a variety of ways, you must know the principal parts of each irregular verb.

Three principal parts of common irregular verbs are given in the following alphabetical list (infinitive, past, and past participle). Use this list for reference. For the principal parts of other irregular verbs, consult a dictionary. Drill exercises on irregular verbs frequently misused are given following the list.

Principal Parts of Irregular Verbs

INFINITIVE	PAST	PAST PARTICIPLE
bear	bore	(have) borne
beat	beat	(have) beaten *or* beat
begin	began	(have) begun
bite	bit	(have) bitten
blow	blew	(have) blown
break	broke	(have) broken
bring	brought	(have) brought
burst	burst	(have) burst
catch	caught	(have) caught
choose	chose	(have) chosen
come	came	(have) come
creep	crept	(have) crept
dive	dived[1]	(have) dived

[1] Informal, *dove.*

INFINITIVE	PAST	PAST PARTICIPLE
do	did	(have) done
draw	drew	(have) drawn
drink	drank	(have) drunk
drive	drove	(have) driven
eat	ate	(have) eaten
fall	fell	(have) fallen
fling	flung	(have) flung
fly	flew	(have) flown
freeze	froze	(have) frozen
get	got	(have) got *or* gotten
give	gave	(have) given
go	went	(have) gone
grow	grew	(have) grown
know	knew	(have) known
lay	laid	(have) laid
lead	led	(have) led
lend	lent	(have) lent
lie	lay	(have) lain
lose	lost	(have) lost
ride	rode	(have) ridden
ring	rang	(have) rung
rise	rose	(have) risen
run	ran	(have) run
say	said	(have) said
see	saw	(have) seen
set	set	(have) set
shake	shook	(have) shaken
shine	shone *or* shined	(have) shone *or* shined
sing	sang *or* sung	(have) sung
sink	sank *or* sunk	(have) sunk
sit	sat	(have) sat
speak	spoke	(have) spoken
steal	stole	(have) stolen
sting	stung	(have) stung
swear	swore	(have) sworn
swim	swam	(have) swum
swing	swung	(have) swung
take	took	(have) taken
tear	tore	(have) torn
throw	threw	(have) thrown
wear	wore	(have) worn
write	wrote	(have) written

26a. Learn the principal parts of common irregular verbs.

To help you learn the correct use of irregular verbs, those which are commonly misused are presented on the following pages in four groups. Memorize the principal parts of the verbs in each group. In doing the exercises, remember that the past participle is used with helping, or auxiliary, verbs: *is, are, was, were, have, has, had, have been,* etc. As you say the principal parts, place *have* before the past participle: *begin, began, have begun.*

Group I

INFINITIVE	PAST	PAST PARTICIPLE
beat	beat	(have) beaten *or* beat
begin	began	(have) begun
blow	blew	(have) blown
break	broke	(have) broken
burst	burst	(have) burst
choose	chose	(have) chosen
come	came	(have) come
do	did	(have) done

EXERCISE 1. Using the Past and the Past Participle Forms Correctly. Number your paper 1–10. After the proper number, write either the past or the past participle of the verb given, whichever will correctly complete the sentence.

EXAMPLE   1. *do*   I —— nothing yesterday.
            1. *did*

1. *begin*   They had —— to argue.
2. *choose* Have the players —— a captain for the basketball team yet?
3. *beat*   You —— me at tennis last Friday.
4. *do*   Has Erica —— her chores yet?
5. *break*   Milt has —— the school track record.
6. *burst*   During the freeze last March, the water pipes at school —— .
7. *blow*   John's shed had been —— over in the storm.
8. *do*   The dancers —— their warm-up exercises.
9. *begin*   I was so scared that I —— to tremble.
10. *come*   Jennifer has —— to spend the weekend.

USAGE

Group II

INFINITIVE	PAST	PAST PARTICIPLE
draw	drew	(have) drawn
drink	drank	(have) drunk
drive	drove	(have) driven
fall	fell	(have) fallen
fly	flew	(have) flown
freeze	froze	(have) frozen
give	gave	(have) given
go	went	(have) gone

EXERCISE 2. Using the Past and Past Participle Forms Correctly.
Number your paper 1–10. Complete each sentence by writing either the past or the past participle of the given verb.

1. *drink*   We have —— spring water for years.
2. *fall*   My ring has —— into the dishwater.
3. *freeze*   They have —— a peck of beans for next winter.
4. *fly*   Have you —— in a helicopter?
5. *drive*   Ellie has never —— a jeep.
6. *draw*   Toni —— pictures on the wall when she was two.
7. *go*   Becky has —— to the rodeo with friends.
8. *drink*   I worked hard, but he —— more water than I did.
9. *go*   He —— out the door before I could stop him.
10. *give*   We should have —— Donna a surprise party.

EXERCISE 3. Using the Past and Past Participle Forms Correctly.
This exercise covers the verbs in Groups I and II. Write a + for each sentence in which the italicized verb is correct; if the verb is incorrect, write the correct form of the verb.

EXAMPLE   1. They *have* often *drove* to the mountains.
　　　　　　1. *have driven*

1. I *gave* her my last dime.
2. They *should have went* to Hawaii for vacation.
3. The guests *have drank* all the punch.
4. It was so cold in the basement, the water *had froze*.
5. Henry *done* his best yesterday.
6. Some of the sketches *were drew* with pen and ink.

7. She wondered if she *had chose* the right one.
8. Why *have* you *came* home so early?
9. During the cold weather the water pipe *had bursted*.
10. Mr. Donahue *flew* to Africa last summer.
11. One of the children *could have fell* down the rickety stairs.
12. The thunder crashed and the lights *begun* to flicker.
13. Our team *has* not *beat* them in three years.
14. I'll never know why he *done* it.
15. The crystal vase *has broke* in a million pieces.
16. They never *would have begun* if you hadn't helped them.
17. The wind *blowed* gently through the pines.
18. At last we *have chosen* a mascot for our club.
19. We *gone* beyond the exit ramp on the highway.
20. The farmer *has drived* that old tractor nearly every day for twenty years.

Group III

INFINITIVE	PAST	PAST PARTICIPLE
grow	grew	(have) grown
know	knew	(have) known
ride	rode	(have) ridden
ring	rang	(have) rung
run	ran	(have) run
see	saw	(have) seen
sing	sang *or* sung	(have) sung
speak	spoke	(have) spoken

EXERCISE 4. Using the Past and Past Participle Forms Correctly.
Number your paper 1–10. Complete each sentence by writing either the past or the past participle of the verb given.

1. *run*   The shortstop —— toward third base.
2. *sing*   Have you ever —— a round before?
3. *speak*   We had —— to the plumber about the leak.
4. *know*   No one could have —— the outcome.
5. *grow*   Our baby hamster has —— rapidly.
6. *see*   We —— the parade on television.
7. *ride*   A few of us had —— on the roller coaster.
8. *ring*   Has the bell —— yet?

USAGE

9. *see* I —— a flash of lightning just now.

10. *ring* If my alarm clock hadn't —— , I would still be sleeping.

Group IV

INFINITIVE	PAST	PAST PARTICIPLE
spring	sprang *or* sprung	(have) sprung
steal	stole	(have) stolen
swim	swam	(have) swum
swing	swung	(have) swung
take	took	(have) taken
tear	tore	(have) torn
throw	threw	(have) thrown
write	wrote	(have) written

EXERCISE 5. Using the Past and Past Participle Forms Correctly.

Number your paper 1–10. Complete each sentence by writing either the past or the past participle of the verb given.

1. *spring* The rabbit had —— out of the bushes.
2. *tear* Why have they —— up the newspapers?
3. *write* Has Penny —— the editorial for the next issue?
4. *throw* Connie finally —— away her old tennis shoes.
5. *swim* She should not have —— so soon after lunch.
6. *take* I wish I had —— your advice.
7. *swing* The trapeze artists —— high above the crowd.
8. *steal* Why would anyone have —— your notebook?
9. *swim* The children were like fish; they —— for hours.
10. *throw* Make a wish after you have —— a coin into the well.

EXERCISE 6. Using the Past and Past Participle Forms Correctly.

This exercise covers the verbs in Groups III and IV. Write a + for each sentence in which the italicized verb is correct; if the verb is incorrect, write the correct form of the verb.

EXAMPLE 1. The bells *rung* loudly two hours ago.
          1. *rang*

1. I *have ran* too far to turn back now.
2. *Had* the children *rang* the bell as a prank?
3. Little Tommy *has growed* two inches taller than I.

4. Ms. Owens *seen* the hit-and-run accident.
5. He *has tore* his shirt on that rusty nail.
6. *Had* she *knew* they were here, she would have stayed home.
7. You *should* not *have took* the biggest slice for yourself.
8. Jory Ann *swung* the lariat and roped the calf.
9. Are you sure he *swum* fifty lengths of the pool?
10. They're sorry they *had* not *spoke* up sooner.
11. He *has* always *rode* the bus to school.
12. I'm afraid the pool *has sprang* a leak.
13. How many times *has* Bobby *stole* second base?
14. The startled burglar *sprang* out of the window.
15. *Has* Gladys ever *sang* a cappella?
16. I *seen* that movie twelve times.
17. Sam *would have wrote,* but he misplaced his address book.
18. The children's choir *sung* as well as could be expected.
19. Who *throwed* out my old comic books?
20. We *were torn* between the two candidates.

EXERCISE 7. Using the Past and Past Participle Forms Correctly.
This exercise covers the verbs in Groups I – IV. Number your paper
1–50. Complete each sentence by writing either the past or the past
participle of the verb at the beginning of the sentence.

1. *burst* The firefighters —— open the door.
2. *freeze* Waiting for the bus, we almost —— .
3. *break* Have the movers —— anything?
4. *fly* They could have —— to Dallas in two hours.
5. *blow* A sudden gust of wind —— out all the candles.
6. *fall* She could not have —— more than two meters.
7. *begin* The networks —— the new season last Monday.
8. *know* We have —— them since grade school.
9. *beat* They —— us fair and square.
10. *ring* I opened the door, but no one had —— the bell.
11. *drive* We were —— by our sense of justice.
12. *ride* Carlton has finally —— in a trolley car.
13. *drink* During the recent flood, we —— bottled water.
14. *run* They —— five miles yesterday evening.
15. *do* Edith and I —— much better than we had hoped.

16. *swim*   Holly has —— the 100-meter butterfly race.
17. *come*   Shortly after you called, Rudy —— home.
18. *steal*   She discovered that the microfilm had been —— .
19. *choose* We should have —— seats closer to the stage.
20. *sing*   I have —— professionally since I was ten.
21. *grow*   The number of entrants in the annual speech tournament has —— tremendously.
22. *speak*   We have —— to the judges on your behalf.
23. *go*   I arrived early, but Gloria had already —— .
24. *see*   Do you think he —— us buying his gift?
25. *give*   What in the world —— them such a crazy idea?
26. *take*   Brenda could have —— a longer vacation.
27. *tear*   I have —— the coupons out of the magazine.
28. *throw*   Greg was furious when Billy —— the golf clubs into the swimming pool.
29. *tear*   The photograph had been —— in half.
30. *write*   Thomas Hardy —— many novels and poems.
31. *throw*   The pitcher has —— six curve balls to me.
32. *go*   I —— to my friend's recital last Sunday.
33. *see*   Haven't you —— the abstract art exhibit?
34. *freeze* Water had —— on the inside of the window.
35. *run*   Time has —— out on the deadline.
36. *come*   When I was sick, Maria —— to the hospital to visit me every day.
37. *write*   How many postcards have you —— ?
38. *drink*   Someone —— the last glass of orange juice.
39. *know*   Iris was never —— for her singing.
40. *break*   The children —— their promise to behave.
41. *begin*   As soon as the play started, Lynne —— to cough.
42. *swim*   It was so hot, the adults —— in the "kiddy" pool.
43. *fall*   We were told that Don had —— off the ladder.
44. *beat*   The blacksmith —— the hot metal into shape.
45. *see*   We —— him perform in the band concert.
46. *throw*   The club has —— its support behind the mayor.
47. *run*   Sue Ann has —— into this problem often.
48. *speak*   They —— to Carolyn about the scholarship.
49. *come*   We have —— to apologize for our rudeness.
50. *write*   You or Beth should have —— the new bylaws.

THREE TROUBLESOME PAIRS OF VERBS

Three pairs of verbs require special study because they are difficult to use correctly. These special verbs are *lie* and *lay, sit* and *set, rise* and *raise*.

Lie and Lay

The verb *lie* means "to assume a lying position" or "to be in a lying position." Its principal parts are *lie, (is) lying, lay, (have) lain*.

The verb *lay* means "to put" or "to place something." Its principal parts are *lay, (is) laying, laid, (have) laid*.

The verb *lie* is intransitive (see page 420); that is, it never has an object. You never "lie" anything down.

The verb *lay* is transitive; that is, it may have an object or be in the passive voice. (See page 420.)

INTRANSITIVE	The pattern **lies** on top of the fabric. [no object]
TRANSITIVE	You **lay** the fabric on a flat surface. [object: *fabric*]
TRANSITIVE	The fabric **is laid** on a hard, flat table. [passive voice]

Memorize the principal parts of these verbs:

INFINITIVE	PRESENT PARTICIPLE	PAST	PAST PARTICIPLE
lie (to recline)	(is) lying	lay	(have) lain
lay (to put)	(is) laying	laid	(have) laid

Take time to think through each form carefully to establish the habit of using the verbs correctly. When faced with a *lie-lay* problem, ask yourself two questions:

1. What is the meaning I intend? Is it "to be in a lying position," or is it "to put something down"?

2. What is the time expressed by the verb and which principal part is required to express this time?

PROBLEM	Ginny (lay, laid) her new dress on the bed.
Question 1	Meaning? The meaning here is "to put." The verb which means "to put" is *lay*.
Question 2	Principal part? The time is past and therefore requires the past form, which is *laid*. [lay, *laid*, laid]
SOLUTION	Ginny **laid** her new dress on the bed.

USAGE

PROBLEM	The cat is (lying, laying) on my good coat.
Question 1	Meaning? The meaning here is "to be in a lying position." The verb which means "to be in a lying position" is *lie*.
Question 2	Principal part? The time here requires the present participle, which is *lying*.
SOLUTION	The cat is **lying** on my good coat.

It will pay you to use this two-question formula each time you are in doubt about a problem in the use of *lie* and *lay*. Of course, you must memorize the principal parts of the verbs before you can use the formula.

Two facts about the use of *lie* and *lay* may be of additional help.

1. Most errors in the use of these verbs are made when the speaker means "to assume or to be in a lying position." When this is the meaning you intend, be especially cautious.

2. When you wish to express the idea of "putting or placing something" in the past tense, always use *laid*.

EXERCISE 8. Using *Lie* and *Lay* Correctly. Number your paper 1–10. After the proper number, write the correct one of the two words in parentheses. Use the two-question formula.

1. If you are sick, you should be (lying, laying) down.
2. They (lay, laid) the heavy crate on the handcart.
3. She had (lain, laid) a great deal of emphasis on usage.
4. Amy (lay, laid) down for a while.
5. I left my gloves (lying, laying) on the counter.
6. She had just (lain, laid) down when the doorbell rang.
7. They (lay, laid) their plans before the committee.
8. The calf (lay, laid) on a pile of straw.
9. She (lay, laid) her pen down and closed her notebook.
10. Don't leave your shoes (lying, laying) under the table.

EXERCISE 9. Using *Lie* and *Lay* Correctly. Choose the correct form of *lie* or *lay* to fill the blank in each sentence. Use the two-question formula.

EXAMPLE 1. I have ——— the ribbons on the counter.
  1. *laid*

1. The letters are ——— on the table for you to read.
2. Why don't you ——— down for a few minutes?
3. Be careful when you are ——— the new carpeting.

4. The mysterious package —— on the park bench.
5. Tomorrow we will —— new tiles in the hallway.
6. After an exhausting day, Carla —— on the sofa.
7. Danny —— the vase down and repaired the crack.
8. She —— on the track while the trainer taped her ankle.
9. The driftwood had —— on the beach for years.
10. Nina had not —— the keys by the telephone.

Sit and Set

Sit usually means "to assume or to be in an upright, sitting position."[1]
The principal parts of *sit* are *sit, (is) sitting, sat, (have) sat. Sit* is almost
always an intransitive verb; it rarely takes an object.

Set usually means "to put, to place something." The principal parts
of *set* are *set, (is) setting, set, (have) set.* Like *lay, set* is a transitive verb;
it may take an object.

Since all forms of *set* are made without changing the vowel, the
problem of using these two verbs is rather simple. When you mean "to
put something down," use *set* or *setting.* For all other meanings, use *sit*
or *sat* or *sitting.*[2]

INFINITIVE	PRESENT PARTICIPLE	PAST	PAST PARTICIPLE
sit (to rest)	(is) sitting	sat	(have) sat
set (to put)	(is) setting	set	(have) set

EXERCISE 10. Using *Sit* and *Set* Correctly. Number your paper
1–10. Write the correct verb in parentheses in each sentence.

EXAMPLE   1. Don't (sit, set) on the wet paint!
          1. *sit*

1. After he had struck out, Pete (sat, set) on the bench.
2. My little sister (sits, sets) quietly when we have company.
3. Where were the packages (sitting, setting) this morning?
4. We had (sat, set) our weary bones in the plush chairs.
5. I never (sit, set) in the balcony at the Bijou.
6. They were (sitting, setting) placemats on the table.
7. It makes no difference to me where you (sit, set).
8. We (sat, set) up folding chairs for the guests.
9. Mr. Han told me to (sit, set) the equipment on his desk.

---

[1] Such expressions as "Sit the baby in the high chair" or "Sit him up" really mean "to put"
or "to place," and these expressions, which are acceptable, are exceptions to the rule.
[2] The expressions "The sun sets," "the setting hen," and "Wait for the cement to set" are
exceptions to the rule.

USAGE

10. I may never know who had (sat, set) on my glasses.

Rise and Raise

The verb *rise* means "to go up." Its principal parts are *rise, (is) rising, rose, (have) risen.* In other words, when the subject of the verb is itself moving upward, use *rise. Rise* is intransitive; it never takes an object.

The verb *raise* means "to force something to move upward." Its principal parts are *raise, (is) raising, raised, (have) raised.* When the subject of the verb is acting on something, forcing it upward, use *raise. Raise* is transitive; it usually takes an object.

INFINITIVE	PRESENT PARTICIPLE	PAST	PAST PARTICIPLE
rise (to go up)	(is) rising	rose	(have) risen
raise (to force up)	(is) raising	raised	(have) raised

EXERCISE 11. Using *Rise* and *Raise* Correctly. Number your paper 1–10. Write the correct verb in parentheses in each sentence.

1. Air bubbles have been (rising, raising) to the surface.
2. Increasing the import duty will (rise, raise) retail prices.
3. The speaker (rose, raised) from her chair and took the mike.
4. This month, the star has been (rising, raising) in the east.
5. The rooster (rises, raises) early.
6. During the Revolutionary War, many American colonists decided to (rise, raise) up against King George III.
7. Balloons can (rise, raise) because they contain heated air, which is less dense than the surrounding air.
8. The Wilsons (rose, raised) six adopted children.
9. Mist was (rising, raising) from the ground.
10. The dough has been (rising, raising) for the past hour.

EXERCISE 12. Using *Lie-Lay, Sit-Set,* and *Rise-Raise* Correctly. For each of the following verbs, write a brief sentence in which the verb is correctly used.

1. lie	3. laying	5. lay (past)	7. rose	9. risen
2. raising	4. raised	6. has laid	8. setting	10. sat

EXERCISE 13. Using *Lie-Lay, Sit-Set,* and *Rise-Raise* Correctly. Number your paper 1–20. Write the correct word in parentheses in each sentence.

USAGE

EXAMPLE   1. Please (sit, set) wherever you like.
    1. *sit*

1. All week that box has (lain, laid) unopened on the desk.
2. We (rose, raised) our hats to salute the astronauts.
3. The injured deer (lay, laid) motionless in the road.
4. Our applications were (lying, laying) in front of the file.
5. Would you please (sit, set) with us?
6. I always (lie, lay) the phone book on this table.
7. We arrived late and had to (sit, set) at the top of the bleachers.
8. Kathy hummed as she (lay, laid) the baby in the crib.
9. Clean up the mess that's (lying, laying) on your floor.
10. Last night's victory really (rose, raised) the team's spirit and confidence.
11. If you (sit, set) the pie on the ledge, it may vanish.
12. Fred should (lie, lay) on his side to stop snoring.
13. After the fire, the museum (lay, laid) in a heap.
14. Tempers (rose, raised) as the debate progressed.
15. The police are (lying, laying) in wait for the crooks.
16. Never (sit, set) anything on the seat next to you.
17. Our St. Bernard often (lies, lays) in my lap.
18. Billows of dust (rose, raised) up from the field.
19. Haven't they (sat, set) down the piano yet?
20. You must (lie, lay) on a padded surface to do exercises.

REVIEW EXERCISE A. Using Verb Forms Correctly.   Number your paper 1–10. In each sentence, identify any verb used incorrectly. Write it on your paper, and next to it write the form of the verb needed to correct the sentence.

EXAMPLE   1. The helicopter raised from the airstrip and headed north.
    1. *raised—rose*

1. As I watched the horror movie, I could feel fear rising in my throat; I knew I had chose the wrong way to relax.
2. Aretha had taken her younger sister to the circus; things went well until the little girl's balloon bursted.
3. When we woke, we saw that the pond was froze.
4. When their parents had went shopping, the twins decided to play some computer games.

USAGE

5. The defendant, who had been found guilty, was brung before the judge for sentencing.
6. After we had donated blood, we laid down for a few minutes and were then given coffee and doughnuts.
7. Before we knew what was happening, Marvin had dove through the ice to rescue the child who had fallen into the lake.
8. If you hadn't been so careless, you wouldn't have broke that vase.
9. While Jessica was in surgery, her concerned parents set in the waiting room and kept their hopes high.
10. Jorge walked up to the door and rung the bell, waiting nervously for the girl he had driven two hours to see.

TENSE

Verbs change in form to show the time of their action or of the idea they express. The time expressed by a verb (present, past, future) is its tense. There are six tenses. As the following conjugations of the verbs *go* and *be* will show you, the six tenses are formed from the principal parts of the verb. Study these conjugations and use them for reference in your work on tense.

26b. Learn the names of the six tenses and how the tenses are formed.

Conjugation of the Verb Go

Present infinitive: *to go*   Perfect infinitive: *to have gone*

Principal Parts

INFINITIVE	PRESENT PARTICIPLE	PAST	PAST PARTICIPLE
go	going	went	gone

Present Tense

Singular	Plural
I go	we go
you go	you go
he, she, it goes	they go

Present progressive: *I am going,* etc.

Past Tense

Singular	Plural
I went	we went
you went	you went
he, she, it went	they went

Past progressive: *I was going,* etc.

Future Tense

(*will* or *shall* + the infinitive[1])

Singular	Plural
I will (shall) go	we will (shall) go
you will go	you will go
he, she, it will go	they will go

Future progressive: *I will* (*shall*) *be going,* etc.

Present Perfect Tense

(*have* or *has* + the past participle)

Singular	Plural
I have gone	we have gone
you have gone	you have gone
he, she, it has gone	they have gone

Present perfect progressive: *I have been going,* etc.

Past Perfect Tense

(*had* + the past participle)

Singular	Plural
I had gone	we had gone
you had gone	you had gone
he, she, it had gone	they had gone

Past perfect progressive: *I had been going,* etc.

Future Perfect Tense

(*will have* or *shall have* + the past participle)

Singular	Plural
I will (shall) have gone	we will (shall) have gone
you will have gone	you will have gone
he, she, it will have gone	they will have gone

Future perfect progressive: *I will have* (*shall have*) *been going,* etc.

[1] For a discussion of the use of *shall* and *will,* see page 613.

USAGE

Conjugation of the Verb **Be**

Present infinitive: *to be*   Perfect infinitive: *to have been*

Principal Parts

INFINITIVE	PRESENT PARTICIPLE	PAST	PAST PARTICIPLE
be	being	was, were	been

Present Tense

Singular	*Plural*
I am	we are
you are	you are
he, she, it is	they are

Present progressive: *I am being*, etc.

Past Tense

Singular	*Plural*
I was	we were
you were	you were
he, she, it was	they were

Past progressive: *I was being*, etc.

Future Tense

(*will* or *shall* + the infinitive)

Singular	*Plural*
I will (shall) be	we will (shall) be
you will be	you will be
he, she, it will be	they will be

Present Perfect Tense

(*have* or *has* + the past participle)

Singular	*Plural*
I have been	we have been
you have been	you have been
he, she, it has been	they have been

Past Perfect Tense

(*had* + the past participle)

Singular	*Plural*
I had been	we had been
you had been	you had been
he, she, it had been	they had been

Future Perfect Tense

(*will have* or *shall have* + the past participle)

Singular	*Plural*
I will (shall) have been	we will (shall) have been
you will have been	you will have been
he, she, it will have been	they will have been

26c. Learn the uses of each of the six tenses.

Each of the six tenses has its own particular uses, some of which require explanation. Study the following explanations, and use them for reference when you are confronted by a problem in your own writing.

(1) The *present tense* is used to express action (or to help make a statement about something) occurring now, at the present time.

EXAMPLES   We **wait** patiently.
We **are waiting** patiently. [progressive form]
We **do wait** patiently. [The verb with *do* or *did* is called the emphatic form.]

☞ NOTE   In all tenses, as in the second example, continuing action may be shown by the use of the progressive form, which ends in *-ing*. The third example illustrates the emphatic form, consisting of a form of *do* plus the first principal part of a verb. The normal way of making a sentence emphatic is to pronounce the helping verb with stress. When there is no helping verb, *do* or *did* is added to carry this stress. These emphatic forms can be used in the present and past tenses only.

The present tense is also used to indicate habitual action.

EXAMPLE   We **wait** for the bus every morning.

The present tense is often used to express a general truth, something which is true at all times.

EXAMPLES   Amy agreed with her mother that honesty **is** [instead of *was*] the best policy.

I have read that Alaska **is** [instead of *was*] the only state without an official nickname.

The present tense is used occasionally to achieve vividness in writing about past events. This use of the present tense is known as the *historical present.*

EXAMPLE   Queen Elizabeth I **strengthens** England's power and **leads** the country through its greatest era.

(2) The *past tense* is used to express action (or to help make a statement about something) that occurred in the past but did not continue into the present. The past tense is formed regularly by adding *-d* or *-ed* to the verb.

EXAMPLES   We **waited** for you yesterday.

We **were waiting** for you yesterday.

We **did wait** for you yesterday.

The past tense may also be shown by *used to:*

EXAMPLE   We **used to wait** for the bus.

(3) The *future tense* is used to express action (or to help make a statement about something) occurring at some time in the future. The future tense is formed with *will* or *shall*.

EXAMPLES   We **will wait** for you tonight.

We **will be waiting** for you tonight.

The future may also be indicated in other ways:

EXAMPLES   We **are going to wait** outside.

We **are about to wait** outside.

We **wait** outside **later.** [present with another word indicating future time]

(4) The *present perfect tense* is used to express action (or to help make a statement about something) occurring at no definite time in the past. It is formed with *have* or *has*.

EXAMPLE   Ted **has waited** for us often.

We **have waited** for them before.

The present perfect tense is also used to express action (or to help make a statement about something) occurring in the past and continuing into the present.

EXAMPLES We **have waited** for an hour. [We are still waiting.]
           We **have been waiting** for an hour. [We are still waiting.]

(5) The *past perfect tense* **is used to express action (or to help make a statement about something) completed in the past before some other past action or event. It is formed with** *had.*

EXAMPLES After we **had waited** for an hour, we **left.** [The waiting preceded the leaving.]
           After we **had been waiting** for an hour, we **left.**

(6) The *future perfect tense* **is used to express action (or to help make a statement about something) which will be completed in the future before some other future action or event. It is formed with** *will have* **or** *shall have.*

EXAMPLES By the time the bus **arrives,** we **will have waited** for an hour. [The waiting precedes the arriving of the bus.]
           By the time the bus **arrives,** we **will have been waiting** for an hour.

EXERCISE 14. Understanding the Uses of the Six Tenses. Explain the difference in meaning between the sentences in the following pairs. The sentences are correct. Then name the tense used in each sentence.

EXAMPLE 1. I met you at 3:00.
            I will have met you at 3:00.
        1. *In the first sentence, the action occurred once and ended. In the second sentence, the action will be completed in the future before another action will be completed.*
          past, future perfect

1. Marga lived in Brazil for eight years.
   Marga has lived in Brazil for eight years.
2. Why had she gone to the theater?
   Why has she been going to the theater?
3. Have the directions been explained clearly?
   Had the directions been explained clearly?
4. Was she driving?
   Had she been driving?
5. As of June 30, they will have raised taxes twice this year.
   As of June 30, they will be raising taxes twice this year.

USAGE

EXERCISE 15. Understanding the Uses of the Six Tenses. In each of the following items you are given the meaning of a sentence. Two sentences then follow. Only one of these sentences matches the given meaning. Number your paper 1–10. Next to the appropriate number, write the *letter* of the sentence that matches the *meaning*. Be prepared to name the tenses used in each sentence.

EXAMPLE 1. *Meaning:* It is not snowing now.
     a. It had been snowing all afternoon.
     b. It has been snowing all afternoon.
   1. a

1. *Meaning:* John still works for Mr. Porzio.
   a. John has worked for Mr. Porzio for a year.
   b. John had worked for Mr. Porzio for a year.
2. *Meaning:* Ann Rosine could be on her way to Worcester right now or could be going later.
   a. Ann Rosine is moving to Worcester, Massachusetts.
   b. Ann Rosine will be moving to Worcester, Massachusetts.
3. *Meaning:* Jaime is still in school.
   a. Jaime has been studying pharmacy since last summer.
   b. Jaime studied pharmacy last summer.
4. *Meaning:* Elena was born on Mary and David's wedding day.
   a. Barbara and Steven had had their first child, Elena, when Mary and David got married.
   b. Barbara and Steven had their first child, Elena, when Mary and David got married.
5. *Meaning:* Sabina will have finished working two jobs by the time she graduates.
   a. When she graduates from college, Sabina will have worked on a farm and in a department store.
   b. When she graduates from college, Sabina will have been working on a farm and in a department store.
6. *Meaning:* Lionel is not in law school yet.
   a. Lionel is going to attend Columbia University Law School in September.
   b. Lionel is attending Columbia University Law School.
7. *Meaning:* Alison takes a bus to work on a regular basis.
   a. Alison takes the bus to work.
   b. Alison is taking the bus to work.

8. *Meaning:* I don't know whether my work has paid off.
   a. After I had passed the test, I knew my work had paid off.
   b. After I pass the test, I know my work will have paid off.
9. *Meaning:* Rayae was a bank officer at the age of twenty-four.
   a. When Rayae turned twenty-five, she had been promoted to the position of bank officer.
   b. When Rayae turned twenty-five, she was promoted to the position of bank officer.
10. *Meaning:* The children will not miss the anniversary celebration.
    a. I'm sure Eva and Claude will celebrate their anniversary when their children come home from college.
    b. I'm sure that Eva and Claude will have celebrated their anniversary when their children come home from college.

WRITING APPLICATION A:
Making Writing Clear Through the Use of Correct Tenses

Time is extremely important in your daily life. When you write, the time your verbs express is equally important. The tense of a verb signals the time for your reader. The incorrect tense can cause considerable confusion.

Writing Assignment

As you near the end of high school, you are probably considering several different options for the future. You may be thinking about a vocational school, college, a job, or the military service. Jot down the steps you plan to take after graduation to reach a long-range goal. Use these notes to write a summary of your plans. Check your paper for correct use of tense.

USAGE

SPECIAL PROBLEMS OF TENSE USAGE

The Past Perfect Tense

The past perfect tense requires special consideration because inexperienced writers frequently fail to use it in expressing two actions that happened at different times in the past. The function of the past perfect tense is to make clear which of the actions came first.

26d. Use the past perfect tense for the earlier of two past actions.

NONSTANDARD Sue mentioned (past) that she invited (past) the neighbors to her party. [The two actions did not happen at the same time. Since the inviting preceded the mentioning, the past perfect form of *invite* should be used.]

STANDARD Sue **mentioned** (past) that she **had invited** (past perfect) the neighbors to her party.

NONSTANDARD There was (past) a parking lot where the brick house was (past). [Since the two verbs in this sentence are in the same tense, the sentence suggests that the lot and the house were there together.]

STANDARD There **was** (past) a parking lot where the brick house **had been** (past perfect). [The past perfect *had been* makes it clear that the house was there before the lot.]

STANDARD There **had been** (past perfect) a parking lot where the brick house **was** (past). [Making the other verb past perfect reverses the time order; the lot preceded the house.]

26e. Avoid the use of *would have* in "if clauses" expressing the earlier of two past actions. Use the past perfect.

NONSTANDARD If he would have taken more time, he would have won.
STANDARD If he **had taken** more time, he would have won.
NONSTANDARD If we would have stopped by, we would have met your cousin.
STANDARD If we **had stopped** by, we would have met your cousin.

EXERCISE 16. Using Tenses Correctly. Correct the following sentences, which all contain errors in the use of tenses. Refer, if necessary, to the tense rules on pages 567–72.

EXAMPLE 1. If I knew the last answer, I would have had a perfect test.
　　　　　　1. *had known*

1. Pam finally appreciated the old saying that every cloud had a silver lining.
2. By the time we graduate in June, Ms. O'Connell will be teaching Latin for twenty-four years.
3. Although Denny's skill was demonstrated during the season, he was not selected to play in the City All-Star game.
4. If they would have called sooner, I would have given them a ride.

5. When I finally got to the dentist, my tooth already stopped hurting.
6. The company hired Ms. Littmann because she lived for many years in Japan.
7. When I presented my speech before the committee, the members previously studied several reports on nuclear waste disposal.
8. Mr. Frey already complained to the neighbors many times before he called the police.
9. By then I will receive my first paycheck.
10. If she forgot the directions, we could have been lost.
11. The judges declared that we made the most interesting exhibit at the science fair.
12. If they had enough money, they could have taken a taxi.
13. As I thought about our argument, I was sure you lost your temper first.
14. By tomorrow we will be living in Los Angeles five years.
15. When we reviewed the videotapes of the game, we saw that the other team committed the foul.
16. The clerk remembered that the manager has ordered the new shipment last Tuesday.
17. How could I have forgotten that Great Britain included England, Wales, and Scotland?
18. We estimate that when we're in our forties, we will be working more than twenty years.
19. If Gary would have read the advertisement, he could have saved a hundred dollars on that camera.
20. Walt would have done much better on the exam if he was present at our study sessions.

Having with the Past Participle

26f. In participial phrases, use *having* with the past participle to express action completed before another action.

NONSTANDARD   Being absent for the midterm exam, I was given a makeup test. [The present participle *being* is incorrectly used to express an action which has obviously been completed *before* the second action in the sentence.]

STANDARD   **Having been** absent for the midterm exam, **I was given** a makeup test.]

NONSTANDARD Choosing a college, Rosa sent her application. [The college had to be chosen *before* she could send an application.]

STANDARD **Having chosen** a college, Rosa **sent** her application. [This idea may also be properly expressed by using the word *after* before the present participle: *After* choosing a college, Rosa sent her application.]

The Present and the Perfect Infinitives

26g. Use the present infinitive (*to go, to see,* etc.) to express action following another action.

NONSTANDARD The dancers were upset because they had planned to have performed for us. [What had the dancers planned, *to have performed* or *to perform?* The present infinitive *to perform* should be used because the action it expresses follows the action of the verb *had planned.*]

STANDARD The dancers were upset because they **had planned to perform** for us.

NONSTANDARD He wanted to have invited all the seniors. [Did he want *to have invited* or *to invite?*]

STANDARD He **wanted to invite** all the seniors.

26h. Use the perfect infinitive (*to have gone, to have seen,* etc.) to express action before another action.

EXAMPLE We **are** happy **to have met** you. [The action expressed by the perfect infinitive *to have met* came before the time of the other verb, *are.*]

EXERCISE 17. Using Verbs Correctly. The sentences in this exercise contain errors in the use of verbs. Correct the sentences according to the rules you have just studied. You will not need to change more than one verb or verbal for each sentence.

1. Spending three hours on a review of chemistry, we then worked on irregular French verbs.
2. I should have liked to have met them.
3. I rewrote the book review that I already typed.
4. We gained two hours when we flew from Missouri to California because the sun rose in the east.
5. We wanted to have avoided any controversy.
6. Sometime before the bus leaves, I will finish packing.

7. They already ate dinner when I stopped by.
8. We were hoping to have had a short-answer test in history instead of an essay exam.
9. If you told me you were going shopping, I would have gone too.
10. By the time dinner was ready, I did all my math homework.

WRITING APPLICATION B:
Using Verb Tenses Consistently for Clarity

A time machine is an intriguing idea. However, do not make your writing a time machine which tosses your readers from past to present to future without reason. Use verb tenses consistently and logically. Otherwise you may lose your readers in your confused world of time.

Writing Assignment

Choose an especially memorable event that has taken place in your senior year. Recreate the event in writing. You might use narration, description, or exposition. Read your writing carefully to make sure that all verb tenses are consistent.

ACTIVE AND PASSIVE VOICE

A verb is in the *active* voice when it expresses an action performed *by* its subject. A verb is in the *passive* voice when it expresses an action performed *upon* its subject or when the subject is the result of the action.

ACTIVE VOICE   The car hit a tree. [subject acting]

PASSIVE VOICE   The tree was hit by a car. [subject acted upon]

All transitive verbs (those that take objects) can be used in the passive voice. Instead of the usual situation in which the verb expresses an action performed by the subject and affecting the object, a passive construction has the subject receiving the action. Compare the following sentences.

                          S   V   O
ACTIVE VOICE   In the novel the spy stole the secrets.

$$\overset{S}{}\qquad\overset{V}{}$$

PASSIVE VOICE   In the novel the secrets were stolen by the spy.

$$\overset{S}{}\qquad\overset{V}{}$$

In the novel the secrets were stolen.

To form the passive construction, the object of the active sentence is moved ahead of the verb and becomes the subject. A form of *be* is added to the verb, and the subject of the active sentence is either expressed in a prepositional phrase or dropped.

Notice that in the passive voice the main verb is always a past participle, and the tense is expressed by an appropriate form of *be*.

ACTIVE   The plumber **fixed** the leaky pipe.
PASSIVE   The leaky pipe **was fixed** by the plumber.

ACTIVE   The captain usually **reads** the lineup.
PASSIVE   The lineup **is** usually **read** by the captain.

The Retained Object

Active sentences that have direct objects often have indirect objects as well. When they do, either the direct or indirect object can become the subject in a passive construction:

$$\overset{S}{}\qquad\overset{V}{}\;\overset{IO}{}\;\;\overset{DO}{}$$

ACTIVE   The company sent us a letter.

$$\overset{S}{}\qquad\overset{V}{}$$

PASSIVE   We were sent a **letter** (by the company).

$$\overset{S}{}\qquad\overset{V}{}$$

PASSIVE   A letter was sent **us** (by the company).

In both of the passive sentences above, one of the objects has been made the subject and the other continues to function as a complement of the verb. In the first sentence the direct object is retained as a complement; in the second it is the indirect object that is retained. The object that continues to function as a complement in a passive construction is called a *retained object*.

Use of Passive Voice

The choice between the active or passive voice is usually a matter of taste, not of correctness. However, it is important to remember that a passive verb is usually less forceful than an active one and that a long succession of passive verbs usually produces an awkward effect.

WEAK PASSIVE   The event was completed when a triple somersault was done by Mario.

ACTIVE   Mario completed the event by doing a triple somersault.

WEAK PASSIVE   Steady rains were hoped for by all of us, but a hurricane was wanted by none of us.

ACTIVE   All of us hoped for steady rains, but none of us wanted a hurricane.

SUCCESSION OF PASSIVES   I *was asked* by Ms. Long to visit her animal shelter for unwanted pets. Rows of cages *had been placed* along both sides of a room. First a large parrot *was shown* to me. Elsewhere, a scrawny puppy *was being comforted* by an assistant. Ms. Long said that so many unwanted pets *had been brought* to her, it was difficult for all of them to *be housed* there. It *was agreed* by us that the responsibility of owning a pet *should be understood* by people before a pet *is bought*.

26i. Use the passive voice sparingly. Avoid weak and awkward passives. In the interest of variety, avoid long passages in which all the verbs are passive.

There are, however, some qualifications of this general rule which should be mentioned. The passive voice is particularly useful in two common situations.

(1) Use the passive voice to express an action in which the actor is unknown.

EXAMPLE   All the tickets **had been sold** many days ago.

(2) Use the passive voice to express an action in which it is desirable not to disclose the actor.

EXAMPLE   Poor judgment **was used** in making this decision.

In some instances the passive voice is more convenient and just as effective as the active voice. The following passive sentences are entirely acceptable.

The laser **was invented** by an American.
The space travelers **were cheered** by the crowds and **praised** by the press.
Ivy Swan, who **is known** by all for her songs, **has been emulated** by many young, hopeful singers.

Remember, however, that the active voice is generally stronger than the passive and less likely to get you into stylistic difficulties.

USAGE

EXERCISE 18. Revising Sentences in the Passive Voice. Revise the following sentences by changing the passive verbs to active verbs wherever you think the change is desirable. If you think the passive is preferable, copy the sentence unchanged.

1. After the computers had been installed by the service reps, a training session was held for us by them.
2. If the children had been enchanted by Mr. Wright's stories before, they would be even more enthralled by his new tale of a fantasy kingdom.
3. A community meeting was held by the area homeowners to discuss the landfill project, which had been proposed by the City Council.
4. The team's code of fair play was agreed to and observed by all the players.
5. While the decorations are being made by Calvin, the buffet will be prepared by Edna.
6. Potatoes had been cultivated by the Incas more than twenty centuries before they were grown by the Europeans.
7. Her ten-speed bike was ridden by her through the country.
8. The lesson on constitutional amendments, which had been assigned to us last week by the teacher, was reviewed by us before the test.
9. Shinae Chun is admired and respected by her colleagues.
10. If the practicality of home robots had been demonstrated by Mike Smith, his request for funding would not have been rejected by the committee.

THE SUBJUNCTIVE MOOD

Verbs may be in one of three moods: *indicative, imperative,* or *subjunctive.* Almost all the verbs you use are in the *indicative mood.* The *imperative mood* is used to express a request or a command.

IMPERATIVE   **Draw** a circle around the verb phrase.
                 Turn off the radio immediately.

The only common uses of the subjunctive mood in modern English are to express a condition contrary to fact and to express a wish. These uses occur mainly in formal standard English and usually apply to only two verb forms—*be* and *were.* The following partial conjugation of *be* will show how the subjunctive mood differs from the indicative.

USAGE

Present Indicative		Present Subjunctive	
Singular	*Plural*	*Singular*	*Plural*
I am	we are	(if) I be	(if) we be
you are	you are	(if) you be	(if) you be
he is	they are	(if) he be	(if) they be

The present subjunctive is used only in certain rather formal situations.

EXAMPLES   We recommended that she **be** invited to speak.
They urged that Thad **be** reinstated.
We move that Alma **be** nominated.

26j. The subjunctive *were* is usually used in contrary-to-fact statements (after *if* or *as though*) and in statements expressing a wish.

CONTRARY TO FACT   If I **were** [not *was*] you, I would be very nervous. [I am not you.]
If Rex **were** [not *was*] thinner, he'd disappear. [He is not thinner.]
Doris teased me as though she **were** [not *was*] my sister. [She is not my sister.]

WISH   I wish I **were** [not *was*] fabulously rich.
I wish Ms. Perkins **were** [not *was*] our coach.

Past Indicative		Past Subjunctive	
Singular	*Plural*	*Singular*	*Plural*
I was	we were	(if) I were	(if) we were
you were	you were	(if) you were	(if) you were
he was	they were	(if) he were	(if) they were

EXERCISE 19. Using the Subjunctive Mood Correctly.   Some of the following sentences contain errors in the use of the subjunctive mood. Others are correct. Number your paper 1–10. If the verbs in the sentence are correct, write a + after the appropriate number. If a verb is incorrect, copy it and write the correct form of the verb next to it.

EXAMPLE   1. If I was you, I would apply for the scholarship.
1. *was—were*

1. Willis insisted that every employee is invited to the company picnic.
2. I'd be a lobster fisherman if I was living on Cape Cod.

3. Gloria was confused all day because it seemed as though it was Friday, but it was only Thursday.
4. Striking out again, Katie moaned, "I wish I was a better hitter!"
5. Vernon lost many of his friends because he acted as if he were better than they.
6. If boxing was less violent, many people would respect it more.
7. "I wish this book was shorter," sighed Sabrena as she turned to page 378.
8. We often complain about working too many hours; but if we were to work fewer, we would be complaining about smaller paychecks.
9. I wish I was able to go to the concert, but I have to work.
10. "I wish it was next year already so that I would be in college," Takala said.

REVIEW EXERCISE B. Using Verbs Correctly. Some of the following sentences contain errors in the use of verbs. Others are correct. Number your paper 1–20. If the verbs in a sentence are correct, place a + after the corresponding number on your paper. If a verb is incorrect, write the correct form after the proper number.

EXAMPLE   1. I drunk more than a gallon of lemonade.
　　　　　　1. *drank*

1. If I was Joan's coach, I'd tell her to relax more.
2. For the holidays they planned to have gone fishing.
3. We swum to shore when we spotted the shark.
4. If you would have written the report yesterday, you could have gone to the concert with us.
5. When the temperature rises, Sid becomes grouchy.
6. As the climbers ascended the mountain, they noticed a shiny object laying on the ledge beneath them.
7. If they weren't too proud to ask, I'd have been glad to help them paint the house.
8. Why don't you ask if they already seen that exhibit?
9. They had forgotten that yesterday was my birthday.
10. As soon as we returned to the campsite, we discovered that someone took our food and gear.
11. If I had begun my chores this morning, I would have finished in time to go to the show.

12. When the news of the explosion come over the radio, Dr. Trimble had already rushed to the site.
13. He swept the floor and then lay the linoleum flooring.
14. If I was more confident, I could try out for the play.
15. If we would have had the engine tuned, I'm sure we would not be stranded on the highway now.
16. We have counted the money and have lain it in the safe.
17. As Ms. Hall interviewed the professor, she realized that the batteries went dead in the tape recorder.
18. In her report Clara explained that shock waves from earthquakes were recorded on seismographs.
19. They wished they were going to the music festival instead of the annual family reunion.
20. Jake, our new supervisor, worked for this company for the past 20 years.

USAGE

CHAPTER 26 REVIEW: POSTTEST

Using Verbs Correctly. Some of the following sentences contain errors in the use of verbs. Others are correct. Number your paper 1–25. If the verbs in a sentence are correct, write a + after the proper number. If a verb is incorrect or awkward, write the correct form after the proper number.

EXAMPLE   1. If she was he, she'd have spoken up.
　　　　　　1. *were*

1. The choir had not sung so well in years.
2. She thought the runners had broke the world record.
3. If we would have checked, we'd have known the store was closed.
4. They were setting on the bench and feeding the ducks.
5. She laid a fire to ward off the cold.
6. We would have preferred to have eaten Chinese food.
7. Mrs. Ames was pleased that when the driver's test was taken by her son, he passed easily.
8. The shoppers laid down their purchases carefully.
9. Cindy retraced her steps and found the café at which she left her credit card.

10. If I was Luis, I would have argued with the umpire.
11. We cheered when the movie finally begun.
12. You should never have lain your radio near the edge.
13. They would have liked to interview the astronauts.
14. I had just laid down on the beach when it started to rain.
15. The ice cubes had not froze in time for the party.
16. Yesterday I swum in the Millers' new pool.
17. Dan worked for this company for eighteen years, longer than any other current employee.
18. The rate of inflation has raised steadily.
19. When they returned to the scene, they discovered that the weapon was taken.
20. I never realized that hurricanes and typhoons were really the same thing.
21. When I enter college, my parents will be married thirty years.
22. The movie was especially liked by Kira and her brother because of the beautiful nature photography.
23. When we saw the group perform, Julia, the lead vocalist, just broke her contract with a big recording company.
24. If we had the chance, we would have stopped by your house.
25. They found the cat laying on the closet shelf.

USAGE

Correct Use of Modifiers

FORMS OF ADJECTIVES AND ADVERBS; COMPARISON

An adjective modifies a noun or a pronoun. An adverb may modify a verb, an adjective, or another adverb. These are familiar statements, but applying them to usage is sometimes difficult. Should you say "tastes strong" or "tastes strongly," "played good" or "played well"? These and other usage problems are discussed in this chapter.

DIAGNOSTIC TEST

Selecting the Correct Modifier.   Number your paper 1–20. Select the correct word in parentheses in each sentence.

EXAMPLE: 1. The hurricane hit the town very (sudden, suddenly).
  1. *suddenly*

1. Some of these plums taste (bitter, bitterly) to me.
2. I didn't do as (good, well) on the test as I thought I had.
3. Have you seen a (friendlier, more friendlier) spaniel than mine?
4. Those imitation diamonds look (real, really) valuable.
5. The weather this afternoon is (pleasanter, more pleasant) than it was this morning.
6. Jan is younger than (anyone, anyone else) in her class.
7. Having tried both brands of glue, I found that Macrogrip is (stronger, strongest).
8. When you get to the stop sign, turn (sharp, sharply) to the left.

9. This is the (baddest, worst) storm this town has ever seen.
10. The room won't look so (bad, badly) after it has been painted.
11. The close of the letter read, "With our (most sincerest, sincerest) thanks."
12. The coast road is more scenic, but Route 180 is (quicker, quickest).
13. The landscape looks (strange, strangely) in this eerie light.
14. The turbostream engine will give better gasoline mileage than (any, any other) engine ever made.
15. We build cars (sturdy, sturdily) enough to last one hundred thousand miles.
16. Rehearsals are going as (good, well) as can be expected.
17. Did you feel (sad, sadly) when you lost your watch?
18. Learning to dance (good, well) takes practice.
19. The lizard turned its head so (slow, slowly) that it looked as if it weren't moving at all.
20. Jeanne looked (casual, casually) in my direction.

ADJECTIVE AND ADVERB FORMS

Before reviewing the usage of adjectives and adverbs, you should make sure that you are able to tell which is the adjective form of a word and which is the adverb form. Most adverbs end in -ly (*clearly*, *happily*, *eagerly*), but not *all* adverbs. Moreover, a few common adjectives end in -*ly*. Some words do have the same form whether used as an adjective or as an adverb.

The following list includes some common adjectives and adverbs with identical forms. It also includes some adjectives ending in -*ly*.

ADJECTIVES	ADVERBS	ADJECTIVES ENDING IN -LY
a *short* race	She stopped *short*.	*nightly* walk
a *close* call	Stand *close* to me.	*bodily* harm
a *high* shelf	She jumped *high*.	*hourly* pay
a *right* answer	Do it *right*.	*unfriendly* man
a *first* time	She left *first*.	*lively* beat
a *hard* problem	He tried *hard*.	*seemly* choice
a *straight* path	Drive *straight*.	*early* class
a *last* chance	We play *last*.	*likely* area
a *fast* start	Walk *fast*.	*weekly* meeting

USAGE

27a. Linking verbs, especially the verbs of sense (*taste, smell, feel,* etc.), are often followed by an adjective. Action verbs are often followed by an adverb.

EXAMPLES   The cider tasted **sweet.** [The adjective *sweet* is correct after the linking verb *tasted.* It modifies the subject *cider.*]
The voices sounded **angry.** [The adjective *angry* is correct after the linking verb *sounded.* It modifies the subject *voices.*]
The man shouted **angrily.** [The adverb *angrily* is correct after the action verb *shouted.* It modifies the verb *shouted.*]

Some verbs may be used as either linking or action verbs. *Look* is one example.

EXAMPLES   Chris looked **happy.** [After the linking verb *looked,* the adjective *happy* is correct. It modifies *Chris.*]
Chris looked **happily** out the window. [After the action verb *looked,* the adverb *happily* is correct. It modifies *looked.*]

When you are not sure whether a verb is a linking verb, try substituting a form of *seem,* which is always a linking verb. If the substitution does not greatly change the meaning of the sentence, the verb is a linking verb and should be followed by an adjective.

EXAMPLES   Chris looked happy. [*Chris seemed happy* has about the same meaning; hence *looked* is a linking verb.]
Chris looked happily out the window. [*Chris seemed happily out the window* does not make sense; hence *looked* is not a linking verb in this sentence.]

27b. In making a choice between an adjective and an adverb, ask yourself what the word modifies. If it modifies a noun or pronoun, choose the adjective. If it modifies a verb, choose the adverb.

PROBLEM   They dug a hole (deep, deeply) enough to plant the tree.
SOLUTION   They dug a hole **deep** enough to plant the tree. [The adjective *deep* modifies the noun *hole.*]

PROBLEM   Has he been studying math (regular, regularly)?
SOLUTION   Has he been studying math **regularly?** [The adverb **regularly** modifies the action verb *has been studying.*]

EXERCISE 1. Selecting Adjectives and Adverbs. Number your paper 1–20. Select the correct word in parentheses in each sentence. If the word modifies the subject, select the adjective; if it modifies the verb, select the adverb. Remember that a linking verb is followed by an adjective.

1. The sled's runners slid (smooth, smoothly) over the ice.
2. The weather outside looks (miserable, miserably).
3. Plan your outline as (careful, carefully) as possible.
4. The official explanation of the budget cut sounds (incredible, incredibly).
5. Why was she looking at me (suspicious, suspiciously)?
6. This apple tastes (peculiar, peculiarly) to me.
7. Don't feel (glum, glumly) about missing the game.
8. You can watch (contented, contentedly) from the sidelines.
9. Dawn goes jogging (regular, regularly).
10. He disappeared (quiet, quietly) behind the curtain.
11. The conference room smelled (stuffy, stuffily).
12. After the first act, we all applauded (enthusiastic, enthusiastically).
13. The stage manager appeared (sudden, suddenly).
14. She spoke (serious, seriously) to the audience.
15. "The leading lady in the play," she said, "is feeling (sick, sickly)."
16. "She is resting (comfortable, comfortably) backstage."
17. "Her understudy will take over the lead (temporary, temporarily)."
18. The understudy seemed (nervous, nervously) to the audience.
19. After a while she was saying her lines (easy, easily).
20. The audience felt (happy, happily) for the understudy.

Bad and Badly

Bad is an adjective modifying nouns and pronouns. *Badly* is an adverb, modifying verbs, adjectives, and adverbs. Since the verbs of sense —*feel, smell, taste, sound*—are followed by an adjective, it is standard English to say *feel bad, smell bad,* etc.

Joan feels bad about the broken vase.

The warped record sounds bad.

The common expression *feel badly*, however, has, through usage, become acceptable English, although ungrammatical. Used with other verbs of sense, *badly* is not yet standard. Do not say *smell badly, taste badly,* etc.

Well and *Good*

Well may be used as either an adjective or an adverb. As an adjective, *well* has three meanings.

1. *To be in good health:*

   He feels **well**.[1] He seems **well**.

2. *To appear well-dressed or well-groomed:*

   She looks **well** in that dress.

3. *To be satisfactory:*

   All is **well**.

As an adverb, *well* means to perform an action capably.

She wrote very **well**.

Good is always an adjective. It should never be used to modify a verb.

NONSTANDARD   The choir sang good at the concert.
STANDARD   The choir sang **well** at the concert.

NONSTANDARD   We bowled very good as a team.
STANDARD   We bowled very **well** as a team.

USAGE

Real and *Really*

Real is an adjective meaning "actual" or "true." *Really* is an adverb and should be used to modify an adjective or another adverb, even though *real* is commonly used in everyday speech.

INFORMAL   Your new car is real nice.
FORMAL   Your new car is **really** nice.

INFORMAL   He played real well in the tryouts.
FORMAL   He played **really** well in the tryouts.

Slow and *Slowly*

Slow is an adjective except in the expressions *Drive slow* and *Go slow,* which have become acceptable because of their wide use on highway signs. *Slowly* is an adverb.

---

[1] *He feels good* is also correct, though its meaning is not limited to health. Example: He feels *good* about the new job offer.

EXERCISE 2. Correcting Errors In the Use of Modifiers. Number your paper 1–10. Some of the sentences contain errors in the use of *bad* and *badly, well* and *good, real* and *really,* and *slow* and *slowly.* If a sentence is correct, write + next to the appropriate number. If a word is used incorrectly, copy it on your paper and next to it write the correct form.

EXAMPLE: 1. After a long rehearsal, the dance troupe performed good.
    1. *good—well*

1. After she had lost the election, Bernadette felt very bad.
2. Charlotte was real happy about getting an *A* on her history test.
3. Ms. Stein is a good teacher who prepares her lessons well.
4. Some shades of blue and green go good together.
5. Let's hope the rest of the day doesn't go this bad.
6. "I'm sure I did good on that test," Anzu confidently remarked.
7. Eating slowly aids digestion.
8. Everyone wondered whether the stone in his ring was a real diamond.
9. "Please speak slow when you give your election speech," Mr. Schmidt advised the nervous candidates.
10. "Life can't be treating you all that bad," I told Walker.

EXERCISE 3. Analyzing the Use of Modifiers. Number your paper 1–20. If the *italicized* modifier in a sentence is correct, write a + after the proper number. If it is incorrect, write the correct form, and after the correct form write the word it modifies.

EXAMPLE 1. Something sounds *strangely* next door.
    1. *strange—something*

1. The players did *good* in the fourth quarter.
2. The bread dough rose too *quick.*
3. I am glad to see you looking *well* after the operation.
4. Limburger cheese smells very *bad.*
5. We walked *slow* on the icy sidewalk.
6. Liz seemed *sad* to hear the news.
7. Sam feels *bad* about forgetting your birthday.
8. Anita is afraid she did *poor* on the test.
9. She sounded very *angrily* on the phone.

10. These new jeans do not fit me *good* at all.
11. Rita answered the questions *precisely*.
12. Fortunately, no one was hurt *bad* in the accident.
13. I could not see the game very *good* from my seat.
14. This old watch has been running fairly *good*.
15. Ms. Tate's company can do the job *efficiently*.
16. The judge rapped the gavel *sharp* to restore order.
17. We didn't win, but we played *well*.
18. My tennis shoes do not look *well* anymore.
19. Jen works *slow* but she is accurate.
20. The whole day has gone *bad* for me.

WRITING APPLICATION A:
Expressing Emotion Through the Use of
Linking Verbs Followed by Adjectives

People often have a hard time expressing emotion, perhaps because they are shy or very private, perhaps because they have never had any practice. Emotions are real and important, however; they indicate that a person is human instead of mechanical, like a robot. The verb *feel* is usually used for expressing emotions. Linking verbs such as *feel* are often followed by adjectives instead of adverbs.

EXAMPLE   Incorrect: I feel *badly* about not making the varsity team. [The adverb *badly* is incorrect after the linking verb *feel*.]

Correct: I feel *bad* about not making the varsity team. [The adjective *bad* is correct after the linking verb *feel*.]

Writing Assignment

The writer E. M. Forster said about the English that they are "afraid to feel." He went on to say that he had been taught at school that the expression of feeling is bad form. How do you view the subject of feelings? Do you express them openly or "bottle" them up? Which feelings do you most often show? Write a paragraph on this subject. At some point, use the verb *feel* followed by an adjective or several adjectives.

USAGE

COMPARISON OF ADJECTIVES AND ADVERBS

27c. *Comparison* refers to the change in the form of adjectives and adverbs when they indicate the degree of the qualities they express. There are three degrees of comparison: *positive, comparative,* and *superlative.*

POSITIVE	COMPARATIVE	SUPERLATIVE
big	bigger	biggest
eager	more eager	most eager
gladly	more gladly	most gladly

Comparative and Superlative Forms

(1) Most adjectives and adverbs of one syllable form their comparative and superlative degrees by adding *-er* and *-est*.

POSITIVE	COMPARATIVE	SUPERLATIVE
neat	neater	neatest
warm	warmer	warmest
fast	faster	fastest

(2) Some adjectives of two syllables form their comparative and superlative degrees by adding *-er* or *-est*; other adjectives of two syllables form their comparative and superlative degrees by means of *more* and *most*. (Sometimes, either method is correct.)

When you are in doubt as to how a word is compared, consult an unabridged dictionary.

POSITIVE	COMPARATIVE	SUPERLATIVE
lively	livelier	liveliest
agile	more agile	most agile

(3) Adjectives of more than two syllables and adverbs ending in *-ly* usually form their comparative and superlative degrees by means of *more* and *most*.

POSITIVE	COMPARATIVE	SUPERLATIVE
delightful	more delightful	most delightful
quietly	more quietly	most quietly

(4) Comparison to indicate less or least of a quality is accomplished by using the words *less* and *least* before the adjective or adverb.

POSITIVE	COMPARATIVE	SUPERLATIVE
weak	less weak	least weak
contented	less contented	least contented
urgently	less urgently	least urgently

Irregular Comparison

Adjectives and adverbs that do not follow the regular methods of forming their comparative and superlative degrees are said to be compared irregularly.

POSITIVE	COMPARATIVE	SUPERLATIVE
bad	worse	worst
good ⎤ well ⎦	better	best
many ⎤ much ⎦	more	most

EXERCISE 4. Using Comparative and Superlative Forms. Write the comparative and superlative forms of the following words. Use a dictionary.

EXAMPLE   1. flat
              1. *flatter, flattest*

1. tiny
2. wistful
3. ill
4. modest
5. curious
6. proudly
7. abruptly
8. good
9. gently
10. thin

Use of Comparatives and Superlatives

27d. Use the comparative degree when comparing two things; use the superlative degree when comparing more than two.

COMPARISON OF TWO THINGS

Although both Laura and Ted wrote on the same topic, Laura's paper was **longer** [not *longest*].

The pitcher threw curveballs and sliders; the curveball was the **more** [not *most*] **successful** pitch.

COMPARISON OF MORE THAN TWO THINGS

Of the **three** routes, the expressway is usually the **most** [not *more*] **congested**.

Which of the **ten** photos is the **most** attractive?

USAGE

☞ USAGE NOTE   Rule 27d is generally observed by writers of formal English. In informal speech and writing, however, the superlative is often used for emphasis, even though only two things are being compared:

INFORMAL   Which park did you like best, Yellowstone or Hot Springs? [formal: *better*]
Of the two operas, Mozart's *The Marriage of Figaro* is the most amusing to me. [formal: *more*]

27e. Include the word *other* or *else* when comparing one thing with a group of which it is a part.

NONSTANDARD   Diamond, a crystalline form of carbon, is harder than any mineral in the world. [Since diamond is also one of the minerals of the world, this sentence says illogically that diamond is harder than itself.]
STANDARD   Diamond, a crystalline form of carbon, is harder than any **other** mineral in the world.
NONSTANDARD   He ran more races than anyone in his club. [He is a member of the club; he cannot run more races than himself.]
STANDARD   He ran more races than anyone **else** in his club.

27f. Avoid double comparisons.

A double comparison is one in which the degree is formed incorrectly by adding *-er* or *-est* in addition to using *more* or *most*.

NONSTANDARD   Alice is a more faster swimmer than I.
STANDARD   Alice is a **faster** swimmer than I.

NONSTANDARD   She is the most friendliest girl in school.
STANDARD   She is the **friendliest** girl in school.

EXERCISE 5. Using Comparatives and Superlatives Correctly.
Number your paper 1–10. Some of the sentences contain errors in the use of the comparative and superlative degrees of adjectives. If a sentence is correct, write + next to the appropriate number. If a comparison is used incorrectly, copy it on your paper and next to it write the correct form.

EXAMPLE   1. That was the most highest grade Oscar ever earned on a Spanish test.
1. *most highest—highest*

USAGE

1. Colleen thought nothing could be as bad as the snow; but when the ice storm arrived, she said, "This weather is even worser!"
2. Both twins, Holly and Julie, have brown eyes, but Holly's are darkest.
3. In each graduating class, the valedictorian is the student whose average is higher than that of any senior.
4. Because he wrote the Declaration of Independence, Thomas Jefferson is regarded as one of the most important Americans in United States history.
5. People need to develop a more clear sense of self-worth.
6. Sue made the mistake of buying a darker shade of paint than she needed for the small room.
7. Performing better than all the gymnasts, Mary Lou Retton was the first American to win an Olympic gold medal in her sport.
8. Myles is taking more classes than I.
9. Dividing the pie in two, Felicia took the least and gave me the larger portion.
10. According to my friend Juan, Houston, Texas, is more interesting and more exciting than any city in that state.

EXERCISE 6. Using Modifiers Correctly. Number your paper 1–20. For each correct sentence, write a + after the proper number; revise each incorrect sentence and write it correctly.

EXAMPLE   1. I am least prepared to take the test than you.
  1. *I am less prepared to take the test than you.*

1. I tried to sing as good as she sang.
2. Josh studied more than anyone in his physics class.
3. I have narrowed my choices to two colleges, and I want to visit them to see which I like best.
4. The shoppers looked oddly at the street musicians.
5. If the dough smells badly, don't bake it.
6. Monica seems good enough to leave the hospital.
7. Mr. Brown is many pounds more heavier than I.
8. The pedestrian stared defiantly at the motorists.
9. He inched very gradual toward the doorway.
10. After a hot day, a cold glass of water tastes good.
11. How did you finish your assignment so prompt?

USAGE

12. The picture on this television set is much more clearer than on that one.
13. Thunderclouds loomed threateningly overhead.
14. We thought Patti was the most talented of all the actors in the community play.
15. They all did well on the test.
16. I read the shorter of the three books for my report.
17. You cheered more often than anyone at the concert.
18. She was less determined to win than her sister.
19. He thought she seemed gracefuller than the other model.
20. Why is she walking so slow toward the house?

USAGE

WRITING APPLICATION B:
Using Comparison to Express Critical Judgment

It is important for readers and viewers to develop critical skills before they attempt to make judgments. You are often asked to compare two or more people, places, or things. In order to express the comparison, you must use adjectives or adverbs in a comparative form.

EXAMPLE Of the three bird prints by Ray Harm, the one entitled *Cardinal* is the *richest* in bright color contrasts. [The superlative form is used because more than two things are being compared.]

Donatello's statue of David is *more realistic* than Michelangelo's *David*. [The comparative form is used because two things are being compared.]

Writing Assignment

Immature readers or viewers are often interested mainly in plot. They value violent action, dangerous missions, close escapes, and so on. More mature critics look for action that is significant. That is, they value action that reveals something meaningful about life or people. Write a comparison of several books or television shows. Judge whether the action is an end in itself or, rather, a means to reveal something significant. Use comparatives and superlatives correctly.

CHAPTER 27 REVIEW: POSTTEST

Identifying the Correct Use of Modifiers. Number your paper 1–25. Some of the following sentences contain errors in the use of modifiers. If a sentence is correct, write + next to the appropriate number on your paper. If the sentence is incorrect, write the incorrect word or words and then write the proper word(s).

EXAMPLE 1. Among my three brothers and sisters, my sister Giselle has the better sense of humor.
     1. *better—best*

1. "This is the most drab outfit I have ever had," said Louise. "Why did I buy it?"
2. Which is widest, the Mississippi River or the Colorado River?
3. My English teacher thinks that Shakespeare is better than any writer who ever lived.
4. My parents read both a morning and an evening newspaper, but I think the morning paper is best.
5. As Mr. Connolly explained the procedure for the experiment, Lisa said to me, "This is going to be real difficult."
6. When the temperature reached 103° in August, the Board of Health warned people to walk slowly when they were outdoors.
7. That paint is the most palest shade of blue I have ever seen.
8. Because the drummer played bad, the band's melody line was drowned out.
9. Pointing to two glasses partially filled with water, the magician asked, "Which glass has the least water?"
10. In preparing for a job interview, you should wear styles and colors of clothing that look attractively on you.
11. Mr. Martinez asked, "Is Donna still feeling badly?"
12. If Mark pedals his bike that slow, he'll never get home.
13. Philadelphia and Atlantic City are the largest cities near my home, but Philadelphia is actually the closest of the two.
14. We found it hard to understand why Randy had spoken as rude as he did in response to a simple question.
15. Has Pete been saving money regular for the trip he wants to take to Alaska?
16. He can't play the guitar too good, but his records sell well.

17. Tommy Lee thinks a vacation in the mountains is peacefuller than any other kind of vacation.
18. The economist said that interest rates would be going up steady for the next five years.
19. Among the Tong triplets, Chi Wan has always been the more industrious one.
20. "Sharon has been working harder than anyone here," I said.
21. My sister's bedroom looked messily this morning.
22. The iced tea tasted too sweetly for me.
23. "Nurse Lopez, I feel remarkably well today, better than I have ever felt before," said Mr. Parker.
24. There is a control on the television set for making the picture a little less brighter.
25. The cheese smells badly but tastes good.

USAGE

Glossary of Usage

COMMON USAGE PROBLEMS

DIAGNOSTIC TEST

Selecting Standard Words and Expressions. The sentences in this exercise contain usage problems discussed in this chapter. Number your paper 1–20. After the proper number, write the standard choice of the two given in parentheses.

EXAMPLE: 1. We were (kind of, rather) disappointed with the results.
1. *rather*

1. After Shirley had starred in our spring play, she acted (like, as if) she were an important and famous movie star.
2. Lionel gave a (credible, credulous) account of how he had spent so much money on his vacation.
3. When we need the tape, we never know where (it's at, it is).
4. At the restaurant where I work, all four of us divide the tips evenly (between, among) ourselves.
5. Neither my parents (or, nor) their friends ever miss watching the Super Bowl game.
6. As I was about to pay for my new jeans, I suddenly realized I (had, hadn't) scarcely any money in my wallet.
7. Because it was (liable, likely) to rain, Lorraine canceled her plans to go swimming.
8. Will you please take your package (off, off of) the table?
9. (Accept, Except) for Carlos and Glenn, everyone went to the fair.

10. The reason we are moving is (because, that) my parents have always wanted to live in Oregon.
11. Whenever I'm not doing (something, nothing) challenging, I grow bored easily.
12. Fairbanks, Alaska, is a long (way, ways) away from Orlando, Florida.
13. Although we do the same type of work, Hasina and I are (affected, effected) differently by it.
14. Whenever we go (anywhere, anywheres), Judy always seems to meet someone she knows.
15. (Bring, Take) the dog with you when you go out for a walk.
16. When I first went (in, into) the principal's office, I felt a little nervous.
17. Marie admitted that if she (had, would have) checked the oil, the engine wouldn't have given her a problem.
18. Looking at the crisp green beans, Rosa said, "(This, Those) kind of beans has always been my favorite."
19. It's an (allusion, illusion) to think you can become successful without hard work.
20. Emily's grandparents (immigrated, emigrated) here from Poland.

Chapters 24 through 27 of this book describe the conventions of standard English usage observed by most careful users of the language. These include subject-verb agreement, pronoun-antecedent agreement, the correct use of pronouns, the correct form and use of verbs, and the correct use of modifiers. In addition to vocabulary, these are the major areas in which standard English differs from nonstandard English.

There are, however, a number of special usage problems that require separate treatment. These are presented here in the glossary.

SUMMARY: LEVELS OF USAGE

Standard English

Informal   The everyday language of people who observe the conventions of English usage, suitable for all but the most formal occasions.

Formal   The language of most serious speakers when they take special pains to say the correct thing; appropriate for all serious writing and speaking, but suitable in any situation.

Nonstandard English

Idiomatic usages and dialects identifiably different from standard English; most often less appropriate than standard English for widespread communication; sometimes suitable for special, but not general, purposes.

If you are not sure of these terms after reading the brief summary, review Chapter 23, in which they are discussed in detail.

In doing the exercises in this chapter, as well as those in other parts of the book, follow the conventions of standard formal English.

The items in this glossary are arranged in alphabetical order, with exercises interspersed. Problems in spelling, such as the difference between *already* and *all ready* and similar words often confused, are taken up on pages 686–92 in the chapter on spelling.

a, an   These short words are called *indefinite articles*. They refer to one of a general group.

> **A** woman bought Larry's car.
> The pioneers came upon **a** herd of buffalo.
> Maria was in **an** accident in her father's car.
> Jonathan fished for **an** hour before he caught that bass.

Use *a* before words beginning with a consonant sound; use *an* before words beginning with a vowel sound. In the examples above, *a* is used before *herd* because *herd* begins with a consonant sound. *An* is used before *hour* because *hour* begins with a vowel sound.

accept, except   *Accept* is a verb; it means "to receive." *Except* as a verb means "to leave out"; as a preposition it means "excluding."

> I **accepted** the gift gratefully.
> Debbie has a perfect attendance record, if you **except** the day she stayed home with the flu.
> We were busy every evening this week **except** Tuesday.

adapt, adopt   *Adapt* means "to change in order to fit or be more suitable; to adjust." *Adopt* means "to take something and make it one's own."

> When it rained on the day of the senior class picnic, we **adapted** our plans.
> The Broadway play was **adapted** from a popular television miniseries.
> The couple who **adopted** the baby read many books and **adopted** some suggestions for infant care.

USAGE

affect, effect *Affect* is usually a verb; it means "to impress" or "to influence (frequently the mind or feelings)." *Effect* as a verb means "to accomplish, to bring about." *Effect* as a noun means "the result of some action."

Try not to let careless remarks **affect** you.
The school board **effected** [brought about] drastic changes in the budget.
The **effects** [results] of the hurricane were shown on the evening news.

all the farther, all the faster Used informally in some parts of the country to mean "as far as, as fast as."

DIALECT Thirty miles per hour was all the faster the first airplane could travel.

STANDARD Thirty miles per hour was **as fast as** the first airplane could travel.

allusion, illusion An *allusion* is a reference to something. An *illusion* is a mistaken idea.

In her essay she made many **allusions** to the American pioneers.
The behind-the-scenes report destroyed her **illusions** of Hollywood.

alumni, alumnae *Alumni (pronounced* ə·lum′nī) is the plural of *alumnus* (male graduate). *Alumnae* (pronounced ə·lum′nē) is the plural of *alumna* (female graduate). The graduates of a coeducational school are referred to (as a group) as *alumni*.

All of my sisters are **alumnae** of Adams High School.
Both men are **alumni** of Harvard.
My parents went to their college **alumni** reunion.

amount, number Use *amount* to refer to a singular word; use *number* to refer to a plural word. (See also **number,** page 611.)

The **amount** of research (singular) on stress is overwhelming.
A **number** of reports (plural) on stress are available.

and etc. Since *etc.* is an abbreviation of the Latin *et cetera*, which means "and other things," you are using *and* twice when you write "and etc." The *etc.* is sufficient.

The new store in the mall sells videotapes, audio cassettes, cameras, radios, electronic games, **etc.** [not *and etc.*]

and which, but which The expressions *and which, but which* (*and who, but who*) should be used only when a *which* (or *who*) clause precedes them in the sentence.

NONSTANDARD Our jazz band was pleased with the audience's enthusiastic response and which we had not expected before the concert.

STANDARD Our jazz band was pleased with the audience's response, **which** was enthusiastic **and which** we had not expected before the concert.

STANDARD Our jazz band was pleased with the audience's enthusiastic response, **which** we had not expected before the concert.

anywheres, everywheres, nowheres Use these words and others like them *without* the final *s*.

I could not find my keys **anywhere**; I looked **everywhere**, but they were **nowhere** in the house.

at Do not use *at* after *where*.

NONSTANDARD Where are they living at now?
STANDARD **Where** are they living now?

EXERCISE 1. Selecting Standard Words and Expressions. The sentences in this exercise contain usage problems presented on the preceding pages in the glossary. Number your paper 1–20. Write the standard choice of the words in parentheses.

1. Some pets find it hard to (adapt, adopt) to city life.
2. This new product has had a harmful (affect, effect) on some people.
3. Does this poem contain any (allusions, illusions) to Homer's *Odyssey*?
4. Jane and Nina are (alumni, alumnae) of our school.
5. I own a large (number, amount) of campaign buttons.
6. During my travels in Europe, I met Americans (everywheres, everywhere).
7. Everyone likes peanut butter (accept, except) you.
8. One line looks longer because of an optical (allusion, illusion).
9. We all (adapted, adopted) the resolution to have a class picnic.
10. A letter went out to all (alumni, alumnae) of the state university.
11. This is (all the farther, as far as) I can run.
12. How does humidity (affect, effect) the speed of sound?
13. Everyone (accept, except) Janet and me applied there.
14. I hope that at least one college will (accept, except) me for admission next year.
15. Ms. Benchley is an (alumna, alumnus) of Reed College.
16. Were any crops (affected, effected) by this year's dry spell?

17. The quiz-show contestant won a large (amount, number) of points by correctly answering questions about geography.
18. The expression "lock, stock, and barrel" is an (allusion, illusion) to the parts of a flintlock rifle.
19. Please (accept, except) my congratulations.
20. The end of the film had a great emotional (affect, effect) on us.

bad, badly   See page 586.

because   The use of *because* after *reason is* ("The reason is because . . .") is common in informal English, but it is generally avoided in formal writing. In a sentence beginning "The reason is . . . ," the clause following the verb is a noun clause used as a predicate nominative. A noun clause may begin with *that* but not with *because,* which usually introduces an adverb clause.

> ACCEPTABLE   The reason she arrived late was **that** [not *because*] her car had a flat tire.
>
> BETTER   She arrived late **because** her car had a flat tire.

WRITING APPLICATION A:
Learning to State Reasons Correctly

In both speaking and writing, you are often asked to defend a position and to give the reasons behind your opinion. Sooner or later, you will be faced with the construction *the reason is. The reason is because* may be acceptable in informal writing, but in formal writing it is not. Instead, you should think of the clause following the verb *is* as a predicate nominative.

> EXAMPLE   The *reason* I object to capital punishment *is* **that it is cruel and unusual punishment.** (In this example, the noun clause following the verb *is* begins correctly with *that*, not *because*.)

Writing Assignment

Take a position on a controversial subject. Be prepared to defend your position with sound and logical reasons. In your topic sentence use either *the reason is* or *the reasons are*. Be sure to follow this construction with a noun clause or several noun clauses beginning with *that*.

USAGE

being as, being that   Nonstandard English when used for *since* or *because*.

> NONSTANDARD   Being as Emily had lived in Montreal for five years, she could speak both French and English.
>
> STANDARD   **Because** Emily had lived in Montreal for five years, she could speak both French and English.

beside, besides   *Beside* means "by the side of" someone or something. *Besides* means "in addition to."

> Who sits **beside** you in English class?
> **Besides** my homework, I have an errand to run.

between, among   The distinction between these words is usually observed in formal English. Use *between* when you are thinking of two items at a time, whether or not they are part of a larger group.

> We have to choose **between** Anne and Lisa.
> I cannot remember the difference **between** a polka, a two-step, and a mazurka. [*Between* is correct because the speaker is thinking of one dance and another dance—*two at a time.*]
> They would know the difference **between** the four teams.

Use *among* when you are thinking of a group rather than of separate individuals.

> She is respected **among** her peers.
> I hated to decide **among** so many qualified applicants.

bring, take   Use *bring* when the meaning is to convey something *to the person speaking.* Use *take* when the meaning is to convey something *away from the person speaking. Bring* is related to *come; take* is related to *go.*

> Remember to **bring** your new albums when you *come* to my house.
> **Take** [not *bring*] your warm jacket when you **go** to the game this afternoon.

can't hardly, can't scarcely   See *The Double Negative* (page 615).

could of   Sometimes carelessly written for *could have*. Do not write *of* for *have*. Similar expressions frequently written incorrectly are *ought to of, might of, must of.*

> NONSTANDARD   Wanda could of told us it wasn't a costume party before we rented these chicken suits.
>
> STANDARD   Wanda could **have** told us it wasn't a costume party before we rented these chicken suits.

USAGE

credible, creditable, credulous Sometimes confused because of their similarity, these words have quite different meanings.

Credible means "believable."

The child gave a **credible** excuse for breaking the window in the kitchen.

Creditable means "praiseworthy."

Her quick thinking and competent action were **creditable.**

Credulous means "inclined to believe just about anything."

The **credulous** woman and her neighbors signed up for the trip to Mars.

data The plural form of the Latin *datum*. In standard informal English, *data* is frequently used, like a collective noun, with a singular pronoun and verb.

INFORMAL   The census data was finally published.

However since *data* has only recently become acceptable as a singular word, you will be safer if, in your writing, you use the word as a plural. See **phenomena.**

FORMAL   The census **data were** finally published.

discover, invent Do not use *invent* to mean "discover." *Invent* means "to make something not known before, to bring something into existence." *Discover* means "to find something that has been in existence but was unknown."

Elias Howe **invented** the sewing machine.
The engineers **discovered** new oil deposits in Michigan.

done Not the past form of *do*. *Done* always needs a helping verb: *has done, was done, will be done,* etc. The past form of *do* is *did.*

NONSTANDARD   We done all our chores in an hour.
STANDARD   We **did** all our chores in an hour.
STANDARD   We **had done** all our chores in an hour.

don't A contraction of *do not, don't* should not be used with a singular noun or the third person of singular pronouns (*it, he, she*). Use *doesn't*. See pages 520–21.

NONSTANDARD   It don't worry us.
STANDARD   It **doesn't** worry us.

effect, affect See **affect, effect.**

emigrate, immigrate *Emigrate* means "to go from a country" to settle elsewhere. *Immigrate* means "to come into a country" to settle.

The war has forced thousands of people to **emigrate** from their homeland to other, more peaceful countries.
Marie's grandparents **immigrated** here in 1950.

etc. See **and etc.**

except, accept See **accept, except.**

famous, notorious *Famous* means "well and widely known." *Notorious* means "widely known" but in an unfavorable sense.

Gloria Steinem and Betty Friedan are **famous** leaders of the women's movement in the United States.
Al Capone was a **notorious** gangster in the 1920's.

farther See **all the farther.**

fewer, less In standard formal English *fewer* (not *less*) is used before a plural noun. *Less* is used before a singular noun.

We printed **fewer** [not *less*] prom tickets this year.
I spent **less** time in the library this morning.

good, well See page 587.

USAGE

EXERCISE 2. Identifying Correct Expressions. The sentences in this exercise contain usage problems explained on pages 602–605. Double negatives and the listed items explained elsewhere in this text are not covered. Number your paper 1–20. Write after the proper number the correct choice of the words in parentheses.

EXAMPLE 1. We could (of, have) taken the bus.
         1. *have*

1. (Being that, Because) Eric is shy, he doesn't say much.
2. When the car broke down, we had only five dollars (between, among) the six of us.

3. (Beside, Besides) our volunteer work, our club sponsors an annual ski trip.
4. Please (bring, take) your guitar when you come to my party.
5. Jon is so (credulous, credible) that he believed your crazy story.
6. They sold (fewer, less) new cars than used cars.
7. In what year was the transistor (invented, discovered)?
8. My reason for missing the rehearsal was not (credulous, credible).
9. Did you (bring, take) your gift back to the store?
10. Basketball is his favorite sport (beside, besides) tennis.
11. I had (fewer, less) cavities than my sister.
12. They (done, did) their best to win the play-offs.
13. Cold weather (don't, doesn't) bother him very much.
14. (Among, Between) the four of us, we can paint the house.
15. If I had known you weren't busy, I would (of, have) asked you to help me.
16. Many people (emigrated, immigrated) to the United States in the nineteenth century.
17. All the critics wrote about Gene Wilder's (creditable, credulous) performance in his most recent movie.
18. Alan Shepard, Jr., became (famous, notorious) as the first American in space.
19. I want to (invent, discover) a fabric that never gets dirty.
20. Angie forgot to (bring, take) her homework assignment when she went to school this morning.

EXERCISE 3. Identifying Correct Expressions. This exercise covers all usage items explained in the glossary to this point. Number your paper 1–20. If a sentence does not contain a usage error, write a + after the proper number. If it does contain an error, write the correct form.

EXAMPLE   1. We excepted the telegram nervously.
    1. *accepted*

1. Frank has less hobbies than his friend.
2. Dr. Nash stopped by to check on my progress, being as she was in the neighborhood anyway.
3. Will the thunderstorms affect the graduation ceremonies?
4. Would you please take this monstrosity out of here?
5. Anyone as credible as you would buy a refrigerator in the Antarctic.

6. Sue Ellen plays and enjoys many sports: baseball, tennis, bowling, field hockey, volleyball, and etc.
7. The reason for the widespread concern for eagles is because many are dying from lead poisoning.
8. The story contains too many allusions to Marie Antoinette.
9. Margie couldn't find her bus pass anywheres.
10. Where will we be staying at on vacation?
11. Six laps of the pool is all the farther I can swim.
12. The manager divided the work evenly between the four of us.
13. We were grateful to our knowledgeable coach and who guided us patiently throughout the year.
14. My aunts, who are identical twins, are both alumnae of Smith.
15. The foreign exchange student has found it difficult to adapt to life in the United States.
16. If I had known you were ill, I could of let you read my notes from physics class.
17. The Russian ballet dancer immigrated from his homeland to find creative freedom.
18. The amount of push-ups that he can do is incredible.
19. To prepare her report, Judy used data that were published by the Department of the Treasury.
20. Even though Roy said it don't matter, I can see that he is angry.

had of   The *of* is superfluous.

NONSTANDARD	If we had of asked permission, we could have used the auditorium for our meeting.
STANDARD	If we **had asked** permission, we could have used the auditorium for our meeting.

had ought, hadn't ought   Do not use *had* with *ought.*

NONSTANDARD	They had ought to be more patient.
STANDARD	They **ought** to be more patient.
NONSTANDARD	I hadn't ought to go to the movies again.
STANDARD	I **ought not** to go to the movies again.

he, she, they, etc.   Do not use unnecessary pronouns after a noun. This error is sometimes called the *double subject.*

NONSTANDARD	My cousin she designs her own clothes.
STANDARD	My cousin designs her own clothes.

hisself, theirselves　These words are sometimes incorrectly used for *himself, themselves.*

　　NONSTANDARD　Lou built the shed hisself.
　　　STANDARD　Lou built the shed **himself.**

illusion, allusion　See **allusion, illusion.**

immigrate, emigrate　See **emigrate, immigrate.**

imply, infer　*Imply* means "to suggest something." *Infer* means "to interpret, to get a certain meaning from a remark or an action."

　Mrs. Hanson **implied** during her lecture that we needed more practice.
　We **inferred** from her comments that we need to practice more.

in, into　In standard formal usage, observe the difference in meaning between these words. *In* means "within"; *into* suggests movement from the outside to the inside.

　　FORMAL　Feeling nervous, I walked **into** [not *in*] the personnel office.
　　INFORMAL　We threw some pennies **in** the well and made a wish.
　　FORMAL　We threw some pennies **into** the well and made a wish.

invent, discover　See **discover, invent.**

kind, sort, type　In standard formal usage the adjectives *this, these, that, those* are made to agree in number with the words *kind, sort, type; this kind, these kinds; that sort, those sorts.*

　We prefer **this kind** of magazines.
　We prefer **these kinds** of magazines.

kind of, sort of　In standard formal usage, avoid using these expressions to mean "rather" or "somewhat."

　　INFORMAL　I feel kind of depressed today.
　　FORMAL　I feel **rather** [somewhat] depressed today.

kind of a, sort of a　The *a* is superfluous.

　What **kind of** [not *kind of a*] sports car is this?

lay, lie　See pages 559–60.

learn, teach *Learn* means "to acquire knowledge." *Teach* means "to dispense knowledge."

If Ms. Green **teaches** [not *learns*] us, we will **learn** more.

leave, let *Leave* (*left*) means "to go away." *Let* means "to allow, to permit."

NONSTANDARD	Leave us finish our dinner.
STANDARD	**Let** us finish our dinner.
NONSTANDARD	He shouldn't have left us borrow his car.
STANDARD	He shouldn't have **let** us borrow his car.

The expressions "Leave me alone" and "Let me alone" are both correct and are commonly used interchangeably. Strictly speaking, "Leave me alone" suggests that you want somebody to go away, leaving you by yourself. "Let me alone" suggests that you want somebody to stop bothering you.

less, fewer See **fewer, less.**

liable See **likely, liable.**

lie, lay See pages 559–60.

like, as *Like* is a preposition and introduces a prepositional phrase. *As* is usually a conjunction and introduces a subordinate clause.

Jo sings **like her sister.** [prepositional phrase]
Jo sings **as her sister does.** [subordinate clause]

Like as a conjunction is commonly heard in informal speech, but it is unacceptable in formal English.

| INFORMAL | She plays golf like the pros do. |
| FORMAL | She plays golf **as** the pros do. |

like, as if *Like* should not be used for *as if* or *as though,* which are conjunctions used to introduce clauses.

| INFORMAL | She looks like she studied all night. |
| FORMAL | She looks **as if** [as though] she studied all night. |

likely, liable These words are often used interchangeably, but some writers of standard formal English prefer to observe the following distinctions: *Likely* is used to express simple probability.

USAGE

Ginny is **likely** to arrive any minute.

Liable is used to express probability with a suggestion of harm or misfortune; it is also used to mean "responsible" or "answerable."

The children playing near the gravel pit are **liable** to get hurt.
Mrs. Lee is **liable** for the damages her daughter caused.

myself, ourselves   Most careful writers of English avoid using pronouns ending in *-self*, *-selves* to replace personal pronouns as subjects or objects. See page 543.

Amy and **I** [not *myself*] are in charge of decorations.
Could you do a favor for Wanda and **me?** [not *myself*]

WRITING APPLICATION B:
Using the Conjunction *As* in a Topic Sentence

Whether you are reading or watching a movie or a television show, you generally want characters who are *credible*. This means that they are believable. A character who is thoroughly evil, for example, is not believable if he suddenly does something kind and unselfish. When you judge whether or not characters are *credible*, you are a literary critic. In a topic sentence about a character's credibility, you might also use the conjunction *as*. This construction, which introduces a subordinate clause, arises as you tell *why* a character is or is not credible. (*Like* is commonly substituted for *as* in this construction, but it is unacceptable in formal English.)

EXAMPLE   In *The Red Badge of Courage,* Henry Fleming is *credible* because he reacts *as* a young, new recruit would in his first battle. [The word *credible* is used correctly. The conjunction *as* is used—not *like*—to introduce the subordinate clause.]

Writing Assignment

Select a character from fiction, the movies, or television who has made an impression on you. Ask yourself if this character is *credible*. Why or why not? Frame a topic sentence similar to the example above. Then write at least one paragraph explaining why the character is or is not believable.

EXERCISE 4. Identifying Usage Errors. The sentences in this exercise cover usage problems explained in the part of the glossary that follows Exercise 3. Number your paper 1–20. If the usage is correct, write a + after the proper number; if it is incorrect, write a 0.

1. In his address to Congress, the President implied that an economic reversal might occur soon.
2. Without any warning, the cat jumped from the chair and leaped in my arms.
3. The children helped themselves to more turkey.
4. When you have time, will you learn me to sew?
5. Leave me figure this problem out by myself.
6. We had ought to have been more considerate.
7. Your room looks as if a tornado had been through it.
8. What am I to imply from your sarcastic remarks?
9. Ben did all the work himself.
10. If you had of asked me, I would have told you.
11. What can you infer from the closing couplet of this sonnet?
12. You hadn't ought to complain so much.
13. Why doesn't he get his work done like he's supposed to?
14. Jane and myself are the editors of our yearbook.
15. We implied from the principal's announcement that our school's administration is becoming stricter.
16. I asked my boss if he would let me have Saturday afternoon off.
17. Some people they're always making a fuss about nothing.
18. Are you implying that I can't read music?
19. Leave them stay if they don't want to join us.
20. We cheered like we never cheered before.

nauseated, nauseous These words do not mean the same thing. *Nauseated* means "sick." *Nauseous* means "disgusting, sickening."

> After riding on the roller coaster, the child became **nauseated.**
> The chemical reaction gave off a **nauseous** odor.

none *None* may be either singular or plural. See pages 513–14.

notorious, famous See **famous, notorious.**

number The expression *the number of* takes a singular verb. The expression *a number of* takes a plural verb. (See page 521, Rule 24s.)

USAGE

The number of candidates **was** surprising.
A number of candidates **were** nominated by the committee.

number, amount See **amount, number.**

of Do not use *of* unnecessarily. See **could of** and **had of.**

off of The *of* is unnecessary.

They pushed us **off** [not *off of*] the raft as a joke.

Do not use *off* or *off of* for *from*.

NONSTANDARD I got some free advice off of the mechanic.
STANDARD I got some free advice **from** the mechanic.

or, nor Use *or* with *either;* use *nor* with *neither.*

Either Gwen **or** Lily will lead the discussion.
Neither Gwen **nor** Lily will lead the discussion.

ought See **had ought, hadn't ought.**

persecute, prosecute Distinguish between these words, which have quite different meanings. *Persecute* means "to attack or annoy someone," often for a person's beliefs. *Prosecute* means "to bring legal action against someone for unlawful behavior."

The old regime **persecuted** those who held opposing views.
The district attorney **will prosecute** anyone caught looting.

phenomena *Phenomena* is the plural form of the word *phenomenon.* Do not use it as a singular noun.

We studied **these** [not *this*] **phenomena** of nature, which **are** [not *is*] rare indeed.
We studied **this phenomenon** of nature, which **is** rare indeed.

politics, mathematics, athletics For the number of these words and other similar words, see page 520.

reason is because See **because.**

respectfully, respectively *Respectfully* means "with respect" or "full of respect." *Respectively* means "each in the order given."

Even though I disagreed, I listened **respectfully** to their side.
Jane Eyre, Emma, and *Adam Bede* were written by Charlotte Brontë, Jane Austen, and George Eliot, **respectively.**

Reverend, Honorable These titles should never be used with a person's last name alone. In addition, the word *the* commonly precedes the titles.

NONSTANDARD   Reverend Becker, the Reverend Becker, Honorable Lugar
STANDARD   the Reverend Mark Becker, the Reverend M. L. Becker, the Reverend Mr. Becker, the Reverend Dr. Becker, the Honorable Richard Lugar.

rise, raise   See page 562.

same, said, such   Avoid such artificial uses of these words as the following:

We worked hard on the props and had **same** guarded against pranksters.
Josie complains about taking care of her young cousin, but she is really fond of **said** cousin.
Steve suggested we skip classes, but I don't approve of **such.**

says   Commonly used incorrectly for *said.*

NONSTANDARD   Doris argued and says, "We should have come earlier."
STANDARD   Doris argued and **said,** "We should have come earlier."

scarcely   See *The Double Negative* (page 615).

shall, will   The old distinction between these words is no longer observed by most people. *Shall,* which was once considered the only correct form for the simple future in the first person, has been replaced by *will* in most speech and writing.

STANDARD   I **shall** be glad to mail your package.
I **will** be glad to mail your package.

In a few expressions *shall* is the only form ever used and so presents no usage problem: *Shall we go? Shall I help you?* To use *will* in these expressions would change the meaning. With the exception of these special uses, *will* is as correct as *shall.*

sit, set   See page 561.

slow, slowly See page 587.

so Avoid using this overworked word too frequently.

POOR The car ran out of gas, so we walked two miles to the nearest service station.

BETTER When the car ran out of gas, we walked two miles to the nearest service station.

BETTER Because the car had run out of gas, we walked two miles to the nearest service station.

some, somewhat Use *somewhat* rather than *some* as an adverb.

FORMAL The rate of inflation in Europe has slowed **somewhat** [not *some*].

take, bring See **bring, take.**

this here, that there The *here* and the *there* are unnecessary.

NONSTANDARD This here shop has the best bargains.

STANDARD **This** shop has the best bargains.

these kind, those kind See **kind, sort, type.**

ways Sometimes used informally for *way* in referring to distance.

INFORMAL At dusk they were still a long ways from the campsite.

FORMAL At dusk they were still a long **way** from the campsite.

well, good See page 587.

when, where Do not use *when* or *where* in writing a definition.

NONSTANDARD A hurricane is when a tropical cyclone has winds faster than 75 miles per hour.

STANDARD A hurricane is a tropical cyclone that has winds faster than 75 miles per hour.

NONSTANDARD An implosion is where something bursts inward.

STANDARD An implosion is a bursting that is focused inward.

where . . . at See **at.**

which, that, who *Which* should be used to refer to things only. *That* may be used to refer to either things or people. *Who* should be used to refer to people only.

I like movies **which** [that] have happy endings.
Debra is an actress **who** [not *which*] inspires admiration.
Debra is an actress **that** inspires admiration.

The Double Negative

A double negative is a construction in which two negative words are used where one is sufficient. Formerly, double negatives were quite acceptable, but now they are considered nonstandard.

can't hardly, can't scarcely The words *hardly* and *scarcely* are negatives. They should never be used with *not*.

NONSTANDARD	It is so dark in here I can't hardly see where I'm going.
STANDARD	It is so dark in here I **can hardly** see where I'm going.
NONSTANDARD	There isn't scarcely enough time to eat lunch.
STANDARD	There **is scarcely** enough time to eat lunch.

can't help but In standard formal English, avoid this double negative.

FORMAL   We **can't help applauding** [not *can't help but applaud*] Ron's positive attitude.

haven't but, haven't only In certain uses *but* and *only* are negatives. Avoid using them with *not*.

FORMAL   They **had** [not *hadn't*] **but** two tickets left.
They **had** [not *hadn't*] **only** two tickets left.

no, nothing, none Not to be used with another negative word.

NONSTANDARD	Haven't you no money?
STANDARD	**Haven't** you **any** money?
STANDARD	**Have** you **no** money?
NONSTANDARD	Carol hasn't said nothing about the picnic.
STANDARD	Carol **has said nothing** about the picnic.
STANDARD	Carol **hasn't said anything** about the picnic.
NONSTANDARD	Joel didn't sell none today.
STANDARD	Joel **sold none** today.
STANDARD	Joel **didn't sell any** today.

EXERCISE 5. Identifying Correct Expressions. The sentences in this exercise cover usage problems explained in the section of the

USAGE

glossary that follows Exercise 4. Number your paper 1–20. Write after the proper number the correct word in parentheses.

EXAMPLE   1. I don't have (any, none) left.

   1. *any*

1. They only had a little (ways, way) left to run in the marathon.
2. Neither the freshman class (or, nor) the sophomore class will have the problems we faced.
3. We were taught to treat our elders (respectively, respectfully).
4. Luis (can, can't) hardly keep from being proud of you.
5. We studied the Mayans, (who, which) had developed a system of writing, as well as an accurate calendar.
6. Ms. Peters explained the (phenomenon, phenomena) of a super-nova.
7. Our enthusiasm has dampened (some, somewhat).
8. Many ancient rulers (persecuted, prosecuted) the people they conquered and made them slaves.
9. I was so sleepy that I (could, couldn't) hardly keep my eyes open.
10. The detectives (haven't, have) no clues in the case.
11. I (had, hadn't) no good reason for being late.
12. In her speech she (says, said) we were at fault.
13. We (had, hadn't) learned anything from the film.
14. The candidates (have, haven't) only three minutes each to state their platforms.
15. She would neither let me tell her the right answer (or, nor) let me give her any other help.
16. We (had, hadn't) but one choice to make.
17. The jazz band and the symphony orchestra will rehearse in rooms 115 and 135, (respectively, respectfully).
18. The manager insisted that there wasn't (any, no) reason for making the customers wait so long.
19. Before we moved, I lived only a little (ways, way) from school.
20. I'm probably getting the flu, because I have felt (nauseous, nauseated) all day long.

REVIEW EXERCISE A. Selecting Appropriate Expressions. The sentences in this exercise contain usage problems presented in the glossary. Number your paper 1–20. If a sentence does not contain a usage error, write a + on your paper. If a sentence does contain a usage error, write a 0. Your teacher may ask you to write the correct form after each 0.

EXAMPLE 1. The amount of voters has grown.
        1. 0 (*number*)

1. Leave us explain our arguments.
2. Eugenia can't hardly wait for vacation to start.
3. Who first discovered the laser?
4. We worked hard to effect a change in the school's policy on flexible lunch hours.
5. Beside your loyalty as a friend, I appreciate your sense of humor.
6. I resent their allusions to my mistakes.
7. The library has a large amount of new books.
8. You would of had trouble driving in Syracuse without snow tires.
9. Being that I'm short, please let me stand in front.
10. Her talk implied that she favored the honor system.
11. The reason you are tired is because we watched the late show.
12. The principal has no patience with those type of behavior.
13. At the supermarket I bought kiwi fruit, papayas, mangoes, and etc.
14. Since Dan started his part-time job, he has had less chances to be with his friends.
15. My parents are members of the alumni association.
16. Bring your riding boots when you go to the stable.
17. Backlighting is when the main source of light is placed behind the subject being photographed.
18. Jody dances as if his feet hurt.
19. Why don't you get some advice off of Rhoda?
20. Thirty feet is all the farther I can throw a football.

REVIEW EXERCISE B. Selecting Appropriate Expressions. The sentences in this exercise contain usage problems presented in the glossary. Number your paper 1–20. If a sentence does not contain a usage error, write a + on your paper. If a sentence does contain a usage error, write a 0.

1. We had to adapt the stage lighting for the rock concert.
2. The mayor made an illusion to our outstanding safety record.
3. A large amount of nails are in the toolbox.
4. Where did you stay at over Thanksgiving?
5. Everyone except Tim has accepted the invitation.

6. Among the two choices, I like the first one better.
7. The data on acid rain are not complete.
8. My mother emigrated to the United States before I was born.
9. Do you know about Bluebeard, who was famous for his cruelty?
10. You are credulous enough to believe the fortuneteller.
11. My sister she attends Iowa State University.
12. We inferred from Rudy's comments that the movie was dull.
13. The Whites grew all the vegetables theirselves.
14. I had ought to spend more time with my friends.
15. He has been the catcher for every game this year, and he is beginning to look kind of tired.
16. Ms. Robinson learned me all I know about public speaking.
17. What kind of a car is that?
18. We spoke respectfully to the Honorable Frank Murphy when he visited our class.
19. There were four freshmen which made the basketball team.
20. A number of suggestions have been submitted to the committee.

CHAPTER 28 REVIEW: POSTTEST

Revising Expressions by Correcting Errors in Usage. The sentences in this exercise cover problems explained in the entire glossary. Number your paper 1–25. If a sentence does not contain a usage error, write a + on your paper. If a sentence does contain a usage error, revise the incorrect portion of the sentence.

EXAMPLE: 1. I was surprised to learn that Robert's parents are wealthy, because he doesn't act like he's rich.
1. *doesn't act as if he's rich.*

1. The form said, "Please enclose a copy of your birth certificate, and we will return said document at a later date."
2. We couldn't help but admire the way the snow lay upon the hills.
3. You hadn't ought to be so careless about your new watch.
4. In a collision the guilty driver is liable for damage to the other car.
5. The weather was kind of muggy as we began to weed the garden.
6. The door scraped loudly because it was off of its hinges.

7. Members of the Student Council tried to effect the faculty's attitude toward the new dress code for school dances.
8. The picture of the notorious discoverer of the cure appeared on the front page of every major newspaper.
9. Theo don't care what others think; he has the courage to say what he believes.
10. Reverend Timothy Butler performed the wedding ceremony.
11. Esperanza and Patrick, respectfully valedictorian and salutatorian, delivered excellent commencement addresses.
12. When our teacher became ill and was replaced by a substitute, we found it difficult at first to adopt to a new routine.
13. Whenever I feel sad, I can't hardly wait to be with my best friend.
14. Arthur Fiedler he made the Boston Pops concerts popular with millions of people all over America.
15. The reason we're so late is because our car wouldn't start.
16. Scientists are still unable to explain fully the phenomena referred to as UFO's.
17. Then Tom says, "Maybe I'll go and maybe I won't."
18. Because Eula made a mistake when she put the film into the camera, none of her pictures could be developed.
19. Three players came off of the bench and ran out onto the field.
20. Even when he is reading difficult material, Mato is very skillful in inferring the main idea of a passage.
21. We plan to visit Tim at Christmas being as we haven't seen him in three years.
22. I have never seen this kind of insect before.
23. Where was Beth at last night when all of us went to the game?
24. Neil is an expert on jazz trumpeters and who are famous.
25. Our teacher said we had done a credible job on our project.

USAGE

Capitalization

STANDARD USES
OF CAPITAL LETTERS

Capital letters serve as an important signal to the reader. They indicate the beginnings of sentences, and they distinguish names and titles. Confusion can easily result if capital letters are not used according to the conventions of standard English.

DIAGNOSTIC TEST

Identifying Standard Uses of Capital Letters.   Number your paper 1–20. In each of the following pairs of items, either item a or item b is correctly capitalized according to standard usage. After the proper number, write the letter of the version containing the standard usage.

EXAMPLE   1. a.   a Movie starring Lena Horne
              b.   a movie starring Lena Horne
           1. *b*

1. a. Resolved: That the dress code should be reinstated.
   b. Resolved: that the dress code should be reinstated.
2. a. a nation in the middle east
   b. a nation in the Middle East
3. a. took courses in English, Spanish, and chemistry
   b. took courses in English, Spanish, and Chemistry
4. a. the crew of the Space Shuttle *Columbia*
   b. the crew of the space shuttle *Columbia*

5. a. at the intersection of Seventh avenue and Market street
    b. at the intersection of Seventh Avenue and Market Street
6. a. a letter of inquiry addressed to American airlines
    b. a letter of inquiry addressed to American Airlines
7. a. a trip to Yosemite National Park
    b. a trip to Yosemite national park
8. a. chief justice Rehnquist
    b. Chief Justice Rehnquist
9. a. fought the Battle of Saratoga during the Revolutionary war
    b. fought the Battle of Saratoga during the Revolutionary War
10. a. enjoyed Hemingway's *the Sun also Rises*
    b. enjoyed Hemingway's *The Sun Also Rises*
11. a. made copies on the xerox machine
    b. made copies on the Xerox machine
12. a. a biography of the American novelist Edith Wharton
    b. a biography of the american novelist Edith Wharton
13. a. a visit to the West Coast of Oregon
    b. a visit to the west coast of Oregon
14. a. a birthday gift from Aunt Madge
    b. a birthday gift from aunt Madge
15. a. freedom to worship god according to personal beliefs
    b. freedom to worship God according to personal beliefs
16. a. Prime Minister Margaret Thatcher of England
    b. prime Minister Margaret Thatcher of England
17. a. a course in World History at Roosevelt high school
    b. a course in world history at Roosevelt High School
18. a. celebrating the fourth of July
    b. celebrating the Fourth of July
19. a. a delicious chinese dinner at Wong's Restaurant
    b. a delicious Chinese dinner at Wong's Restaurant
20. a. birds migrating across the strait of Gibraltar
    b. birds migrating across the Strait of Gibraltar

MECHANICS

In the use of capital letters, as in all matters pertaining to language usage, variations are common. In standard usage, for instance, the names of the seasons are not capitalized, but some newspapers do capitalize them. Newspapers may also adopt what they call the "down style" of capitalization, in which words like *avenue, university,* and *library* are not capitalized as they are in standard usage when used with a particular name.

STANDARD USAGE	"DOWN STYLE"
Fifth Avenue	Fifth avenue
Brandeis University	Brandeis university
Detroit Library	Detroit library

The usage described in this book is standard ("up style") usage, which is generally followed in books and magazines.

29a. Capitalize the first word in a sentence.

If you do not always use a capital letter at the beginning of a sentence, review Chapter 10 to make sure that you can recognize the end of one sentence and the beginning of the next.

(1) Capitalize the first word of a formal statement following a colon.

EXAMPLE   The committee included the following statement: In light of these statistics, we recommend that four-way stop signs be installed.

(2) Capitalize the first word of a resolution following the word *Resolved*.

EXAMPLE   Resolved: That government support of the arts be increased.

(3) Capitalize the first word of a direct quotation.

EXAMPLE   Ms. Simpson said, "Your sister is a born leader."

Do not capitalize the first word of a quoted sentence fragment.

EXAMPLE   I agree with Ms. Simpson's comment that my sister is a "born leader."

(4) Capitalize the first word of a statement or question inserted in a sentence without quotation marks.

EXAMPLE   My question is, Will this action solve the problem?

☞ NOTE   Traditionally, poets capitalize the first word in a line of poetry. This use of capitals, although by no means as common today as it once was, is still often found.

MECHANICS

Recognized sections of the country or the world the South, the Northwest, the Far East

> ☞ **NOTE** Do not capitalize *east, west, north*, and *south* when they indicate direction. Do capitalize them when they refer to recognized sections of the country.

EXAMPLES At the corner, turn west, and you will see the museum on the south side of the street.
Is the Midwest the "heart" of the country?

The modern tendency is to write nouns and adjectives derived from *East, West, North*, and *South* without capital letters (a *southerner, southern* hospitality, *midwestern* customs), but the capitalization of such words is also correct.

Adjectives specifying direction are not capitalized unless they are part of the name of a country: **n**orthern Utah, **w**estern United States, but **E**ast Germany, **W**estern Samoa.

> ☞ **NOTE** Some nouns and adjectives derived from proper names are no longer capitalized: **m**ackintosh, **m**acadam, **m**orocco leather, **c**hina dishes. Most such words may be written with or without capital letters, however: **r**oman (**R**oman) numerals, plaster of **p**aris (**P**aris), **v**enetian (**V**enetian) blinds, **t**urkish (**T**urkish) towel, **g**othic (**G**othic) style, etc. When you are in doubt about the capitalization of words of this kind, refer to your dictionary.

EXERCISE 1. Identifying Standard Uses of Capitalization.

Number your paper 1–20. After the proper number, write the letter of the standard form (*a* or *b*). In two of the items, both forms are correct; write both *a* and *b*.

1. a. the Nile river
   b. the Nile River
2. a. She said, "Tell me, too."
   b. She said, "tell me, too."
3. a. Bering strait
   b. Bering Strait
4. a. Fifty-Second Street
   b. Fifty-second Street
5. a. Hoover Dam
   b. Hoover dam
6. a. Charles Adams, Jr.
   b. Charles Adams, jr.

7. a. We heard him say he was "pleased to be here."
   b. We heard him say he was "Pleased to be here."
8. a. Swedish immigrants
   b. Swedish Immigrants
9. a. an American Citizen
   b. an American citizen
10. a. Los Angeles County highways
    b. Los Angeles County Highways
11. a. east of the river
    b. East of the river
12. a. the Iberian peninsula
    b. the Iberian Peninsula

13. a. people of the Far East
    b. people of the far east
14. a. the Brooklyn Bridge
    b. the Brooklyn bridge
15. a. an Irish setter
    b. an Irish Setter
16. a. a westerner
    b. a Westerner
17. a. New Jersey Turnpike
    b. New Jersey turnpike
18. a. Eastern seaports
    b. eastern seaports
19. a. Georgia O'keeffe
    b. Georgia O'Keeffe
20. a. Sixty-sixth street
    b. Sixty-sixth Street

EXERCISE 2. Using Standard Capitalization. Write the following names, terms, and phrases, using capital letters wherever they are required in standard usage.

1. cook county
2. an african village
3. four miles south
4. ranching in the south
5. forty-ninth street
6. olympic national park
7. a city like new orleans
8. a popular spanish singer
9. an arabian stallion
10. james o'toole, jr.

(3) Capitalize names of organizations, business firms, institutions, and government bodies.

Organizations Spanish Club, League of Women Voters, Humane Society

Business firms Delta Airlines, Procter and Gamble Company, Control Data Corporation, International Business Machines, Grand Hotel, Fox Theater

Institutions Loyola University, First Baptist Church, Biology Department

Government bodies Congress, House of Representatives, Federal Aviation Administration, Department of Commerce, Internal Revenue Service

☞ NOTE The names of government bodies are capitalized when they are exact names. Do not capitalize such general names as the following: *the state legislature, the latest department meeting, commission agenda.*

> ☞ NOTE Do not capitalize words such as *hotel, theater, church, high school, college,* and *university* unless they are part of a proper name.

EXAMPLES Chelsea Hotel   a hotel in New York
Webster High School   a nearby high school
United States Postal Service   the local post office

(4) Capitalize the names of historical events and periods, special events, and calendar items.

Historical events American Revolution, Renaissance, Civil War, Vietnam War

Special events Special Olympics, Conference on World Hunger, Kentucky Derby, Senior Prom

Calendar items Monday, June, Halloween, Professional Secretaries' Week

> ☞ NOTE The names of the seasons are not capitalized unless the seasons are personified.

EXAMPLES an early winter
Summer's royal progress

(5) Capitalize the names of nationalities, races, and religions.

EXAMPLES Caucasian, Semitic, Roman Catholic, Baptist, Congregationalist, Korean, Romanian, Afro-American

(6) Capitalize the brand names of business products.

EXAMPLES Mazola, Xerox, Polaroid, Atari

> ☞ NOTE A common noun that often follows a brand name is not capitalized except in advertising displays.

EXAMPLES Phillips screwdriver, Campbell's soup, Waring blender

(7) Capitalize the names of ships, planes, monuments, awards, and any other particular places, things, or events.

MECHANICS

EXAMPLES   the *Merrimac* (ship), Vietnam Memorial, Nobel Prize, Academy
Award, Statue of Liberty

☞ NOTE   Do not capitalize the names of school subjects, except for the
names of languages and for course names followed by a number.

EXAMPLES   English, Latin, Italian, math, art, chemistry, Chemistry II, Art 102

☞ NOTE   Rooms and some other nouns identified by a numeral or letter
are capitalized.

EXAMPLES   Room 31, Parlor B, School District 18, Chapter 4

☞ NOTE   Names of school classes may or may not be capitalized, but the
modern tendency is to capitalize them; however, the words *senior, junior,*
sophomore, freshman are not capitalized when used to refer to a student.

EXAMPLE   The senior agreed to speak before the Sophomore Class. [or sophomore class]

EXERCISE 3. Using Standard Capitalization.   Number your paper
1–20. Rewrite each item using correct capitalization. Write *C* after the
number of a correct item.

1. itawamba junior college
2. a hotel across town
3. central high school
4. She is a junior.
5. the swiss people
6. a royal typewriter
7. winter blizzard
8. the barclay hotel
9. trigonometry
10. physics I
11. labor day
12. history department
13. apple computer
14. two high-school seniors
15. bureau of the census
16. *zephyr* (train)
17. the crusades
18. the world series
19. newport athletic club
20. an italian restaurant

EXERCISE 4. Using Standard Capitalization.   List the words that
should be capitalized in each sentence. When the words make up a

phrase, write them as a phrase: *Sunshine Skyway, National Gallery of Art.* Indicate the number of the sentence in which each word or word group appears.

EXAMPLE   1. When my family lived in mexico city, we often had picnics in chapultepec park.
1. *Mexico City*
Chapultepec Park

1. One of our science teachers, ms. stephens, took her biology II classes to winslow marsh to study snails and collect water samples for testing in the high-school laboratory.
2. The massachusetts institute of technology campus in cambridge extends for more than a mile along the charles river.
3. Iowa department of education planners agreed with franklin county leaders that the new community college should be built in an urban location to make it accessible to many residents.
4. The explorers' club from my high school in bond, kansas, visited the jones fire science training center, where they watched a demonstration of rappelling, the skill of descending a sheer wall with the aid of a double rope.
5. In 1754 columbia college, then called king's college, stood next to trinity college, near the corner of broadway and wall street.
6. Mr. samuel reynolds, jr., my history teacher, captivated his audience of high school seniors as he vividly described the battle of britain during world war II.
7. Just west of fernandina beach, highway a1a crosses the amelia river and then curves by the entrance to fort clinch state park.
8. The denson hotel and the star theater, at the corner of river avenue and twenty-first street, are being renovated as part of the city's efforts to improve the area tourists first see when they enter the city.
9. Kathleen o'brien, who still has her native irish accent, read some of william butler yeats's poems to our english class on wednesday.
10. Sara turner, owner of turner's nutrition now, a chain of health food stores known for the development of ultravita yogurt, endowed memorial hospital's new wing, which was built this spring on the block between the hospital and finley mall.

29d. Capitalize titles.

(1) Capitalize the title of a person when it comes before a name.

EXAMPLES   Superintendent Davis, Dean Williams, President Robinson, Prime
Minister Shamir

**(2) Capitalize a title used alone or following a person's name only if it
refers to a high government official or someone else to whom you want to
show special respect.**

EXAMPLES   Dr. Glenda Davis, superintendent of schools; Ms. Williams, dean of
women; Marie Robinson, class president; *but* Neil Goldschmidt,
Governor of Oregon; Thurgood Marshall, Justice of the Supreme
Court [titles of high government officials]
the Senator, *but* the work of a senator; the General's orders, *but* the
insignia of a general; the Chief Justice, the Secretary of State, the
Prince of Wales.

☞ NOTE   When used to refer to the head of a nation, the word *president*
is usually capitalized. Two capitals are required in *vice-president* when it
refers to the vice-president of a nation. The words *ex-* and *-elect* used with
a title are not capitalized: *ex*-President, Governor-*elect*.

☞ NOTE   When a title is used in place of a person's name, it is usually
capitalized.

EXAMPLES   Goodbye, Professor.
Yes, Senator, please ask about it.

**(3) Capitalize a word showing family relationship when the word is used
with a person's name but *not* when it is preceded by a possessive (unless
the possessive is part of the name).**

EXAMPLES   Uncle Juan, Cousin Nora, my cousin Nora, your mother, *but* my
Aunt Sandy (when "Aunt Sandy" is considered her name)

☞ NOTE   Words of family relationship are usually, but not always,
capitalized when used in place of a person's name.

EXAMPLE   I think someone told Grandma.

(4) Capitalize the first word and all important words in titles of books, periodicals, poems, stories, articles, documents, movies, paintings, and other works of art, etc. [The important words are the first word and all other words except articles (*a, an, the*), coordinating conjunctions, and prepositions of fewer than five letters.]

EXAMPLES   *Great Expectations, Fortune,* "The Force That Through the Green Fuse Drives the Flower," Bill of Rights, *Bird in Space* [sculpture]

☞ NOTE   The words *a, an, the* written before a title are capitalized only when they are part of the title. Before the names of magazines and newspapers, they are not capitalized.

EXAMPLES   *The Count of Monte Cristo, A Farewell to Arms* [*The* and *A* are parts of the titles.]
Have you read the *Collected Stories* by Jean Stafford? [*The* is not part of the title.]
the *Science Digest,* the *St. Louis Dispatch*

(5) Capitalize words referring to the Deity.

EXAMPLES   God, the Almighty, Lord

Pronouns referring to God (*he, him,* and rarely, *who, whom*) are often capitalized.

EXAMPLE   Grace asked God to bring peace to His earth.

The word *god* when used to refer to the gods of ancient mythology is not capitalized.

EXAMPLE   Cassandra could foretell the future but was condemned by the god Apollo never to be believed.

EXERCISE 5. Using Standard Capitalization.   Number your paper 1–20. After the proper number, rewrite each item using standard capitalization. Write *C* after the number of a correct item.

1. captain Ahab
2. *guërnica* [painting]
3. Ms. Solomon, the center director
4. the club president
5. aunt Betty
6. senator Dole
7. mayor Fulton of Nashville
8. *down and out in paris and london* [book title]

MECHANICS

9. the speaker of the House of Representatives
10. Rabbi Klein, a military chaplain
11. ex-president Carter
12. the leader of a brass band
13. a sergeant in an army
14. the lord in his wisdom
15. the magna carta
16. your aunt
17. the *Los Angeles times*
18. duties of a legislator
19. Mildred Zaharias, former national golf champion
20. "the world is too much with us" [poem]

WRITING APPLICATION B:
Using Capitalization Correctly to Make Your Writing Clear

By using capitalization correctly, you enable your reader to understand your meaning. Compare the following examples:

EXAMPLES   I concocted my formula for white peanut butter while I was living in west Virginia.
I concocted my formula for White peanut butter while I was living in West Virginia.

In the first example, the reader would naturally think that the writer had developed peanut butter that is white while living in the west part of the state of Virginia. The second example makes it clear that the writer is using a brand name and referring to a different state.

Writing Assignment

After an absence of ten years, you have returned to town to attend the tenth reunion of your graduating class. The organizers of the reunion have asked everyone in the class to write a personal sketch for inclusion in a booklet to be distributed at the banquet. Write the sketch, using capitalization correctly; tell where you have been during the last ten years and what you have done.

REVIEW EXERCISE. Using Standard Capitalization.   This exercise covers all of the capitalization rules in the chapter. List in order the words that should be capitalized in each sentence.

1. The civitan club of midland township meets once a month in the restaurant next to the plaza theater.

2. As I started to laugh, aunt Dora and uncle John simultaneously asked, "you did what?"
3. In their english classes this term, the juniors have read *o pioneers!,* a novel by willa cather about swedish immigrants in nebraska.
4. A report from the secretary of labor included this statement: most of the new jobs in the next decade will be in service fields.
5. According to professor De La Rey, Tennyson's *idylls of the king* was published in 1859, the same year that saw the publication of Darwin's *origin of species,* FitzGerald's translation of omar khayyam's *rubaiyat,* and Dickens' *a tale of two cities.*
6. In "canto I" the poet Ezra Pound describes an ominous sea voyage to the same mythical land of the dead visited by the hero Odysseus in the *Odyssey,* an epic by the greek poet Homer.
7. The president joined the secretary of state at Dulles international airport for their trip to south america for a conference.
8. Speaking to a reporter from the *County Clarion,* coach Sheila Kim explained the drafting of a team resolution, which read, in part, "Resolved: that we will win all of our games next year."
9. After high school, my cousin Joe completed additional courses at Thompson vocational center and took a job with the Boone electronics company, which makes the electrowhiz circuit board.
10. When one student at Sunrise preschool woefully remarked that he was "tired of resting," the other children quickly agreed.
11. My grandparents lived for many years in the middle west, but when they retired they moved to southern California, finally settling in mecca, a town between palm springs and the salton sea.
12. In ancient egypt the people worshiped many gods equally until the sun god Ra became the principal deity.
13. The Raffles hotel in singapore, a base for many explorers' adventures in the far east, is named after sir Thomas Raffles, who founded the island country as a british colony in 1819.
14. Dr. Bruce Jackson, jr., principal of the high school, formerly taught mathematics I classes and an introductory class in computer science offered to freshmen and sophomores.
15. From the St. Croix island national monument in Maine to the Huleia wildlife refuge in Hawaii, public lands managed by the federal government, including the military, equal a third of the nation's total acreage.

MECHANICS

16. Susan o'Rourke, president of the jogging club, has an exercise route that takes her three times a week through Myers park, down Carriage street, and then back west to Dean avenue.
17. The vice-president of the United States automatically takes over if the president dies in office.
18. Shea stadium, near the site of the New York world's fair, is the home of the mets, the national league baseball team in New York.
19. My aunt, who spent some years in the south when she was younger, likes spicy Texas chili.
20. The will of the swedish industrialist and inventor of dynamite, Alfred Nobel, established the Nobel prize to honor those who have benefited the world in the areas of literature, medicine, physics, chemistry, and peace; a prize in economics was added in 1969.

CHAPTER 29 REVIEW: POSTTEST

Identifying Standard Uses of Capital Letters.   Number your paper 1–20. Many of the following sentences contain errors in standard capitalization. If a sentence contains an error, write the corrected word, term, or phrase after the proper number. If the sentence is correct as written, write *C* after the proper number.

EXAMPLE   1. Manolo Cruz will be attending Stanford university in the Fall.
                    1. *University   fall*

1. I am studying russian, English, and Art this Semester.
2. Go north for two Streets and then turn east on Central Avenue.
3. The Mountain Ranges in the Western states offer a variety of hiking and hunting experiences for those who love the outdoors.
4. For most Americans, Thanksgiving day is one for family gatherings.
5. Last summer I enjoyed reading *To Kill A Mockingbird* by Harper Lee, a southern writer.
6. HOMES is an acronym for the great lakes: Huron, Ontario, Michigan, Erie, and Superior.
7. Salt Lake City, Utah, is the headquarters of the Church of Jesus Christ of Latter-Day Saints, commonly called the mormon church.
8. Despite their political differences, my mother, a Democrat, and my father, a Republican, work together to increase voter registration.

9. Born in Mississippi, William Faulkner won the Nobel prize in 1949.

10. In the History of the United States, only one person, Gerald R. Ford, has held the nation's highest office without being elected either president or Vice-President.

11. Among the items on display at the Smithsonian institution in Washington, D.C., is the armchair used by Archie Bunker in the comedy series *All in the Family*.

12. The senior class will hold its Prom on Friday, May 14.

13. George Strum, Mayor for two terms, has announced that he will be a candidate again next November.

14. The first American woman in space, Sally Ride, was a member of the crew aboard the space shuttle *challenger* launched from cape Canaveral, Florida, on June 18, 1983.

15. Aldous Huxley's novel *Brave new World,* published in the 1930's, foreshadowed many of the moral dilemmas that would accompany the development of Genetic Engineering in the 1970's and 1980's.

16. My sister Eartha attends Boston University, and my brother Bayard attends the university of Notre Dame.

17. Henry David Thoreau, the New England writer, immortalized a small Massachusetts Pond in *Walden,* an autobiographical account of his two years alone at Walden Pond.

18. Because Mike's letter was addressed to 730 Lexington Place instead of to 730 Lexington Court, it was delayed for six days.

19. America's political and economic interests are closely tied to those of its northern neighbor, Canada, and to those of its southern neighbors, the central American countries.

20. When she came to Washington High School earlier this year, Ms. Morales, our new Principal, quickly earned a reputation as a good Administrator and a caring person.

MECHANICS

SUMMARY STYLE SHEET

Kansas City	a city in Kansas
Frederick Douglass National Park	our national parks
Thirty-first Street	across the street
Shell Lake	a shallow lake
North America	northern Wisconsin
the Toastmasters' Club	a public-speaking club
Boeing Company	an aircraft company
Lakeland High School	a new high school
Black Hawk College	
the American Revolution	a successful revolution
the Chrysler Building	a New York City building
the Fourth of July	the fifth of July
the Senior Prom	a prom given by seniors
the Junior Class	junior classes
English, French, Latin	social studies, art, biology
History II	a course in world history
Fall's coat of many colors	spring, summer, winter, fall
Dean Marsh	Mrs. Marsh, the dean
the President (U.S.)	the president of our club
Mayor Smith	a mayor's duties
May God go with you.	tribal gods of the Cherokees
the South	a mile south (north, east, west)
Tell Mother (or mother).	Tell my mother.
Uncle Joe	my uncle
Prell shampoo	
a Methodist, an Arab	
The Pickwick Papers	
the *Saturday Evening Post*	

Punctuation

END MARKS AND COMMAS

Punctuation helps make the meaning of a sentence clear to the reader. Some marks of punctuation indicate in writing the pauses and stops that the voice makes in speaking. They indicate not only where a pause should come but also how long the pause should be—the comma standing for a slight hesitation, the period for a longer one. Other vocal inflections are conveyed by the question mark and the exclamation point.

DIAGNOSTIC TEST

Correcting Sentences by Adding or Deleting End Marks and Commas. Number your paper 1–20. After the proper number, write all words that are followed by incorrect punctuation, and add or delete end marks and commas in accordance with the standards of written English. If a sentence is correct as written, write C.

EXAMPLES 1. We went to the mall, to the movies, and to our favorite restaurant, this afternoon.
　　　　　1. *restaurant*
　　　　　2. Well I think it's a good idea.
　　　　　2. *Well,*

1. Mr. Stanton will you please give me a reference?
2. The students the teachers and the administrators are looking forward to the long Memorial Day weekend.

3. Jenny Ho will be valedictorian, and Abe Gehrke will be salutatorian.

4. On the first day of the second semester of the school year Botow Okamoto drove up in a sleek red car.

5. Students who do well in academic subjects should in my opinion be commended by their school administrators.

6. When she took her first ride in a hot-air balloon. she experienced the amazing silence half a mile above the surface of the earth.

7. Lisa and Conrad arrived on time but everyone else was late.

8. No Sandy will not leave until the fifth of August.

9. Because I need exercise I ride my bicycle six miles each day.

10. Although Alan had worked very hard on his essay Mr. Burar felt it needed more revision.

11. Dolores Garcia a former Olympic swimmer is going to coach at our school next year.

12. Look at the size of the fish I caught.

13. On January 1 2000 my niece will celebrate her twenty-first birthday.

14. Mom or Dad or Uncle Paul will cook dinner tonight.

15. Tomorrow morning before school, the juniors will prepare juice, toast, and ham, and eggs for the seniors.

16. As I looked at the traffic which was backed up as far as I could see I decided to leave the highway and drive along local streets.

17. Please address all complaints to Joseph Redwing Jr Department of Consumer Affairs 4749 Cole Street Eugene OR 97401.

18. In San Francisco the summer temperatures often go no higher than sixty-eight degrees but in nearby San Jose the thermometer often climbs above eighty degrees in the summer.

19. Having suffered from headaches for ten days Mida decided to consult her family physician.

20. My grandmother a maid all her life saved her money and put both of her children through college.

This chapter and the one that follows describe the conventions for punctuating sentences according to the standards of written English and provide exercises to help you fix these uses in your mind. Punctuating exercises is at best an artificial activity, however, and you must be very careful to carry these punctuation principles over into your writing.

Do not overpunctuate. Use a mark for punctuation for only two reasons: (1) because meaning demands it, or (2) because conventional usage requires it.

END MARKS

30a. A statement is followed by a period.

EXAMPLE Spring break begins April 10.

30b. An abbreviation is followed by a period.[1]

EXAMPLES Blvd.   Oct.   B.C.   Messrs.

☞ NOTE Abbreviations in the metric system are often written without periods.

30c. A question is followed by a question mark.

(1) Distinguish between a statement containing an indirect question and a sentence that asks a question directly.

EXAMPLES Susan wants to know when the first match starts. [a statement containing an indirect question—followed by a period]

Do you know when the first match starts? [a direct question —followed by a question mark]

(2) Polite requests in question form (frequently used in business letters) may be followed by a period; a question mark is also correct.

EXAMPLES Would you please correct my account in this amount.

Would you please correct my account in this amount?

(3) A question mark should be placed inside quotation marks when the quotation is a question. Otherwise, it should be placed outside the quotation marks.

EXAMPLES Harold asked, "Have you heard from Dolores?" [The quotation is a question.]

Could I say, "I just don't want to go"? [The quotation is not a question. The sentence as a whole, however, is a question.]

---

[1] For a fuller discussion of abbreviations see page 32.

MECHANICS

30d. An exclamation is followed by an exclamation point.

EXAMPLES   What a wonderful idea!   You're joking!

How lovely!   Congratulations!

(1) Many exclamations begin with either "What a . . ." or "How . . ." as in two of the preceding examples. When you begin a sentence with these words, check the end mark carefully.

(2) An interjection at the beginning of a sentence is usually followed by a comma.

CUSTOMARY   Ah, there you are!

RARE   Ah! There you are!

(3) An exclamation point should be placed inside quotation marks when the quotation is an exclamation. Otherwise, it should be placed outside the quotation marks.

EXAMPLES   "What a good movie!" exclaimed Mary as she left the theater.
Don't say "It can't be done"!

30e. An imperative sentence may be followed by either a period or an exclamation point, depending upon the force intended.

EXAMPLES   Please write me a letter.

Hold that line!

EXERCISE 1. Correcting a Passage by Adding End Marks. Many periods and all exclamation points and question marks have been omitted from the following passage. Copy in a column on your paper all words that should be followed by end marks. After each word, write the end mark required. If a new sentence should begin after the end mark, write the first word of the sentence, giving it a capital letter. Before each word, write the number of the line in which it appears.

EXAMPLE   1. How glad I was to see him alas, he seemed not so glad, but did
2. greet me with, "What a surprise" and asked, "How are you" it
3. had been a long time . . .
1. *him! Alas*
2. *surprise! you?" It*

1   Lynn Block, Ph D, Director of Research for the Hubert F
2   Langston Soap Company, looked at her calendar. "Oh, no" she

3 groaned. Today she must conduct interviews to hire a new secre-
4 tary. "How nerve-racking it is when an applicant is unprepared"
5 Nonetheless, she was ready for the 9:00 A.M. interview when 9:00
6 came, however, the applicant had not arrived.
7   At 9:35 A.M., the receptionist ushered in the late arrival. "Oh,
8 dear" thought Dr Block as she surveyed the young man's torn
9 jeans, unironed T-shirt, and shaggy hair. To questions about his
10 qualifications, the young man answered only yes or no, and he did
11 not apologize for his lateness when asked about it, he mumbled
12 something about oversleeping. "Gee," Dr. Block puzzled, "this
13 person has good experience and typing skills, but he certainly
14 doesn't seem to want the job."
15   The next applicant, Ms Smith, was early. In walked a young
16 woman wearing a professional tool belt with well-cared-for carpen-
17 try tools around her waist. She said, "I'm so sorry to disturb you I
18 must have taken a wrong turn when I got off the elevator I'm
19 interested in the maintenance position being advertised."
20   "I'll say" exclaimed Dr. Block. She directed the woman to the
21 maintenance office on the Sixth St side of the building and wished
22 her luck. To herself, she mused, "Whew at this rate, I may never
23 get a secretary." By then the next interviewee had arrived—on
24 time. "Now what" wondered Dr. Block. Looking up to see a neatly
25 dressed young man, she asked, "Are *you* sure you're in the right
26 place it's been a highly unusual morning so far."
27   He replied, "Oh, yes I'm applying for the secretarial position.
28 I'm very much interested in it" Dr. Block smiled, and the interview
29 proceeded. He gave brief, helpful explanations and asked appropri-
30 ate questions about the job. About his future career plans, he said
31 "I would someday like to be an office manager I like office work
32 and believe good management is vital to a smooth operation."
33   "You're right about that" exclaimed Dr. Block. After the
34 interview ended, Dr. Block pondered her choices. She thought,
35 "Well, he doesn't have as much experience or quite as high a typing
36 rate as the first interviewee, but I know whom I'm going to hire"

THE COMMA

The comma—the most frequently used mark of punctuation—is used
mainly to group words that belong together and to separate those that
do not. Certain other uses have little to do with meaning but are
standard ways of punctuating sentences.

MECHANICS

Items in a Series

30f. Use commas to separate items in a series.

EXAMPLES She had been a correspondent for the wire service in London, Paris, Rome, and Madrid.

There were books on the desk, posters on the wall, and clothing on the floor.

☞ NOTE Do not place a comma before the first item or after the last item in a series.

INCORRECT The students in the auto mechanics class learned, to replace the spark plugs, adjust the points, and change the oil, in three different makes of automobiles.

CORRECT The students in the auto mechanics class learned to replace the spark plugs, adjust the points, and change the oil in three different makes of automobiles.

It is permissible to omit the comma before the *and* joining the last two items in a series if the comma is not needed to make the meaning clear. There are some constructions in which the inclusion or omission of this comma affects the meaning of the sentence.

Timepieces may be classified in the following categories: sundials, hourglasses, clocks, watches and chronometers. [four categories]

Timepieces may be classified in the following categories: sundials, hourglasses, clocks, watches, and chronometers. [five categories]

☞ NOTE Words customarily used in pairs are set off as one item in a series: *bag and baggage, pen and ink, hat and coat, pork and beans,* etc.

For supper they served a tossed salad, spaghetti and meatballs, garlic bread, milk, and fruit.

(1) If all items in a series are joined by *and* or *or*, do not use commas to separate them.

EXAMPLE We can go under or over or around it.

(2) Independent clauses in a series are usually separated by a semicolon; however, short independent clauses may be separated by commas.

EXAMPLE   We talked, we walked, we laughed, and we sang.

30g. Use a comma to separate two or more adjectives preceding a noun.

EXAMPLES   She is a creative, intelligent executive.

How can you watch that boring, silly, worthless program?

(1) Do not use a comma before the final adjective in a series if the adjective is thought of as part of the noun.

INCORRECT   It was a crisp, clear, invigorating, fall day.

CORRECT   It was a crisp, clear, invigorating fall day. [*Fall day* is considered one item. The adjectives modify *fall day*, not *day*.]

CORRECT   She hung small, round, delicate Chinese lanterns. [*Chinese lanterns* is thought of as one word.]

(2) If one of the words in a series modifies another word in the series, do not separate them by a comma.

EXAMPLE   Why did he wear a bright red cap?

Comma Between Independent Clauses

30h. Use a comma before *and, but, or, nor, for, so,* and *yet* when they join independent clauses, unless the clauses are very short.

EXAMPLES   Monday's meeting had gone smoothly, yet I felt a controversy brewing.

I'll go this way and you go that way. [independent clauses too short to require punctuation]

When the conjunction joins two verbs, not two main clauses, a comma is not used.

EXAMPLES   Geraldo gave me some good advice and got some from me in return. [The conjunction joins the verbs *gave* and *got*.]

Geraldo gave me some good advice, and I gave him some in return. [The conjunction joins two independent clauses.]

> ☞ NOTE   Many writers use the comma before these conjunctions only when necessary to keep the meaning clear.

MECHANICS

NOT CLEAR   We didn't know whether to stay for the weather forecaster had predicted rain.

CLEAR   We didn't know whether to stay, for the weather forecaster had predicted rain.

As you can see from this example, a reader may easily be confused if the comma is omitted. This is especially true of the comma before the conjunction *for,* which should always be preceded by a comma when it means *because.*

EXERCISE 2. Correcting Sentences by Adding Commas. The following sentences cover rules 30f–h. Number your paper 1–10. For each sentence, write the words that should be followed by a comma, placing the comma after the word. Be prepared to explain the punctuation you use.

1. The police searched everywhere but there were no fingerprints.
2. Albert Levin ordered salad juice and macaroni and cheese.
3. States along the Continental Divide include New Mexico Colorado Wyoming Idaho and Montana.
4. I played the melody on the guitar and the electric bass provided the rhythm.
5. She is a bright charming young woman.
6. We are learning more and more about space through our new and stronger telescopes our huge radar installations and our instrument-packed space probes.
7. At the airport I lost my luggage hat and coat and briefcase.
8. They are responsible for the confusion arose because of statements they made.
9. Young children do not use capital letters consistently and their punctuation is frequently unconventional.
10. The smoke choked us the odor sickened us and the wind chilled us.

Nonessential Elements

30i. Use commas to set off nonessential clauses and nonessential participial phrases.

A nonessential (nonrestrictive) clause is a subordinate clause that is not essential to the meaning of the sentence but merely adds an idea.

MECHANICS

NONESSENTIAL   Carla Harris**, who was offered scholarships to three colleges,** will
go to Vassar in the fall.

The basic meaning of this sentence is *Carla Harris will go to Vassar in the fall.* The subordinate clause does not affect this basic meaning; it merely adds an idea to the sentence. It is a nonessential clause because it does not limit in any way the word it modifies—*Carla Harris.* Clauses that modify proper nouns are nearly always nonessential.

The opposite of a nonessential clause is an essential (restrictive) clause.

ESSENTIAL   Carla Harris is the only senior **who won scholarships to three colleges.**

Here the subordinate clause is essential to the sentence, for without it the sentence would mean something else: *Carla Harris is the only senior.* The subordinate clause limits the meaning of *senior* to [*that*] *senior who won scholarships to three colleges.*

Study the following examples of essential and nonessential clauses until you understand the terms. Note the punctuation: *essential—no punctuation; nonessential—set off by commas.*

ESSENTIAL   New Orleans is the city **that interests me the most.**
NONESSENTIAL   Pierre**, which is the capital of South Dakota,** is on Lake Sharpe in the center of the state.

ESSENTIAL   The man **who said that** is my English teacher.
NONESSENTIAL   Mr. Gerz**, who is my English teacher,** said that.

☞ NOTE   Many writers prefer to use *that* rather than *which* to introduce an essential clause that modifies a thing; *which* is acceptable, however.

Sometimes a clause may be interpreted as either essential or nonessential. In such instances the writer must decide which interpretation to give the clause and punctuate it accordingly.

EXAMPLES   Dave took his problem to the librarian who is an authority on reference books. [interpreted as essential]

Dave took his problem to the librarian, who is an authority on reference books. [interpreted as nonessential]

Since the punctuation of the first sentence indicates that the clause is essential, the reader assumes that there is more than one librarian. Dave chose the one who is an authority on reference books. From the punctuation of the second sentence, the reader assumes that there is only one librarian and that the librarian is an authority on reference books.

EXERCISE 3. Identifying Essential and Nonessential Clauses.
Some of the sentences in this exercise contain essential clauses; others contain nonessential clauses. Number your paper 1–10. If the italicized clause is essential, write *E* after the proper number; if it is nonessential, write *C* to indicate that you would use commas in the sentence.

1. Employees *who always have a ready smile* make the job seem easier.
2. She is wearing the shirt *that she received for her birthday.*
3. Her new shirt *which was a birthday gift* is in her favorite color.
4. People *who are overly nervous* may not make good drivers.
5. Adults *whose development has been studied and recorded* continue to mature, usually in predictable stages, after the age of eighteen.
6. Cities *that seem alike* bear a closer look.
7. School boards *that need to build new facilities* often ask voters to pass a bond issue.
8. The Suez Canal *which is 103 miles long* connects the Mediterranean Sea and the Red Sea.
9. That law *which may have met a real need one hundred years ago* should be repealed or rewritten to deal with today's situation.
10. The Federal Reserve System *which is the central bank of the United States* monitors money and credit growth.

A participial phrase is a group of related words containing a participle (see page 449). Present participles end in *-ing;* past participles of regular verbs end in *-ed* or *-d.*

Like a nonessential clause, a nonessential participial phrase is set off by commas.

NONESSENTIAL My baby brother**, frightened by thunder,** climbed into my lap.
ESSENTIAL A child **frightened by thunder** often needs reassurance.
NONESSENTIAL The scattered band members came together suddenly**, quickly arranging themselves into the first formation.**
ESSENTIAL I watched the scattered band members **quickly arranging themselves into the first formation.**

EXERCISE 4. Correcting Sentences by Adding Commas. This exercise covers all comma rules given up to this point in the chapter.

After the proper number, write all words in the sentence that should be followed by a comma. Add the comma after each word. Be prepared to explain your answers.

1. Any student who wishes to join the gymnastics team will have to excel in floor exercises on the balance beam and on the uneven parallel bars.
2. The sophomores decorated the gym the juniors provided the refreshments and the seniors took care of the tickets.
3. Anyone taking the basic photography course will learn how to shoot close-ups portraits and still lifes.
4. The judge leaving her chambers stopped to talk to some court reporters who had gathered around her.
5. We got encouragement from everyone but our parents helped us most of all.
6. Careful writers distinguish between *uninterested* which means "indifferent" and *disinterested* which means "unbiased."
7. Any student wishing to sing or act or perform on Class Day should sign up before tomorrow which is the deadline.
8. Governor Quigley whose speeches are filled with clichés appeared on television last night asking people to "tighten their belts bite the bullet pull their own weight and give till it hurts."
9. A mongrel which had followed me halfway home suddenly trotted up to me and staring at me soulfully started to lick my hand.
10. A story that appeared in yesterday's newspaper was about the Toronto Maple Leafs which is my favorite hockey team.

Introductory Elements

30j. Use a comma after certain introductory elements.

(1) Use a comma after words such as *well, yes, no,* and *why* when they begin a sentence.

EXAMPLES   Well, what do you think?

Yes, you are welcome to join us.

Why, the whole story sounds suspicious!

(2) Use a comma after an introductory participial phrase.

MECHANICS

EXAMPLE   **Giggling like a child,** he wrapped the last present.

☞ NOTE   Do not confuse a gerund ending in -*ing* and used as the subject of the sentence with an introductory participial phrase.

EXAMPLES   **Cleaning and painting my room** was hard but fun. [gerunds used as compound subject—not followed by a comma]
Cleaning and painting my room, I ran across a favorite ring of mine. [introductory participial phrase—followed by a comma]

(3) Use a comma after a succession of introductory prepositional phrases.

EXAMPLE   **At the end of the block next to the old railroad station in Mill Heights,** my grandparents own a small house.

☞ NOTE   A single introductory prepositional phrase need not be followed by a comma unless it is parenthetical (*by the way, on the contrary,* etc.) or the comma is necessary to prevent confusion.

EXAMPLES   **By the way,** I heard from Grace Lee yesterday.
With athletes, injuries can end careers.
In the evening I like to visit friends.

(4) Use a comma after an introductory adverb clause.

EXAMPLE   **While Sal put on his tuxedo,** the flute player checked the sheet music.
As soon as we left the house, we heard the phone ring.

EXERCISE 5. Correcting Sentences by Adding Commas. This exercise covers all comma rules to this point in the chapter. Number your paper 1–10. Write the words in each sentence that should be followed by a comma, placing a comma after each word.

1. One draft is not enough for most writers can improve their work by revising it.
2. When they finished playing the drums were moved offstage to make room for the dancers.

3. By the end of the second day of school all students seemed to have found their correct classrooms teachers and lockers.
4. Oh if it's all right with you I'll ask Gloria and Agnes or Leo.
5. In the second half of the third period Johnson evaded the defense caught a twenty-yard pass and raced into the end zone.
6. Speaking at the forum Kay Stone described her experience as head of a household civic fund-raiser and business owner.
7. After a lengthy discussion the committee whose members were not satisfied voted to reject both of the two themes proposed for the prom and seek fresh ideas.
8. Many of those in the long winding ticket line had arrived just within the past hour but we having arrived before dawn held places near the sales window.
9. Regional theaters are prospering in many cities but the Broadway stage is still the goal of most young actors dancers and musicians.
10. As Phil began climbing the ladder began to slip out at the bottom and I immediately grabbed it to keep it in place.

WRITING APPLICATION A:
Using Commas Correctly to Make Your Writing Clear

Introductory participial phrases and adverb clauses lend variety to sentences, helping you avoid a monotonous tone. Unless these introductory elements are punctuated correctly, however, your reader may misread the sentence. Compare the following examples:

EXAMPLES We finished eating. The table was cleared. We played *Monopoly*.
When we finished eating the table was cleared for a game of *Monopoly*.
When we finished eating, the table was cleared for a game of *Monopoly*.

Writing Assignment

Select a famous person who particularly interests you. Write an account of this person's life, including material that is lively and interesting as well as factual. Use introductory participial phrases and adverb clauses to add variety to your writing. Proofread your paper to make sure you have used commas correctly.

MECHANICS

Interrupters

30k. Use commas to set off an expression that interrupts a sentence.

Use two commas to set off an expression unless the expression comes first or last in the sentence.

(1) Appositives and appositive phrases are usually set off by commas.

An appositive is a word—with or without modifiers—that is set beside a noun or pronoun and identifies or explains it. An appositive phrase consists of an appositive and its modifiers.

EXAMPLE   An interview with Florence Cohen, **the noted landscape architect,** will appear Sunday in the *Herald*, **our local paper.**

When an appositive is so closely related to the word it modifies that it appears to be part of that word, no comma is necessary. An appositive of this kind is called a restrictive appositive. Usually it is one word.

EXAMPLES   Her cousin **Rita**

The novel *Arrowsmith*

The preposition *with*

(2) Words used in direct address are set off by commas.

EXAMPLES   Do you know, **Lena,** where your brother is?

Jerry, please see about this.

You seem upset, **my friend.**

(3) Parenthetical expressions are set off by commas.

The following expressions are commonly used parenthetically: *I believe (think, know, hope,* etc.), *I am sure, on the contrary, on the other hand, after all, by the way, incidentally, in fact, indeed, naturally, of course, in my opinion, for example, however, nevertheless,* and *to tell the truth.*

EXAMPLES   The train will, **I am sure,** be on time.

On the contrary, exercise is relaxing.

That clever Jameson was the first to solve the puzzle, **naturally.**

Knowledge of this rule and of the expressions commonly used parenthetically is helpful in punctuating, but in many instances your intention is what determines the punctuation that you use. If you want the reader to pause, to regard an expression as parenthetical, set it off; if not, leave it unpunctuated. Sometimes, however, the placement of the expression in the sentence determines the punctuation.

EXAMPLES   That is **indeed** startling news. [no pause]

That is**,** **indeed,** startling news. [pause]

Indeed, that is startling news. [comma required by placement]

I hope this report will help clarify the situation for you. [no comma because of placement]

This report will**,** **I hope,** help clarify the situation for you. [comma required by placement]

EXERCISE 6. Correcting Sentences by Adding Commas. The following exercise covers all comma rules to this point in the chapter. Number your paper 1–10. After the proper number, write the words in each sentence that should be followed by a comma, placing a comma after each word. Write *C* if the item is correct.

1. The plot of that book a murder mystery is in my opinion far too complicated.
2. Polish workers however did not seem to agree with government labor policies for many tried to organize their own trade unions.
3. The nineteenth-century book *El Jíbaro* which was written by Manuel A. Alonso is considered the first Puerto Rican classic.
4. If you quickly get your application in our office will be able to process it before the deadline which is this afternoon.
5. Please understand friends that as much as I would like to I cannot be at the picnic the game and the track meet at the same time.
6. The people riding in the front of the roller coaster were the ones who screamed the most loudly.
7. Looking for economical transportation Harry who had never bought a car before nervously scouted the possibilities at Country Motors which sells used sedans station wagons and pickup trucks.
8. In spite of an initial lack of support Armanda and Julie who were very determined continued their campaign to clean up the vacant lots a task they admitted would take some time.
9. Before you start putting that jigsaw puzzle together Rosa I hope you are sure that it will when completed fit on the table.
10. When Jamie had finished the chicken and potatoes were all gone and the beans carrots and salad had been left untouched.

WRITING APPLICATION B:
Using Commas to Make Your Writing Clear

Like blinking yellow lights at an intersection, the commas before and after certain parenthetical expressions signal the reader to prepare for a change—in this case, a change in the direction of the writer's presentation. Notice in the following example how the commas that set off the parenthetical expression *however* prepare you for the information in the second sentence.

EXAMPLE   Leontyne Price's world-famous soprano voice was still powerful and still drew capacity crowds. In 1985, however, she decided to end her operatic career.

Writing Assignment

Write a composition discussing the advantages and disadvantages of the college you will attend or the job you will look for after you graduate from high school. Proofread your paper carefully to make sure you have used commas correctly with parenthetical expressions.

Conventional Uses

30l. Use a comma in certain conventional situations.

(1) Use a comma to separate items in dates and addresses.

EXAMPLES   Hawaii achieved statehood on August 21, 1959, becoming the fiftieth state.

Write to me at 423 Twentieth Street, Salt Lake City, UT 84101, after the first of May. [*Two-letter postal abbreviation used with ZIP code. There is no comma between the state and ZIP code.*]

EXAMPLES   Their twins were born on Saturday, March 6, 1982, in Detroit, Michigan.

☞ NOTE   When only the month and day or only the month and year are given, no punctuation is necessary.

EXAMPLES   It was on June 20 that we began rehearsals.
A severe storm hit much of western Europe in January 1985.

MECHANICS

When the items are joined by a preposition, do not use commas.

EXAMPLE   Joanna lives at 301 Green Street in San Diego, California.

(2) Use a comma after the salutation of a friendly letter and after the closing of any letter.

EXAMPLES   Dear Angela,   Sincerely yours,

(3) Use a comma after a name followed by *Jr., Sr., Ph.D., etc.*

EXAMPLES   Peter Grundel, Jr.   Lorraine Henson, Ph.D.

> ☞ NOTE   If these abbreviations are used within a sentence, they are followed by a comma as well:
> Hazel Sellers, M.D., will be the guest speaker.

Unnecessary Commas

30m. Do not use unnecessary commas.

The tendency of modern writers is to use commas sparingly. You should be able to show either that the commas you use help the reader to understand what you have written or that they are required by standard usage—as in a date or address, for example. Unnecessary commas are just as confusing to the reader as the absence of necessary ones.

REVIEW EXERCISE. Correcting Sentences by Adding End Marks and Commas.   This exercise covers end marks and all comma uses. Rewrite the sentences so that they are punctuated correctly.

1. Stalled in the traffic jam the motorcyclists Carl and Lou who were on their way home settled in to wait.
2. According to that book the history of fine arts is divided into the following periods: classical medieval renaissance baroque neoclassical and modern.
3. Our apartment at 310 Columbia Avenue Fort Wayne Indiana was cozy but I also enjoyed living at 2125 West Third Street in Omaha Nebraska.

MECHANICS

4. Jay Carson Jr a senior with good organizational skills arranged for the benefit concert setting the date and ticket sales hiring the musical talent and handling the publicity.

5. In 1936 the library staff at the *Tribune* began recording the newspaper on microfilm and now the library has microfilm copies of every issue from October 14 1858 up to the most recent one.

6. When Jolene who was taking her road test got behind the wheel her mother smiling proudly looked on attentively.

7. On the spur of the moment Lily who was known for her thoughtfulness decided against going to the party and went instead to see Jan her friend who had been hospitalized with appendicitis.

8. As the students watched Dr. Stanford an expert in distillation and a widely published author was demonstrating how to set up the special separation process explaining each step carefully.

9. Our company which we started as high-school seniors can provide all types of home office and factory cleaning services.

10. How disappointed we were to find that our research papers on which we had worked for weeks had been destroyed in the school fire, and Ms Harper had not even had a chance to read them

11. When the doctor informed me that on the one hand only a very small percentage of people suffer a bad reaction to the vaccine and that on the other hand the disease it prevents is nearly always fatal what could I do but agree to have the shot

12. In an address delivered on Tuesday August 3 in Phoenix Arizona she said that the way to peace is through international economic cooperation political understanding and disarmament.

13. Having found a good home the scrawny undernourished kitten had grown into a cat that was small but glossy and beautiful.

14. At the edge of the deep woods along the shore of Goose Lake they made camp for the night.

15. Well if I had wanted to go I would have said so.

16. Surprisingly the secondhand clothes were not torn or dirty or out of style.

17. Why I think it's remarkable that you have already completed the project for the others started before you did

18. The island of Tierra del Fuego named the Land of Fire by the explorer Ferdinand Magellan because of its many Indian bonfires lies off the southern tip of South America in a cold windy climate.

19. Benjamin Banneker a noted inventor astronomer and mathematician served on the commission that surveyed and laid out Washington DC

20. I beg your pardon sir but do I know you

CHAPTER 30 REVIEW: POSTTEST

Correcting Sentences by Adding or Deleting End Marks and Commas. Number your paper 1–25. Most of the following sentences contain errors in the use of end marks or commas. After the proper number, write all words that are followed by incorrect punctuation, adding or deleting end marks and commas in accordance with the standards of written English. If a sentence is correct, write *C*.

EXAMPLE 1. My best friend has moved to 712, Mills Avenue, Orlando, FL 32806.
   1. 712

1. Marilyn and Antonio who work at a local child care center greatly enjoy inventing, and playing games with the children.
2. Unfolding solar panels placing satellites into orbit and conducting medical experiments kept the space shuttle crew busy and interested throughout their space flight.
3. Because we had to rekindle the fire our cookout was delayed.
4. Well if you want to apply for admission to eight colleges you will surely have to pay a large sum in application fees.
5. On the beaches of Louisiana Florida and Georgia this has been a summer of boating fishing and swimming.
6. "It is my pleasure to introduce Cranston Fellows Jr. who has recently returned from a visit to Sydney Australia," said Adele Peters president of the Students' Foreign Exchange League.
7. The diplomats both educated at American University in Washington DC received posts in Athens Greece and Nicosia Cyprus.
8. "The house is on fire" shouted my father. "Everyone out."
9. On the far wall to the right of the main entrance you will see a striking oil painting done in matte black, neutral gray and ash white.
10. "November 30 will be the deadline for submitting outlines note cards and thesis paragraphs for your papers," said Ms. Walsh.

11. Coming home from the football game we were delighted to be greeted by the fragrant spicy aroma of Ned's spaghetti sauce.

12. Studying *Beowulf* for the first time the class enjoyed Grendel the grim gruesome monster.

13. The treasurer's report did I believe make it clear that the Senior Class has been very successful in its fund-raising activities this year.

14. Interrupting his friends Philip asked, "Are you ready to leave"?

15. My aunt and uncle who have been married for twenty-five years plan to visit Egypt Kenya and Sierra Leone next October.

16. Joanne moaned, "Oh this weather is terrible"!

17. We spent the morning cleaning the basement and sorting boxes but in the afternoon we rode our bicycles along lovely country roads.

18. This is an emergency; I need to see a doctor immediately.

19. Naturally the seafood that I like best lobster is also the most expensive.

20. "Mr. President" said the Secretary of State "here is the preliminary draft of the treaty"

21. We have already decided to hold our class reunion on July 4 2008 at the Hyatt Regency Hotel in San Francisco California.

22. Professor Dimitri Pantermalis a Greek archaeologist recently announced the excavation of a rare mosaic dating from the second century AD when Greece was under Roman rule.

23. Much to my delight the festival offered jazz country rock and classical music.

24. Using hyperbole the store took out a full-page newspaper ad reading "World's Most Spectacular Labor Day Sale"!

25. When they went to the prom Martha wore a white lace gown and George wore a light blue tuxedo.

MECHANICS

SUMMARY OF USES OF END MARKS AND COMMAS

30 a. Use a period at the end of a statement.

30 b. Use periods with abbreviations.

30 c. Use a question mark at the end of a question.

30 d. Use an exclamation point at the end of an exclamatory sentence.

30 e. Use either a period or an exclamation point at the end of an imperative sentence, depending on the force intended.

30 f. Use commas to separate items in a series.

30 g. Use a comma to separate two or more adjectives preceding a noun.

30 h. Use a comma before *and, but, or, nor, for, so,* and *yet* when they join independent clauses, unless they are very short.

30 i. Use commas to set off nonessential clauses and nonessential participial phrases.

30 j. Use a comma after certain introductory elements.
    (1) After words such as *well, yes, no, why,* etc., when they begin a sentence
    (2) After an introductory participial phrase
    (3) After a succession of introductory prepositional phrases
    (4) After an introductory adverb clause

30 k. Use commas to set off expressions that interrupt the sentence.
    (1) Appositives
    (2) Words in direct address
    (3) Parenthetical expressions

30 l. Use a comma in certain conventional situations.
    (1) To separate items in dates and addresses
    (2) After the salutation of a friendly letter
    (3) After a name followed by *Jr., Sr., Ph.D.,* etc.

30m. Do not use unnecessary commas.

MECHANICS

Punctuation

OTHER MARKS OF PUNCTUATION

Although the marks of punctuation treated in this chapter are used less frequently than the period and comma, they are often important. Just as you have learned to follow certain conventions in grammar and usage and spelling, you should observe the conventional uses of the punctuation marks described in this chapter.

DIAGNOSTIC TEST

Correctly Using Punctuation Marks Other Than End Marks and Commas. Number your paper 1–20. Each of the following sentences contains an error in punctuation. Proofread each sentence, and, after the proper number, write as much of the sentence as is necessary to correct the punctuation.

EXAMPLE 1. Looking at Paulas pictures of our Senior Class trip, we felt as though we were back in Washington, D.C.
    1. *Paula's*

1. Labor Day traffic was rerouted from the washed-out bridge consequently, a massive backup of cars developed.
2. Who is your favorite mystery writer on the following list, Agatha Christie, P. D. James, Wilkie Collins, or Edgar Allan Poe?

3. One of my favorite Biblical passages is the story of Jesus and the Samaritan woman in John 4-5.

4. Since Lydia visited Europe last summer, she has been using foreign expressions such as bonjour and ciao constantly.

5. The class judged the commercials to have little appeal for teenagers or adults, that is, they considered the ads suitable only for children younger than thirteen.

6. "How long will it take for the pictures of the class play to be developed"? I asked.

7. Our English class agreed that Richard Connell's short story The Most Dangerous Game is one of the best we have ever read.

8. The confusion occurred because I thought the gift was your's instead of Dorothy's.

9. "Because we have recorded a twenty three percent increase in productivity," stated the factory owner to his employees, "each of you will receive a bonus in your next paycheck."

10. Its anyone's guess who will win the election for student council officers next week.

11. Please turn down the radio I'm getting a headache from the vibrations.

12. Outstandingly successful people, whether they excel in politics, sports, or the arts, share a common trait: they are self motivated.

13. We might and according to the tour schedule should have a free afternoon in Rome.

14. Juanita asked the librarian for: the *Readers' Guide to Periodical Literature* and the latest *World Almanac*.

15. According to my sister, a college sophomore, her sociology professor expects his students to read "The New York Times" each day before attending class.

16. When we finish school at 2-15, I'll drive you home.

17. "You may not realize that auto mechanics are skilled specialists", said Mr. Busch on our first day in Auto Mechanics I.

18. Because I have spent so many happy times there, I love to visit my grandmother's and grandfather's house.

19. "The second string team will begin practice as soon as the varsity players have left the field," announced Coach Carberry.

20. Since I am on a tight budget, I was glad to see the ad announcing a special sale on mens' jeans.

MECHANICS

THE SEMICOLON

31a. Use a semicolon between independent clauses not joined by *and, but, or, nor, for, yet,* or *so.*

EXAMPLES   Three candidates have filed for the new commission seat; none of them have any previous experience in public office.

Read all the choices; don't write the first answer that seems correct.

You must have some basis for deciding whether to express two independent clauses with a semicolon between them, or two sentences with a period (and capital letter). In most writing, the division into sentences is preferable. A semicolon is used only when the ideas in the two clauses are so closely related that a period would make too distinct a break between them.

31b. Use a semicolon between independent clauses joined by such words as *for example, for instance, that is, besides, accordingly, moreover, nevertheless, furthermore, otherwise, therefore, however, consequently, instead,* or *hence.*

EXAMPLES   Everyone in this area takes visitors to our local tourist attraction; **for instance,** I went there just last Sunday with my visiting aunt.

The speech was long and repetitious; **consequently,** listeners fidgeted in their seats and whispered among themselves.

When the connectives mentioned in this rule are placed at the beginning of a clause, the use of a comma after them is frequently a matter of taste. When they are clearly parenthetical (interrupters), they are followed by a comma. The words *for example, for instance,* and *that is* are always followed by a comma. The word *however* is almost always followed by a comma.

EXAMPLES   Leaders of the two countries saw no hope for a settlement; **that is,** each claimed the other was stubborn and unwilling to compromise.

Leaders of the two countries saw no hope for a settlement; **however,** they were willing to meet again. [. . . they were willing, *however,* to meet again.]

Most of the words listed in this rule, however, are rarely used at the beginning of a clause. They are usually placed later in the clause.

EXAMPLE   The situation is intolerable; we **therefore** need to take immediate action.

31c. A semicolon (rather than a comma) may be needed to separate independent clauses joined by a coordinating conjunction when there are commas within the clauses.

EXAMPLE   Super Stop, the store on Falk Avenue, sells not only groceries but also prescription drugs, cosmetics, hardware, garden supplies, and sportswear; and its first shoppers, interviewed on the news last week, seemed very pleased with the convenience the store offers.

> ☞ NOTE   As suggested in Rule 31c by the words "may be needed," you are allowed considerable leeway in applying this rule. When there are only one or two commas in the independent clauses, the semicolon is not needed. It is required when there are so many commas, as in the example above, that the sentence would be confusing without the semicolon.

31d. Use a semicolon between items in a series if the items contain commas.

EXAMPLE   Winners in the competition were Alene Murphy, first place; Jeff Bates, second place; Ed Davis, third place; and Nancy Green, who, as a member of the Student Council, had proposed the contest.

WRITING APPLICATION A:
Using Semicolons to Make Your Writing Clear

Determining the amount of information to include in a single sentence is an important part of writing clearly. You can help your reader understand that ideas are closely related by using semicolons to join independent clauses. In the following example the semicolon links two independent clauses, signaling the reader that the ideas are closely related:

EXAMPLE   I am much more tolerant than I used to be; for example, my little brother's teasing no longer bothers me.

Writing Assignment

Write a composition comparing and contrasting yourself as you are now—not just physically, but intellectually and emotionally—and as you were three years ago. Proofread it carefully to make sure you have used semicolons correctly to join independent clauses expressing closely related ideas.

MECHANICS

THE COLON

31e. Use a colon to mean "note what follows."

(1) Use a colon before a list of items, especially after expressions like *as follows* and *the following.*

EXAMPLES Amazingly enough, the small bag held everything: shirts, pants, sweaters, a jacket, shoes, underwear, nightclothes, toiletries, and a present for my hosts.

Be prepared to answer the following questions: What was your last job? Why did you leave it? What other experience have you had? [list introduced by "the following"]

☞ NOTE When a list constitutes the direct object of a verb or the object of a preposition, do not use a colon.

EXAMPLES We **collected** blankets, canned goods, medical supplies, and clothing for the flood victims. [list is direct object]

Dan has always been interested **in** snakes, frogs, lizards, and other reptiles. [list is object of preposition *in*]

(2) Use a colon before a long, formal statement or quotation.

EXAMPLE Dr. Stafford made the following observation: Cooperation between the leading nations of the world is essential to the survival of the planet. [Note that a formal statement of this kind need not be enclosed in quotation marks.]

(3) Use a colon between independent clauses when the second clause explains or restates the idea in the first.

EXAMPLE Those hanging lamps are the most popular kind: they are inexpensive, come in many colors, and are easy to install.

31f. Use a colon in certain conventional situations.

(1) Use a colon between the hour and the minute when you write the time.

EXAMPLE 8:00 A.M.

(2) Use a colon between chapter and verse in referring to passages from the Bible.

EXAMPLE Proverbs 3**:**3

(3) Use a colon between volume and number or between volume and page number of a periodical.

EXAMPLES *Harper's* 203**:**16 [volume and number]
Harper's 203**:**16-19 [volume and page numbers]

(4) Use a colon after the salutation of a business letter.

EXAMPLES Dear Ms. Ayala**:**   Gentlemen**:**   Dear Sir or Madam**:**

WRITING APPLICATION B:
Using Colons Correctly to Make Your Writing Clear

Since the semicolon and the colon serve completely different purposes, it is important to distinguish between them in your writing. Your reader relies on these marks to know whether to expect, for example, an independent clause closely related to the preceding one (after a semicolon) or a list (after a colon). In the first example, below, the misuse of a semicolon for a colon is misleading.

EXAMPLES Three committees were set up for the banquet**;** awards, decorations, and food.
Three committees were set up for the banquet**:** awards, decorations, and food.

Writing Assignment

You are serving on the awards committee for a banquet to honor outstanding writers in the senior class. Decide what kind of awards to present and how many, and write a letter ordering the items. Proofread it carefully to make sure that you have used colons correctly.

UNDERLINING (ITALICS)

31g. Use underlining (italics) for titles of books, films, plays, television programs, periodicals, works of art, ships, etc.

MECHANICS

EXAMPLES   The Old Man and the Sea

the San Diego Tribune, or the San Diego Tribune

the Senior Scholastic

the View of Toledo, Appalachian Spring, The Thinker

the Norway, the Garden State Special, the Columbia

The use of quotation marks for titles is now generally limited to short compositions such as short stories, short poems, parts of publications and episodes of television programs; the titles of the publications and television programs themselves are underlined. (Compare page 668.)

EXAMPLE   Read Chapter 39, "Americans in the Second World War (1941–1945)," from Rise of the American Nation.

☞ NOTE   When set in type, underlined words are italicized.
The Old Man and the Sea   the *Senior Scholastic*

The words *a, an, the,* written before a title, are underlined only when they are part of the title. Before the names of magazines and newspapers, they are not underlined.

EXAMPLE   I found some good ideas for my paper in my text, The History of the Americas, and in several back issues of the New York Times.

31h. Use underlining (italics) for words, letters, and figures referred to as such and for foreign words not yet adopted into English.

EXAMPLES   The most common English word is the; the letters used most frequently are e and t; and numbers often confused are 7 and 9.

I know the Latin phrase ab initio—it reminds me of all the setbacks I've ever had—but the saying ad astra per aspera gives me hope.

EXERCISE 1. Using Colons, Semicolons, and Italics Correctly. Number your paper 1–10. After the proper number, write the words and numbers that should be followed by a semicolon or a colon, and write the appropriate punctuation after each. Write and underline all words that should be italicized.

1. From 1970 to 1981, one-parent families doubled in number however, two-parent families in 1981 still comprised nearly 80 percent of families with children.

2. Performers in the show included the following band members playing two instruments apiece Tony Fleming, trumpet and trombone Donna Bryant, clarinet and saxophone and Phyllis Ward, drums and steel guitar.

3. Our local paper, the Morning Ledger, always carries these features comics, advice columns, and a crossword puzzle.

4. Interesting stories are plentiful in the Bible two of my favorites are the battle between David and Goliath in I Samuel 17 4–57 and the story of the good Samaritan in Luke 10 25–37.

5. Groups of art students, all going to see Egyptian, Assyrian, and Greek exhibits, boarded the buses at 8 30 but the buses did not leave until 9 00, when the parking lot was finally cleared and the last stragglers had boarded.

6. Ms. Bell often assigns reading in current magazines for instance, our latest one runs as follows The Atlantic, 218 33–44 U.S. News and World Report, 26 5 Changing Times, 8 62–67.

7. According to historians, Michelangelo always thought of himself first as a sculptor his sculpture the Pietà is the only work he ever signed.

8. She revised her report three times first, for content second, for organization and third, for style.

9. Legislators were in a difficult position they had to finance demand for increased services without calling for increased taxes.

10. While downtown, I bought several gifts a cookbook for my father a print of Rousseau's The Jungle for my mother and for my sister, the album featuring the soundtrack of Annie.

QUOTATION MARKS

31i. Use quotation marks to enclose a direct quotation—a person's exact words.

DIRECT QUOTATION   My sister said, "My favorite singer is Lena Horne."

Do not use quotation marks to enclose an indirect quotation—one that does not give a person's exact words.

INDIRECT QUOTATION   My sister said her favorite singer is Lena Horne.

Enclose means to place quotation marks at both the beginning and the end of a quotation. Omission of quotation marks at the end of a quotation is a common error.

(1) A direct quotation begins with a capital letter.

EXAMPLE   She told me, "Finish this assignment first."

Exception: If the quotation is only a fragment of a sentence, do not begin it with a capital letter:

EXAMPLE   A reviewer called the movie "**a** futile attempt to trade on his reputation as a maker of blockbusters."

(2) When a quoted sentence is divided into two parts by an interrupting expression such as *he said* or *Mother asked,* the second part begins with a small letter.

EXAMPLE   "Take care," he warned, "**t**hat you don't spill anything."

If the second part of a divided quotation is a new sentence, it begins with a capital letter.

EXAMPLE   "Don't open the door," he pleaded. "**W**e're developing the film."

(3) A direct quotation is set off from the rest of the sentence by commas or by a question mark or an exclamation point.

EXAMPLES   Flo said**,** **"**We could send them a telegram."

"What would you say to that**?"** she asked.

> ☞ NOTE   If the quotation is only a phrase, do not set it off by commas.

EXAMPLE   For him, **"**one for all and all for one**"** is the key to a successful club.

(4) Other marks of punctuation, when used with quotation marks, are placed according to the following rules:

   1. *Commas and periods are always placed inside the closing quotation marks.*

EXAMPLE   **"**I'm sure**,"** said Joe, **"**that we'll be finished by Friday.**"**

2. *Semicolons and colons are always placed outside the closing quotation marks.*

EXAMPLES "Eva," my grandmother said, "you should keep up with your chores"; then she reminded me that it was my turn to wash the dishes.

Gail Sloan describes the following as "deserted-island reading": *An Encyclopedia of World History,* the complete works of Shakespeare, and *Robinson Crusoe.*

3. *Question marks and exclamation points are placed inside the closing quotation marks if the quotation itself is a question or an exclamation; otherwise they are placed outside.*

EXAMPLES "Is everyone present?" asked the teacher.

"How perceptive you are sometimes!" she exclaimed.

Were you surprised when he said, "You win"?

Stop saying "You know"!

No more than one comma or one end mark is used at the end of a quotation.

INCORRECT Who said, "No one can make you feel inferior without your consent."? [two end marks, period and question mark]

CORRECT Who said, "No one can make you feel inferior without your consent"?

INCORRECT Did you ever ask yourself, "Where will I be ten years from now?"?

CORRECT Did you ever ask yourself, "Where will I be ten years from now?"

(5) When you write dialogue, begin a new paragraph every time the speaker changes.

EXAMPLE "Hi, guys. Look what I just got!" said Jessie as she came up to her friends Mark and Sue. She was cradling a sophisticated new 35mm camera in her hands.

"That's beautiful!" said Sue.

Raising his eyebrows, Mark said, "Where did you get it?"

"Oh, I got a great deal at the camera shop—and a loan from my mother."

"How," they both asked at once, "will you pay her back?"

"Well, I have my part-time job," said Jessie. "I'm also going to take pictures for people—at a modest price, of course. Say," she added, "wouldn't you two like to have your pictures taken?"

MECHANICS

(6) When a quoted passage consists of more than one paragraph, place quotation marks at the beginning of each paragraph and at the end of the entire passage, not at the end of each paragraph.

> ☞ NOTE   Usually such a long quotation is set off from the rest of the paper by indentation and single spacing. In such a case, no quotation marks are necessary.

(7) Use single quotation marks to enclose a quotation within a quotation.

EXAMPLE   What she said was, "For Tuesday read Masefield's poem 'Sea Fever.' "

31j. Use quotation marks to enclose titles of short works such as poems, short stories, articles, songs, and individual episodes of television programs; and of chapters and other parts of books.

EXAMPLE   Read Chapter 19, "The Progressive Movement."
My favorite episode of *Star Trek* is "The Trouble with Tribbles."

> ☞ NOTE   Book titles and names of magazines are indicated by underlining (italics) (see page 663).

31k. Use quotation marks to enclose slang words, technical terms, and other expressions that are unusual in standard English.

Use this device sparingly.

EXAMPLES   I don't think he is a "nerd."

The names Kansas and Arkansas are derived from the Sioux Indian word for "downstream people."

EXERCISE 2. Using Punctuation Marks Correctly.   Rewrite the following sentences, inserting quotation marks, other required punctuation, and capitalization.

1. How many of you Mrs. Martinez asked have studied a foreign language for more than two years.
2. Nice try Donna was what the coach said.
3. We should have started our homework earlier said Beth we have answered only three questions so far.

4. Where have you been she asked.

5. Someone once asked George Bernard Shaw how old he was, and he answered I'm as old as my tongue and a few years older than my teeth.

6. To whom was Stendhal referring asked Mrs. Ross when he dedicated his novels to the happy few.

7. Was it Elizabeth Browning asked Sandra who wrote the poem Shall I Compare Thee to a Summer's Day?

8. Cast off shouted the captain we're bound for Rio.

9. Would you let us hand in our research papers next week Ms. Lewis we asked none of the books we need are in the library.

10. Alice whispered thank you for lending me the article Is There Life on Other Planets?

THE APOSTROPHE

31l. To form the possessive case of a singular noun, add an apostrophe and an *s*.

EXAMPLES   Dora's choice   Kelly's coat   Ross's sleeve

In words of more than one syllable that end in an *s*-sound, it is permissible to form the singular possessive by adding the apostrophe without the *s*. This is done to avoid too many *s*-sounds.

EXAMPLES   the seamstress' work   Odysseus' travels

> ☞ NOTE   Since the use of the apostrophe varies among writers, it is not possible to make a hard and fast rule about the apostrophe in singular words ending in *s*. Thus *Hughes' poetry* and *Hughes's poetry* are equally acceptable. Punctuate according to pronunciation. If you say a word as "Hugheses" or "McCullerses," write "Hughes's" and "McCullers's." If you say "Hughes" poems or "McCullers" novels, write "Hughes'" and "McCullers'."

(1) To form the possessive case of a plural noun ending in *s*, add only the apostrophe.

EXAMPLES   girls' team   the Millses' back yard

MECHANICS

> ☞ NOTE   The few plural nouns that do not end in *s* form the possessive by adding the apostrophe and an *s* just as singular nouns do.

EXAMPLES   women's tournament
children's playground

(2) Personal pronouns in the possessive case (*his, hers, its, ours, yours, theirs,* and the relative pronoun *whose*) do not require an apostrophe.

INCORRECT   We thought the top score was her's.
CORRECT   We thought the top score was **hers.**

INCORRECT   I have witnessed democracy at it's best.
CORRECT   I have witnessed democracy at **its** best.

INCORRECT   Who's notebook is this?
CORRECT   **Whose** notebook is this?

(3) Indefinite pronouns (*one, everyone, everybody,* etc.) in the possessive case require an apostrophe and an *s*.[1]

EXAMPLES   **Everyone's** vote counts equally.
She consented to **everybody's** request for a class meeting.

EXERCISE 3. **Proofreading Possessives.**   Number your paper 1–20. If the possessive case for each item in the list has been correctly formed, write *C* after the proper number. If it has been incorrectly formed, write the correct form.

1. everyone's share
2. bus' windows
3. children's books
4. this school's reputation
5. pants' cuffs
6. Is this your's?
7. a girl's or a boy's bike
8. opened it's covers
9. flower's bud
10. The loss is our's.
11. a street of lawyer's offices
12. at the Gibb's home
13. that nation's debts
14. women's objections
15. found it's way home
16. travelers' briefcases
17. soldiers knapsacks
18. did its best
19. babie's toys
20. the poets' works

[1] Note the correct form of such words used with *else: everyone else's; somebody else's.* Note that there is no apostrophe in *oneself.*

MECHANICS

(4) In hyphenated words, names of organizations and business firms, and words showing joint possession, only the last word is possessive in form.

HYPHENATED   **father-in-law's** hobby

ORGANIZATIONS   The **Economic and Social Council's** members
                   Black and Decker's tools

JOINT POSSESSION   **Dotty and Fay's** report

Exception: When the second word is a possessive pronoun, the first word is also possessive.

INCORRECT   Dotty and my report
CORRECT   **Dotty's and my** report

(5) When two or more persons possess something individually, each of their names is possessive in form.

EXAMPLE   **Tom's** and **Bill's** jackets

(6) The words *minute, hour, day, week, month, year,* **etc., when used as possessive adjectives, require an apostrophe. Words indicating an amount in cents or dollars, when used as possessive adjectives, require apostrophes.**

EXAMPLES   a minute's work, five minutes' work

            a day's rest, three days' rest[1]

            one cent's worth, five cents' worth

EXERCISE 4. Revising Phrases by Forming Possessives. In the following list, the possessive relationship is expressed by means of a phrase. Revise each item so that the possessive case of the noun or pronoun is used to express the same relationship.

EXAMPLE   1. a vacation of two weeks
               1. *a two weeks' vacation*

1. hats of Carol and Pat
2. dressing room of the men
3. job of my sister-in-law
4. character of a person
5. business of Jorge and Ralph
6. speech of the governor-elect
7. a pause of a moment
8. worth of two cents
9. highlights of the film
10. shoes of the women
11. insignia of the sergeant-at-arms

[1] Also correct: a three-day rest, etc.

MECHANICS

12. worth of four dollars
13. catalog of Lord and Taylor
14. prize of Ralph Bunche
15. sides of it
16. remarks of the judges

17. trip of Maria and Alma
18. a wait of an hour
19. heat of the sun
20. albums of Simon and Garfunkel

31m. Use an apostrophe to show where letters have been omitted in a contraction.

A contraction is a word made up of two words combined into one by the omission of one or more letters.

EXAMPLES For *do not,* the contraction is *don't.* [The letter *o* is omitted.]
For *it is,* the contraction is *it's.* [The letter *i* is omitted.]
For *they are,* the contraction is *they're.* [The letter *a* is omitted.]

☞ NOTE The most common error in the use of the apostrophe comes from the confusion of *it's,* which means *it is,* with the possessive form *its* (*its* appearance). Another common error is the insertion of the apostrophe in the wrong place: *does'nt* for *doesn't,* etc. Also note that *let's* in an expression such as "Let's go!" is a contraction of *let us* and requires an apostrophe.

31n. Use the apostrophe and *s* to form the plurals of letters, numbers, and signs, and of words referred to as words.

EXAMPLES *Hawaii* is spelled with two *i*'s.
He correctly placed the decimal before the two *6*'s.
Don't you need +'s in that equation?
Try not to use so many *very*'s in your writing.

EXERCISE 5. Proofreading Possessives and Contractions and Revising Phrases by Forming Possessives.
Number your paper 1–20. Write the following phrases and sentences, inserting apostrophes where they are needed and changing the phrases to possessive forms. If an item is correct, write *C.*

1. womens sports
2. statements of a mayor-elect
3. Its great, isn't it?
4. sand in its gears
5. Its still early, Im sure.

6. If he lets us, well go too.
7. Her cousins choices were the same as hers.
8. Lets see whats going on.
9. I've found its no help.

MECHANICS

10. firm of Dun and Bradstreet
11. Whats its title?
12. on a minutes notice
13. locker of Frank and Carlos
14. Whos on Vickys bicycle?
15. this pianos keys
16. How many *is* are there in *Mississippi*?
17. childrens magazine
18. Her scores were a 9.0 and two 8.5s in the freestyle event.
19. books of Woodward and Bernstein
20. office of the principal

THE HYPHEN

31o. Use a hyphen to divide a word at the end of a line.

Try to avoid dividing words at the end of a line in order to maintain an even margin unless it is necessary. For rules that will help you in deciding where to place the hyphen, see page 33.

31p. Use a hyphen with compound numbers from *twenty-one* to *ninety-nine* and with fractions used as adjectives.

EXAMPLES **forty-two** applicants
a **two-thirds** majority, *but* **two thirds** of the voters

31q. Use a hyphen with the prefixes *ex-, self-, all-;* with the suffix *-elect;* and with all prefixes before a proper noun or proper adjective.

EXAMPLES   ex-mayor   non-European
               self-controlled   anti-Fascist
               all-star   pro-Canadian
               president-elect   Pan-American

Variant spellings exist (*reelect, re-elect, reëlect*), but the modern tendency is to close up most other prefixes (*reelect*).

31r. Hyphenate a compound adjective when it precedes the word it modifies.

EXAMPLE   well-liked author   The author is well liked.

> ☞ NOTE   Do not use a hyphen if one of the modifiers is an adverb ending in *-ly*.

MECHANICS

EXAMPLES   highly polished surface   quickly done task

31s. Use a hyphen to prevent confusion or awkwardness.

EXAMPLES   re-collect [prevents confusion with *recollect*]
anti-icer [avoids the awkwardness of *antiicer*]

THE DASH

31t. Use a dash to indicate an abrupt break in thought.

EXAMPLES   He might—if I have anything to say about it—change his mind.

The truth is—and you probably already know it—we can't do it without you.

31u. Use a dash to mean *namely, in other words,* or *that is* before an explanation.

EXAMPLE   It was a close call—the sudden gust of wind pushed the helicopter to within inches of the power line. [The dash means *that is.*]

In this use, the colon and the dash are frequently interchangeable.

EXAMPLE   It was a close call: the sudden gust of wind pushed the helicopter to within inches of the power line.

PARENTHESES

31v. Use parentheses to enclose incidental explanatory matter that is added to a sentence but is not considered of major importance.

EXAMPLE   Former Representative Jordan (Texas) was on that committee.

The population of the United States is shifting (see Chart B) to the South and the Southwest.

> ☞ NOTE   Commas, dashes, and parentheses are frequently used interchangeably to set off incidental matter.

(1) Be sure that any material within parentheses can be omitted without changing the basic meaning or structure of the sentence.

IMPROPER USE OF PARENTHESES   Tina had been shopping (in that store) most of her life. [The idea in parentheses is too important to the meaning of the sentence to be placed in parentheses.]

(2) Punctuation marks are used within parentheses when they belong with the parenthetical matter. Punctuation marks that belong with the main part of the sentence are placed after a closing parenthesis.

EXAMPLES   Fred Bates asked us (What a silly question!) if we really thought we could do it.

If the committee is headed by Alison (Is she here?), the student council will probably support it.

BRACKETS

You will seldom have a use for brackets. Commas, dashes, and parentheses are preferable as means of setting off parenthetical matter.

31w. Use brackets to enclose explanations within parentheses or in quoted material when the explanation is not part of the quotation.

EXAMPLES   Ms. Gray was quoted as saying in her acceptance speech: "I am honored by it [the award], but I would like to share the recognition with those who made my work possible."

By a vote of 5–4, the Supreme Court overturned the lower court's ruling. (See page 149 [Diagram A] for a chronology of the case.)

REVIEW EXERCISE. Proofreading Passages for Punctuation and Capitalization.   Most of the necessary punctuation and capitalization has been omitted from the following passages. Rewrite the passage, proofreading it carefully and preparing a version that uses the conventions of standard English. The only changes you need to make in paragraphing are those required by dialogue. Some of the existing punctuation is incorrect, but in most instances you need only *add* punctuation and capitals.

1

No discussion of Americas outstanding sports figures would be complete without reference to Jim Thorpe who was voted in 1950 the greatest athlete of the centurys first half. His feats in football track and baseball remain unique and his strength and speed are legendary born of irish french and indian heritage and reared in prague oklahoma Thorpe began earning honors early in his life he was an all american halfback for two years while playing for the local indian school and broke all previous records in winning the gold medals for the pentathlon and the decathlon at the 1912 olympic games where he was hailed as the greatest athlete in the world. Because hed already begun playing professional baseball however he was forced to return his medals a year later (They were restored posthumously in 1982) Thorpe spent six outstanding years in professional baseball but he became best known as a football player who could do everything well run pass catch punt and more. He played professional football for over ten years with great ability in 1969 sixteen years after his death and on the national football leagues fiftieth birthday Thorpe was named to footballs all time all professional team.

2

Roger Morton sat back for a moment feeling slightly proud of himself. Have you finished those sample business letters yet asked Ms Zimsky the typing teacher. Yes Roger replied quickly. I think Ive improved on the format too. Look how much space ive saved on each page Ms Zimsky glanced down These arent done the way they are in the book. Just do them that way for now though you need to finish this chapter today or youll be way behind. Theres no time to talk about format. Embarrassed and tired Roger later told his friend Annette about the incident. Your problem she mused isnt that you improved the letters its the same one I had once on my job at bartons shop. I learned that any time you want to change a procedure no matter how great an improvement it is you should first talk it over with the person who will need to approve it. Try discussing your idea again when Ms Zimsky has more time. Roger went back to the typing classroom after school and Ms Zimsky listened thoughtfully to all his suggestions Oh I see what youre doing here she said. Its really a very good idea in fact I think Ill share it with the whole class. See you tomorrow then Roger Yes said Roger with a smile and thanks for listening Ms Zimsky.

CHAPTER 31 REVIEW: POSTTEST

Using Punctuation Correctly.   Number your paper 1–25. Each of the following sentences contains at least one error in the use of punctuation or italics. Rewrite the sentence correctly.

EXAMPLE   1. Why did you let your work go until the last minute asked my friend Tanya when I told her my problem?

   1. *"Why did you let your work go until the last minute?" asked my friend Tanya when I told her my problem.*

1. When I read The Hobbit, my favorite chapter was the one in which Bilbo meets Gollum.
2. Among the members of the Fine Arts Commission meeting in New York City were several talented people Diane Keaton actress Paul McCartney musician Paul Taylor choreographer and Lee Krasner artist.
3. My brothers and sisters and I have been encouraged to be self reliant since we were children.
4. The origin of the bacterial infection see note below and its cure posed a grave puzzle to the medical experts.
5. Shakespeares Hamlet is a popular play because it involves a ghost murder and romance.
6. I believe we will win this game, said the soccer coach to the newspaper sportswriter.
7. Paulette sent in my application before the deadline however she neglected to put a stamp on the envelope.
8. After we had returned from our class trip to Houston, our teacher Ms Ryan said "we were the most well behaved group she had ever chaperoned."
9. When a graduate of our high school appeared on television playing Scott Joplin's Maple Leaf Rag, a new interest in ragtime music blossomed at Franklin High School.
10. "These packages are your's arent they" asked Tamala as she nearly tripped.
11. Although the oil contract had not been renewed, the oil company made a delivery the customers complained when they received the bill.
12. The mayor elect met today with members of the Allentown Youth Council see picture on page 40.
13. When asked her opinion, the president of the brokerage firm said I favor purchasing blue chips those with a history of steady earnings and stable prices.
14. Monicas noisy muffler makes it impossible for her to drive down the street without attracting attention.
15. Suspending students from school for cutting classes creates a Catch-22 situation, said education consultant Cho Yin Lum.
16. In a stunning upset, said the radio announcer the Liberals have defeated the Conservatives!

MECHANICS

17. At Book Lore the bookstore where I work sale's have increased twenty seven percent since last month.
18. Do you know that Europeans write their 7s differently from the way Americans do asked Estrella?
19. Ill never forget the first time I read Walt Whitmans poem When Lilacs Last in the Dooryard Bloom'd said Megan it made me feel the tragedy of Abraham Lincolns death.
20. Have you read this months issue of Seventeen?
21. During the pep rally and even after it had ended the cheerleading captain, Teresa Suarez, led the students in enthusiastic cheering.
22. Within the next three weeks, new television stations will begin broadcasting from the following cities Salinas California Kalamazoo Michigan and Fairbanks Alaska.
23. George Gershwins Rhapsody in Blue is probably the best-known American composition in the world.
24. January 3 is the birthday shared by two world famous writers Cicero and J. R. R. Tolkien.
25. Helena knew it would be a less than perfect day when she heard herself saying Don't forget to dot your ts and cross your is.

CHAPTER 32

Spelling

IMPROVING YOUR SPELLING

This chapter suggests a number of things you can do to improve your spelling:

1. Be careful.
2. Use the dictionary.
3. Keep a list of your own spelling errors.
4. Learn to spell words by syllables.
5. Learn a few helpful spelling rules.
6. Learn to distinguish between words that sound alike.
7. Learn lists of commonly misspelled words.

GOOD SPELLING HABITS

1. *Be careful.* Care in writing and in proofreading your compositions will eliminate errors in the spelling of simple words like *to, there,* and *its,* which account for so many of teachers' corrections on students' themes.

2. *Use the dictionary.* Some students would rather take a chance on guessing than expose themselves to the truth. But the only sure way to find out how to spell a word is to look it up.

3. *Keep a list of your own spelling errors.* We do not all misspell the same words. The habit of recording in your notebook the words you misspell in your compositions will pay you a large return on the investment of a little time and patience.

4. *Learn to spell words by syllables.* This is the "divide and conquer" technique used with success by invading armies. It is equally effective in attacking a long and troublesome word. Dividing a long word into

syllables gives a number of short parts; hence you can simplify your spelling problem by acquiring the habit of dividing words into syllables and spelling them part by part.

Two common causes of spelling mistakes are the omission of a letter or syllable and the addition of an extra letter or syllable. A student who spells *probably* as though it were *probaly* has made the first kind of mistake. If you spell *lightning* as though it were *lightening*, you have made the second kind. Errors like these stem from errors in pronunciation, which, in turn, are the result of not knowing the exact syllables in the word.

EXERCISE 1. Spelling Words by Syllables. Write each of the following words in syllables—place a hyphen between syllables. When you have completed the exercise and studied the words, take a test on them from dictation. Whether your divisions correspond exactly with the dictionary syllabication is not important, provided the words are divided into pronounceable parts and all letters are included and no letters are added.

1. modern
2. similar
3. library
4. surprise
5. athletics
6. disastrous
7. government
8. privilege
9. perspiration
10. boundary
11. candidate
12. equipment
13. recognize
14. business
15. representative
16. entrance
17. accidentally
18. sophomore
19. quiet
20. mischievous

SPELLING RULES

5. *Learn a few helpful spelling rules.* Although some spelling rules are hopelessly complicated, a few are simple enough and important enough to justify the effort required to master them. Study the following rules and apply them whenever possible in your writing.

ie and *ei*

32a. Write *ie* when the sound is *ē,* except after *c.*

EXAMPLES   believe, thief, fierce   ceiling, receive, deceive
EXCEPTIONS   seize, either, weird, leisure, neither

Write *ei* when the sound is not *e*, especially when the sound is *a*.

EXAMPLES   freight, neighbor, weigh, height
EXCEPTIONS   friend, mischief

EXERCISE 2. **Spelling *ie* and *ei* Words.** Write the following words, supplying the missing letters (*e* and *i*) in the correct order. Be able to explain how the rule applies to each.

1. for...gn	6. n...ce	11. sl...gh	16. w...rd
2. br...f	7. c...ling	12. ach...ve	17. rec...pt
3. rel...ve	8. gr...f	13. handkerch...f	18. bel...f
4. conc...ve	9. p...ce	14. perc...ve	19. f...nd
5. v...l	10. retr...ve	15. s...ge	20. l...sure

–cede, –ceed, and –sede

32b. Only one English word ends in *–sede: supersede;* only three words end in *–ceed: exceed, proceed, succeed;* all other words of similar sound end in *–cede.*

EXAMPLES   precede, recede, secede, accede, concede

Adding Prefixes

A *prefix* is one or more than one letter or syllable added to the beginning of a word to change its meaning.

32c. When a prefix is added to a word, the spelling of the word itself remains the same.

il + legal = **il**legal	a + moral = **a**moral
in + elegant = **in**elegant	mis + spell = **mis**spell
im + movable = **im**movable	re + commend = **re**commend
un + necessary = **un**necessary	over + run = **over**run

Adding Suffixes

A *suffix* is one or more than one letter or syllable added to the end of a word to change its meaning.

32d. When the suffixes *–ness* and *–ly* are added to a word, the spelling of the word itself is not changed.

MECHANICS

EXAMPLES   mean + ness = mean**ness**
               final + ly = final**ly**

EXCEPTIONS   Words ending in *y* usually change the *y* to *i* before *–ness* and *–ly:*
               ready—read**ily**; heavy—heav**iness**; happy—happ**iness**. One-
               syllable adjectives ending in *y*, however, generally follow Rule
               32d: dry—dry**ness**; shy—shy**ly**.

EXERCISE 3. Spelling Words with Prefixes and Suffixes. Spell correctly the words indicated.

1. *rate* with the prefix *over*
2. *habitual* with the suffix *ly*
3. *green* with the suffix *ness*
4. *material* with the prefix *im*
5. *appoint* with the prefix *dis*
6. *apprehend* with the prefix *mis*
7. *practical* with the suffix *ly*
8. *abated* with the prefix *un*
9. *natural* with the prefix *un*
10. *stubborn* with the suffix *ness*
11. *legible* with the prefix *il*
12. *appropriate* with the prefix *in*
13. *appear* with the prefix *dis*
14. *movable* with the prefix *im*
15. *construct* with the prefix *re*
16. *animate* with the prefix *in*
17. *similar* with the prefix *dis*
18. *keen* with the suffix *ness*
19. *avoidable* with the prefix *un*
20. *merry* with the suffix *ly*

32e. Drop the final *e* before a suffix beginning with a vowel.

EXAMPLES   care + ing = car**ing**   use + able = us**able**

EXCEPTIONS   Keep the final *e* before *a* or *o* if necessary to retain the soft sound
               of *c* or *g* preceding the *e:* noticeable, courageous

32f. Keep the final *e* before a suffix beginning with a consonant.

EXAMPLES   care + ful = care**ful**   care + less = care**less**

EXCEPTIONS   true + ly = tru**ly**   argue + ment = argu**ment**
               acknowledge + ment = acknowledg**ment** [more usual spelling]

32g. With words ending in *y* preceded by a consonant, change the *y* to *i* before any suffix not beginning with *i*.

EXAMPLES   funny—funnier; hurry—hurried; hurry—hurrying

32h. Double the final consonant before a suffix that begins with a vowel if both of the following conditions exist: (1) the word has only one syllable or is accented on the last syllable; (2) the word ends in a single consonant preceded by a single vowel.

EXAMPLES   plan + ing = planning [one-syllable word]

forget + ing = forgetting [accent on last syllable; single consonant and single vowel]

cancel + ed = canceled [accent not on last syllable]

prefer + able = pref′erable [accent shifts; not on last syllable]

EXERCISE 4. **Spelling Words with Suffixes.** Write correctly the words formed as follows:

1. defer + ed
2. defer + ence
3. hope + ing
4. approve + al
5. benefit + ed
6. nine + ty
7. prepare + ing

8. profit + ing
9. write + ing
10. propel + ing
11. desire + able
12. control + ed
13. hope + less
14. move + ing

15. true + ly
16. run + ing
17. singe + ing
18. fame + ous
19. name + less
20. red + est

The Plural of Nouns

32i. Observe the rules for spelling the plural of nouns.

(1) The regular way to form the plural of a noun is to add *s*.

EXAMPLES   chair, chairs   book, books

(2) The plural of some nouns is formed by adding *es*.

The *e* represents the extra sound heard when -*s* is added to words ending in *s, sh, ch,* and *x*.

EXAMPLES   dress, dresses   birch, birches
                 box, boxes   bush, bushes

(3) The plural of nouns ending in *y preceded by a consonant* is formed by changing the *y* to *i* and adding *es*.

EXAMPLES   fly, flies   enemy, enemies   lady, ladies

(4) The plural of nouns ending in *y preceded by a vowel* is formed by adding an *s*.

EXAMPLES   monkey, monkeys   donkey, donkeys

(5) The plural of most nouns ending in *f* or *fe* is formed by adding *s*. The plural of some nouns ending in *f* or *fe* is formed by changing the *f* to *v* and adding *s* or *es*.

EXAMPLES   Add *s*: roof, roofs   dwarf, dwarfs   chief, chiefs

               Change *f* to *v* and add *s* or *es*:
                   knife, knives   calf, calves
                   loaf, loaves   wharf, wharves

(6) The plural of nouns ending in *o preceded by a vowel* is formed by adding *s*. The plural of nouns ending in *o preceded by a consonant* is formed by adding either *s* or *es*.

EXAMPLES   *o* following a vowel:
                 rodeo, rodeos   radio, radios

              o following a consonant:
                 hero, heroes   potato, potatoes
                 mosquito, mosquitoes

EXCEPTIONS   Words of Italian origin ending in *o* that refer to music form the plural by adding *s*: piano, pianos; soprano, sopranos; solo, solos.

(7) The plural of a few nouns is formed by irregular methods.

EXAMPLES   child, children   mouse, mice   ox, oxen
               woman, women   tooth, teeth   goose, geese

(8) The plural of compound nouns written as one word is formed by adding *s* or *es*.

EXAMPLES   cupful, cupfuls
               leftover, leftovers
               strongbox, strongboxes

(9) The plural of compound nouns consisting of a noun plus a modifier is formed by making the noun plural.

In the following examples, the phrases *in-law* and *of-war* and the adjectives *martial, general,* and *by* are all modifiers. It is the nouns modified by them that are made plural.

EXAMPLES   mother-in-law, mothers-in-law
               man-of-war, men-of-war
               court martial, courts martial
               secretary-general, secretaries-general
               passer-by, passers-by

MECHANICS

(10) The plural of a few compound nouns is formed irregularly.

EXAMPLES   drive-in, drive-ins
tie-up, tie-ups
six-year-old, six-year-olds

(11) Some nouns are the same in the singular and the plural.

EXAMPLES   sheep, deer, trout, species, Chinese

(12) The plural of some foreign words is formed as in the original language.

EXAMPLES   alumnus (*man*), alumni (*men*)
alumna (*woman*), alumnae (*women*)
datum, data
crisis, crises

(13) The plural of other foreign words may be formed either as in the foreign language or by adding *s* or *es*.

EXAMPLES   index, indices *or* indexes
appendix, appendices *or* appendixes

☞ NOTE   In certain words the English plural is the preferred one; for example, *formulas* not *formulae*. Whenever there is any doubt about which plural to use, consult the dictionary.

---

(14) The plural of numbers, letters, signs, and words considered as words is formed by adding an apostrophe and an *s*.

EXAMPLES   If you think there are ten 5's in that column, you'd better count again.
There are two *s*'s in *necessary*.
My last paper was full of 0's, not +'s.
Don't use too many *I*'s in writing your paper.

EXERCISE 5. Writing the Plural Form of Nouns.   Write the plural form of each of the following nouns. Be able to explain your spelling on the basis of the rules.

MECHANICS

1. candy	8. chief	15. bench
2. sheep	9. tomato	16. editor in chief
3. piano	10. gas	17. spoonful
4. valley	11. fly	18. hero
5. alumnus	12. alto	19. knife
6. cameo	13. brother-in-law	20. goose
7. torch	14. shelf	

EXERCISE 6. Explaining the Spellings of Words. By referring to the rules on the preceding pages, explain the spelling of each of the following:

1. misstate	5. alumnae	9. roofs
2. stubbornness	6. leisure	10. weigh
3. peaceable	7. occurred	
4. ladies	8. writing (*e* dropped)	

WORDS THAT SOUND ALIKE

6. *Learn to distinguish between homonyms, words that sound alike.* These words present problems because they sound alike but have different meanings and different spellings. You probably have had trouble distinguishing between *principle* and *principal, capital* and *capitol,* and other such pairs. Most of the paired words in the following lists sound alike. Some pairs, however, are confused even though they are not pronounced exactly alike.

already	*previously* I had *already* seen the movie twice.
all ready	*all are ready* (or *wholly ready*) Give the signal when you are *all ready*.
all right	[This word really does not belong in this list, but it is included here because many persons think there is a word spelled *alright,* as though *all right* did have a homonym. There is no word *alright*. The correct spelling is always *all right*.]
altar	*a table or stand in a church or a place for outdoor offerings* The priest was standing beside the *altar*.
alter	*to change* If we are late, we will *alter* our plans.

MECHANICS

altogether	*entirely* She doesn't *altogether* approve of me.
all **together**	*everyone in the same place* We were *all together* at Christmas.
born	*given birth* When were you *born*?
borne	*carried* He has *borne* his hardships bravely.
brake	*device to stop a machine* A defective *brake* caused the accident.
break	*to fracture, shatter* Try not to *break* any dishes.
capital	*city; money or property;* also, as an adjective, *punishable by death* or *of major importance* Washington is the *capital* of this country. Killing a police officer is a *capital* offense. That is a *capital* idea.
capitol	*building* The *capitol* faces a park.
cloths	*pieces of cloth* Try the new cleaning *cloths*.
clothes	*wearing apparel* Her *clothes* are expensive.

MECHANICS

EXERCISE 7. Selecting Correct Spelling Words to Complete Sentences. Number your paper 1–10. Write after the proper number the correct one of the words given in parentheses in the sentences below.

1. Mother was (all together, altogether) too surprised to protest.
2. Events have (born, borne) out my predictions.
3. If you (brake, break) a window, you will pay for it.
4. When you are (already, all ready) I will help you.
5. Was her work (alright, all right)?
6. We polished the car with (cloths, clothes).
7. We will (altar, alter) the building to suit tenants.

8. The dome on the (capital, capitol) is illuminated at night.
9. The club members were (all together, altogether) only once.
10. When did the Supreme Court rule on (capital, capitol) punishment?

---

coarse   *rough, crude*
He wore a suit of *coarse* cloth and used *coarse* language.

course   *path of action; part of a meal; a series of studies*
The golf *course* is outside of town.
Soup was the first *course*.
I am taking a *course* in cooking.

---

complement   *something that completes or makes perfect*
The *complement* of 50° is 40°. [*completes* a 90° angle]
His part of the job *complements* mine. [Together they *complete* the job.]

compliment   *a remark that says something good about a person; to say something good*
I am pleased by your *compliment*.
She *complimented* me on my backhand.

---

consul   *representative of a foreign country*
The American *consul* in Quito helped us during our visit.

council, councilor   *a group called together to accomplish a job; a member of such a group is a councilor*
The *council* met to welcome a new *councilor*.

counsel, counselor   *advice; the giving of advice; one who gives advice is a counselor*
I accepted the wise *counsel* of my *counselor*.

---

des'ert   *a dry region*
We flew across the *desert*.

desert'   *to leave*
She *deserted* her friends in their time of need.

dessert'   *the final course of a meal*
The *dessert* was ice cream.

---

formally   *conventionally or properly, according to strict rules*
She spoke *formally* and with great dignity.

formerly   *in the past, previously*
I was *formerly* a member of that club.

MECHANICS

its	[possessive] The village is proud of *its* school.
it's	*it is* *It's* a long way.

later	*more late* We will arrive *later*.
latter	*the second of two* When given the choice of an apple or an orange I chose the *latter*.

lead	[present tense] *to go first* You *lead* and we will follow.
led	[past tense] She *led* the team to victory.
lead	[pronounced **led**] *a heavy metal*, also *graphite in a pencil* The industrial uses of *lead* are many.

EXERCISE 8. Selecting Correct Spelling Words to Complete Sentences. Number your paper 1–10. Write after the proper number the correct one of the words given in parentheses in the sentences.

1. Our (consul, counsel) in Romania has returned to Washington.
2. I enjoyed the dinner but not the (dessert, desert).
3. Avoid (course, coarse) language.
4. I do not enjoy parties conducted as (formally, formerly) as this one.
5. We are not sure which (course, coarse) to follow.
6. Are you sure (its, it's) not too late?
7. I spent five summers working as a camp (councilor, counselor).
8. I spoke to the mayor and the superintendent; the (later, latter) was more helpful.
9. Albert (lead, led) the team to a championship.
10. These shoes (complement, compliment) my blue dress.

loose	*free, not close together* The animals broke *loose*. They stumbled in the *loose* sand.
lose	[pronounced **lo͞oz**] *to suffer loss* When did you *lose* your books?

MECHANICS

miner	worker in a mine A *miner's* job is sometimes dangerous.
minor	*under legal age; less important* A *minor* cannot marry without a parent's or guardian's consent. They raised only *minor* objections.

moral	*good; also a lesson of conduct* His good conduct showed him to be a *moral* person. The class understood the *moral* of the story.
morale	*mental condition, spirit* The *morale* in our school is excellent.

passed	*verb* The Fiat *passed* me at the finish line.
past	*noun or adjective or preposition* Some persons prefer to live in the *past* (n.) because *past* (adj.) events seem more interesting than present ones. I went *past* (prep.) your house without realizing it.

peace	*opposite of strife* Everyone prefers *peace* to war.
piece	*a part of something* They ate every *piece* of cake.

personal	*individual* He gave his *personal* opinion.
personnel	*a group of people employed in the same place* The *personnel* of the company ranged in age from 16 to 64.

plain	*not fancy; also a flat area of land; also clear* She lives in a very *plain* home. We crossed the *plains* in two days. Our problem is *plain*.
plane	*a flat surface; also a tool; also an airplane* *Plane* geometry is a study of imaginary flat surfaces. The carpenter used a *plane*. A *plane* circled the airport.

principal	*head of a school; also the main one of several things* They went to the *principal's* office. The *principal* cause of accidents is carelessness.

MECHANICS

principle   *a rule of conduct;* also *a main fact* or *law*
The judge accused the criminal of having no *principles.*
She understands the *principles* of mathematics.

---

quiet   *still, silent*
A study hall should be *quiet.*

quite   *completely, wholly;* also *to a great extent or degree*
I had *quite* forgotten her advice.
Angela is *quite* tall.

EXERCISE 9. Selecting Correct Spelling Words to Complete Sentences. Number your paper 1–10. Write after the proper number the correct one of the words given in parentheses in the sentences that follow.

1. All three nations signed a (peace, piece) treaty.
2. Do these printed instructions seem (plain, plane) to you?
3. This store's sales (personal, personnel) are very helpful.
4. The (principal, principle) of solar energy is easy to understand.
5. If you (loose, lose) your concentration, you might (loose, lose) the tennis match.
6. Can you tell the (principal, principle) parts of the verb "to shrink"?
7. Students should remain (quiet, quite) during a study period.
8. Does every fable have a (moral, morale)?
9. On my way to school I always walk (passed, past) the bakery.
10. If you can vote, you are officially no longer a (miner, minor).

---

stationary   *in a fixed position*
The classroom desks are *stationary.*

stationery   *writing paper*
I received three boxes of *stationery* at Christmas.

---

than   conjunction
I am stronger *than* she.

then   adverb meaning *at the time*
Wear a green hat; *then* I'll recognize you.

---

there   *a place;* also used as an expletive (see pages 434–35)
We were *there* at two o'clock.
There were four of us.

MECHANICS

their	[possessive] The pupils bring *their* own lunches.
they're	*they are* *They're* going with us.

---

to	a preposition or part of the infinitive form of a verb Give the book *to* me, please. We will have *to* leave early.
too	adverb meaning *also* or *too much* George is a sophomore, *too*. It is *too* late to go now.
two	*one plus one* We had only *two* dollars.

---

waist	*middle part of the body* She wore a wide belt around her *waist*.
waste	*unused material; also to squander* Pollution can be caused by industrial *wastes*. Don't *waste* your time.

---

who's	*who is, who has* *Who's* coming? *Who's* been here?
whose	[possessive] *Whose* coat is this?

---

your	[possessive] Is this *your* coat?
you're	*you are* *You're* a true friend.

EXERCISE 10. Selecting Correct Spelling Words to Complete Sentences. Number your paper 1–10. Write after the proper number the correct one of the words given in parentheses in the following sentences:

1. They had neglected to lock (there, their) lockers.
2. I wanted to go to camp, (to, two, too).
3. Tie the rope around your (waist, waste).
4. The platform, we discovered when we tried to move it, was (stationary, stationery).

5. No one could remember (whose, who's) name had been drawn first.
6. As soon as (their, they're) printed, we will ship the books.
7. Write your letters on business (stationary, stationery).
8. (Your, You're) lucky to have such a good job.
9. I cannot do any more (then, than) I have done.
10. I was surpised at (you're, your) taking that attitude.

REVIEW EXERCISE. Selecting Correct Spelling Words to Complete Sentences. Number your paper 1–25. After the proper number, write the correct one of the words in parentheses in the following sentences:

1. Columbia is the (capital, capitol) of South Carolina.
2. Have you discussed this problem with your guidance (councilor, counselor)?
3. The vegetation in the (dessert, desert) surprised us.
4. Mrs. Crane (formally, formerly) taught here.
5. Every nation must conserve (its, it's) resources.
6. My companion (lead, led) me down a dark passage.
7. We were (all ready, already) to start before dawn.
8. Try not to (lose, loose) your keys.
9. Success is the best (moral, morale) builder.
10. The new (altar, alter) is made of white marble.
11. I have read Murdoch and Spark, and I prefer the (later, latter).
12. (Its, It's) time to think about getting a job.
13. There was (all together, altogether) no truth in the report.
14. Members of the (counsel, council) are elected annually.
15. (Course, Coarse) wood absorbs more paint than fine-grained wood.
16. My red tie (complements, compliments) my blue suit.
17. Jack (past, passed) the ball to Joe.
18. When you are (all together, altogether), I'll take a group picture.
19. The mission was completed with no loss of (personal, personnel).
20. We prefer (stationary, stationery) seats in our classrooms.
21. There's a student (whose, who's) going to succeed.
22. His act was not outstanding, but it was (alright, all right).
23. The (principals, principles) of democracy are admired.
24. Do you know (they're, their, there) new address?
25. Mrs. Starkey gave our play (complimentary, complementary) reviews.

MECHANICS

COMMONLY MISSPELLED WORDS

7. *Learn lists of commonly misspelled words.* Frequent short spelling tests are an effective means of fixing correct spellings in your mind. On the following pages you will find a list of 300 commonly misspelled words. Taking no more than twenty at a time, have these words dictated to you. Study the ones you miss and record them in your list of spelling errors. When you have studied them (divided them into syllables and practiced writing each word several times), write them again from dictation. Spelling tests should be written, not oral.

Three Hundred Spelling Words[1]

abundant	apparatus	carburetor
academically	apparent	caricature
accelerator	arousing	catalog
accessible	arrangement	catastrophe
accidentally	atheistic	cellar
acclimated		cemetery
accommodation	attendance	changeable
accompaniment	awfully	chassis
accomplishment	ballet	Christianity
accuracy	bankruptcy	circumstantial
	barbarian	
acknowledge	basketball	colossal
acquaintance	beggar	communist
adequately	behavior	comparative
admission	beneficial	competition
admittance	bibliography	complexion
adolescent		conceivable
advantageous	biscuit	connoisseur
aerial	blasphemy	conscientious
allege	boulevard	consciousness
allegiance	bracelet	consistency
	buffet	
alliance	bureaucrat	controlling
allotting	burial	controversy
annihilate	calculation	cruelty
anonymous	camouflage	curriculum
apologetically	capitalism	debacle

[1] The list does not include the homonyms listed on pages 686–92.

decadent	forfeit	magnificence
deceitful	fulfill	maintenance
deference	fundamentally	malicious
descendant	gaiety	manageable
desirable	galaxy	maneuver
despair	gauge	marriageable
detrimental	grammatically	martyrdom
devastation	guidance	materialism
devise	harassment	meadow
dilemma	hereditary	mediocre
diligence	hindrance	melancholy
disastrous	horizontal	melodious
disciple	hospital	metaphor
discrimination	hygiene	miniature
diseased	hypocrisy	mischievous
dissatisfied	ideally	misspelled
division	idiomatic	mortgage
ecstasy	incidentally	mosquito
efficiency	independent	municipal
embarrassment	indispensable	mysterious
emperor	inevitable	naive
emphasize	influential	necessity
endeavor	ingenious	neurotic
enormous	initiative	noticeable
entertainment	innocent	novelist
enthusiastically	inoculate	nucleus
entrance	institution	nuisance
environment	intellectual	nutritious
espionage	interference	obedience
exhaustion	irrelevant	occasionally
exhibition	irresistible	occurrence
exhilaration	kerosene	omitting
expensive	laborious	opportunity
exuberant	larynx	orchestra
familiarize	leisurely	outrageous
fascination	license	pageant
fascism	liquor	pamphlet
feminine	livelihood	paralysis
financier	luxurious	parliament
fission	magistrate	pastime

MECHANICS

peasant
pedestal
penicillin
perceive
permanent

permissible
persistent
perspiration
phenomenon
physician
picnicking
playwright
pneumonia
politician
precede

presence
prestige
presumption
prevalent
privilege
procedure
propaganda
propagate
prophesy
prove

psychoanalysis
pursue
quietly
rebellion
receive
recommendation
reference
referred
rehearsal
relieve

reminiscent
remittance
representative
resources
responsibility
reveal
safety
seize
separation
sergeant

siege
significance
souvenir
specimen
sponsor
statistics
strategic
stubbornness
succeed
succession

summed
superintendent
supersede
suppress
surroundings
susceptible
symbolic
symmetrical
symphonic
synonymous

tariff
temperament
temperature
tendency
theoretical

tolerance
tomorrow
tortoise
traffic
tragedy

transcend
transparent
tried
twelfth
tyranny
undoubtedly
universal
unmistakable
unnatural
unnecessary

unscrupulous
vaccine
vacuum
valedictory
variation
vaudeville
vehicle
vengeance
versatile
vigilance

villain
vinegar
visage
welcome
whisper
whistle
withhold
yacht
yawn
yield

MECHANICS

PART FOUR

RESOURCES FOR WRITING AND STUDYING

CHAPTER 33

The Library

ARRANGEMENT AND RESOURCES

Libraries, or media centers, as they are now frequently called, are sufficiently alike so that when you become familiar with one library, you can easily find your way in others. You should understand the following:

1. The arrangement of books in the library
2. The uses of the card catalog
3. The names and functions of the parts of a book
4. The use of the *Readers' Guide*
5. The use of the vertical file
6. The location of items in your library

If the library owns a book you cannot find, ask the librarian about it. It may be checked out, or it may be "on reserve" for various reasons. The librarian might place your name on a waiting list and notify you when it's available.

ARRANGEMENT OF BOOKS IN THE LIBRARY

33a. Learn the arrangement of books.

Fiction

By this time you know that books of fiction are usually arranged alphabetically by authors' last names. If your library contains numerous books by the same author, they are alphabetized by their titles, in that author's space.

Nonfiction: The Dewey Decimal System

All nonfiction books receive numbers in a classification system developed by the American librarian Melvil Dewey.[1] There are ten numerical subject classifications, with decimal points allowing an unlimited number of subdivisions. The value of this system is that all books on one subject are given the same number and are located together on the shelves. Dewey's broad classifications are shown below.

000–099	General Works (encyclopedias, periodicals, etc.)
100–199	Philosophy (includes psychology, conduct, etc.)
200–299	Religion (includes mythology)
300–399	Social Sciences (economics, government, law, etc.)
400–499	Language (dictionaries, grammars, etc.)
500–599	Science (mathematics, chemistry, physics, etc.)
600–699	Technology (agriculture, engineering, aviation, etc.)
700–799	The Arts and Recreation (sculpture, painting, music, photography, sports, etc.)
800–899	Literature (poetry, plays, orations, etc.)
900–909 ⎤ 930–999 ⎦	History
910–919	Travel
920–929	Biography (arranged alphabetically by name of subject of biography)

Books having the same class number may be distinguished from one another by the author's name. For instance, all books on aviation are given the number 629.1. This number appears on the spine of the book.

---

[1] The Library of Congress system of cataloging, used in many public libraries but not commonly used in high-school libraries, classifies all books, both fiction and nonfiction. Each general subject category (Philosophy, Science, etc.) is assigned a code letter. In addition, whole categories are often subdivided by adding a second code letter to the first. Thus, the letter *P* (which designates Literature) may be followed by the letter *S* to specify American literature. Call numbers include the letter codes, followed by a series of numbers that identify specific books within a category. For example, the book *Responses: Prose Pieces 1953–1976,* by Richard Wilbur, an American author, has the Library of Congress call number PS 3545. A complete schedule of Library of Congress categories is usually available in any library using this system.

With the number appears the first letter of the author's name: if the author is Hood, the book's complete number is $\dfrac{629.1}{H}$. This number, including the first letter of the author's name, is known as the book's *call number.* To find the call number of a book, you look up the book in the card catalog.

LOCATING INFORMATION IN THE LIBRARY

The Card Catalog

Undoubtedly you have used the card catalog in your school or town library. You may not, however, know as much about it as you need to know in order to get the most help from it.

33b. Learn the uses of the card catalog.

In most libraries, the catalog cabinet holds at least three cards for each book in the library: at least one *author card,* the *title card,* and at least one *subject card.*

```
808.8  Warren, Barbara, 1947–    comp.                                author
         The feminine image in literature.  Rochelle Park, N. J.,     card
    808.8  feminine image in literature, The.
    Warren, Barbara, 1947–    comp.                                   title
                                                                      card
       808.8  Women - Literary collections.

       Warren, Barbara, 1947–    comp.
            The feminine image in literature.  Rochelle Park, N. J.,  subject
       Hayden Book Co. ₍1973₎                                         card
          266 p.  23 cm.  (Hayden humanities series)
          Includes bibliographical references.


          1. Women—Literary collections.    I. Title.
       PN6071.W7W3              806.8′0352           73–11928
       ISBN 0–5104–5068–2                                MARC
       Library of Congress         74 ₍4₎
```

The Author Card

The *author card* has the name of the author at the top. When there is joint authorship, there is a card for each author. Since the cards for all books by an author are placed together, you are able to find out what other books by the author the library owns. Cards for books *about* an author follow the cards for books *by* an author.

The Title Card

The quickest way to find a book in the catalog is to look it up under its title. Cards for books whose titles begin with *a, an,* or *the* are arranged alphabetically by the second word in the title.

The Subject Card

Subject cards are invaluable when you wish to find a number of books on a subject but do not know specific titles or authors. Under the subject heading "Political parties—United States," for instance, you will find a card for every book in the library on this subject. In fact, you may find a card for every book that contains as little as one article or chapter on United States political parties, so thoroughly is the cataloging done.

Information Given on a Catalog Card

A brief study of the sample catalog cards reproduced on page 701 will show you that a complete card gives a great deal of information. In addition to giving the title, author, and call number of a book, the card may give the following information:

    1. *Facts about authorship:* full name of the author; names of joint authors and illustrators, if any.
    2. *Facts about publication:* the place of publication; the name of the publisher; the date of publication.
    3. *Facts about the book:* number of pages; whether the book contains illustrations, diagrams, etc.

"See" and "See Also" Cards

When you look for a certain subject, you may find a "see" card referring you to another heading. The "see" card tells you, in effect, "There is nothing here. You will find what you want under this other heading."
    A second type of cross-reference card is the "see also" card, which refers you to another heading in the catalog where you may find additional titles on your subject.

```
WORLD WAR I: see
European War 1914-1918
```

```
DETECTIVES: see also
Police
Secret Service
```

Sample Cross Reference Cards

EXERCISE 1. Using the Card Catalog. Using the card catalog in your library, write the title, author, and call number for the following books.

1. A history of American literature
2. A book about South America
3. A book by Edith Wharton
4. A book giving information about Edith Wharton
5. A book about space exploration

Using the card catalog, find answers to the following questions. Write the answers.

6. Does the library own any books by Willa Cather? If so, give the title and call number of one of them.
7. Give the title, author, publisher, and publication date of a book about George Washington Carver.
8. Does the library own the complete plays of Shakespeare in one volume? If so, give the exact title and the publisher of the book.
9. Give the title, author, and date of publication of a book of American poetry.
10. Does the library own a copy of Charlotte Brontë's *Jane Eyre*? If so, give the publisher.

The Parts of a Book

Once you have found the right book, you need to know the important parts of a book and the uses of each.

33c. Learn the names and functions of the parts of a book.

The Frontispiece

The frontispiece is a full-page illustration. If the book has a frontispiece, it faces the title page.

The Title Page

The first important page in a book, the title page gives the complete title, any subtitle, the name of the author or editor, the name of the publisher, and the place of publication.

The Copyright Page

The reverse side of the title page is the copyright page. Here you find the year in which the book was registered in the government copyright office in Washington. Before publishers release a new book, they send two copies to the United States Copyright Office. The office then issues a copyright, which gives to the copyright owner exclusive right to print the book or any part of it during the lifetime of the author and for a period of fifty years after the author's death. Sometimes publishers secure a copyright in their own name, sometimes in the name of the author.

Often you will find more than one date listed on the copyright page: "Copyright 1946, 1949, 1955." This means that the first edition of the book was copyrighted in 1946. In 1949 and 1955 new material was added and a new copyright secured to cover the new material. In books published since September 1957, the international copyright symbol is used: © 1980. The date of copyright is very important when you wish to know whether the material in a book is sufficiently up-to-date to be reliable.

Publishers sometimes indicate on this page which printing of the book this particular volume represents. Note the distinction between a new copyright date and a new printing date. The former tells when the book was last revised; the latter notes when it was merely reprinted.

The Preface, Foreword, Introduction

These terms are now used interchangeably to refer to remarks at the beginning of a book in which the author, editor, or publisher explains the purpose of the book, gives information that aids the reader in understanding the book, acknowledges credit and inspiration, etc.

The Table of Contents

The table of contents appears at the front of the book and consists of a list of the chapters and subdivisions with their page numbers. It provides a quick view of the content and organization of the entire book.

List of Illustrations (Maps, Diagrams, Charts, etc.)

Such a list cites illustrations with their page numbers and generally follows the Table of Contents. A very long list may appear at the end of a book.

The Appendix

The appendix contains additional information that the author did not include in the body of the book. It may include long quotations from other works on the subject, lists, diagrams and tables, etc.

The Glossary

A glossary is usually a list of definitions of technical or foreign language words used in the book. It is placed near the close of the book.

The Bibliography

The bibliography is a list of books consulted by the author in writing the book or recommended to the reader who wishes more information.

The Index

The index is an alphabetical list of topics treated in the book, given with page numbers. It is much more detailed than the table of contents. When you have found a book that seems likely to provide information on your topic, the index will tell you how much information there is and exactly where to find it.

The End Papers

The pages pasted inside the front and back covers of the book are the end papers. Sometimes they are used for a map or an illustration or to give a summary of the contents.

The *Readers' Guide*

A large part of the library reference work you will do in high school will deal with subjects of a contemporary rather than a historical nature. The best source of information, indeed very often the only source of information on truly current subjects, is a magazine. Without some sort of guide, you would have to spend hours hunting through magazines in search of articles on a subject. However, the *Readers' Guide to Periodical Literature* solves this problem for you.

33d. Learn how to use the *Readers' Guide to Periodical Literature.*

In the *Readers' Guide*, articles from some 170 magazines are indexed alphabetically by subjects and by authors. You may look up the subject in which you are interested and find the articles that have been written on it and the magazines in which they appeared.

Magazine stories are listed by title and by author; the complete entry is given with the author listing only. Poems and plays are listed by author.

Articles *about* moving pictures and plays are listed under the subject headings MOVING PICTURE PLAYS and DRAMAS, beneath the subheading **Criticisms, plots, etc.**

The *Readers' Guide* is published in paperbound pamphlets twice a month from September to June and monthly in July and August. Occasionally during the year a cumulative issue is published which includes the articles listed in preceding months as well as those for the current month. At the end of a year, a large volume is published containing all entries for the year, and every two years a volume covering a two-year period is published.

When you are taking down references from the *Readers' Guide*, you need to know what magazines your library has. You should know, too, whether the library has kept back issues of all these magazines or only of certain ones and for how many years back it has the magazines.

A sample excerpt from the *Readers' Guide* is reproduced on page 707. You can probably understand the many abbreviations used, but if you cannot, you will find them explained in the front of the *Readers' Guide* itself.

BALL, George Wildman	author entry
Options on Iran. por Newsweek 95:43 Ap 7 '80	article by author
Question of oil [interview by R. Christopher] por Macleans 93:50 Ja 7 '80	
about	article about author
Mr. Ball's world. E. N. Luttwak. New Repub 182:12-14 Ap 5 '80 •	
BALL, Leslie D. See Waldron, D. jt auth	"see" cross reference to joint author
BALLANTINE, H. Thomas, Jr	
Role of government in health-care delivery in the 1980s [address, January 16, 1980] Vital Speeches 46:258-60 F 15 '80	
BALLANTINE, Ian	
Uses and abuses of enchantment. [D. Weinberger. il Macleans 93:45-5 Ja 28 '80 •	title of article
BALLERINAS. See Dancers	
BALLET	title and issue of magazine
See also	
Choreography	subject entry
Cleveland Ballet Company	
Dance Theatre of Harlem	
Houston Ballet Company	
Joffrey Ballet	
Maryland Ballet	
Merce Cunningham & Dance Company	
Metropolitan Opera Ballet	
Motion pictures—Dance films	
New York City Ballet	
Pittsburgh Ballet Theatre	
Television broadcasting—Dance programs	"see" cross reference
Dance. J. Maskey. See issues of High fidelity [and Musical America	
Domestic reports: news and views from across the country. See issues of Dance magazine	
Editor's log. W. Como. See issues of Dance magazine	
Opera ballet:	
Taming the two-headed monster. B. Laine. Dance Mag 54:51-3 F '80	volume number
Presstime news. See issues of Dance magazine	
Reviews:	
Ballet Metropolitan of Columbus. A .Barzel. Dance Mag 54:51-3 F '80	page reference
Dance Ring. A. Barzel. Dance Mag 54:44-6 F '80	
Louisville Ballet. A. Barzel. Dance Mag 54:50-1 F '80	date of issue
Ohio Ballet. W. Salisbury. Dance Mag 54:116+ F '80	
Tulsa Ballet Theatre: old world style for a new frontier. J. Pikula. il pors Dance Mag 54:62-5 F '80	illustration reference
Bibliography	
Dance. books. il Dance Mag 54:106+ Ja; 121 F; 121 Mr '80	
Directories	
Dance directory. See issues of Dance magazine	
International aspects	
Foreign reports: news and views from around the world. See issues of Dance magazine	secondary subject heading
Study and teaching	
Education briefs [ed by M. Pierpont] See issues of Dance magazine	
Australia	
Dance in Australia. A. Brissenden. il Dance Mag 54:12 F '80	
Canada	
See also	"see also" cross reference
National Ballet of Canada	

EXERCISE 2. **Using the *Readers' Guide*.** Write answers to the following questions.

1. Where are the bound magazines stored in your library?
2. What is the date of the latest *Readers' Guide* in your library? What period does it cover?
3. Select a prominent musician of today and look for an article about the person in the *Readers' Guide*. Give the complete listing.
4. Find and copy a "see" reference from the *Readers' Guide*.
5. Copy from the *Readers' Guide* the complete listing of a review of a motion picture.

Information Files

33e. Learn the nature and proper use of the vertical file.

Useful information on current topics is often found in pamphlets published by government agencies, industrial concerns, museums, colleges and universities, radio stations, welfare organizations, etc. Many libraries store such publications, as well as clippings and pictures from newspapers and magazines, in a special cabinet referred to as the vertical file. Consult the librarian to see if a file folder is available on the topic you are studying.

33f. Use microfilm and microfiche to find information.

Many libraries store some publications on microfilm or microfiche. *Microfilm* is a roll or reel of film; *microfiche* is a small sheet of film. Both types of film contain photographically reduced material which can be enlarged to readable size by special projectors. Consult your librarian for instructions.

33g. Use computers to find information.

Many media centers now store their lists of books and periodicals on computers. Instead of using the card catalog or the *Readers' Guide,* you type the information you need into a computer. You might have to read the list of available materials from the screen, or you might be able to get a printout. The librarian can provide information on the center's computer systems.

33h. Learn the location of resources in your library.

Your use of a library will be more efficient if you know the exact location of the principal items you may wish to use. If you will remember the information the following exercise calls for, you will save both the librarian and yourself a great deal of time.

EXERCISE 3. **Locating Items in Your Library.**   Be prepared to state where each of the following items is located in your school or public library.

1. The card catalog
2. The *Readers' Guide*
3. The magazine rack and the newspaper rack
4. The pamphlet file
5. The fiction shelves
6. The encyclopedias
7. The biography shelves
8. The unabridged dictionaries
9. The computers
10. The microfilm and microfiche projectors

CHAPTER 34

Reference Books

SPECIAL SOURCES OF INFORMATION

Some media centers have bigger collections of reference books than others, but almost any media center will have most of the standard reference books described here. It may surprise you to find how quickly and easily you can locate needed facts, once you know that a reference book specifically made to supply them is in a nearby library. Familiarity with a library's reference books will increase your efficiency in looking up information.

ENCYCLOPEDIAS

34a. Get acquainted with encyclopedias: their plan, content, and indexes.

You have probably been using an encyclopedia in your schoolwork for some time. You know that it is a collection of articles in alphabetical order on nearly all fields of knowledge. Although written by experts with a high level of factual accuracy, the articles only give overall views, with details limited by space.

In any encyclopedia, the index or index-volume is important. If you looked in the *Enclyopedia Americana* under the entry "Olympic Games," you would find an article several columns long. But in the index, you would find the volumes and page numbers of more than twenty other entries with information about the games. If you had not used the index, you would not have known about these other entries.

When using the *Encyclopaedia Britannica,* you should usually check the *Micropaedia* first. These first ten volumes contain shorter articles, with cross-referencing to the remaining nineteen volumes, called the *Macropaedia,* which have much longer treatments. Several encyclopedias publish yearbooks, which contain statistics, important events, and developments in every field pertaining to the year just preceding. Check these annuals if your topic involves a rapidly changing field.

Encyclopedias in Many Volumes

Collier's Encyclopedia
> 24 volumes
> Bibliography and Index in Volume 24
> Publishes *Collier's Yearbook*

Encyclopedia Americana
> 30 volumes
> Index in Volume 30
> Publishes the *Americana Annual*

Encyclopaedia Britannica
> 30 volumes
> Cross-referencing throughout *Micropaedia*
> Publishes the *Britannica Book of the Year*

World Book Encyclopedia
> 22 volumes
> Research Guide and Index in Volume 22
> Publishes an annual supplement

One- and Two-Volume Encyclopedias

Very often a brief, handy account of a subject is enough. For this purpose, a one- or two-volume "desk" encyclopedia is adequate. There are three well-known works of this kind. The *New Columbia Encyclopedia* and the *Random House Encyclopedia* are arranged alphabetically like dictionaries. The *Lincoln Library of Essential Information* has two volumes arranged in broad fields of knowledge with many subdivision articles and an index.

GENERAL REFERENCE BOOKS

Almanacs and Yearbooks

Although almanacs come out annually to cover a one-year period, many of their statistics include data for preceding years. Remember that an almanac tells about the year before its date: data for 1980 should be sought in the 1981 issue.

World Almanac and Book of Facts

Most popular of the handy annual reference books on the world today, the *World Almanac* gives facts and figures that are needed very often. Typical items are census tables, production quantities, export and import figures, election results, officeholders, sports records, Nobel and other prize-winners, and a summary of notable events. A full index is in the front.

Information Please Almanac

This almanac covers much of the same ground as the *World Almanac*, but in a different arrangement. Its full index is in the back. The *Information Please Almanac* covers fewer subjects, but its informal style is easy to follow and its articles are sometimes fuller.

The International Yearbook & Statesmen's Who's Who

The International Yearbook & Statesmen's Who's Who includes up-to-date information on international organizations and political, statistical, and directory information about each country of the world. A biographical section gives sketches of world leaders in government, religion, commerce, industry, and education.

Atlases

Don't think of an atlas as just a collection of maps. It contains information of many kinds: climate, rainfall, crops, topography, population, some history, etc.

Find out which atlases your library has and where they are kept. Because our day is marked by amazing numbers of new nations, an atlas even a few years old may be significantly inaccurate. To find out how up-to-date an atlas is, check its copyright date in the opening pages.

A few of the reliable atlases are listed here.

General Atlases

Hammond Contemporary World Atlas
National Geographic Atlas of the World
New York Times Atlas of the World

Historical atlases help us to visualize history by showing the world, or a region of it, as it was in one or more past periods.

Historical Atlases

The American Heritage Pictorial Atlas of United States History
Rand McNally Atlas of World History
Shepherd, William, *Historical Atlas*

BIOGRAPHICAL REFERENCE BOOKS

34b. Learn to use these handy biographical reference tools.

Many of the biographical reference works discussed here are likely to be on your library's shelves. Since their functions differ, be sure to find out what each can do for you.

General Biography

Biography Index (1946 to date)

This work, as its name implies, is not a collection of biographies, but an index that tells you where to find material on the life of nearly anyone about whom a book or an article has been published. It indexes current biographical books and biographical material in periodicals, in much the same manner as the *Readers' Guide to Periodical Literature*. Like the *Readers' Guide*, the *Biography Index* is published regularly and in cumulative editions.

Dictionary of American Biography

This monumental work provides authoritative articles on notable Americans no longer living, from the earliest times virtually to the present. Individual articles are more detailed than those in any encyclopedia. The complete set of fifteen volumes includes a one-volume index, as well as updating supplements.

The New Century Cyclopedia of Names (3 volumes)

As the title may imply, this work deals with proper names of all sorts, including real, legendary, and mythological persons, places, and events, as well as literary works and characters and works of art—100,000 in all. Names hard to find elsewhere are often at hand in it, and historians commend its accuracy.

Webster's Biographical Dictionary

In this book, over 40,000 concise biographies appear in alphabetical order. Care has been taken to give the correct pronunciation of each name. Though the dictionary offers some details, it is not intended to provide the complete life of any person.

Who's Who, Who's Who in America, and *The International Who's Who*

These standard books, found in most libraries, give essential facts about notable *living* persons. Note that these are books of *facts;* they do not summarize the subject's life in any detail. Typical entries list parentage, place and date of birth, educational background, positions held, important achievements, writings and their dates, awards, religious and political affiliations, and present address.

Who's Who gives information about notable British persons and some famous persons in other countries. It comes out yearly.

Who's Who in America gives facts about notable Americans. It comes out every two years. Although persons listed in *Who's Who in America* are dropped after they die, entries for the most important persons thus dropped are preserved in a volume entitled *Who Was Who in America.*

The International Who's Who might prove useful to you in locating material on persons not listed in the above-mentioned sources. Well-known educators, artists, diplomats, etc., from various parts of the globe are included here.

Current Biography

Like the *Who's Who* books above, this monthly serial is concerned with *living* people. Each issue contains short, informal biographies of those currently prominent in the news. A picture of the person is often included. The scope is international.

Annually, articles in the twelve issues are put in alphabetical order in one bound volume. Currently, its cumulative index locates articles from 1971 on. A separate index covers those from 1940 through 1970. Biographies are also indexed by professions.

Books About Authors

Although the lives of authors are included in all biographical reference books and in the encyclopedias, the following books treat authors only. *The Writers Directory* briefly lists 18,000 of today's writers. It comes out every two years. Articles in the others are informal, longer, and include authors' pictures.

> *American Authors 1600–1900* by Kunitz and Haycraft
> *American Writers* by Unger
> *British Authors Before 1800* by Kunitz and Haycraft
> *British Authors of the Nineteenth Century* by Kunitz and Haycraft
> *Contemporary Authors: First Revision,* Gale Research Company
> *Dictionary of Literary Biography,* Gale Research Company
> *The Writers Directory,* St. James Press, London/St. Martin's Press, N.Y.
> *Twentieth Century Authors* by Kunitz and Haycraft
> *World Authors* by Wakeman

Magill's *Cyclopedia of World Authors* is a popular reference that includes authors from all over the world. It gives biographical facts for each author and a critical sketch characterizing his or her works.

LITERATURE REFERENCE BOOKS

34c. Develop the habit of using reference books on literature.

You were just introduced to some standard reference books on authors. For information on literary works and their plots, characters, sources, quotations, etc., the following books are useful.

General

Benét's *The Reader's Encyclopedia*

This book describes itself aptly as "an encyclopedia of all the things you encounter in reading." It does have great variety: plots and characters, summaries of poems, allusions to myths and to the Bible, and descriptions of works of art, music, and so on. Though the Second Edition best meets today's interests, either is good.

Books of Quotations

At times you may want to find the source or exact wording of a quotation. Because books of quotations differ in arrangement, you need to learn how to find what you want in the one you are using.

Bartlett's *Familiar Quotations*

Bartlett's is probably the best known. It provides four kinds of information about quotations: (1) the author; (2) the source; (3) the exact wording; (4) famous lines by any author.

Stevenson's *Home Book of Quotations* and *Home Book of Proverbs, Maxims, and Familiar Phrases*

Using a different type of arrangement, these books group quotations according to subject matter, not by author. This plan is convenient when you want quotations on a particular subject—success, love, duty, etc.

H. L. Mencken's *New Dictionary of Quotations*

The choice of numerous quotations marked by epigrammatic wit or satire makes this collection unusual.

Magill's *Quotations in Context*

This book of quotations includes the contexts of the quotations.

Indexes and Collections of Poetry

Stevenson's *Home Book of Verse* and *Home Book of Modern Verse*

When you want to find a popular poem, it is a good idea to look for it first in these two big anthologies. The poems are arranged by subjects. Since the books are indexed in three ways—by author, by title, and by first line—you should have no trouble finding the poem you want if it is in either book.

Granger's Index to Poetry (sixth edition)

When you want to find a particular poem, *Granger's Index* can lead you quickly to a collection that includes it. It has three listings for each poem: by author, by title, and by first line. Whichever you use will give you the same information as the other two do.

Remember that the *Index* does not print any whole poems, but its listings are quick poem-locators for almost any poem you want to find.

Other Indexes

Other useful indexes include the following ones: *Short Story Index, Play Index*, and *Essay and General Literature Index*.

OTHER REFERENCE BOOKS

If you are researching a topic within one of these broad fields, check your library for the following reliable resources.

Literature

 American Authors and Books by W. J. Burke and W. D. Howe, augmented and revised by Irving Weiss
 Book Review Digest
 Bulfinch's Mythology
 Cambridge History of American Literature
 Cambridge History of English Literature
 Cyclopedia of Literary Characters
 Contemporary Literary Criticism
 Encyclopedia of World Literature in the Twentieth Century
 Guide to Great Plays by J. T. Shipley
 The New Century Classical Handbook
 Nineteenth Century Literary Criticism
 Oxford Companion to American Literature
 Oxford Companion to English Literature
 Oxford Companion to French Literature
 Oxford Companion to Classical Literature
 Oxford Companion to the Theatre
 Thirteen Hundred Critical Evaluations of Selected Novels and Plays

Grammar and Usage

 The Careful Writer: a Modern Guide to English Usage by Theodore M. Bernstein
 A Dictionary of Contemporary American Usage by Bergen and Cornelia Evans

History and Social Studies

 Cambridge Modern History
 Dictionary of American History by J. T. Adams
 The Dictionary of Dates by Helen R. Keller
 Encyclopedia of American History by R. B. Morris
 Encyclopedia of the Social Sciences
 Encyclopedia of World History by W. L. Langer

Great Events from History
Statistical Abstract of the United States
Webster's New Geographical Dictionary

Science and Mathematics

Chambers Dictionary of Science and Technology
McGraw-Hill Encyclopedia of Science and Technology

Music and Art

Encyclopedia of World Art
Encyclopedia of the Arts, edited by Herbert Read
Grove's Dictionary of Music and Musicians
The Harvard Dictionary of Music, first edition, edited by Willi Apel. (The second edition contains additional and updated entries but abbreviates the first listings considerably. An abridged paperback edition is also available: *The Harvard Brief Dictionary of Music.*)
The International Cyclopedia of Music and Musicians
The McGraw-Hill Encyclopedia of World Art
The New College Encyclopedia of Music, edited by J. A. Westrup and F. L. Harrison (the handiest and best one-volume popular work)
Vasari's Lives of the Painters, Sculptors, and Architects, new edition in four paperback volumes

Colleges and Universities

American Universities and Colleges, American Council on Education
Barron's Profiles of American Colleges
Comparative Guide to American Colleges, edited by James Cass and Max Birnbaum
Lovejoy's College Guide

EXERCISE 1. Explaining the Uses of Specific Reference Books.
Be able to explain the principal uses of each of the following resource books, its advantages and its limitations.

1. An encyclopedia

2. Yearbooks

   World Almanac and Book of Facts
   Information Please Almanac
   The International Yearbook & Statesmen's Who's Who
   Collier's Yearbook

3. An atlas

4. Biographical reference books

> *Biography Index*
> *Webster's Biographical Dictionary*
> *Who's Who, Who's Who in America, Who Was Who in America*, and *The International Who's Who*
> *American Authors 1600 - 1900*

5. Literature reference books

> Bartlett's *Familiar Quotations*
> Stevenson's *Home Book of Quotations*
> Stevenson's *Home Book of Verse* and *Home Book of Modern Verse*
> Granger's *Index to Poetry*

EXERCISE 2. Distinguishing Between Specific Reference Books. Answer in writing the following questions.

1. Distinguish between a world atlas and a historical atlas.
2. List three books that contain information about events of the past year.
3. Which literature reference book would you use to find the author of a poem whose title you know?
4. Arrange the following titles in order according to the frequency of their publication, listing the most frequently published first: *Who's Who in America, Who's Who, Current Biography*.
5. Contrast the arrangements of Bartlett's *Familiar Quotations* and Stevenson's *Home Book of Quotations*.

EXERCISE 3. Selecting Reference Books to Find Specific Information. Number your paper 1–10. From the books and reference works given in brackets, write the one you would use to get the specified information. Be prepared to explain your choices.

1. Names of the senators in Congress from your state. [encyclopedia, *Who's Who in America, World Almanac*]
2. Books in your library about reptiles. [*Readers' Guide*, card catalog, vertical file]
3. Life of the Secretary-General of the United Nations. [*Current Biography, Dictionary of American Biography, Webster's Biographical Dictionary*]

4. International records in track events. [*Information Please Almanac, Who's Who in America, Readers' Guide*]
5. The source of the common expression "All the world's a stage." [Stevenson's *Home Book of Verse, Webster's Dictionary of Synonyms,* Bartlett's *Familiar Quotations*]
6. Titles and authors of biographies of the President. [*Biography Index, Who's Who in America, Webster's Biographical Dictionary*]
7. A quotation about youth. [Bartlett's *Familiar Quotations, World Almanac,* Stevenson's *Home Book of Quotations*]
8. The body of water into which the Suwannee River flows. [*The International Yearbook & Statesmen's Who's Who, World Almanac,* atlas]
9. A picture of an author who came into prominence during the past six months. [encyclopedia, *Current Biography, Who's Who*]
10. Leaflets recently published by the National Safety Council. [card catalog, *Readers' Guide,* vertical file]

EXERCISE 4. Using Library Tools or Reference Books to Find Specific Information. Which library tool or reference book, including the encyclopedia, would you use to find the following items of information? Write your first choice. Be able to explain.

1. Titles of recent magazine articles on the latest fashions in dress
2. The special power that the mythological character Clotho had
3. The title of a book, owned by your library, on conservation
4. An account of the climate of Tahiti
5. The native state of the Vice-President of the United States
6. The ten most populous cities in the United States
7. An illustrated article on the Navajo Indians
8. Pamphlets published by the Foreign Policy Association
9. Any books the library may have on stamp collecting
10. Officials of the present government of Pakistan

CHAPTER 35

The Dictionary

CONTENT AND
USES OF DICTIONARIES

Although dictionaries differ from one another in number of entries and method of presenting information, they all provide a report on the way language is used. Dictionary makers do not by themselves decide what words mean or how they should be pronounced and spelled. As a result of careful research, dictionary makers are able to record the way the majority of educated people use the language: the meanings such people apply to words and the ways they pronounce and spell words.

To people who want to make themselves understood and who wish to understand what they read, such a reliable report on language practice is of obvious value. No speaker of English knows all the words. Everyone needs help sometimes with the meaning, spelling, pronunciation, and use of a particular word.

KINDS OF DICTIONARIES

35a. Know the kinds of dictionaries.

Excluding the many special dictionaries—dictionaries of scientific terms, foreign-language dictionaries, etc.—there are two main kinds of dictionaries with which you should be familiar: the large *unabridged* dictionary, which you will probably use mainly in libraries; and the "college-size" dictionary, which you should have when you study.

College Dictionaries

The most practical dictionary for everyday use is the college dictionary, which usually has from about 100,000 to about 160,000 entries. Material in the front and the back often includes guides to punctuation, usage, and preparing research papers, and may contain other information useful to students. Because it is frequently revised, a college dictionary is likely to be more nearly up-to-date than an unabridged.

The four listed below are well known and reputable.

The American Heritage Dictionary of the English Language, Houghton Mifflin Co., Boston

The Random House College Dictionary, Random House, New York, N.Y.

Webster's New Collegiate Dictionary, G. & C. Merriam Co., Springfield, Mass.

Webster's New World Dictionary of the American Language, Second College Edition, William Collins Publishing Co., Cleveland, Ohio

Unabridged Dictionaries

The largest dictionaries—containing over 300,000 entries—are called *unabridged* dictionaries. *Unabridged* in this context means only "not cut down from a bigger one." Three (two American and one British) are listed below:

The Random House Dictionary of the English Language, Random House, New York, N.Y.

Webster's Third New International Dictionary, G. & C. Merriam Co., Springfield, Mass.

The Oxford English Dictionary, Oxford University Press, New York, N.Y.

An unabridged dictionary has two or three times the number of entries in a college dictionary. Many entries are likely to be more detailed and to give more facts. An unabridged dictionary is more likely to contain a rare or very old word, a dialect or regional word. *Webster's* and the *Oxford* use many actual quotations from named writers to show words in certain senses.

CONTENT AND ARRANGEMENT OF DICTIONARIES

35b. Familiarize yourself with the kinds of information in your dictionary and learn where and how each kind is given.

Although people most commonly use the dictionary to look up the spelling and meaning of words, to use it only for these purposes is to miss its many other kinds of information. The following study materials and exercises will help you discover the full resources of your dictionary and may lead you to refer to it more often and more efficiently.

Although all good dictionaries contain essentially the same facts, material may be arranged and handled quite differently. For example, some list items such as notable persons and places in the main alphabetical listing; others put them in separate sections. The location of abbreviations and foreign phrases may also differ.

EXERCISE 1. Understanding the Content and Arrangement of Your Dictionary.   Using the dictionary with which you have been provided, write the answers to the following questions. Use the table of contents whenever it is helpful.

1. What is the full title of your dictionary?
2. Who is the publisher?
3. What is the latest copyright date? (Look on the back of the title page.)
4. Where does the complete key to pronunciation appear?
5. Is there a shorter key on each page? On every other page?
6. On what page do the explanatory notes on pronunciation begin?
7. On what page does the introductory article describing and explaining the dictionary begin?
8. What special articles are there on the history of the language, grammar, etc.?
9. On what page are abbreviations used in the dictionary listed?
10. Are the other abbreviations, such as A.D., C.O.D., and UNESCO, explained in the body of your dictionary or in a separate section at the back?
11. Are guides to spelling, punctuation, and capitalization given? If so, list the page on which each begins.
12. Is there a section giving the meaning of commonly used signs and symbols? If so, give the page it begins on.
13. Are the names of important people and places listed in the body of your dictionary or in a separate section?
14. Does your dictionary provide derivations of words? If so, do they appear near the beginning or at the end of an entry?

15. Are the names of literary, mythological, and Biblical characters listed in the body of your dictionary or in a special section? To find out, look up Hamlet, Poseidon, and Deborah.

EXERCISE 2. Using Your Dictionary to Find Specific Information. Look up in your dictionary the answers to the following questions and write the answers in a column on your paper. *After each answer write the page number on which you found it.* If any of the items are not in your dictionary, write the number of the question and leave a blank space.

1. What was the occupation of Maria Mitchell?
2. Give the meaning of the French phrase *comme il faut.*
3. Give the spelling rule for retaining the silent final *e* on a word when you add a suffix.
4. In what play is Iago the villain?
5. Where is Prince Edward Island?

A Dictionary's Information About a Word

Definitions

The main function of a dictionary is to give the meanings of words. Since a single word may have many meanings, an entry covering it must have a matching number of definitions. In some dictionaries, all definitions are simply numbered in sequence. In others, small subdivisions of meaning within a numbered definition are headed by letters in sequence.

Some dictionaries still put definitions in historical order, the earliest meaning first, the latest last. Others base order on frequency of use, the most common meaning first, the least common last. The first entry below shows historical order; the second, frequency of use.

> **mas·ter·piece** \'mas-tər-,pēs\ *n* (1605)   **1** : a piece of work presented to a medieval guild as evidence of qualification for the rank of master   **2** : a work done with extraordinary skill; *esp* : a supreme intellectual or artistic achievement

From *Webster's Ninth New Collegiate Dictionary.* © 1986 by Merriam-Webster Inc., publisher of the Merriam-Webster® Dictionaries. Reprinted by permission of Merriam-Webster Inc.

> **mas·ter·piece** (mas′tər pēs′, mä′stər-), *n.*   **1.** a person's most excellent production, as in an art.   **2.** any production of masterly skill.   **3.** a piece made by a journeyman or other craftsman aspiring to the rank of master in a guild or other craft organization as a proof of his competence. [MASTER + PIECE, modeled on D *meesterstuk,* G *Meisterstück*]

A label usually shows the part of speech of the word being defined. For example, *n.* stands for noun, *v.* for verb, and so on. (Abbreviations used are explained in a dictionary's front matter.) In older dictionaries, a word used as more than one part of speech was given a new entry for each one. Now these once-separate entries are usually gathered into one main entry, with definitions still grouped and labeled by part of speech—noun definitions together, verb definitions together, etc. Definition numbers commonly start over for each new part of speech. College-size and bigger dictionaries cling to these practices.

When you look up a word's meaning, read all its definitions. Unless you do, you can't be sure that the meaning you select best fits the context in which the word is used.

Even though you have looked up the meaning, you should be wary of using a word you have encountered only once. A great many English words not only have more than one meaning, but they also have *implied* or *connotative* meanings, which are not given in a dictionary. Furthermore, there may be idiomatic uses of which a young student speaker or writer is not aware.

Spelling

The boldfaced word at the very beginning of a dictionary entry tells you the accepted spelling. When there are two or more acceptable spellings, the various spellings are given. Any spelling given has enough standing to justify use of it if you prefer it.

If grammatical change in the form of a word is likely to raise spelling problems, *inflectional* forms are given. (These are forms of a word resulting from its habitual usage, like the principal parts of verbs or the comparative and superlative forms of adjectives.) A dictionary is the best reference work to consult if you are uncertain about doubling a consonant, changing an *i* to a *y*, and so on.

Both the principal parts of irregular verbs you may have difficulty remembering and the spelling of frequently misspelled words can be found in any good dictionary. Think of the dictionary as the place to find the proper spelling (and forms) of:

    a. the plural of a word, if the plural is formed irregularly
    b. the feminine form of a foreign word: **alumnus; alumna,** fem.
    c. the principal parts of an irregular verb
    d. comparative and superlative forms of irregular adjectives and adverbs
    e. case forms of pronouns: **who;** *possessive* **whose;** *objective* **whom**

Syllable Division

When a word must be divided at the end of a line, it should be divided between syllables. Syllable division is indicated in the boldfaced entry word and often in inflectional forms. The break is usually shown by a centered dot (**bas•ket**). In some dictionaries it is indicated by a space (**bas ket**). Look at the various sample entries throughout this chapter to see the different ways each dictionary shows syllable division.

Capitalization

Proper nouns and adjectives, commonly written with initial capital letters, are entered in most dictionaries with the usual capitals. *Webster's Third,* however, prints the entry word in small letters followed by a brief note such as: *usu cap* or *often cap,* short for *usually capitalized* or *often capitalized.*

Sometimes a word not capitalized in most of its meanings should be capitalized when used in one sense, or perhaps more than one. The abbreviation *cap.* following a definition number indicates that the word is capitalized when used in that sense.

EXAMPLE

cap•i•tol \'kap-ət-ºl, 'kap-tºl\ *n* [L *Capitolium,* temple of Jupiter at Rome on the Capitoline hill] (1699) **1 a** : a building in which a state legislative body meets   **b** : a group of buildings in which the functions of state government are carried out   **2** *cap* : the building in which the U.S. Congress meets at Washington

From *Webster's Ninth New Collegiate Dictionary.* © 1986 by Merriam-Webster Inc., publisher of the Merriam-Webster® Dictionaries. Reprinted by permission of Merriam-Webster Inc.

Pronunciation

Ordinary spelling cannot show the sounds of words precisely. Dictionary pronunciations respell each word, using one fixed symbol for each of the 42 or 43 common sounds of English. Most of the symbols look like ordinary letters of the alphabet, some with special marks added, but they work differently: each one stands exclusively and consistently for only one sound.

Each dictionary explains its symbols in a key, usually in the front of the book, and also prints a shortened key at the foot of each pair of facing pages. The key shows each symbol tied to its sound *as heard in one or two familiar words.*

In long words, one syllable, or sometimes more than one, may be spoken with more stress or force than the others. This stress is shown by accent marks: heaviest stress by a heavier mark, lighter stress by a lighter mark. The marks may be either slanted or straight, either above or within the line of type, and either before or after the syllable involved.

EXAMPLES   **tax·i·cab:**   tak' se kab'

                     'tak se kab

                     ták se kăb

When a word has more than one recognized pronunciation, all of the pronunciations are given. You will have to study your dictionary's way of giving pronunciations, since each of the most available dictionaries differs from the others in the system it uses.

Etymologies, or Word Histories

Most dictionaries show, by means of abbreviations and symbols, what language a word originally came from and what its original meaning was. They also explain the source of recently coined words, such as *quark*.

The abbreviations used to indicate the languages from which words derive are explained in the front of your dictionary. The following examples show how dictionaries vary in where they position an etymology within an entry. The symbol < means "from," like the abbreviation *fr.*

EXAMPLE   ¹**book** \'bùk\ *n* [ME, fr. OE *boc;* akin to OHG *buoh* book; perh. akin to OE *bōc* beech (prob. fr. the early Germanic practice of carving runic characters on beech wood tablets) — more at BEECH] (bef. 12c)

From *Webster's Ninth New Collegiate Dictionary.* © 1986 by Merriam-Webster Inc., publisher of the Merriam-Webster® Dictionaries. Reprinted by permission of Merriam-Webster Inc.

Restrictive Labels

Most of the words defined in a dictionary are part of the general vocabulary. Some, however, have to do with a special field or are used almost exclusively in a single region or are used at only one level of usage.

To indicate these words, dictionaries use restrictive labels—*subject labels* such as *Law, Med.* (medicine), *Chem.* (chemistry), etc.; *area labels* such as *southwest U.S.;* and *usage labels* such as *informal, slang,* or *dialect.*

Usage labels provide a good general guide to usage, but all writers must learn to make judgments about these matters on the basis of their own observations. Assigning a label such as *slang* or *informal* is necessarily a subjective judgment on the part of a definer, and not all dictionaries agree about labeling the same word. Your knowledge of the connotations of a word and the situation in which you want to use it should be your guide in choosing or rejecting a particular word or meaning.

Synonyms and Antonyms

Dictionaries often list other words of similar meaning (synonyms) and sometimes also words of opposite meaning (antonyms) at the end of an entry. At times they also append a slightly longer note comparing two or more words with similar meanings, showing fine shades of differences as well as similarities.

In the following example, synonyms (SYN) are discussed in detail, and antonyms (ANT) are also given.

EXAMPLE **brave** (brāv) *adj.* [Fr. < It. *bravo*, brave, bold, orig., wild, savage < L. *barbarus*, BARBAROUS] **1.** willing to face danger, pain, or trouble; not afraid; having courage **2.** showing to good effect; having a fine appearance **3.** fine, grand, or splendid *[a brave new world]* —*n.* **1.** any brave man ✩**2.** [< 17th-c. NAmFr.] a North American Indian warrior **3.** [Archaic] a bully —*vt.* **braved, brav′ing 1.** to face with courage **2.** to defy; dare **3.** [Obs.] to make splendid, as in dress —*vi.* [Obs.] to boast —**brave′ly** *adv.* — **brave′ness** *n.*
SYN.—**brave** implies fearlessness in meeting danger or difficulty and has the broadest application of the words considered here; **courageous** suggests constant readiness to deal with things fearlessly by reason of a stout-hearted temperament or a resolute spirit; **bold** stresses a daring temperament, whether displayed courageously, presumptuously, or defiantly; **audacious** suggests an imprudent or reckless boldness; **valiant** emphasizes a heroic quality in the courage or fortitude shown; **intrepid** implies absolute fearlessness and esp. suggests dauntlessness in facing the new or unknown; **plucky** emphasizes gameness in fighting against something when one is at a decided disadvantage —*ANT.* craven, cowardly

Encyclopedia Entries

Besides giving information about words, the college dictionaries listed in this chapter (but not some unabridged dictionaries) give facts about many people and places. These may appear as entries in the body of the dictionary or in special sections at the back.

Important Persons

A dictionary usually covers these items about a person:

1. *Name:* spelling, pronunciation, and given names
2. *Date of birth (and death if deceased)*

3. *Nationality (and country of birth if different)*
4. *Why famous*

Dictionary information about contemporaries soon goes out of date. It may be safer to refer to *Who's Who* or *Who's Who in America* for up-to-date facts.

Important Places

In treating a geographical entry, a dictionary usually gives the following information:

1. *Name:* spelling, pronunciation
2. *Indentification:* city, nation, lake, river, etc.
3. *Location*
4. *Size:* population, as of a city; area, as of a state, body of water, etc.; length, as of a river; height, as of a mountain
5. *Political importance:* If a city is capital of a state or nation, the fact will be noted, and the city may be named in the entry for the state or nation.
6. *Historical or other interest:* as Yorktown, site of surrender of the British
7. *Controlling country:* as in Guam, a United States possession

Be sure that a dictionary uses the latest census for its (undated) population figures before you trust them. Old data can be seriously misleading.

SPECIAL DICTIONARIES

35c. Learn the use of special dictionaries.

Along with general dictionaries, there are dictionaries of the special vocabularies of law, medicine, slang, and so on.

Books of synonyms are useful to people who do much writing. They help writers to vary their choice of words and to find the exact word needed.

Roget's Thesaurus of English Words and Phrases

This is the classic book of synonyms, over a century old. Originally, its words were grouped by classes and subclasses of meaning, with a huge index attached. Some recent editions retain this ingenious format. Others put the material in dictionary form—straight alphabetical order.

Funk and Wagnalls Standard Handbook of Synonyms, Antonyms, and Prepositions

This is also a standard book, listing in alphabetical order most of the words you might want to use and giving synonyms and antonyms for them.

Webster's Dictionary of Synonyms

This is valued especially for its able discussion of distinctions between words of similar meaning.

EXERCISE 3. Using Your Dictionary to Find Information About Words. This exercise is designed to test your knowledge of the information given about a word in the dictionary. With your dictionary before you, begin work at the teacher's signal. Look up the answers to the following questions. While your speed indicates to some degree your efficiency in using the dictionary, accuracy is the more important consideration.

1. Which is the more usual spelling: *judgment* or *judgement?*
2. In the first pronunciation for *research,* is the accent on the first or second syllable?
3. Copy the correct pronunciation of the word *comely,* using the respelling and symbols.
4. Copy the word *automatic,* dividing it correctly into syllables.
5. How many different meanings are given in your dictionary for the word *run* as an intransitive (*v.i.*) verb?
6. What restrictive label is given the word *shank* when used in the expression "the shank of the evening"?
7. Distinguish between the meaning of *councilor* and *counselor.*
8. What is the origin of the word *candidate?*
9. In what literary work does the character Mrs. Malaprop appear? For what was she noted?
10. Tell the story of Hero and Leander as given in your dictionary.

EXERCISE 4. Using Your Dictionary to Find Information About Words. Like the preceding exercise, this exercise will test your knowledge of the information given in a dictionary and your familiarity with the location of this information in the dictionary. At the teacher's signal look up the answers to the following questions. Accuracy is more important than speed, but speed is important.

1. Find two synonyms for the word *cowardly*.
2. Write the plural of *analysis*.
3. Write the comparative and superlative forms of *ill*.
4. What city is the capital of Burma?
5. What is the population of Dallas, Texas?
6. When did Queen Victoria reign?
7. What was George Eliot's real name?
8. What is the meaning of the symbol AA used by a doctor in writing a prescription?
9. Write two acceptable plurals of *octopus*.
10. What is the meaning of the Latin phrase *caveat emptor*?

CHAPTER 36

Vocabulary

MEANING THROUGH CONTEXT AND WORD ANALYSIS

Although it is likely that this may be your last year of systematic vocabulary study, the number of English words you know and are able to use will continue to be important throughout your life. Most immediately, you will see that a good vocabulary will help you to succeed in college or at a job. More important, however, your general knowledge or your knowledge of a specific field cannot be very deep or impressive unless you have a considerable stock of words at your command. The number of words you know is one indication of the pride you take in your mind. You owe it to yourself to have a vocabulary that fairly reflects your interests and abilities.

DIAGNOSTIC TEST

Selecting the Closest Meaning   Number your paper 1–20. After the proper number, write the letter of the word or expression that comes closest to the meaning of the italicized word.

1. to *augment* the budget
   a) increase
   b) examine closely
   c) reduce
   d) disapprove of

2. to *ascertain* the facts
   a) cover up
   b) review
   c) find out
   d) testify to

3. a king known
   for his *avarice*
   - a) wisdom
   - b) vanity
   - c) deceitfulness
   - d) greed

4. a *biennial* event
   - a) twice yearly
   - b) every two weeks
   - c) every two years
   - d) twice daily

5. a *blithe* mood
   - a) bitter
   - b) proud
   - c) angry
   - d) carefree

6. an offer to
   capitulate
   - a) confer
   - b) mediate
   - c) compromise
   - d) surrender

7. a suspicion of
   collusion
   - a) robbery
   - b) foolishness
   - c) mistrustfulness
   - d) agreement to
     deceive

8. to *conjecture*
   about the facts
   - a) talk
   - b) lie
   - c) guess
   - d) conceal the truth

9. to *corroborate*
   testimony
   - a) testify about
   - b) confirm
   - c) deny
   - d) question

10. to act under
    duress
    - a) compulsion
    - b) misunderstanding
    - c) difficulties
    - d) bribery

11. an imposing
    edifice
    - a) natural wonder
    - b) manner
    - c) speech
    - d) building

12. a leader's
    foible
    - a) weakness
    - b) habit
    - c) example
    - d) follower

13. an *interminable*
    show
    - a) worthless
    - b) endless
    - c) tedious
    - d) difficult to describe

14. to *nurture* a
    child
    - a) neglect
    - b) give medicine to
    - c) scold
    - d) feed and bring up

15. a sign of
    opulence
    - a) poverty
    - b) health
    - c) wealth
    - d) generosity

16. a *prosaic* sight
    - a) commonplace
    - b) solemn
    - c) stirring
    - d) peaceful

17. a *prudent* action
    - a) unexpected
    - b) ill-mannered
    - c) sensible
    - d) foolish

18. good-natured
    raillery
    - a) scuffling
    - b) boisterousness
    - c) competition
    - d) banter

19. a well-deserved
    reproof
    - a) promotion
    - b) reprimand
    - c) apology
    - d) recognition

20. a *volatile*
    temperament
    - a) changeable
    - b) disagreeable
    - c) sluggish
    - d) easygoing

CONTEXT CLUES

36a. Find clues to meaning in context.

The words that surround a particular word in a sentence or paragraph are called the *verbal context* of that word. Consider this sentence, for example:

> Although she continued to predict victory, Captain Winters was really not *sanguine* about her team's prospects.

If you are not sure of the meaning of *sanguine*, the rest of this sentence provides some important clues. The first part suggests that there is something contradictory about the captain's predicting victory when she is not sanguine about her team's chances. From the whole sentence, you may reasonably conclude that *sanguine* must mean "hopeful" or "optimistic." Sometimes, of course, such reasoning will lead you into a wrong guess; but more often than not you will be right.

In addition to the other words, the situation itself often provides clues to the meaning of a word. In the example above, you would expect a captain to be concerned about her team's success. Thus, you would not suppose that *sanguine* meant "bored" or "disinterested." Clues provided by the situation being discussed often help in deciding between two very different meanings of the same word or of words that have the same spelling. For example, if you are reading about an argument, *retort* is likely to mean "a ready and effective reply." In a description of a scientific experiment, on the other hand, *retort* would probably mean "a vessel used in distilling."

EXERCISE 1. Using Context Clues to Determine Meanings of Words.

Number your paper 1–10. After each number, write the italicized word in the sentence and write a short definition based on the clues you find in context. You may check your definitions with the dictionary later.

1. After listening to a good deal of coaxing, the mother finally *acceded* to her children's request.
2. After a *hectic* year in the city, George was glad enough to return to the peace and quiet of the country.
3. Although the risks were great, the dissatisfied officers met and formed a *cabal* against the commander-in-chief.

4. The last two lines of the poem are so *cryptic* that no two readers can agree about what they mean.
5. Any person who was not entirely *devoid* of honor would have been outraged at the suggestion.
6. The loud, *raucous* laughter of the troop irritated the lieutenant.
7. A large constrictor grabs its prey in its mouth and quickly coils itself around the victim to *immobilize* it. The harder the animal struggles, the tighter the snake constricts.
8. Eventually, the criminal *expiated* this murder and many other crimes on the gallows.
9. According to Bacon, scientists should learn about nature through *empirical* observations based on experiments and on careful study of the greatest possible amount of evidence.
10. Despite the awesome *fecundity* of certain species of fish, the balance of nature limits the population.

Common Clues to Meaning

Although a sentence may provide clues to the meaning of a word in a variety of ways, there are four kinds of context clues that are particularly helpful. Learning to recognize these four kinds of clues will help you determine the meanings of many of the unfamiliar words you encounter.

Synonym

Often writers use synonyms in sentences for variety. In such cases the meaning of one word is the clue to the meaning of the other word. In the following example, notice that the writer uses the word *avoid* as a synonym for *eschew* so that *eschew* does not have to be repeated in the sentence.

> A person on a reducing diet is expected to *eschew* greasy foods and, especially, to *avoid* sugar.

Example

Another technique that writers may employ to clarify meaning is including examples of an important word in a sentence. Expressions such as *for example, for instance, such as,* and *especially* will often indicate an example. In the following sentence, you can probably guess that the word *charlatan* means "a person who claims to have a skill which he doesn't really have" from the examples in the sentence.

> When hiring someone to do home repairs, be wary of charlatans such as carpenters or plumbers who do not have any references or tools.

Comparison or Contrast

The comparisons or contrasts used by writers often supply clues to meaning by pairing an unfamiliar word with a common word or phrase. Look for expressions such as *like, as, similar to,* or *in the same way* to precede comparisons. In the following sentence, the comparison of the word *buffoon* to the word *clowns* illustrates how comparison can be a good context clue.

> At parties William is a buffoon, just *like* all the other clowns in the class.

Contrasting meanings are often signaled by such words as *but, not, although, rather than,* and *however.* In the following example, notice that the word *dirge* is contrasted with *wedding march.*

> We were surprised at the bride's choice of music, for the processional sounded like a dirge *rather than* a wedding march.

Because it is contrasted to the wedding march, you can guess that a *dirge* is a music type that is not appropriate for a wedding. However, you might have to check your dictionary to discover that a *dirge* is specifically "a funeral hymn." Comparison or contrast clues will help you guess a word's meaning, but to be absolutely certain, look up the word in a dictionary.

Definition

When writers anticipate that their readers may not know the meaning of an important word, they often provide a definition. They may introduce the definition with an expression such as *in other words* or *that is,* or they may slip it in as an appositive without calling attention to it. The definitions or explanations in the following examples are italicized, and the words defined are in boldfaced type.

> The painting clearly shows the **aegis**, or *shield*, of Athena.
>
> A word is often defined by a **synonym**—that is, *a word of similar meaning.*
>
> His *observation* was *too obvious to mention*—a **truism**. [Notice that the explanation comes before the word defined in this example.]

People do not go to the trouble of explaining things unless they want to be understood. Be on the lookout for definitions of difficult words.

EXERCISE 2. Using Context Clues to Determine Meanings of Words. Number your paper 1–10 and after each number write the italicized word. Give a brief definition in your own words, based on the context.

1. Along with the discovery of the properties of poisons came the discovery of substances that had properties of combating the effects of poisons. These early *antidotes* were strange mixtures.
2. The border rebellion, *quiescent* during the winter months, broke out in renewed violence in the spring.
3. To the rest of us, the outlook just then seemed more ominous than *propitious*.
4. Most snakes are meat eaters, or *carnivores*.
5. The *salutary* effect of the new drug was shown by the rapid improvement in the patient's condition.
6. *Subterranean* temperatures are frequently higher than those above the surface of the earth.
7. Because the official could not attend the meeting herself, she had to send a *surrogate*, or deputy.
8. The method of reasoning from the particular to the general—the *inductive* method—has played an important role in science since the time of Francis Bacon.
9. If the leaders felt any *compunction* about planning and carrying out unprovoked attacks on neighboring countries, they showed no sign of it.
10. Formerly, a doctor who found a successful cure often regarded it as a trade secret and refused to *divulge* it to others.

EXERCISE 3. Using Context Clues to Determine Meanings of Words. Read the following passage and then write your own definitions for the italicized words. Consult your dictionary only after you have written your own definitions from context.

Most of the doctors who had treated cases of the peculiar disease were almost certain by then that the characteristic initial (1) *lesion* was the bite of some (2) *minute* creature, but they had little reason to suspect mites of being the guilty parties. At the time, it was generally believed that mites could transmit only two serious (3) *febrile* diseases— Japanese river fever and endemic typhus. Both of these are rarely found in the United States, and anyway both had been eliminated from consideration in this instance by laboratory tests. Moreover, the mouse, unlike the rat, had never been proved to be a reservoir for disease-bearing parasites. Mr. Pomerantz admits that hitting upon the mouse as the probable (4) *host* was largely intuitive. He is persuaded, however, that in singling out mites as the carriers—or (5) *vectors*, as such agents are known—of the disease he was guided entirely by (6) *deduction*.

Mites are insectlike organisms, closely related to ticks. Both are members of the Arachnida, a class that also includes spiders and scorpions. Compared to a tick, a mite is a minute animal. A mite, when fully (7) *engorged*, is about the size of a strawberry seed. In that state, it is approximately ten times its usual, or unfed, size. So far, science has classified at least thirty families of mites, most of which are vegetarian and indifferent to man and all other animals. The majority of the (8) *parasitic*, blood-sucking mites have to feed once in every four or five days in order to live. Most mites of this type attach themselves to a host only long enough to engorge, and drop off, (9) *replete*, after fifteen or twenty minutes. No one ever feels the bite of a mite—or of a tick, either, for that matter—until the animal has dropped off. Entomologists believe that both creatures, at the instant they bite, (10) *excrete* a fluid that anesthetizes a small surrounding area of the body of the host. Mites are only infrequently found in this country and until recently were practically unknown in New York City. Consequently, very few Americans, even physicians and exterminators, have ever seen a mite. Mr. Pomerantz is one of those who have. He came across some in line of duty on three occasions in 1945.

BERTON ROUECHÉ

36b. Look up unfamiliar words in your dictionary.

For those words that context does not make sufficiently clear, the dictionary will provide you with the help you need. But here, too, context is important. Most words have a number of different meanings. To find the one you want, you will need to keep in mind the context in which you originally encountered the word. Once you have found the meaning you want, read on through the whole definition. Most words have a range of different meanings; to know the word well, you should know more than one of its meanings. Moreover, learning the pronunciation, the derivation, and related forms of the word will help you to remember it. Once you take the trouble to go to the dictionary, you may as well get as much information as possible from it.

WORD ANALYSIS

36c. Use your knowledge of prefixes, suffixes, and roots.

In general, English words are of two kinds: those that can be analyzed into smaller parts (*unworkable, impolitely*) and those that cannot (*stone, money, winter*). The words of the first kind, those that can be divided, are made up of parts called prefixes, roots, and suffixes. Because these parts have broad, general meanings that remain essentially the same in different words, knowing something about word analysis can help you figure out the meaning of an unfamiliar word. However, there are some difficulties that make it unwise to depend entirely on word analysis for clues to meaning. It is not always easy to tell whether a particular group of letters is really the prefix or suffix it appears to be. The *-er* in *painter* is a suffix, but the *-er* in *winter* is not. To be certain, you have to know something about the origin of the word. Moreover, the original force of a combination of word parts may no longer have much to do with the modern meaning of a word. For these and other reasons, absolute dependence on word analysis would lead you to make as many bad guesses as good ones.

There are, however, some good reasons for having a general knowledge of the way English words are formed. Word analysis helps you to understand the peculiarities of English spelling and the connection between the related forms of a particular word. (Knowing about related forms often enables you to learn four or five new words as easily as one.) Also, word analysis gives you useful practice in taking a close look at words. In reading, you pass very quickly over words, hardly noticing more than their general shape. This is all very well for words you know well, but close examination is called for with unfamiliar ones. Most important of all, word analysis offers the key to the origin of English words. The fact that many different cultures have contributed to the vocabulary of English is one of its particular strengths. Educated people should know something about the history as well as the use of their words.

How Words Are Divided

Words that can be divided have two or more parts: a core called a *root* and one or more parts added to it. The parts that are added are called *affixes*—literally, "something fixed or attached to something else." An affix added before the root is called a *prefix;* one added after the root is called a *suffix.* A word may have one or more affixes of either kind, or several of both kinds. A root with no affixes at all is incapable of being divided. A word consisting of a root only is one like *stone* or *money,* to which word analysis does not apply.

The following table shows some typical combinations of affixes (prefixes and suffixes) and roots.

PREFIX[ES]	ROOT	SUFFIX[ES]	EXAMPLE
un-	work	-able	unworkable
post-	-pone		postpone
	friend	-ly	friendly
	fright	-en, -ing	frightening
il-	-leg-	-al	illegal
under	take	-er	undertaker
	truth	-ful	truthful
	child	like	childlike

Some of the affixes and roots in English are recognizable as complete words in themselves (*fright* in *frighten; child* and *like* in *childlike*). Most other affixes and roots were also once separate words, though the original words may no longer exist in our modern language. For example, *post* in *postpone* was a Latin word meaning *after,* and *pone* (*pono, ponere*) was the Latin word for *put.*

The Origins of English Words

In the lists that appear later in this chapter, prefixes and roots are grouped according to the language in which they originated: Old English, Latin (or Latin-French), and Greek.

Old English, or Anglo-Saxon, is the earliest recorded form of the English language. It was spoken from about A.D. 600 until about A.D. 1100, and most of its words had been part of a still earlier form of the language. Many of the common words of modern English, like *home, stone,* and *meat,* are native, or Old English, words. Most of the irregular verbs in English derive from Old English (*speak, swim, drive, ride, sing*), as most of our shorter numerals (*two, three, six, ten*) and most of our pronouns (*I, you, we, who*). Many Old English words can be traced back to Indo-European, a prehistoric language that was the common ancestor of Greek and Latin as well. Others came into Old English as it was becoming a separate language.

As the speakers of Old English became acquainted with Latin, chiefly through contact with Christianity, they began to borrow Latin words for things for which no native word existed. Some common words borrowed at this time were *abbot, altar, candle, temple, fever,* and *lettuce.*

Many other Latin words came into English through French. In 1066, toward the end of the Old English period, the French under William the Conqueror invaded England and defeated the Anglo-Saxons under King Harold. For the next three hundred years, French was the language of the ruling classes in England. During this period, thousands of new words came into English, many of them words relating to upper-class pursuits: *baron, attorney, ermine, luxury.* English has continued to borrow words from French right down to the present, with the result that over a third of our modern English vocabulary derives from French.

Many words from Greek, the other major source of English words, came into English by way of French and Latin. Others were borrowed directly in the sixteenth century when interest in classical culture was at its height. Directly or indirectly, Greek contributed *athlete, acrobat, elastic, magic, rhythm,* and many others.

In the modern period, English has borrowed from every important language in the world. The etymologies in your dictionary trace the origins of words, often providing insights into their present meanings and into history as well.

EXERCISE 4. Finding the Etymologies of Words. Find out from your dictionary the origins of each of the following words. (For help in interpreting the etymology, see page 727 of this book.)

abscond	demon	quart
air	legal	tyrant
chase	loyal	votary

Prefixes

English borrowed not only independent words from Greek, Latin, and French, but also a number of word parts from these languages for use as affixes and roots. These sources are indicated in the following list of prefixes and in the list of roots on pages 748–51.

Prefixes have broad general meanings like *not, under,* and *against,* and a particular one of them may appear in hundreds of different words. In general, a knowledge of prefixes will help you to know when to double consonants in such words as *misspell* and *overrun*; when you are not sure, however, be sure to check a dictionary. Many prefixes have several different spellings in order to fit with various roots.

PREFIX	MEANING	EXAMPLES
Old English		
a-	in, on, of, up, to	afoot, awake
be-	around, about, away	beset, behead
for-	away, off, from	forsake, forget
mis-	badly, poorly, not	mismatch, misspell
over-	above, excessively	oversee, overdo
un-	not, reverse of	untrue, unfold
Latin and Latin-French		
ab-, a-, abs-	from, off, away	-abduct, absent
ante-	before	antedate
bi-	two	bimonthly, bisect
circum-	around	circumnavigate
com-, co- col-, con-, cor-	with, together	compare, coexist, collide, convene, correspond
contra-	against	contradict
de-	away, from, off, down	defect, desert
dis-, dif-	away, off, opposing	dissent, differ
ex-, e-, ef-	away from, out	excise, efface
in-, im-	in, into, within	induct, impose
in-, im-, il-, ir-	not	incapable, impious, illegal, irregular
inter-	among, between	intercede, intersperse
intro-, intra-	inward, to the inside, within	introduce, intravenous, intramural
non-	not	nonentity, nonessential
post-	after, following	postpone, postscript
pre-	before	prevent, preclude
pro-	forward, in place of, favoring	produce, pronoun, pro-American
re-	back, backward, again	revoke, recede, recur
retro-	back, backward	retroactive, retrospect
semi-	half	semiannual, semicircular

PREFIX	MEANING	EXAMPLES
Latin and Latin-French (continued)		
sub-, suf-, sum-, sup-, sus-	under, beneath	subjugate, suffuse summon, suppose, suspect
super-	over, above, extra	supersede, supervise
trans-	across, beyond	transfuse, transport
ultra-	beyond, excessively	ultramodern, ultraviolet
Greek		
a-	lacking, without	amorphous, atheistic
anti-	against, opposing	antipathy, antithesis
apo-	from, away	apology, apocrypha
cata-	down, away, thoroughly	cataclysm, catastrophe
dia-	through, across, apart	diameter, diagnose
eu-	good, pleasant	eulogy, euphemism
hemi-	half	hemisphere, hemiplegic
hyper-	excessive, over	hypercritical, hypertension
hypo-	under, beneath	hypodermic, hypothesis
para-	beside, beyond	parallel, paradox
peri-	around	periscope, perimeter
pro-	before	prognosis, program
syn-, sym-, syl-, sys-	together, with	synchronize, sympathy, syllable, system

EXERCISE 5. Understanding Prefixes in Words. Divide the following words into prefix and root, putting a slant line (/) at the point of division. Then give the meaning of the English word. Be ready to explain the connection between the meaning of the prefix and the present meaning of the word.

EXAMPLE 1. amnesia
1. a/mnesia *(loss of memory)*

1. absolve
2. amorphous
3. antipodes
4. biennial
5. circumspect
6. compunction
7. excise
8. hypodermic
9. impolite
10. subordinate

EXERCISE 6. Writing Words with Specific Prefixes. Find and write on your paper two words that contain each of the following prefixes: *de-, dia-, dis-, eu-, ir-, mis-, pro-, re-, syn-, ultra-.*

Suffixes

Suffixes, you will recall, are affixes added after the root, or at the end of a word. There are two main kinds of suffixes: those that provide a grammatical signal of some kind but do not greatly alter the basic meaning of the word and those that, by being added, create new words. The endings -*s*, -*ed*, and -*ing* are suffixes of the first kind; by adding them to *work (works, worked, working)* we indicate something about number and tense, but we do not change the essential meaning of the word. This kind of suffix is a *grammatical* suffix.

Grammatical suffixes are important in grammar, but in vocabulary we are more concerned with the second kind of suffixes—those that make new words. By adding -*ful* to *thank*, we get a different word: *thankful*. Adding -*hood* to *girl* gives us *girlhood*, again a different word. Suffixes that change meaning in this way are called *derivational* suffixes. Notice in the following examples that the addition of a derivational suffix often gives a new part of speech as well as a new meaning.

ROOT	DERIVATIONAL SUFFIX	RESULT
acid (n. or adj.)	-ity	acidity (n. only)
free (adj.)	-dom	freedom (n.)
accept (v.)	-ance	acceptance (n.)

Since derivational suffixes so often determine the part of speech of English words, we can conveniently classify them according to parts of speech. The meanings given for the suffixes are very broad. Often they have little connection with the meaning of the resulting word.

NOUN SUFFIXES	MEANING	EXAMPLES
Old English		
-dom	state, rank, condition	freedom, wisdom
-er	doer, maker	hunter, writer, thinker
-hood	state, condition	childhood, statehood
-ness	quality, state	softness, shortness
Foreign (Latin, French, Greek)		
-age	process, state, rank	passage, bondage
-ance, -ancy	act, condition, fact	acceptance, vigilance, hesitancy
-ard, -art	one that does (esp. excessively)	coward, laggard, braggart

NOUN SUFFIXES	MEANING	EXAMPLES
Foreign (Latin, French, Greek) (continued)		
-ate	rank, office	delegate, primate
-ation	action, state, result	occupation, starvation
-cy	state, condition	accuracy, captaincy
-ee	one receiving action	employee, refugee
-eer	doer, worker at	engineer, racketeer
-ence	act, condition, fact	evidence, patience
-er	doer, native of	baker, westerner
-ery	skill, action, collection	surgery, robbery, crockery
-ess	feminine	waitress, lioness
-et, -ette	little, feminine	islet, cigarette, majorette
-ion	action, result, state	union, fusion, dominion
-ism	act, manner, doctrine	baptism, barbarism, socialism
-ist	doer, believer	monopolist, socialist, capitalist
-ition	action, state, result	sedition, expedition
-ity	state, quality, condition	paucity, civility
-ment	means, result, action	refreshment, disappointment
-or	doer, office, action	elevator, juror, honor
-ry	condition, practice, collection	dentistry, jewelry
-tion	action, condition	creation, relation
-tude	quality, state, result	fortitude, multitude
-ty	quality, state	novelty, beauty
-ure	act, result, means	culture, signature
-y	result, action, quality	jealousy, inquiry

ADJECTIVE SUFFIXES	MEANING	EXAMPLES
Old English		
-en	made of, like	wooden, golden
-ful	full of, marked by	thankful, masterful
-ish	suggesting, like	childish, devilish
-less	lacking, without	helpless, hopeless
-like	like, similar	childlike, dreamlike
-ly	like, of the nature of	friendly, cowardly
-some	apt to, showing	tiresome, lonesome
-ward	in the direction of	backward, homeward
-y	showing, suggesting	hilly, sticky, wavy

ADJECTIVE SUFFIXES	MEANING	EXAMPLES
Foreign		
-able	able, likely	capable, affable, changeable
-ate	having, showing	animate, separate
-escent	becoming, growing	obsolescent, quiescent
-esque	in the style of, like	picturesque, statuesque
-fic	making, causing	terrific, soporific
-ible	able, likely, fit	edible, flexible, possible, divisible
-ose	marked by, given to	comatose, bellicose
-ous	marked by, given to	religious, furious

ADJECTIVE OR NOUN SUFFIXES	MEANING	EXAMPLES
-al	doer, pertaining to	rival, animal, autumnal
-an	one belonging to, pertaining to	human, European
-ant	actor, agent, showing	servant, observant, radiant
-ary	belonging to, one connected with	primary, adversary, auxiliary
-ent	doing, showing, actor	confident, adherent
-ese	of a place or style, style	Chinese, journalese
-ian	pertaining to, one belonging to	barbarian, reptilian
-ic	dealing with, caused by, person or thing, showing	classic, choleric
-ile	marked by, one marked by	juvenile, servile
-ine	marked by, dealing with, one marked by	marine, canine, divine
-ite	formed, showing, one marked by	favorite, composite
-ive	belonging or tending to, one belonging to	detective, native
-ory	doing, pertaining to, place or thing for	accessory, contributory

VERB SUFFIXES	MEANING	EXAMPLES
Old English		
-en	cause to be, become	deepen, darken

VERB SUFFIXES	MEANING	EXAMPLES
Foreign		
-ate	become, form, treat	populate, animate
-esce	become, grow, continue	convalesce, acquiesce
-fy	make, cause, cause to have	glorify, fortify
-ish	do, make, perform	punish, finish
-ize	make, cause to be	sterilize, motorize

Some of the words in the above lists make independent sense without the suffix (*employee, employ*). Others, however, do not (*delegate, deleg-*).

Because the English language has been exposed to so many different influences, the pattern of adding suffixes to form related words is often inconsistent. Things made of wood are *wooden*, but things made of stone are not *stonen*. We do have some regularities: verbs ending in *-ate* usually have a related noun ending *-ation* (*prostrate, prostration*). We have such regular patterns as *differ, difference, differential, exist, existence, existential*, etc., but we have many other examples that are not so systematic. This irregularity is one reason why it is so important to learn related forms of the new words you add to your vocabulary. You cannot derive the noun form of *reject* (*rejection*) by knowing the noun form of *accept* (*acceptance*). You have to learn it separately. In a sense, you do not really know a word until you know its important related forms.

EXERCISE 7. Writing Related Nouns of Specific Verbs. What nouns, if any, are companion forms of the following verbs? Write the noun after the proper number. Do not use gerunds.

EXAMPLES   1. convene   2. decode
           1. *convention* 2. *decoder*

1. cavil
2. collate
3. demur
4. disburse
5. intercede
6. intervene
7. prescribe
8. proscribe
9. stultify
10. verify

EXERCISE 8. Writing Related Verbs for Specific Nouns. Number your paper 1–10. Give a related verb for each noun below if there is one. If there is no verb form, write 0 after the proper number.

1. asperity
2. austerity
3. complaisance
4. defection
5. notation

6. raillery
7. remission
8. remuneration
9. turpitude
10. verification

EXERCISE 9. Writing Related Adjectives for Specific Nouns and Verbs.

Number your paper 1–10. Give a related adjective for each of the following nouns and verbs.

1. austerity
2. complaisance
3. deduce
4. increment
5. environment

6. essence
7. excess
8. prescience
9. prescribe
10. vituperate

Roots

A root is the core of a word—the part to which prefixes and suffixes are added. To find the root, you have only to remove any affix there may be. For example, removal of the affixes *a-* and *-ous* from *amorphous* leaves us with *-morph-*, a root meaning "form or shape." The root *-clysm*, meaning "falling," remains after we remove the prefix *cata-*, meaning "down," from *cataclysm*.

Roots have more specific and definite meanings than either prefixes or suffixes and appear in fewer different words. The following list contains some of the common foreign roots in English words.

ROOT	MEANING	EXAMPLES
Latin		
-ag-, -act-	do, drive, impel	agitate, transact
-agr-	field	agriculture, agrarian
-am-, -amic-	friend, love	amatory, amicable
-aqu-	water	aquatic, aqueduct, aquarium
-aud-, -audit-	hear	audible, auditorium
-ben-, -bene-	well, good	benefit, benediction
-brev-	short, brief	abbreviate, breviary
-cand-	white, glowing	candor, incandescent
-capit-	head	capital, decapitate
-cent-	hundred	century, centennial
-cid-, -cis-	kill, cut	suicide, regicide, incision

ROOT	MEANING	EXAMPLES
Latin (continued)		
-clin-	bend, lean	decline, inclination
-cogn-	know	recognize, cognizant
-cred-	belief, trust	incredible, credulity
-crypt-	hidden, secret	crypt, cryptic
-culp-	fault, blame	culpable, exculpate
-duc-, -duct-	lead	educate, conductor
-equ-	equal	equation, equanimity
-err-	wander, stray	erratic, aberration
-fac-, -fact-, -fect-, -fic-	do, make	facile, manufacture, defective, efficient
-fer-	bear, yield	transfer, fertile
-fid-	belief, faith	fidelity, perfidious
-fin-	end, limit	final, indefinite
-frag-, -fract-	break	fragment, fracture
-fus-	pour	transfuse, effusive
-gen-	birth, kind, origin	generate, generic
-jac-, -ject-	throw, hurl, cast	adjacent, eject
-jud-	judge	prejudice, adjudicate
-jug-	join, yoke	conjugal, conjugate
-junct-	join	junction, disjunctive
-jur-	swear, plead	adjure, perjury
-leg-, -lig-, -lect-	choose, read	eligible, legible, lectern
-loc-	place	locus, locale
-loqu-, -loc-	talk, speech	colloquial, locution
-magn-	large	magnitude, magnify
-mal-	bad	malady, malevolent
-man-, -manu-	hand	manicure, manual
-mit-, -miss-	send	remit, emissary
-mor-, -mort-	die, death	mortuary, immortal
-omni-	all	omnipotent, omniscient
-ped-	foot	pedal, quadruped
-pend-, -pens-	hang, weigh	appendix, suspense
-pon-, -pos-	place, put	postpone, interpose
-port-	carry, bear	transport, importation
-prim-	first, early	primitive, primordial
-punct-	point	punctuation, punctilious
-reg-, -rig-, -rect-	rule, straight, right	regent, incorrigible, rectangular
-rupt-	break	rupture, interrupt

ROOT	MEANING	EXAMPLES
Latin (continued)		
-sang-	blood	sanguine, consanguinity
-sci-	know, knowledge	omniscient, prescience
-scrib-, -script-	write	inscribe, proscribe, manuscript
-sent-, -sens-	feel	presentiment, sensitive
-sequ-, -secut-	follow	sequel, persecute, consecutive
-son-	sound	consonant, sonorous
-spir-	breath, breathe	expire, inspiration
-strict-, -string-	bind tight	constrict, stricture, stringent
-tract-	draw, pull	traction, extractor
-uni-	one	unity, universe
-ven-, -vent-	come	intervene, supervene
-verb-	word	verbal, verbiage
-vid-, -vis-	see	evident, television
-vit-	life	vitality, vitamin
Greek		
-anthrop-	man	anthropology, misanthropic
-arch-	ancient, chief	archaeology, monarch
-astr-, -aster-	star	astronomy, asterisk
-auto-	self	automatic, autonomy
-bibli-	book	bibliography, bibliophile
-bio-	life	biology, autobiography
-chrom-	color	chromatic, chromosome
-cosm-	world, order	cosmos, microcosm
-cycl-	wheel, circle	cyclone, bicycle
-dem-	people	democracy, epidemic
-gen-	kind, race	eugenics, genesis
-geo-	earth	geography, geology
-gram-	write, writing	grammar, epigram
-graph-	write, writing	orthography, geography
-hydr-	water	hydrogen, dehydrate
-log-	word, study	epilogue, theology, logic
-micr-	small	microbe, microscope
-mon-	one, single	monogamy, monologue
-morph-	form	amorphous, metamorphosis
-neo-	new	neologism, neolithic
-orth-	straight, correct	orthodox, orthography
-pan-	all, entire	panorama, pandemonium
-path-	feeling, suffering	apathy, pathology, sympathy

ROOT	MEANING	EXAMPLES
Greek (continued)		
-phil-	like, love	philanthropic, philosophy
-phon-	sound	phonology, euphony
-poly-	many	polygon, polygamy
-proto-	first	prototype
-psych-	mind	psychology, psychosomatic
-soph-	wise, wisdom	philosophy, sophomore
-tele-	far, distant	telegram, telepathy
-zo-	animal	zoology, protozoa

EXERCISE 10. Writing Words with Specific Roots. List two English words (other than those given as examples above) containing each of the following Latin roots.

EXAMPLES   1. -verb-
            1. *adverb, verbose*

1. -aud- (hear)
2. -crypt- (hidden, secret)
3. -duc- (lead)
4. -fin- (end, limit)
5. -junct- (join)
6. -man-, -manu- (hand)
7. -mor-, -mort- (death)
8. -port- (carry)
9. -vid-, -vis- (see)
10. -vit- (life)

EXERCISE 11. Writing Words with Specific Roots. Follow the instructions for Exercise 10 for the following Greek roots.

1. -arch- (chief)
2. -auto- (self)
3. -bio- (life)
4. -chron- (time)
5. -cycl- (wheel, circle)
6. -dem-, -demo- (people)
7. -gram- (write, writing)
8. -hydr- (water)
9. -mega- (large)
10. -poly- (many)

Limitations of Word Analysis

Knowing something of the way in which prefixes, suffixes, and roots combine to form words provides insights into the history of our words and into their meanings. However, it would be misleading to suggest that the original meanings of the parts are always clearly reflected in a modern word.

It may happen that following the method of word division will lead you to a meaning that is so far from the modern one as to be of little help. For example, the words *admonition* and *monetary* have an element

(*-mon-*) in common. The first means "warning" and the second "pertaining to money." What is the connection? There is one, but it is remote: in ancient Roman times, money was coined in or near a temple of Juno, a goddess known as "the warner." This is interesting, but not much of a clue if you do not already know the meaning of both words. Word analysis can often help you to make a plausible guess at what a word may mean; it can rarely be absolutely depended upon.

Semantic Change

One obvious reason that word analysis does not always work as a way of finding meaning is that words change their meanings. This change in meaning—called *semantic change*—is extremely common.

There are several ways in which this change comes about. Sometimes a word that has had a general meaning comes to have a specific meaning. The word *starve* once meant "to die." It only later took on the special meaning of "to die from lack of food." In Old English, any crawling creature—including the dragon in *Beowulf*—could be called a *worm*. Now the word is used only to mean earthworms and the like.

Words also take on new meanings in the opposite way—from specific to general. Originally *barn* meant "a storage place for barley," and *lord* meant "loaf guard or bread keeper."

When a word acquires a new meaning, it may lose the old meaning, as *worm, starve,* and *lord* have. When this situation takes place, the word has become detached from the root meaning, although it retains the original root form. The *-jure* of *adjure* is related to *jury* and originally had to do with swearing in a legal sense. But usually the word now means "to entreat," and the meaning connection with the root has been lost.

Sometimes both old and new meanings are retained. Indeed, often it works out that a word will have six, eight, or ten meanings. Some of these meanings may be close to the original meanings of the word elements; some may vary from them considerably. The word *aegis* meant originally a shield or breastplate, especially one associated with the goddess Athena; then it also came to mean "protection" and "patronage, sponsorship." Depending on the context, it can mean any of these things in modern English. As a result, we may say that a lecture or exhibit is held under either the auspices—originally, bird watching— or the aegis—originally, shield—of a certain group. *Insular* means "pertaining to an island," but it has also come to mean "isolated, detached" and also "narrow, provincial." *Sanguine* may retain the root meaning and indicate "bloody," but it is more likely to mean "quite optimistic." Because there are so many situations involving semantic change, careful use of context clues or steady use of the dictionary is likely to give a more accurate sense of word meanings than word analysis alone.

EXERCISE 12. Writing the Original Meanings of Specific Words. List the following words and write after each its original meaning as given in the dictionary: *abeyance, challenge, derive, detriment, dirge, farce, lampoon, melancholy, monster, pedigree.*

Synonyms

Word borrowing, word derivation by affixes and roots, semantic change, and other processes keep going on all the time, making English rich in synonyms. Synonyms are words that may be interchanged in given contexts. We can say "a hard task" or "a difficult task," because *hard* and *difficult* are synonyms. We can say that New York is a large city or a metropolis, and *city* and *metropolis* are therefore synonyms.

It is often said that there are very few pairs of words in English that are entirely interchangeable, because there are usually slight but important differences between synonyms. Sometimes one synonym is noticeably more learned than another; *edifice* is more learned and pretentious than *building, domicile* more so than *home* or *residence. Daily* is the ordinary English word, *diurnal* and *quotidian* quite learned. Sometimes one of a pair of synonyms is noticeably informal; *smidge* or *smidgeon* is less formal than *particle.* Often learned words are rather specific in their suggestions; the sphere in which they can be used is narrow. It is possible to analyze both *terrestrial* and *mundane* as "pertaining to the world." But *terrestrial* is likely to suggest contrast between our world and other heavenly bodies, described by words like *lunar* and *solar;* and *mundane* carries with it suggestions of the practical, routine, everyday affairs of this world, as contrasted with more spiritual matters. Synonyms may differ, too, in expressing value judgments; to be *resolute* is a virtue; and to be *obstinate* is a fault.

The wealth of synonyms in English gives us a variety of ways of expressing ourselves, but challenges us to decide on the most appropriate of them.

EXERCISE 13. Understanding the Difference Between Pairs of Synonyms. Use each of the following words in a sentence which illustrates the specific meaning of each synonym.

1. donation, gift
2. venomous, toxic
3. reverent, pious
4. lean, gaunt
5. meditate, ruminate

6. vapid, inane
7. void, vacuum
8. gracious, cordial
9. congenital, hereditary
10. handle, manipulate

REVIEW EXERCISE. Selecting the Definitions of Words.
Number your paper 1–20. After the proper number, write the letter of the word or expression that comes closest to the meaning of the italicized word.

1. *amorphous* clouds
   a) formless
   b) romantic
   c) jar-shaped
   d) commonplace

2. under the *auspices* of the state
   a) protests
   b) sponsorship
   c) opposition
   d) observation

3. struggle for *autonomy*
   a) fair treatment
   b) self-esteem
   c) survival
   d) self-rule

4. the last chance to *capitulate*
   a) turn the tide
   b) surrender
   c) negotiate
   d) compromise

5. *circumspect* behavior
   a) improper
   b) cautious
   c) surprising
   d) praiseworthy

6. to *collate* two documents
   a) preserve
   b) seal up
   c) duplicate
   d) compare

7. feeling no *compunction*
   a) satisfaction
   b) ambition
   c) remorse
   d) pride

8. to *conjecture* about a motive
   a) guess
   b) mislead
   c) lie
   d) find out

9. the soldier's *defection*
   a) weakness
   b) decoration
   c) desertion
   d) wound

10. not daring to *demur*
    a) whisper
    b) appear
    c) object
    d) tell the truth

11. *devoid* of sympathy
    a) full
    b) without a trace
    c) deserving
    d) undeserving

12. without *divulging* the answer
    a) guessing
    b) revealing
    c) suspecting
    d) peeking at

13. to *expiate* a crime
    a) profit from
    b) witness
    c) atone for
    d) facilitate

14. a *judicious* choice
    a) illegal
    b) required by law
    c) wise
    d) laughable

15. a *minute* creature
    a) short-lived
    b) quickly moving
    c) very small
    d) very young

16. *mundane* concerns
    a) worldly
    b) tedious
    c) religious
    d) dishonest

17. *parasitic* followers
    a) loyal
    b) living off others
    c) disloyal
    d) fanatical

18. a *propitious* start
    a) proper
    b) false
    c) sudden
    d) favorable

19. an unusual *pseudonym*
    a) last name
    b) antonym
    c) pen name
    d) honorary title

20. an act of *temerity*
    a) cowardice
    b) rage
    c) uncertainty
    d) foolish daring

Word List

In many of the following vocabulary words you will recognize the Old English, Latin, and Greek word parts you have just studied. Make it a habit to learn unfamiliar words from this list regularly; ten each week is a practical number. When you consult a dictionary for the meaning of an unfamiliar word, make sure you find the meaning that fits the context you have in mind, or ask your teacher to verify the meaning.

aberration	ascetic	buffoon
abeyance	ascribe	bullion
abject	aspersion	burnish
abnegation	assiduous	cadaverous
abscond	assimilate	cajole
absolve	atrophy	calumny
abstruse	augury	candor
acrimonious	auspices	capitulate
adjudge	austerity	capricious
adjure	avarice	captivate
admonish	aver	caricature
adroit	banal	cessation
affront	bauble	charlatan
allay	bellicose	chastise
amorphous	benevolence	chauvinism
anarchy	biennial	chicanery
antipathy	blazon	choleric
antipodes	bode	circumvent
apostasy	bravado	civility
artifice	broach	clandestine

coerce
cognizant
colloquy
commensurate
commiserate
commodious
conciliate
confer
configuration
connoisseur

consign
consternation
contingency
copious
corollary
corroborate
cosmopolitan
dearth
decorum
deduce

demagogue
denizen
deplore
desist
detriment
devoid
differentiate
dirge
discrepancy
discursive

disparity
dissent
distraught
diurnal
doggerel
dogma
duress
effusion
elegy
elicit

elocution
emaciate
emanate
empirical
engender
enigma
ennui
epitome
equanimity
equivocal

erudite
esoteric
espouse
ethereal
ethnology
eulogy
euphemism
euphony
evanescent
exhilaration

exhort
expatriate
expound
extant
extenuate
extol
extort
extraneous
extricate
facetious

facile
farcical
feign
festoon
fiasco
finesse
firmament
fissure
foible
foment

fortuitous
fresco
frugal
gambol
gauntlet
germane
glib
gratuitous
gregarious
guffaw

guile
hackneyed
harbinger
herculean
hiatus
homily
homogeneous
humdrum
hyperbole
idiosyncrasy

ignominy
illicit
immutable
impair
impassive
impeccable
incarcerate
incognito
inconsequential
incorrigible

indigent
indulgent
inexorable
infringe
ingenuous
iniquity
inordinate
inscrutable
intercede
introvert

inundate
inveigle
iridescent
irrevocable
lampoon
litigation
longevity
loquacious
ludicrous
lugubrious

magnanimous
maim
malign
malinger
maudlin
menial
mercurial
mesmerism
mete
misnomer

mollify
moot
mottled
mundane
munificent
nadir
nebulous
nefarious
nemesis
nettle

nondescript
nonentity
obese
obnoxious
obsequious
officious
omniscient
opulence
ostensible
pallor

paragon
parsimonious
patrimony
pecuniary
perfidious
pervade
pestilence
phlegmatic
poignant
precocious

precursor
predispose
prerogative
prevaricate
primordial
proffer
progeny
prognosis
promontory
propitious

proponent
propriety
prosaic
protégé
pseudonym
punctilious
purloin
quell
querulous
quiescent

rampant
recant
refute
regimen
remonstrate
remuneration
renounce
repository
reprisal
residual

restitution
retaliate
retroactive
retrospect
revile
sagacity
salient
saline
sanguine
scathing

scrupulous
scurrilous
sedentary
seraphic
solicitous
sonorous
specious
strident
subjugate
subversion

sumptuous
sundry
tacit
taciturn
temerity
tenable
tenuous
tenure
terra firma
testimonial

treatise
truism
usury
venal
venerate
vestige
vindicate
virulent
vociferous
voluminous

CHAPTER 37

Studying and Test Taking

WRITING TO LEARN AND TAKING TESTS

The writing requirements you face as a student might be even more complex than you have considered. They require a fairly wide range of skills.

Basically, you are called upon to summarize material, to take tests, and to write essays, either at home or during your exams. These activities require you to be good at comprehending what you read. You must have a good vocabulary and be a good speller, and you must know about such things as synonyms, antonyms, and verbal analogies. You must be able to recognize and correct errors, and you must be competent at revising sentences and organizing paragraphs.

WRITING THE PRÉCIS

A précis is a summary. It shortens some piece of writing—a passage, a chapter, an article, a report—to its bare essentials. In other words, the précis dispenses with all the examples, illustrations, quotations and other elements that fill out an author's basic points. It leaves only the central points themselves.

Précis-writing is an especially effective tool for sharpening your writing skills. It is also one of the best avenues to more attentive reading, since you must thoroughly understand material before you can summarize it.

In writing a précis, observe these rules:

1. *Be brief.* A précis is seldom more than a third as long as the material being summarized. It is often less than a third.

2. *Don't paraphase.* If you merely put each sentence of the original version in slightly different words, you will wind up with as much material as you had in the beginning.

3. *Stick to the central points of the material.* Avoid examples, illustrations, unnecessary adjectives, and repetitions.

4. *Use your own wording* instead of lifting phrases or sentences from the original.

5. *Be faithful to the author's points and views.* Don't insert your own ideas or comments, and don't use such expressions as "The author says" or "The paragraph means."

This is how to proceed with a précis:

1. Read carefully the material you are about to summarize. Keep reading it until you know precisely what it says. Look up any words or references you don't understand.

2. Write a brief sentence, in your own words, for each important point the author makes.

3. When you have gone all the way through the material, use your collection of sentences to write the rough draft of your précis.

4. Compare your rough draft with the original material, making sure you have accurately covered the important points.

5. Revise your draft until it is as concise and readable as you can make it.

Read the following paragraph two or three times. Then read the four précis of it given below. Each of them illustrates one major error in précis writing.

> The first thing that strikes the critical minority, as it looks at the whole cultural picture, is that ours is a nation of new-rich people, well washed, all dressed up, rather pathetically unsure just what it is washed and dressed up for; a nation convinced that a multitude of material goods, standardized, furiously and expensively advertised by appeals to greed and vanity, will in themselves make life worth the living. Because we are new-rich, we overvalue possessions. Almost any individual who makes a great deal of money very rapidly supposes that mere possession of wealth is evidence of worth. He also is apt to imagine that with his means he can buy happiness. These mistakes usually seem folly to the old-rich, to one who was born to property, whose father and mother were bred with it. Such a one knows that merely because he or his friends have it, it is no sign that they are worth it, but quite commonly the contrary. He has learned through experience that

money is not in itself very valuable stuff. Happiness, which is what all men desire, cannot be purchased; it is an illusive something not for sale. The old-rich know these things well enough, but the new-rich rarely discover them until they too have grown accustomed to possessions. So it seems to be with our society. We go in, almost without question and in all classes, for the sordid nonsense of supposing that externalities possessed ennoble the owners, that a full fist invariably indicates a fine spirit.   [255 words]

Faulty Précis

1. <u>Ours is a nation of new-rich people convinced</u> that material goods will in themselves <u>make life worth the living.</u> Any individual who makes a great deal of money <u>rapidly supposes</u> that <u>wealth is evidence of worth.</u> He imagines that with his means he can <u>buy happiness.</u> These mistakes <u>seem folly</u> to one <u>born to property.</u> He knows that because he or his friends have it, it is <u>no sign that they are worth it. Happiness, which all men desire, cannot be purchased.</u> We go in for the <u>nonsense that a full fist indicates a fine spirit.</u>   [96 words]

phrases and sentences merely copied from original

2. On the whole we are a nation of new-rich people who are well washed and well dressed, but <u>we don't know what we're washed and dressed for. Our material goods are all standardized</u> and expensively advertised. Advertisers appeal to our greed and vanity. We think these material goods are the means to wealth and happiness. <u>The old-rich know that their friends aren't worth the money they have,</u> but the new-rich don't know this until they have been rich for a while.   [81 words]

précis misses point of original and emphasizes unimportant points

3. First, the critical minority says that we are a nation of new-rich people all dressed up with no place to go. We think the material goods advertised by appeals to our greed and vanity are what make life worth living. Anyone who makes a lot of

money thinks his money shows his worth and
believes that it will make him happy. The old-rich,
however, think that these ideas are foolish. Born
into a rich family with property, these people know
that money and property don't make them any
better people. They know that the opposite is
frequently true. They know that money in itself
isn't worth much and that it won't buy happiness,
which is the thing everyone wants. The new-rich,
however, don't know these things until they have
been rich long enough to find them out. Almost
everyone, regardless of social class, believes that
possessions make their owners better, and the
more you have the more worthy you are. This is
nonsense.   [163 words]

précis too long—nearly two-thirds the length of original

4. The critical minority says we are a nation of
new-rich people who are victims of newspaper,
magazine, and television advertising which, by
appealing to our greed and vanity, tries to convince
us that all we need for happiness is a lot of
possessions. We don't need most of the advertised
stuff such as appliances, cars, and fur coats, but the
rest of the world judges our worth by what we
have. In many other countries, people don't have
the material goods we have. We can't all be as
lucky as the old-rich, who don't have to worry
about money because they already have it.   [104
words]

writer of précis injected own ideas

Acceptable Précis

Critics of American culture see us as a new-rich
people who, because we are new-rich, think that
material goods make life worth living. We think
that money is an indication of worth and that
wealth brings happiness. The old-rich know better.

ideas stated in précis writer's words

Born to property, they do not believe that just
because they have it, they are worth it. They know
that happiness cannot be bought. The new-rich,
however, mistakenly believe that possessions indicate the worth of their owner.   [78 words]

less than one-third
the length of original

EXERCISE 1. Writing Précis. As your teacher directs, use the
following passages for practice in précis writing.

1

   Rapidity in reading has an obvious direct bearing on success in college
work, because of the large amount of reading which must be covered in
nearly all college courses. But it is probably also a direct measure of the
special kind of aptitude which I am calling bookish, because rapidity of
reading usually correlates with comprehension and retention. Generally
speaking, the more rapidly a reader reads, the more effectively he grasps
and retains. The median reading speed of college freshmen has been found
to be around 250 words a minute on ordinary reading matter, and a student
who reads more slowly than that will certainly have difficulty in completing
his college tasks within reasonable study periods. To be a really good college
risk under this criterion one should readily and habitually cover not fewer
than 300 words a minute on ordinary reading matter.   [143 words]

2

   The major struggle between writer and subject is fought here, in the
arena of reputation. A biographer may or may not choose to reveal the
intimate, amorous details of a life, but he must, if he is good at what he
does, probe beneath its public self. The doubts and vulnerabilities, the
meannesses, ambitions, and private satisfactions that are hidden within a
social personality yield him his greatest insights. Seeking to reveal what his
subject filters out as unworthy or perhaps only as uninteresting, he becomes
for him, we have seen, an adversary to be frustrated, coopted, or even
outsmarted ("It will read charmingly in your biography," Jane Carlyle wrote
bitingly of an insincere letter from her husband). A life taken only at its own
crafted word is imperfectly and even unjustly rendered. Fine biography
challenges the pose to find the personality.   [145 words]

3

   Ever since a group of men first developed a government, there have
been opposing ideas of the relation between the state and its members. One
view puts the state above the individual. The individual has no existence
except as a member of the community, carrying out its will, living for its
welfare, ready to die in its service. He is not supposed to separate his

identity or his personal profit from that of the nation. The community has a right to interfere in his affairs; he has no private life in which it is bound not to interfere. The state is more than the sum of its members. Its continuance must be assured at whatever cost. The state is a *totality* in which they are completely submerged. This view of the state is held by all absolute rulers, including modern dictators. We usually speak of it as *totalitarianism* or *fascism*. It prevails over a large part of the world.

The other view puts the individual above the state. The state exists for the individual, not the individual for the state. The government has no other purpose than to serve the people; they may alter its form or, if need be, revolt against it, should it fail to carry out their wishes. Public and private life are quite distinct. The state may not interfere with the individual's private life so long as he does no injury to others. The individual has numerous rights which the state may not restrict except to protect the rights of other individuals. This view came to be widely held in England and northern Europe in the 1600's and 1700's; from there it spread to the New World. It took shape in the democratic form of government.   [295 words]

4

What is strange about this new passivity, regarding both travel and broadcasting, is that not so long ago the reverse was considered normal; that is, flying was once a highly participatory activity—as was automobile driving, as was broadcasting. Thirty-five years ago, the driver of an ordinary car was intimately involved with the event of driving, by means of direct access to his steering wheel, brakes, transmission, and the outside environment. In the same period, a listener to Edward R. Murrow's broadcasts from London was directly involved with the event of broadcasting as well as the events of the Second World War that Murrow was describing. Since then, however, the automobile driver has given up his direct involvement in favor of power controls, automatic transmissions, and sealed-in passenger interiors, while the television audience has largely given up its involvement with drama and news in favor of undemanding, mechanical entertainment and uninvolving news. Nowadays, only aggressive people insist on direct, or participatory, driving, by means of sports cars; at least they are owned by people who are willing to appear aggressive. And only an aggressive minority, perhaps of a different, cultural, nature, appears to prefer participatory television, such as the music and serious drama programs that now and then are shown on public television.   [215 words]

WRITING IN OTHER COURSES

37a. Use writing to explore concepts and topics in your science courses.

Writing about concepts and topics from a content-area subject, such as a science course, can enable you to understand the class better. Book reviews and journals are two forms of writing you can use to improve how you learn course content.

A book review examines and evaluates the contents of a book. You can write book reviews about fiction or nonfiction works that discuss scientific periods, discoveries, figures, or events. By doing so, you combine your scientific understanding and your judgment of how well a writer treats a particular concept.

Like other kinds of critical reviews, a book review in a science course should discuss the work's major points. It should also present your evaluation of the work's strengths and weaknesses, supported by specific details from the work itself and from reference works. Begin your work on a review by doing a close reading of the book. As you read, take careful notes about important details and concepts in the book. Decide which major points you should discuss, and decide what your evaluation of the work is. Review your notes to locate specific details that support your views. You should also consult reference works and other sources on the same subject to check the accuracy of the book you are reviewing. Then, write your book review, answering any one of the following questions: *How does this book broaden your knowledge or understanding of science? How does this work enable you to better grasp the content of your science course? Does the author present a biased, or slanted, view of the subject—and if so, how is this bias justified? In a fictional work, how probable and believable is the role of science and technology?* After you write your review, evaluate, revise, and proofread it—just as you would with any other piece of writing. (See also critical reviews, pages 154–60.)

If you want to write a book review about a fictional work, remember that science fiction is especially appropriate for a book review in a science course. For example, you might consider reviewing works by Isaac Asimov, Arthur C. Clarke, and Ursula K. LeGuin. If you choose to review a nonfiction work, you will find many possible choices, including works like Tracy Kidder's study of computers, *The Soul of a New Machine,* and Lewis Thomas's collection of essays, *The Lives of a Cell: Notes of a Biology Watcher.* Whether you review a fiction or a nonfiction work, try to select a book that has some relation to the content of your science course.

Another way to use writing in a science course is to keep a journal, just as you might keep a writer's notebook in an English class (see page 14). For example, as you conduct an experiment, you can record the specific procedures you follow, the results you observe, and your reactions to each phase of the experiment. You can also discuss why procedures succeeded or failed, and you can try to account for unexpected results. Journal entries like these can provide the information for a laboratory report about the experiment, using the format your science teacher provides. You can also use your journal to record field studies, demonstrations, and other class activities.

You can also use your journal to discuss the scientific concepts and topics you are studying. For example, you might write a journal entry about any of the following concepts:

1. Explain the differences between nuclear fission and nuclear fusion.
2. Describe the process of mitosis.
3. Discuss three practical applications of the laws of aerodynamics.

By writing about these concepts, you can organize your thoughts and discover where your understanding needs to be improved. You can also practice applying your knowledge of expository writing to answering essay questions or to writing compositions in your science courses.

This book also discusses specific expository writing assignments that are well suited to writing in science courses. In Chapter 4, see the discussion of "Exposition That Informs," "Exposition That Explains," "Explaining Cause and Effect," "Essays of Classification," and "Essays of Definition" (pages 123–29, 135–51). No matter what kind of writing you do in science class, or in any other course, apply your knowledge of description, narration, exposition, and persuasion (Chapters 3–5), and of the structure and development of paragraphs and compositions (Chapters 2 and 3). In addition, use your understanding of the writing process (see Chapter 1) to improve your writing in all your content-area subjects.

EXERCISE 2. Writing in Science.   Following the steps in the writing process, complete one of the activities below.

1. Write a book review of a fiction or nonfiction work about a scientific concept, event, or figure. In your review, answer at least one of the questions on page 764.
2. For several days, keep a journal about the progress of an experiment, field study, or class demonstration. Write a brief essay that summarizes the procedures and results of the experiment and the specific ways that this activity added to your scientific knowledge.
3. Prepare a journal entry about any concept you are studying. Use one of the above three concepts or one your teacher suggests.

TAKING TESTS

No matter what your plans for the years following high school, you will most likely be asked to "take some tests." The most commonly administered tests include measures of verbal fluency, reading comprehension, and/or grammar and composition.

Among the tests of this type used for college entrance, the best known are probably the *Scholastic Aptitude Test—Verbal,* or SAT—V, (including the *Test of Standard Written English,*), and the *English Composition Test,* or "English Achievement" test. Both are administered by the College Entrance Examination Board. Another well-known test is the *American College Testing Program* (ACT) *Assessment Test.*

Some schools and colleges do *not* require tests for admission but do administer tests for placement in courses and for guidance purposes. The military and other employers may also administer tests of English language skills for certain jobs.

Tests with the word *aptitude* in their titles are used mainly to predict future success, whether in school or on the job. They do not, on the whole, measure what you have learned in particular courses. They measure the language skills which you have been developing all your life. *Achievement* tests, on the other hand, concentrate on specific skills and information which you have learned in academic courses.

Cramming is *not* an appropriate or helpful way to prepare for tests of this nature. There are, however, a number of good test-taking practices that will help you to do your best on any examination. These may be summarized as follows:

SUMMARY OF TEST-TAKING PRACTICES

1. Take a positive approach to the test.
   a. Try to do your best even though you may be nervous. Don't panic.
   b. Regard lapses of memory as normal. If you "block" on a certain question, go on and come back to it later if you can.
   c. Don't expect to answer every question correctly. Some of the tests are built so that the average student will answer only about half of the questions correctly.

2. Use your time wisely.
   a. Look over the test before you start to work. Get a feel for its length and difficulty.

   b. Plan your time. If you have a time limit of 20 minutes for a 40-question test, check that you are on or beyond question 21 after 10 minutes. But avoid too much clock-watching; it uses up your time and heightens anxiety.
   c. Work rapidly but carefully. Answer the easy questions first. If you don't know an answer right away, leave it and go on.
   d. If you have time after finishing the test, try some of the questions you left out the first time. (On the ACT, you are not penalized for guessing.)
3. Avoid careless errors.
   a. Pay close attention to directions. Do the sample questions even though you're sure you understand the task.
   b. Read each question carefully. Be sure you know exactly what it is asking you to do.
   c. Look at all the choices before you answer. In many cases the correct answer is not *absolutely* correct; it is the *best* among the choices.
   d. Avoid careless mistakes in marking the answer sheet. Keep it lined up with the booklet if possible. The scoring machine can't tell when you were "off" by one question or one row.
   e. If you change an answer, be sure you erase the first answer thoroughly. If the machine "reads" both marks, it will count the question as unanswered.

One of the best ways to prepare for any test is to become familiar with the types of tasks you will be asked to perform. Many test questions will be familiar, while others may be new to you. The purpose of this chapter is to show you some of these question types.

TESTS OF WORD KNOWLEDGE OR VOCABULARY

Vocabulary tests measure your understanding of the meanings of words, either in isolation or in context. Often, the relationships among words—the way they are related in meaning—will be tested. Examples of three types of vocabulary questions follow.

Word Meanings

The simplest type of vocabulary question asks you the meaning of a word. Usually, the format is an incomplete statement to which you add one of several choices to complete the meaning. The following is a sample question of this type.

EXAMPLE   **A** To whet one's appetite is to ——

       a wean it
       b salve it
       c sharpen it
       d appease it
       e dampen it

Answer:[1]

A ⓐ ⓑ ● ⓓ ⓔ

Some questions of this type ask for a choice between *phrases* explaining the word's meaning or use; others offer *single words* and ask you to choose a synonym of the key word.

EXERCISE 3. Choosing the Correct Meaning.   Read the beginning of each sentence below and the choices that follow it. Choose the answer which best completes the sentence.[2]

1 A person who is talkative is ——

    a fervent
    b reticent
    c jocular
    d loquacious

2 To be nimble is to be ——

    a gracious
    b agile
    c numb
    d earthy

3 Material you can see through is called ——

    a opaque
    b potential
    c imaginary
    d transparent

---

[1] Answer: © *sharpen it.* When you have marked your answer sheet for ©, this is the way it will look. You will black in the circle containing the letter of the correct answer. Answers are shown this way for all sample test items throughout this chapter.
[2] Answers for this and all the following exercises will be found on page 787.

4 Something that is powerful must be ——

    a lavish
    b lenient
    c potent
    d malicious

5 To condense something is to ——

    a abridge it
    b accelerate it
    c abolish it
    d acclaim it

Synonyms and Antonyms

In a test on synonyms or antonyms you are asked to select, from four or five choices, the word *most similar* in meaning (synonym) to the word given *or* the word *most nearly opposite* in meaning (antonym). *Pay attention!* These are sometimes mixed together. There are few true synonyms or antonyms in English; the "correct" answer, therefore, is the one most nearly the same or most nearly the opposite in meaning.

    Following are two sample questions in which you are to find the word *most similar* in meaning (synonym) to the underlined word.

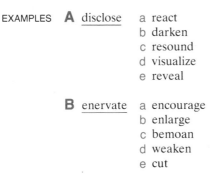

EXAMPLES **A** <u>disclose</u>   a react
                  b darken
                  c resound
                  d visualize
                  e reveal

        B <u>enervate</u> a encourage
                    b enlarge
                  c bemoan
                  d weaken
                  e cut

Answer:

The last question includes a common misconception of the word's meaning among the choices. Many people are confused as to whether *enervate* means to take "nerve" away or to give it; hence *encourage* is given as an incorrect choice.

EXERCISE 4. Choosing the Antonym. For each of the following questions, choose the word *most nearly opposite* in meaning (antonym) to the underlined word.

1 abstract
    a extract
    b general
    c concrete
    d ideal
    e difficult

2 chronic
    a occasional
    b habitual
    c public
    d unimportant
    e healthy

3 detriment
    a complement
    b loss
    c damage
    d attribute
    e benefit

4 abate
    a fall
    b shrink
    c subside
    d increase
    e release

5 transient
    a swift
    b permanent
    c polite
    d sure
    e passenger

Verbal Analogies

Analogies measure your understanding of relationships among words. Here is a sample set of directions and one question.

EXAMPLE   In the items below, the first and second words are related in a certain way. The third word is related in the same way to one of the four words which follow it. You are to choose the word related to the third word in the same way that the second word is related to the first.

A *Inch* is to *foot* as *ounce* is to ——

   a weight
   b meter
   c yard   Answer:
   d pound   **A** ⓐ ⓑ ⓒ ⬤

In this sample question, the relationship tested is that of a unit of measurement to a larger unit in the same scale. An inch is a division of a foot. The correct answer is *pound,* since an ounce is a division of a pound.

   Analogies may also be presented as shown in the following example:

EXAMPLE   Below is a list of five pairs of related words. Choose the pair of words whose relationship is most like that of the first pair.

A INCH : FOOT ::

   a quart : measure
   b weight : peck
   c ounce : pound
   d mile : length   Answer:
   e meter : yard   **A** ⓐ ⓑ ⬤ ⓓ ⓔ

Again, *ounce* is related to *pound* as *inch* is related to *foot*. But here you are to find the whole pair. In the first example, the first part of the second pair was given to you. It may help to turn them into sentences such as the one in the first example.

   Suppose the first pair of words were *glance* and *gaze*. Both name ways of looking at something. But a *glance* is a quick look, while *gaze* has the idea of a long or thoughtful look. Which of these pairs of words, then, has the most similar relationship?

EXAMPLE   **A** GLANCE : GAZE ::

   a blink : scowl
   b glimpse : stare
   c observe : note
   d skim : peek   Answer:
   e peruse : study   **A** ⓐ ⬤ ⓒ ⓓ ⓔ

Option b presents the pair which completes the analogy, since *glimpse* also implies a quick once-over and *stare* gives the notion of a long and concentrated look. Another way to check your understanding of the analogy is to compare the first and third parts, and then check to see if the second and fourth parts have the same relationship. In the original example, this check would take the form: "*Inch* is to *ounce* as *foot* is to —— ?"

EXERCISE 5. Completing Analogies. In the items below, the first and second words are related in a certain way. The third word is related in the same way to one of the five words which follow. Choose the word related to the third word in the same way as the second word is related to the first.

1 *Clear* is to *cloudy* as *definite* is to ——

    a sunny
    b vague
    c bright
    d positive
    e short

2 *Reckless* is to *cautious* as *rash* is to ——

    a hasty
    b impudent
    c careless
    d prudent
    e smooth

3 *Gaggle* is to *goose* as *pride* is to ——

    a lion
    b vain
    c king
    d bear
    e eagle

4 *Calm* is to *storm* as *quell* is to ——

    a traffic
    b crowd
    c ink
    d riot
    e nerve

5 *Encourage* is to *scold* as *chide* is to ——

    a punish
    b praise
    c query
    d insult
    e forbid

In the following items, choose the pair of words whose relationship is most similar to that of the first pair given.

6 LIMP : WALK ::

   a snore : sleep
   b walk : ride
   c whistle : sing
   d stutter : speak

7 QUARRY : STONE ::

   a rock : mineral
   b mine : ore
   c soil : field
   d oil : drill

8 SALVE : WOUND ::

   a eraser : pencil
   b drink : thirst
   c save : money
   d sword : scabbard

9 LAVISH : STINGY ::

   a quick : average
   b late : earlier
   c bright : brightest
   d profuse : grudging

10 RELEVANT : PERTINENT ::

   a wasteful : efficient
   b thoughtful : reasonable
   c implicit : explicit
   d quiet : slow

READING ACHIEVEMENT

Your grasp of the meaning of what you read is often measured in tests for school or vocational guidance. Reading abilities are usually measured in one of the two ways described below.

Sentence Completion

This question format could be called "fill in the blanks." Sentences are presented with one or two blanks, each indicating that a word has been left out. You are to choose the word which fits best in the sentence.

EXAMPLE **A** We laughed at the clown —— he performed funny tricks.

     a but
     b until
     c because
     d unless
     e although

Answer:

The sentence clearly calls for a conjunction, but the only one that makes any sense is *because*. Questions like this look for your ability to recognize the logic and coherence of the sentence—one aspect of comprehension.

Reading Comprehension

Reading tests are not concerned with testing whether you understand, word by word, what you have read, but rather how well you can draw conclusions and make judgments about what you read. The questions about the passage you read should not require outside information, but should be based upon the information within the passage itself. Here is a sample passage followed by three questions.

EXAMPLE   Two days after his sudden death on June 9, 1870, Charles Dickens was honored in a *New York Times* obituary covering more than five of the seven long columns on the front page. The length of this article accurately reflected Dickens' position among the American reading public of a century ago, when entire households waited anxiously from month to month to discover the fate of Little Nell, or Oliver Twist, or whichever Dickensian hero figured in the novel currently being serialized for United States audiences. In later years, the novelist's reputation diminished; critics dismissed him as a "popular" writer rather than a true craftsman. His remarkably vivid characterizations were considered caricatures, even though numerous outstanding writers such as Feodor Dostoevski, Joseph Conrad, and Henry James expressed their indebtedness to "the master." But during the 1940's, writers like Franz Kafka and Edmund Wilson brought readers to a fresh awareness of Dickens' unforgettable delineations of personalities whose very names—Scrooge, for instance—have assumed an independent meaning for people around the world. Readers today are also impressed by Dickens' vision, more than 100 years ago, of what the modern city was to become. For Dickens' London was a place of smoke and filth and a decaying social fabric, rather than the rich, bustling, upper-class London of virtually all his contemporaries.

A The main thrust of this article has to do with ——

    a modern attitudes towards Dickens
    b Dickens' descriptions of London
    c changes in Dickens' literary reputation
    d Dickens' treatment of fictional characters

B Dostoevski, Conrad, and James indicated that ——

    a their writing was influenced by Dickens
    b Dickens wrote for a lower-class public
    c they had learned about London from Dickens
    d Scrooge was a caricature

C Apparently other British authors of Dickens' day ——

    a were upper-class Londoners
    b ridiculed Dickens' London
    c believed Dickens an expert on city life
    d pictured London as an attractive place to live

Answer:

These sample questions illustrate several types that may be asked. Question A, for example, asks for the main idea of the passage. Question B asks for a restatement of an idea clearly stated in the passage. And question C asks for an inference which the reader must draw from the passage. Other types of questions may ask for the meaning of a term or phrase as used in the passage, a recognition of the author's intent, or the identification of bias, exaggeration, or value judgments.

EXERCISE 6. Drawing Conclusions from Reading.
After reading the following passage, answer the questions given at its conclusion.

    The computerized age in which we live, while enabling us to land people on the moon and accomplish vast feats of arithmetical figuring in seconds, has raised many new problems. One of these, according to Dr. Lee McMahon, a psychologist at the Bell Tele-
5   phone Laboratories, is the need for communication between computers and between humans and computers. In order to facilitate such communication, Dr. McMahon developed, in 1966, a new

"language" designed to eliminate computer confusion about the relation of words in a sentence. The language is called FASE, for
10 Fundamentally Analyzable Simplified English, and although at first it appears indistinguishable from ordinary English prose, it is actually quite different, for FASE reduces English to a strict form in which syntax is absolutely clear and free of ambiguity. The resulting
15 grammatical structures can be broken down easily by a computer, while ordinary English cannot. For example, consider how a computer would interpret the phrase "time flies." The computer would have to decide whether this meant "time speeds by" or "clock the speed of certain insects," and such a choice, unaccom-
20 panied by human guidance, is beyond the capacity of even the most advanced computers. But a computer programmed to "read" FASE would have no trouble with the phrase, for FASE is based on a strictly maintained sequence of subject, verb, and object, with other parts of speech falling regularly into line. FASE lacks the
25 beauty of English, then, and its spontaneity, but can be very useful in indexing scientific documents, which would be punched on cards and stored in a computer until needed. Locating a particular subject would be a comparatively simple matter for the computer, since there would be no ambiguity of meaning. "Time flies," for
30 instance, would be "FASE-indexed" under time, rather than speed or insects.

1 FASE was developed by a ——

  a psychologist
  b computer programmer
  c physician
  d linguist

2 A FASE-programmed computer could correctly interpret the phrase "time flies" because ——

  a the phrase is an idiom
  b computers work so speedily
  c the phrase contains a verb
  d the subject comes before the verb

3 Sentences written in FASE are probably rather ——

  a ambiguous
  b idiomatic
  c boring
  d spontaneous

4 The writer implies that a computer's ability to make decisions is ——

    a unlimited
    b limited to choices about grammar
    c nonexistent, even in sophisticated machines
    d controlled by the use of FASE

5 In which of the following lines is a value judgment expressed?

    a lines 24–25
    b lines 27–28
    c line 7
    d line 16

STANDARD WRITTEN ENGLISH

The best way for someone to "test" your ability to write standard English is to have you write. This is not always practical, so multiple-choice tests have been developed to measure your knowledge of correct spelling and usage, your skill in organizing material, and your sensitivity to nuances of tone, style, and choice of words. The paragraphs which follow give examples of some of the more commonly used methods of testing skills in standard written English.

Spelling

Spelling may be tested in any number of ways. One of the most common formats consists of four words, one of which may be misspelled. You are to indicate the word spelled incorrectly or mark a choice indicating no errors. Another type of question involves the misuse of homonyms —words which sound alike but differ in spelling and meaning, such as *to, too*, and *two*. In this sort of test question, four phrases with different homonyms are usually given, and you are asked to choose the phrase in which a homonym is used correctly or incorrectly.

EXAMPLE   **A**   a *too* hot
            b grizzly *bear*
            c *peace* of pie
            d rough *seas*

Answer:

A ⓐ ⓑ ● ⓓ

EXERCISE 7. Identifying Misspellings. For each of the following questions, choose the one word that is misspelled. If no word is misspelled, mark the answer N for no error.

1
a seize
b percieve
c righteous
d salutary
N

2
a ruse
b laughter
c explannatory
d traveler
N

3
a bumble *bee*
b *bowl* weevil
c string *bean*
d acting *troupe*
N

4
a bare *feet*
b boat's *sail*
c *bail* of hay
d filet of *sole*
N

5
a pint of *beer*
b carving *board*
c *right* to work
d wild *hoarse*
N

Error Recognition

Error recognition questions ask you to detect or correct errors in written passages. Some questions ask you only to indicate that an error is present; others ask you to specify the type of error it is. Here are samples of three types of questions.

EXAMPLES TYPE 1.

Mark the letter of the line containing an error in spelling, punctuation, capitalization, grammar, or usage. If there is no error, mark N for no error.

A
a Actually, bats are fascinating
b animals. They are the only Mammals
c living today that are able to fly.
N

Answer:

A ⓐ ● ⓒ Ⓝ

TYPE 2

Mark the letter of the underlined part that must be changed in order to make the sentence correct. (Be sure to note whether underlining includes the punctuation.) If there is no error, mark *e*.

B During <u>the colonel period</u>, many colonies had
         a

<u>their own flags,</u> the <u>earliest of which</u> was based on
     b   c

<u>the British flag.</u> <u>No error</u>
     d   e

Answer:

B ● ⓑ ⓒ ⓓ ⓔ

TYPE 3

Some of the sentences below contain errors; others are correct as they stand. For each sentence, mark your answer sheet:

 a —if the sentence contains an incorrect choice of words (error in diction)
 b —if the sentence is wordy (verbose or redundant)
 c —if the sentence contains an overworked expression (cliché) or mixed metaphor
 d —if the sentence contains an error in grammar or structure
 e —if the sentence is correct as it stands

1 Each day it was a daily occurrence to see the mail truck arrive.

2 The mass of detail is not penitent to the question at hand.

3 The young man was fit as a fiddle as he started work.

Answer:

EXERCISE 8. Identifying Errors in Written English.   Following the appropriate set of directions, record your answers to each of the following questions.

TYPE I.   Mark the letter of the line containing an error in spelling, punctuation, capitalization, grammar, or usage. If there is no error, mark N for no error.

1 a Russias woman astronaut may have been
   b the first woman to explore outer space,
   c but she wasn't the first woman explorer.
   N

2 a As long ago as 1805, woman were helping
   b men find their dangerous way across
   c the uncharted Rocky Mountains.
   N

3 a Sacajawea whose name means "Bird Woman," was
   b only 13 when she was captured by a tribe of
   c enemies.
   N

4 a She was living with them in North Dakota
   b when Lewis and Clark asked her help
   c in accomplishing this difficult feat.
   N

5 a Charbonneau, her French-Sioux husband,
   b was hired in the autumn of 1804
   c as a guide for the exposition.
   N

TYPE II. Mark the letter of the underlined part that must be changed in order to make the sentence correct. (Be sure to note whether the underlining includes the punctuation.) If there is no error, mark *e*.

6 <u>Sacajawea's</u> geographical knowledge and
    a

<u>her usefulness as</u> a guide <u>was limited</u> to
      b   c

her native region of <u>western Montana</u>.   <u>No error</u>
                d   e

7 <u>Nevertheless</u>, she traveled all the way from
    a

<u>Fort Mandan, N.D.</u>, to the <u>Pacific Ocean</u> and
      b   c

back <u>again with the exploring</u> party.   <u>No error</u>
            d   e

8 The <u>first-hand reports</u> of the expedition
        a

by <u>Lewis, Clark, Gass, and</u> <u>others praised</u>
      b   c

her highly <u>but, not her husband</u>.   <u>No error</u>
              d   e

9 Shortly before the expedition <u>left to find</u>
                      a

<u>its way</u> to the coast, a <u>healthy son</u> was born
  b   c

to Sacajawea on <u>February 11, 1805</u>.   <u>No error</u>
               d   e

10 Her son, who was given the name
　　　　　　a

Jean-Baptiste Charbonneau made the entire
　　　　　　　　　　　b

trip with his mother and father.　　　　　　　　　No error
　c　　　　d　　　　　　　　　　　　　　　　　　　e

TYPE III. Some of the sentences below contain errors; others are correct as they stand. For each sentence, mark your paper with one of the following letters as appropriate:

　　a—if the sentence contains an incorrect choice of words (choice in diction)
　　b—if the sentence is wordy (verbose or redundant)
　　c—if the sentence contains an overworked expression (cliché) or a mixed metaphor
　　d—if the sentence contains an error in grammar or structure
　　e—if the sentence is correct as it stands

11 Charbonneau was given five hundred dollars for his services as a guide, but Sacajawea received no pay.

12 It was generally agreed by the leaders of the project, Charbonneau mistreated his wife and was unworthy of his pay.

13 Their son returned back to St. Louis, Missouri, with William Clark, who brought him up and paid for his education.

14 After all was said and done, Sacajawea faded from view and, to make a long story short, it is not known what fate befell her in her later years.

15 Though it is a mistake to say that she guided the expedition, it is entirely possible that the roll played by Sacajawea made the difference between its success and its failure.

Error Correction

Error correction questions indicate the inappropriate part of the sentence and ask you to choose a suitable correction from the choices provided. Here are some samples.

EXAMPLE　**A** Eating, drinking, and *to stay up* late at night were among her pleasures.

　　　　　　a correct as it stands
　　　　　　b she liked staying up
　　　　　　c staying up
　　　　　　d to remain up

B *On the snow-covered branch, two sparrows, they huddled close together.*

a correct as it stands

b On the snow-covered branch, two sparrows huddled close together.

c On the snow-covered branch, two sparrows, huddled close together.

d Closely, on the snow-covered branch, huddled the two sparrows together.

Answer:

Sentence Revision

This type of question requires you to mentally restate a *correct* sentence, using a given phrase. Using the phrase will require change in other parts of the sentence as well. Then you must choose, from among the choices given you, a word or phrase that will appear somewhere in the restated sentence. (It may not necessarily follow directly after the given revision.) Study the sample given below.

EXAMPLE **A** Sentence: When night came and the temperature fell, my father lit the fire in the bedroom.

Revision: Begin with *"Each night . . ."*

a that the temperature

b upon the temperature's

c because the temperature

d when the temperature

Answer:

A ⓐ ⓑ ⓒ ●

There will often be several ways in which the new sentence could be completed. If none of the choices given is in your revised sentence, think of another way to rephrase the sentence, and check the choices again. But be sure not to change the meaning of the original sentence when you revise it.

EXERCISE 9. **Selecting the Best Revision.**   Following the appropriate directions, answer each of the following questions.

Error Correction. Choose the letter which indicates the best correction for the underlined part of each sentence. If the sentence is correct as it stands, mark *a*.

1 Traffic on the highway was blocked for an hour, <u>this causing</u> many drivers to have cold suppers.

a correct as it stands
b causing
c thus having necessitated
d which was responsible for

2 I <u>haven't but</u> a few more pages to write for this report.

a correct as it stands
b have scarcely
c haven't any except
d have only

3 <u>Everyone due to the continued storm sat and sang around the fireplace.</u>

a correct as it stands
b Sitting and singing around the fireplace were everyone, while the storm continued.
c The storm continued while everyone sits and sings around the fireplace.
d Everyone sat around the fireplace and sang while the storm continued.

4 Harry, although tired, worked late, <u>typed long</u> into the quiet summer evening.

a correct as it stands
b lengthily typing
c and he typed late too
d typing long

5 Suppose you tell us exactly where you hid <u>and a thorough report of your precise reasons for doing it.</u>

a correct as it stands
b and a report on why.
c and give us a report of your reasons.
d and precisely why you did it.

Sentence Revision. Mentally revise each of the following sentences according to the instructions given for each. Then choose the letter of the phrase most likely to occur in the sentence as revised.

6 Sentence: Leaning on the arm of her granddaughter, the old woman slowly entered the room.

Revision: Begin with: *The old woman leaned*

    a so that she could
    b for her entrance
    c as she
    d to slowly enter

7 Sentence: Aside from his dread of snakes, he was afraid of almost nothing.

Revision: Begin with: *He had a dread*

    a but otherwise
    b still
    c outside of that fear
    d and so

8 Sentence: What have we been doing all week but preparing for the holidays?

Revision: Change to a declarative sentence.

    a had done
    b anything all week more thàn
    c nothing all week but
    d does

9 Sentence: Bonnie told me she hadn't been there and didn't find out about what had happened until long after all of the excitement was over.

Revision: Change the indirect quote to a direct quote.

    a told me, "I'd never been there and didn't find out
    b told me, "I wouldn't have gone and
    c told me, "I wasn't there. I didn't find out
    d told me, "I won't go. I'm not going to find out

10 Sentence: She leapt to her feet and yelled, "I heard you say, 'What are they really worth?'"

Revision: Make the last direct quote an indirect quote.

    a "I heard you say What are they really worth?"
    b "I heard you ask what they're really worth."
    c "I heard you ask What they're really worth."
    d "I heard you say what they're really worth."

Organizing Paragraphs

Another writing skill often tested is organization. The most frequent exercise designed to measure organizational ability is the scrambled paragraph. This exercise takes a paragraph and presents the sentences in random order. Your job is to figure out the order that will make a well-knit paragraph.

Here is the way the directions are likely to go:

DIRECTIONS   Each group of sentences in this section is a paragraph presented in scrambled order. Each sentence in the group has a place in the paragraph; no sentence is to be left out. You are to read each group of sentences and decide the best order in which to put the sentences so as to form a well-organized paragraph.

Before trying to answer the questions, jot down the correct order of the sentences in the margin of the test book. Then answer each of the questions by blackening the appropriate space on the answer sheet. Remember that you will receive credit only for answers marked on the answer sheet.

A sample paragraph follows:

EXAMPLE   P As you read, however, concentrate only on main ideas; don't try to remember everything.

Q If you develop an interest in what you read, you are more likely to remember the factual information in a passage.

R Finally, when you have completed the passage, pause to summarize the main ideas in your mind.

S You will have an even stronger motive for remembering those facts if you understand their importance to you.

1 Which sentence did you put first?

a sentence P

b sentence Q

c sentence R

d sentence S

2 Which sentence did you put after sentence S?

a sentence P

b sentence Q

c sentence R

d None of the above. Sentence S is last.

3 Which sentence did you put after sentence **Q**?

   a sentence **P**

   b sentence **R**

   c sentence **S**

   d None of the above. Sentence **Q** is last.

Answer:

Note the use of words such as *finally, however,* and *even stronger.* These words refer to previous statements. You may also find clues in sentences using pronouns or adjectives clearly referring to some noun in a previous sentence (*those* facts). Before you answer any of the questions, determine the correct order for all the sentences and write it down for your own reference. Most tests, however, will not ask you to give that order all at once. They will be designed so as to give you credit for each correct relationship you detect between the individual sentences.

EXERCISE 10. Organizing Paragraphs. Read the following sentences carefully and write down their correct order before answering the questions. Then choose your answer for each question that follows.

P Swim out and approach the victim from behind in order to avoid struggling.

Q Then go into the special procedure called a "carry," and swim back to shore with the victim.

R In order to save a drowning person, you must jump into the water, keeping your eye on the victim at all times.

S Bring the victim into a horizontal position by pulling back on the chin and resting the body on your hip, using your arms as a lever.

T Stick your elbow in the middle of the victim's back and cup the chin with your hand.

1 Which sentence did you put first?

   a sentence **P**

   b sentence **Q**

   c sentence **R**

   d sentence **S**

   e sentence **T**

2 Which sentence did you put after sentence **P**?

a sentence **Q**

b sentence **R**

c sentence **S**

d sentence **T**

e None of the above. Sentence **P** is last.

3 Which sentence did you put after sentence **Q**?

a sentence **P**

b sentence **R**

c sentence **S**

d sentence **T**

e None of the above. Sentence **Q** is last.

4 Which sentence did you put after sentence **R**?

a sentence **P**

b sentence **Q**

c sentence **S**

d sentence **T**

e None of the above. Sentence **R** is last.

5 Which sentence did you put after sentence **T**?

a sentence **P**

b sentence **Q**

c sentence **R**

d sentence **S**

e None of the above. Sentence **T** is last.

Answers to Exercises

Ex. 3, p. 768	Ex. 4, p. 770	Ex. 5, p. 772	
1-d	1-c	1-b	6-d
2-b	2-a	2-d	7-b
3-d	3-e	3-a	8-b
4-c	4-d	4-d	9-d
5-a	5-b	5-b	10-b

Ex. 6, p. 775	Ex. 7, p. 777	Ex. 8, p. 779		
1-a	1-b	1-a	6-c	11-e
2-d	2-c	2-a	7-b	12-d
3-c	3-b	3-a	8-d	13-b
4-c	4-c	4-N	9-e	14-c
5-a	5-d	5-c	10-b	15-a

Ex. 9, p. 782		Ex. 10, p. 786
1-b	6-c	1-c
2-d	7-a	2-d
3-d	8-c	3-e
4-d	9-c	4-a
5-d	10-b	5-d

ESSAY TESTS

Essay questions require that you organize and write down your under-standing and analysis of a specified subject in a set time. Your answer is considered deficient if it is not organized according to the directions provided, not supported with sufficient detail, or is incomplete in the treatment of the subject matter.

Studying for Essay Tests

The best preparation for an essay test is to write out your own questions. In doing this, you must review the material and identify the most important points. Once you have written several questions, close the book and outline the answers. You will be testing your command of the material and exercising the skills you need in the actual test.

Scheduling Your Test Time

Always scan the complete test before you begin to work. Note the number and types of questions to be answered in the time allowed as well as the point value of each section. Then schedule your time accordingly. As a general rule, count on about two minutes of planning and one minute of revising for each five minutes of actual writing.

Analyzing the Question

Always read an essay question carefully and thoughtfully before you begin your answer. You usually have some choice about what to include;

however, teachers often specify the following ways in which you are to treat the material.

Identify Key Terms

Key terms indicate the organizational pattern you are expected to use. Answers that do not use the approach specified in the question may be evaluated as incorrect, even if the information given is correct. For example, if you have been asked to compare two characters in a short story, you must talk about two characters in terms of their similarities and differences. Your discussion of how one character was developed in the story might be accurate, but it would not show the comparison that was asked for.

The chart below gives the four main patterns of exposition and key terms associated with each.

PATTERN	KEY TERMS
1. Comparison and contrast	compare, contrast, show the differences, have in common, find likenesses, in what way are . . . similar/dissimilar
2. Cause and effect	analyze, explain, criticize, defend, show why, give factors that lead to, tell the effect of
3. Sequence or placement	list and discuss, trace, review, outline, give the steps, locate
4. Description	describe, identify, give examples of, write the characteristics of, define

Identify Specific Points to Be Included

Most essay questions require that you complete more than one task. Take time to note exactly what points you must include in your answer.

EXAMPLE   In literature, as in life, there are many forms of heroism. One fictional character is a hero because of a single act of valor. Another is heroic because of living a life of quiet endurance. Sometimes the heroic act is one of physical strength and stamina. In other stories, the hero manifests moral courage. How do you define heroism? Choose two characters, each from a different short story read this semester. Evaluate each character in terms of the characteristics of heroism that you included in your definition of a hero. Show by contrast that one character is a hero and the other is not. Use specific details to support your evaluation.

In your answer you must write a definition of a hero which makes clear the characteristics that you consider essential to heroism. You must evaluate two short story characters (each from a different story) in terms of your definition. You must contrast the characters, explaining why one is a hero and the other is not. You must use specific details from each story to support your evaluation.

EXERCISE 11. Analyzing Essay Questions. Read through the following essay questions for a one-hour test on computer use. For each (a) tell how much time should be scheduled for the answer; (b) list the key term or terms and identify the pattern of organization called for; (c) identify the number and kinds of examples or support that must be included.

1. (15 points) Discuss the technical developments that resulted in powerful, small-sized computers.
2. (10 points) List three to five ways a computer might be used in a small business office.
3. (15 points) Show the advantages of word processing programs over traditional typewriters. Include at least three specific points in your comparison.
4. (30 points) Describe how either programmed learning or simulation games take advantage of the computer's capacities. Include three or more examples of specific programs.

Writing Essay Answers

Do not leave out any of the stages of the writing process.

1. Plan your answer by formulating a thesis statement and very briefly outlining your major points of support.

2. Write your answer in complete sentences. Judge from the amount of time available whether you should write a single paragraph or develop each of your main points in a paragraph of its own. Be sure to include specific examples or details to support your thesis.

3. Read through your answer to make sure you have covered all the points specified in the question. Proofread your paper carefully.

EXERCISE 12. Planning and Writing an Essay Answer. Following your teacher's directions, compose your own essay question on a topic you are studying in one of your classes. Assign it a point value in a test meant to take 40 minutes. Exchange questions with another student, or answer your own question.

PART FIVE

SPEAKING AND LISTENING

CHAPTER 38

Discussion and Debate

TYPES OF DISCUSSION;
ELEMENTS OF DEBATING

It is natural for people to talk things over, either to exchange information or to dispute. The common kinds of discussion and debate are treated in this chapter.

GROUP DISCUSSION

Societies of every kind—school clubs, civic organizations, labor unions, legislative assemblies—use discussion as a means of arriving at a solution to a problem or of airing members' opinions before making a decision. This method of problem solving gives each member a voice.

38a. Learn how discussion differs from conversation and debate.

Although conversation, discussion, and debate are similar, there are marked differences.

A *conversation* is unplanned and private. It ranges over many topics, casually touching on each. It may have no purpose other than fellowship, or it may aim to entertain, instruct, or persuade.

A *discussion* is planned and public. It focuses on one topic, which participants examine in depth under the direction of a discussion leader. Its purpose is to consider a problem, evaluate proposed solutions, and arrive at the best solution.

A *debate* considers two sides of a problem. The supporters of each side attempt to defeat their opponents by setting forth arguments in carefully reasoned and extended speeches. A debate usually follows a formal procedure and involves a decision by judges.

Types of Group Discussion

38b. Learn the various types of group discussion.

Among the many types of group discussion, the most common are the *round table,* the *forum,* the *symposium,* and the *panel.*

A *round table* is an informal discussion in which the participants exchange views under the direction of a discussion leader. The number of participants usually does not exceed a dozen. Members of the group speak without rising and without being recognized by the chair.

The most common example of round-table discussion is the committee meeting. Many organizations conduct their business through committees. A committee considers business referred to it and reports its findings and recommendations to the entire organization.

A *forum* is any type of speaking program that is followed by audience participation. For example, a lecture followed by questions from the audience is a forum.

A *symposium* involves several formal speeches on a single topic followed by audience participation. When the audience is large, audience participation is sometimes limited to questions; expressions of opinion from the floor are usually not allowed.

A *panel* is a discussion among a selected group of persons under the direction of a moderator. The speakers represent different viewpoints. There are usually no set speeches, but sometimes speakers are asked to set forth their viewpoints in brief preliminary statements. The moderator keeps the discussion moving forward and invites the audience to join in. At the conclusion of the discussion, the moderator summarizes what has been said and thanks the participants and audience.

The purpose of a panel is to get important facts and opposing opinions into the open, stimulate audience thinking, and lay a basis for wide audience participation.

EXERCISE 1. Identifying Types of Group Discussion. Listen to a radio or television group discussion. Identify the type of discussion and observe how the discussion was conducted. Summarize your findings in a brief paragraph.

Preparing for Group Discussion

38c. Select a topic that lends itself to profitable group discussion.

The success of a group discussion depends on the topic. Before selecting a topic, ask yourself the following questions:

1. Is it sufficiently limited for the time allowed?
2. Is it related to the needs, interests, and experience of the listeners and speakers?
3. Is it timely?
4. Is it controversial?
5. Is it many-sided?
6. Is it stated clearly?

What are good sources of topics for group discussion? Books, magazine articles, newspapers, movies, and television programs can often stimulate discussion. The discussion of controversial current events can capture and hold an audience's attention.

A topic for discussion should be a question of policy rather than fact. "Have we a supply of energy?" is a question of fact. The only appropriate reply is a direct, factual answer. "Should we control the use of energy?" is a question of policy which should stir discussion. For suggestions on choosing topics, see page 171.

EXERCISE 2. **Selecting Topics for Group Discussion.** List five topics suitable for group discussion. Test yours and those submitted by classmates against the criteria listed above. The topics may relate to school, state, national, or international affairs.

38d. Prepare by thinking, talking, and reading about the topic.

Many discussions fail because of insufficient preparation by the participants. When the topic is announced, do your own thinking. Make sure that there is sufficient evidence to substantiate the truth of every major point. Think things through and avoid making rash or erroneous judgments.

Talk to others about the topic. Discuss it with your friends and parents. Discuss it with someone who is an authority on the topic. Be ready to modify your previous opinion.

Consult reference books, recent publications, magazine articles, and editorials. Inform yourself as thoroughly as you can about the topic. Investigate the facts before arriving at a decision. For other strategies on gathering information, see pages 12–18.

38e. Follow the steps of logical thinking.

In preparing for and participating in a group discussion, follow the steps of logical thinking. When confronted by a problem, you follow certain logical steps. For example, if your ball-point pen fails to write, you ask yourself:

1. What is the trouble? [You define the problem.]
2. What *might be* the cause? [You mentally list various causes: clogged point, defective mechanism, exhausted ink cartridge.]
3. What *is* the cause? [You consider each of the previously listed possibilities. The point is not clogged, the mechanism works smoothly, the cartridge is used up.]
4. What should be done about it? [Obviously you need a new cartridge or a new pen.]

This simple example illustrates the steps in problem solving.

    I. Define the problem.
      A. Limit the problem.
      B. Phrase the problem.
   II. Find the possible causes.
  III. Propose and examine possible solutions. [What would be the effects of each? To what extent would each solve the problem?]
  IV. Select the best solution.
   V. Put the best solution into operation. [What obstacles will be encountered and how will they be overcome?]

When participants are familiar with these five steps and follow them in their individual and group thinking, an orderly, purposeful discussion results.

EXERCISE 3. Analyzing a Television or Radio Discussion. Listen to a television or radio discussion program and report on it orally to your class. Did the discussion follow the steps in problem solving listed above? If not, what order or sequence did it follow?

Participating in Group Discussion

The success of a group discussion depends on the attitudes of the participants and the quality of their participation, the guidance of the discussion leader, and the response of the audience.

38f. Learn the responsibilities of a speaker in a group discussion.

As a speaker in a group discussion, you should have a cooperative attitude. Recognize that the good of the group supersedes your own concerns.

Know your topic well. To have an adequate knowledge of the topic, prepare by reflecting on it and by talking and reading about it.

Contribute willingly. Some of your ideas will come from previous reflection, and others will come on the spur of the moment, stimulated by what someone else has said. Don't hesitate to express tentative ideas, for these ideas may be just what are needed. Everyone should have a chance to be heard; do not monopolize the discussion.

Listen intelligently. When you agree with another speaker, listen to increase your store of information. When you disagree, listen to accept a different viewpoint if it is supported by sufficient evidence or to refute it by sound reasons if it is fallacious.

Speak so that all can hear—not only the participants but the audience too, if there is one. Be courteous always. Sarcasm and ridicule are out of place. Self-control is a mark of maturity. Disagree reasonably— and with reasons.

38g. Learn the responsibilities of a leader of a discussion.

If you are chosen to lead a discussion, familiarize yourself with the topic and the special interests and backgrounds of the participants. If the discussion is to be held before an audience, arrange a preliminary meeting of the speakers to decide on procedure and the order in which the various aspects of the topic will be discussed.

Decide on the seating plan. "Set the stage" with an arc of chairs and tables on a slightly raised platform close to the audience.

Introduce the speakers to the audience, telling something of each one's background or point of view. Arouse the audience's interest in the topic by a brief introductory statement. Say just enough to spotlight the problem and then ask the first question.

Address your questions to the group as a whole; don't question individual members. Let participation be as free and spontaneous as possible. Ask challenging questions—not the *yes* and *no* kind, but *why?* and *how?* Dig out points of difference in a friendly, united pursuit of a solution.

Take time for occasional summaries. People like to know what progress is being made. In your final summary, mention the loose ends, if any.

Be impartial and keep your own viewpoint out of the discussion. Break in only to ask clarifying questions, bring the discussion back on the track, advance to the next point, or summarize.

Invite audience participation at a point of high interest. Speakers from the floor may describe their own experiences or state their opinions. Refer questions to the panel.

Before closing, be sure to thank the speakers and the audience.

38h. Learn the responsibilities of a member of the audience.

By listening attentively, asking questions, and making clarifying statements, members of an audience can help make a group discussion stimulating. As a member of the audience, you also have an obligation to prepare for the discussion by thinking, talking, and reading about the topic.

Listen with an alert mind. Ask yourself: "What proof is offered in support of each important argument?"

Join in when the discussion leader invites the audience to participate. Speak freely, briefly, sincerely.

Focus on the main issues. Minor points of fact or opinion should be overlooked.

Speak audibly. While your remarks are addressed to the chair, speak so that all can hear.

EXERCISE 4. Conducting a Round-Table Discussion. Conduct a round-table discussion on a topic concerning all the participants. The discussion leader, appointed beforehand, will end the discussion after twenty minutes and summarize. Suggested topics:

1. City vs. country living
2. Improving student government
3. The school yearbook
4. Assembly programs
5. Building school spirit

EXERCISE 5. Conducting a Forum or a Symposium. Conduct a forum or a symposium on discipline. The speakers in the symposium should represent the viewpoints of a young person, a parent, a law enforcement officer, an educator, and a community leader.

EXERCISE 6. Presenting a Panel Discussion. Divide the class into groups. Each group will select a discussion leader and present a panel discussion before the class on any one of the following topics or a topic of its own. Each panel should meet beforehand to settle matters of procedure and scope. Suggested topics:

1. Modern manners
2. Choosing a career
3. The honor system of conducting examinations
4. Professional vs. amateur sports
5. Vandalism

6. How to overcome prejudice
7. The kind of world I'd like to live in
8. Our foreign policy
9. Problems of the farmer
10. Ways of preventing war

Nonverbal Communication

As you may have noticed in your conversations and discussions with others, people often gesture with their hands or use facial expressions to convey meaning. These body movements are examples of nonverbal communication.

Discussion skills should include effective nonverbal habits. For example, hand gestures should not distract listeners; they should support what you are trying to say. Be sure that the gestures you use convey specific meaning to your listeners.

Listening

As a member of the audience, you must be able to understand and evaluate the ideas of others in the discussion.

38i. Learn to listen efficiently.

Studies show that the average listener recalls only a little more than half of what a speaker says. By understanding and applying the following points, you can close this gap between speaker and listener.

Listen to acquire information and evaluate it. As you hear a speaker present ideas, you interpret them and pass judgment on them as sound or weak. Ask yourself: "Has the speaker presented enough evidence to justify these opinions? Is the evidence from reliable sources?"

Listen with the right attitude. To listen efficiently, you must be unbiased and cooperative. People with fixed ideas find it difficult to listen to viewpoints different from their own. An intelligent listener, on the other hand, is fair-minded and receptive to all ideas that are supported by convincing evidence.

Do not strongly agree or disagree with a speaker early in a talk. Withhold final judgment until the topic is developed.

Listen with attention. Concentration is hard work. We all have a tendency to listen for a few minutes, daydream for a while, and then turn our attention again to the speaker. Make an effort to concentrate continuously on the speaker's message. .

Listen for the main ideas. Usually only a few main points are presented in a discussion. Listen to discover the central ideas and fasten attention upon them.

Listen for supporting information. A speaker should support assertions by offering evidence in the form of facts, statements of authorities, and logical reasoning.[1] The evidence must be sufficient to justify what has been said; otherwise the assertion fails for lack of proof.

Listen for faulty reasoning. In Chapter 5 you learned about errors in reasoning, such as hasty generalizations, cause-and-effect fallacies, and only cause fallacies. As you listen to a discussion, you may hear faulty reasoning for this mistake is more common in oral than in written presentations.

Listen for loaded words.[2] The use of emotionally loaded words is natural in a discussion, particularly when the speakers are committed to a viewpoint. The active listener discounts arguments that are directed at emotions, not reason.

EXERCISE 7. Listening Critically to a Radio or Television Discussion. Report on a radio or television discussion on a controversial question. Did the speakers present both sides of the question fairly? What evidence did they offer to support their opinions? What objections can you pose?

Evaluating Group Discussion

By considering the merits and deficiencies of a group discussion after it is over, you can learn to improve future discussion programs. In your evaluation, consider the group as a whole, the individual participants, the discussion leader, and the outcome of the discussion.

38j. Evaluate a group discussion by asking key questions about it.

The following questions will help you estimate the worth of a group discussion.

---

[1] For a discussion of evidence, see pages 179–81.
[2] For a discussion of loaded words, see pages 324–25.

1. Was the discussion purposeful? Were the causes of the problem considered? Were various solutions proposed and analyzed? If the discussion was concerned with solving a problem, did it follow the steps of logical thinking?

2. Was the outcome worthwhile? A group discussion need not reach a solution or agreement. It may be successful if it brings areas of disagreement into the open.

3. Were the participants familiar with the problem? Did they present facts, statements of competent authorities, and statistics to support their opinions?

4. Was the discussion lively? Was there a give-and-take of opinion in an atmosphere of mutual respect? Did all participate? Did anyone monopolize the meeting?

5. Were the audience's questions thought provoking? Did the speakers answer them directly and fully?

6. Was the discussion courteous? Did each speaker exercise self-control by refraining from interrupting when another was speaking?

7. Was the discussion leader competent? Did the introductory remarks arouse interest? Did the discussion avoid pointless digressions? Was everyone encouraged to join in? Was there a summary?

EXERCISE 8. Preparing and Using a Rating Sheet. Prepare a rating sheet for group discussions. Use it to evaluate one of the panel discussions conducted in Exercise 6.

DEBATING

A debate is a form of argument in which two teams publicly dispute a question in a systematic way. Debating focuses attention on controversial questions, particularly those affecting the public interest. It stimulates thinking, develops speaking ability, provides training in research, and encourages the habit of suspending judgment until all facts are at hand.

The team supporting the question, or *proposition,* is called the affirmative; the opposing team, the negative. Each team consists of two (or rarely, three) speakers, who are called *first affirmative* (or *negative*), *second affirmative,* etc.

A debate is divided into two parts. During the first part (constructive speeches), both sides present their arguments for or against the proposition. After an intermission, both sides try to refute (with rebuttal speeches) the opposing arguments.

The order of speaking may be as follows:

1. CONSTRUCTIVE SPEECHES	2. REBUTTAL SPEECHES
a. First affirmative	a. First negative
b. First negative	b. First affirmative
c. Second affirmative	c. Second negative
d. Second negative	d. Second affirmative

Notice that the affirmative side opens and closes the debate and that the first rebuttal is made by the negative side.

The Proposition

The characteristics of a proposition are discussed in Chapter 5, pages 172–74. The following review recalls the main points in that discussion.

38k. A proposition is a topic stated in debatable form.

It may be phrased either as a question or as a resolution.

EXAMPLES   Should football be prohibited as a high-school sport?
         Resolved: Football should be prohibited as a high-school sport.

(1) A proposition should contain only one central idea.

NOT DEBATABLE   *Resolved:* Fraternities and sororities should be banned in high schools, and every high-school student should be required to participate in at least one extracurricular activity. [two ideas]

DEBATABLE   *Resolved:* Fraternities and sororities should be banned in high schools.

DEBATABLE   *Resolved:* Every high-school student should be required to participate in at least one extracurricular activity.

(2) A proposition should be debatable. It should have two sides.

NOT DEBATABLE   *Resolved:* The automobile has greatly affected the way we live. [This is so obviously true that it cannot be debated.]

DEBATABLE   *Resolved:* Everyone should know how to drive a car.

(3) A proposition should be stated fairly.

UNFAIR   *Resolved:* That the unjust and harmful cutbacks in school aid should be rescinded. [This assumes what has to be proved—that school aid cutbacks are unjust and harmful.]

FAIR   *Resolved:* That the cutbacks in school aid should be rescinded.

(4) A proposition should be timely.

There are hundreds of vital questions relating to young people, schools, local conditions, and state, national, and international affairs that stimulate controversy.

(5) A proposition should be stated affirmatively.

CONFUSING *Resolved:* Capital punishment should not be abolished. [The affirmative side would have to argue, "Yes, it should not be abolished," a confusing position.]

CLEAR *Resolved:* Capital punishment should be abolished.

(6) A proposition should put the burden of proof on the affirmative.

Anyone who makes an assertion should be ready and able to prove it. The affirmative side, which asserts the truth of a proposition, must present enough proof to establish its case beyond a reasonable doubt.

The affirmative side must show a need for a change; for example, that high-school football should be prohibited. Existing conditions—called the *status quo*—are presumed to be satisfactory until the affirmative offers sufficient proof to show that a change is necessary.

NOT DEBATABLE *Resolved:* That our government should continue to support wildlife conservation. [This makes the affirmative defend the *status quo* and the negative advocate a change.]

DEBATABLE *Resolved:* That our government should stop supporting wildlife conservation.

The negative has only to prove that the affirmative case is false or unsound. It does not have to offer an alternative solution.

(7) A proposition should contain no words of uncertain meaning.

For example, "*Resolved:* That oil is more valuable than steel in modern civilization" is not debatable because "valuable" has no exact meaning. Does it mean essential? Costly? Efficient? Useful?

EXERCISE 9. Composing Propositions for Debates. Compose five propositions for class debate. Be sure that each of your propositions satisfies all the preceding requirements. If your teacher agrees, you and a classmate may evaluate each other's propositions, using items 1-7 above and on page 802 as criteria.

The Issue

38l. An issue is a point of disagreement.

The points in a debate on which there are clashes of opinion are called *issues*.[1] A proposition rests on several issues. If they are proved, the proposition is proved. An issue is stated as a question which can be answered by *yes* or *no*.

PROPOSITION   *Resolved:* That students should participate in the process of selecting high-school principals.

ISSUE   Is the present method of selecting principals faulty?

Issues often deal with the need for a change, the practicability of a proposed solution, and the desirability of adopting a different solution.

EXERCISE 10. Listing Issues for a Proposition.   List at least three issues for one of the propositions you submitted in Exercise 9.

The Brief

In Chapter 5, you learned the principles of argumentation. Those principles are as valid in debating as in writing.

38m. A brief is an outline for debate.

In a debate, arguments are prepared in a detailed logical outline called a *brief*. A brief is an orderly arrangement of all the arguments needed to prove or disprove a proposition. All the statements in a brief are complete sentences.

The introduction summarizes the history of the questions and defines terms. Sometimes, it sets forth issues and mentions any matters that are excluded from discussion by mutual agreement. In the brief proper, the issues are taken up one by one, and the evidence in support of each is given in the form of facts, figures, examples, authority, and logical reasoning. The conclusion summarizes the main arguments and reasserts or denies the proposition.

The partial example that follows illustrates the form and content of a brief.

Model Brief

Resolved: That the jury system in the United States should be significantly changed.

---

[1] An *issue* in debate corresponds to the minor proposition in other kinds of argument.

Affirmative

I. Jury trials in civil cases cause unfair delay and clog court calendars.
   A. Court calendars are crowded because only a few jury cases can be heard at a time while many others await trial. A national survey by the Institute of Judicial Administration showed that the average delay was 13.3 months.
   B. Delay is a great aid to wrongdoers.
      1. It erases the memories of witnesses.
      2. It may cause wronged parties to give up their cases.
   C. Delay inflicts hardship on the innocent, who have to wait before they can clear themselves.
II. Jury trials waste time and money.
   A. They take up the time of the courts, participants, and jurors.
   B. They increase the cost of court administration, including the payment of jurors' fees.
   C. In New York City alone, jury service each year is equivalent to taking 50,000 people away from their jobs for ten days—an enormous loss of time and money to the jurors' businesses.
III. Juries should be composed of fewer than twelve members.
   A. There is no sound reason for the number twelve.
   B. Many states have smaller juries, sometimes eight, often six, and the administration of justice has not suffered.
   C. If juries were smaller, fewer jurors would have to be challenged, expenses would be cut, and verdicts could be reached more quickly.

Negative

I. Court congestion is not caused by jury trial alone but by
   A. Increasing population.
   B. Failure of public authorities to create sufficient judgeships and to provide enough court facilities.
II. The jury system does not waste time, money, and human energy.
   A. Compared with what we spend on education, defense, and other aspects of government, the jury system costs little.
   B. In the Federal courts, jury expenditures constitute only $\frac{1}{170}$ of 1% of total costs. (If you paid an income tax of $17,000, only one dollar of it would go to support the jury system.)
   C. A University of Chicago study found that 94% of those who served on juries wanted to serve again, 3% more were willing to do so, and only 3% were unwilling to serve again.
III. The proposal to reduce the size of juries is fraught with danger.
   A. It would be the first step in doing away with juries entirely.
   B. It diminishes the protection given to those in the minority.
   C. It substantially reduces the likelihood of representation by people of diverse ethnicity.

    D. It would lower public confidence in jury verdicts.

    E. Innocent persons are more likely to be convicted if a jury is composed of fewer than twelve.

The Rebuttal

38n. Plan the rebuttal while preparing the debate.

The rebuttal tests a debater's ability to analyze and answer an opponent's arguments. To refute effectively, a debater must be able to think quickly and speak extemporaneously.

    Prepare for the rebuttal weeks before the debate at the time you are gathering material and thinking about your case. Your success as a debater may rest on your ability to answer your opponents' arguments. As you prepare your brief, consider the arguments they will use, confer with your colleagues about them, and assemble arguments to refute them. Summarize each opposing argument and your answer to it on a separate card. Have your cards available for reference during the debate.

    Refutation can start during the constructive speeches. Reply to your opponent's arguments when your turn comes to speak. When refuting, state your opponent's arguments clearly and fairly, quoting your opponent's words if possible. Then present evidence to show that the argument is illogical, misleading, or unproved.

    In rebuttal, limit yourself to the main arguments of the opposition. If you can demolish the opposition's main contentions, the minor arguments can be ignored.

Participating in Debate

38o. Observe the conventions of debate.

Address the chair as "Mr. Chairman" or "Madam Chairman." Refer to the judges as "Honorable judges."

    Instead of referring to participants by name, use the customary terms: "The first affirmative speaker," "My worthy opponents," "My colleagues," or "My teammates."

    Ridicule, sarcasm, and personal attacks have no place in debating. A debate should be won or lost on the basis of reasoned argument and convincing delivery.

38p. The judges' decision is based on the skill of the debaters, not on the truth or falsity of the proposition.

The most common method of determining the winner of a debate is by decision of three appointed judges. The judges base their decision on the merits of the debate and not on their own views of the question.

Another method is by decision of a critic judge who announces the winning team and gives the reasons for the decision.

A third method is by means of a shift-of-opinion poll. Before the debate, ballots are distributed to listeners to record their opinions regarding the proposition. At the end of the debate another ballot is taken. Only ballots showing a change of opinion are counted. The decision is awarded to the team that caused the greater number of listeners to change their opinion.

EXERCISE 11. Preparing for a Debate; Presenting a Debate.
Divide the class into groups of four or six. Each group will decide on a proposition for debate, divide into affirmative and negative teams, prepare briefs, and on the appointed date present the debate in class under the direction of a leader appointed by the teacher or elected by the class. If desired, another class may be invited to attend the debate. The following topics, which should be phrased as propositions, are only suggestions.

1. Jury system
2. Tipping
3. Freedom of the press
4. Abolition of football
5. Government support of TV
6. Electoral college
7. Compulsory voting
8. Eleven-month school year
9. Elective courses
10. Nuclear energy
11. Federal aid to schools
12. Censorship of movies
13. Raising the driving age
14. Energy conservation
15. Ecology
16. Compulsory military service
17. Lagging school spirit
18. Reorganization of Congress
19. A permanent site for the summer Olympics
20. Mass transit

CHAPTER 39

Public Speaking

PREPARING, DELIVERING, AND EVALUATING AN INFORMAL SPEECH

Informal speaking situations will frequently arise in the course of your life. For example, you may give an informal, personal speech at a committee meeting, in a working session of a task group, or even in a small gathering of friends and acquaintances. To prepare an informal, personal speech, you follow many of the same steps as you do in the writing process.

PREPARING THE SPEECH

In some speaking situations, such as reporting on an interview, the topic is already determined. In others, you must choose and limit a subject, gather information, and organize the information in a logical and interesting manner.

39a. Analyze the occasion, the interests of your listeners, and your personal interests and experiences when you choose a subject.

Consider the occasion. The purpose of the occasion may suggest subjects to you. When you think about the occasion, also consider the number of speakers in the group and the time limit for each speech.

Consider the interests of your listeners. People like to listen to subjects that already interest them. Analyze the interests and concerns of your audience before you choose a subject.

Consider your personal interests and experiences. Writers are often advised to write about what they know best. Likewise, as a speaker, you can speak enthusiastically and convincingly if your subject is one you know well.

EXERCISE 1. Choosing a Subject for an Informal Speech. For each of the following occasions and purposes, select a subject suitable for a speech. Be prepared to discuss your choices.

1. *Occasion:* Adventure Club meeting; *Purpose:* to decide on a field trip
2. *Occasion:* social service committee meeting; *Purpose:* to establish guidelines for choosing a Volunteer of the Year
3. *Occasion:* Career Day committee; *Purpose:* to organize a school assembly on career choices
4. *Occasion:* Youth Task Force meeting; *Purpose:* to identify problems in the school and community
5. *Occasion:* weekly discussion group; *Purpose:* to share personal experiences

39b. Limit your subject so that you may treat it adequately and achieve your purpose.

An informal speech usually has a time limit, expressed officially or unofficially. Limit your subject so you can cover the important points or main ideas in the time allowed. For specific suggestions on how to limit a subject, see pages 9–11 of Chapter 1.

The purpose of your speech will also help you limit your subject. There are four purposes of public speaking: to inform, to convince, to entertain, and to move to action. For example, if your speech is on volunteer work at a hospital, you might vary the subject to suit each purpose as follows:

TO INFORM	Discuss the duties of a volunteer worker.
TO CONVINCE	Advocate that everyone volunteer to serve at the hospital.
TO ENTERTAIN	Talk about humorous experiences at the hospital.
TO MOVE TO ACTION	Urge students to work five hours a week at the hospital.

Write down your purpose in sentence form on a card and use it as a temporary title of your speech. This statement will help clarify your thinking, focus your attention, and guide you in selecting ideas. The following sentences are typical titles:

Local businesses need dependable part-time workers. [to inform]
Foreign languages should be required subjects. [to convince]
Flunking your driver's test isn't the end of the world. [to entertain]
Write to the television networks to end violence on TV programs. [to move to action]

EXERCISE 2. Developing a Topic for an Informal Speech. Suppose you were asked to speak to a small group of classmates on one of the following subjects. Decide on a purpose for your talk and limit the subject to three topics. For each topic, write three points you might include in your informal speech.

1. Careers
2. Art
3. Singing
4. Ecology
5. Camping
6. Community service

39c. Gather information from your own experiences, from interviews, and from printed materials.

Your own experiences, knowledge, and background are an important source of information for an informal speech. Use an information-gathering technique such as brainstorming or clustering to delve into your personal storehouse of information.

Share your thoughts with others in informal conversations. Often, other people can give you a fresh perspective on the topic and prepare you for listeners' reactions to your ideas. These informal interviews will help you sharpen your thinking and adapt the topic to your audience.

Check the library for sources of information to support your main points. Magazines, newspapers, and brochures can give you the most recent information on a topic. Reference books can provide an overview and help identify authorities in the field. Remember to take notes on information you have gathered from printed materials. Include all the details of the source of your information, such as the title, author, page number, and date of publication.

EXERCISE 3. Gathering Information for an Informal Speech. Select a topic for a three-minute speech to give to a small group of classmates. Make a list of the information-gathering strategies you will use and the sources you intend to consult. Use one of the following topics or choose your own.

---

[1] Information-gathering strategies used in the writing process also apply to preparing a speech. Refer to pages 12–18, Chapter 1.

1. The best place for a senior trip
2. How to combine work and study
3. Why I hate (love) Saturday mornings
4. A fund-raising project for our organization
5. Why I'm not nervous about job interviews

39d. Write an outline of your informal speech.[1]

After you have gathered information, write an outline of the main points you can cover within the time limit. Below each main point, write at least two supporting ideas. Analyze your outline to determine if the arrangement you have chosen is the most logical.

EXERCISE 4. Preparing an Outline for Your Informal Speech. Use the topic and sources you developed in Exercise 3 to prepare an outline for your three-minute speech. Analyze the effectiveness of the arrangement of your ideas.

39e. Prepare an introduction that will capture your listeners' interest and lead into your topic.

An effective, interesting beginning to a speech will arouse your listeners' interest and curiosity, making them more receptive to your ideas. Do not be afraid to try something different to begin your speech. If everyone else begins by saying "I would like to recommend . . . " or "I think we should . . . " your listeners will welcome a fresh, thought-provoking beginning.

Consider the following approaches to beginning an informal speech.

A STRIKING STATEMENT
Imagine you are sitting in a small rubber boat only thirty feet from an enormous gray whale.

A QUESTION
Why are we burying our heads in the sand while vandals are destroying our school?

A COMMAND
Learn to recognize and deal with stress now—before it kills you.

AN ANECDOTE
Mr. X is forty-five years old, has a wife and three children, and works on a factory assembly-line. Thanks to the tutoring of a dedicated senior, Mr. X has learned to read.

[1] For information on outlining, see pages 98–101, Chapter 3.

39f. Develop your main and supporting ideas logically and effectively.

Many informal speeches present information that people must use for making decisions. The following methods will help you develop your main and supporting ideas effectively.

EXPLANATION

Acid rain results from the mixture of sulfur and nitrogen oxides with water vapor and oxygen in the atmosphere. The sulfur and nitrogen are released into the air by smoke from coal-burning furnaces and power plants. The fifty-year-old power plant that heats our school and keeps us warm is also destroying the environment.

STATISTICS

Eight out of ten households in our community have a dog or a cat. The average cost of boarding a pet at the local kennels during the summer is ninety dollars a week. I propose that we raise funds by setting up a pet-sitting service this summer and charging sixty dollars a week.

EXAMPLES

Our book sale last year was a failure; only seventy-five people attended. Central High held a book and bake sale that attracted over a thousand people. Their organizing committee sent out news releases, distributed posters and brochures, and asked a rock band to volunteer their services as entertainment. Our committee should follow their example to make our sale a success this year.

PROBLEM-SOLVING

If we go on our field trip during Memorial Day weekend—as we always have—only ten of us will be free to go. However, if we plan our trip for spring vacation, only one person will not be able to go. We should break with tradition this year so that more of us can participate.

39g. Prepare a conclusion that will impress the central idea of your speech on the listeners.

Conclude by summarizing the main points of your informal speech. To add force to your conclusion, you may end with an appropriate quotation, an emotional appeal for action, or a thought-provoking question.

EXERCISE 5. Preparing an Introduction and Conclusion for Your Informal Speech. Use the outline of the speech you developed for Exercise 4 and write at least two possible introductions and conclusions. Read them to your classmates and discuss why they are or are not effective.

DELIVERING THE SPEECH

Four methods of presenting a speech—impromptu speaking, extemporaneous speaking, memorized speaking, and a composite method—are most commonly used in delivering a personal, informal speech.

Impromptu speaking often occurs in small groups when each member is asked to state an opinion or give an immediate analysis of data. The speaker has no advance warning and must prepare and organize the speech on the spur of the moment.

Extemporaneous speaking allows time for preparation and development of the speech, often in outline form. The speaker does not memorize the speech, but he or she is familiar with the main and supporting points and is flexible enough to adapt the speech to listeners' reactions.

Memorized speaking is written and learned word for word. Because it usually results in a rigid, artificial-sounding talk, memorization is only advised for introductions and conclusions.

The *composite method* is a combination of two or more methods, such as memorizing an opening quotation and speaking extemporaneously.

39h. Use nonverbal communication effectively.

Most informal speeches are given in small- to medium-size groups in which the speaker is near the listeners. When you give an informal speech, you must adapt nonverbal, or unspoken, communication to the size of the group and the physical surroundings.

1. *Maintain good posture.* Whether you deliver your speech standing or sitting, keep your body in a comfortable but alert position.

2. *Establish and maintain good eye contact.* Through eye contact, you can make each listener feel that you are speaking directly to him or her. This helps you stay in control of your speech, and it helps your listeners pay close attention to your words.

3. *Gesture naturally and comfortably.* In smaller groups, make your gestures sparingly and effectively. Also, pay attention to audience reaction. If some listeners start daydreaming, take a few steps or shift your weight while you are standing, or stand up from a sitting position.

EXERCISE 6. Using Effective Nonverbal Communication. Use the speech you developed in Exercises 4 and 5. Practice delivering the speech while sitting down and while standing up. Then deliver your speech to a small group of classmates and adapt your gestures and position to your listeners' reactions.

EVALUATING AN INFORMAL SPEECH

To evaluate a speech, you must listen attentively and courteously. In real-life situations, you may be asked to make a decision based on the information you receive from informal speeches.

39i. Learn how to evaluate an informal speech.

In any speaking situation, you should listen to learn information, to appreciate and understand the viewpoints of others, and to analyze the content and delivery of the speech. When you evaluate speeches, listen constructively and objectively to your classmates to help them improve. They, in turn, will evaluate your speech with the same purpose in mind.

Focus on the points listed in the following sample evaluation sheet as you listen to speeches given in class. Use the section for comments to cite specific examples of strengths and weaknesses.

EVALUATION SHEET

Speaker: Topic:

Evaluator: Purpose of Speech:

	Very Good	Good	Fair	Weak
Speech				
Introduction				
Organization				
Conclusion				
Choice of subject				
Preparation and knowledge of subject matter				

	Very Good	Good	Fair	Weak
Use of standard English				

Delivery

Nonverbal communication: Posture				
Eye contact				
Gestures				
Relation of speaker to listeners: Direct and sincere				
Conversational				
Communicative				
Confident				
Voice, enunciation, pronunciation				

Comments:

An evaluation of a classmate's speech should be friendly, helpful, and honest. If the purpose of the speech was to convince or to move to action, let the speaker know if the main and supporting points were persuasive or if the use of an example, anecdote, or statistic was appropriate. If the purpose of the speech was to entertain, tell the speaker if it held your interest and give examples. If the purpose was to inform, let the speaker know if you learned something new or if something needs to be clarified. The constructive information you give in an evaluation helps your classmates improve as speakers and helps you become a knowledgeable, alert listener.

EXERCISE 7. Analyzing a Speech.   Listen to a small-group discussion, a panel discussion, or an informal speech given in your community, on television, or on radio. Evaluate each speaker's presentation, using the sample evaluation sheet.

REVIEW EXERCISE A. Delivering an Informal Speech. Expand the outline you prepared in Exercise 4 to apply to a five-minute speech. Deliver your speech in class. Use the evaluation sheets prepared by your listeners to analyze your strengths and weaknesses.

REVIEW EXERCISE B. Delivering an Informal Extemporaneous Speech. Choose a local, state, or national issue that is important to you and prepare a five-minute extemporaneous speech to convince or to move to action. Prepare an outline. You may memorize your introduction and conclusion. Use the evaluations you receive to analyze your strengths and weaknesses.

REVIEW EXERCISE C. Delivering an Impromptu Speech. Use one of the following topics or make up one of your own to deliver a two- to three-minute impromptu speech. You may take a few minutes to think of two or three main points and to develop an interesting introduction and conclusion.

1. How I plan to spend my summer
2. Why first impressions are (are not) reliable
3. The first day of work on a part-time job
4. Why music (a sport, a hobby) is important to me
5. Three ways to improve your memory

INDEX

Index

D

INDEX

K 4 5
L 6
M 7
N 8
O 9

INDEX

NOTES

NOTES

NOTES